Advanced Woodwork and Furniture Making

4th Edition, 2nd Revision

The manufacturer uses the raw materials from our forests and with modern technology including mass production methods produces quality furniture.

Advanced Woodwork and Furniture Making

4th Edition, 2nd Revision

John L. Feirer
Head, Industrial Education Department
Western Michigan University
Kalamazoo, Michigan

and

Gilbert R. Hutchings, Professor
Industrial Education Department
Western Michigan University
Kalamazoo, Michigan

Bennett Publishing Company, Peoria, IL 61615

Library of Congress Catalog Card Number: 80-70160
PRINTED IN THE UNITED STATES OF AMERICA

ISBN 87002-341-1

Preface

ADVANCED WOODWORK AND FURNITURE MAKING has been widely used in schools for basic courses in machine woodworking and furniture construction. Before this revision was made, industrial education teachers were questioned concerning their recommendations for changes, additions, and modifications. This new edition is written largely on the basis of those suggestions and with a view to the changes taking place in the woodworking field.

Major features of the original edition are retained. The organization is essentially the same, and the book continues to emphasize the visual approach to instruction. However, the fourth edition incorporates the following important changes:

1. New section on upholstery which is an important part of completing many furniture pieces.
2. Additional technical information on wood and wood products.
3. Almost all new illustrations on furniture design.
4. Second color throughout the book, used as a teaching aid both in illustrations and text.
5. Full-color illustrations which show the beauty of wood and furniture design.
6. Additional and updated illustrations and instruction on many of the basic woodworking machines.
7. A major unit on mass production to give students an insight into the furniture industry and how it functions.
8. A unit on careers, to provide an occupational orientation.
9. A unit on metrics in furniture construction.

This second revision of the fourth edition includes a unit on repairing and refinishing wood furniture.

ADVANCED WOODWORK AND FURNITURE MAKING is planned for use in woodworking classes in high schools, vocational schools, and teacher education institutions. The book is written at high school reading level.

Acknowledgments

Personal

Melvin Anderson
Robert Colpetzer
Robert Compsmith
Jerry E. Door
Michael Fortenbacher
William K. Purdy

Corporations and other organizations

Adjustable Clamp Company
Ajax Hardward Corporation
Ethan Allen Furniture Company
Allis-Chalmers Manufacturing Company
American Forest Products Industries
American Hardboard Association
American of Martinsville
American Plywood Association
Anka Web Spring Company
Auto-Nailer Company
Baumritter Corporation
Black and Decker Manufacturing Company
Blade Manufacturing Company
Boice-Crane Company
The Brandt Cabinet Works, Incorporated
British Columbia Industrial Design Committee
Buss Machine Works, Incorporated
Clausing Corporation
Cleveland Twist Drill Company
Columbia Fastener Company
Comet Industries Corporation
Condé Nast Publications Incorporated
Cornell University
Curtis Companies
Dansk Designs, Incorporated
DeVilbiss Company
Disston Saw Company
Dodds Machinery Company
Duo-Fast Corporation
Drexel Furniture Company
Dunbar Furniture Corporation
Dux, Incorporated
Fastener Corporation
Foley Manufacturing Company
Franklin Glue Company
General Electric Company
General Finishes and Sales Service Company, Div. W. H. Pipcorn Company
General Motors Corporation
Globe Furniture Company
B. F. Goodrich Company
Greenlee Bros. and Company
Hardwood Plywood Manufacturers Association
Hekman Furniture Company
Heritage Furniture Company
Arvids Iraids Multi-Purpose Spring Clamps
Kay Manufacturing Corporation
Jens Risom Design, Incorporated
Karges Furniture Company, Incorporated
Knoll Associates, Incorporated
Kroehler Company
Lane Company, Incorporated
Latex Foam Rubber Council
Lehigh Furniture Corporation
Masonite Corporation
Mattison Machine Works, Incorporated
Howard Miller Clock Company
Millers Falls Company
Mohawk Finishing Products, Inc.
George Mount Company
National Particleboard Association
R. A. Ness and Company
Newman Machine Company, Incorporated
Northfield Foundry and Machine Company
No Sag Spring Company
Oliver Machinery Company
Onsrud Machine Works, Incorporated
Panelyte Division, St. Regis Paper Company
Frank Paxton Lumber Company
Pennsylvania House
Perkins Glue Company
Pirelli Limited
C. O. Porter Machinery Company
H. K. Porter Company
Powermatic Incorporated
Rockwell Manufacturing Company
Sellstrom Manufacturing Company
Senco Products, Incorporated
Sherwin-Williams Company
Simonds Saw and Steel Company
Singer Company
Skil Corporation
Sprague and Carleton, Incorporated
Stanley Tools
Star Chemical Co., Inc.
John Stuart, Incorporated
Thonet Industries, Incorporated
Timesavers Sanders, Incorporated
Tomlinson Furniture Company
United Gilsonite Laboratories
United States Plywood Corporation
United States Rubber Company
Upholstery Supply Company of Grand Rapids
Warren Dado Sawing Company
Watco-Dennis Corporation
Western Wood Products Association

Contents

Contents

Contents

Designing and Planning

Examples of furniture and art objects which show good design in home furnishings. Many materials are represented. (Baumritter Corporation)

UNIT 1 Building Good Furniture

The secret of success in building good furniture is to follow such steps as the ones outlined below. All instructions necessary to completion of each step will be found in this book. While not all pieces of furniture are constructed in the same manner, you can achieve good results by following these steps:

1. Select a good design that fits your needs

It is always best to choose something that is really useful. Remember your ability, however, and don't start making a chest of drawers, for instance, if you're in the lamp or tray (beginner's) "stage." Fig. 1-1. Make a working drawing for the product.

2. Select the right kinds of materials

Decide on the kind of furniture wood, plywood, and other materials that will best suit the project. Remember, however, that *working qualities of furniture woods and*

Each of these three furniture pieces was designed and built by a student craftsman and each won a prize for good design. These pieces show that good design and craftsmanship can be combined in the learning of woodworking skills.

1-1a. The grand prize winner was this beautifully executed desk. Detail emphasis on the drawer fronts was thoughtfully done. The utility area above the drawers imparts a light, airy feeling to the design. Suitability of materials, good construction, fine workmanship, and exceptional finish brought this project a close-to-perfect rating.

1-1c. This stool with upholstered seat won recognition in the junior division. It is well designed and shows good workmanship.

1-1b. This coffee table was selected best in its division. Note the excellent proportion and location of the legs in relationship to the top.

1-2. This Early American cabinet of birch can be built only if the cutting tools on the machine are sharp. The overall size is 34″ wide x 18½″ deep x 31½″ high.

1-3. Well-chosen hardware gives the finishing touch to this maple night table. It measures 25″ wide x 16″ deep x 26″ high.

plywoods differ greatly. It is easier to work (cut, shape, sand, etc.) mahogany than oak or birch, for example. If you don't have a planer available, you should buy surfaced lumber (S2S). Fig. 1-2.

3. Make an accurate bill of materials

Have a drawing or design and from this make a list of all of the materials (lumber and plywood) you will need as well as the supplies (dowel rod, screws, glue, finishing material, and hardware). Fig. 1-3.

4. Have the correct equipment

It is difficult to do a job without the right machines and tools. Of course, any step that is done on a machine can also be done by hand. The time it takes is so much greater, however, that sometimes the beginner becomes discour-

aged, especially if he is building a large furniture piece.

5. Make an accurate layout

Work slowly and carefully as you measure and mark out the pieces to be cut. A common error is cutting the pieces too small. When furniture woods are used, this can be a costly mistake. Fig. 1-4.

1-4. A contemporary table of fine walnut that is 36″ in diameter and 16″ high. When working with fine cabinet woods, one cannot afford to make a mistake.

6. Cut the parts to the correct shape

This will include rough cutting to size, squaring up and cutting out the design.

7. Make the joints accurately

A sign of good furniture construction is good, sturdy joints of the right kind. A sloppy dado or a poor-fitting mortise and tenon will make a weak piece. Fig. 1-5.

1-5. Good joints are a key item in chair construction. Note the clean-cut lines and Contemporary styling of this piece. The wood is teak.

1-6a. Note the use of a square to check the table as it is being assembled.

8. Assemble carefully

Make sure that all parts are completed and carefully sanded. Then glue up the project square and true. A poor job of clamping and gluing weakens an otherwise good piece. Fig. 1-6.

9. Apply the proper kind of finish

A poor finish can ruin a piece that is perfect in every other respect. Be very sure that the finish you select is appropriate and is one that you can apply with relative ease. Today's craftsman has a distinct advantage since excellent finishes are available. Some can be applied simply with cloths, others with a brush, and still others by spraying. Fig. 1-7.

1-6b. Each part must be carefully made so that it will fit into the assembly.

1-6c. This hi-fi cabinet was made by an advanced student of furniture making. The project is elegant in its simplicity. A large piece such as this requires careful workmanship and good planning since it must be designed around the component parts of the stereo.

1-7. A fine finish is a highly important part of any quality furniture piece. The top, sides, and drawer fronts of this commode are of cherry veneer. The top is 27″ x 22″ and the piece is 21″ high.

UNIT 2 Furniture Styles and Periods

The history of furniture is the history of the world. Each era had a different style of furniture. Study the early history of Europe and the Near East. You'll find many interesting ways in which the furniture of each period reflected the way people lived. Oftentimes, for instance, a ruler would dictate a new furniture style and then everyone throughout the country would imitate it. As a matter of fact, many of the furniture styles are named after

2-1a. English or Traditional: This pleasant sitting room has classic English designs. All of the pieces are mahogany with a handsome 18th-Century warm brown finish. Among the designs are a Sheraton flip-top card table, 18th Century pie-crust table of Chippendale design, and a Sheraton chest on a Hepplewhite desk.

kings, queens and rulers such as Louis XIV and Queen Anne.

The story of furniture fills many sets of books. In your study of history, you might be interested in looking up the style of furniture accepted in each period. Do you know, for example, what kind of furniture Napoleon liked? You should be interested in the styles of furniture that people buy today. You ought to be able to distinguish the different styles and recognize quality furniture. Various qualities of furniture are made in each style. Below this are cheaper grades, such as commercial furniture, that have no particular style.

There are six main styles of furniture: English or Traditional, French Provincial, Early American or Colonial, Contemporary, Italian Provincial, and Spanish or Mediterranean.

English or Traditional

This is actually a group of styles. Until recent years this was the most popular kind of furniture. Among the Traditional styles the most popular is called *18th Century*. Fig. 2-1. This name is given to furniture that combines

2-1b. A beautiful breakfront in 18th-Century style.

2-2. A chair in 18th-Century style.

brothers, and Sheraton—are responsible for the greatness of this era. All of these gifted men lived and worked in and around London. Their designs are very superior and you should know something about their work.

Thomas Chippendale was known as a designer, wood-carver, cabinetmaker and manufacturer of furniture. He was extremely intelligent and made use of all the known designs of furniture, making improvements on them. He designed many different styles. Some were influenced by the French, others by the Chinese and still others by the early English designs. Fig. 2-3. He was renowned as a builder of chairs. His most famous chair is the ladder back. Fig. 2-4 and Fig. 2-5. He used many different shapes of feet on his chairs but his most popular was the "claw and ball" foot. Fig. 2-6. Mahogany was his favorite wood. Fig. 2-7.

the best design characteristics of the 18th century. Fig. 2-2. The efforts of the "big four" among 18th century designers—Chippendale, Hepplewhite, the Adam

2-4. Chippendale ladderback chair.

2-3. This Chippendale coffee table reflects Chinese influence. It is 18″ high and the top is 21½″ x 38½″.

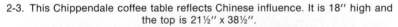

2-5. Chippendale characteristics—solidity, firmness, no undue refinements.

2-6. The claw-and-ball foot.

2-7. A Chippendale table showing the use of claw-and-ball foot.

2-8. Notice the simple lines of this Hepplewhite table. It is 18″ high and the top is 22″ x 36″.

2-9. Hepplewhite characteristics—simplicity, little ornamentation, tapered legs.

George Hepplewhite was also a London cabinetmaker and an original designer of furniture. In later life he established his own furniture factory. All of his furniture pieces were slender and well proportioned. Fig. 2-8. He did not like the heavy, massive furniture of early England. He permitted little or no carving but used painting and inlay. Fig. 2-9. He preferred mahogany and satinwood for his furniture. His most famous design is the shield-back chair. Fig. 2-10.

Robert and James Adam were architects and designers but not craftsmen as were Chippendale and Hepplewhite. They designed both homes and furniture for other people to build. They developed a style that was adapted from ancient Roman architecture. The legs were straight and tapered with very slender refinements of

2-10. The shield-back chair design, used frequently by Hepplewhite.

17

2-11. Adam characteristics—low relief carving, vertical lines, geometric ornaments.

2-12. This end table has the rectangular top and drop leaf which are characteristics of Sheraton.

all parts. Grooving and fluting was used on the legs and some carving was done. Fig. 2-11.

Thomas Sheraton was a designer and cabinetmaker and was the last of the great men of the golden age of furniture. Besides designing and building furniture, he was a publisher, preacher, author, and drawing teacher. However, he was a very poor businessman and died penniless. Sheraton used simple, straight lines, as shown in his rectangular table tops with drop leaves, and square-back chairs. Figs. 2-12 and 2-13.

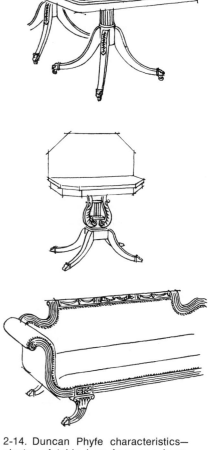

2-13. Sheraton characteristics—delicate, tapered legs; rectangular chair backs.

2-14. Duncan Phyfe characteristics—cluster of table legs from one base; modified curve of chair legs, with little or no carving.

2-15. This Duncan Phyfe end table shows the pedestal with four legs.

graceful curves. Fig. 2-14. Some of his best known pieces are tables with a pedestal and three or four legs. Fig. 2-15. A feature of these tables is the bronze claw at the end of the leg. Another of his best known designs is the lyre-back chair. Fig. 2-16. His furniture had some carving and considerable reeding. The construction of all his pieces was excellent, for Phyfe was not only a designer but a master cabinetmaker.

French Provincial

While this is another of the Traditional designs, it is usually classified separately because it has such a distinct style.

What is French Provincial? During the reigns of Louis XV and Louis XVI, great progress was

2-16. A lyre-back dining chair.

We see in stores today modifications of the work of each of these men. For example, you might see a Sheraton desk or a Hepplewhite table. Most manufacturers have combined the features of all and called the furniture 18th Century.

Do you know who Duncan Phyfe was? You should, for he was the only American cabinetmaker for whom a period or style of furniture is named. His designs were so fine that they have lived on and are still favorites with many people. Duncan Phyfe worked near the close of the 18th century in and around New York City. At one time over 100 men made furniture by hand in his factory.

As a designer he was a master of the elegant style of simple

2-17a. French Provincial. This bedroom set in French Provincial has the lovely cabriole leg and delicate carving. While this furniture often has a natural finish with a distressed surface, it is equally suitable in the off-white color with gold trim shown here.

2-17b. Notice the beautiful curved legs and form of the French Provincial table.

2-18b. Note the easily identified cabriole leg.

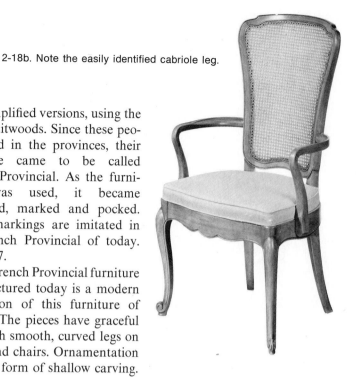

very simplified versions, using the local fruitwoods. Since these people lived in the provinces, their furniture came to be called French Provincial. As the furniture was used, it became scratched, marked and pocked. These markings are imitated in the French Provincial of today. Fig. 2-17.

The French Provincial furniture manufactured today is a modern adaptation of this furniture of France. The pieces have graceful lines with smooth, curved legs on tables and chairs. Ornamentation is in the form of shallow carving.

made in furniture design. These kings loved rich living and commissioned the best craftsmen to develop extremely ornate furniture with heavy carving and gorgeous curves. Lesser officials who lived in the countryside wanted copies of this furniture. Their local cabinetmakers could make only

HOW TO IDENTIFY FRENCH PROVINCIAL FURNITURE:

One of the most distinguishing features of French Provincial is the cabriole leg—(**a**) a furniture leg shaped in a double curve with the upper part swelling out. Early, formal French Provincial can be recognized by the scroll work (**b**) that adorns the cabriole leg. The heavier Provincial pieces, such as cabinets and chests (**c**), have short legs which suggest either the upper part of the cabriole leg (**d**), or a straight outside with a continuation of the curve pattern adorning the bottom of the piece (**e**).

2-18a. Chest of oak showing the fine carving frequently done in French Provincial furniture.

2-19a. French Provincial.

20

2-19b. French Provincial chest of cherry.

2-20. *Early American or Colonial.* This dining room suite features many of the basic pieces and characteristics of this style. Maple and birch are the basic materials. Often reed seats are also featured. Note the delightful turned legs and the simple designs on the door fronts.

Fig. 2-18. Woods used are mostly cherry and walnut. A characteristic is the presence of small black scratches. This is called a "distressed" finish and is purposely done to imitate wear marks found in the original furniture. The finish applied today is called fruitwood to imitate the appearance of the original natural fruitwoods used.

French Provincial is difficult to manufacture and almost impossible to make in the ordinary shop. Fig. 2-19.

Early American or Colonial

The first furniture made in America was different from all others. The early settlers needed simple, useful, sturdy pieces. They used the native woods available—oak, pine, and maple. Instead of nails they assembled the parts with wooden pegs. The earliest pieces had hand-whittled legs in-stead of turned legs. They also had flat, sturdy surfaces instead of ornamental carvings. Early American was such a functional, useful style that it is still very popular today. Characteristics of the style are the many turned parts and simple curves. Fig. 2-20.

Later, the colonists began to be interested in making a furniture that was a little more decorative.

Fig. 2-21. This became known as Colonial. The Colonial (later called Federal) furniture was somewhat more ornate and was influenced by the French designers. Colonial furniture was made from maple, pine, oak, and walnut. Characteristic pieces are the hutch cabinet, cobbler's bench and Windsor chair and desk. Fig. 2-22. See page 25.

A BASIC AMERICAN FURNITURE VOCABULARY

PERIOD DEFINITIONS

Colonial: The American period extending from the time of the earliest 17th Century settlements to the Revolution. (The term is frequently but improperly applied to most American furniture up to 1850.) The more primitive styles were developed in New England and the Pennsylvania Dutch area. The more elegant styles, in large cities north and south, were greatly influenced by English cabinetmakers, but American designers adapted and embellished with great success on their own.

Federal: The American period coincidental with early years of the Republic, 1780 to 1830. Duncan Phyfe was the outstanding designer.

BEDS

Bonnet: Has a short extended canopy on tall head-board posts.

Bunk: Single bed with matching bed fitted on top (with ladder). Some types can be rearranged into a trundle or twins.

Cannonball: Large balls cap each of its four low posts.

Canopy (or Tester): Tall four-poster with fabric-covered wood frame over it. Originally had vertical hangings to keep out drafts.

Poster: Has four tall posts, decoratively turned.

Spindle: Has decorative turnings, like some chair backs. (Right)

Spool: Its turnings are shaped like thread spools.

Trundle: Low bed on rollers which fits under a single bed.

STORAGE PIECES

Apothecary Chest: Chest with many small (or simulated) drawers adapted from early American druggists' chests.

Bachelor's Chest: Small-scale chest of drawers.

Chest-on-Chest: Two-sectioned chest, one mounted on top is usually slightly smaller.

Cheval Mirror: Mirror that swings between posts and is adjustable. Small versions, often with drawers in base, are used on chests or tables.

Commode: Originally an enclosed bedroom "chamber box," later combined with a wash stand. Now the term means night stand or console chest.

Credenza: Buffet-like storage cabinet, usually with doors.

Dry Sink: Originally water was added for washing dishes. Today's version: cupboard with open well in top, often lined with copper tray.

Highboy: Tall chest of drawers on legs (usually cabriole legs).

Hutch: Open-shelved storage piece on a base with cupboards and/or drawers.

Secretary: Desk with drawers below, open or closed bookshelves above.

CHAIRS

Captain's Chair: Type of Windsor, with saddle seat; often with low bentwood back and arms. Once used on ships, later in taverns. (Right)

Comb-back: Type of Windsor with spindles resembling an old-fashioned high comb.

Duxbury: See Windsor.

Hitchcock: Named for early Connecticut chair maker. Derives from a Sheraton design called "fancy chair"; usually has an oval top rail. Many are painted and decorated with stencils.

Ladder-Back: Popular design from 1750 to 1800. Back is ladder-shaped, with horizontal slats.

Lawson: Upholstered. Low-backed; arm is often set back at the front to accommodate a "T" cushion (seating cushion that extends forward and across front of arm). (Right)

Mate's Chair: Smaller than a Captain's style, with shorter arms.

Saddle Seat: Scooped away to side and back from central ridge, for more comfort. Resembles the pommel of a saddle.

Settle: All wood, often of Windsor design. In reality, a bench with arms, sometimes called a "Deacon's bench."

Tub: Upholstered. Small circular chair, rather like half a barrel.

Tuxedo: Upholstered. Arms are same height as back.

Windsor: Characterized by slender turned spindles, wooden saddle seat and turned, splayed or raked legs usually joined by stretcher at bottom. Also referred to as "Duxbury." (Right)

Wing: Upholstered. High side pieces (once used to ward off drafts).

TABLES

Butterfly: Has rounded drop leaves supported by wing brackets. (Right)

Candlestand: Small tripod, pedestal, or four legged table, used to hold candles and their drippings.

Cobbler's Bench: Originally a shoemaker's work seat with drawers for tools. Copied for cocktail and coffee tables.

Doughbox: Deep slope-sided box, once used for "raising" bread, adapted for occasional table with roomy storage compartment.

Drum: Round library or lamp table. Deep open or closed top (that suggests a drum) sometimes revolves on a pedestal base.

Gateleg: Has two drop leaves. Legs swing out like a gate to support the leaves when extended.

Harvest: Very long drop leaf table, usually with narrow leaves running entire length. Originally used for feeding harvest "hands."

Lazy Susan: Round, revolving wood tray for center of dining table.

Pedestal: Single turned center pedestal supports table, or pedestal may have tripod base. Extension tables often have two pedestals for firm support when extended.

Pembroke: Small rectangular table with two drop leaves, shallow drawer.

Step: Originally made to reach high bookshelves. Adapted today, keeping the steps, as two- or three-level end table.

Trestle: Long rectangular top on two vertical supports. Informal.

DESIGN ELEMENTS

Apron: Structural support placed at right angles to underside of table or chair for decorative trim and to increase support.

Broken Pediment: A triangular top, from classical architecture, sometimes used on headboard, mirrors, tall chests or cabinets. Its sloping lines stop short of the peak, leaving a gap for an ornamental finial such as a turned knob or urn shape. (Above)

Cabriole Leg: Shape has a graceful "S" curve. (Right)

Cornice: A projecting molding used to give an architectural finish to the top edge of a chest, dresser or cabinet.

Dentil: A small rectangular block. Used in a row projecting like teeth under a cornice. A classic Greek form of ornamentation. (Above)

Fiddleback: Chair or bed back whose splat resembles a violin.

Fluting: Vertical channels carved into columns, as seen in ancient Greek architecture.

Gallery: Decorative railing around edge of table, shelf or tray.

Grill: Can be metal or wood, combined with glass for some cabinet doors.

Louvers: Fixed, shutter-like slats used for decorative door panels.

Mullion: Slender moulding dividing the panes of glass of doors.

Ogee Bracket Foot: Shaped like a bracket, with a double curve. (Right)

Spoonfoot: Simple flattish end of a cabriole or turned leg.

Stenciling: Pattern applied to furniture by painting over thin metal or heavy paper cut-outs.

Stretcher: Support connecting legs of any piece of furniture; frequently turned for decorative interest.

FINISH

Antiquing and/or Distressing: Method of treating wood to lend an old appearance or "patina." This may be done with chemicals, paint or stain. It adds a worn-away look to the color and reduces the brilliance of the surface. Specking adds a soft look instead of continuous color.

CONSTRUCTION

Center Drawer Guide: Channel under center of the drawer rides over a guide on the case frame to prevent jamming and insure smooth operation.

Dovetail: Joint made by flared tongues of wood that interlock with shaped pieces of wood to hold front and back drawer corners securely. (Right)

Dowel: Round peg of wood that fits into corresponding hole to form a strong joint. Used originally instead of nails.

Floating Construction: Used for furniture made of solid woods; it permits top and side panels to expand or contract with changes of temperature and humidity, thus avoiding warping or cracking.

Mortise and Tenon: A tongue or projecting part of wood that fits into a corresponding rectangular hole or mortise (one of the most important joints in woodworking).

HARDWARE

Back Plate: A metal mount or escutcheon, on which the drawer handle or pull is mounted.

Bail Handle: Made of metal in the form of a half-loop.

Drop Handle: Pear- or tier-shaped pull, usually brass.

H and L Hinge: An early design, resembling the letters H and a connecting L, made originally of iron or brass.

2-21a. This Early American server with hutch top is typical of the furniture pieces of this period.

2-21b. A captain's chair with many turned parts.

HOW TO IDENTIFY COLONIAL FURNITURE:

One of the quickest ways to identify Colonial pieces is by the presence of turned elements, almost always in the legs (**a**). Simple balusters and the vase turnings found in Windsor chairs (**b**) are also good identification keys. Heavier pieces, such as the Goddard-type chest, (**c**) used short, thick legs with the curve on both the inside and outside. However, earlier pieces of this weight (**d**) had a simple variation of this leg with a curve on the inside only (**e**). Four-poster beds (**f**) are still popular in Colonial reproductions.

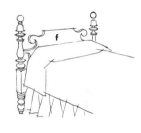

2-21c. Colonial furniture.

2-22a. The furniture in this Colonial dining room is made of maple and birch.

2-22b. A magazine-rack end table with an interesting design including a lift-top storage unit.

2-23a. The simple study is typical of Italian Provincial design. Desk and chairs are good illustrations of the leg design most commonly applied to this style. The simple curved arch in the book storage cabinet is also another characteristic.

2-24a. Note the marble inserts in this table top.

Italian Provincial

Italian Provincial is another style that is easily identified as a distinct grouping. Fig. 2-23. It gets its style from the craftsmen of the Italian provinces of the 18th and 19th centuries. The distinguishing feature is the square, tapered leg. In appearance, Italian Provincial has more in common with English or Traditional than with French Provincial. Marble is often used for table tops, and there are also some inlay, overlay, and fluting. Fig. 2-24. Common woods are

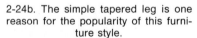

2-24b. The simple tapered leg is one reason for the popularity of this furniture style.

2-23b. This Italian Provincial dining room illustrates the delicate carving and clean, simple lines of this furniture style.

cherry and walnut, frequently finished with a distressed fruitwood appearance.

Spanish or Mediterranean

Spanish or Mediterranean furniture reflects the artistry of the Romance countries during the 17th and 18th centuries, with the added characteristics of Moorish Spain. Fig. 2-25. This style has many geometric shapes and unique design motifs. In addition to wood, Mediterranean and Spanish furniture utilizes a wide variety of materials such as leather, glass, metal, and ceramics.

2-25b. Spanish or Mediterranean design:
(a) Note the influence of Spanish knights in this accent design. (b) Fretwork (delicate cut-out surfaces) is shown in this chest. (c) Note the arched top of the headboard. (d) Metal is a common accent. (e) This chair is covered with leather and has a slightly heavy appearance. (f) This chest shows the use of geometric forms. (g) A simple table. (h) Table with a marble top. (i) Note the somewhat heavy appearance of this arm chair. (j) A good example of geometric design. Many such designs are popular in this furniture style.

a

b

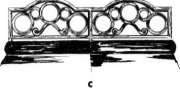

c

2-25a. Spanish or Mediterranean. This living-dining area shows the strong geometric shapes that are common to Spanish or Mediterranean furniture.

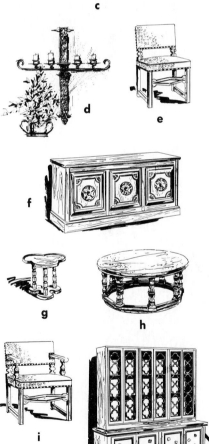

d

e

f

g

h

i

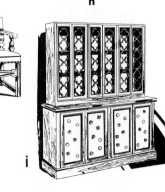

j

2-26. This Mediterranean table is completely covered with leather and has metal corners. It is a typical Moorish piece.

2-27. The arches of this snack table give it a Spanish appearance.

2-28. Much heavy carving is used on this book-shelf end table. Note the interesting hardware accents.

Fig. 2-26. There is a good deal of fretwork and other ornamentation. The most commonly used wood is pecan, finished in dark brown. Designs are borrowed from castles and old buildings of Spain and southern Italy. Shaped arches are used on mirrors, doors, and other parts to impart the Moorish appearance. Fig. 2-27. Carved door fronts, drawers, and frame openings look as if they came from age-old cathedrals. Fig. 2-28.

Modern or Contemporary

These terms can be confusing. One problem is that every style was modern or contemporary at one time. Furniture which is now described by these terms will seem the very opposite of modern at some time in the future. Another problem is that some authorities use the terms "Modern" and "Contemporary" to mean the same thing, while others do not. Despite these handicaps, this book will attempt to define and use these terms as precisely as possible.

The furniture which is often called Modern first became popular in the United States around the middle of the 1920's. The earliest Modern furniture had many harsh, square lines, and sharp angles. There were also round, inserted corners. The fronts of chests and beds often featured the "waterfall" design. This is the furniture we have come to think of as "modernistic."

Many would say that this early

2-29a. This colorful living room is a good illustration of Contemporary style. Clean-cut lines of tables and storage cabinet are examples of functional simplicity. The chair is Danish in influence with soft-curved back and interesting upholstered seat and back.

2-29b. A handsome combination display cabinet and desk. The chair shows the influence of the Danish design.

2-29c. A Contemporary two-drawer table desk made of teak.

2-29d. This Modern table with its clean lines is notable for its quiet elegance.

Modern style has already become dated. However, designers have improved upon the harshness of those early pieces and have developed a style which is widely accepted in America today. It is easy to see why this furniture fits our way of life. It is functional, simplified, and informal. Fig. 2-29. Pieces can be adapted to many different uses. For instance, a chest might be used in the living room, dining room, bedroom, or den. Heights, depths, and other measurements have been standardized so that many different arrangements can be made using the same pieces. Most good Modern is not sold in sets. Pieces can therefore be purchased as needed. It is most important to recognize *good* Modern because, unfortunately, there is a great deal of poor Modern on the market. Fig. 2-30.

HOW TO IDENTIFY MODERN FURNITURE:

Clean, unadorned legs are one of the most distinguishing characteristics of modern furniture. The tapered, round leg (**a**) is found quite often on sofas, chests and larger pieces. Tubular steel legs and supports (**b**) are used on occasional chairs and various forms of angle steel have been employed for pieces that are available in sections (**c**). Preformed wood and plastic seats and backs (**d**) are symbols of modern, as are heavy, plate glass (**e**) table tops that reveal underside construction. Sculptured lines (**f**) are becoming more evident in modern, too.

2-30. Modern furniture.

2-31a. A Contemporary office.

Some characteristics of good Modern are simple lines, excellent construction, good wood, and fine finish. Little or no ornamentation is to be found. Modern furniture is made from walnut, cherry, oak, and mahogany as well as a great variety of other woods. Often the woods are finished natural or with a soft hue or tone.

As mentioned, some authorities use the terms Modern and Contemporary to describe somewhat different furniture styles. Contemporary (with capital C) furniture would have some of the same characteristics as Modern—simplicity, informality—but it would show the influence of other cultures and traditions. Fig. 2-31. Scandinavian furniture, with its clean, functional lines, is an illustration of this. Fig. 2-32. (The popular style commonly called

2-31b. Note the variety of shapes and designs in Modern or Contemporary furniture.

2-32. A lounge chair and ottoman distinctly Danish in flavor.

Danish Modern would actually be classed as Contemporary.) French or Italian influences are also found in some Contemporary pieces. The style shown in Fig. 2-33 has heavy hardware. There are deep picture-frame moldings on otherwise straight-line cases and a play of dark and light tones in the glowing finish of the pecky pecan veneers. Italian elements can be seen in its design. Notice the similarities (such as use of rectangles) and differences between this Contemporary piece and the Italian Provincial table (Fig. 2-24).

Some Contemporary furniture, influenced by Chinese, is rich in Oriental design. Fig. 2-34. Still other pieces express informality together with elements borrowed from the American and Mediterranean design. All Contemporary designs are functional. As with Modern, some pieces such as chests can be interchanged among different types of rooms.

2-33. Here a Contemporary piece borrows much of its interest from the Italian style influence.

2-34. These tables show Chinese influence.

UNIT 3 Furniture Design

Furniture must be well designed if it is to be *useful, attractive,* and *convenient.* Fig. 3-1. The furniture products shown in this book are good examples of well-designed products. Some are student designed and built while others are examples of what the best industrial furniture designers have produced. Fig. 3-2. Look carefully at each of the illustrations, for in doing so you will be studying good design.

Basic Rules of Good Design. It is almost impossible to give specific rules that will insure good design in a piece of furniture. Often, the mere use of rules will fail to produce a well-designed piece. The *taste* or *feeling* for good design can be acquired by observing quality in all manufactured products and by adhering to certain fundamentals.

3-1. Good design in Contemporary furniture. Note the simplicity of design. The table is 29″ high, the top 32″ x 32″. The side chairs are 19″ wide, 22″ deep, and 31½″ high.

3-2. One of these tables was made by student craftsmen; the other by a commercial manufacturer. They are both of good design. Can you tell which one is a school product?

3-3. This combination desk and storage unit was designed for usefulness. Note the built-in telephone. This is truly a functional piece.

The first point to remember is that an article is well designed only if it meets the needs for its intended use. Fig. 3-3. For example, a chair must be comfortable to sit in and a table must be the right size and height for its particular use. There are standards for most of these measurements.

A second point is that the materials selected must be appropriate. Fig. 3-4. Certain kinds of furniture woods possess excellent qualities of beauty and durability. Other materials are satisfactory only for the internal parts of furniture.

A third point is that the methods of construction must be fundamentally sound. Flimsy construction is in itself poor design.

3-4a. This chest of drawers is made of several different materials. The base can be of aluminum or bronze. The front, sides, and back can be of oiled teak, oak, or rosewood; and the top can be of stone or leather insert. The basic dimensions are 91¾'' wide x 22¾'' deep x 28⅛'' high.

3-4b. Note the many different materials effectively used in this desk and chair. Wood, plastic laminates, metal, and leather are only a few of the basic materials.

33

3-5a. This slide-top cabinet displays not only good quality materials but also fine construction. Its overall size is 75″ long x 21″ wide x 28″ high.

A chair that wobbles or a table that tips is of little use. Fig. 3-5.

A fourth point is the appearance or visual aspect of the piece. Fig. 3-6. This varies greatly, as explained in the previous unit, on furniture styles. Fig. 3-7. If the pieces are true to their style, they are likely to be attractive and to represent the principles of good design. When a questionable or non-existent style is concocted, however, a poor design usually results.

3-5b. Note the fine construction of the slide top with the hanging file detail.

3-5c. Here you see the adjustable shelf compartment in the slide-top cabinet.

3-5d. The removable tray detail of the slide-top cabinet. Note the exposed finger joints at the corners. These joints add both beauty and strength to the product.

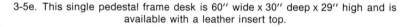

3-5e. This single pedestal frame desk is 60″ wide x 30″ deep x 29″ high and is available with a leather insert top.

3-5f. Drawer construction in the desk. Note the vinyl-covered pencil tray and the metal side guide and slide.

3-7a-b. Compare these candlestick tables. They are designed for the same use or function; however, one is Early American or Colonial in design, the others Contemporary. While the use is the same, the appearance is very different.

3-6a-b-c. Three styles of record cabinets of identical size and shape. Each is given a different style by changing the fronts and the construction of the legs or base.

Elements of Design

Browse through this book and look at some of the examples of fine furniture and accessories. While all appear different in design and beauty, they have certain things in common. These are the elements of design that you or the furniture designer must use in designing a piece of furniture.

Lines. In design, lines are what you must put on a piece of paper in order to illustrate what you have in mind. A line is the path of a point as it moves through space. Lines can be straight, curved, S-shaped, circular, or spiral. Fig. 3-8. Lines can give a feeling of action or motion. Fig. 3-9. They also give shape to a product. Fig. 3-10.

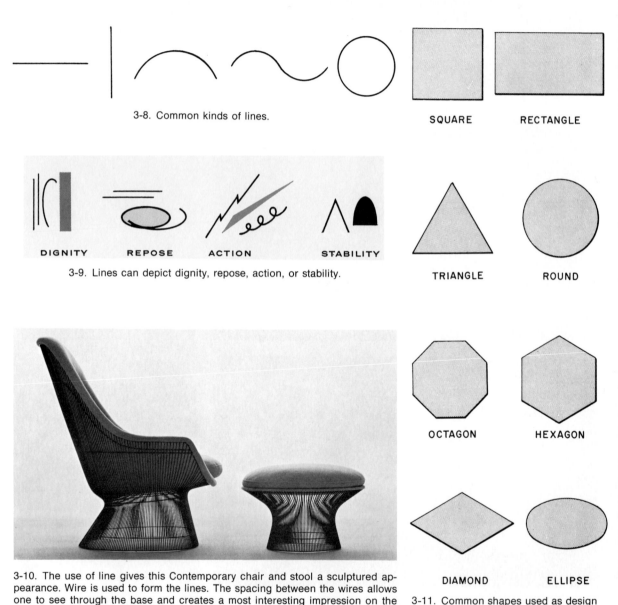

3-8. Common kinds of lines.

SQUARE   RECTANGLE

DIGNITY   REPOSE   ACTION   STABILITY

3-9. Lines can depict dignity, repose, action, or stability.

TRIANGLE   ROUND

OCTAGON   HEXAGON

3-10. The use of line gives this Contemporary chair and stool a sculptured appearance. Wire is used to form the lines. The spacing between the wires allows one to see through the base and creates a most interesting impression on the eye.

DIAMOND   ELLIPSE

3-11. Common shapes used as design elements in furniture.

3-12a. Common shapes for table tops: square, round, and rectangular.

3-12b. Here the triangle is used as a basic shape for tables.

Shapes. An understanding of shapes is basic to furniture design. The common shapes are square, rectangular, round, triangular, diamond, elliptical, hexagonal, and octagonal. Fig. 3-11. We see all of these represented in fine furniture. Fig. 3-12. There are also many irregular shapes that can be used to enrich a furniture design.

Mass (or Solids) and Form. Lines and shape make up mass and form which give an object the three-dimensional appearance. Fig. 3-13. All of the basic materials you work with—lumber, plywood, hardboard, and plastic laminates—have solid shapes. Shapes produce the form of a product.

3-12c. This unusual table of wood and glass is made with parts that are irregular in shape.

3-13. Simple shapes, such as the square and circle, make up this cube-form occasional table.

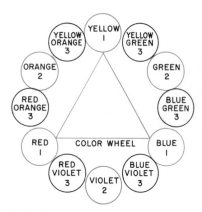

3-14. The color wheel. Note the primary (No. 1), secondary (No. 2), and tertiary colors (No. 3). Colors that are next to each other on the wheel are called analogous colors. Sometimes an eye-pleasing color scheme can be arranged simply by using neighboring colors. At other times contrasting colors from across the wheel are introduced. Study the examples in the following full-color illustrations. What you learn can be put to use in selecting wood-finish tones and upholstery fabrics.

3-15b. This room is dominated by the red side of the color wheel. It uses accents from across the wheel. Colors directly across the wheel from each other, such as red and green, are called complementary colors.

Color. Color creates a mood or atmosphere and is a most important element of furniture design. It can be natural or applied. Colors can be added to wood and are also used in upholstery, hardware, and other furnishings. A color wheel shows the basic primary, secondary, and tertiary colors. Fig. 3-14. All colors or hues are blends of the primary and secondary colors. Color schemes may be of three types—namely, contrasting, similar, or monochromatic (in which the various values and hues of one color are used). Color, when properly used, has great aesthetic value. Fig. 3-15.

Tone and Texture. Tone is a contrast between light and dark, or shadows and brightness, on a surface. When we look at an object, what we really see is light reflected from it. Fig. 3-16. Texture is the way a surface feels to the touch and how it reflects color. Fig. 3-17. Every material has a natural texture. Textures can also be added to a surface by carving or by applying paints, finishes, or overlay materials. Fig. 3-17.

3-15a. In this room yellow and green are the predominating colors. Used as accents are yellow-orange (gold) which is analogous to yellow, and red, which is directly across the color wheel from green.

3-15c. Blue walls and accents in this room are strikingly contrasted with furniture and carpet in tones almost directly across the color wheel.

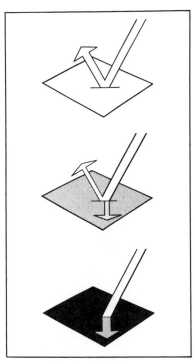

3-16. Reflection and absorption of light by white, gray, and black surfaces. The darker the color, the greater the absorption of light.

3-15d. This room is done chiefly in tones from red through yellow-green. These colors are grouped around less than half of the color wheel and involve some analogous combinations such as the yellow lamp with the yellow-green sofa, and the red-orange china with the red walls and chair.

3-17a. Different materials such as wood, cloth, and metal reflect light in different ways.

3-17b. The hand-carved drawer fronts of this chest give unusual texture to the product.

table with bulky ones is in poor proportion. Sometimes only a slight variation in the size of parts will influence proportion.

● *The parts must be in harmony with one another.* Many times different materials are combined, or different shapes are put together. However, the finished article must appear to be made up of parts that belong together naturally. *Unity* is another term that is often used to express this idea. Fig. 3-19.

● *Each furniture piece needs a point of emphasis.* This may be the over-all appearance of the piece itself, the fine finish, a simple piece of hardware, or some point in its construction. Fig. 3-20.

Whenever possible, good design usually takes advantage of the natural texture of materials. Texture in woods can also be achieved by sandblasting the surface. Sometimes natural defects like knots, holes, and other irregularities add interest to the wood texture.

Principles of Design

All good design follows a few basic rules:

● *The parts must be in balance.* Balance is achieved when the object appears to have equal weight on either side. If parts are *symmetrical*, the result is *formal balance.* If the parts are not symmetrical but still the piece has the appearance of *being at rest,* this is called *informal balance.* Fig. 3-18.

● *The article must be in good proportion.* A large chair with spindly legs or a dainty coffee

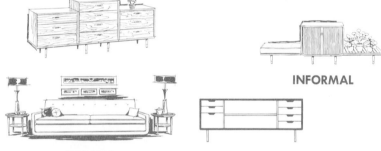

INFORMAL

FORMAL

3-18a. These drawings illustrate formal and informal balance.

3-18b. Table and chairs which illustrate pure formal balance.

40

3-18c. This wall cabinet is a good illustration of informal balance. Note that the overall appearance is one of equal weight on either side although different shapes and kinds of cabinets are used.

Common Mistakes

The most common mistakes made in furniture design in the home and school shop which result in a homemade appearance are:

• *A definite style of furniture is not selected.* Too often an individual will design a piece that represents no style but is rather a combination of many styles.

• *A basic principle of design is ignored.* If a part is out of balance or proportion, the total effect is spoiled.

• *A poor selection of materials is made.* It is difficult to make quality furniture from cheaper woods. Only good furniture woods should be chosen. It is usually faddish and cheap to combine woods of highly contrasting color quality.

3-19. Two entirely different kinds of chairs. However, both have harmony and are equally suitable for rest.

41

The wood must also be chosen for a particular style of furniture. For example, Early American is made of cherry, birch, maple, or pine.

• *The beginner often over-decorates.* Surface decoration should be used sparingly. Most modern pieces have little or no surface decoration but depend upon the natural beauty of the wood. Grooving, beading, fluting, inlaying, and other embellishments are most effective when used sparingly and in their proper places.

• *The finish is often poor.* A smooth, even finish is a characteristic of good furniture. One which is applied irregularly or which unintentionally leaves an uneven color or surface texture is definitely defective. (Some finishes, such as distressing, are intended to leave the surface uneven, but this must be done carefully or the result will look amateurish.)

3-20. The point of emphasis on this clock is obvious. The face and hands are what attract the eye.

3-21. A one-piece dip tray 12½" in diameter.

3-24. A contemporary table or bench of leg-and-rail construction; it is 54" long x 21" wide x 15" in height.

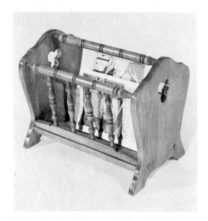

3-22. Notice the number of duplicate parts in this magazine rack. The size is 18" long x 12½" wide x 15" high.

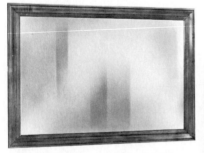

3-23. This mirror frame is typical of frame construction.

3-25. These record cabinets are good examples of the box.

Types of Furniture Construction

When you observe many pieces of furniture and accessories, you find that they can be classified into a few basic types. These are as follows:

● *One-Member Piece.* The simplest of all is the one-member accessory such as a turned bowl, a cutting board, or a carved ornament. Fig. 3-21.

● *Duplicate Part.* This type has two or more identical parts. Sometimes they can be cut and shaped simultaneously, or one part can be made first and then duplicated. Fig. 3-22. A tray with identical sides or ends, and a simple whatnot shelf are common examples.

● *Frame.* The frame is an assembly of four parts used for picture frames, mirrors, bulletin boards, and in many parts of furniture. It is joined together at the corners with reinforced miter or lap joints. Fig. 3-23.

● *Skeleton or Leg and Rail.* Most chairs and tables are of this kind of construction, usually consisting of four legs and four or more rails. Fig. 3-24. The rails are joined to the legs with a dowel-butt joint or mortise-and-tenon joint.

● *Box.* The box is made up of four sides with a bottom and a top. The corners may be joined with a simple butt, rabbet, or variation of the miter joint. The space inside a box may be divided by partitions. A drawer is a simple box. Fig. 3-25.

● *Case Construction.* This is simply a box turned on its side or end. Almost all bookcases, radio cabinets, and most built-ins are of case construction. The back is usually installed by cutting a rabbet around the inside. The front sometimes is trimmed with molding. If solid shelves are installed, a form of dado joint is made. Doors can be hung in the openings. Fig. 3-26.

● *Carcass.* This consists of an enclosed cabinet usually having one or more doors and drawers. Parts are often of panel construction. Fig. 3-27.

3-26. This bookcase is 32″ wide x 11″ deep x 51″ in height.

3-27. Early American server. It is 17½″ deep x 33″ wide x 31″ high.

UNIT 4 Designing a Product

4-1a. This modern office desk is made of black walnut. The simple lines illustrate the good characteristics of this furniture style.

The first question that comes to mind is "What style of furniture should I build?" Too much of what is made by the beginning craftsman has no style, design, or character. Strangely enough, it is just as easy to build good, high-quality furniture as it is to make junk.

The craftsman must first decide on the style or period, as explained in Unit 2. Figures 4-1 through 4-5 show examples of well-designed pieces in several of the most important styles. The architectural style of a home will influence the decision about the style of furnishings for the home.

43

CONTEMPORARY HOME

TRADITIONAL HOME

RANCH STYLE HOME

4-1c. The design of furniture should match the style of the home in which it will be used.

4-1b. This Contemporary desk has both wood and metal construction.

4-2. The characteristics of good Modern in a lamp table. Top is 30″ x 30″, height is 21″.

4-3. A Contemporary table which is a good example of the influence Chinese culture has had on furniture styling.

4-4. This four-drawer, Early American desk is well designed. Top is 48″ x 18½″ and it is 30″ in height.

4-6. This oiled walnut clock case is both an interesting and useful accessory.

4-5. French Provincial, Mediterranean and many of the Traditional styles feature curves and carved work that make them very difficult to construct in the small cabinet shop. This globe stand with underparts of selected solid oak illustrates the complexity of this type of construction.

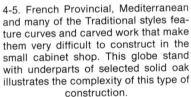

4-7. An Early American drop-leaf table.

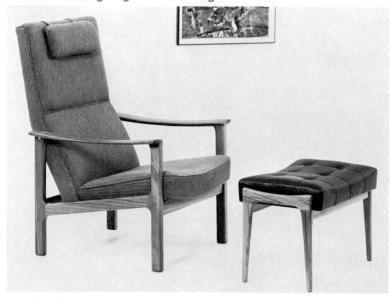

4-8. High back chair and ottoman of teak.

Kinds of Items to Build

The second question that comes to mind is "What should I build?" Items that can be built may be grouped as follows:

1. ACCESSORIES. These include trays, lamps, small shelves, clocks, carved ornaments, shadow boxes. Fig. 4-6.

2. TABLES, including coffee or cocktail, end, game, lamp, snack, dining. Fig. 4-7.

3. STOOLS, benches, and chairs. Fig. 4-8.

4. BOOKCASES. Fig. 4-9.

5. CABINETS, including dish, radio, television, storage, and all-purpose. Fig. 4-10.

6. CHESTS AND DESKS. Fig. 4-11.

There are many others, of course, but these are the ones with which we will be concerned here. The *beginner* will probably want to start by making some accessory. The *craftsman with some experience* will probably tackle a simple table, bookcase, or cabinet. The *more advanced woodworker* may try a chair, chest, or desk. Several suggestions for each of these groups can be found in this book.

Another question often asked is, "Should I design my own furniture?" *When making your first*

4-9. These book storage cases possess great simplicity of design.

4-10. This Early American maple and birch dry sink measures 40″ wide x 20″ deep x 35″ high.

pieces, it is probably better to follow some existing design, in some cases making small changes or adaptations to fit particular needs. The size may be changed slightly, for example, provided that the change does not upset the proportion of the piece. For the *more advanced craftsman,* the answer to that question would be to design your own furniture. With close attention to the principles of good design, you can achieve very satisfying and individual results. To help in designing your own furniture, Figs. 4-12a and b show the standard sizes of certain pieces.

Sometimes you will see a picture of a furniture piece you would like to make. With careful planning you can design one that is very similar to it, following this procedure:

1. Make a full-size outline of the over-all size of the piece

In most cases, the width, length, and height will be available. This outline can be made in the same way as you would start an orthographic projection, cabinet, or isometric drawing.

2. Determine the approximate scale of the picture or sketch

By measuring the full-size outline and then the actual picture, the approximate scale can be determined. For example, if the over-all height of the object is 36 inches, and the height on the picture measures $1\frac{1}{2}$ inches, the scale is about $\frac{1}{2}$ inch to the foot. This scale can then be followed to determine the approximate size of all the major parts. Remember, however, that these dimensions

4-11. Bedroom and study in Early American with highly functional desks and chests.

will be only approximate. You yourself will need to figure out the exact size of the furniture in order to insure good proportion in the finished piece.

Another method of determining size is with the following procedure. In most cases, the three major dimensions of height, depth, and width are given. Proceed as follows:

● Fasten the picture to the left side of a piece of paper. Fig. 4-12c. See page 49.

Item	Height	Depth–Width	Length
Tables			
Coffee or Cocktail	14″ to 18″	18″ to 24″	36″ to 60″
Card	29″	30″	30″
Game	30″	30″	30″
Writing	30″	24″	36″ to 40″
Kitchen	30″	30″	42″
End	27″	15″	24″
Dining	29″ to 32″	42″	42″ to 70″
Chairs			
Desk	16½″	15″ to 18″	15″ to 18″
Dining	16″ to 18″	15″ to 18″	15″ to 18″
Cabinets			
Sectional	30″	12″ to 14″	Any
China Storage	54″ to 60″	20″ to 22″	Any
Kitchen	36″	12″ to 24″	Any
Chests	32″ to 54″	24″	Any
Bookcases	32″ to 82″	18″	Any
Desks	30″	24″ to 30″	40″ to 60″

4-12a. Chart of typical furniture sizes.

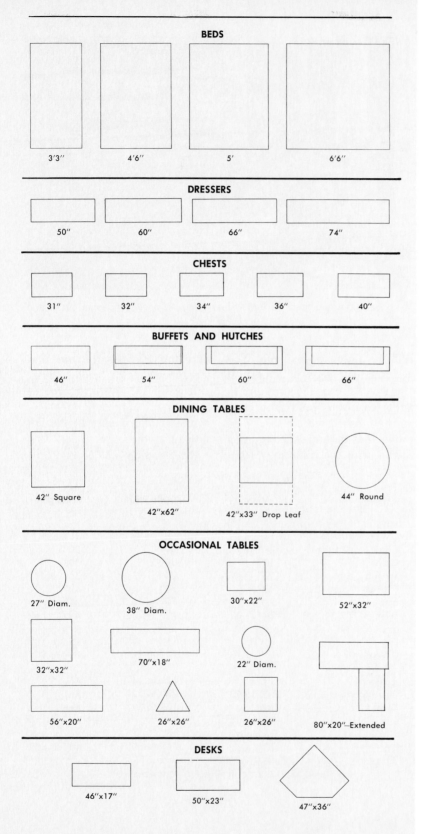

BEDS

3'3"   4'6"   5'   6'6"

DRESSERS

50"   60"   66"   74"

CHESTS

31"   32"   34"   36"   40"

BUFFETS AND HUTCHES

46"   54"   60"   66"

DINING TABLES

42" Square   42"x62"   42"x33" Drop Leaf   44" Round

OCCASIONAL TABLES

27" Diam.   38" Diam.   30"x22"   52"x32"

32"x32"   70"x18"   22" Diam.

56"x20"   26"x26"   26"x26"   80"x20"—Extended

DESKS

46"x17"   50"x23"   47"x36"

4-12b. Typical furniture sizes related to shapes.

• Use a T-square to project straight lines from the edges of the furniture piece.

• Assume that the overall height is 30″. Select a scale in which 30 units in length will fit diagonally between the two horizontal lines. Place the first division point of the scale on the top line and the last on the bottom line.

• Project lines from the photo until each line intersects the diagonal line for each dimension needed. This will give you an easy count of the number of units or inches for that part.

• The same method can be used to secure the width dimensions.

• The depth dimension, such as the depth of a chest, is usually a single measurement.

• *Make a working drawing* of the product to be built.

• Complete a *materials list* and a *plan of procedure.*

• *Lay out the sizes of each part on the full-size drawing.* Determine the best method of joining the various parts, remembering that there are many kinds of woodworking joints.

• Now, *"Plan your work, and then work your plan,"* as described in the following sections of the book.

In designing a piece of furniture for yourself, follow these simple rules:

1. Determine your needs. (What is the function of the furniture?) Make only what you can use. Is your real need a table, desk, or bookcase? Remember, a need must exist. Fig. 4-13.

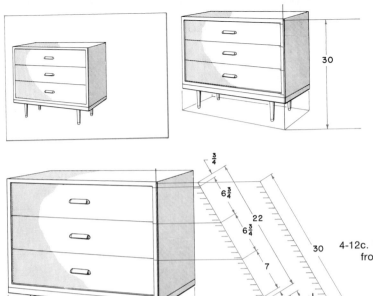

2. Make sketches of the product. The designer (you) dreams and draws (sketches). Fig. 4-14. The designer must understand furniture styles, materials, and construction. Fig. 4-15. See page 50.

3. Select the best idea from the sketches.

4. Develop the final sketch into a working drawing and/or model.

4-12c. Determining the size of an object from a photograph or sketch.

4-13. Perhaps you would like to build a new coffee table for a room such as this one. Fig. 4-17 suggests a table you might build.

4-14. When you design, you must put your ideas on paper.

4-15a. A table can be square, round, rectangular, or almost any shape.

4-15b. If you decide to design a square, Contemporary coffee table, you might want to make sketches of different ones.

Fig. 4-16. A model provides an opportunity to study the piece for possible revisions. Also develop a plan of procedure. Fig. 4-17.

5. Select the materials (woods, wood products, metals, plastics, hardware, etc.) and the finishes to be used.

6. Construct the product following good techniques.

7. Apply a good finish.

8. Judge the article to determine if it fits your needs and is satisfactory in every other respect.

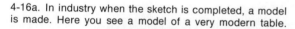

4-16a. In industry when the sketch is completed, a model is made. Here you see a model of a very modern table.

4-16b. The table (Fig. 4-16a) might look like this when it is built.

4-17a. A sketch of the table selected.

PROCEDURE:
1. Cut the top to size.
2. Cut the rails to size, miter the ends and cut the groove for the top, making sure the groove allows at least ⅟₃₂″ clearance for expansion of the top.
3. Chamfer the top of the rails on a jointer, then drill the holes for the dowels.
4. Assemble top and side rails, gluing the corner joints and clamping firmly. Do not glue the top.
5. Taper the inside of the legs on a saw, using a taper fixture, and taper the leg thickness on a jointer.
6. Cut the legs to exact length and angle, and cut the dadoes for the corner blocks.
7. Cut the corner blocks and glue blocks to correct shape. Fasten the corner blocks and legs in place with glue and screws. And glue three glue blocks to each rail.
8. Sand thoroughly and apply oak finish.

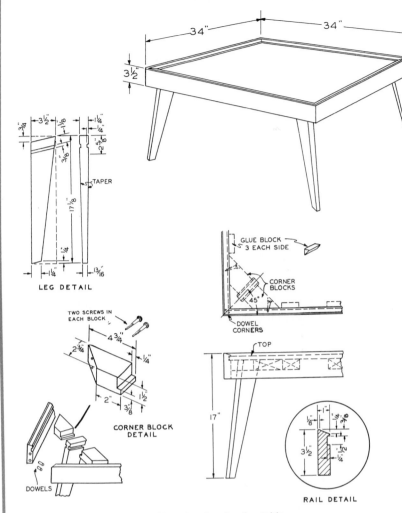

4-17b. Working drawing for the table.

IMPORTANT: All dimensions listed below, except for length of dowel, are FINISHED size.

No. of Pieces	Part name	Thickness	Width	Length	Wood
1	Top	½″	32⁷⁄₁₆″	32⁷⁄₁₆″	Oak Plywood
4	Rails	1″	3½″	34″	Oak
4	Legs	1¼″	3½″	17⅛″	Oak
8	Corner Blocks	1½″	2¾″	4¾″	White Pine
12	Glue Blocks	¾″	1½″	2½″	White Pine
1	Dowel	½″		12″	
16	1¾″-12 Flat-Head Wood Screws.				

4-17c. Bill of materials and procedure for making the table.

4-17d. Here the table has fulfilled its need.

UNIT 5 Occupations in the Furniture Industry

The furniture industry offers a wide variety of opportunities for anyone interested in working with tools, materials, machines, and ideas to produce the furniture needed in such places as homes, offices, and laboratories.

Furniture building is a big business with over four billion dollars' worth produced each year. Approximately one-third of a million people produce this furniture in over 5,500 plants throughout the United States. Over two-thirds of all these furniture factories employ fewer than twenty persons. Fig. 5-1.

The fifty largest furniture companies in the United States produce over one-third of all the case goods, one-quarter of the upholstered, and over fifty percent of all the metal furniture. Most furniture manufacturers are located in the South Atlantic states and in the East, North, and Central areas of the United States.

The wide variety of occupations in the furniture industry can be seen by the following list:

ADJUSTER
ANTIQUER
ARM MAKER
ART METAL-CHAIR ASSEMBLER
ASSEMBLER, METAL FURNITURE
ASSEMBLY INSPECTOR
ASSEMBLY-LINE INSPECTOR
BABY-CARRIAGE ASSEMBLER
BACK MAKER
BACK PADDER (UPHOLSTERER HELPER)
BACK-PANEL PADDER
BAND EDGER (VENEER-EDGE BANDER)
BANDING-MACHINE OPERATOR (BANDER)
BASE ASSEMBLY MAN
BENCH HAND
BENCH-SHEARS OPERATOR
BOXING-MACHINE OPERATOR
BRUSH STAINER
CABINET ASSEMBLER I
CABINET ASSEMBLER II

CARVER, HAND (WOOD CARVER, HAND)
CASE FITTER
CHAIR ASSEMBLER
CHAIR CANER
CHAIR INSPECTOR
CHAIR MAKER
CHAIR UPHOLSTERER (CHAIR TRIMMER)
CHUCKING-AND-BORING MACHINE OPERATOR
CLEANER, FURNITURE
CORNER-BRACE-BLOCK MACHINE OPERATOR
COVER INSPECTOR
COVER MAKER
CUPBOARD BUILDER
CUSHION-COVER INSPECTOR
CUSHION MAKER
DECORATOR
DESK ASSEMBLER
DIPPER AND DRIER
DISTRESSER
DOOR MAKER
DOUBLE-END-TRIMMER AND BORING-MACHINE OPERATOR
DRAWER BUILDER
EXAMINING-CHAIR ASSEMBLER
FINISHED-STOCK INSPECTOR
FINISH INSPECTOR
FINISH PATCHER
FITTER
FIXTURE DESIGNER
FOREMAN
FORMICA TABLE-TOP-MOLDING WRAPPER
FRAME MAKER
FURNITURE ASSEMBLER
FURNITURE DESIGNER
FURNITURE REPRODUCER
GLASS INSTALLER
GLUE-JOINTER HELPER
GLUE-SIZE-MACHINE OPERATOR
GRAINING-ROLLER MAKER
HARDWARE ASSEMBLER
HIGHLIGHTER
HYDRAULIC-CHAIR ASSEMBLER

5-1. Many people work in business and office occupations in the furniture industries.

INSPECTOR

LAMINATING-MACHINE
  OPERATOR

LAMINATOR, HAND

LEATHER TOOLER

LOCK ASSEMBLER

MARQUETRY WORKER

MODEL BUILDER

OVEN TENDER

PADDER, CUSHION

PAINTER, PANEL EDGE

PANEL MAKER

PATTERNMAKER

PLASTIC-TOP INSTALLER

RADIO-AND-TELEVISION-CABINET
  INSPECTOR

RAIL MAKER

RATTAN WORKER

REED WORKER

REPAIRMAN, WOOD FURNITURE

RIPPER

SATIN FINISHER

SEAT ASSEMBLER

SEWING-MACHINE OPERATOR

SHAPER

SHELLAC PATCHER

SIDE-PANEL PADDER

SKIRT MAKER

SLIP-SEAT COVERER

SMALL PARTS ASSEMBLER

SOFA INSPECTOR

SORTER, UPHOLSTERY PARTS

SPRING ASSEMBLER

SPRING COVERER

SPRINGER

STAINER

STAIN WIPER

STAPLER, MACHINE

STEAM CLEANER

STENCILER

STOCK-PARTS INSPECTOR

SUBASSEMBLY MAN (TABLE-TOP
  ASSEMBLER)

TABLE AND DESK FINISHER

TABLE ASSEMBLER

TABLE MAKER

TRIMMING ASSEMBLER

UPHOLSTERER

UPHOLSTERY CLEANER

UPHOLSTERY CUTTER

UPHOLSTERY REPAIRMAN

UPHOLSTERY TRIMMER

VACUUM-SPINDLE SANDER

VARNISH DIPPER

VARNISH PATCHER

VENEER MATCHER

WASHCOAT WIPER

WEBBING TACKER

WELT SEWER

WICKER SORTER

WICKER WORKER

WILLOW WORKER

WIPER

WIRE-BORDER ASSEMBLER

ZIPPER SETTER

Following are brief descriptions of a few of the major occupations. (For more detailed descriptions, refer to the *Dictionary of Occupational Titles,* published by the United States Government.)

A. Professional

FURNITURE DESIGNER. Fig. 5-2. Designs a line of furniture or individual pieces for manufacture, according to knowledge of design

5-2a. The furniture designer is responsible for developing ideas into a line of furniture acceptable to the public. He or she must understand tools, materials, processes, and products.

53

5-2b. Several designers worked long hours to develop this beautiful line of furniture inspired by Spanish Mediterranean influence.

trends, offerings of competition, production costs, capability of production facilities, and characteristics of company's traditional market.

WOOD TECHNOLOGIST. Conducts research in seasoning, preservation, and utilization of wood and its by-products.

FURNITURE REPRODUCER. Prepares working drawings and templates of antique or custom furniture to facilitate reproduction.

B. Skilled Trades and Technical Occupations

CABINETMAKER. Fig. 5-3. Constructs and repairs wooden articles, such as store fixtures, office equipment, cabinets, and high-grade furniture, using woodworking machines and handtools.

FURNITURE FINISHER. Fig. 5-4. Finishes or refinishes damaged, worn, or used furniture or new high-grade furniture to specified color or finish, utilizing knowledge of wood properties, finishes, and furniture styling.

5-3. A cabinetmaker is an all-around skilled woodworker.

5-4. Furniture finishers must know how to apply all types of finishes.

5-5. An upholsterer finishing a furniture piece.

5-6. A millwright using special equipment to sharpen a circular saw blade.

5-7. People who feed materials into machines have relatively routine jobs in the furniture industry.

FURNITURE UPHOLSTERER (furniture repairer; upholsterer; upholstery repairer). Fig. 5-5. Repairs and rebuilds upholstered furniture, using hand tools and knowledge of fabrics and upholstery methods.

MILLWRIGHT. Installs machinery and equipment according to layout plans, blueprints, and other drawings in an industrial establishment. Also sharpens saws and other cutting tools. Fig. 5-6.

CARVER, HAND. Carves ornamental designs into wooden furniture parts, using hand tools and woodworking machines.

C. Semi-Skilled Jobs

WOODWORKING-MACHINE FEEDER. Fig. 5-7. Feeds wood stock on conveyors, into hoppers, or between rollers of woodworking machines that saw, sand, bore, or shape wooden articles.

WOODWORKING-MACHINE OPERATOR. Fig. 5-8. Operates one or more hand- or power-fed woodworking machines to surface, size, or joint lumber or to cut tongues, grooves, bevels, beads, or molding patterns.

5-8. Machine operators have an opportunity to gain experience which will qualify them for more challenging jobs.

DISCUSSION TOPICS

Section One—DESIGNING, AND PLANNING

Unit 1. Building Good Furniture

1. List the steps to be followed in building good furniture.

2. Discuss the differences in working qualities between furniture woods and plywoods.

3. Why is an accurate bill of materials necessary in planning good furniture?

4. Tell why it is important to have the right kinds of machines and tools for making furniture.

5. What happens when a piece of wood for furniture is cut too small?

6. Why does today's craftsman have an advantage over the craftsman of earlier years in finishing his furniture piece?

Unit 2. Furniture Styles and Periods

1. Why are many of the period pieces of furniture named after kings and queens?

2. Name the "big four" of the 18th century designers.

3. Which Traditional furniture design was made by an American cabinetmaker? Explain.

4. Why does French Provincial furniture have small scratches in the finish?

5. Explain why it is difficult to construct French Provincial furniture.

6. What were the common woods used in Early American and Colonial furniture?

7. What are the identifying characteristics of Colonial furniture?

8. What is the difference between Modern and modernistic furniture?

9. Is Modern furniture sold in sets, such as a bedroom or dining room set? Explain.

10. What are the characteristics of Italian Provincial furniture?

11. Why are many different materials used in Spanish furniture?

Unit 3. Furniture Design

1. Explain why the first principle of good design is that an article be functional or made for use.

2. Should a piece of Modern furniture be made of pine? Why?

3. What is the difference between formal and informal balance?

4. List some of the common mistakes found in furniture made in home and school shops.

5. What are the elements of design?

6. What kind of furniture construction is a carved wall ornament?

7. A knick-knack shelf with sides that are identical represents what kind of furniture?

8. The frame around a bulletin board takes what kind of joint?

9. Give another name for leg-and-rail construction.

10. A silver chest is a good example of what kind of construction?

11. When a box is turned on its side or end it is called what kind of construction?

12. The most complicated construction involves a furniture piece with drawers and doors. Name it.

Unit 4. Designing a Product

1. Name the most popular woods for Modern furniture manufacture.

2. List five different furniture items that can be built.

3. What is the correct height for a card table?

4. What is the range in height for a good dining-room table?

5. Are dining-room chairs all the same height? Explain.

6. Tell how to design a piece of furniture from a picture or sketch.

Unit 5. Occupations in the Furniture Industry

1. How many people are employed in the furniture industry?

2. Where are most furniture factories located?

3. Describe the work of a furniture designer.

4. What does a cabinetmaker do?

5. Name two semi-skilled jobs in the furniture industry.

EXTRA CREDIT ACTIVITIES

1. Write a report on the history of a furniture style.

2. Design an accessory such as a basic wall shelf in each of the four main styles of furniture.

3. Report on the work of one of the leading furniture designers in the United States.

Section

2

Materials

The basic raw material for most furniture is typified by this cedar log. From it, not only the lumber, but plywood, veneer, particle board, and hardboard are produced. All the beautiful wood furniture shown in this book began as logs. (Evans Products Company)

UNIT 6 Materials for Furniture Construction

Three basic materials are used in the manufacture of furniture, namely, wood, plastic, and metal. Fig. 6-1. However, wood is used almost universally for fine furniture because:

- It is easily worked.
- It is highly decorative.

- It is a poor conductor of heat; therefore, normal changes in air temperature do not make wood unpleasantly hot or cold to the touch.
- It is comparatively noiseless under movement or impact.
- It is easily repaired.

- Wood pieces can be easily fastened together with nails, screws, dowels, and glue.

Parts of a Tree

The three main parts of a tree are roots, trunk, and crown. Fig. 6-2. The trunk is cut into logs which are further processed into solid lumber and veneers for plywood. Other parts of the tree are cut into chips for making particle board and hardboard.

Parts of a Log. Fig. 6-2 shows the parts of a log. The center is called the pith. Around this are annual rings which form the grain of the lumber. The dark rings show the *summer growth*, when the tree grows slowly; the light rings show the *spring growth*, when the tree grows rapidly. The center part of the log around the pith is called the *heartwood*, which is darker in color, while the outer area is called the *sapwood*, which is lighter in color. The rays running at tangents from the center or pith are called *medullary rays*. These are prominent in some woods—oak for instance—while in others they are less noticeable. The outside of the log, of course, is the *bark*.

The structure of the tree itself is composed of long, narrow tubes or cells which are lined with fine, spiral strands of cellulose. The tubes are held together with a substance that is called *lignin*. Fig. 6-3. In some woods these tubes are relatively large, making an open-grain wood, while in other, closed-grain woods the tubes are very small. It is plain to see why it is easier to work (cut, shape, form, etc.) *with* the grain than

6-1. This modern office furniture combines many different kinds of materials, particularly wood, metal, and plastic. In addition, the top of the chest is cork and the table top is fine marble. See how all of these different materials blend.

HOW A TREE GROWS

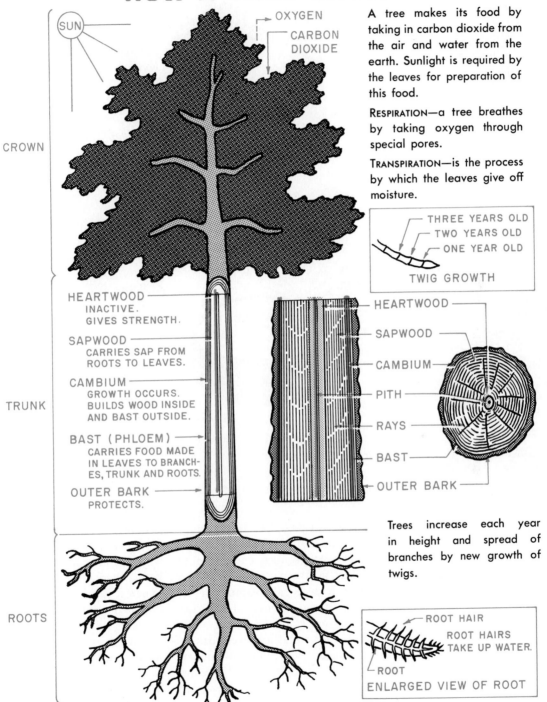

A tree makes its food by taking in carbon dioxide from the air and water from the earth. Sunlight is required by the leaves for preparation of this food.

RESPIRATION—a tree breathes by taking oxygen through special pores.

TRANSPIRATION—is the process by which the leaves give off moisture.

SUN

OXYGEN

CARBON DIOXIDE

CROWN

THREE YEARS OLD
TWO YEARS OLD
ONE YEAR OLD

TWIG GROWTH

HEARTWOOD
INACTIVE.
GIVES STRENGTH.

SAPWOOD
CARRIES SAP FROM
ROOTS TO LEAVES.

CAMBIUM
GROWTH OCCURS.
BUILDS WOOD INSIDE
AND BAST OUTSIDE.

BAST (PHLOEM)
CARRIES FOOD MADE
IN LEAVES TO BRANCH-
ES, TRUNK AND ROOTS.

OUTER BARK
PROTECTS.

TRUNK

HEARTWOOD

SAPWOOD

CAMBIUM

PITH

RAYS

BAST

OUTER BARK

Trees increase each year in height and spread of branches by new growth of twigs.

ROOTS

ROOT HAIR
ROOT HAIRS
TAKE UP WATER.
ROOT

ENLARGED VIEW OF ROOT

6-2. How a tree grows.

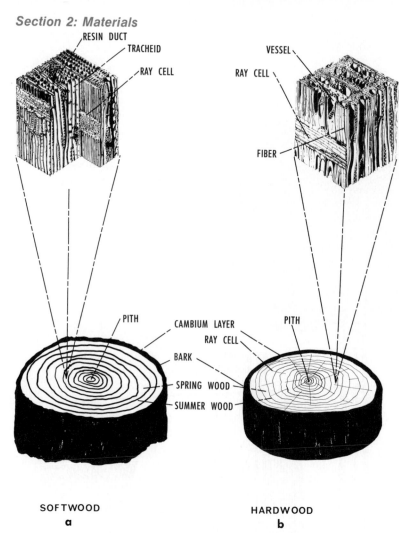

6-3. Enlarged view showing the cell structure of hardwoods and softwoods.

classification, many of the so-called softwoods are harder than some of the hardwoods!

For purposes of use, woods are classified according to their *actual hardness* or *ability to resist wear*. In this method, which is most practical for the woodworker to follow, we have the following classifications:

HARD
    Ash
    Beech
    Birch
    Cherry
    Maple
    Oak, red
    Oak, white
    Pecan
    Walnut
MEDIUM HARD
    Gum
    Mahogany, true
    Mahogany, Philippine
SOFT
    Basswood
    Pine, Ponderosa
    Pine, Sugar
    Poplar
    Redwood
    Willow

Method of Cutting Lumber

Boards are cut from logs in two major ways. The most economical way is called *plain-sawed* (when it is a hardwood tree) or *flat-grained* (when it is a softwood tree). The log is squared and then given a series of lengthwise cuts.

Advantages of plain-sawing:
● Method is cheaper and less wasteful.
● Lumber is easier to kiln dry.
● Boards average greater widths.
    Quarter-sawed (for hardwood)

across it. Fig. 6-3 points out some of the structural differences between softwoods and hardwoods. Resin ducts are not found in hardwoods, but they are present in many softwoods, such as pine, spruce, larch, and Douglas fir.

Classification of Woods

There are several ways of classifying woods into hard and soft. One of the most common is to divide all trees into two classes:

those that shed their leaves annually and those which are "ever" green or produce cones. Those which shed their leaves—including such trees as oak, walnut, maple, ash, basswood, birch, cherry, and gum—are called *hardwoods.* Fig. 6-4. Those that are evergreen or produce cones (conifers)—including such trees as fir, pine, cedar, spruce, and redwood—are called *softwoods.*

However, in this method of

or *edge-grained* (for softwood) is a more expensive method of cutting. It shows a better grain pattern especially in oak and other hardwoods.

Advantages of quarter-sawing are that the lumber shrinks, twists, and cups less and there is less checking and splitting.

A third but less common method of cutting is called rift-sawing. The boards are sawed at not less than 35 degrees nor more than 65 degrees to the annual rings. Fig. 6-5.

Methods of Drying

When a tree is first cut down, it contains from 30 to 300 percent more moisture than it will after the wood has been oven dried. An oven-dried piece of wood contains almost no moisture. The moisture in this green wood exists in two conditions: as free water in the cell cavities and as water absorbed

LUMBER IS OBTAINED FROM TWO GROUPS OF TREES

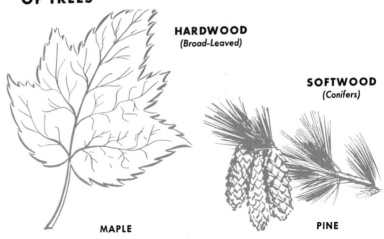

HARDWOOD
(Broad-Leaved)

SOFTWOOD
(Conifers)

MAPLE

PINE

6-4. Trees are divided into two main classes—namely, hardwood and softwood.

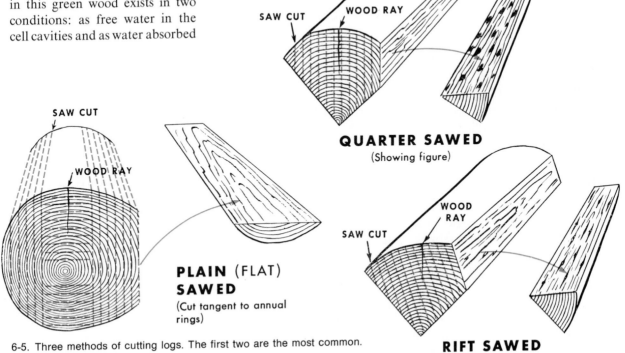

WOOD RAY

SAW CUT

QUARTER SAWED
(Showing figure)

SAW CUT

WOOD RAY

PLAIN (FLAT) **SAWED**
(Cut tangent to annual rings)

WOOD RAY

SAW CUT

RIFT SAWED
(Showing a pencil line grain)

6-5. Three methods of cutting logs. The first two are the most common.

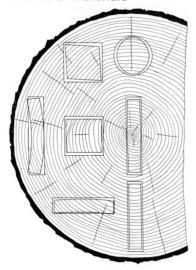

6-6. Shrinkage of lumber takes place in various ways depending upon how it is cut from the log.

in the cell walls. When wood is dried, the free water is removed first. When wood contains just enough water to saturate the cell fibers, it is said to be at the *fiber saturation* point which is approximately 23 to 30 percent moisture content.

The removal of free water does not change the size of the wood. However, during further drying, the shrinkage that occurs *after* the saturation point is about in proportion to the amount of moisture lost. The exact amount that the wood shrinks depends on the kind of wood and how it is cut from the log. One percent loss in moisture below the fiber saturation point causes the wood to shrink about one-thirtieth in width.

Wood shrinks very little in length. This is due to the makeup of the wood cells. For all practical purposes, the length of the piece of wood (with the grain) will not

be affected by a change of moisture content.

Shrinkage across the grain is much greater. The amount of shrinkage across the grain depends, to some degree, on the way the wood has been cut. Flat-grained or plain-sawed lumber will change almost twice as much in width as quarter-sawed or edge-grained stock. The way shrinkage affects lumber cut from different sections of a log is shown in Fig. 6-6.

There are two common methods of drying. *Air drying* is a method in which lumber is stacked with space between the boards in the open air or in sheds. This lumber is allowed to dry until it has a moisture content of 12 to 15 percent. *Kiln drying* lumber is an artificial method. The lumber is placed in an enclosed kiln and hot air is circulated around it until the moisture content is about 6 to 12 percent. Always specify kiln-dried wood when ordering for furniture making.

Effect of Climate Changes on Furniture

Furniture takes on and gives off moisture as temperature and humidity change. This is true, regardless of the quality of the wood or how well it is selected, seasoned, machined, assembled, and finished. In other words, even a completed piece of furniture shrinks and swells.

In buildings which are heated during the winter, the humidity indoors may be as low as 8 to 10 percent, which is drier than the Sahara Desert. In the summer, indoor humidity is often 75 per-

cent or higher. A wooden article in a heated home will have a moisture change during one season of as much as 12 percent of its own weight. The moisture content of a finished furniture piece may vary from about 4 percent in the winter, when the building is heated, to about 8 percent in the summer, slightly more during damp weather. When the humidity is high, doors stick and drawers may not open. A finish reduces the rate of absorption somewhat but does not entirely eliminate it.

A finish cannot keep out the moisture completely. This is why it is important to apply finish to both the upper and lower surfaces of furniture pieces, even though some of the hidden parts do not show. For example, a table top with a good finish on the top but none on the lower surface will warp, especially if it is made of solid wood rather than plywood. For best results, furniture wood should have a moisture content of about 6 percent at the time it is made into the finished piece. Such furniture will shrink very slightly in the winter in a heated building and swell a little bit in the summer. However, this shrinking and swelling will not seriously affect the piece if it is well made.

In storing furniture parts, make sure that you do not expose them to extremely dry air, to moist air, or to a sudden change in humidity. Careful seasoning methods, the use of quarter-sawed lumber and good plywood, and proper finishing techniques will eliminate to a large degree the problems that exist in moisture changes in furniture.

STANDARD HARDWOOD GRADES[1]

Grade and lengths allowed (feet)	Widths allowed	Surface measure of pieces	Amount of each piece that must work into clear-face cuttings	Maximum cuttings allowed	Minimum size of cuttings required
Firsts: [2]	Inches	Square feet	Percent	Number	
8 to 16 (will admit 30 percent of 8- to 11-foot, ½ of which may be 8- and 9-foot).	6+	4 to 9 . . . . . . 10 to 14 . . . . . 15+	91⅔ 91⅔ 91⅔	1 2 3	4 inches by 5 feet, or 3 inches by 7 feet.
Seconds: [2] 8 to 16 (will admit 30 percent of 8- to 11-foot, ½ of which may be 8- and 9-foot).	6+	4 and 5 . . . . . . 6 and 7 . . . . . . 6 and 7 . . . . . . 8 to 11 . . . . . . 8 to 11 . . . . . . 12 to 15 . . . . . 12 to 15 . . . . . 16+	83⅓ 83⅓ 91⅔ 83⅓ 91⅔ 83⅓ 91⅔ 83⅓	1 1 2 2 3 3 4 4	4 inches by 5 feet, or 3 inches by 7 feet.
Selects: 6 to 16 (will admit 30 percent of 6- to 11-foot, ⅙ of which may be 6- and 7-foot).	4+	2 and 3 . . . . . . 4+	91⅔ (3)	1	4 inches by 5 feet, or 3 inches by 7 feet.
No. 1 Common: 4 to 16 (will admit 10 percent of 4- to 7-foot, ½ of which may be 4- and 5-foot).	3+	1 . . . . 2 . . . . 3 and 4 . . . . . . 3 and 4 . . . . . . 5 to 7 . . . . 5 to 7 . . . . 8 to 10 . . . . . . 11 to 13 . . . . . 14+	100 75 66⅔ 75 66⅔ 75 66⅔ 66⅔ 66⅔	0 1 1 2 2 3 3 4 5	4 inches by 2 feet, or 3 inches by 3 feet.
No. 2 Common: 4 to 16 (will admit 30 percent of 4- to 7- foot, ⅓ of which may be 4- and 5-foot).	3+	1 . . . . 2 and 3 . . . . . . 2 and 3 . . . . . . 4 and 5 . . . . . . 4 and 5 . . . . . . 6 and 7 . . . . . . 6 and 7 . . . . . . 8 and 9 . . . . . . 10 and 11 . . . . 12 and 13 . . . . 14+	66⅔ 50 66⅔ 50 66⅔ 50 66⅔ 50 50 50 50	1 1 2 2 3 3 4 4 5 6 7	3 inches by 2 feet.

[1] Inspection to be made on the poorer side of the piece, except in Selects.

[2] Firsts and Seconds are combined as 1 grade (FAS). The percentage of Firsts required in the combined grade varies from 20 to 40 percent, depending on the species.

[3] Same as Seconds.

6-7. Hardwood grading chart.

Grades of Lumber

The so-called softwoods are graded into three groups: yard, factory or shop and structural lumber. Yard lumber, the kind usually available from lumberyards, is divided into two classes, *select* and *common*. Only select would be satisfactory for furniture. There are four grades of select, ranging from *A* to *D*. *A* is practically clear and *D* contains knots and other defects. Factory or shop (common) lumber is intended for manufacturing, such as in making windows and doors. This is available in two grades, *No. 1* and *No. 2*, of which No. 1 is the better. The third group is *structural lumber*, with which the woodworker is not concerned.

Hardwoods are available in three grades, *firsts and seconds* (FAS), *select,* and *No. 1 common*. Generally, firsts and seconds are used for furniture construction.

Grading rules for hardwood lumber have been established by the National Hardwood Lumber Association. Each different kind of hardwood lumber has a slightly different grading standard. To get an idea of lumber grades, look at the chart of standards shown in Fig. 6-7. This chart shows that if a 12-board-foot piece of 4/4 (four quarter or 1") hardwood is to fall into grade firsts and seconds (FAS), it must:

● Yield $91\frac{2}{3}$ percent of its entire volume.

● Have not more than two clear-face cuttings.

● Meet the clear-face standards on both sides. (*Clear face* means unblemished by knots or other defects.)

Selects are the same as FAS except that the clear face is required on only one side. The reverse side can be of lower standard.

Lumber Defects

A lumber buyer needs to know many terms (Fig. 6-8), including those relating to lumber defects. The most common defect is warp. This is defined as any variation from a true or plane surface. Kinds of warp include crook, bow, cup, and twist. A warped board is likely to have more than one of these defects, in any combination. Bow and crook are similar.

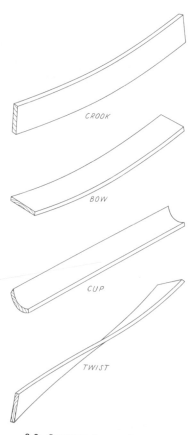

CROOK

BOW

CUP

TWIST

6-9. Common types of warp.

(See the next page.) As Fig. 6-9 shows, both are deviations from a straight line drawn from one end of a piece of lumber to the other. Cup is the most common defect that results from uneven drying.

Lumber Sizes

Some lumber is purchased just as it comes from the sawmill with the surface rough (rgh). Before it can be used, this lumber must be smoothed by running it through a planer or surfacer. Most lumber is dried, then dimensioned (run through a surfacer) at the mill. The dressed or surfaced (actual) size is smaller than the rough (nominal) size. Lumber sizes are based on the rough green dimensions. For example, a 1" hardwood piece, when surfaced, is reduced to $\frac{13}{16}$". Fig. 6-10a on page 66.

Softwood lumber standards have been established by the U. S. Department of Commerce. Under the current standards, softwood is divided into two classifications—*dry* lumber with 19 percent or less in moisture content, and *green* or *unseasoned* lumber with over 19 percent moisture content. For example, standard 1" boards would measure $\frac{3}{4}$" dry, and $\frac{25}{32}$" thickness for green boards. Fig. 6-10b.

In lumber dimensions, the first figure is always the thickness, the second the width, and the third the length. The two charts in Fig. 6-10 show the rough or nominal thickness as well as the dressed or surfaced thickness and width for both hardwood and softwood. Softwoods are cut to standard thickness, width, and length.

Air-drying. (AD) Method of drying lumber by permitting air to circulate around the lumber through spaces provided when it is piled.

Band Sawn. Saw blade tooth markings (on face) are at right angle to edge of board.

Board Foot. A piece of lumber 1 in. thick, 12 in. wide, and 1 ft. long, or its equivalent.

Check. A lengthwise separation of the wood.

Circular Sawn. Saw blade tooth markings are curved on face of board.

Collapse. A seasoning defect resulting in the breakdown of wood cells, caused by too hasty or improper seasoning.

Decay. Disintegration of wood substance due to the action of wood-destroying fungi.

End Check. The separation of the wood fibers at the end of a board.

Flat-sawed. (Same as plain-sawed.)

Growth Rings. New wood formed by the annual growth of a tree. (Also called annual rings.)

Heartwood. The central part of the trunk of a tree, consisting of matured wood in which practically no further change will occur.

Honeycomb. A defect of lumber in which wood is eaten away by insects, giving it the appearance of honeycomb. This term also loosely used to describe internal, open checking, usually in 1½″ and thicker lumber, caused by improper kiln drying.

Kerf. The path that any saw makes in the process of cutting.

Kiln-drying. Artificial method of drying lumber by forcing heated air to circulate around the lumber. (Abbreviated KD).

Knot. A portion of a branch of a tree that forms a mass of woody fiber running at an angle to the grain of the main stock and making a hard place in the timber.

Linear Foot. A piece of board one foot in length, regardless of width or thickness.

Logging. The process of cutting trees and moving the logs to the sawmill.

Medullary Rays. The cellular tissue in wood, extending from the pith, or heart, to the bark.

Pith. The small soft core occurring in the structural center of a log.

Plain-sawed. Lumber that has been sawed in a plane approximately perpendicular to a radius of the log.

Quarter-sawed (Edge-grained). Lumber that has been sawed so that the wide surfaces extend approximately at right angles to the annual growth rings.

R.W.&L. Random widths and lengths.

Resin. A vegetable liquid or semi-liquid which exudes from certain species of trees, particularly the pine tree. Pine resin is the source of tar, pitch, turpentine, and similar products.

RGH. Rough, i.e., as the board comes from the saw, not surfaced.

S2S. Surfaced on two sides; edges rough.

S4S. Surfaced all four sides.

SND. Sap no defect.

Sapwood. The outer part of the trunk of the tree through which the sap flows most freely.

Shake. A lengthwise separation of the wood, the greater part of which occurs between the growth rings. Shakes are differentiated from checks by the fact that they occur in the timber before it is cut into lumber, usually resulting from violent storms or in felling the log.

Split. A lengthwise break in a board.

Square Foot. A piece of board one foot square, or its equivalent, regardless of thickness.

Stain. Discoloration in lumber. Also, a substance for coloring wood.

Steamed. This term, when applied to walnut lumber, refers to a special process in which the green lumber is steamed in vats for the purpose of darkening the sapwood.

Surface Check. The separation of the wood fibers, producing small checks or cracks on the surface of a board.

T&G. Tongued and grooved on sides of board; otherwise D&M—i.e., dressed and matched.

T&G&EM. Tongued and grooved and end matched—i.e., tongued and grooved on all four edges of piece, as in oak flooring.

Wane. The presence of bark, or the lack of wood from any cause on the edge or corner of a piece of lumber.

Warp. Any variation from a true or plane surface.

W.H.N.D.&W.H.A.D. Worm hole no defect and Worm hole a defect.

6-8. Common terms used in selecting and buying lumber.

Thickness (Widths vary with Grades)		
Nominal (Rough)	Surfaced 1 Side (S1S)	Surfaced 2 Sides (S2S)
3/8″	1/4″	3/16″
1/2″	3/8″	5/16″
5/8″	1/2″	7/16″
3/4″	5/8″	9/16″
1″	7/8″	13/16″
1 1/4″	1 1/8″	1 1/16″
1 1/2″	1 3/8″	1 5/16″
2″	1 13/16″	1 3/4″
3″	2 13/16″	2 3/4″
4″	3 13/16″	3 3/4″

6-10a. Standard thicknesses of surfaced lumber-hardwoods.

Thickness (Inches)			Width (Inches)		
	Minimum Dressed			Minimum Dressed	
Nominal	Dry	Green	Nominal	Dry	Green
1	3/4	25/32	2	1 1/2	1 9/16
1 1/4	1	1 1/32	3	2 1/2	2 9/16
1 1/2	1 1/4	1 9/32	4	3 1/2	3 9/16
2	1 1/2	1 9/16	5	4 1/2	4 5/8
2 1/2	2	2 1/16	6	5 1/2	5 5/8
3	2 1/2	2 9/16	7	6 1/2	6 5/8
3 1/2	3	3 1/16	8	7 1/4	7 1/2
4	3 1/2	3 9/16			

6-10b. Standard thicknesses and widths of softwood.

Nominal widths are 4″, 6″, 8″, 10″ and 12″. The standard lengths of softwoods are from 8′ to 20′ increasing at intervals of 2′. Hardwood lumber is generally available in standard thickness, but because of its high cost it is cut to whatever widths and lengths are most economical and convenient.

To one not working regularly in fine woods, the fact that hardwoods are almost always offered in a random width and length (RW&L) assortment presents something of a mystery. You may wonder, "Why don't they make birch, oak and walnut in convenient dimensional sizes like pine, redwood and fir?"

The answer: Markets for hardwoods and softwoods are entirely different. Softwoods are used mainly for construction, while most hardwoods go into furniture, fixtures, and moldings.

Hardwood lumber is cut to yield the maximum of usable material. Each board is sawed as wide and long as the log allows, then trimmed just enough to make the edges and ends square.

This production method satisfies the major hardwood markets, at the same time limiting waste and reducing costs.

Both widths and lengths are, of necessity, random, and even the best grades allow an occasional defect.

Measurement of Lumber

A *board foot* of lumber is a piece 1 inch thick, 12 inches wide, and 1 foot (12 inches) long. The board foot is the standard unit of measurement used in lumber yards. Lumber less than 1 inch thick is figured as 1 inch. This is a way to figure board feet: Multiply the thickness in inches by the width in feet by the length in feet. For example, a 2 by 4 inch piece that is 12 feet long would be 8 board feet: $2 \times 4/12 \times 12 = 8$. The width (4 inches) is divided by 12 to change it to feet.

A simpler way to figure board feet for products is as follows: Board feet equals the thickness in inches times the width in inches times the length in feet over 12.

$$\text{Board Feet (BF)} = \frac{T \text{ (in inches)} \times W \text{ (in inches)} \times L \text{ (in feet)}}{12}$$

For example: How many board feet are there in a piece of birch 1 inch by 7 inches by 6 feet?

$$BF = \frac{1 \times 7 \times 6}{12}, \text{ or } 3\frac{1}{2} \text{ board feet.}$$

For very small pieces you can figure board feet this way: Board feet equals the thickness in inches times the width in inches times the length in inches divided by 144. There are 144 cubic inches in one board foot.

$$\text{Board Feet (BF)} = \frac{T \times W \times L \text{ (all in inches)}}{144}$$

For example: How many board feet are there in a piece of walnut 1/2 inch thick, 9 inches wide and 28 inches long? (Remember that stock less than 1 inch thick is figured as 1 inch).

$$BF = \frac{1 \times 9 \times 28}{144} \text{ or } 1\frac{3}{4} \text{ board feet.}$$

Lumber is sold by the board foot, by the hundred board feet, or by the thousand board feet (M). For example, if lumber sells for $350.00 per M, it would cost you $35.00 for 100 board feet and 35 cents for one board foot. Some lumber less than 4 inches wide, especially moldings, is sold by the linear foot or running foot.

Writing Hardwood Lumber Specifications

When ordering hardwood for furniture, specify *quantity, thickness, kind of wood, grade, surface, condition of seasoning,* and *widths and lengths.* Here is a typical order (with explanation added in parentheses).

500 Bd. Ft. (board feet), 1″ or ⁴⁄₄ (thickness is expressed in inches or in fractions of an inch), African

mahogany, FAS (firsts and seconds), Rgh (rough), KD 5–8% (kiln dried to a specific percentage), RW & L (random widths and lengths).

Remember these points when ordering:
● Be thorough. Omit nothing important.
● Use standard terms and abbreviations.
● Order lumber rough if a surfacer or planer is available. Otherwise order it surfaced two sides (S2S).
● Indicate the percentage of moisture content, not just "kiln dried."
● If the job permits, order random widths and lengths, as this costs less.

Plastics in Furniture

Plastic materials are widely used in the furniture industry. Plastic is a synthetic material and is of two types: *thermoplastics* (soft when heated) and *thermosetting* which cannot be reshaped. Common thermoplastics include vinyl, polyethylene, and acrylic. The more common thermosetting plastics include phenolic, melamine-amino, and polyester.

Common uses for plastics include plastic laminates for tops of tables, dressers, and counters; vinyl fabrics for upholstery covering; urethane foams for cushioning; resins to bond wood flakes together to make hardboard and particle board; and polyvinyl glues for assembling. Many plastics are also used in wood finishing. In addition to this, plastic parts are also being used in furniture in combination with wood.

6-11b. Wood or plastic? Would you have guessed that this furniture piece is made from plastic if you could not see the mold marks on the inside of the panel?

Many of the ornate decorative items for drawers, doors, and picture or mirror frames are made of molded plastic. Fig. 6-11. Molded plastic legs that look like wood are also being produced. Fig. 6-12.

6-12a. A plastic resin coating is applied to a molded plastic table leg. The coating can be covered to give it the exact appearance of natural wood.

6-11a. These decorative designs simulate wood carving but are actually made of plastic. The reproductions are made of durable, flexible plastic resin that imitates the appearance, feel, and heft of wood grain and carving details.

6-12b. The finished table is a combination of plastic (legs) and the natural hardwood (cabinet). With plastic legs, quality items can be made much more economically.

6-13a. Many parts of this storage cabinet are made of aluminum. Others are wood, plastic laminates, and hardboard.

Metals in Furniture

All of the common metals including steel, aluminum, copper, and brass are used in a wide variety of ways in wood furniture. Fasteners such as corner braces, table leaf supports, and brackets are but a few of the pieces for which metal is used. Some styles of furniture such as Spanish and Contemporary make use of metal for structural parts and for decoration. Fig. 6-13. Not only are metals being used in furniture that is primarily of wood, but also a great deal of furniture, particularly for offices, is made entirely of metal.

6-13b. This Mediterranean-style furniture features metal inserts in the door fronts.

UNIT 7 Kinds of Woods

There are over a thousand kinds of species of woods. A great many of these, however, have limited commercial value. Eight kinds of wood are basic to the furniture industry, comprising over 95 percent of all the fine hardwoods used in furniture manufactured in the United States. This unit deals primarily with those eight woods —birch, cherry, true mahogany, Philippine mahogany, hard and soft maple, oak (red and white), pecan, and walnut.

Fig. 7-1 lists the properties of these woods as well as certain other species which have less prominence in the furniture industry.

Birch

GENUS: *Betula.* Principal lumber species: *lutea* (yellow birch); *lenta* (sweet, black, or cherry birch); and *papyrifera* (paper, canoe, or white birch).

GENERAL CHARACTERISTICS: Moderately heavy, hard and strong. Ex-

cellent machining and finishing characteristics. Tree deciduous; wood diffuse porous, with little contrast between spring and summer wood, although annual growth is well marked. Heartwood reddish brown, sapwood yellowish white with a trace of pink. Weight kiln dried about 3.7 lbs. per board foot.

Growing in southeastern Canada, the Lake States, New England and the Appalachian region as far south as Georgia, yellow birch is the most important commercially of the birches. The sweet birch is found from Newfoundland and Ontario through New England to the southern Appalachians. It is a little denser and deeper in color than yellow birch, although, where cut together, the two are sold simply as birch.

When considering birch as a decorative wood, the paper birch should be disregarded entirely. It grows in much the same range as sweet birch, with the commercial center in Maine.

7-1. Characteristics of common hardwoods and softwoods. (Right)

SPECIES	Comparative Weights[1]	Color[2]	Hand Tool Working	Nail Ability[3]	Relative Density	General Strength[4]	Resistance to Decay[5]	Wood Finishing[6]	Cost[7]
HARDWOODS[8]									
APITONG............	Heavy	Reddish Brown	Hard	Poor	Medium	Good	High	Poor	Medium High
ASH, brown.......	Medium	Light Brown	Medium	Medium	Hard	Medium	Low	Medium	Medium
ASH, tough white.....	Heavy	Off-White	Hard	Poor	Hard	Good	Low	Medium	Medium
ASH, soft white.......	Medium	Off-White	Medium	Medium	Medium	Low	Low	Medium	Medium Low
AVODIRE..........	Medium	Golden Blond	Medium	Medium	Medium	Low	Low	Poor	High
BALSAWOOD........	Light	Cream White	Easy	Good	Soft	Low	Low	Medium	Medium
BASSWOOD.........	Light	Cream White	Easy	Good	Soft	Low	Low	Easy	Medium
BEECH............	Heavy	Light Brown	Hard	Poor	Hard	Good	Low	Easy	High
BIRCH............	Heavy	Light Brown	Hard	Poor	Hard	Good	Low	Easy	Medium
BUTTERNUT........	Light	Light Brown	Easy	Good	Soft	Low	Medium	Medium	Medium
CHERRY, black.......	Medium	Medium Reddish Brown	Hard	Poor	Hard	Good	Medium	Easy	High
CHESTNUT..........	Light	Light Brown	Medium	Medium	Medium	Medium	High	Poor	Medium
COTTONWOOD.......	Light	Greyish White	Medium	Good	Soft	Low	Low	Poor	Low
ELM, soft grey......	Medium	Cream Tan	Hard	Good	Medium	Medium	Medium	Medium	Medium Low
GUM, red...........	Medium	Reddish Brown	Medium	Medium	Medium	Medium	Medium	Medium	Medium High
HICKORY, true.......	Heavy	Reddish Tan	Hard	Poor	Hard	Good	Low	Easy	Low
HOLLY............	Medium	White to Grey	Medium	Medium	Hard	Medium	Low	Easy	Medium
KORINA...........	Medium	Pale Golden	Medium	Good	Medium	Medium	Low	Medium	High
MAGNOLIA..........	Medium	Yellowish Brown	Medium	Medium	Medium	Medium	Low	Easy	Medium
MAHOGANY, Honduras	Medium	Golden Brown	Easy	Good	Medium	Medium	High	Medium	High
MAHOGANY, Philippine	Medium	Medium Red	Easy	Good	Medium	Medium	High	Medium	Medium High
MAPLE, hard.........	Heavy	Reddish Cream	Hard	Poor	Hard	Good	Low	Easy	Medium High
MAPLE, soft........	Medium	Reddish Brown	Hard	Poor	Hard	Good	Low	Easy	Medium Low
OAK, red (average)....	Heavy	Flesh Brown	Hard	Medium	Hard	Good	Low	Medium	Medium
OAK, white (average)..	Heavy	Greyish Brown	Hard	Medium	Hard	Good	High	Medium	Medium High
POPLAR, yellow.......	Medium	Light to Dark Yellow	Easy	Good	Soft	Low	Low	Easy	Medium
PRIMA VERA.........	Medium	Straw Tan	Medium	Medium	Medium	Medium	Medium	Medium	High
SYCAMORE..........	Medium	Flesh Brown	Hard	Good	Medium	Medium	Low	Easy	Medium Low
WALNUT, black.......	Heavy	Dark Brown	Medium	Medium	Hard	Good	High	Medium	High
WILLOW, black.......	Light	Medium Brown	Easy	Good	Soft	Low	Low	Medium	Medium Low
SOFTWOODS[9]									
CEDAR, Tennessee Red	Medium	Red	Medium	Poor	Medium	Medium	High	Easy	Medium
CYPRESS............	Medium	Yellow to Reddish Brown	Medium	Good	Soft	Medium	High	Poor	Medium High
FIR, Douglas........	Medium	Orange-Brown	Medium	Poor	Soft	Medium	Medium	Poor	Medium
FIR, white..........	Light	Nearly White	Medium	Poor	Soft	Low	Low	Poor	Low
PINE, yellow longleaf..	Medium	Orange to Reddish Brown	Hard	Poor	Medium	Good	Medium	Medium	Medium
PINE, northern white.. (Pinus Strobus)	Light	Cream to Reddish Brown	Easy	Good	Soft	Low	Medium	Medium	Medium High
PINE, ponderosa......	Light	Orange to Reddish Brown	Easy	Good	Soft	Low	Low	Medium	Medium
PINE, sugar.........	Light	Creamy Brown	Easy	Good	Soft	Low	Medium	Poor	Medium High
REDWOOD..........	Light	Deep Reddish Brown	Easy	Good	Soft	Medium	High	Poor	Medium
SPRUCES (average)....	Light	Nearly White	Medium	Medium	Soft	Low	Low	Medium	Medium

[1]Kiln dried weight.

[2]Heartwood. Sap is whitish.

[3]Comparative splitting tendencies.

[4]Combined bending and compressive strength.

[5]No wood will decay unless exposed to moisture. Resistance to decay estimate refers to only heartwood.

[6]Ease of finishing with clear or "natural" finishes.

[7]Prices for best grade.

[8]Leaf bearing tree.

[9]Cone and needle bearing trees.

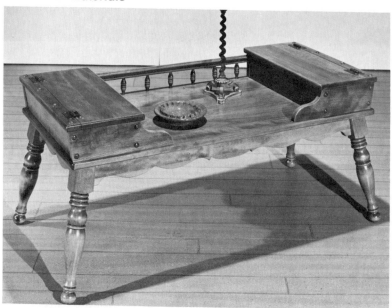

7-2. This coffee table is made of high quality birch. Birch is particularly suited for turned parts. The table is 42″ x 18″ by 18″ high.

longs to the rose family. Prunus serotina is a small, scrubby tree in poor situations but in the rich, moist soil of the Appalachian regions it may reach a height of 100 feet or more, with diameters of four to five feet.

Many connoisseurs of fine cabinet woods regard cherry as of top value as a furniture species, ranking in this country second only to walnut. Factory produced cherry furniture is usually stained a deep red color. This practice is so common that people often think of cherry as really of that color. Actually, the light, reddish brown wood is much more beautiful if finished with clear varnish or lacquer and allowed to age naturally. It will in a few years deepen to a rich, golden luster which cannot be duplicated by other means.

The uses of cherry are those of any fine cabinet wood, limited now because of its relative scarcity. The fine large timber once available has largely been cut, so that cherry lumber of top quality is practically unobtainable and the woodworker must face the necessity of careful fabrication to dispose of knots and other defects. Cherry lumber has one outstanding industrial use: it is a valuable stereotype or electrotype wood, its unusual stability making it desirable for that purpose.

The wood from any of our fruit trees is sometimes called "fruitwood." As a rule this term refers to cherry. Fig. 7-3.

Paper birch is valuable for the sapwood, which constitutes the greater part of the tree of moderate size, and is ideally suited for turnery. Moderately hard, uniform in texture and fine grained, it is one of our best woods for dowels, spools, bobbins, handles, etc. Other uses include toothpicks, clothespins and shoepegs.

Birch lumber as a decorative species is the delight of the architect, who often seems willing to specify it for almost any purpose. Due to the diminishing supply of good birch timber, difficult specifications in this wood can be the despair of both the lumber merchant and his customer, who is to do the work. Unless too much is asked, however, birch is still one of our most versatile and useful hardwoods. It machines and sands beautifully and can be stained to simulate any of the darker woods of value.

Birch is especially popular for furniture, fixtures, fine cabinets, flooring, doors and interior trim. Although sometimes available as "selected white birch" (all sapwood one face),

and "selected red birch" (all heartwood one face), the majority of users prefer unselected birch, which contains portions each of heartwood and sapwood. Despite its ability to receive stains of every hue, your true lover of fine woods also prefers this one in its natural color. Fig. 7-2.

In addition to its usefulness as lumber, Birch is the most popular of the decorative woods of value in plywood form. Vast quantities of birch plywood are consumed every year.

Cherry

GENUS: *Prunus*. Only lumber species; *serotina*.

GENERAL CHARACTERISTICS: Moderately heavy and hard, strong. Machines and sands to glasslike smoothness. Tree is deciduous; wood diffuse porous, close grained; annual growth visible but not pronounced; exceptional stability. Heartwood reddish brown, sometimes with greenish cast; sapwood yellowish. Weight about 3.4 lbs. per board foot kiln dried.

Like all our fruit trees, cherry be-

7-3. This lamp commode is made of selected cherry veneer with a base of solid cherry.

Mahogany

GENUS: *Swietenia* (American mahogany); and *Khaya* (African mahogany). Principal lumber species: S. *macrophylla*—Mexican, Central and South American mahogany. S. *mahagoni*—West Indian mahogany. K. *ivorensis*—African mahogany.

GENERAL CHARACTERISTICS: Moderate density and hardness. Strength factor high in comparison to weight. Unsurpassed working and finishing characteristics. Polishes to high luster. Stability excellent; durable in situations favoring decay. Tree is deciduous, although virtually an evergreen; wood is diffuse porous. Pores are open, requiring filling in conventional type finishes. Texture even; annual growth visible. Color medium reddish brown; much lighter than most persons suppose, although the wood will darken considerably with the years. Weight about 2.7 lbs. per board foot, kiln dried.

There may be some differences of opinion on this point, but most woodworkers regard mahogany as the premier cabinet wood of the world. It has everything to recommend it for fine furniture, fixtures, interior trim, cabinets and other objects intended to have beauty as well as utility. It turns and carves beautifully.

The two types mentioned in the heading are usually considered the genuine mahoganies. The African genus is related botanically to the American types and the two woods are very similar in appearance. Only an expert can identify small individual pieces of the two, although as a rule African mahogany is slightly coarser in texture than American.

African mahogany develops more figured wood than the American varieties, thus is preferred for veneers. Most mahogany faced plywood is African unless otherwise stipulated. The ribbon stripe seen in some mahogany is obtained by quarter sawing or slicing, while the plain figure develops from tangential cutting.

While mahogany is used in our country principally for the uses al-

7-4. A Sheraton table of solid mahogany with a top center fitted with genuine black leather.

ready mentioned, it is one of the best of all materials for the construction of boats and many of the finest boats contain a heavy proportion of this wood.

The bulk of the mahogany lumber consumed in the United States is from Mexico and British Honduras. Some mahogany of species macrophylla is reaching us from the upper Amazon region, in Peru. It is closely similar to Honduras mahogany. West Indian mahogany no longer appears in the United States market, as the production is limited and most of it is needed at home. The West Indian is somewhat denser, harder and heavier than that from other localities, and was preferred by some famous furniture makers when the wood was obtainable. African mahogany is largely from Ghana, French Equatorial Africa and Nigeria. Fig. 7-4.

Philippine Mahogany

GENUS: *Shorea* and *Parashorea.* Principal lumber species: S. *polysperma* (Tanguile and Bataan); S. *negrosensis* (Red Lauan); S. *eximia* (Almon); and P. *malaanonan* (Bagtican).

GENERAL CHARACTERISTICS: Medium density and hardness. Dark red varieties somewhat firmer in texture than light red. Strong in comparison to weight. Machining and finishing properties excellent. Luster high; texture fine and uniform. Diffuse porous, but pores are moderately prominent and require filling in conventional type finishes. Durable in situations favoring decay. Color of dark red types: dark brownish red. Color of Light Red types: light yellowish red. Weight about 3.6 lbs. per board foot, kiln dried.

There are a number of species comprising the Philippine mahogany group; of which those listed supply most of the Philippine mahogany lumber sold in the United States. The wood of these trees is often mixed as to species, but almost always divided for color, and sold as either dark red or light red Philippine mahogany. Tanguile, bataan and red lauan are the dark red varieties; Almon and Bagtican, the light red. While the properties of all these species are quite similar, dark red types are firmer in texture and command somewhat higher prices in the market.

Compared to the prices of other woods of lesser intrinsic value, Philippine mahogany, either light or dark red, is the most reasonably priced fine cabinet wood on the market today. It lacks in some respects the value of the genuine mahoganies and is a little more difficult to finish, but this is a difference of degree only. Philippine mahogany does not suffer at all by comparison with the average good cabinet timber.

The uses of Philippine mahogany are those common to other good cabinet woods. It is an excellent wood for furniture, fixtures, residence and office building trim, mouldings, wall paneling. Philippine mahogany plywood is available at moderate cost, and the two color types lend great flexibility in finishing to any of the popular wood colors.

Hard Maple

GENUS: *Acer*. Principal lumber species: *saccharum* (sugar maple); and *nigrum* (black maple). Some botonists consider nigrum only a variety of saccharum. For all practical purposes, they may be regarded as one species.

GENERAL CHARACTERISTICS: Hard, heavy and strong. Famous for resistance to abrasive wear. Odorless and tasteless. Tree is deciduous; wood diffuse porous; annual growth visible, but inconspicuous. Very fine texture and grain; does not require filling. Heartwood very light brown or tan, sometimes with darker mineral streaks. Sapwood white or off-white. Weight about 3.7 lbs. per board foot, kiln dried.

Hard maple is the most valuable member of the maple family, and the most plentiful. Its range includes most of the hardwood region of the eastern United States and Canada, but in the United States, the best stands are near the Great Lakes and in the St. Lawrence Valley and northern New England.

The excellent technical properties of hard maple have recommended it for a wide number of industrial uses. Its superiority in wearing quality makes it the leader in woods for flooring in residences, dance halls, schools, skating rinks, bowling alleys and shops. Furniture of hard maple, if well made, may be expected to outlast the owner, and at the same time serve the esthetic sense as well as the practical.

Hard maple is the standard wood for cutting boards in packing plants, restaurants and homes, as it imparts no taste to food and holds up well. Some trees develop a figure of a special type, such as curly grain, fiddleback, mottle and bird's-eye. The cause of bird's-eye figure is not known, but we do know it is not caused by birds, bird pecks or any of the causes to which it is popularly attributed.

The tree is called sugar maple for the sweet sap, which flows profusely in early spring and is the source of syrup and sugar of considerable economic value. Fig. 7-5.

Soft Maple

GENUS: *Acer*. Principal lumber species: *rubrum* (red or swamp maple); and *saccharinum* (silver or white maple).

GENERAL CHARACTERISTICS: Medium density, hardness and strength. Machining and finishing properties good; stability good. Fine texture; close grained; wood does not require filling. Annual growth inconspicuous. The color of heartwood varies greatly, from pale tan to reddish gray, sometimes streaked. Sapwood is white to off-white. Weight about 3.2 lbs. per square foot.

The term "soft maple" is a little misleading, as the wood is not really soft. Its density is similar to that of magnolia and gum, and the name was intended primarily to distinguish it from hard maple. The range of the soft maples includes almost the entire eastern United States, the area of greatest commercial importance including the Atlantic coast region from southern Virginia through the Carolinas. Silver maple is less abundant than red maple, although in the Mississippi Valley, it is the predominant of the two.

The most important use of soft maple is in the furniture industry, which consumes large quantities of it. Much of the medium priced Colonial maple furniture is of soft maple.

Where the wood is to be stained, especially to the conventional red maple finish, soft maple is a satisfactory and economical substitute for the costlier hard maple. It is not difficult to work, is easily polished to high luster and receives stains of different colors acceptably. A further recommendation is the fact that it holds its place well in the finished product.

The Oaks

GENUS: *Quercus*. Principal lumber species: So many different species of oaks are cut for lumber that it seems pointless to list them. It would be difficult if not impossible to purchase oak lumber in the market according to species.

GENERAL CHARACTERISTICS: Very hard, heavy and strong. Fairly easy to work, density considered. Turns, carves and bends well. Sanding and finishing qualities excellent; stability excellent. Except for the live oaks, which are not a factor in the lumber industry, the oaks are deciduous and the wood ring porous. Color of heartwood in red oaks is reddish or light reddish brown; in white oaks light tan or brown. Weight kiln dried about 4 lbs. per board foot.

7-5. Maple and birch are combined in the Early American furniture in this study.

The oaks comprise the most important group of hardwood timber trees in the United States. None is better known or more widely used. Fig. 7-6.

As explained earlier, there are many separate species cut and marketed as oak lumber. The genus Quercus seems to have a distinct tendency to variation for no apparent reason. Oak lumber is sold as either red oak or white oak, with no attempt to separate or identify the different species. There are certain important distinctions which cause this separation, however, which may be of interest.

Red Oaks

1. Color of heartwood tends to be reddish.
2. Because of internal structure, this wood is not waterproof.
3. Freshly cut wood has a sour, often unpleasant odor.
4. Pores in summer wood few. Can be counted under a hand lens.
5. Annual rings usually widely separated, resulting in coarser textured woods.
6. Heartwood not particularly durable under conditions favoring decay.

White Oaks

1. Color of heartwood tends to be tan or brownish.
2. Because of internal structure, this wood is waterproof.
3. Freshly cut wood has a distinct but not unpleasant odor.
4. Pores in summer wood numerous and small. Cannot be counted even with a hand lens.
5. Annual rings usually compact, resulting in finer textured wood.
6. Heartwood quite durable under conditions favoring decay.

The oaks are related to the beech and chestnut, but in some ways the Quercus family is unique. It is the only tree bearing acorns, certain species of which are edible. It is one of the few groups including both evergreen and deciduous trees (the live oaks are evergreens). Its range is probably greater than that of any

7-6. This coffee table has a top of selected oak veneer on plywood banded with solid oak. The under parts are also solid oak. The top is 54" x 22"; the table is 16" high.

other of our important hardwoods. It is found all over the United States east of the great plains, and on the West Coast.

The uses of oak lumber are almost too numerous to permit listing. Almost any article which can be made of wood has, at one time or another, been manufactured from oak. So long as those responsible for design and finish are alert to the possibilities of this fine material, oak will always be a popular furniture wood. Few woods are more beautiful when skillfully handled, and few can be finished in so many attractive ways. There can be no doubt about the serviceability of oak furniture; it will last for generations with ordinary care.

Pecan

GENUS: *Hicoria* (listed as Carya in some tree books). Principal lumber species: *pecan* (sweet pecan); *aquatica* (bitter pecan); *cardiformis* (bitternut hickory) and *myristicaformis* (nutmeg hickory).

GENERAL CHARACTERISTICS: Very heavy, hard, elastic and strong. Next to true hickory, toughest and strongest American wood in common use. Machines and turns well; steam bends well. Tree deciduous; wood ring porous. Annual growth rings

distinct. Color of heartwood, light to dark reddish brown, sapwood white. Weight kiln dried: about 4.2 lbs. per board foot.

Although the range of one of the pecan species, the bitternut hickory, includes most of the eastern United States, pecan is essentially a southern wood. It is at its best in Louisiana, eastern Texas, Mississippi, Arkansas, and throughout the Delta region. From here it ranges through the Gulf States to Florida.

Although the pecans are all hickories and their characteristics are similar in most respects, there are slight differences which apply in general. Pecan is not quite as hard and tough as hickory, but is still harder than other commercial species. The color of the heartwood will vary, but, in the main, pecan is a little darker than hickory and inclined to display a slightly more reddish hue. Unless the use is an extremely difficult or technical one, pecan will serve the purpose as well as hickory.

Pecan furniture is produced in large quantities. The wood is very serviceable for this purpose, satisfying all requirements of strength, hardness and rigidity. Fig. 7-7. A relative of walnut, the grain of pecan and walnut are similar, and a piece of pecan

73

7-7. Serving cabinet made of pecan.

most of the lumber produced is from six to ten feet in length. Top grades are 5″ and wider, averaging about seven inches in width. The small size of the timber does not permit the removal of the sapwood, which is nearly white when freshly cut. Mills specializing in the production of walnut lumber place the stock directly from the saw into steaming pits. Here it is covered with walnut sawdust and other refuse of the mill and steamed until the color of the sapwood is brought as closely as possible to that of the heart. This process still leaves some contrast between heartwood and sapwood, but it is diminished to the point where a skillful finisher can blend the two perfectly.

The beauty of walnut is admired by almost everyone, and there are few homes in the land which do not possess at least one article made of it. Its unsurpassed finishing properties are so inherent that even an amateur finisher can expect excellent results with it. It is one of our best woods to carve, and few woods respond more agreeably to both hand and machine tools. The wood is durable and offers a very high degree of dimensional stability.

The principal uses of walnut are in fine furniture, gun stocks, interior trim, fine cabinets, fixtures, radio and television cabinets, musical instrument cases and the like. Much walnut is made into veneers for walnut faced plywood.

The bulk of the yield is in plainsawn lumber and plain-sliced veneers. Occasionally one sees walnut quarter-sawn or sliced. This is usually called "pencil stripe" walnut, as this method of cutting displays the edge of the annual growth rings as a series of narrow bands or lines. Walnut crotches and stumps close to the roots are valuable for the highly figured stock produced from them. Crotch and stump walnut is never seen as solid wood, but always in veneered panels. This is true also of burl walnut. The tree sometimes produces burls large enough to be sliced into veneers.

wood skillfully stained to walnut color will defy identification by all but the most expert. It is attractive as wall paneling and used in a variety of planing mill products, vehicle parts, heavy baseball bats, camp cots, folding chairs, and similar items.

Walnut

GENUS: *Juglans.* Principal lumber species: *nigra.*

GENERAL CHARACTERISTICS: Moderately dense and hard. Strong in comparison to weight. Excellent machining properties. Superb finishing qualities. Tree is deciduous; wood ring porous. Open pores require filling in conventional finishing. Annual growth clearly marked; texture fine and even. Polished to high luster.

Color of heartwood: variegated dark, chocolate brown, sometimes with a purplish cast. Sapwood nearly white. Weight kiln dried about 3.5 lbs. per board foot.

Walnut is the most valuable furniture and cabinet timber of the United States. It is found as scattered specimens and in small groves over the entire United States east of the great plains but is best developed in the middle-west, the Mississippi and Ohio valleys, Tennessee and the lower Appalachian mountains. Fig. 7-8.

Walnut is found as isolated trees in forest and farm lots, never in dense stands. The logs are hauled, sometimes over long distances, to the mills, adding to the cost of the lumber. The walnut log is relatively short, so that

7-8. American walnut was the choice for construction of this Modern office desk.

UNIT 8 Plywood

Plywood consists of an odd number of layers of veneer and/or wood joined together by an adhesive. Fig. 8-1. The grain of each layer or ply is approximately at right angles to the grain of the adjacent ply or plies. The exterior face of the plywood may be either softwood or hardwood. Common hardwood plywood comes with an exterior face of oak, walnut, elm, cherry, maple, birch, gum, teak, rosewood, or mahogany. Common softwood plywoods have an exterior face of fir or pine. The better surface ply is called the *face veneer*. The other surface ply is called the *back veneer*. (Sometimes both surfaces are of equal quality.) The innermost ply is called the *core*. All other plies between the core and face plies are called *crossbands*. Plywood is usually made with 3, 5, 7, or 9 plies, with 3 or 5 the most common. Three common types of plywood construction are:

● *Veneer Core*—The core is made of thick wood veneer. Most softwood plywoods are this type of construction. Fig. 8-2.

● *Lumber Core*—The core consists of strips of lumber bonded together. Good woods for lumber core plywood are basswood and chestnut. Fig. 8-3.

● *Particle-Board Core*—The core is made of particle board which is a wood composition material sometimes referred to as flakeboard or chipboard. This kind of plywood is commonly used for the

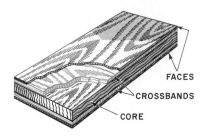

5-PLY

8-1. Plywood is a wood product made of layers of veneer and/or lumber bonded together with adhesive (glue). A veneer is a thin sheet or layer of wood $\frac{1}{100}''$ to $\frac{1}{4}''$ thick that has been sliced or peeled from a log.

tops of tables and cabinets because it is very stable. Fig. 8-4.

Manufacture of Plywood

Veneers are thin sheets of wood usually cut from the trunk of the tree. Some species produce choice and unusual figures. Fig. 8-5. See page 76.

The three principal methods of cutting veneer are:

● Rotary cutting, Fig. 8-6, page 76.

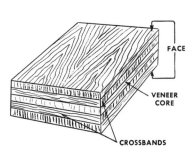

8-2. Veneer-core construction is used for most softwood plywood. The plastic resin glues of today generally make plywood stronger than solid lumber.

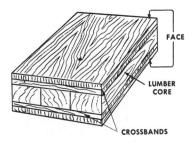

8-3. Lumber-core plywood is used to a large degree in furniture production.

● Flat slicing.
● Quarter slicing.

Steps in manufacturing plywood are shown in Fig. 8-7, page 77.

Hardwood Plywood

There are five categories of hardwood plywood. The top two groups are both considered No. 1 grade. Fig. 8-8a. A brief description of the five categories follows:

Premium grade comprises a very special selection of wood. The face veneer may be made from more than one piece of high quality. Only very minor defects are allowed. It is commonly used for fine furniture and interior paneling. (Continued on pages 77, 79.)

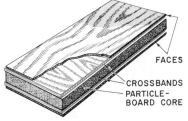

5-PLY WITH PARTICLE-BOARD CORE

8-4. Plywood made with a particle-board core simplifies production problems and makes for a very stable panel. Particle-board core is particularly suited to table and cabinet tops because it does not warp, even on large surfaces.

8-5. The veneers for the top of this unusual round dining table were cut and matched from Persian walnut, using veneers from the crotch of the tree.

8-6. The three principal methods of veneer manufacture.

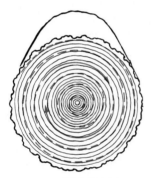

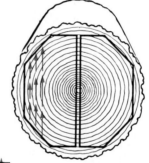

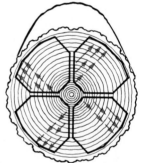

ROTARY CUTTING

Put on a lathe and revolved against knife. Veneer is un-wound like paper from a roll.

KNIFE
STATIONARY

FLAT SLICING

Log HALVED and sliced parallel to axis of tree Clamped onto slicer moving up and down against knife, cutting veneer on downstroke.

KNIFE
STATIONARY

QUARTER SLICING

Log QUARTERED and sliced radially to growth of tree.

KNIFE
STATIONARY

GRAIN CHARACTERISTICS

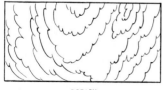

ROTARY

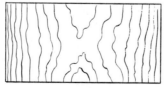

FLAT SLICED

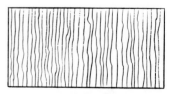

QUARTER SLICED

Manufacture of Hardwood Plywood

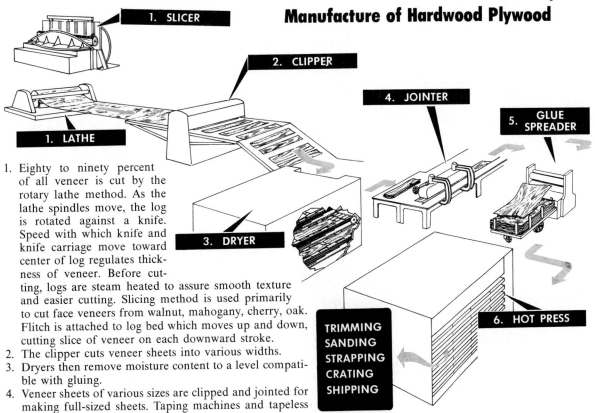

1. Eighty to ninety percent of all veneer is cut by the rotary lathe method. As the lathe spindles move, the log is rotated against a knife. Speed with which knife and knife carriage move toward center of log regulates thickness of veneer. Before cutting, logs are steam heated to assure smooth texture and easier cutting. Slicing method is used primarily to cut face veneers from walnut, mahogany, cherry, oak. Flitch is attached to log bed which moves up and down, cutting slice of veneer on each downward stroke.

2. The clipper cuts veneer sheets into various widths.

3. Dryers then remove moisture content to a level compatible with gluing.

4. Veneer sheets of various sizes are clipped and jointed for making full-sized sheets. Taping machines and tapeless splicers may be used.

5. Veneers are then coated with liquid glue, front and back, with a glue spreader.

6. Heat and pressure applied in the hot press bonds the veneers into plywood famous for strength, beauty and versatility. Panels are trimmed, sanded and stacked for conditioning and inspection, after which they are ready for grading, strapping and shipping.

8-7. Steps in the manufacture of hardwood plywood.

HARDWOOD PLYWOOD STANDARD GRADES

Grade	Face Veneer	Allowable Defects	Grade	Face Veneer	Allowable Defects
1	PREMIUM—Book or slip matched for pleasing effect	Burls, pin knots, slight color streaks and inconspicuous small patches in limited amounts.	2	SOUND—Free from open defects; a painting grade.	All appearance defects permitted so long as smooth and sound. Smooth patches permitted.
1	GOOD—Unmatched, but sharp contrasts in color, grain and figure not permitted	Burls, pin knots, slight color streaks and inconspicuous small patches in limited amounts.	3	UTILITY	All natural defects; including open knots, wormholes and splits, maximum size of which are defined.
			4	BACKING	Defects practically unlimited; only strength and serviceability are considered.

8-8a. Grading standards for hardwood plywoods.

INTERIOR TYPE GRADES

| Panel Grade Designations | Minimum Veneer Quality | | | Surface |
	Face	Back	Inner Plies	
N-N	N	N	C	Sanded 2 sides
N-A	N	A	C	Sanded 2 sides
N-B	N	B	C	Sanded 2 sides
N-D	N	D	D	Sanded 2 sides
A-A	A	A	D	Sanded 2 sides
A-B	A	B	D	Sanded 2 sides
A-D	A	D	D	Sanded 2 sides
B-B	B	B	D	Sanded 2 sides
B-D	B	D	D	Sanded 2 sides

VENEER QUALITY

N	Intended for natural finish. Selected all heartwood or all sapwood. Free of open defects. Allows some repairs.
A	Smooth and paintable. Neatly made repairs permissible. Also used for natural finish in less demanding applications.
B	Solid surface veneer. Repair plugs and tight knots permitted. Can be painted.
C	Sanding defects permitted that will not impair the strength or serviceability of the panel. Knotholes to $1\frac{1}{2}''$ and splits to $\frac{1}{2}''$ permitted under certain conditions.
C plugged	Improved C veneer with closer limits on knotholes and splits. C plugged face veneers are fully sanded.
D	Used only in Interior type for inner plies and backs. Permits knots and knotholes to $2\frac{1}{2}''$ in maximum dimension and $\frac{1}{2}''$ larger under certain specified limits. Limited splits permitted.

TYPICAL WOOD SPECIES

Group 1	American Birch, Douglas Fir, Sugar Maple and Southern Pine
Group 2	Cypress, White Fir, Western Hemlock, Philippine Mahogany, Black Maple, Red Pine and Yellow Poplar
Group 3	Red Adler, Alaska Cedar, Eastern Hemlock, Jack Pine, Redwood, and Black Spruce
Group 4	Quaking Aspen, Western Red Cedar, Eastern Cottonwood and Sugar Pine
Group 5	Basswood, Balsam Fir and Balsam Poplar

TYPICAL GRADE MARKING

(Also available in Groups 2, 3 and 4)

8-8b. Grading standards for construction and industrial plywood.

Good grade has a matched grain for pleasing effect and is designed to take a natural finish. *Sound grade* is designed for a smooth paint surface. *Utility grade* is a less desirable grade for painting. *Backing grade* is used for the backs of cabinets, crates, and similar pieces.

Hardwood plywood is made with three types of glue. *Type* I is for boat building and exterior use. *Type* II is a weather-resistant bond, and *Type* III is for interior use only.

Construction and Industrial Plywood

Formerly called softwood plywood, these panels are now made from seventy species including softwoods and hardwoods. These plywoods, of veneer-core construction, are manufactured in two basic types, namely *exterior* with waterproof glue and *interior* with moisture-resistant glue. For furniture construction (including built-ins and paneling) the interior grades ranging in quality from N-N to A-B are used. Thicknesses range from $\frac{1}{4}''$ to $1\frac{1}{4}''$, widths from 36″ to 60″ and lengths from 60″ to 144″ in 12″ increments. Plywood is ordered by group number, type, grade, and size. A typical order might be: Group 2, interior type, A-B grade, $\frac{1}{2}'' \times 48'' \times 96''$. Fig. 8-8b and 8-9.

Treating the Edges of Plywood

One of the problems of using plywood in furniture construction is that the edges must be treated. The simplest way is to apply a veneer edge using the same veneer as the plywood face. This veneer

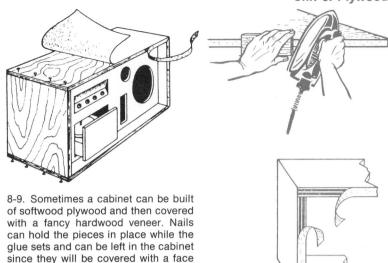

8-9. Sometimes a cabinet can be built of softwood plywood and then covered with a fancy hardwood veneer. Nails can hold the pieces in place while the glue sets and can be left in the cabinet since they will be covered with a face veneer.

edging material can be obtained either with an adhesive already on it or as a plain veneer that can be attached with contact cement. Fig. 8-10. Also see Unit 16.

Purchasing Furniture Made of Plywood

Many people think that best quality furniture is made only of solid lumber. Actually, for wide surfaces such as the tops of tables, desks, and chests, plywood is often

8-10. The simplest method of covering the edge of plywood is with a wood tape veneer that has an adhesive on the back. An iron can be moved along to set the adhesive.

better than solid wood; it shrinks and swells less than solid wood. If furniture is advertised as of a certain solid wood (such as solid maple), all exposed surfaces must be made of lumber. No plywood can be used. Fig. 8-11. If it is

8-11. This dining room table is solid maple. A solid wood top like this must be attached in a way that permits expansion and contraction to take place without causing the top to warp. This is called "floating construction."

advertised only as *genuine* walnut, mahogany, or some other type of hardwood, then it can be made of both solid wood and hardwood plywood. Fig. 8-12. However, furniture that is made with some Philippine mahogany plywood (which is actually lauan) cannot be sold as genuine mahogany. The lauan tree is not genuine mahogany.

8-12. This credenza has a walnut veneer top with a pecan veneer border. The door frames and moldings are solid pecan. This piece could not be sold as genuine walnut, although it is a most excellent example of fine cabinetmaking. Pecan and walnut go very well together and are widely used in fine furniture.

UNIT 9 Hardboard and Particle Board

Two man-made materials widely utilized in furniture construction are hardboard and particle board. Both are members of the family of forest products. Both are made from wood particles, flakes, or individual wood fibers that are combined with resin binders and other chemicals. Some people have the notion that these materials denote lower-cost furniture. However, this is completely false. For many furniture parts, these materials are superior to both solid lumber and plywood. Fig. 9-1. Hardboard is frequently used for drawer bottoms and for the backs of chests and cases because it is more stable than either solid wood or plywood. Particle board is widely used as the core of good hardwood plywood or for plastic laminates.

Particle Board

Particle board is made by combining wood particles with resin binders and hot pressing them into panels. Fig. 9-2. It is made in a wide variety of sizes and thicknesses. Certain types of particle board are called flakeboard.

It is best to check with a lumber yard or supplier as to the best kind of particle board to purchase for your own use. The largest single use for particle board is as core material for various types of furniture, case goods, and built-ins.

9-1. In fine quality furniture, such as the pieces displayed in this showroom, cores of large surface areas often are made of particle board or hardboard.

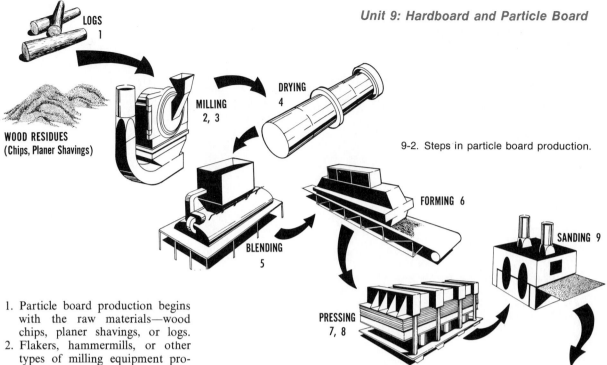

9-2. Steps in particle board production.

1. Particle board production begins with the raw materials—wood chips, planer shavings, or logs.
2. Flakers, hammermills, or other types of milling equipment produce the desired types of tiny wood particles.
3. Screens classify the particles into the proper mixture of sizes.
4. Dryers remove excess moisture and uniformly control the moisture content to the desired level.
5. Resin binders and other chemicals are sprayed onto the wood particles at a controlled rate in a blending operation.
6. Forming machines deposit the treated particles onto belts or metal cauls forming mats.
7. Particle mats are consolidated and the binders are cured in heated hydraulic presses with temperatures up to 400°F and pressures up to 1,000 p.s.i.
8. After pressing, boards are trimmed to the desired length and width.
9. Sanding in high speed belt sanders produces the smooth surfaces and accurate thickness tolerances characteristic of particle boards.

Furniture designers have incorporated particle board into almost all popular furniture styles. It is useful when a flat, true surface is needed. Because it takes plastic laminate so well, particle board is very popular for furniture that has this kind of top. See Unit 16. Particle board is usually covered with wood veneer or plastic laminate. Fig. 9-3. Because it is available in a wide variety of densities, particle board is used not only for home furniture but also for office and commercial furniture.

9-3a. The tops of desks are often made of particle board covered with wood veneer or plastic laminate.

9-3b. Here particle board has been covered with a wood veneer. Note the miter spline joint that will fasten the pieces together in the corner.

9-3c. Soft edging with wood or plastic veneers results in attractive surfaces. Veneer can be glued to a particle board edge in the same way it is applied to the surface.

Hardboard

Hardboard is one of the more popular materials for cabinet-making and furniture construction. Its name is an excellent description since it is very hard and is truly a board. Fig. 9-4. It is much harder than particle board and has many of the excellent working properties of wood. It also looks like wood but never splits, cracks, or splinters. Hardboard has a light, natural wood color that is excellent for furniture fabrication. Fig. 9-5. It is made in a wide variety of types, textures, and sizes. The most common is called *standard hardboard.* By adding chemicals to standard

1. Logs are conveyed from storage yards to huge chippers which reduce the wood to clean, uniformly sized chips.
2. The chips are then reduced to individual wood fibers by either the steam or the mechanical defibering processes.
3. Fibers are put through certain mechanical processes varying with the method of manufacture, and small amounts of chemicals may be added to enhance the resulting board properties.
4. The fibers are interlocked in the felter into a continuous mat and compressed by heavy rollers.
5. Lengths of mat, or "wetlap," are fed into multiple presses where heat and pressure produce the thin, hard, dry board sheets.
6. Leaving the press, moisture is added to the board in a humidifier to stabilize it to surrounding atmospheric conditions.
7. The board is trimmed to standard specified dimensions, wrapped in convenient packages, and readied for shipment.

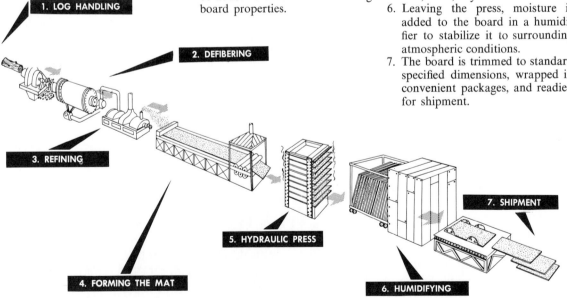

9-4. Steps in the manufacture of hardboard.

9-5. Drawer bottoms and the back of this Contemporary desk are made of hardboard.

hardboard and applying a heat-treating process, the product takes on added stiffness and hardness and is called *tempered hardboard.* Hardboard is manufactured with one or both surfaces smooth which is referred to as S1S or S2S. The S1S hardboard has one smooth face with a back of screened or rough appearance.

Hardboard is made in several different thicknesses, the most common being $\frac{1}{8}$″, $\frac{3}{16}$″, and $\frac{1}{4}$″. The panel measures 4′ x 8′, although it is available in standard lengths of 4′, 6′, 8′, 10′, 12′, and 16′.

Specialty Hardboards

Because hardboard is a manufactured product, it can be made in many different shapes, sizes, and surfaces. Thus it is able to meet the needs of many types of construction and industrial uses, including a wide variety of uses in furniture construction and cabinetmaking. For example, perforated panels are available in a variety of sizes and styles with round, diagonal, or square holes. Fig. 9-6. Wood-grained hardboards have a printed grain which matches the color and texture of walnut, oak, and other woods.

Many other types of panel woods are designed primarily for the building construction industry.

9-6. The sliding fronts of this cabinet are made of perforated hardboard.

DISCUSSION TOPICS

Section Two—MATERIALS

Unit 6. Materials for Furniture Construction

1. List the major parts of a tree.
2. What is the difference between open- and closed-grain wood?
3. Name the two common methods of cutting lumber.
4. Why should kiln-dried lumber be used for furniture making?
5. Does air-dried lumber have a higher moisture content than kiln-dried?
6. Discuss the hardwood grades of lumber.

7. What is the most important use of factory or shop lumber?

8. What is the surfaced or dressed thickness of 1″ hardwood?

9. Name five common lumber defects.

10. What is a board foot of lumber?

11. Explain the meaning of the term S2S.

12. What are the two major kinds of plastics?

13. Discuss the use of metal in furniture construction.

Unit 7. Kinds of Wood

1. Approximately how many kinds or species of wood are there?

2. Name six common hardwoods used in furniture making.

3. Name three hardwoods that are difficult to work with hand tools.

4. What are some of the light-weight hardwoods?

5. What hardwood is used as a substitute for walnut?

6. Discuss the difference between white oak and red oak.

7. Is Philippine mahogany a true mahogany? Explain.

Unit 8. Plywood

1. Describe the three principal methods of cutting veneer.

2. Describe the five grades of hardwood plywood.

3. Explain the steps in the manufacture of hardwood plywood.

4. What are the advantages of plywood over glued-up lumber for large surfaces in furniture?

Unit 9. Particle Board and Hardboard

1. Describe how particle board is manufactured.

2. Why is particle board often used as a base for plastic laminates?

3. Explain the manufacture of hardboard.

4. Describe some of the common kinds of hardboard.

EXTRA CREDIT ACTIVITIES

1. Prepare a visual aid showing the construction of plywood.

2. Prepare a research paper on the manufacture of plywood.

3. Examine the design and construction of several pieces of furniture and discuss the materials used.

First Steps in Furniture Construction

Before you can build beautiful furniture like this, you must have a drawing, a bill of materials, and proper know-how. (Baumritter Corporation)

UNIT 10 Reading a Drawing

Drawings for furniture and accessories are available from many sources. Examples of a few of these drawings are shown in this book. Others can be secured from magazines, project books, and commercial companies. Fig. 10-1.

In some cases, a full-size pattern drawing is available in which the parts are drawn to full size and dimensioned so that the pattern can be laid directly on the wood. However, most furniture drawings found in books are made to scale. Use the dimensions indicated on the drawing to make up the bill of materials, the stock cutting list, and the layout.

If the drawing contains irregularly shaped parts, it is frequently shown cross-sectioned in order that these parts can be enlarged to full size and the pattern thus duplicated.

Kinds of Drawings

There are three kinds of drawings commonly used in furniture construction: orthographic projection, isometric and cabinet. In

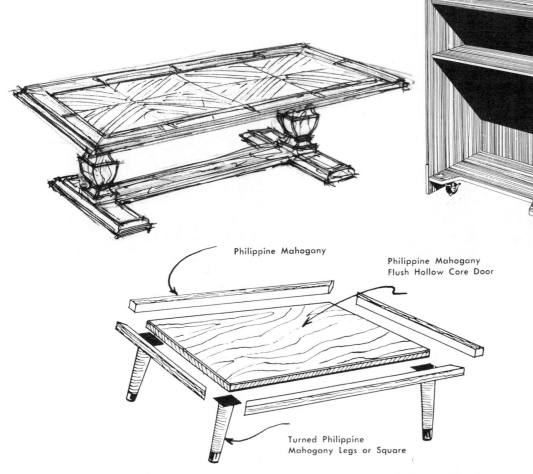

Philippine Mahogany

Philippine Mahogany
Flush Hollow Core Door

Turned Philippine
Mahogany Legs or Square

10-1. Pictorial drawings can be used to show the general shape of furniture.

orthographic projections, (sometimes called multiview drawings) two or more views are shown, usually three, which are most frequently the front, top, and right side or end view of a project. Fig. 10-2. This kind of drawing shows the true shape of all parts. Fig. 10-3. An *isometric* drawing is one in which the sides are drawn at an angle of 30 degrees to the horizontal and all views are shown as one drawing. Fig. 10-4. A *cabinet* drawing is one in which the front view is exactly like that of the orthographic projection, but the sides are drawn at an angle of 45 degrees. Fig. 10-5. These sides are foreshortened to *half their true length,* giving the object the proportions it would have in a photograph. Fig. 10-6, page 92.

When the isometric or cabinet drawing is used, additional details are usually needed to show construction techniques. These two kinds of drawings are most often used for modern furniture pieces, so that a "picture" of the piece can be combined with dimensioning.

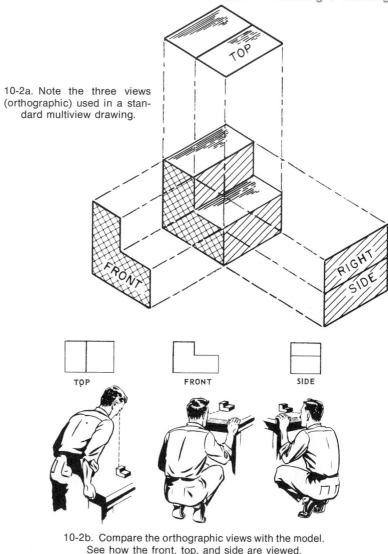

10-2a. Note the three views (orthographic) used in a standard multiview drawing.

TOP   FRONT   SIDE

10-2b. Compare the orthographic views with the model. See how the front, top, and side are viewed.

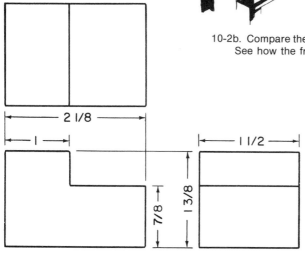

2 1/8

1

1 1/2

7/8

1 3/8

10-2c. The standard orthographic views as they appear.

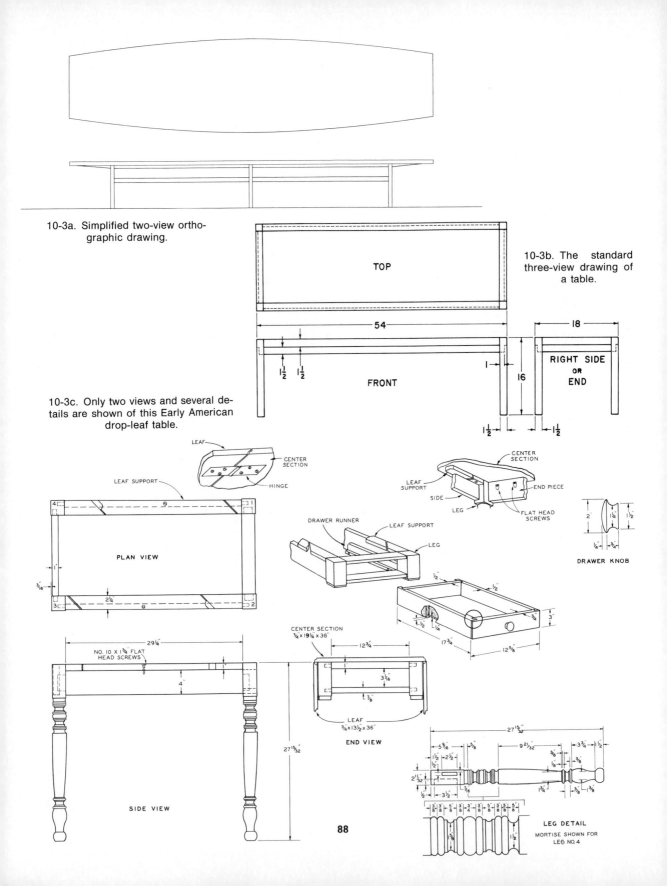

10-3a. Simplified two-view orthographic drawing.

10-3b. The standard
three-view drawing of
a table.

TOP

54

FRONT

RIGHT SIDE
OR
END

18

16

$1\frac{1}{2}$ $1\frac{1}{2}$

$1\frac{1}{2}$ $1\frac{1}{2}$

1

10-3c. Only two views and several details are shown of this Early American
drop-leaf table.

LEAF

CENTER
SECTION

LEAF SUPPORT

HINGE

CENTER
SECTION

LEAF
SUPPORT

END PIECE

SIDE

LEG

FLAT HEAD
SCREWS

4

1

PLAN VIEW

1"

$\frac{3}{16}$"

$2\frac{1}{4}$

3

2

DRAWER RUNNER

LEAF SUPPORT

LEG

$\frac{1}{2}$"

$\frac{1}{2}$"

$\frac{1}{2}$"

$\frac{1}{4}$"

$\frac{3}{4}$"

3"

$17\frac{3}{4}$"

$12\frac{5}{8}$"

2"

$1\frac{1}{8}$"

$1\frac{1}{2}$"

$\frac{1}{4}$"

$\frac{3}{4}$"

DRAWER KNOB

$29\frac{1}{4}$

NO. 10 X $1\frac{3}{4}$" FLAT
HEAD SCREWS

4"

CENTER SECTION
$\frac{3}{4}$ x $19\frac{1}{4}$ x 36"

$12\frac{3}{4}$"

$3\frac{1}{16}$"

$\frac{7}{8}$"

LEAF
$\frac{3}{4}$ x $13\frac{1}{2}$ x 36"

END VIEW

$27\frac{15}{32}$

SIDE VIEW

$27\frac{15}{32}$"

$5\frac{5}{16}$" $\frac{5}{8}$" $9\frac{21}{32}$" $3\frac{3}{4}$" $1\frac{1}{2}$"

$1\frac{1}{2}$" $2\frac{1}{2}$" $\frac{3}{8}$" $\frac{3}{8}$"

$2\frac{11}{32}$" $\frac{1}{8}$" $\frac{3}{8}$"

$\frac{1}{2}$ $3\frac{1}{2}$" $\frac{7}{8}$" $1\frac{3}{4}$" $3\frac{3}{8}$" $1\frac{3}{8}$"

$\frac{3}{8}$" $\frac{3}{4}$" $\frac{5}{8}$" $\frac{3}{8}$" $\frac{3}{8}$" $\frac{3}{4}$" $\frac{5}{8}$" $\frac{3}{8}$"

$1\frac{1}{2}$"

LEG DETAIL
MORTISE SHOWN FOR
LEG NO. 4

88

BILL OF MATERIALS

All Dimensions Are Finished Size

No. Pieces	Thickness	Width	Length	Description
4	$2^{11}/_{32}''$	$2^{11}/_{32}''$	$27^{15}/_{32}''$	Leg
2	$1''$	$4''$	$31\frac{3}{4}''$	Side Rails
1	$1''$	$5''$	$14\frac{3}{4}''$	End Rail
1	$1''$	$2\frac{1}{4}''$	$14\frac{3}{4}''$	Top End Rail (for drawer)
1	$\frac{7}{8}''$	$2\frac{1}{4}''$	$14\frac{3}{4}''$	Bottom End Rail (for drawer)
2	$1''$	$2\frac{1}{4}''$	$29\frac{1}{4}''$	Leaf and Table Supports
2	$1''$	$2''$	$29\frac{1}{4}''$	Drawer Runners
2	$\frac{1}{2}''$	$3''$	$17\frac{3}{4}''$	Drawer Sides
1	$\frac{1}{2}''$	$3''$	$12\frac{1}{8}''$	Drawer Back
1	$\frac{3}{4}''$	$3''$	$12\frac{5}{8}''$	Drawer Front
1	$\frac{1}{4}''$	$12\frac{1}{8}''$	$17\frac{1}{8}''$	Drawer Bottom
1	$\frac{3}{4}''$	$19\frac{1}{4}''$	$36''$	Top-Center Section
2	$\frac{3}{4}''$	$13\frac{1}{2}''$	$36''$	Leaves
4				Hinges
1	$2''$ dia.	——	$1''$	Drawer Knob

10-3d. A bill of materials and photograph of the table. (See next unit for fuller explanation of bill of materials.)

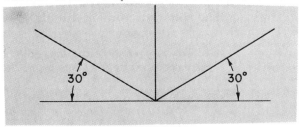

10-4a. The isometric drawing is started as shown here.

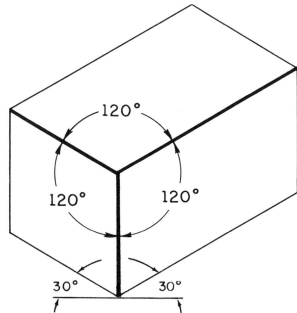

10-4b. An isometric drawing is always enclosed in a box that is drawn with the lines 120° apart.

LUMBER LIST
Desk

Pieces or quantity	Description	Wood	Thick	Wide	Long
1	Top	Philippine Mahogany	1⅜"	2'	6'8"
1	Typewriter Shelf	Philippine Mahogany	¾"	14½"	1'2"
4	Ends	Philippine Mahogany	¾"	23¼"	1'6"
2	Bottom	Philippine Mahogany	¾"	23¼"	1'3½"
2	Back	Philippine Mahogany	¾"	15½"	1'5¼"
1	Door	Philippine Mahogany	¾"	18"	1'5"
1	Drawer Front	Philippine Mahogany	¾"	4½"	1'5"
1	Drawer Front	Philippine Mahogany	¾"	13½"	1'5"
2	Drawer Sides	Philippine Mahogany	½"	4"	1'10½"
2	Drawer Sides	Philippine Mahogany	½"	12"	1'10½"
1	Drawer Back	Philippine Mahogany	½"	3⅛"	1'2¼"
1	Drawer Back	Philippine Mahogany	½"	12"	1'2¼"
2	Drawer Bottoms	Philippine Mahogany	½"	22½"	1'4¼"
4	Glue Cleats	Philippine Mahogany	¾"	¾"	1'

Letter Pigeon Holes

Pieces or quantity	Description	Wood	Thick	Wide	Long
2	Ends	Philippine Mahogany	¾"	12"	8¾"
1	Top	Philippine Mahogany	¾"	12"	3'11¾"
1	Bottom	Philippine Mahogany	¾"	11¼"	3'11¾"
1	Back	Philippine Mahogany	¾"	4"	3'11¾"
1	Apron Facia	Philippine Mahogany	¾"	4"	3'11¾"
4	Dividers	Philippine Mahogany	¾"	4"	11¼"

Note: Unless otherwise specified, material to be solid Philippine Mahogany.

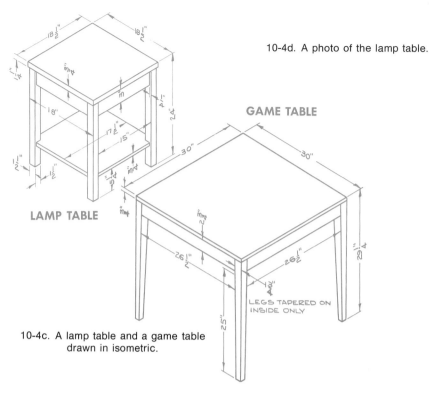

10-4d. A photo of the lamp table.

LAMP TABLE

GAME TABLE

LEGS TAPERED ON INSIDE ONLY

10-4c. A lamp table and a game table drawn in isometric.

10-4e. A game table made of oak. The top is upholstered with plastic leather.

10-4f. Construction details of a desk. Note how some parts of the desk are moved away from the base so that you can see the details. This is called an "exploded" isometric.

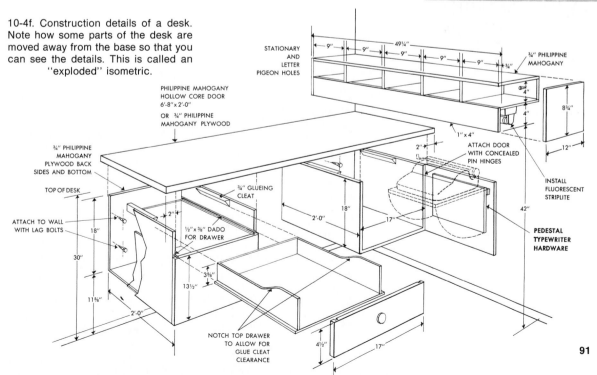

STATIONARY AND LETTER PIGEON HOLES

¾" PHILIPPINE MAHOGANY

PHILIPPINE MAHOGANY HOLLOW CORE DOOR 6'-8" x 2'-0"
OR ¾" PHILIPPINE MAHOGANY PLYWOOD

ATTACH DOOR WITH CONCEALED PIN HINGES

¾" PHILIPPINE MAHOGANY PLYWOOD BACK SIDES AND BOTTOM

TOP OF DESK

¾" GLUEING CLEAT

INSTALL FLUORESCENT STRIPLITE

ATTACH TO WALL WITH LAG BOLTS

½" x ⅜" DADO FOR DRAWER

PEDESTAL TYPEWRITER HARDWARE

NOTCH TOP DRAWER TO ALLOW FOR GLUE CLEAT CLEARANCE

91

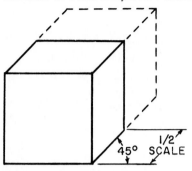

10-5a. A cabinet drawing is made with the inclined side one-half the true length. The dotted lines show how it would appear in true length.

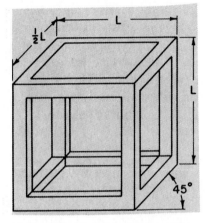

10-5b. Notice that the drawing of this cube-shaped table made in cabinet form appears to be a cube.

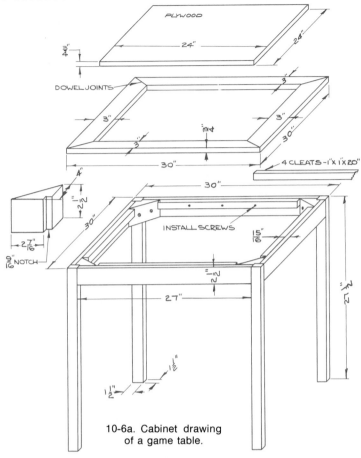

10-6a. Cabinet drawing of a game table.

10-6b. This game table is made of mahogany and has a top with a leather insert.

How to Read a Drawing

In reading a drawing, you will derive a certain meaning from each line. Fig. 10-7. These are:

1. *Visible line.* Body or outline of the object.

2. *Invisible line.* Indicates a part that cannot be seen from the surface.

3. *Center line.* Divides the drawing into equal or symmetrical parts.

4. *Extension line.* Extends out from the solid line to provide lines between which dimensions can be shown.

5. *Dimension lines.* Have arrowheads at one or both ends and line is broken in the center. These lines run between the extension lines.

It is extremely important in reading a drawing to observe the dimensions carefully. Never measure the drawing directly. Every part on the drawing should be dimensioned to show its thickness, width, and length. Frequently, however, the length will not include the stock needed to make the joints. For example, when a rail has been dimensioned, the length is frequently shown from leg to leg. Add an amount to provide for the joints.

Woodworking Drawings

Notice that furniture drawings, especially those found in books and magazines, do not follow the strict standards of machine drawing. Some characteristics of furniture drawings are:

● Several types of drawings are used to show the product. Some of the views may be orthographic while others may be isometric or cabinet drawings. Fig. 10-8.

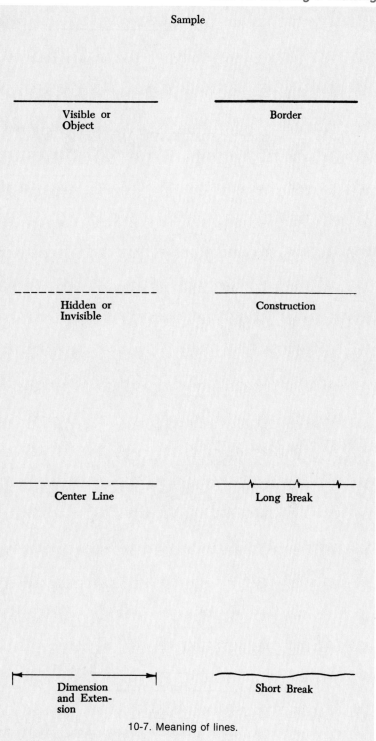

Sample

Visible or Object

Border

Hidden or Invisible

Construction

Center Line

Long Break

Dimension and Extension

Short Break

10-7. Meaning of lines.

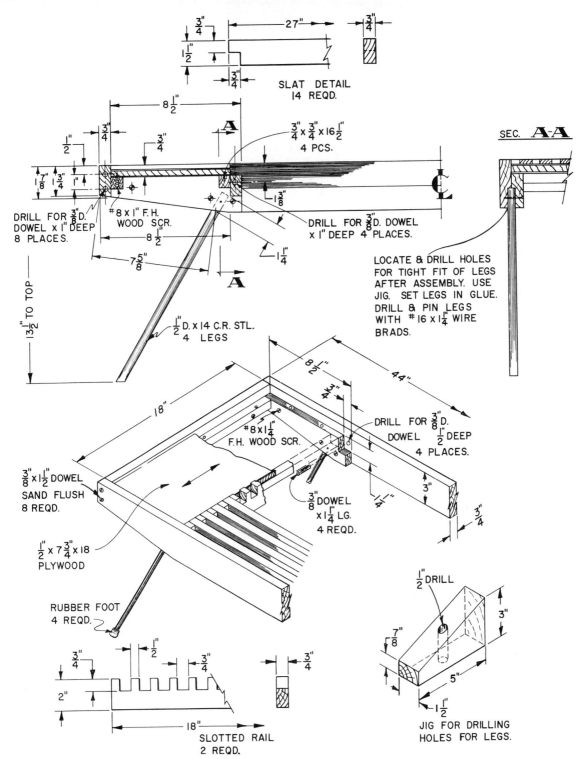

$\frac{3}{4}$"

27"

$\frac{3}{4}$"

$1\frac{1}{2}$"

$\frac{3}{4}$"

SLAT DETAIL
14 REQD.

$8\frac{1}{2}$"

$\frac{1}{2}$"

$\frac{3}{4}$"

$\frac{3}{4}$"

A

$\frac{3}{4}$" x $\frac{3}{4}$" x $16\frac{1}{2}$"
4 PCS.

SEC. A-A

$1\frac{7}{8}$" $1\frac{3}{4}$" 1"

C

$1\frac{3}{8}$"

DRILL FOR $\frac{3}{8}$"D.
DOWEL x 1" DEEP
8 PLACES.

#8 x 1" F.H.
WOOD SCR.

DRILL FOR $\frac{3}{8}$"D. DOWEL
x 1" DEEP 4 PLACES.

$8\frac{1}{2}$"

$7\frac{5}{8}$"

$1\frac{1}{4}$"

A

LOCATE & DRILL HOLES
FOR TIGHT FIT OF LEGS
AFTER ASSEMBLY. USE
JIG. SET LEGS IN GLUE.
DRILL & PIN LEGS
WITH #16 x $1\frac{1}{4}$" WIRE
BRADS.

$13\frac{1}{2}$" TO TOP

$\frac{1}{2}$"D. x 14 C.R. STL.
4 LEGS

$8\frac{1}{2}$"

44"

$\frac{3}{4}$"

18"

#8 x $1\frac{1}{4}$"
F.H. WOOD SCR.

DRILL FOR $\frac{3}{8}$"D.
DOWEL $\frac{1}{2}$" DEEP
4 PLACES.

$\frac{3}{8}$" x $1\frac{1}{2}$" DOWEL
SAND FLUSH
8 REQD.

$\frac{3}{8}$"DOWEL
x $1\frac{1}{4}$" LG.
4 REQD.

3"

$\frac{1}{4}$"

$\frac{3}{4}$"

$\frac{1}{2}$" x $7\frac{3}{4}$" x 18
PLYWOOD

RUBBER FOOT
4 REQD.

$\frac{1}{2}$"DRILL

3"

$\frac{3}{4}$"

$\frac{1}{2}$"

$\frac{3}{4}$"

$\frac{3}{4}$"

$\frac{7}{8}$"

2"

5"

$1\frac{1}{2}$"

18"

SLOTTED RAIL
2 REQD.

JIG FOR DRILLING
HOLES FOR LEGS.

10-8a. Note how a combination of drawings is used for this Contemporary coffee
table.

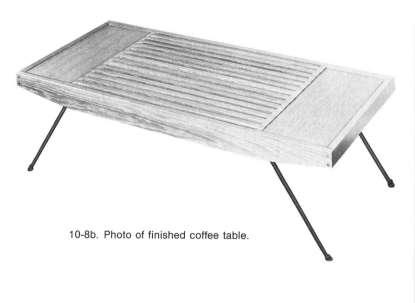

10-8b. Photo of finished coffee table.

1. Cut all pieces to size on circular saw.
2. With the aid of a taper jig on a circular saw, cut tapers on side rails and side cleats.
3. Set saw arbor to proper angle and cut angle on bottom edge of end rails.
4. Lay out and bore all dowel holes.
5. Lay out notches for slats on center rails. Cut notches with dado head on circular saw.
6. Cut dowels to length and glue up all rails.
7. Notch ends of slats and side cleats with dado head.
8. Drill screw shank holes in all cleats and countersink or counterbore holes as required. Drill anchor holes in rails and top panels.
9. Glue slats into place.
10. Attach all cleats with glue and F. H. Wood Screws.
11. Fit and attach top panels with F. H. Wood Screws.
12. Bore holes for tight fit of legs. A boring jig will aid in boring holes for the slanting legs. Cut a hardwood block 1½" x 3" x 5". Center and bore a ½" hole thru the width of the block. Cut an angle on the block so that it measures 3" wide at one end and ⅞" wide on the other. Clamp this jig in place and bore holes.
13. Cut legs to length. Chamfer and smooth bottoms of all legs.
14. Set all legs in glue. Drill and pin all legs in place with No. 16 x 1¼" wire brads.
15. Finish sand entire project.
16. Apply desired finish.
17. Paint legs coach (dull) black.
18. Reshape ½" black rubber crutch tips. Chuck a short length of ½" dowel in drill press. Slip crutch tip on dowel and file and sand off ribs. Mount a tip on each leg.

No. of Pieces	Part Name	Thickness	Width	Length	Material
	IMPORTANT: All dimensions listed below are FINISHED size.				
2	Side Rails	¾"	3"	44"	White Oak
2	End Rails	¾"	1⅞"	18"	White Oak
2	Center Rails	¾"	2"	18"	White Oak
4	Side Cleats	¾"	2¼"	8½"	Hardwood
4	Panel Cleats	¾"	¾"	16½"	Hardwood
2	Panels	½"	7¾"	18"	Comb Grain White Oak Plywood S1S
14	Slats	¾"	1½"	27"	White Oak
8	Dowels	⅜" dia.		1½"	White Oak
4	Dowels	⅜" dia.		1¼"	Hardwood
4	Legs	½" dia.		14"	Cold Rolled Steel
4	Rubber Feet				
32	No. 8 x 1¼" F. H. Wood Screws				
12	No. 8 x 1" F. H. Wood Screws				
4	No. 16 x 1¼" Wire Brads				

10-8c. Bill of materials.

10-8d. Procedure for making coffee table. (See next unit for fuller explanation of a plan of procedure.)

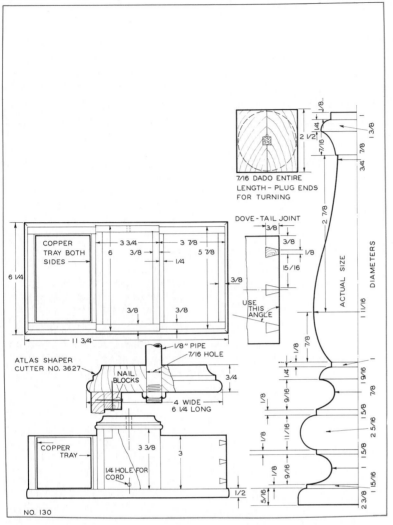

7/16 DADO ENTIRE LENGTH – PLUG ENDS FOR TURNING

DOVE-TAIL JOINT

USE THIS ANGLE

ACTUAL SIZE

DIAMETERS

COPPER TRAY BOTH SIDES

ATLAS SHAPER CUTTER NO. 3627

NAIL BLOCKS

1/8" PIPE
7/16 HOLE

4 WIDE
6 1/4 LONG

COPPER TRAY

1/4 HOLE FOR CORD

NO. 130

10-9a. Note how the views of this lamp are placed on the sheet for convenient layout.

10-9b. Planter lamp.

• If an orthographic drawing is used, the views may not be in their correct location. The views are often arranged for the convenience of page layout and do not follow standard view placement. Fig. 10-9.

• Not all of the information is shown. For example, joint construction is sometimes not shown since it is assumed that the craftsman will work this out for himself.

• Sections are used to show the inside of the object. Sometimes these are enlarged to show a part in greater detail.

• Inch marks (″) are often used even though this is not standard drafting practice. Fig. 10-10.

Enlarging a Pattern and Transferring a Design

Many product designs are available in full-size patterns that can be transferred directly to the lumber. More often, though, in books and magazines, the irregular shapes are drawn in some smaller size and you must enlarge them. Fig. 10-11. This can be done very simply as follows:

1. Check the drawing to see how much it must be enlarged. Most irregular shapes are covered with squared lines, and the size of square indicates the size for a full-size pattern. Usually the drawing will show ½-inch or 1-inch squares.

2. Secure a piece of paper large enough for a full-size pattern and lay out squares of the required size. This can be done on a piece of wrapping paper.

3. Start at the lower lefthand corner of the original drawing to letter each horizontal line a, b, c,

96

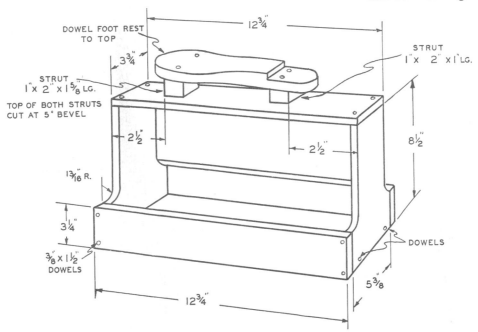

10-10. Inch marks (″) are shown on many woodworking drawings.

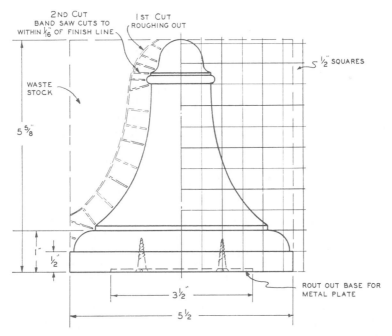

10-11. An enlargement of this bookend would have to be made before it could be transferred to the wood and cut out.

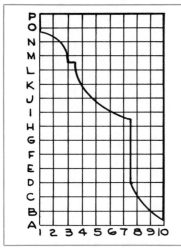

THE ENLARGING OF A DESIGN

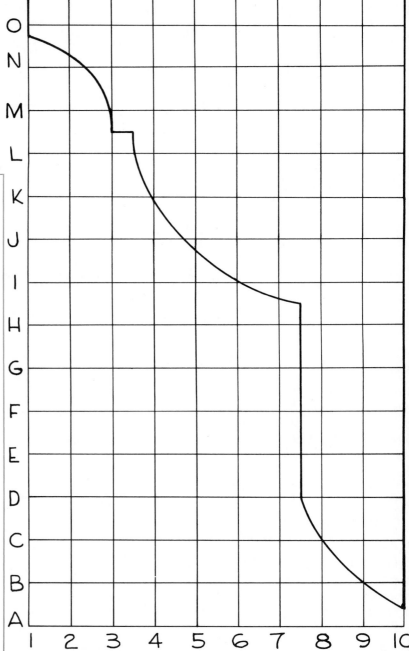

etc., from bottom to top. Number each vertical line from left to right 1, 2, 3, etc. Fig. 10-12.

4. Letter and number the lines on the full-size pattern in the same manner. Now locate a point on the original drawing and transfer it to the full-size pattern. Continue to do this until enough points have been located to draw in the lines for the full-size pattern. Usually a drafting tool called a *French curve* is used to draw in the curves. Another method is to bend a piece of wire solder to follow the points and then draw in the lines by tracing along the wire.

5. The pattern can then be transferred to the stock by one of the following methods:

a. Place the pattern over the stock with carbon paper underneath it and trace a design.

b. Cut out the pattern. Place it over the stock and trace around it.

c. If many parts of the same design are to be made, it may be a help to make a plywood template or pattern.

10-12. Procedure for enlarging a drawing.

98

UNIT 11 Making a Materials Bill and Plan of Procedure

When you have selected the furniture design and the drawing or sketch is at hand, you must make a materials bill. Fig. 11-1. In some cases you will find the bill of materials listed with the project design. The exact arrangement of this form varies somewhat. Fig. 11-2. But in every case it includes such items as number of pieces, names and sizes of the parts, and kinds of wood.

It is a good idea first to make the lumber specifications for the project, indicating the finished size and the cutout size. The cutout size is the same as the finished size with amounts added to the thickness, width, and length for rough-cutting the pieces to size and for extra material for joints. Usually $\frac{1}{16}''$ to $\frac{1}{8}''$ is added to the thickness, about $\frac{1}{4}''$ to the width, and about $\frac{1}{2}''$ to the length. Allowances for cutout sizes will vary with finished sizes. Larger pieces such as cabinet sides and tops will require larger allowances than legs and rails.

Once the cutout size has been determined, it is necessary to make a lumber order. Instead of figuring the board feet and cost for each item, determine the sizes of boards from which the cutout-size pieces can be cut. For example, the items should be grouped so that all pieces of the same thickness and kind of material are together.

After this is done, it is frequently necessary to determine whether some rough lumber must be "glued up" in order to obtain the required finished size. For example, if the legs of a table are $1\frac{1}{2}'' \times 1\frac{1}{2}''$, perhaps 1'' rough stock should be ordered and pieces of it glued together face-to-face to form the larger size.

Pieces can also be glued edge-to-edge to form larger surfaces.

In making the lumber specifications and lumber order, it is well to keep in mind the standard sizes of lumber and plywood that are available. Remember that most hardwood lumber can be ordered to the exact thickness, but that it is usually cheaper to order material in random widths and lengths (R W & L). If the parts are made of plywood, standard size

BILL OF MATERIALS
IMPORTANT: All dimensions listed below are FINISHED size.

No. of Pieces	Part Name	Thickness	Width	Length	Material
1	Top	$\frac{3}{4}''$	$27\frac{3}{4}''$	$27\frac{3}{4}''$	Comb Grain White Oak Plywood
2	Shelves	$\frac{3}{4}''$	$11\frac{1}{4}''$	$28\frac{1}{2}''$	Comb Grain White Oak Plywood
1	Corner Shelf Support	$\frac{3}{4}''$	$7''$	$7''$	Comb Grain White Oak Plywood
1	Corner Shelf Support	$\frac{3}{4}''$	$6\frac{3}{4}''$	$7''$	Comb Grain White Oak Plywood
2	End Shelf Support	$\frac{3}{4}''$	$9\frac{1}{2}''$	$7''$	Comb Grain White Oak Plywood
2	Top Cleats	$1''$	$2\frac{1}{2}''$	$32''$	White Oak
2	Top Cleats	$1''$	$2\frac{1}{2}''$	$27\frac{3}{4}''$	White Oak
2	Shelf Cleats	$\frac{3}{4}''$	$2\frac{1}{2}''$	$11\frac{1}{2}''$	White Oak
4	Side Rails	$\frac{3}{4}''$	$2\frac{1}{2}''$	$23\frac{3}{8}''$	White Oak
4	Stretchers	$\frac{3}{4}''$ dia.		$26\frac{1}{8}''$	White Oak
4	Legs	$1\frac{3}{4}''$	$1\frac{3}{4}''$	$16\frac{1}{8}''$	White Oak
7	Facings	$\frac{1}{8}''$	$\frac{3}{4}''$	$7''$	White Oak
2	Facings	$\frac{1}{8}''$	$\frac{3}{4}''$	$17''$	White Oak
2	Facings	$\frac{1}{8}''$	$\frac{3}{4}''$	$28\frac{3}{8}''$	White Oak
40	Dowels	$\frac{3}{8}''$ dia.		$1\frac{1}{2}''$	Hardwood
16	No. 10 x $1\frac{1}{2}$ F. H. Wood Screws				

11-1a. This bill of materials (or materials bill) shows the dimensions in finished sizes. You must convert these to the cutout sizes for determining the lumber order. Note also that the bill of materials does not include a list of the finishing materials needed.

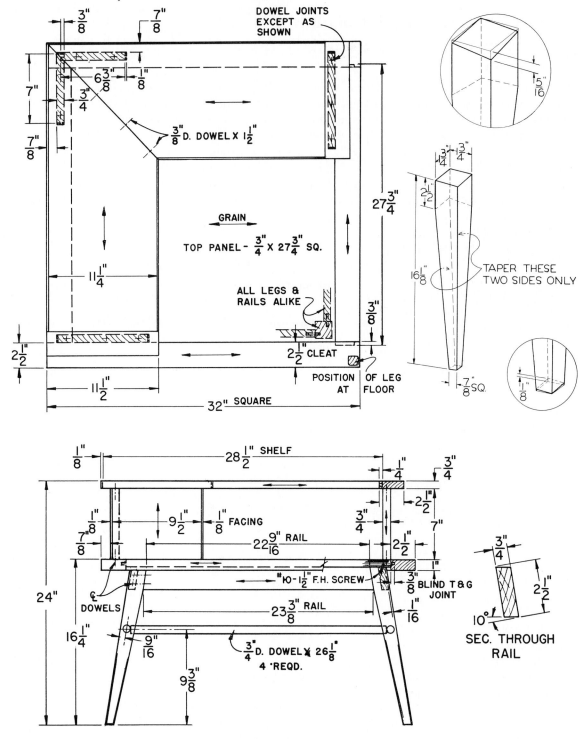

11-1b. Drawing of a corner table.

is 4' x 8' sheets, although 4' x 4' sheets can be purchased. In addition to the lumber specification and lumber order, a list of other supply costs should be included. Such items as plastics, metal fittings, fastening devices, finishing materials, and others must be included. Once this is completed, a plan of procedure is made (if not already supplied). Fig. 11-3. This describes the processes, the tools, and the machines that will be required. See page 103.

11-1c. A corner table made of white oak.

1. Cut all pieces to size on circular saw.
2. Taper two adjoining sides of each leg on circular saw with a taper jig, or on a jointer.
3. Cut angle on ends of side rails on circular saw. Cut 10° angle on top and bottom edges on a circular saw, or on a jointer.
4. Bore all dowel holes in side rails and legs. Drill and countersink screw holes in side rails for mounting top.
5. Sand all members of the base and assemble.
6. Cut tongue on four sides of top panel, one end of each shelf member, and one edge of one corner shelf support. Also, cut tongue on both ends of two top cleats.
7. Using dado head or moulding head on circular saw, cut groove in all top and shelf cleats. Groove should stop ½" from each end on shelf cleats and two top cleats for blind tongue and groove joint. Also, groove one corner shelf support.
8. Assemble top. Locate and drill anchor holes in top for mounting on base.
9. Glue cleats onto shelf members.
10. Glue facings on shelf members and all shelf supports.
11. Carefully miter one end of each shelf member.
12. Bore dowel holes for doweled miter joint. Assemble shelf.
13. Locate and bore all dowel holes in shelf, top and shelf supports.
14. Assemble corner shelf support.
15. Carefully sand top, shelf and supports. Assemble.
16. Attach top assembly on to base with No. 10 F. H. Wood Screws.
17. Apply an oak finish.

11-1d. Plan of procedure for building the corner table.

MATERIALS BILL

LUMBER SPECIFICATIONS

Name of Part or Article	Kind of Wood	No. of Pieces	Cutout Size			Finished Size		
			T	W	L	T	W	L

(See charts on the next page.)

(*Charts continued from previous page.*)

LUMBER ORDER

Instead of figuring bd. ft. and cost for each individual item in the materials bill (page 101), determine the size of boards from which the *Cutout Size* pieces can be cut. Figure bd. ft. and cost of these boards.

No. of Pieces	T	W	L	Kind of Wood	No. of Bd. ft.	Cost Per Bd. ft.	Total Cost	Instr's O.K.

Total Cost ____________

OTHER SUPPLY COST

(Metal, Plastic, Hardware, Finishing Materials, etc.)

Item	Quan.	Size	Unit Cost	Total Cost	Instr's O.K.

COST SUMMARY

Lumber Cost ____________
Supply Cost ____________
Total Cost ____________
Less Allow. ____________
Amount Due ____________
Date Paid ____________

11-2. You can make up blank forms like these when you need to make a materials bill or to order lumber and other supplies. (*Do not write in this book.*)

PLAN OF PROCEDURE

Description of the Processes	Tools or Machines

11-3. You can make a plan of procedure based on this blank form when you are preparing to build a furniture piece. (*Do not write in this book.*)

UNIT 12 Getting Out Stock

The first step in the actual building of a piece of furniture is *cutting the stock to rough* (stock-cutting) size. Fig. 12-1. In getting out the stock, always cut the pieces of like thickness before going on to the next. Fig. 12-2. Regardless of whether the stock is Rgh (rough) or surfaced (S2S or S4S), first examine the end of the board to see if it is split, checked, or otherwise imperfect. If necessary, trim off a small amount to remove any imperfection and to square off the end. Now examine both surfaces of the board for any serious imperfections such as a knot, split, check, or dry rot. With proper layout, only small areas need to be wasted, even if there is an imperfection.

When making duplicate parts, you should perform the same operation on all parts before starting a new step. Most hardwood stock for furniture is purchased rough, so first you must get the stock and square it up. The steps needed to bring it to finished size are described here. For most cabinet-making, stock is brought to correct thickness and width by planing and jointing, and to correct length by sawing. If end grain is exposed, it may be necessary to plane the ends. Before stock is rough cut to length, it should be checked for warp. (Review Unit 6 for discussion of warping.)

In general, when boards are first cut at the saw mill, the faces are flat and the edges straight. However, during air and kiln drying, various forms of crookedness develop such as bow, crook, cup, and twist. There is little difficulty with bow and crook, but *cup* and *twist* present a greater problem. Fig. 12-3. Cupping is usually caused when one surface absorbs more moisture than the other. For example, if the bottom face takes up more moisture than the top, the bottom will swell causing it to cup upward. Cupping happens more often with plain-sawed wood than with quarter-sawed lumber. Neither cup nor twist can be removed by surfacing on the planer alone; therefore it is always important that the first working surface be "trued up" on a jointer before squaring up the board.

Always surface a board *with the grain*. Fig. 12-4. Planing against the grain roughens the surface. It may be difficult to see grain direction on a rough board; however, jointing will make it easier to see.

Rough cut the pieces to length, allowing enough material for squaring up. This can be done on a *radial arm* or *circular saw*. Fig.

12-1. To build any product such as this Contemporary table, the first step is rough cutting the stock to size.

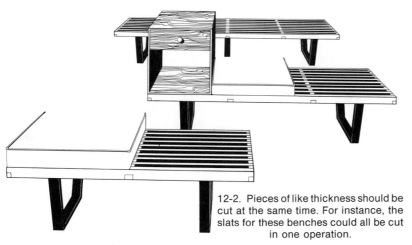

12-2. Pieces of like thickness should be cut at the same time. For instance, the slats for these benches could all be cut in one operation.

12-5. Now check each piece of stock to determine which appears to be the best side. Arrange the lumber so the best side will appear on the exterior of the furniture piece. Frequently, the first side that is surfaced will be the poorer side, but this will always be called the *face surface*. The first edge to be surfaced will be called the *face edge*. These must be the most accurate, so, when laying out joints, always mark from the face surface and face edge.

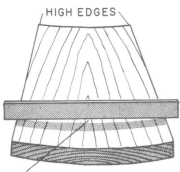

12-3a. Cupping is caused by uneven shrinkage.

DIRECTION OF GRAIN

12-4. Grain direction.

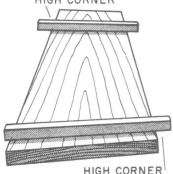

12-3b. These two sticks placed at the ends of a piece of stock show twist in the board. This is the most difficult defect to remove.

12-5. Cutting to length with a radial arm saw. See Unit 26. Allow about ½″ more than desired final length, for squaring.

The common procedure for squaring up rough stock (six steps) is:

1. *True up one face.* Plane the face surface on the jointer to smooth the stock and remove any warp. Fig. 12-6a.

2. *True up one edge.* Joint the first edge by holding the face surface against the fence of the jointer. Fig. 12-6b. Mark the face surface and edge. Fig. 12-6c.

3. *Plane to thickness.* Use a thickness planer if one is available. If not, buy S2S lumber as suggested in Unit 6. Fig. 12-6d.

4. *Cut and plane to finished width.* Adjust the fence of the circular saw to cut about $\frac{1}{16}''$ to $\frac{1}{8}''$ over finished width and then rip. Plane to finished width on a jointer. Fig. 12-6e.

5 and 6. *Cut and/or plane to finished length.* Cut one end square on the circular saw. Lay out the correct length and cut to finished length. Remember to allow enough for joints. If the end grain must be exposed, cut one end square and surface it on the jointer. Then cut the other end $\frac{1}{16}''$ too long and surface to exact length on the jointer. Fig. 12-6f.

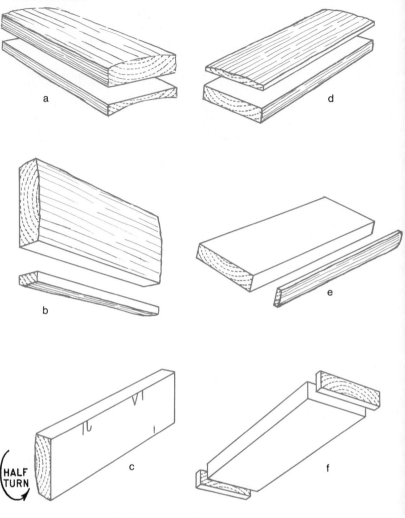

12-6. Steps in squaring up stock.

UNIT 13 Gluing Up Stock

Large surfaces for furniture can be made by using plywood or other panel stock, by building a frame and panel, or by gluing up solid stock. Fig. 13-1. If the furniture is to be made of solid wood, as is frequently done for Early American or Colonial, one of the first steps is to edge-glue material for large parts such as table tops, cores, or drawer stock. Also, for almost every type of furniture, thicker pieces for legs and posts must be glued up with the surfaces face-to-face. Fig. 13-2.

Kinds of Wood Adhesives or Glues

The term *adhesive* is used to describe materials that will hold together other materials by surface attraction. Common adhesives include glues, cements, pastes, and mucilage. However, the term

13-1a. When using solid stock to make certain furniture parts, such as those with large surfaces, an early step is to glue up the stock. The cabinet sides were glued up. Can you see other items in this fine dining room set which were made of pieces glued edge-to-edge or face-to-face?

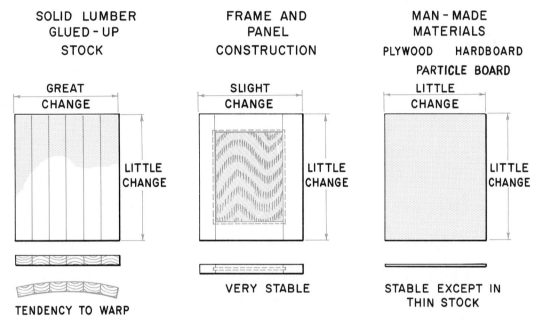

SOLID LUMBER
GLUED-UP
STOCK

GREAT
CHANGE

LITTLE
CHANGE

TENDENCY TO WARP

FRAME AND
PANEL
CONSTRUCTION

SLIGHT
CHANGE

LITTLE
CHANGE

VERY STABLE

MAN-MADE
MATERIALS
PLYWOOD   HARDBOARD
PARTICLE BOARD

LITTLE
CHANGE

LITTLE
CHANGE

STABLE EXCEPT IN
THIN STOCK

13-1b. Here you see the three basic methods of large surface construction and how these react to moisture content changes which result in warpage, expansion, and contraction.

13-2. The two common methods of gluing up materials: edge-gluing and face-gluing.

Type	Description	Recommended Use	Care in Using	Correct Use	70° Clamping Time	
					Hardwood	Softwood
Liquid Hide Glue	Liquid, ready-to-use brown animal glue. Reliable. Comes in flakes to be heated in water or in prepared form as liquid hide glue. Very strong, tough, light color.	Excellent for furniture and cabinetwork. Gives strength even to joints that do not fit very well.	Not waterproof; do not use for outdoor furniture or anything exposed to weather or dampness.	Apply glue in warm room to both surfaces and let it become tacky before joining.	2 hours	3 hours
Casein	From milk curd. Comes in powdered form. Must be mixed with water.	For inside and woodwork. Almost waterproof. Good for oily woods. Inexpensive. Good for heavy wood gluing.	Some types require bleaching. Will deteriorate when exposed to mold.	Mix with water to creamy consistency. For oily woods, sponge surfaces with dilute caustic soda one hour before gluing. Apply with brush. Clamp and allow to dry.	2 hours	3 hours
Plastic Resin Glue	Comes as powder to be mixed with water and used within 4 hours. Light colored. Very strong if joint fits well.	Good for general wood gluing. First choice for work that must stand some exposure to dampness, since it is almost waterproof.	Needs well-fitted joints, tight clamping, and room temperature 70° or warmer.	Make sure joint fits tightly. Mix glue and apply thin coat.	16 hours	16 hours
Resorcinol Waterproof Glue	Comes as powder plus liquid, must be mixed each time used. Dark colored, very strong, completely waterproof.	This is the glue to use with exterior type plywood for work to be exposed to extreme dampness.	Expense, trouble to mix and dark color make it unsuitable to jobs where waterproof glue is not required.	Use within 8 hours after mixing. Work at temperature above 70°. Apply thin coat to both surfaces.	16 hours	16 hours
White Glue Liquid Resin	Comes ready to use at any temperature. Clean working, quick setting. Strong enough for most work, though not quite as tough as hide glue.	Good for indoor furniture and cabinetwork. First choice for small jobs where tight clamping or good fit may be difficult.	Not sufficiently resistant to moisture for outdoor furniture or outdoor storage units.	Use at any temperature but preferably above 60°. Spread on both surfaces, clamp at once.	1 hour	1½ hours
Contact Cement	Comes in a can as a light tan liquid.	Excellent for bonding veneer, plastic laminates, leather, plastics, metal foil, or canvas to wood.	Adheres immediately on contact. Parts can't be shifted once contact is made. Position accurately. Temperature for working must be 70° F. or above.	Stir cement. Apply two coats to both surfaces. Brush on a liberal coat. Let dry for 30 minutes. Apply second coat. Allow to dry for not less than 30 minutes. Test for dryness by pressing wrapping paper to surface. If paper doesn't stick, the surfaces are dry and ready for bonding.	No clamping. Bonds instantly.	
Epoxy Cement	Comes in two tubes, or cans, that must be mixed in exact proportions.	Excellent for attaching hardware and metal fittings to wood. Good for extremely difficult gluing jobs. Will fill large holes.	Epoxies harden quickly. Mix only what can be used in half hour. Use at temperatures above 60 degrees. Keep epoxy compounds separate. Don't reverse caps.	Mix small amounts. Clean and roughen the surfaces. Remove oil, dirt, and other loose matter. Apply to surfaces with putty knife. Clean tools immediately. Press parts together.	No clamping. Dries faster with heat.	

13-3. Common kinds of glues for furniture making.

O—Best Product for This Use X—Acceptable for This Use Adhesive	Wood to Wood and Plywood	Wood Veneering	Plastic Laminates to Wood	Wood Boats and Marine Uses	Wood for Outdoor Use	Metal to Wood	Metal to Metal	Paper to Paper or Cloth	Leather to Leather or Wood	Rubber to Wood or Metal	Cloth to Cloth or Wood	Plywood Panels to Frame or Stud
Liquid Hide Glue	X	X	X					X	O		X	
Casein	X	X	X									
Plastic Resin	X	O	X		X							
Waterproof Resorcinol	X	X	X	O	O							
Liquid Resin White Glue	X	X	X					O	X		X	
Contact Cement		X	O				X		X	O	X	O
Epoxy Cement						O	O					

13-4. Glue and cement selection chart.

"gluing" is often used loosely to mean assembling parts with any type of adhesive, not just glue. Some of the more common kinds of wood adhesives or glues are discussed in Fig. 13-3. In selecting an adhesive, it is important to choose the right kind for the job. Select one that will provide a strong bond for the materials you are working with and will meet your needs for assembly time. Fig. 13-4. *Assembly time* means the total amount of time between the spreading of the adhesive and the application of clamps. *Open assembly time* refers to the time after spreading the glue and before the surfaces are placed together.

Closed assembly time indicates the amount of time the glue joint has to stand before pressure is applied with clamps. Assembly time varies with such factors as the types of glue, kind of spread, temperature, moisture content of the wood, and amount of air circulation. Open assembly time should be about one-third that allowed for closed assembly time. When using cold ready-to-use glues, such as white glue, pressure should be applied right after spreading. If glue squeeze-out occurs when pressure is applied, then the maximum assembly time hasn't been exceeded.

When edge-gluing and face-

gluing, you don't proceed the same way as when gluing for assembly. Not only the glues but also the techniques are different. For example, the parts do not need to be protected as they would in assembly gluing, and you don't need to be as careful about the amount of glue applied since you are not working with finished surfaces. The best glue for edge- and face-gluing is liquid hide glue. The glue must be rigid to resist the stresses applied to the glue line by moisture change. Properly made joints will be stronger than the wood itself and will last for the life of the furniture.

HINTS FOR GLUING

The surfaces must be clean and dry.

The joints should be properly made.

The correct kind of glue should be selected.

The correct mixture should be used. Follow manufacturer's directions on each can. Never vary the amounts.

Mix only enough glue for one job. Most glues deteriorate with age.

Make sure the temperature is correct. Some glues must be used only at 70 degrees or above. Others can be used at any temperature.

Mark the pieces to be glued with corresponding numbers.

Have the proper clamps ready and set.

Apply glue with stick, brush, or squeeze bottle.

Glue may be spread on only one surface (called single spreading) but double spreading results in much better gluing. When gluing end grain stock, apply a thin coat, let it become tacky, and then apply a second coat before joining the parts.

Clamp all parts properly. Do not apply so much pressure that all the glue squeezes out. This may create a glue-starved joint that is very weak.

Remove excess glue before it dries with a damp sponge or rag.

Allow the assembly to dry thoroughly as recommended by the manufacturer.

When dry, remove bits of glue with a small chisel or knife. *Never try to remove this by planing or surfacing.*

If glue stains are present around the joint, bleach with oxalic acid before applying finish.

Clamps and Clamping

Clamps are needed to apply pressure to the joint so that a thin, uniform glue line is produced and the parts are held in position until the glue dries. Fig. 13-5. Enough clamps must be used to give uniform pressure along the glue line. Clamps should be evenly tightened so that pressure is about 150 psi (pounds per square inch). Usually if you tighten the clamps with one hand you will apply about the right amount of pressure. Tightening hard with both hands often results in too much pressure, which causes a starved joint. See pages 111, 112 and 113.

HINTS FOR CLAMPING

Always select the correct size and number of clamps needed.

Always open the clamps slightly wider than necessary before beginning the assembly work.

Always place protective pieces of scrap wood on the finished surface of stock when using C or bar clamps.

When using several, fasten clamps on alternate sides of the stock to equalize the pressure.

Gluing Up Stock Edge-to-Edge

If the stock is 8″ or more in width, cut it into narrow strips about 4″ to 6″ wide. Plane one surface and two edges of each piece. The jointed edges should be square with the face. Arrange pieces, keeping in mind the following:

1. Make sure the grain runs in the same direction on all pieces.

2. Match the color and grain so there is not a light piece right next to a darker one.

3. Arrange adjoining pieces with the annual rings on the ends facing in opposite directions. This will help to prevent the surfaces from warping after they are glued up. Fig. 13-6. See page 114.

4. Check the assembly to make sure the pieces fit properly by placing one board in a vise with the joint edge up and stacking the other ones on this. Observe the following:

a. Touch the upper boards to make sure they don't rock.

b. Look along the edge of each board to see that the edges are tight along the entire length of the stock.

c. Hold a straightedge against the face surface to see that the boards form a flat surface.

d. Push lightly on the ends of the boards to see that they are tight.

After doing this, mark each adjoining surface with a matching number so that you can easily identify the pieces when gluing up. If added strength is needed, insert dowels or a spline in each joint.

If an extremely wide board is needed and the planer is too narrow, it may be wise to glue up the piece in two sections. Surface both sections to finish size. Glue the two sections together taking special care to align the surfaces. After gluing a light cut can be made with a hand plane to smooth the surface. (See page 114.)

CLAMP SELECTION CHART and PARTS GUIDE

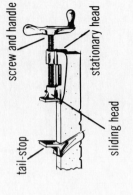

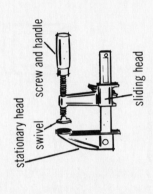

CLAMP FIXTURES
To Be Mounted on Wood Bars

For those who prefer the qualities and economy of wood bars, even though sacrificing some of the rigid strength and rapid action of steel bar clamps. Light in weight with a minimum of exposed metal parts. Used for fine cabinet work.

Steel Bar Clamps
SLIDING HEAD TYPE
Screw Is in the "Sliding" Head

All adjustment is in the sliding head for convenience in close quarters. Widely used in place of "C" Clamps because of instant adjustment to work. "Multiple-Disc-Clutch" permits zip adjustment to work—holds securely—releases easily.

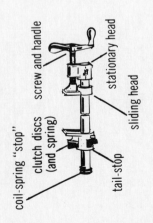

CLAMP FIXTURES
To Be Mounted on Black Pipe

Make economical, instant-acting bar clamps. No tools required to assemble on threaded pipe. "Multiple-Disc-Clutch" permits zip adjustment to work—holds securely—releases easily.

Clutches encircle pipe, hold top and bottom—will not crush pipe or fill up with filings. Clutches are reversible.

Easy to mount on different lengths of pipe to fit the job.

HOLD-DOWN CLAMPS

For Regular Service

Mount to hold work in any location—in the middle or along the edge of work surface—a distinct advantage over conventional clamps and vises which function only near the edge of a work-bench or table. Slides "on" and "off" prespotted holding-bolt (furnished) in wood or metal bench. "T"-slot or machine table.

Feature easy installation, fast adjustment, secure hold.

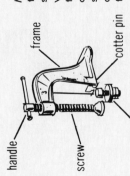

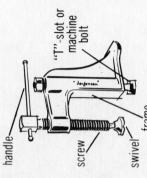

For Heavy-duty Service

Simplify holding any object on machine or bench for drilling, milling, welding or other fabricating or assembly operation. Ideal in jig or fixture set-ups. Eliminates complicated arrangements of steps, block and other accessories. Easy to install, fast to adjust, hold securely.

Furnished complete with both "T"-slot and machine bolts. Final tightening is accomplished at the top of the clamp where it is convenient to use a wrench.

13-5. Kinds of clamps. (Continued on pages 112, 113.)

CLAMP SELECTION CHART and PARTS GUIDE

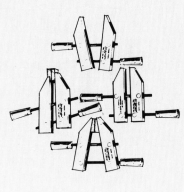

"end" spindle

handle

nuts (rh & lh)

jaws

"middle" spindle

HANDSCREWS

Most satisfactory device for holding wood, metal, plastics, fabrics—all materials. Will hold round or irregular shapes. Jaws adjust to angles to hold uneven work—hold more securely than metal clamps—will not crawl or twist. Broad area pressure reduces tendency to mar work. Jaws provide greater "reach" over the work. Also available in "non-adjustable" design if specified.

locking cam

bolt-head

head

band

BAND CLAMPS

For Light Service

For clamping irregular shapes such as chairs, drum tables, and picture frames; also used as a strapping device for securing loads, bundles, cartons, luggage, etc., for transport. Nylon band, 1″ wide, is furnished in 15-ft. length.

Band encircles work, is pulled tight through self-locking cam so that it cannot slip. Final tightening is accomplished by a few turns of a small wrench (furnished) or screwdriver.

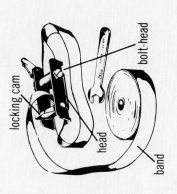

screw and handle

cams

roller

head

base

band

For Heavy-duty Service

For clamping irregular shapes such as furniture frames, assemblies, tanks, or columns.

Canvas or steel band encircles the work, is drawn tight by screw action. Canvas band, 2″ wide, is used for all ordinary applications and is always furnished unless steel band is specified. Steel band, 1¾″ wide, should be used on round shapes only.

Self-locking cams hold the band securely up to the strength of the band itself—approximately 2,800 lbs. Cam-extensions provide for convenient, easy release with only fingertip pressure.

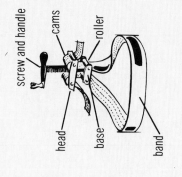

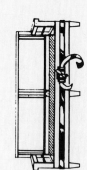

CLAMP SELECTION CHART and PARTS GUIDE

Steel Bar Clamps
HINGED TYPE

Steel bar clamps with swivel-plate at foot-end. Can be mounted anywhere—swing in arc up to or away from work. Prepositioned clamps swing up to work when wanted—out of the way when not in use. Ideal for production jigs and fixtures—handy on any bench or saw-horse.

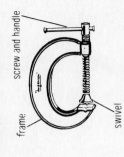

screw and handle

sliding head

stationary head

swivel

swivel plate

Track for Hinged Clamps

Special track permits "sideways" adjustment along length of track.

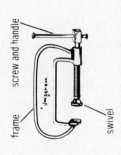

Steel Bar Clamps
Screw Is in the "Fixed" Head

The most widely used general-purpose type of steel bar clamps.

stationary head

sliding head

screw and handle

tail-stop

SPRING CLAMPS

Convenient, inexpensive, spring-operated, spring-operated jaws hold any material quickly, efficiently. Hand pressure opens the jaws—spring pressure grips the work. Very rapid action. Used wherever relatively light pressure is adequate and where speedy application and removal are important.

Opening capacities—1", 2", 2¾" and 4". Some sizes can be furnished with poly-vinyl protected tips and/or handles.

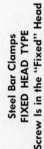

handles

spring

jaws

jaw tips

rivet

C or Carriage

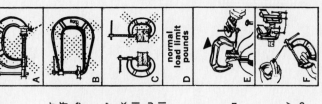

normal load limit pounds

screw and handle

frame

swivel

screw and handle

frame

swivel

SPECIFIC SUGGESTIONS FOR SELECTING, USING, AND CARING FOR "C" CLAMPS

Use the proper size "C" clamp. A "large" clamp on "small" work throws an abnormal bending strain onto the clamp screw and frame (see drawing A).

Use "C" clamps having as small a depth of throat, or "reach," as your work will permit. The greater the depth of throat, the greater the leverage on the clamp frame by the same force at the screw (see drawing B).

Specify "full length" screws on the larger sizes of "C" clamps only when unusual conditions require them. On work of the proper size for a "large" clamp, the longer screw will extend out so far as to be a distinct annoyance. Also, you will not be burdened with the 20% extra-charge for such "full length screws" (see drawing C).

Select "C" clamps designed to take the load intended.

Any student can wreck the best clamp made—if he uses a wrench or bar long enough! (see drawing E).

A drop of oil on the clamp screw now and then, and handy storage racks for clamps not in actual use, will do much to prolong clamp life (see drawing F).

In comparing original cost, or "price," of the "C" clamps you are going to order, make "ultimate value" the basis for final selection. "Cheap" clamps usually turn out to be the most expensive ones!

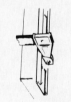

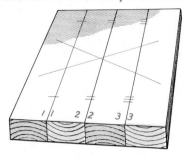

13-6. Pieces arranged with the annual rings in opposite directions.

13-7a. Note that the clamps should be alternated, one from one side and the next from the opposite side.

Proceed with the gluing as follows:

1. Make sure that you have enough clamps of the right size and kind. There should be a bar clamp at least every 15 inches. Fig. 13-7. On wide assemblies, cut some cleats or battens that are long enough to go crosswise at either end to hold the assembly flat. Fig. 13-8. It is a good idea to hold the bar clamps in a simple jig when gluing up. Open the clamps slightly wider than the stock to be glued up.

2. Mix the glue and have everything ready.

3. Hold the two matching edges together or clamp them in a vise. If dowels or splines are being used, dip half in the glue and drive into one edge. Cover both edges and exposed dowel or spline evenly with a thin coating of glue. *Do not apply too much.* Work quickly and accurately.

4. Slip these pieces together and then proceed with the other edges in a similar manner. If necessary, use a rubber or wooden mallet to bring the pieces into place.

5. Tighten all the bar clamps slowly and evenly, a little at a time. Fig. 13-9. When several bar clamps are used, put them on alternately from opposite sides.

6. Place the wooden cleat or batten across either end with a piece of paper underneath and clamp in place with a C clamp or hand screw. Wipe off any excess glue immediately with a damp cloth.

7. Allow the wood to dry a sufficient length of time. Sometimes a wide surface is run through the planer too soon after gluing, resulting in a *sunken joint*.

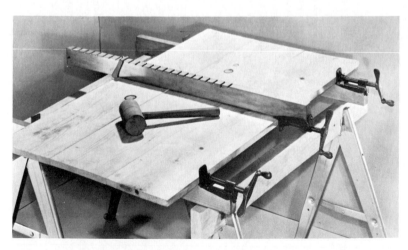

13-7b. Clamp fixtures mounted on wood bars are sometimes used since there is less chance to damage the surface of the wood.

When a water-based adhesive is used for gluing, it swells the wood along the glue line. If planing is done too soon, the surface will be true at first. However, the swollen wood along the glue line will continue to dry out and shrink the wood, resulting in a depressed area along the glue line. This will show up, particularly when a glossy finish is applied to the surface. It is especially noticeable on a table top. Fig. 13-10.

13-8. Fastening cleats to glued up stock to keep the surface true.

13-9. Gluing up a wide assembly. Notice that the clamps are alternated.

JOINT EXPANDED BY MOISTURE IN GLUE.

WOOD SURFACED BEFORE WOOD IS DRY.

13-10. Note what will happen if a glued-up panel with a raised glue line is surfaced.

SUNKEN WOOD JOINT WHEN DRY.

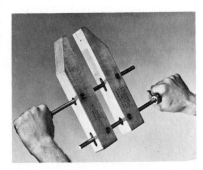

13-11a. Opening or closing a hand screw. To adjust a hand screw, grasp the handle of the middle spindle in one hand and the handle of the end spindle in the other. Revolve the spindles in the same direction: in one direction to open and the other to close. If the jaws aren't parallel, adjust one spindle until they are.

13-11b. Correct and incorrect ways of clamping with a hand screw. On the left the clamps are not parallel; therefore they will not hold properly. When tightening a hand screw, always tighten the middle spindle first and then the end spindle.

13-11c. A large number of hand screws used to glue up laminated stock. This is necessary to equalize pressure throughout the length of the stock.

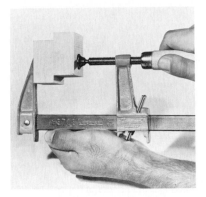

13-11d. This quick clamp can be used in place of a C clamp for many kinds of small clamping operations.

13-12. Stock glued up face to face with C clamps. Note the cauls (protective pieces of wood) between the clamps and the stock. (Cauls are also called cleats or battens.)

Gluing Up Stock Face-to-Face

When gluing up stock for legs or similar parts, plane the *face surfaces* of the two pieces that are to be glued together. If more than two pieces are needed, the inside stock should be squared up so that both face surfaces are true and the stock is of equal thickness throughout. Apply glue evenly to both surfaces and clamp together with hand screws or clamps. Fig. 13-11. See illustrations on page 115, and to the left on this page.

If C clamps are used, place wooden cleats or battens across the stock to equalize the pressure. Fig. 13-12.

DISCUSSION TOPICS

Section Three—FIRST STEPS IN FURNITURE CONSTRUCTION

Unit 10. Reading a Drawing

1. Name the three kinds of drawings most commonly used in furniture construction.
2. List five common kinds of lines used in making a working drawing.
3. Why is it important to observe the dimensions carefully when reading a drawing?
4. Explain how to enlarge a design.

Unit 11. Making a Materials Bill and Plan of Procedure

1. Discuss the four major parts of a materials bill.
2. What is a stock-cutting list?
3. Why should all pieces for an item of furniture be grouped as to the thickness and kind of material?

Unit 12. Getting Out Stock

1. List the common procedure for squaring up rough stock.
2. What are the kinds of saws used to cut stock to length?

Unit 13. Gluing Up Stock

1. Why should wide stock be cut into narrower strips before gluing?
2. List three points to observe when making a joint.
3. What should be the spacing for bar clamps used in gluing up stock?
4. Describe the procedure for gluing up stock.
5. Which glue is made from milk curd?
6. What are the advantages and disadvantages of animal glue?
7. Which type of glue is the most nearly waterproof?
8. Describe the common methods of applying glue.

EXTRA CREDIT ACTIVITIES

1. Write a report on one type of glue.
2. Glue several test pieces of the same kind of wood together, using different kinds of glue, clamp, let set, and then try to break open the joints. Write a report on the results.
3. Make a full-size design of a table leg.

Fundamentals of Furniture Construction

The construction of fine furniture, as shown in this room, requires knowledge and skill in many of the fundamental areas discussed in this section. Note the fine workmanship and authentic design.
(Baumritter Corporation)

UNIT 14 Making Joints

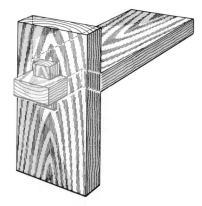

Most furniture pieces are constructed of several parts, held together with joints. Fig. 14-1. The joint is held secure with glue or other adhesive and, in some cases, with fastening devices such as dowels, nails, or screws. Joints serve two basic purposes. First, once the cuts for the joints have been correctly made you have an accurate guide to the way the parts fit together. Second, the joints hold the parts together securely. Two key points to observe for obtaining strong joints in furniture construction are:

• Surfaces to be glued together must be wide enough so that a sufficient amount of adhesive can be applied.
• Certain types of joints with fastening devices must be so designed that they will lock in place. A keyed (pinned) mortise-and-tenon joint is a good example. In this joint parts will lock together before the glue is added. Fig. 14-2.

In selecting joints for furniture, make sure that they are easy to make and assemble. The mortise-and-tenon joint requires a great deal of time, especially without

14-2. A keyed joint of this type does not have to be glued. It is sometimes used in furniture that must be taken apart.

specialized equipment. A simple joint is the butt joint with dowels added to give it strength. The strength of a glue joint depends to a large degree on the grain of the two members of the joint. If end grain is glued to edge grain (like a miter joint), the joint will be quite weak unless it is strengthened by fastening devices. However, edge grain to edge grain makes a relatively strong joint even without extra strengthening devices.

There are over 100 different varieties of joints but most of them are adaptations of eight basic ones which will be discussed in this unit. There are four steps in the construction of all joints and, while the procedure for each varies, these four steps should be followed carefully and in order.

STEP 1. MAKING THE LAYOUT

1. Make sure that you have accurate instruments—rule, try square, marking gage, etc.—and a sharp pencil or knife. It is extremely important that the layout

14-1. Many different types of joints are required for assembling this fine furniture. The more common ones are edge joint strengthened with dowels, mortise-and-tenon, dovetail, and butt joint strengthened with dowels and corner blocks.

118

be accurate. A knife can be used whenever a line is to be cut. A sharp pencil can be used for all layouts but especially when only part of the area is cut away.

2. Select the wood for the joint carefully and make sure that the grain runs in the right direction. Certain kinds of joints can be made only across grain, since they would break out otherwise.

3. Make all your measurements from a common starting point, edge, or surface. Start from one end of the piece. Always measure from this point for each joint, never from the next mark.

4. Always use the *superimposing method* of laying out the joint. That is, mark one location of the joint and then hold the second part over it to mark the width and/or length. Fig. 14-3.

5. Lay out all identical joints at the same time. Sometimes this can be done by clamping the pieces of stock together and marking across all of them. Fig. 14-4.

6. Always identify the two

14-4. Marking the location of dowels for joint construction.

members of each joint with a pencil mark (*1–1, 2–2,* etc.) so they can be quickly identified during assembly.

STEP 2. CUTTING THE JOINT

1. Use the right machine for making each cut. Most cuts are made on the circular saw with or without a dado head. Others are cut on the shaper, on a drill press with a mortising attachment, on a router, on a jointer, and even on the band saw or jig saw. Often there is more than one way of making the cut.

2. Always make the cuts in the waste stock just inside or outside the layout line. A tenon, for example, should be cut outside the line and a dado inside the line.

3. When necessary, trim out the joint with a router plane or chisel.

STEP 3. FITTING THE JOINT

1. A well-fit joint is one that can be assembled with hand pressure but is not so loose that it falls apart by itself.

2. If a joint must be trimmed, always remove the stock from the

piece fitting into the second member. Trim the tenon, for example, not the mortise.

STEP 4. ASSEMBLING THE JOINT

1. Always choose the proper kind of clamping devices.

2. Cut enough scrap blocks to go between the clamps and the project to protect it when using C or bar clamps.

3. Make a trial assembly to make sure that each joint fits properly.

4. Determine the correct method of fastening: glue, nails, screws, dowels, splines, keys, corrugated fasteners, or a combination of two or more.

5. Mix just enough glue for the one job. Apply the glue carefully with a stick or brush. *Do not apply too much.* If the wood is to be bleached, use a glue that will not stain. If pounding must be done, use a rubber mallet.

6. Check to see that the product is square and aligned before it is dry. This often requires a little pounding or shifting of clamps. Make several measurements with a try square and rule.

7. On a complicated product, glue up sub-assemblies and then the final product. On many tables, for instance, it is well to glue up the ends, allow them to dry, and then glue up the entire product.

Methods of Strengthening Joints
Dowels

Many types of joints—especially the edge, the butt, the miter, and the mortise-and-tenon—are strengthened by installing dowels. Dowel rod is made of birch or maple and can be purchased in

14-3. Marking the wood for a rabbet by superimposing one piece over the other. This insures accuracy.

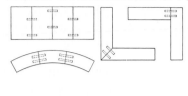

14-5. Common uses of dowels for joint construction.

diameters from $\frac{1}{8}''$ to $1''$, in 3-foot lengths, with either a plain or grooved surface. Small dowel pins with beveled ends can be purchased. Fig. 14-5. The grooved surface allows the glue to run more freely into the joint. Install dowels as follows:

1. Locate accurately the position of the dowel holes in the two adjoining surfaces. To do this, mark the location of the dowels on the surface of the two adjoining pieces. Fig. 14-6. Then with a try square mark a line across the edges and/or end.

2. With a marking gage set at half the thickness of the stock, mark a line along the edge or end that will intersect the other line to locate the center of the hole. This step is unnecessary when using a doweling jig or a fence on a drill press. Fig. 14-7.

3. In selecting the size dowel rod to use, a general rule to follow is that the diameter should be not more than half the thickness of the stock. The depth of the hole will vary with the kind of joint. The length of the dowel rod should be cut about $\frac{1}{8}''$ to $\frac{1}{4}''$ shorter than the total of the two holes. The ends of the dowel pins

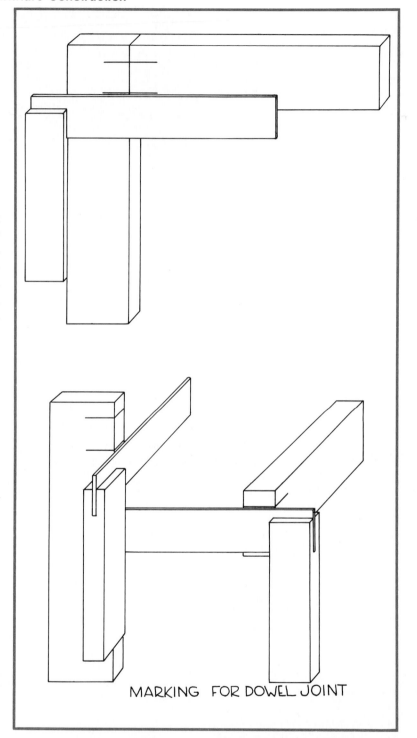

MARKING FOR DOWEL JOINT

14-6. Marking the location for dowels on an edge-butt joint.

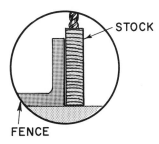

STOCK

FENCE

14-7. By putting the fence on the drill press, all holes will be centered without marking.

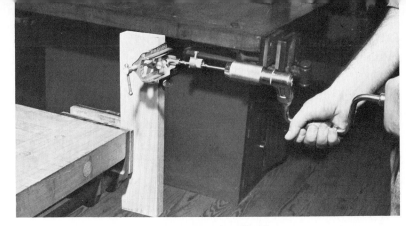

14-10. Using a doweling jig.

14-8. A dowel pointer. This tool is used in a brace to bevel the ends of the dowel.

14-9. Doweling jig. There are several types available.

should be cut with a bevel. Use a dowel pointer or sand the bevel. Fig. 14-8.

4. The holes can be bored with an auger bit and brace, but this requires careful sighting and ex-

tremely accurate work. A doweling jig is a device that can be used for locating the position of the holes and guiding the auger bit accurately for boring. Fig. 14-9. This jig has several guide rods for different diameter bits. This guide rod can be adjusted to center on any thickness of stock. The jig is then clamped over the stock and aligned with the cross line. Fig. 14-10. Always remember to place the jig on the stock with the solid side against the face surface. A stop is clamped to the auger bit to control the depth of the hole. Dowel holes can also be made on a drill press as shown in Fig. 14-11.

Splines

A *spline* is a thin strip of wood inserted in a groove cut in the two adjoining surfaces of a joint. Fig. 14-12. It is used extensively on edge and miter joints. The groove is cut on a circular saw or shaper to a specific width and depth. A thin piece of stock is then cut to fit into this groove. This stock should be cut so the grain runs at right angles to the grain of the joint.

14-11. Drilling dowel holes with the table turned to a vertical position.

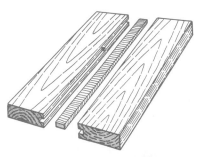

14-12. A spline used to strengthen an edge joint.

Feather and Key

A key or *feather* is a small piece of wood inserted in one or both members of a joint to hold it firmly together. This is commonly used for miter joints. A key in a mortise-and-tenon joint is commonly used in Early American furniture and in some kinds of Modern ranch-type furniture.

Kinds of Joints

Edge Joints

The first basic joint is the *plain-edge* joint (also called the *square-edge* joint). Fig. 14-13. Adaptations of this are the *dowel, spline, tongue-and-groove,* and *rabbet-edge* joints. The edge joint is constructed whenever it is necessary to make up larger surfaces such as tops for tables, desks, and other large parts. Fig. 14-14. Added strength can be secured by installing several dowels or a spline along the adjoining edge. A tongue can be cut on one adjoining edge and a groove on the other on the shaper. This kind of joint is often used when paneling a surface. Cutting a rabbet on either adjoining edge provides greater gluing area and strengthens the joint.

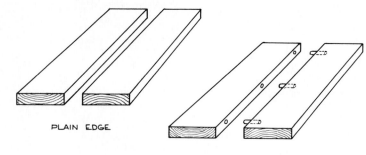

PLAIN EDGE

DOWEL EDGE

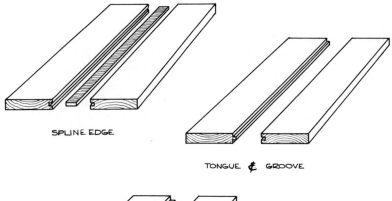

SPLINE EDGE

TONGUE & GROOVE

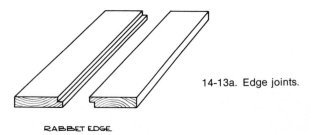

RABBET EDGE

14-13a. Edge joints.

Butt Joints

A butt joint is found in simple box construction, bookcases, cabinets, inexpensive door and frame construction, to name but a few. Fig. 14-15. In a butt joint, the square end of one member fits against the flat surface, edge, or end of the second member. Fig. 14-16. A simple butt joint can be made on edge or flat. The corner of a butt joint can be strengthened by installing glue blocks or dowels. The *end butt with dowels* is a joint in which two ends are joined together to lengthen a board. The *middle-rail butt with dowels* is used to install shelves and partitions in box and case work. The *frame butt with dowels* is used for making a frame. The *rail-to-leg butt with dowels* is often found in furniture to replace mortise-and-tenon joints. Fig. 14-17.

14-13b. Details of a dowel-edge joint.

14-14. This drop-leaf extension table is made of solid wood. The top is glued together of strips of wood, using an edge joint.

14-15. This drawer is assembled with simple butt joints.

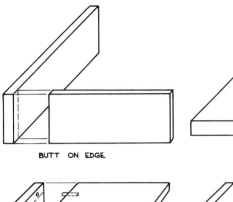

BUTT ON EDGE

BUTT – FLAT

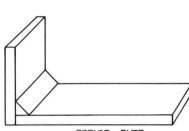

CORNER BUTT WITH DOWELS

CORNER BUTT WITH GLUE BLOCK

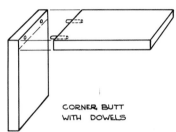

END BUTT WITH DOWELS

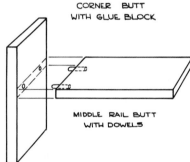

MIDDLE RAIL BUTT WITH DOWELS

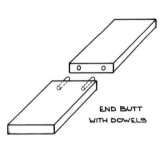

FRAME BUTT WITH DOWELS

RAIL-TO-LEG BUTT WITH DOWELS

BUTT JOINTS

14-16. Types of butt joints. Dowels and corner blocks give additional strength to the joints.

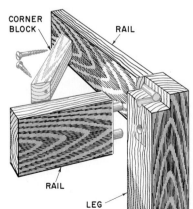

CORNER BLOCK

RAIL

RAIL

LEG

14-17. The butt joint with dowels is given added strength by means of a corner block. Glue and wood screws hold the parts permanently together.

14-18. This table is assembled with butt joints strengthened with dowels.

To make a butt joint, cut the end accurately to fit against an edge or surface. Dowels are installed as described previously. A corner block is used to give added strength. Fig. 14-18.

Rabbet Joints

The rabbet joint is one in which a rabbet is cut in the end or edge of one board and a second member fit into it. Fig. 14-19. The rabbet is found in simple corner construction for cabinets, bookcases, and drawers. Fig. 14-20. It is also used to install a top or bottom to a box or case. The rabbet can be made on edge or flat. A *back-panel rabbet joint* is commonly used to install a panel in the back of case construction. A rabbet is cut around the back and on all four sides, and a panel installed.

To lay out a rabbet joint, hold one edge of the second member over the end or side of the first and mark the width of the rabbet. For casework draw a line down the sides or end and measure one-half to two-thirds the thickness of the first member as the depth of the rabbet. The cuts can

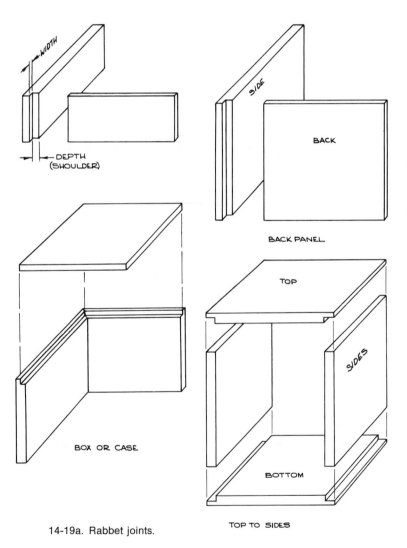

14-19a. Rabbet joints.

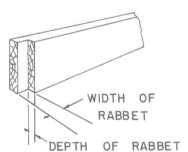

14-19b. Correct shape for a strong rabbet joint.

be made on the circular saw, jointer, or shaper.

Dado Joints

Dado joints are used primarily to install shelves, partitions, or steps in bookcases, chests, cabinets, and the like. Fig. 14-21. A dado joint is one in which a dado is cut in one member and a second member fit into it. Fig. 14-22. A *plain dado* is one which has a rectangular groove cut across grain. A *dovetail dado* is one in which a dovetail is cut across grain and notches cut in the end of the second piece to fit into this dovetail. A *blind dado* is one in which a dado is cut only partway across the first member and a corner cut out of the second member to fit into it. This is found frequently in better furniture construction when the joint should not be visible from the front edge. A *corner dado* has a rectangular groove cut cornerwise across one member and a corner cut off the second member to fit into the first. This is constructed frequently for installing a lower shelf in many different types of tables.

Make a *plain dado* as follows:

1. Mark a line across the stock to indicate one side of the dado.

2. Hold the second member over it and mark the width of the dado. Draw a line across either edge and mark the depth of the dado. This is usually one-fourth to one-half the thickness of the stock.

3. Cut the dado on a circular saw with or without a dado head, on a shaper or with a router attachment. Remember always to cut the dado in the waste stock.

14-20. The rabbet joint is used in fastening the top to the sides of this spice case.

14-21. The shelves of this breakfront are joined to the sides by means of blind dado joints.

125

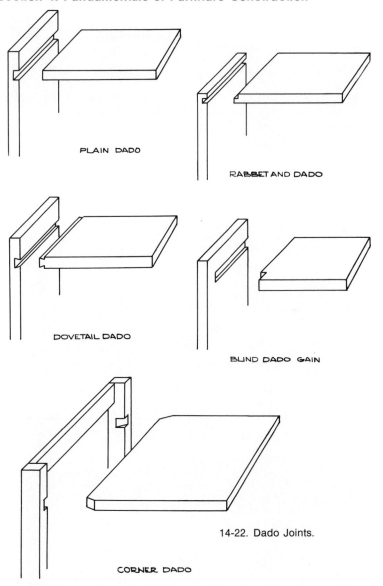

PLAIN DADO

RABBET AND DADO

DOVETAIL DADO

BLIND DADO GAIN

CORNER DADO

14-22. Dado Joints.

of the cut or, better still, cut a square hole with a mortising attachment. See page 318.

3. Cut up to the hole with a dado head. See page 291. If a round hole has been bored, the corner must be trimmed out by hand.

4. Cut a notch in the second member to fit into the blind dado.

The *rabbet-and-dado joint* is a combination of these two. A dado is cut in one member and a rabbet cut on the end of the second. The dado is cut equal to half the thickness of the stock and to a depth equal to one-fourth to one-half the thickness. This joint is frequently used for joining the back to the sides of drawers, or for bookcases and cabinets, since, by its very construction, it holds the two pieces square.

Miter Joints

A miter joint is an angle joint that hides the end grain of the two members. The common angle is 45 degrees. Fig. 14-23. It is found in modern furniture construction in the corners of cabinets, frames, boxes, moldings, and other things. Fig. 14-24. The simple miter can be cut flat by adjusting the miter gage to 45 degrees or can be cut on edge by setting the miter gage at 90 degrees and tilting the blade to 45 degrees. The simple miter is not very strong, because both pieces are cut on the *end* grain. It must be strengthened by dowels, splines, or keys. A spline can be cut along the ends for either a flat miter or a miter on edge. One or more dowels can be installed across the corner. The holes for these can be drilled

The dovetail dado must be cut with a router or router attachment. When a dado is cut with a single saw blade, several passes should be made through the waste stock and then the excess trimmed out with a router plane or chisel. When many dados are cut at one time, it is simpler to fit the saw with a dado head to make the correct width of dado. See page 291.

Make a *blind dado* as follows:

1. Lay out in the same general manner as a simple dado, indicating the length of the blind dado from the back edge.

2. Bore a round hole at the end

as shown in Unit 30. A feather miter is another method of strengthening the corner. A *miter with half lap* is an adaptation of the miter and lap joint which gives added strength to a corner. A *miter with rabbet* is one that combines the features of the rabbet joint with the miter joint. Polygon miters are those cut at an angle more or less than 45 degrees. Fig. 14-25. A compound miter, or hopper, joint is used to make such projects as picture frames and shadow boxes. To cut a compound miter with the sides at a slope (work angle) of 45 degrees, set the miter gage to an angle of $54\frac{3}{4}$ degrees and tilt the blade to an angle of 30 degrees. For other slopes see Fig. 14-26, page 128.

Lap Joints

The lap joint is found in simple furniture legs, frames, tables, and chairs, as well as many other pieces. Fig. 14-27. The basic one is the *cross-lap* or *middle-half-lap*. Adaptations of this are the *edge-lap, middle-* or *tee-lap, end-lap,* and *half-lap.* The cross lap is one in which two pieces cross with the surfaces flush. They may cross at 90 degrees or any other necessary angle. On modern furniture, for example, they frequently cross at 45 degrees. Fig. 14-28, page 129.

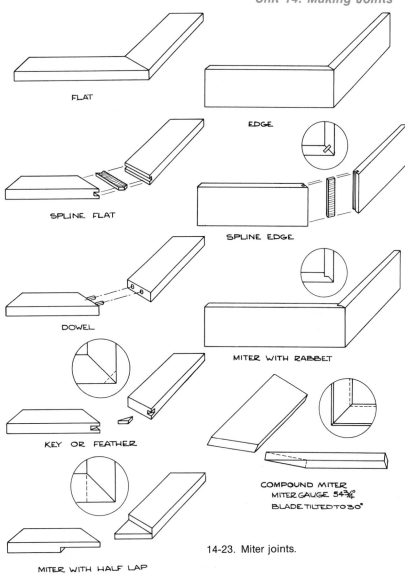

FLAT

EDGE

SPLINE FLAT

SPLINE EDGE

DOWEL

MITER WITH RABBET

KEY OR FEATHER

COMPOUND MITER
MITER GAUGE 54¾°
BLADE TILTED TO 30°

MITER WITH HALF LAP

14-23. Miter joints.

14-24. The tops of these modern tables are joined with a right angle miter joint.

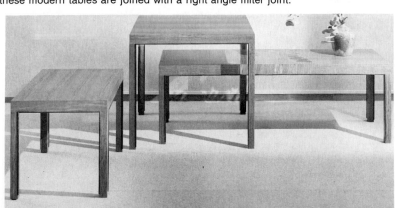

14-25a. An octagonal coffee table with a glass top.

THREE	SIDES	=	30.	DEGREES
FIVE	SIDES	=	54.	DEGREES
SIX	SIDES	=	60.	DEGREES
SEVEN	SIDES	=	64.3	DEGREES (APPROX.)
EIGHT	SIDES	=	67.5	DEGREES
NINE	SIDES	=	70.	DEGREES
TEN	SIDES	=	72.	DEGREES

14-25b. Correct angles for common polygons. To find the correct angle setting in degrees, divide 180 by the number of the sides, and then subtract this amount from 90°.

Tilt of Work	4-Side Butt		4-Side Miter	
	Blade Tilt	Miter Gauge	Blade Tilt	Miter Gauge
5 degrees	½°	85°	44¾°	85°
10 degrees	1½°	80¼°	44¼°	80¼°
15 degrees	3¾°	75½°	43¼°	75½°
20 degrees	6¼°	71¼°	41¾°	71¼°
25 degrees	10°	67°	40°	67°
30 degrees	14½°	63½°	37¾°	63½°
35 degrees	19½°	60¼°	35¼°	60¼°
40 degrees	24½°	57¼°	32½°	57¼°
45 degrees	30°	54¾°	30°	54¾°
50 degrees	36°	52½°	27°	52½°
55 degrees	42°	50¾°	24°	50¾°
60 degrees	48°	49°	21°	49°

14-26. Tables for compound miter cuts.

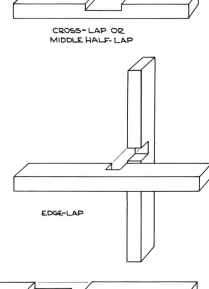

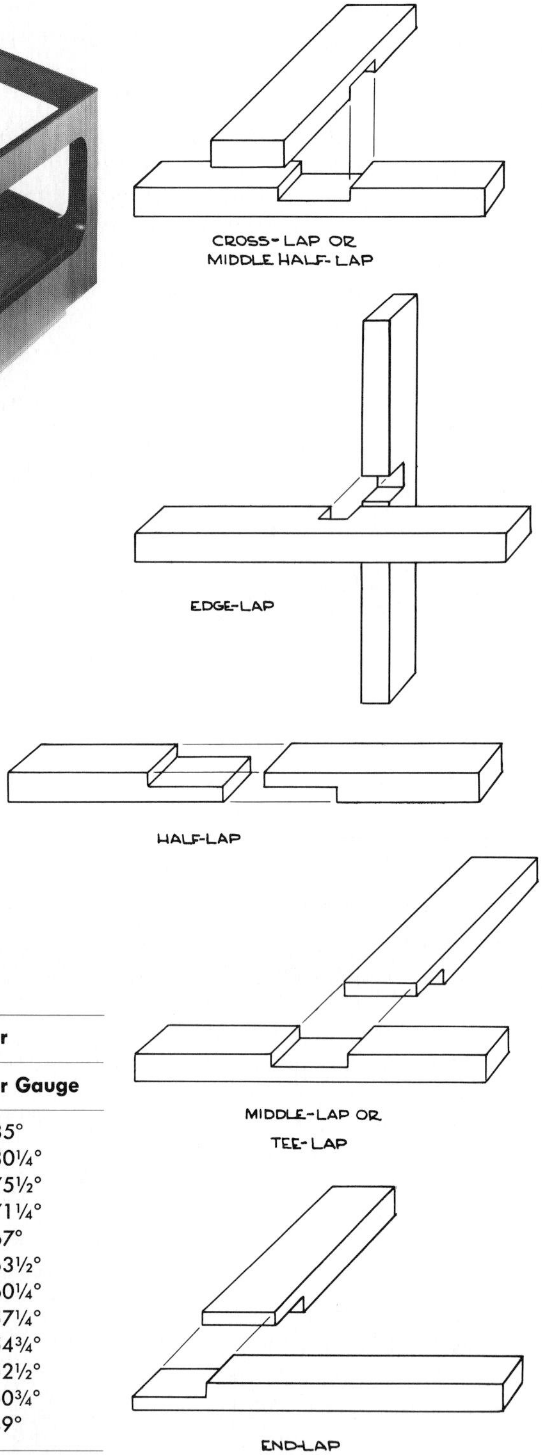

CROSS- LAP OR MIDDLE HALF- LAP

EDGE-LAP

HALF-LAP

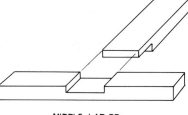

MIDDLE-LAP OR TEE-LAP

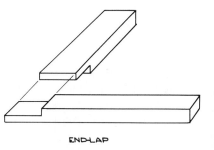

END-LAP

14-27a. Lap joints.

Make a *cross-lap joint* as follows:

1. Mark a line across one surface of one member to indicate one side of the dado. Place the second member over it and mark the width.

2. Invert the pieces and mark the width on the second member.

3. Draw lines down the edges of both pieces and mark the depth of the dado, which should be one-half the thickness of the pieces.

4. Make the cut in the same way as a dado, which it actually is.

The edge-lap joint is identical except that the members cross on edge. The middle-lap or tee is made with one member exactly like the cross-lap and the second member cut as a rabbet. The end-lap joint, which is used in frame construction, is made by laying out and cutting both pieces as rabbets. The half-lap is cut in the same way except that the pieces are joined end to end.

Mortise-and-Tenon Joints

The mortise-and-tenon joint is one of the best, primarily used in leg and rail construction for tables, chairs, and benches, as well as for installing stretchers and making frames. Fig. 14-29.

There are many kinds of mortise-and-tenon joints. The *blind mortise-and-tenon*, which is found in leg-and-rail construction, has a mortise cut in the leg and a tenon on the rail. Fig. 14-30. The *bare-faced mortise-and-tenon* is similar to a blind except that all the stock for making the tenon is removed from one surface and

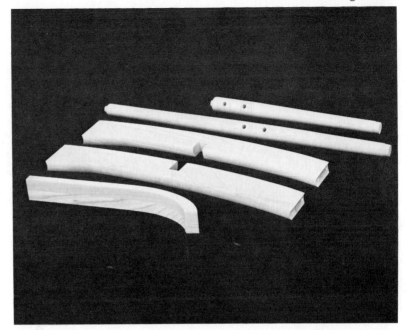

14-27b. Machine parts for a chair. Note the cuts on the second and third pieces to make an edge-lap joint.

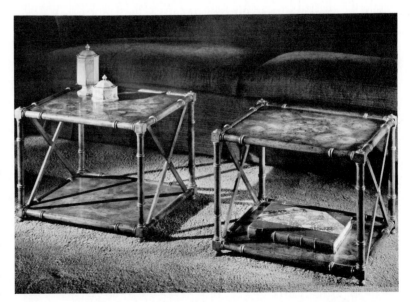

14-28. A cross-lap joint is used on the crosspieces at the ends of these coffee tables.

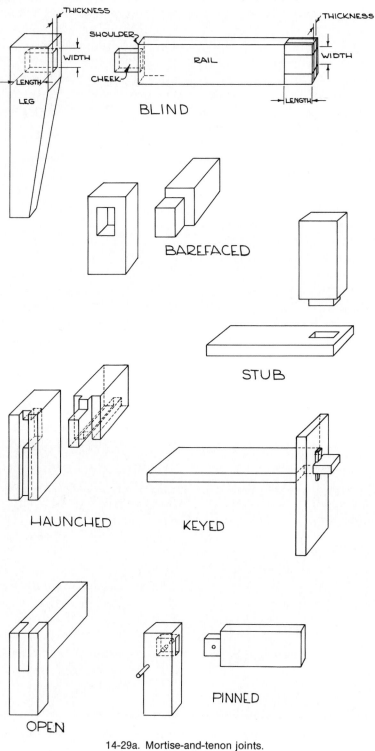

THICKNESS

SHOULDER

WIDTH

LENGTH

CHEEK

RAIL

THICKNESS

WIDTH

LENGTH

LEG

BLIND

BAREFACED

STUB

HAUNCHED

KEYED

OPEN

PINNED

14-29a. Mortise-and-tenon joints.

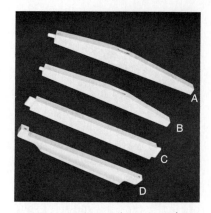

14-29b. Note the mortise cut on pieces A and B. Piece C has tenons cut on each end. Piece D shows the use of dowel holes for A and B.

14-30. Mortise-and-tenon joints are frequently used in joining parts in Early American furniture.

one edge; the surfaces of the rail and leg are flush. This is most common in modern furniture. A *frame (stub) mortise-and-tenon* is simply a short tenon that fits into a second member. This is often used in frame construction. Fig. 14-31. The *haunched mortise-and-*

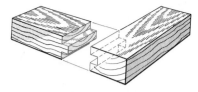

14-31. The stub mortise-and-tenon joint.

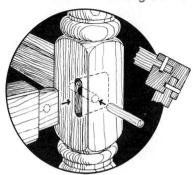

14-32a. Note the dowels sometimes used to lock a mortise-and-tenon together.

tenon is used primarily in panel construction. A groove is cut in one member and a mortise cut deeper in the same member, the same width as the groove. A tenon with the corner notched out is cut in the end of the second member to fit this. The *keyed mortise-and-tenon* is found in Early American and ranch-type furniture. An *open mortise-and-tenon joint* is used often in simple frame construction when a mortiser is not available. A *pinned mortise-and-tenon* is one in which a dowel rod is installed through the mortise and tenon to strengthen it. Fig. 14-32.

It is usually necessary to make eight mortise-and-tenon joints to join the four legs and rails. Hold the legs and rails up as they will be in the finished article, with the face side and edge of the legs in and the face side of the rails also in. Mark each adjoining rail and leg 1-1, 2-2, etc., so they can be easily identified. Place those numbers so that they will not be removed when cutting the joints.

Laying out and cutting the mortise:

When a mortising attachment or a mortising machine is used, it is necessary to lay out only one mortise in each location, because the machine is set. All similar cuts are made with the same set-up.

1. Mark a line in from the face edge of the leg to indicate one side of the mortise. Mark a second line to indicate the thickness of the mortise. The thickness of the mortise is the same as the thickness of the tenon. The distance to the mortise from the outside of the leg should equal the amount of stock removed from one side of the tenon plus the amount the rail is to set back from the leg. When the leg and rail are to be flush, the mortise is set in a distance equal to only the amount of stock

14-32b. For added strength, mortise-and-tenon joints that are pinned are sometimes used, even in Contemporary furniture. This is particularly true on a chair such as this, on which the back legs join the rails and are subject to a great deal of pressure.

removed from the outside surface of the rail.

2. From the end of the leg, mark two lines to indicate the width of the tenon.

3. Select a mortise bit of the correct size and cut the mortise as described in the section on MORTISERS AND MORTISING AT-TACHMENTS, pages 317–320. The mortise can be cut by hand by boring a series of holes in the waste stock and trimming out the joint with a chisel. The mortise should always be cut first.

Laying out and cutting the tenon:

1. Measure the length of the tenon from the end of stock and draw a line completely around the stock, using a try square. Do this on both ends of all rails and then check the length of the rails from shoulder to shoulder to make sure they are exactly the same. This is the important dimension since it will determine the final size of the product.

2. Lay out a line across both edges and ends to indicate the amount of stock to be removed on each side of the tenon. Hold a marking gage against the face surface to make these measurements. If not otherwise specified, the tenon should be about half the thickness of the stock. In all cases, however, it should be some standard thickness such as $\frac{1}{4}$″, $\frac{3}{8}$″, $\frac{1}{2}$″, etc., so that it will fit into a standard mortise opening. In making a bare-faced mortise-and-tenon, remove all of the stock from one side.

3. Determine the amount of stock to be removed from each edge to form the width of the tenon. This is usually $\frac{3}{16}$″ to $\frac{3}{8}$″. With a marking gage held against the face edge, mark a line across each surface and end to indicate the amount of stock to be removed.

4. Cut the tenon on a circular saw. Fig. 14-33. Fit the tenon into the mortise.

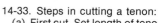

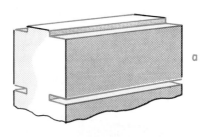

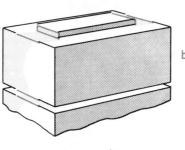

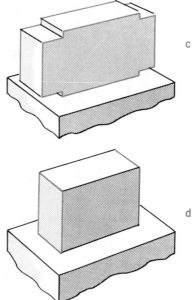

14-33. Steps in cutting a tenon:
(a) First cut. Set length of tenon from fence to outside of saw blade. Adjust saw depth on end as shown and then cut to proper length and depth.

(b) Second cut. With same fence setting, turn stock on edge and adjust to proper depth of cut in the same way as in first cut.

(c) Third cut. Change fence setting and saw depth. By standing stock on end, make cheek cut, adjusting the fence until the proper width is secured. Be sure the waste stock is outside the saw cut. Use a tenoning attachment on the circular saw to do this. See Unit 29.

(d) Fourth cut. At the same saw depth as for third cut, change the fence setting to make the final cuts. This time have the waste between the saw and the fence, thus providing a better bearing to prevent twist. The stock is guided with the miter gage and supported with a piece of scrap wood screwed or clamped to the miter gage. The scrap stock should extend to the fence (beyond the saw blade). Thus the pieces cut off will be carried through the saw to prevent kickback.
RULE: The shoulder should be at least $\frac{1}{4}$″ to facilitate a groove for a panel.

Making other kinds of mortise-and-tenon joints:

1. The open mortise-and-tenon joint is made very simply because both the mortise and the tenon can be cut on the circular saw. One member of the open mortise is simply a deep dado.

2. The keyed mortise-and-tenon joint is made by cutting a square opening completely through the first piece. A notch is cut out of each side of the rail or stretcher so that the tenon slips completely through the mortise, with part of the tenon extending beyond. A square hole is cut in the tenon, through which a key is fastened.

Dovetail Joints

The dovetail joint is found in the finest quality drawer and box construction. Fig. 14-34. The common types are the lap, stopped-lap, and blind miter or secret dovetail. These are so difficult to make by hand, however, that most hand craftsmen never do it. With a portable router and a dovetailing attachment, the dovetail joint can be made very quickly as described in the section on ROUTERS. See page 346.

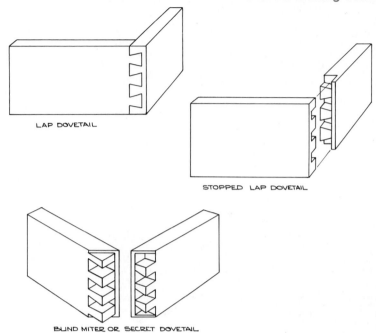

LAP DOVETAIL

STOPPED LAP DOVETAIL

BLIND MITER OR SECRET DOVETAIL

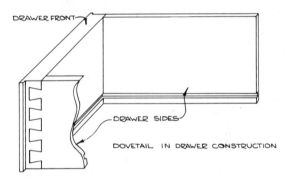

DRAWER FRONT

DRAWER SIDES

DOVETAIL IN DRAWER CONSTRUCTION

14-34. Dovetail joints. The dovetail joint is the best one for joining the front of a drawer to the sides.

UNIT 15 Tables and Chairs

As a rule, tables and chairs are made with skeleton or leg-and-rail construction. Fig. 15-1. A table is generally much simpler to construct than a chair. Sometimes an occasional table may consist of only four legs, four rails (sometimes called aprons), and a top. Fig. 15-2. More complicated tables vary widely in design and construction. Fig. 15-3. Benches and ottomans are similar to tables in construction. Fig. 15-4.

Few pieces of furniture are more difficult to construct than chairs. The reason for the difficulty of construction is that chairs are nonrectangular in structure.

15-1a. Beautiful tables of Early American and Colonial design. Note the many turned parts.

15-2. A simple contemporary table consisting of four legs, four rails, and a top.

15-1b. Traditional tables of excellent design.

Tables

The most common table types are occasional, kitchen, dining, and end tables. These are made in a variety of common geometric shapes including round, square, rectangular, triangular, hexagonal, and many others, Fig. 15-5, and in many different styles. The style can usually be identified by the shape of the legs. Fig. 15-6.

Most Contemporary occasional tables, which are used as end, coffee, lamp, and corner tables, are relatively simple to build. They usually consist of four legs and four rails (aprons) as the base, with a top of hardwood plywood or particle board, covered with veneer or plastic laminate. Some Early American tables have tops of solid stock. Fig. 15-7. Sometimes one or more extra rails, called *stretchers,* are added for strength to the underside of the structure. Fig. 15-8. Shelves or drawers are sometimes added.

15-3. Tables of unusual design.

BENCHES AND OTTOMANS

15-4. Benches and ottomans are similar to tables in construction.

15-5. Common table shapes.

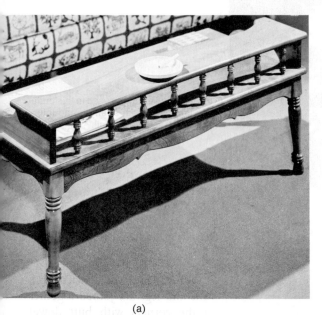

(a)

15-7. This Early American table is made of solid antique pine.

(b)

15-6. Note that the legs help to identify the style of table: (a) Early American or Colonial. (b) Contemporary. (c) French Provincial. (d) Italian Provincial.

(c)

(d)

137

15-8a. The stretchers used in this butler tray table add both strength and interesting detail.

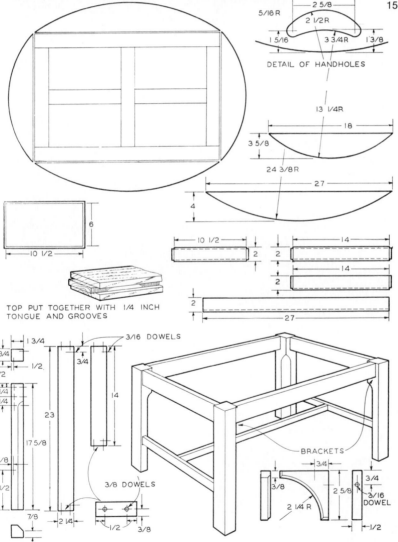

15-8b. Working drawing of a butler table with a single stretcher.

2 5/8
5/16 R
2 1/2R
1 5/16   3 3/4R   1 3/8
DETAIL OF HANDHOLES

13 1/4R

18
3 5/8

24 3/8R

27
4

10 1/2   14
2   2
14
2
2
27

6
10 1/2

TOP PUT TOGETHER WITH 1/4 INCH
TONGUE AND GROOVES

1 3/4
1 3/4
1/2.
3/4
3/16 DOWELS
1/2
1 1/4
1 1/4
14
23
17 5/8
3/8
5 1/2
3/8 DOWELS
7/8
2 1/4
1/2   3/8

BRACKETS

3/4
3/8   2 5/8   3/4
3/16 DOWEL
2 1/4 R   1/2

Fig. 15-9. In most construction, rails and legs are joined together at the corners with butt dowel joints, while the corners are strengthened with corner blocks. Fig. 15-10. Mortise-and-tenon joints are frequently used in construction of traditional styles. Fig. 15-11. For a larger table surface, drop leaves can be added. Fig. 15-12. The drop leaves are attached to the top with hinges. The leaves are supported by either a wood or a metal table-leaf support. Fig. 15-13. Tops of solid wood should generally be avoided because of the problems of shrinking and swelling. Plywood is almost always used, with the edges covered in some way.

Some details of table construction, including edge trimming, installing corner blocks, fastening tops to tables, and using commercial legs, are included in this unit.*

*More complicated tables, such as extension dining room tables, are explained in greater detail in the textbook CABINET-MAKING AND MILLWORK, by John L. Feirer.

15-9. Solid cherry and cherry veneer have been combined to make this coffee table with one drawer. The top is 54″ x 22″ and the height is 15¾″.

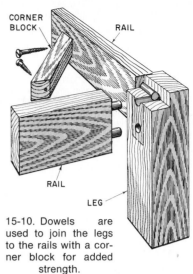

15-10. Dowels are used to join the legs to the rails with a corner block for added strength.

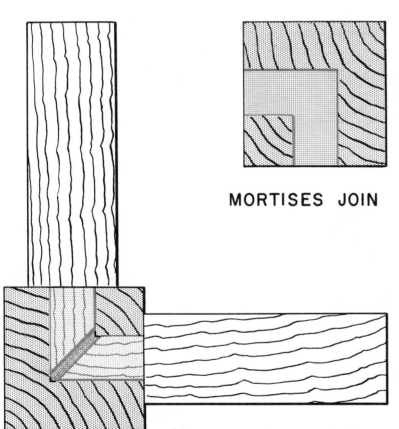

MORTISES JOIN

TENONS HAVE CLEARANCE AT ENDS

15-11. Mortise-and-tenon joint.

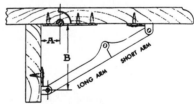

15-12. Drop leaves are used to make larger tops for many tables.

Dimension A (inches)	Dimension B (inches)		
	6″ Size	8″ Size	10″ Size
½	3½	3½	5
1	3¼	3³⁄₁₆	4¹¹⁄₁₆
1½	2¹³⁄₁₆	2⅞	4⁷⁄₁₆
2	2½	2½	4
2½	2⅛	2⅛	3⁹⁄₁₆

15-13a. Directions for mounting a table-leaf support.

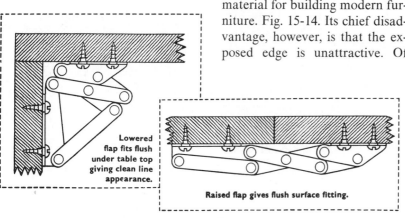

Lowered flap fits flush under table top giving clean line appearance.

Raised flap gives flush surface fitting.

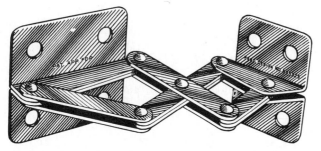

15-13b. Many Contemporary tables have flat table hinges which eliminate the unsightly gap formed by butt hinges. The flat table hinge provides a flush, clean-cut appearance.

Treating the Edge of Plywood

Plywood is a very desirable material for building modern furniture. Fig. 15-14. Its chief disadvantage, however, is that the exposed edge is unattractive. Of course, this exposed edge can be covered with filler during the finishing process to blend with the remainder of the piece. There are several better methods of covering it, however:

• A thin veneer can be glued to the edge with a miter joint at each corner.

• A solid piece of stock can be glued to the edge.

• A piece of molding of any desired shape and size can be glued and/or nailed in place.

• A solid wood piece can be joined to the edge with a tongue-and-groove joint.

• A spline can be inserted between the plywood and solid wood edging. Fig. 15-15.

Installing Corner Blocks

Corner blocks are installed on chairs, tables, and other furniture pieces to strengthen corners which are the weakest points. Fig. 15-16. For wood corner blocks, select stock at least 2″ to 2½″ in thickness, of some softwood such as pine or poplar. For square tables, cut the block as in Fig. 15-17.

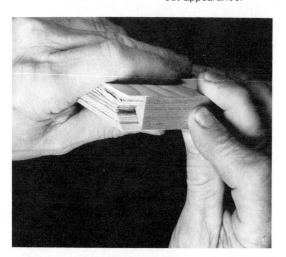

15-14. A handsome plywood edge can be obtained by cutting a V-groove and then inserting a matching wood strip. Thin strips of veneer edge banding can also be used to cover the edges of plywood.

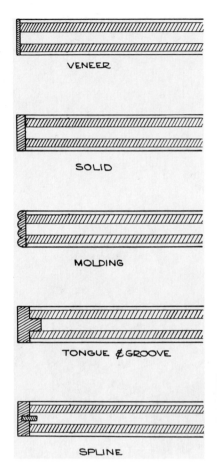

VENEER

SOLID

MOLDING

TONGUE & GROOVE

SPLINE

15-15. Methods of treating the edges of plywood.

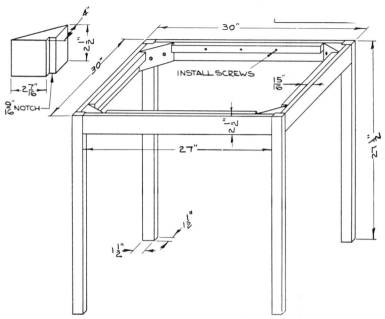

INSTALL SCREWS

15-17. Wood corner blocks on a table.

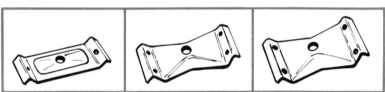

15-18. Metal corner braces.

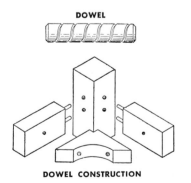

DOWEL

DOWEL CONSTRUCTION

15-16. Wood corner block.

Make sure that the corners fit perfectly. Notch out the corner so the block fits around the leg and against the rail. Drill at least two holes on either side and fasten firmly with screws.

On chairs and other objects that are not perfectly square, the correct included angle can be secured by holding a sliding T bevel over the flat pattern layout or over the object itself. Divide this angle in half for adjusting the circular saw, and cut a piece of wood to fit the corner. Metal corner supports can also be used. Fig. 15-18.

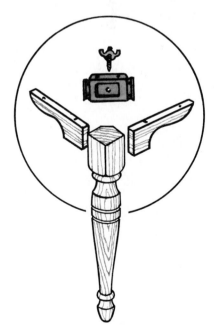

141

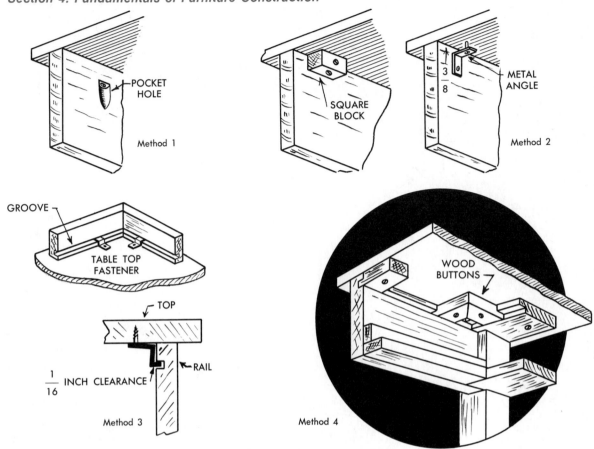

15-19. Methods of fastening tops to tables.

Fastening Tops to Tables and Desks

There are several methods of permanently fastening the top to a piece of furniture that is made with leg-and-rail construction. Fig. 15-19.

METHOD 1: To install the top with flathead screws, drill a tapered hole from the inside of the rail to the upper edge. Enlarge the lower end of the hole to a size equal to that of the screw head. Fasten rail to top with screws.

METHOD 2: Cut four wood cleats about ¾″ square to go along the sides and ends. Drill a series of holes from two directions in the piece. Fasten the cleat first to the rail, and then fasten the top by installing screws from the bottom of the cleat, or use metal angles.

METHOD 3: Cut a groove around the inside of the rail about ½″ down from the upper edge. Use metal fasteners that slip into this groove, and screw them to the top.

METHOD 4: The same method described in No. 3 can be followed by cutting a slightly wider groove. Then cut small blocks of wood, called buttons, with a rabbet on the ends to slip into the groove.

Screw the buttons to the top. Use wood buttons or metal tabletop fasteners if the top is of solid wood. These will make it possible for the top to shrink and swell without buckling.

Commercial legs are available in a wide variety of styles, materials, and lengths. Fig. 15-20. Some are one-piece units that fit directly to the base of a table. Others have metal attaching brackets into which the legs are fastened. Some of these brackets are made in such a way that the legs can be fastened either in a vertical position or at a slight

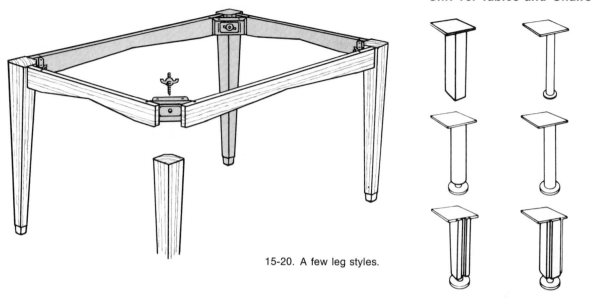

15-20. A few leg styles.

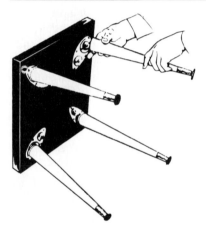

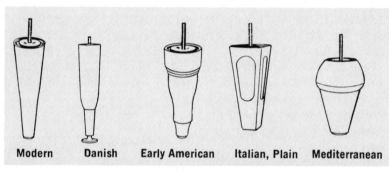

Modern   Danish   Early American   Italian, Plain   Mediterranean

15-22. A few varieties of commercial legs.

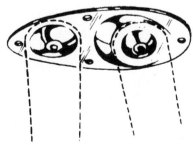

FOR VERTICAL STYLE   FOR FLARED STYLE

15-21. Note that with metal brackets the legs can be installed vertically or at a slight angle.

angle. Fig. 15-21. For heavy furniture it is best to install a one-piece leg. In selecting commercial legs, consider the following:

● *Style*—Legs are available in Modern or Contemporary, Early American, Traditional, and other styles. Fig. 15-22.

● *Kind and Material*—Most one-piece legs are metal. Those with a set of brackets are available in wood, metal, or plastic.

● *Finish*—Wood legs can be purchased unfinished or in a variety of common finishes. Most plastic legs are prefinished.

● *Size*—The length is important to the design of the product. Fig. 15-23. See the next page.

15-23. Metal legs are available in a wide variety of lengths.

Making a Coffee Table

The coffee table in Fig. 15-24 is typical of the type of item that can be made in machine woodworking. It is similar to all standard tables and chairs that can be made and therefore will be described in some detail.

Four basic kinds of joints were used in making this table, including *edge joint* strengthened with dowels, *mortise-and-tenon joint*, *miter joint* strengthened with dowels, and *corner dado joint*. It also shows typical *leg and rail* construction, *frame* construction and *table leaf* construction.

Here are the steps:

1. *Select or design the project.* This was designed by the author to fit into a modern, mahogany-trimmed room. The size of the top and the height of the table are typical of modern coffee table designs.

2. *Make a sketch and a bill of materials.* The sketch of the project should show the correct dimensions and the kinds of joints to be used. In making a bill of materials, determine the amount of stock of each different thickness needed. In the case of this table, stock 1″ thick and 2″ thick is needed. If necessary, the legs can be made from 1″ stock by gluing the pieces face to face. This coffee table required 9 board feet of 1″ mahogany and 4 board feet of 2″ mahogany.

3. *Lay out and cut the rough stock to size.* Trim off the end of the stock. Then cut lengths for the rails and frame that are about $\frac{1}{4}″$ wider and $\frac{1}{2}″$ longer than the finished size. In cutting the rails to length, remember that material is needed to make the tenons. Also cut the stock for the legs, shelf, and table leaves.

4. *Square up the stock.* Use the jointer and circular saw (planer also if one is available) to square up the stock for the legs, rails, and frame. Surface one face and two edges of the stock that are to be used for the shelf and the leaves. Try to use the poorer surface as the face surface.

5. *Glue up the stock for the shelf and leaves.* It will be necessary to glue up stock to form a piece wide enough for the shelf and leaves. If the stock from which the parts are cut is over 8″ wide, it is a good idea to re-cut the board again into strips not over 4″ to 6″ in width.

15-24a. A Contemporary coffee table with Early American influence as shown by the functional drop leaves.

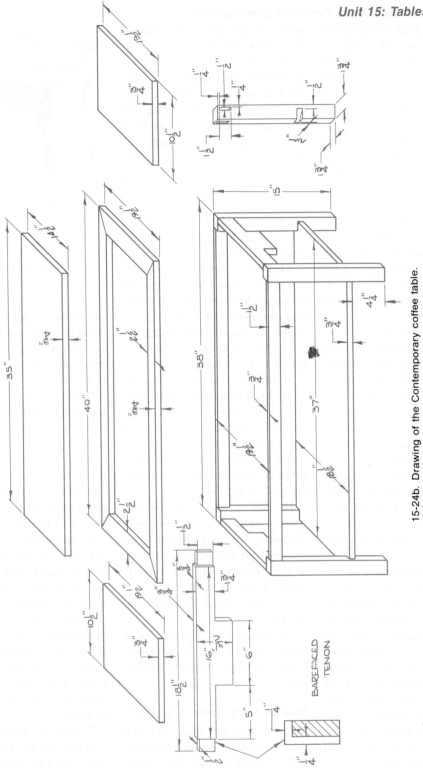

15-24b. Drawing of the Contemporary coffee table.

BAREFACED
TENON

Make an edge joint strengthened with dowels. Glue and clamp the boards together to make the shelf and leaves. Then square up these pieces to size.

6. *Make the mortise-and-tenon joints.* Carefully lay out the location of the mortises and the size of the tenons. Cut the mortises on a mortising machine or with a mortising attachment on the drill press, or, if necessary, by hand. Cut the tenons on the circular saw. Fit the tenons into the mortises and, as each one is finished, mark the upper edge of the rail and the top of the leg 1–1, 2–2, etc., so these will be assembled correctly later.

7. *Cut the corner dados on the legs and shelf.* Locate the position of the corner dado and cut it as shown in Fig. 29-55. Also cut the corners on the shelf to fit into the corner dado.

8. *Sand all parts thoroughly.* Do not, however, sand off the marks necessary for assembly.

9. *Glue up the two ends of the table.* Use scrap blocks when clamping the legs and end rails together. Check to see that the legs are parallel and square with the rails.

10. *Make the miter frame with dowels for the table top.* Cut the mitered corners on the ends of the frame. Be very careful that the two opposite sides are exactly the same length and that the miter is exactly 45 degrees. It is a good idea to lay the frame out on the table and check these joints carefully. Locate the position for two dowels on each corner. Drill or bore the dowel holes on a drill press or with the dowel jig attach-

ment. Cut the dowel and point the ends. Glue up the frame.

11. *Glue the side rails and the shelf to the end assemblies to form the bottom of the table.* Be especially careful that the entire unit is square. Measure across from corner to corner and check with the square at several points. Remove any excess glue from the assembly before it gets hard.

12. *Cut the corner blocks for strengthening the corners.* Cut and install these corner blocks as described on page 140.

13. *Make the wood cleats to fasten the frame to the bottom assembly.* Method 2, in Fig. 15-19, was followed for fastening the frame to the bottom assembly.

14. *Re-sand all parts.* Fasten the frame to the base.

15. *Fasten the leaves to the table.* Two butt hinges and a single table leaf support are used at either end. The hinges are fastened flat against the bottom of the frame and leaf, and the table leaf support is installed from under the leaf to the end rail.

16. *Cut a piece of plywood slightly smaller than the opening in the frame.* Cut two support strips that will go across the underside of the frame to support the plywood. Screw these in place.

17. *Apply the desired finish to the table.*

18. *Cover the plywood with leather and insert it in the frame.* Fasten in place from the underside.

Modern Lamp Table, Fig. 15-25.

1. Cut out the back and two side rails; miter the ends of these.

2. Cut out the two short front

15-25a. Lamp table.

rails and the drawer front, taking them from the same piece of stock so the grain will match. Cut a miter on one end of each front rail.

3. Cut $\frac{5}{8}'' \times \frac{1}{2}''$ rabbets on the lower inside edge of the back and front rails, to receive the drawer slides.

4. Cut spline slots in the mitered ends of the rails. For strength, cut the splines with the grain running the short way, as shown in the drawing.

5. Assemble all rails with splines, glue and clamps. A piece of scrap stock clamped to the outside of the two front rails will help to space and align them.

6. Make the legs, cutting the face taper on a jointer and the inside taper on a circular saw with taper jig. Cut the tops and bottoms of the legs to the correct angle. Cut two dadoes at the top of each leg.

7. Cut the corner blocks. Note that the blocks which fit against the front rails must be cut and

All Dimensions Listed Are Finished Size

No. of Pieces	Part Name	Thickness	Width	Length	Wood
2	Side Rails	¾″	3½″	21″	White Oak
1	Back Rail	¾″	3½″	21″	White Oak
2	Front Rails	¾″	3½″	4½″	White Oak
1	Drawer Front	¾″	3½″	12″	White Oak
1	Top	½″	20¾″	20¾″	Plywood
4	Legs	1¼″	2½″	24¾″	White Oak
2	Drawer Slides	½″	2¼″	20¾″	White Oak
2	Drawer Guides	½″	¾″	19½″	White Oak
2	Drawer Sides	⅜″	3″	15″	White Oak
1	Drawer Back	⅜″	3″	11¼″	White Oak
1	Drawer Bottom	¼″	11½″	14⅜″	Plywood
8	Corner Blocks	1⅝″	2″	3⅜″	White Oak
4	Splines	⅛″	3½″	½″	White Oak
6	Glue Blocks	¾″	1″	2½″	Pine

15-25b. Bill of materials.

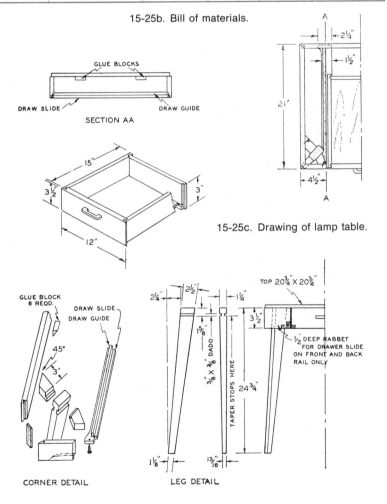

SECTION AA

15-25c. Drawing of lamp table.

CORNER DETAIL

LEG DETAIL

installed individually. They meet the rails at about 71 degrees, while the others are cut at 45 degrees.

8. Assemble the legs, corner blocks and rails, using glue and screws.

9. Construct the drawer, using the joints in the drawing. Note that the drawer front is designed to have a ½″ overhang at the bottom and a ⅛″ overhang at each end.

10. Cut out the drawer slides and guides and fasten together with small screws. Install with screws, and adjust so the drawer will slide easily.

11. Cut the table top to size and clamp to rails until the glue blocks are thoroughly dry.

12. Finish as desired.

13. Install drawer pull.

Other sample table ideas are shown in Figs. 15-26 and 15-27.

15-26. Step table.

15-27. Contemporary coffee tables.

Wood Chairs

No other item of furniture varies so much in design and construction as chairs. This variation in construction is due not only to external appearance but to the actual method of construction.

Most chairs are of the *box-seat type,* which is somewhat similar in construction to the table. In other words, the basic chair consists of rails, legs, and posts (the vertical back parts). A post differs from a leg in that it extends well above the rail. Fig. 15-28. Sometimes stretchers are installed below the rails for added strength. The seat for a box chair is added after the chair is built.

The *Windsor chair,* on the other hand, is entirely different in construction. The basic feature is the wood seat. The legs have round tenons that fit into the underside of the seat, while the stretchers fit between the legs. The back posts are joined to the upper part of the seat with round tenons that fit into the round holes at the seat. Fig. 15-29.

The *ladder-back chair* is similar to the box seat in construction. Its posts and legs are joined by stretchers that are usually turned. Fig. 15-30. There are many other styles of chairs including the bentwood chair. All chairs are difficult to construct for the following reasons:

● A chair is not rectangular in construction like most tables; therefore all of the rails must be joined at an odd angle (not 90 degrees) to legs and posts. Fig. 15-31.
● Chairs take more abuse than any other kind of furniture. While

15-28. A Contemporary box seat chair.

15-29. A modern version of the Windsor chair.

15-30. A ladder-back chair.

most chairs are not designed for it, people tilt back on the back legs, putting extraordinary strain between the legs and the rails. For this reason extra strength must be added at these points.

● Chairs must be designed for many uses such as relaxing, writing, playing games, and dining. The same kind of chair cannot be used for all of these purposes. As a result, basic design details must be varied. For example, the seat may be as low as 12″ from the floor for a relaxing chair or as high as 15″ for a writing chair.

Because of these great variations, it is impossible to give specific instructions on how to build a chair, but the following are suggested:

● Use dowel joints for most chair construction. While some mortise-and-tenon joints are still used, dowel construction is far simpler. Generally, at least two dowels should be installed at each joint.

15-31. Note the variety of styles in these side and arm chairs.

149

Dowels can be installed with greater ease when the end of the rail must be cut at an angle. It is relatively easy to bore two holes at right angles to the end grain of a rail and into the edge grain of a leg so that the legs fit exactly. The two parts to be joined can be at any angle. A dowel joint also makes it possible to assemble the parts with greater precision.

● Corner blocks should be installed at all four corners of the chair to increase its strength. Fig. 15-32. These blocks must be cut to fit the angle between the side and back or front rail. They should be made of softwood and installed with glue and screws. Metal corner blocks are not strong enough for chairs.

● The back posts of a chair run from the floor to the total height. These oftentimes must be cut at a slight curve. When this is necessary, the post should be thick enough so it won't split. The back panels between the two posts are made in a variety of designs. Sometimes solid wood is cut on a slight curve while, in other cases, bent plywood is used. Many chair designs allow stretchers to be installed below the rails which increase the rigidity of a chair. Arms are sometimes part of the design of certain dining and relaxing chairs. Most box-type chairs have a slip seat added after the chair is constructed. Frequently this slip seat is made by cutting plywood to size and then upholstering it with foam rubber and a cloth cover. The complete slip seat is attached to the chair from underneath with wood screws through the corner blocks.

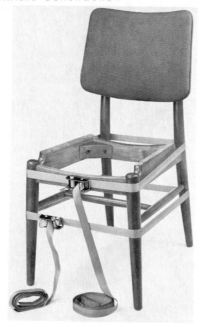

15-32. Corner blocks must be added to a chair for strength.

In building a simple chair, one of the first steps is to make a full-size seat plan. From this, the angle at which the rails fit to the legs can be determined. Also a full-size plan of the back and sides of the chair must be made. This will determine the angle at which the rails meet the back legs.

Modern Desk Chair, Fig. 15-33.

1. Cut out the stock for the front legs. Taper the inside and back of each, using a jointer or a taper jig on a circular saw.

2. Next make an accurate full-size drawing of the seat plan and a paper pattern of the back post profile.

3. Cut out the back posts with a band saw. Then, using a jointer, taper the inside faces from the seat level to each end.

4. Cut the mortises for the rails in all four legs, making use of the seat plan drawing for angles of the side rails.

5. Cut out four rails. Cut tenons to fit the legs.

6. Saw out the pieces for the chair back, cut the notches for the halved joints, and drill for dowels.

7. Make a sub-assembly of the two back posts, back seat rail and chair back members. Glue and clamp until dry.

8. Make a sub-assembly of the two front legs and front rail. Glue and clamp until dry.

9. Join the two sub-assemblies with the two side rails, glue and clamp together.

10. Cut out corner blocks, glue and screw in place.

11. Clean off all excess glue and sand thoroughly.

15-33a. Modern desk chair.

12. Finish as desired.

13. Cut panel for slip seat out of ½" plywood, and round the edges with a plane and sandpaper.

14. Cover the seat with a piece of chair covering such as tapestry or mohair and filling such as 1" foam rubber.

IMPORTANT: All dimensions listed below, except for length of dowel, are FINISHED size.

No. of Pieces	Part Name	Thickness	Width	Length	Wood
2	Front legs	1⅝"	1⅝"	17"	White Oak
2	Back posts	1¼"	4"	32½"	White Oak
1	Front rail	¾"	2¼"	15¾"	White Oak
2	Side rails	¾"	2¼"	15¼"	White Oak
1	Back rail	1"	2⅝"	14"	White Oak
1	Horizontal Back strip	¾"	1"	16"	White Oak
1	Horizontal Back strip	¾"	1"	13⅝"	White Oak
1	Horizontal Back strip	¾"	1"	12⅞"	White Oak
1	Horizontal Back strip	¾"	1"	12"	White Oak
2	Vertical Back strips	¾"	1"	12⅜"	White Oak
4	Corner blocks	1"	2"	5½"	Pine
1	Seat panel	½"	14¾"	17"	Fir Plywood
1	Dowel	⁵⁄₁₆"		18"	Hardwood
12	1¼"-10 Flat-head wood screws				

15-33b. Bill of materials for the desk chair.

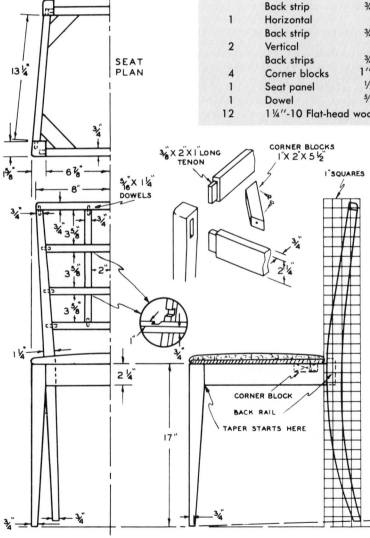

15. Place the final cover face down on a clean work surface. Position the plywood base with the filling material attached upside-down and centered on the final cover. Tack the cover in place as described in Unit 44, Making A Pad Seat.

16. Trim the surplus fabric. Then cut a piece of black poster board about ½" smaller than the outline of the plywood. Center it on the bottom and tack it in place to conceal the irregular fabric edges.

17. Fasten the seat to the chair with four wood screws up through the corner blocks.

15-33c. Drawing of desk chair.

UNIT 16 Plastic Laminates

Plastic laminate surfacing materials combine beauty with exceptional durability. Fig. 16-1. In the making of these laminates, layers of craft paper impregnated with phenolic resins are covered with melamine-resin-saturated pattern paper. Then they are topped by a protective sheet coated with additional melamine. Fig. 16-2. These are cured under intense heat and pressure to form a single hard-surface sheet.

Plastic laminates are used widely for the tops and other wearing surfaces of furniture. They come in solid colors, wood grain, and a wide variety of other patterns. Fig. 16-3. In normal use, the material is virtually inde-structible since it resists high heat, stains, and impact. Fig. 16-4. It won't crack or chip and it maintains its initial luster and finish throughout the lifetime of the product. Since no finishing is ever required, it is used most frequently for the tops of furniture which take excessive wear.

Working Plastic Laminates

Plastic laminates can be worked with standard woodworking or metalworking tools. However, if a great deal of production is to be done, carbide-tipped tools are recommended. For handwork, a brace and bit, boring brace bits, files, and other standard tools can be used. Some common standards that should be followed in using plastic laminate include the following:

● Chamfer all exposed edges by filing to prevent possible damage by chipping.

● Seal exposed edges with some kind of banding, including the band of plastic laminate, solid wood, metal, or veneer.

● Avoid making miter joints at 45 degrees for outside corners since a miter joint is easily damaged by a sharp blow.

The following tools and materials are necessary: a 2" bristle brush, small hand roller, hand plane, flat mill file, hammer, several scraps of plastic laminates each slightly longer than the width of the plastic laminate top, block of wood, contact bond cement, and abrasive paper. Obtain a piece of $\frac{3}{4}$" plywood or particle board of the correct size for the table. The plywood or particle board should be about $\frac{1}{8}$" to $\frac{1}{4}$" smaller than the plastic laminate. Fig. 16-5. Select the best surface for the top. If there are imperfections in the surface, fill with wood filler and smooth the surface by sanding.

16-1. Tables of varying design with plastic laminate tops.

152

MELAMINE OVERLAY
PATTERN SHEET
7 LAYERS OF CRAFT PAPER
BACKING

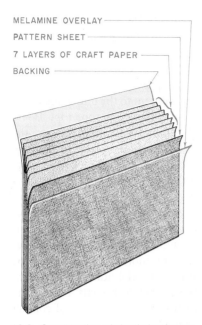

16-2. Construction of plastic laminates.

16-3. The checkerboard design on this card table is plastic laminate.

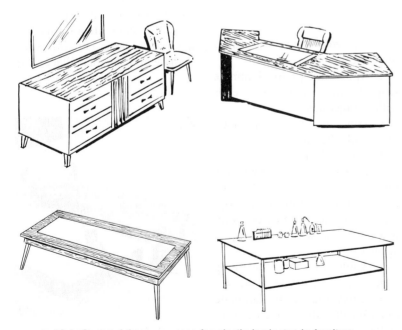

16-4. Some of the many uses for plastic laminates in furniture.

16-5. Particle board makes a good base for plastic laminate. Here laminate sheets are being glued to particle board with an adhesive that must be clamped. Contact cement requires no clamping.

Edge Treatments

- Wood Tape or Veneer

1. Obtain wood tape or veneer $\frac{1}{8}''$ or $\frac{1}{4}''$ wider than the thickness of the top. Fig. 16-6.

2. Apply tape with contact cement to the two opposite edges.

3. Trim the excess material flush with the core.

4. Trim the top and bottom with a razor blade.

5. Apply the tape to the two remaining edges, and repeat steps 3 and 4.

6. Apply the plastic laminate to the core.

7. Sand all edges.

- Plain Facing. Fig. 16-7.

1. Apply plastic laminate to core.

2. Cut lumber to length with 45 degree miters at each end.

3. Apply the edging to the core with glue and clamps.

4. Remove all machine marks with abrasive cloth.

- Bevel. Fig. 16-8.

1. Set the saw blade at the proper angle and cut bevels on all four edges.

2. Apply plastic laminate to table. Then trim any laminate that hangs over edge.

3. Fill edge grain of plywood with wood filler.

4. Remove all machine marks with abrasive paper.

- Self-Edging. Fig. 16-9. In most self-edging applications an extra piece of lumber or plywood is fastened to the underside of the core and flush with the outside edges to give the edge a heavier appearance.

1. Obtain strips of plastic laminate $\frac{1}{4}''$ longer than the core and

16-6. Wood tape or veneer edge.

16-7. Plain facing.

16-8. Bevel edge.

16-9. Self edge.

$\frac{1}{8}''$ to $\frac{1}{4}''$ wider than the thickness of the top.

2. Apply the plastic laminate strips to the two opposite ends with contact cement.

3. Trim the plastic laminate flush with the core.

4. Use a block plane or file to trim the plastic edge flush with the top and bottom. Hold the file parallel to the top during this operation to insure a good joint when the plastic laminate top is applied.

5. Apply the two remaining edge strips and repeat 3 and 4.

6. Apply the plastic laminate top after the edges have been installed on the core.

Applying the Contact Cement

Clean the surface of the core and apply a heavy, uniform coat of contact cement with a brush. Also apply a uniform film of contact cement to the underside of the plastic laminate top. Fig. 16-10. When a glossy film covers the entire surface, this indicates you are using enough adhesive. Any dull spots which appear after drying indicate that the coat is uneven. These spots must be recoated. Usually one coat is enough, but some porous surfaces require more; in that event be sure to let the adhesive dry completely between coats. Follow the instructions on the can of contact cement.

Make sure the adhesive is dry. This can be checked by applying a piece of craft paper to the surface and pressing lightly. If it does not stick, the adhesive is ready to receive the plastic laminate.

Use extreme care in aligning the plastic laminate and the core material, because bonding is immediate upon contact. Place scrap

16-10. Applying contact cement.

strips of plastic laminate with the smooth side down on top of the plywood. Fig. 16-11. Align the plastic laminate and the plywood so that an equal amount of laminate hangs over all four sides of the core. Now gently slip the center piece of scrap from beneath the plastic laminate, leaving the other scrap pieces in place. The two adhesive surfaces will come in contact with one another. Then remove the other scraps one at a time. Be careful not to jar the work as you move the scraps because the two pieces will bond immediately. *There will be no chance to move the material once the contact is made.*

With a small roller, roll the surface from the center toward the edges in both directions. If a small roller is not available, use a block of soft wood. Place this on the center and work toward the edges, tapping sharply with a hammer. Fig. 16-12. Tap or roll every inch of the surface to insure complete bond.

Use a hand plane to remove the excess plastic laminate which overhangs the edges of the plywood core.

File the edges smooth with a flat mill file. If the edges have already been applied, hold the file at a 20- to 30-degree angle to the edge. Fig. 16-13. Use long, smooth, downward strokes. If the edge has not been applied, care must be taken to file the plastic laminate flush with the plywood core. This leaves a sharp corner at the top to insure a good joint between the edges to be applied and the plastic laminate. Clean off the excess cement.

16-11. Removing one piece of scrap from under the plastic laminate. Always work from the center towards the ends.

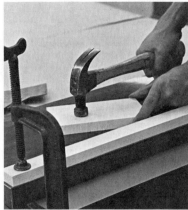

16-12. Tapping a block of wood with a hammer to make sure the plastic laminate is firmly in place.

Building a Coffee Table,
Fig. 16-14.

MATERIALS:

16—$\frac{3}{8}$" x 2" dowel pins
12—$\frac{1}{4}$" x 1$\frac{1}{2}$" dowel pins
4—$\frac{5}{8}$" single prong furniture glides
1 piece plastic laminate 24" x 36"
4 legs—1-$\frac{1}{4}$" x 1-$\frac{1}{4}$" x 14"
2 rails—$\frac{3}{4}$" x 1-$\frac{3}{4}$" x 15-$\frac{1}{2}$"
2 rails—$\frac{3}{4}$" x 1-$\frac{3}{4}$" x 27-$\frac{1}{2}$"
2 side stretchers $\frac{3}{4}$" x 1-$\frac{3}{4}$" x 27-$\frac{1}{2}$"
1 center stretcher $\frac{3}{4}$" x 3-$\frac{3}{8}$" x 17-$\frac{1}{4}$"
2 pieces top edging $\frac{3}{4}$" x 2" x 36" (Note: these pieces must be the same thickness as the $\frac{3}{4}$" plywood)
2 pieces top edging $\frac{3}{4}$" x 2" x 24" (Note: these pieces must be the same thickness as the $\frac{3}{4}$" plywood)
1 piece fir plywood AD $\frac{3}{4}$" x 20" x 32"
104" of spline material $\frac{1}{4}$" x $\frac{7}{16}$"

16-13. Filing the edge of plastic laminate at an angle.

PLAN OF PROCEDURE

1. Machine all stock to finished dimensions.

2. Cut a rabbet on the inside of the two side stretchers $\frac{1}{16}$" deep x $\frac{7}{16}$" wide.

3. Cut a rabbet on each end of the center stretcher $\frac{1}{2}$" deep x $\frac{7}{16}$" long.

16-14a. A Contemporary coffee table with a plastic laminate top.

4. Cut a groove ¼″ x ¼″ in the center of all four edges of the plywood top.

5. Cut a groove ¼″ x ¼″ in the center of one edge of each piece of the top edging.

6. Cut 45° miters on the ends of the top edging so it will accurately fit around the edge of the plywood top.

7. Apply glue; insert the spline

16-14b. The trays for the Contemporary table are reversible, with different colored plastic laminate on each side.

material and clamp the top edging.

8. When the glue has cured sufficiently, sand the top surface smooth. Special care should be taken in sanding to be certain there is no ridge at the joint between the plywood and the edging and that a flat surface is maintained.

9. Tilt the circular saw blade to 15° off the vertical (on most saws this will be 75°) and adjust the fence to within ⅜″ of the saw blade at the table. (The blade must tilt away from the fence.) On some circular saws, the fence must be placed on the opposite side of the blade from which it is normally used. Raise the blade to about 1½″ above the table. When you are certain the saw is set up properly, place the table top on its edge with the top surface against the fence and make a cut on each of the four edges.

10. Lay out and bore all dowel holes.

11. Drill and countersink screw holes in the edges of the rails for attaching the top.

12. Set up a taper jig and cut the tapers on the legs (Note: Only the sides of the legs which have dowel holes bored in them are to be tapered, as per the drawing).

13. Set up a taper jig and cut the taper on the side stretcher.

14. Plane, scrape, and sand to remove all machine marks from exposed surfaces.

15. Glue and clamp each of the sides of the table together using the legs, rails, and side stretchers. Remove from clamps when the glue has cured.

16. Glue and clamp the two side units together, using the end rails and center stretcher. Remove from clamps when the glue has cured.

17. Apply the plastic laminate to the top, using contact cement.

18. Trim the edges.

19. Carefully remove all excess glue from the table.

20. Attach the top to the table legs using eight 2″ #8 flathead wood screws.

21. Finish-sand entire project.

22. Finish as desired.

23. Attach glides to the bottoms of the table legs.

REVERSIBLE TRAYS

These trays have a dual function. First, they can be used for shelf storage of books or magazines as a part of the table. Second, they can be removed when it is desired to use them as serving trays. The plastic laminate surfaces are stain- and water-proof. The trays and table make a handsome living room piece.

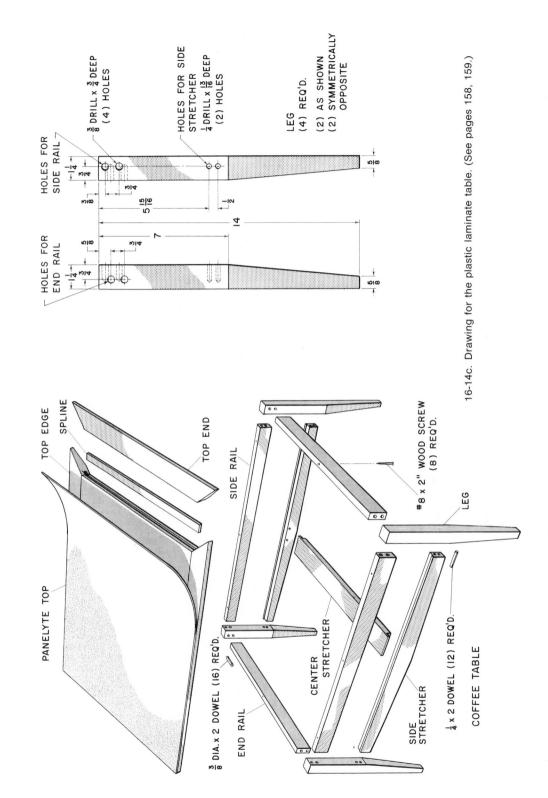

HOLES FOR
SIDE RAIL

$\frac{3}{8}$ DRILL x $\frac{3}{4}$ DEEP
(4) HOLES

HOLES FOR SIDE
STRETCHER
$\frac{1}{4}$ DRILL x $\frac{13}{16}$ DEEP
(2) HOLES

LEG
(4) REQ'D.

(2) AS SHOWN
(2) SYMMETRICALLY
OPPOSITE

$1\frac{1}{4}$
$\frac{3}{4}$
$\frac{3}{4}$
$3\frac{1}{8}$
$5\frac{15}{16}$
$\frac{1}{2}$
$\frac{5}{8}$

HOLES FOR
END RAIL

$\frac{5}{8}$
$\frac{3}{4}$
7
14
$1\frac{1}{4}$
$\frac{3}{4}$
$\frac{5}{8}$

16-14c. Drawing for the plastic laminate table. (See pages 158, 159.)

TOP EDGE
SPLINE
TOP END

PANELYTE TOP

SIDE RAIL

#8 x 2" WOOD SCREW
(8) REQ'D.

LEG

$\frac{3}{8}$ DIA. x 2 DOWEL (16) REQ'D.

CENTER
STRETCHER

END RAIL

SIDE
STRETCHER

$\frac{1}{4}$ x 2 DOWEL (12) REQ'D.

COFFEE TABLE

157

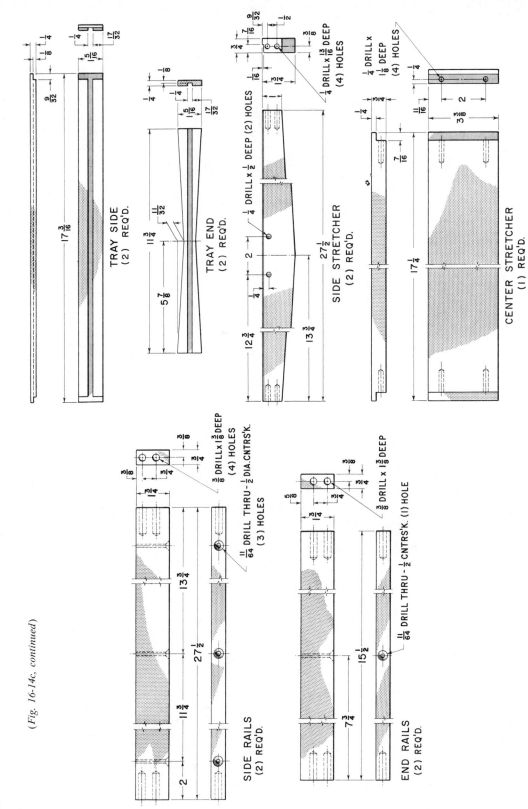

TRAY SIDE
(2) REQ'D.

TRAY END
(2) REQ'D.

SIDE STRETCHER
(2) REQ'D.

CENTER STRETCHER
(1) REQ'D.

SIDE RAILS
(2) REQ'D.

END RAILS
(2) REQ'D.

$\frac{1}{4}$ DRILL x $\frac{1}{2}$ DEEP (2) HOLES

$\frac{1}{4}$ DRILL x $\frac{13}{16}$ DEEP (4) HOLES

$\frac{1}{4}$ DRILL x $1\frac{1}{8}$ DEEP (4) HOLES

$\frac{3}{8}$ DRILL x $1\frac{3}{8}$ DEEP (4) HOLES

$\frac{11}{64}$ DRILL THRU - $\frac{1}{2}$ DIA.CNTRS'K. (3) HOLES

$\frac{3}{8}$ DRILL x $1\frac{3}{8}$ DEEP (1) HOLE

$\frac{11}{64}$ DRILL THRU - $\frac{1}{2}$ CNTRS'K. (1) HOLE

(Fig. 16-14c, continued)

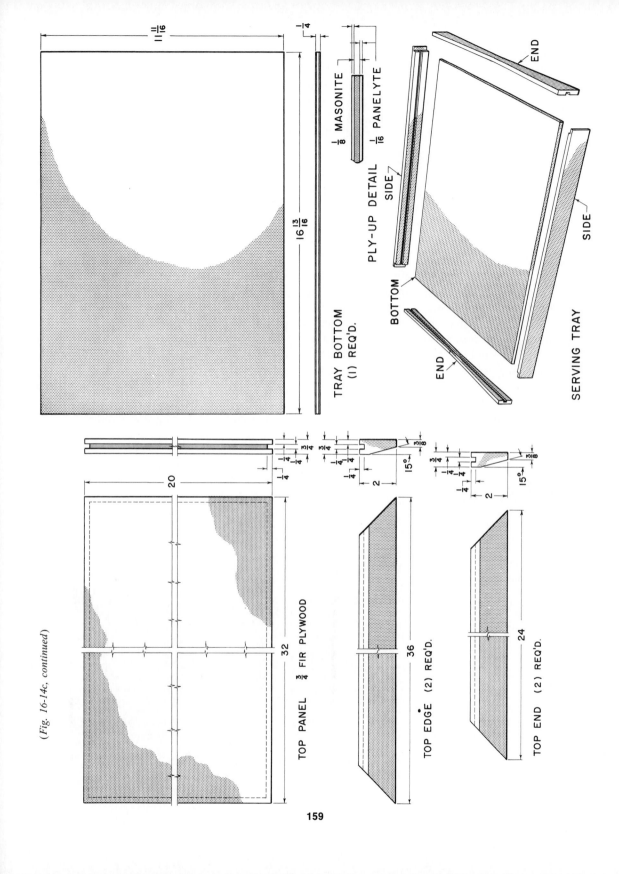

(*Fig. 16-14c, continued*)

$11\frac{1}{16}$

$\frac{1}{4}$

$16\frac{13}{16}$

$\frac{1}{8}$ MASONITE

$\frac{1}{16}$ PANELYTE

TRAY BOTTOM
(1) REQ'D.

PLY-UP DETAIL

SIDE

END

BOTTOM

END

SIDE

SERVING TRAY

20

32

TOP PANEL $\frac{3}{4}$ FIR PLYWOOD

$\frac{1}{4}$

$\frac{3}{4}$

$\frac{1}{4}$ $\frac{1}{4}$

$\frac{3}{4}$

$\frac{1}{4}$ $\frac{1}{4}$

$\frac{3}{8}$

15°

2

36

TOP EDGE (2) REQ'D.

$\frac{3}{4}$

$\frac{1}{4}$ $\frac{1}{4}$

$\frac{3}{8}$

15°

2

24

TOP END (2) REQ'D.

MATERIALS (ROUGH SIZE)

1 piece hardboard, ⅛″ x 12″ x 17″

4 pieces plastic laminate, 12″ x 17″

2 pieces (sides and ends), ¼″ x 1½″ x 30″

Contact cement

Glue

PLAN OF PROCEDURE

1. Obtain stock for tray bottom: one piece, rough size ⅛″ hardboard, 12″ by 17″.

2. Fasten a piece of plastic laminate to each side with contact cement. NOTE: Place the plastic laminate surface on a piece of scrap plywood when cutting to size on the circular saw; this will prevent scratching the plastic laminate.

3. Cut the tray bottom to finished size, 11¹¹⁄₁₆″ by 16¹³⁄₁₆″.

4. Obtain stock for sides and ends: ¼″ by 1½″ by 30″ (rough width and length).

5. Rip to width allowing for a jointer cut to remove the saw marks (1⁵⁄₁₆″ finished).

6. Cut off the pieces to finished length. One side and one end can be obtained from each piece. Ends, finished length, 11¾″— sides, finished length, 17³⁄₁₆″.

7. Cut a groove (to receive the hardboard and plastic laminate tray bottom ⅛″ deep) in each piece. As a safety factor and to insure great accuracy, it is recommended that two feather boards be used when grooving. Clamp one feather board to the fence to hold the stock down; the second should be clamped to the table to hold the stock tightly against the fence.

8. Cut the rabbets on the end-pieces immediately after grooving, using the same depth of cut as for grooving. Cut the rabbet about ¹⁄₃₂″ longer than the necessary ¼″. This will permit the joint to be sanded flush after the tray has been glued up.

9. Lay out the desired finger-grip contour line on the end pieces and cut them out. Both pieces may be sawn at the same time, holding them together by driving some ½″ wire brads into the waste stock.

10. Drawfile the sawed edges to the line.

11. Sand the inside area of all pieces before the pieces are assembled.

12. Assemble the tray dry and make sure all joints fit properly.

13. Assemble, glue, and clamp.

14. Completely sand the outside surfaces and edges.

15. Finish as desired.

UNIT **17** Casegoods

In the furniture industry the term "casegoods" includes all types of bookcases, cabinets, chests, and other furniture pieces intended for storage. Fig. 17-1. Complicated casegoods items, which have both drawers and doors, are sometimes said to be of *carcass construction*. Figs. 17-2 and 17-3.

The first step in building a case is to determine how the body will be constructed. Top, bottom, and sides of the body can be of all plywood or some other panel stock, of frame-and-panel construction, or of open-frame construction covered with panels. Fig. 17-4. Various types of corners can be used to fasten the top and bottom to the sides. Fig. 17-5.

17-1a. A very practical, open bookcase with small drawers measuring 30″ x 18″ x 30″ in height.

17-1b. A relatively simple hi-fi cabinet.

17-1c. This small, solid oak chest has a top that is 34″ x 21″ and 18½″ high.

17-2. These beautiful, tall cabinets represent excellent quality furniture making.

17-1d. This cherry, slant-top desk was made by a high school student. It displays a high degree of craftsmanship. It is an illustration of complicated casework.

17-3. Casework of this type can be made only when the manufacturer has all of the industrial production equipment.

17-4a. The sides and top of this case are made of lumber-core plywood.

17-4b. The sides and doors of this cabinet are of frame-and-panel construction.

17-4c. This shows a dresser frame which is made in a skeleton form. Some kind of panel material will be attached to the outside.

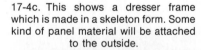

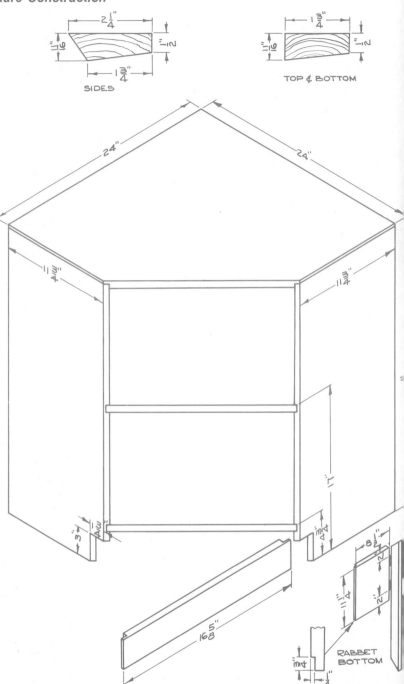

17-5a. The corners of the sides and top of this simple bookcase are joined with rabbet joints.

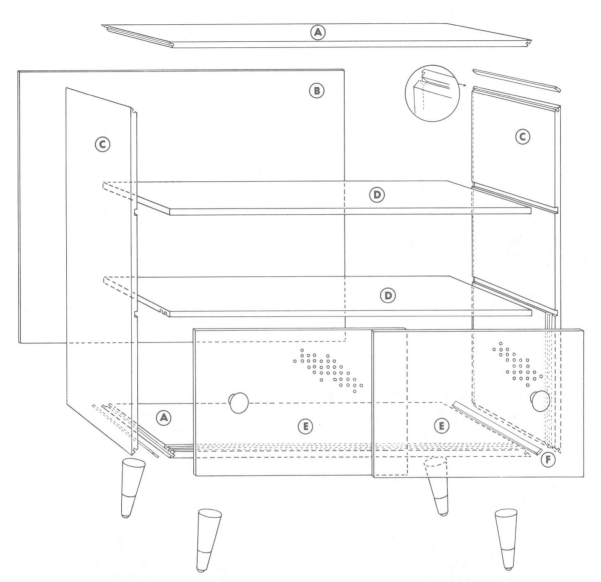

17-5b. This combination storage cabinet and bookcase has corners joined with spline miters. The parts include: (A) top and bottom, (B) back, (C) sides, (D) shelves, (E) perforated hardwood door, and (F) commercial legs.

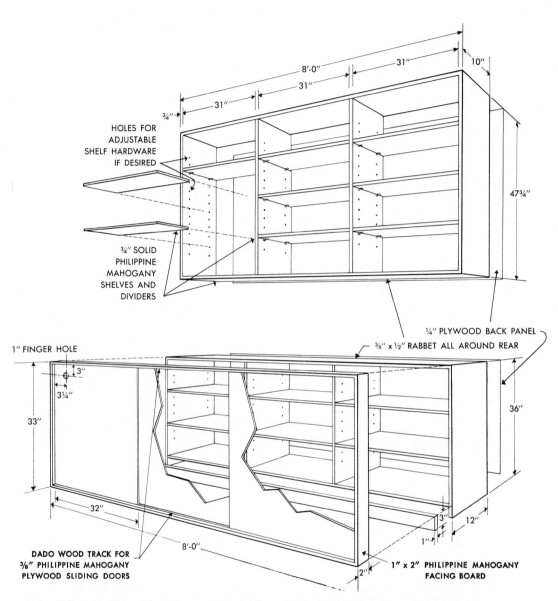

HOLES FOR
ADJUSTABLE
SHELF HARDWARE
IF DESIRED

¾" SOLID
PHILIPPINE
MAHOGANY
SHELVES AND
DIVIDERS

8'-0"

31"

31"

31"

10"

¾"

47¾"

¼" PLYWOOD BACK PANEL

⅜" x ½" RABBET ALL AROUND REAR

1" FINGER HOLE

3"

3¼"

33"

36"

32"

8'-0"

DADO WOOD TRACK FOR
⅜" PHILIPPINE MAHOGANY
PLYWOOD SLIDING DOORS

1" x 2" PHILIPPINE MAHOGANY
FACING BOARD

3"

12"

1"

2"

17-5c. This cabinet can be used as a room divider or bookcase. All dimensions are figured for butt joints.

LUMBER LIST
Bookcase & Room Divider

Upper Case:

Pieces or Quantity	Description	Wood	Thick	Wide	Long
2	Ends	Philippine Mahogany	¾″	10″	3′11¾″
2	Top & Bottom	Philippine Mahogany	¾″	10″	7′10½″
2	Dividers	Philippine Mahogany	¾″	9½″	3′10¼″
9	Adjustable Shelves	Philippine Mahogany	¾″	9⅜″	2′6⅞″
3	Back	Philippine Mahogany	¼″	31¾″	3′11″

Lower Cabinet:

Pieces or Quantity	Description	Wood	Thick	Wide	Long
2	Ends	Philippine Mahogany	¾″	12″	3′
2	Top & Bottom	Philippine Mahogany	¾″	12″	7′10½″
2	Dividers	Philippine Mahogany	¾″	11½″	2′7½″
6	Adjustable Shelves	Philippine Mahogany	¾″	11⅜″	2′6⅞″
3	Backs	Philippine Mahogany	¼″	31¾″	2′8¼″
1	Kickboard	Philippine Mahogany	¾″	3″	7′10½″
2	Front Verticals	Philippine Mahogany	¾″	2″	2′9″
2	Rails	Philippine Mahogany	¾″	2″	7′10½″
3	Sliding Doors	Philippine Mahogany	⅜″	32″	2′8″

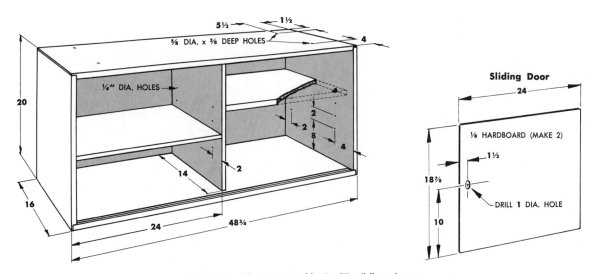

17-5d. A wall storage cabinet with sliding doors.

165

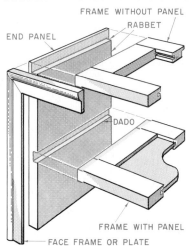

17-6a. Note how the sides and frames of this cabinet are joined with a dado joint. A dado is cut in the sides into which the frame fits.

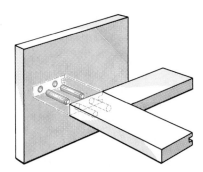

17-6b. Here the dowel joint is used.

If the case is to include drawers, then dividers or frames are installed between the sides. These are made of plywood and are either dadoed into the side or installed with a dowel. Fig. 17-6. Frames can be either open or enclosed with a panel of hardboard or plywood. Fig. 17-7. The dust frame serves as a base for drawer guides.

The backs of casegoods are usually made of thin plywood or hardboard. Fig. 17-8a. A rabbet

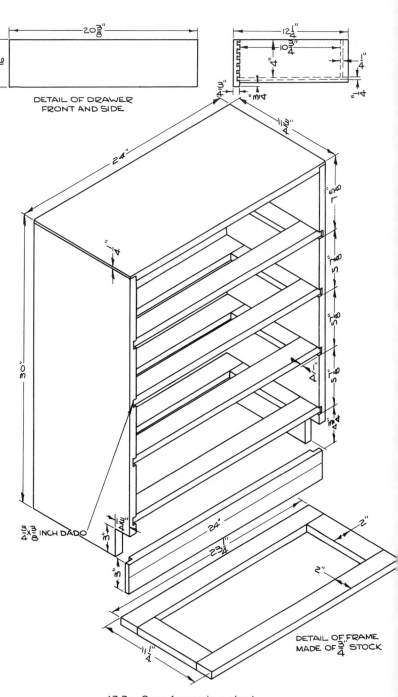

DETAIL OF DRAWER FRONT AND SIDE

17-7a. Open frames in a chest.

DETAIL OF FRAME MADE OF 3/4" STOCK

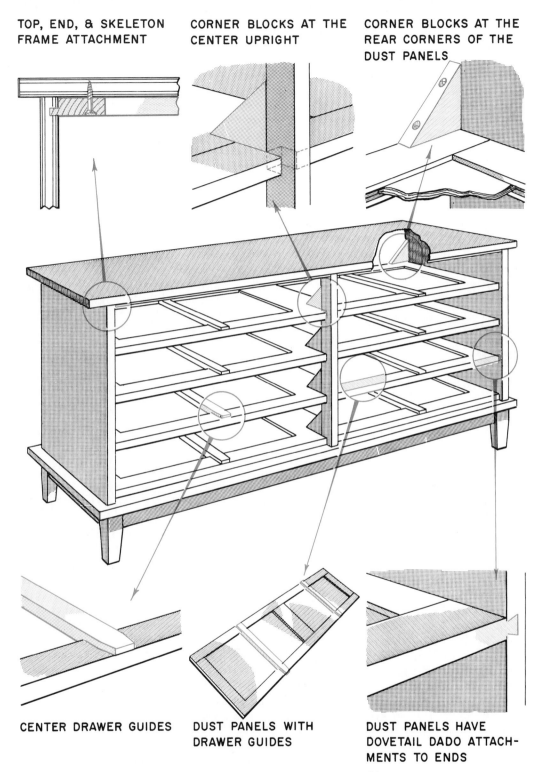

TOP, END, & SKELETON
FRAME ATTACHMENT

CORNER BLOCKS AT THE
CENTER UPRIGHT

CORNER BLOCKS AT THE
REAR CORNERS OF THE
DUST PANELS

CENTER DRAWER GUIDES

DUST PANELS WITH
DRAWER GUIDES

DUST PANELS HAVE
DOVETAIL DADO ATTACH-
MENTS TO ENDS

17-7b. Dust frame and panel with drawer guides.

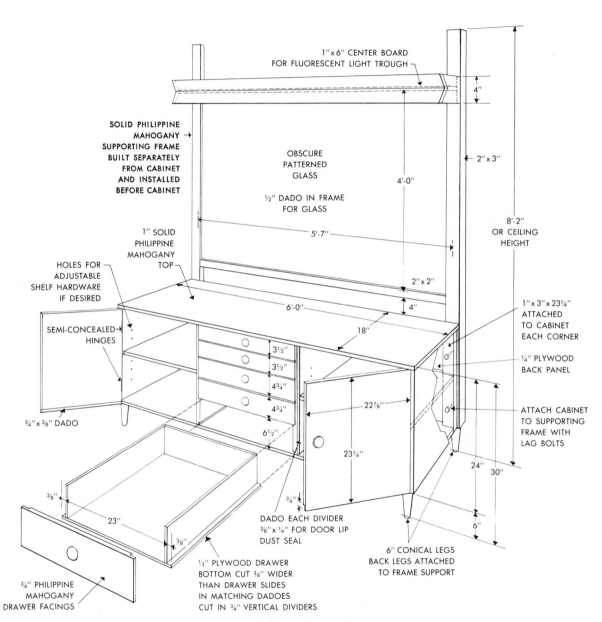

1"x 6" CENTER BOARD
FOR FLUORESCENT LIGHT TROUGH

4"

SOLID PHILIPPINE
MAHOGANY →
SUPPORTING FRAME
BUILT SEPARATELY
FROM CABINET
AND INSTALLED
BEFORE CABINET

OBSCURE
PATTERNED
GLASS

½" DADO IN FRAME
FOR GLASS

4'-0"

2" x 3"

8'-2"
OR CEILING
HEIGHT

1" SOLID
PHILIPPINE
MAHOGANY
TOP

5'-7"

HOLES FOR
ADJUSTABLE
SHELF HARDWARE
IF DESIRED

2" x 2"

4"

1" x 3" x 23¼"
ATTACHED
TO CABINET
EACH CORNER

SEMI-CONCEALED →
HINGES

6'-0"

18"

¼" PLYWOOD
BACK PANEL

3½"

3½"

4¾"

4¾"

ATTACH CABINET
TO SUPPORTING
FRAME WITH
LAG BOLTS

¾" x ⅜" DADO

22⅞"

6½"

23¼"

24"

30"

23"

⅜"

⅜"

DADO EACH DIVIDER
⅜" x ¼" FOR DOOR LIP
DUST SEAL

¾"

6"

6" CONICAL LEGS
BACK LEGS ATTACHED
TO FRAME SUPPORT

¾" PHILIPPINE
MAHOGANY
DRAWER FACINGS

½" PLYWOOD DRAWER
BOTTOM CUT ⅜" WIDER
THAN DRAWER SLIDES
IN MATCHING DADOES
CUT IN ¾" VERTICAL DIVIDERS

17-7c. Drawers are installed in this dresser without dust frames. Note how the bottom of the dresser acts as a drawer guide.

LUMBER LIST
Dresser or Buffet

Pieces or Quantity	Description	Wood	Thick	Wide	Long
2	Vertical Frame	Philippine Mahogany	1⅝″	3″	8′2″
1	Top Rail	Philippine Mahogany	1⅝″	4″	5′6″
1	Bottom Rail	Philippine Mahogany	1⅝″	2″	5′6″
2	Light Box Ends	Philippine Mahogany	¾″	4″	8″
2	Facia	Philippine Mahogany	¾″	2½″	6′
1	Light Board	Philippine Mahogany	¾″	5½″	5′10½″
2	Ends	Philippine Mahogany	¾″	18″	1′11¼″
1	Bottom	Philippine Mahogany	¾″	17⅜″	5′10½″
2	Dividers	Philippine Mahogany	¾″	17⅜″	1′10½″
2	Adjustable Shelves	Philippine Mahogany	¾″	16⅞″	1′10½″
2	Doors	Philippine Mahogany	¾″	23¼″	1′10⅞″
1	Top	Philippine Mahogany	1″	18″	6′
1	Back	Philippine Mahogany	¼″	24½″	1′11¼″
2	Backs	Philippine Mahogany	¼″	23″	1′11¼″
2	Cabinet Supports	Philippine Mahogany	¾″	3″	1′11¼″
4	Conical Legs	Philippine Mahogany	2½″	2½″	6″
2	Drawer Fronts	Philippine Mahogany	¾″	3½″	2′ ½″
2	Drawer Fronts	Philippine Mahogany	¾″	4¾″	2′ ½″
1	Drawer Front	Philippine Mahogany	¾″	6½″	2′ ½″
4	Drawer Sides	Philippine Mahogany	½″	3″	1′5″
4	Drawer Sides	Philippine Mahogany	½″	4¼″	1′5″
2	Drawer Sides	Philippine Mahogany	½″	5¼″	1′5″
2	Drawer Backs	Philippine Mahogany	½″	3″	1′10″
2	Drawer Backs	Philippine Mahogany	½″	4¼″	1′10″
1	Drawer Back	Philippine Mahogany	½″	5¼″	1′10″
5	Drawer Bottoms	Philippine Mahogany	½″	17″	2′ ½″

17-8a. Note how a rabbet is cut around the back of the piece. Then the back can fit into this recess.

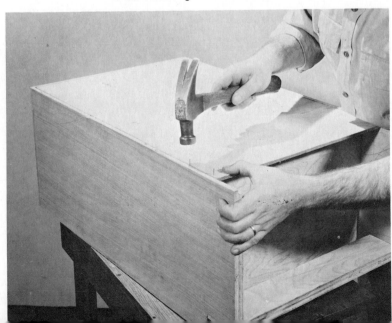

17-8b. Attaching the back to a case.

17-9. If the back is exposed, then the same kind of veneer or wood should be used for the back as for the rest of the furniture piece.

17-10a. Note that the legs have been added to this casework piece.

is cut around the back of the case frame and the back panel is nailed or stapled into the groove. If the case is an open piece such as a bookcase or china cabinet, a good quality hardwood plywood is needed since the back must be finished the same as the rest of the unit. Fig. 17-9. For other case-goods, however, a less expensive material such as hardboard is an excellent choice. Legs may be built in or added onto the case. Fig. 17-10. Sometimes the lower part is made of leg-and-rail construction and acts as a stand for the case. Fig. 17-11. Some case-goods pieces have a separate base (plinth) that may or may not be recessed to act as a kick rail. Fig. 17-12. It is also possible to add some kind of commercial legs and/or casters to the case. Fig. 17-13.

17-10b. The legs of this hall bench are an integral part of the design.

17-11. A base of leg-and-rail construction is used under this chest.

17-12b. The base under this chest is recessed.

17-12a. Note the separate base on this tall clock.

17-13a. A cedar chest with casters for moving it about.

17-13b. Metal legs that are commercially available are installed on this desk.

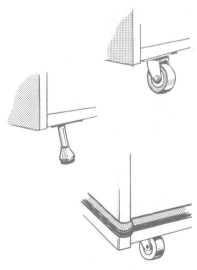

17-13c. Casters and commercial legs can be used.

17-14a. This relatively simple casework item is made of softwood plywood.

17-14b. A combination bed-and-chest made of hardwood plywood.

17-14c. This fine library unit is made from a variety of materials, and the construction includes frame and panel work.

Casegoods are constructed in so many different ways and of so many different quality materials that it is difficult to describe exactly how to put any individual piece together. Each manufacturer follows a different type of construction, depending on the style and quality of his casework. All manufacturers follow drawings and specifications in building casework, since it is very important that all of the parts fit together. This is particularly true if the case includes doors and drawers. Fig. 17-14.

Frame-and-Panel Construction

Frames are used for interior casework construction as part of the exterior sides and tops; sometimes they are also used for covered doors. Exterior frame-and-panel construction for the sides, doors, and drawers of casework is quite difficult; therefore it is not covered in this text except for the very simplest frame-and-panel door.

The two basic types of interior frames are *skeleton* and *dust* frames.

Skeleton Frame

Skeleton frame—sometimes called a rib, open, false, or web frame—consists of two longer members called stiles and two shorter ones called rails. It is open in the center. The simplest open type frame is often joined in the corners with dowels. Fig. 17-15. Other joints that can be used include the stub mortise-and-tenon, the haunched mortise-and-tenon, and the dowel joint. Fig. 17-16. Frames are installed in the inte-

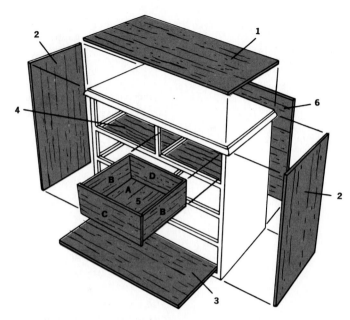

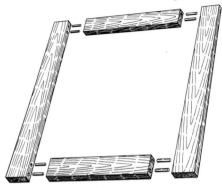

17-15. The simplest type of open or web frame can be joined with dowels at each corner.

17-14d. A typical furniture cabinet might contain these items of hardwood plywood: (1) cabinet tops; (2) side panels; (3) bottom panels; (4) dust partitions; (5) drawer parts—(A) bottoms, (B) laminated sides, (C) fronts, (D) backs; (6) casebacks. Companies that manufacture such cabinets use various construction methods.

rior of casework to add stability to the unit, to provide horizontal support for the drawers, and as a means of fastening the tops to some kinds of cases. Fig. 17-17, page 174.

Dust Frame

Better quality casework makes use of a dust or panel frame. This is a web frame with a center of plywood or hardboard. Frame-and-panel construction, when used for exterior surfaces, adds a decorative note to the case. This construction method is used most often for Early American, French Provincial, Italian Provincial, and English furniture. This type of construction requires careful fitting and accurate workmanship.

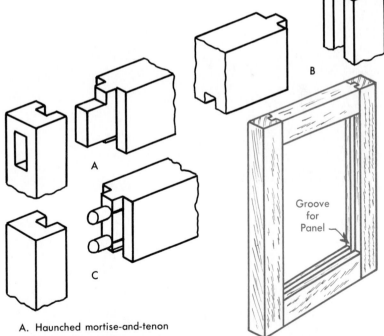

A. Haunched mortise-and-tenon
B. Stub mortise-and-tenon
C. Stub mortise-and-tenon with dowel

17-16. Common methods of joining the corners of frames.

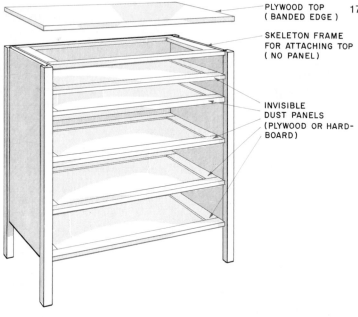

PLYWOOD TOP
(BANDED EDGE)

SKELETON FRAME
FOR ATTACHING TOP
(NO PANEL)

INVISIBLE
DUST PANELS
(PLYWOOD OR HARD-
BOARD)

17-17. Note the interior construction of this case. The frames serve as base for drawer guides.

Since it is rather complicated, it is not usually done in beginning furniture making.

Good examples of frame-and-panel construction are shown in Fig. 17-18.

Steps in Building a Frame and Panel

The advantage of panel construction is that the complete unit does not warp as badly as a solid piece of similar size. Fig. 17-19. *Stiles* run the full length of the frame, and the *rails* run between the stiles. There may be two or more rails, depending on how many panels are to be installed in a single unit. The rails are joined to stiles with either dowels, a stub mortise-and-tenon joint (sometimes called tongue-and-groove), or a haunched mortise-and-tenon joint.

1. Determine the size of the frame. The stiles are cut to the exact length and the rails are cut to provide sufficient material for the tenon as needed.

2. Square up the stock.

3. Select the panel that is to be installed in the frame and decide on the method of installation. Usually a $\frac{1}{4}''$ or $\frac{3}{8}''$ panel is used. Remember that the panel must be

17-18a. The chests at the bottom of this page and the top of the next page are the same size. However, the styling has been changed by different kinds of door and drawer fronts. All of the fronts are of frame-and-panel construction.

17-18b. The sides, doors, and drawers of this buffet cabinet are of frame-and-panel construction.

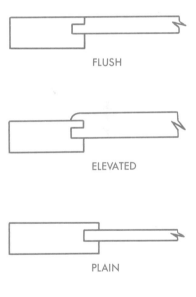

FLUSH

ELEVATED

PLAIN

RAISED

17-19. Common types of panels.

cut large enough to cover the opening and to fit into the groove.

4. Lay out and cut a groove on all edges in which the panel is to be fit. The groove is cut as deep as or slightly deeper than it is wide. This can be done on a circular saw or shaper.

5. Make the joint for joining the rails to the stiles. In making a stub mortise-and-tenon, the thickness of the tenon is the same as the width of the groove, and the length of the tenon is the same as the depth of the groove. In making a haunched mortise-and-tenon joint, the thickness of the mortise should be the same as the width of the groove. The mortise should be started far enough away from the ends of the stiles to prevent breaking out. The width and depth of the mortise should be about two-thirds the width of the rail. The length of the tenon should be equal to the depth of the mortise plus the depth of the groove. Cut a notch in the tenon so that the long part of the tenon will fit into the mortise opening and the short part will fit into the groove.

6. Make a trial assembly of the panel in the frame. Then take it apart and wax the edge of the panel. In gluing up the panel, apply the glue to the joint itself but *never to the edge of the panel or to the groove.*

7. In some panel construction, a rabbet is cut around the inside edge of the frame so that this side of the door is flush. In such a case, the panel must be glued or fastened in place. Sometimes glass or expanded metal is fitted into the opening.

Making Chests.

Chest construction is a type of carcass work which includes making a case, drawers, and drawer guides and runners. Fig. 17-20. In making a chest, proceed as follows:

1. Determine the width, height and depth of the chest. Then decide on kind of construction and the joints to be used. Cut the sides, top, and bottom. Sometimes a bottom piece is unnecessary.

2. Determine the kind of joints that will be used to join the sides to the top and bottom. The most common ones are the rabbet, miter, or dado, or an adaptation of one of these.

3. Make the joints to assemble the chest. Cut a rabbet around the inside back edge of the sides, top, and bottom to install a panel.

4. Determine the location of the drawers and cut dadoes, either plain or stop, in the sides to receive the frames.

5. Make the frames that separate the drawers. Fig. 17-21. The frames themselves are made with a dowel butt joint, a miter butt joint, or a mortise-and-tenon joint. On superior drawer construction, these frames are made as in panel construction to prevent the accumulation of dust in the drawers. If the front of the frame is to be exposed, it should be made of the same wood as the exterior of the chest. If not, the frames can be made of some good, clear softwood. Assemble the frames. Fasten the exterior to the frames.

6. Make the drawers. Cut the stock for the drawer fronts to cover the openings. Build the drawer as desired. Make the drawer guides and runners. Install

17-20. This modern chest is a good example of simplicity in design and construction. Its beauty lies in this very simplicity.

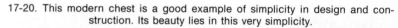

17-21. The interior construction of a chest.

17-22a. This shows how a glue block would be positioned to reinforce the interior of a cabinet.

17-22b. Corner blocks are similar to glue blocks except that they are larger in size.

these guides and runners to fit the drawers.

7. Install the back panel.

Using Glue Blocks

Glue blocks are small, triangular pieces of wood that are installed along the edges of two adjoining pieces to strengthen them. Fig. 17-22a. For example, when a frame is to fit around the front of a case or cabinet, glue blocks are usually installed along the inside corners between the frame and case. Cut these three-cornered blocks in the same manner as corner blocks. Apply glue to the two edges and clamp in place with hand screws, or install nails or brads. Sometimes corner blocks are also used to give rigidity to the case. Fig. 17-22b.

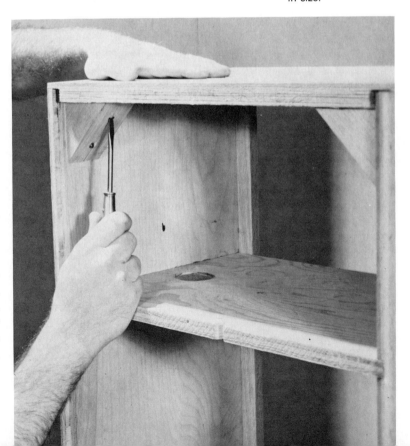

Fixed shelves are usually installed with some type of dado joint. Fig. 17-23.

Installing Shelves

Modern furniture is flexible and therefore most shelves are made to be adjustable. There are several methods of doing this: Fig. 17-24.
• Lay out a vertical line about 1″ to 2″ from both edges of the sides of the bookcase or shelf. Determine the spacing between the shelves and mark the location for a series of holes. Select suitable dowel rod and cut pins about 1″ long. Drill or bore holes of this same size along the inside of the sides. Always place a stop on the drill or bit to avoid cutting a hole through the sides.

17-23a. The simple dado joint can be used for fixed shelves.

17-23b. The combination rabbet and dado joint can also be used for shelves, particularly the bottom shelf.

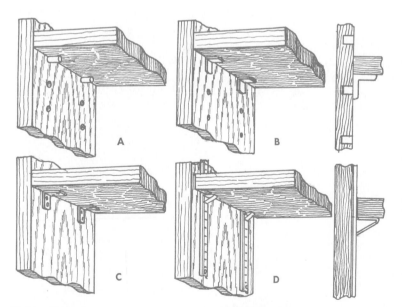

17-24a. Methods of installing shelves: (A) dowel pins, (B) metal shelf pins, (C) metal corner braces, and (D) shelf standard and support clip.

17-24b. Installing metal pins in holes for shelves.

17-25a. Plastic shelf pins.

17-25b. Plastic shelf pins are particularly good when the shelves are glass.

- Follow the same method of drilling holes and install commercial adjustable shelf pins of metal or plastic. Fig. 17-25.
- Permanently fasten the shelves with shelf brackets.
- Use adjustable shelf brackets with snap-on clips. These can be obtained in any length. Two pieces are needed for either side. Install with screw-type nails. Cut shelves to length and then cut out small slots at the locations for the bracket strips. Ends of the shelves can be straight. For neater appearance, cut vertical grooves into which the brackets fit. Then the shelves do not have to be notched.

Adding Facing and Molding (Face Frames)

When a case is made of plywood, the edge must be treated. A common way is to add a face frame or piece of solid stock. The corners can be joined with some kind of butt or miter joint. After the frame is built, it is attached by gluing and/or nailing and stapling it in place. Fig. 17-26. To enrich a simple case, a molding can be added. Fig. 17-27. Moldings come in a wide variety of shapes. The common method of attaching molding to a case is with staples, glue, nails, and/or screws. Fig. 17-28. See pages 180, 181.

17-26a. Sectional furniture.

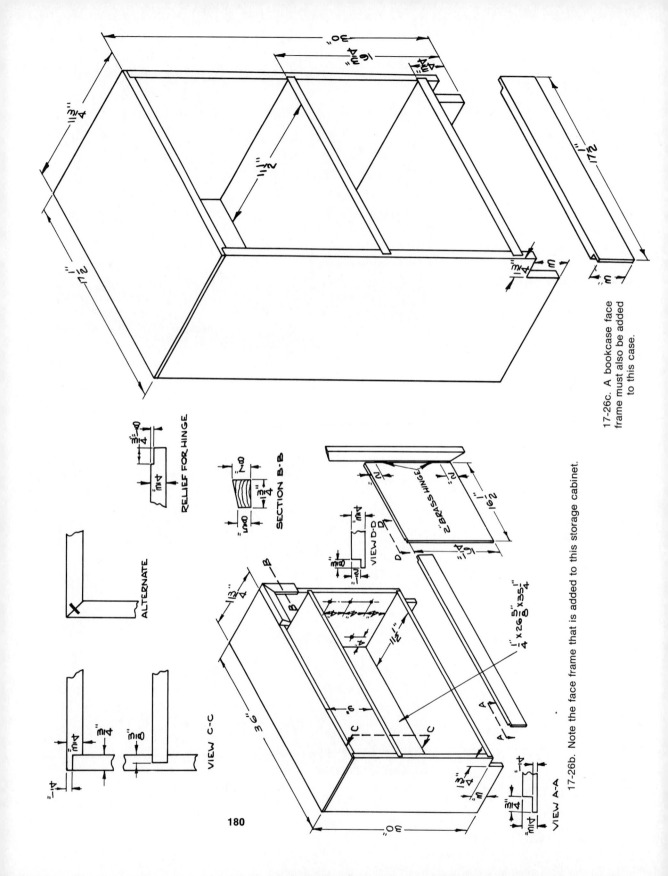

RELIEF FOR HINGE

SECTION B-B

ALTERNATE

VIEW C-C

VIEW D-D

2" BRASS HINGE

VIEW A-A

1" x 26⅝ x 35¾"

17-26b. Note the face frame that is added to this storage cabinet.

17-26c. A bookcase face frame must also be added to this case.

180

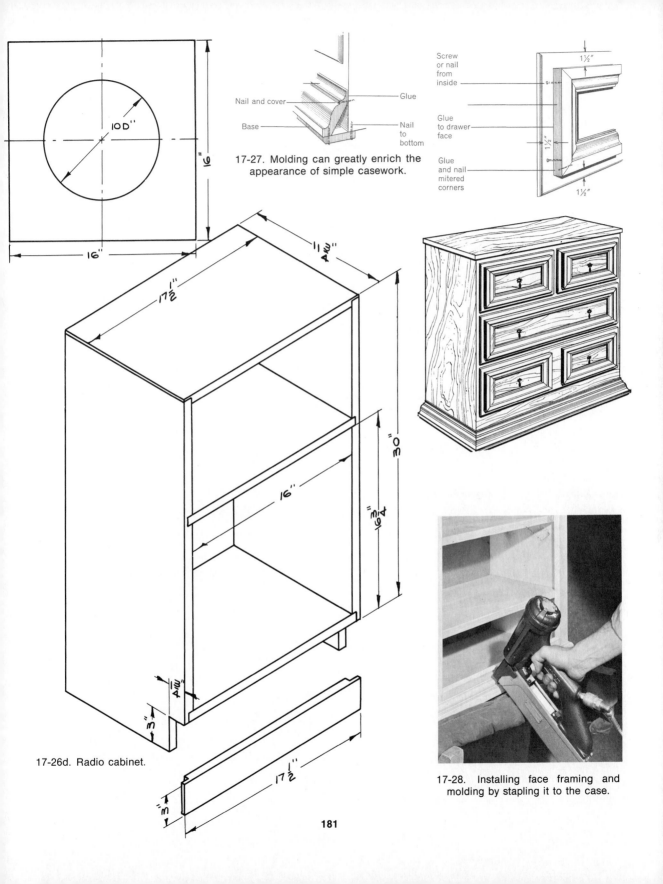

10 D"

16"

16"

Nail and cover
Base

Glue

Nail
to
bottom

17-27. Molding can greatly enrich the appearance of simple casework.

Screw
or nail
from
inside

1½"

Glue
to drawer
face

Glue
and nail
mitered
corners

1½"

1½"

17½"

11½"

30"

16"

6¾"

3¾"

3"

17½"

3"

17-26d. Radio cabinet.

17-28. Installing face framing and molding by stapling it to the case.

Drawers are a necessity in many casegoods items. Fig. 18-1. They must slide in and out of the cases freely and easily. A drawer actually is a box without a top. Drawers vary from the very simple type shown in Fig. 18-2 to a fine furniture drawer which is always assembled with dovetail joints. Fig. 18-3.

Types of Drawer Fronts

There are three basic types of drawer fronts. The *flush* drawer fits exactly into the opening of the case. The drawer edges do not

18-1a. A lip drawer in an Early American coffee table.

18-1b. Lip drawer in a china cabinet.

18-1c. Flush drawers beautifully fitted into a Colonial writing desk.

extend beyond the case front. This type must be carefully fitted so there will be sufficient clearance for smooth operation, but no unsightly space between the drawer front and case. Fig. 18-4.

The *lip* drawer has a rabbet, usually $\frac{3}{8}$" deep, cut around the inside edge of the drawer front to cover part of the frame. Fig. 18-5a. The front edge of the lip drawer is usually rounded and treated with a fancy edge. Fig. 18-5b. This drawer can be fitted a little looser since the crack between drawer and case will be covered by the lip.

The *overlap* or *overlay* drawer is designed so that the front covers the sides of the case. Sometimes the frame just below or above the drawer front is also covered. This

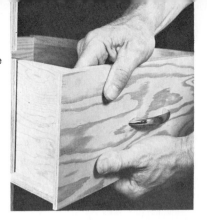

18-2a. A very inexpensive and simple drawer made of plywood.

type of drawer is sometimes found in Contemporary furniture. Fig. 18-6, page 185.

Parts of a Drawer

A basic drawer consists of five parts: front, back, two sides, and bottom. Fig. 18-7. Drawer fronts are usually $\frac{3}{4}$" thick and made of solid wood or plywood. The drawer sides should be at least $\frac{1}{2}$" thick, although material as thick as $\frac{3}{4}$" may be used if a side guide and runner are installed. Usually a relief cut is made in the top edge of each side. (A relief cut on drawer sides is a depression along most of the top edge to make the drawer operate more smoothly.)

18-2b. Inexpensive lip drawers in a plywood case.

18-3a. This chest has drawers of high quality.

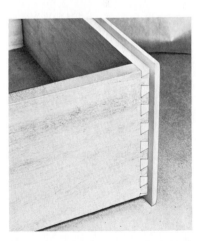

18-3b. Drawer front and side joined with dovetail joint.

18-4a. The drawers in this fine furniture are of the flush type.

18-4b. One can imagine the careful fitting required for these flush drawers.

18-5a. A small night table of maple and birch. The drawer has a machined edge to make it more attractive.

18-5b. Excellent examples of lip drawers are found in the dresser and the chest-on-chest shown in this illustration.

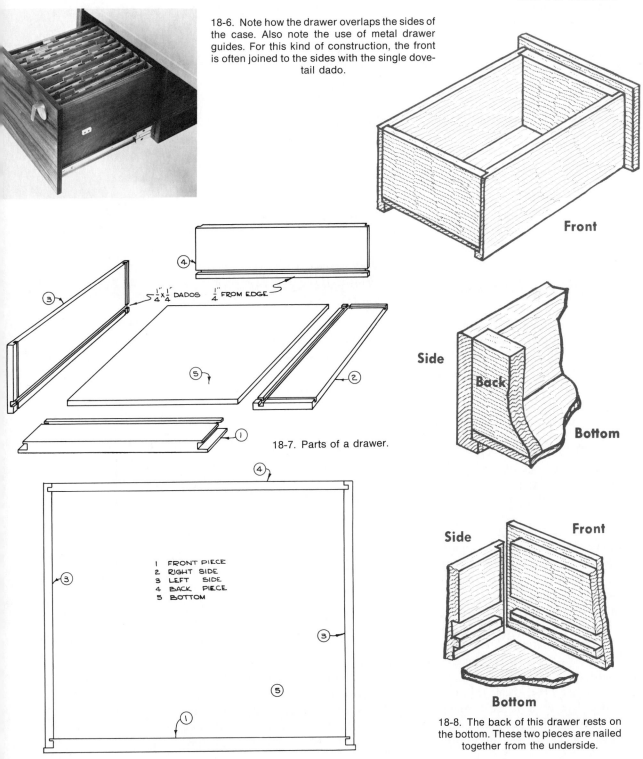

18-6. Note how the drawer overlaps the sides of the case. Also note the use of metal drawer guides. For this kind of construction, the front is often joined to the sides with the single dovetail dado.

Front

$\frac{1}{4}$" x $\frac{1}{4}$" DADOS $\frac{1}{4}$" FROM EDGE

Side   **Back**   **Bottom**

18-7. Parts of a drawer.

1 FRONT PIECE
2 RIGHT SIDE
3 LEFT SIDE
4 BACK PIECE
5 BOTTOM

Side   **Front**

Bottom

18-8. The back of this drawer rests on the bottom. These two pieces are nailed together from the underside.

185

These edges are then rounded to reduce friction. The back of the drawer is made in one of two ways. Sometimes the bottom of the drawer is nailed to the back as shown in Fig. 18-8. For better quality drawers the bottom is fitted into a groove in the back as well as the sides and front. This type is called a "boxed-in" drawer and is generally found in commercial furniture. Fig. 18-9.

The drawer bottom is usually made of $\frac{1}{4}$" plywood or hardboard. Hardboard is excellent since it will not shrink or swell in any direction.

Making Drawers and Drawer Guides

1. Determine the size of the drawer. Measure the opening (both height and width) into which the drawer will fit. There should be a clearance of about $\frac{1}{16}$" on either side and $\frac{1}{16}$" for height. Also measure the depth of the drawer. Fig. 18-10.

2. Choose the wood for the drawer. The front should match the rest of the project and should be as thick or slightly thicker than the other parts. Usually the front is $\frac{3}{4}$" thick. The sides and back should be about $\frac{1}{2}$" thick in a clear lumber such as birch, sycamore, oak, or maple. Sycamore is used quite often in industry because it is inexpensive, has nice texture, and is easily machined. The drawer bottom is most often made of $\frac{1}{4}$" plywood or hardboard.

3. Select the front drawer joints. The three most common joints for joining the front to the sides are the rabbet, the drawer corner joint (rabbet and groove), and the dovetail.

a. The *rabbet* is made by cutting a recess on the inside of each end of the front. The width of the rabbet should equal two-thirds the thickness of the front. The depth should be slightly more than the thickness of the sides to allow for clearance. Fig. 18-11.

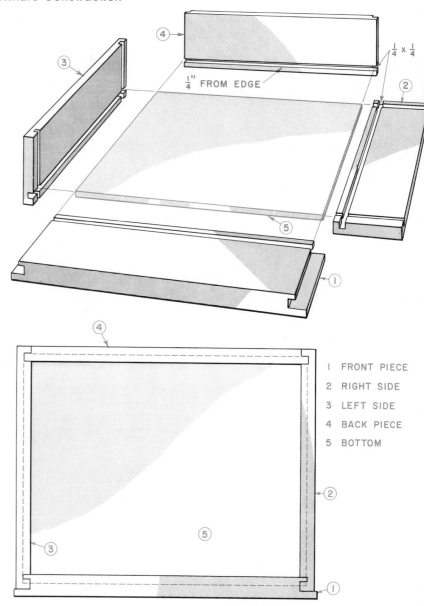

1 FRONT PIECE
2 RIGHT SIDE
3 LEFT SIDE
4 BACK PIECE
5 BOTTOM

PARTS OF A DRAWER

18-9. Boxed-in drawer construction. This is used in many better quality drawers.

186

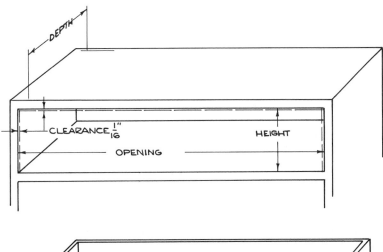

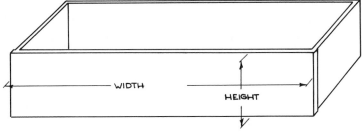

18-10. Measuring the size of the drawer front.

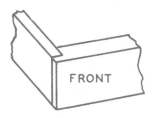

18-11. A simple rabbet joint is a good choice for elementary drawer construction.

b. The drawer corner (dado-rabbet) joint is often used to fasten the sides to the front because it is a strong joint that is easy to make on the circular saw. Fig. 18-12 shows this joint made with a ¾″ drawer front and ½″ sides.

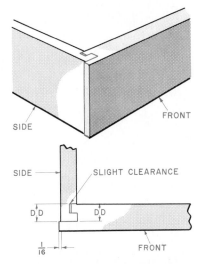

18-12. A drawer corner joint (dado and rabbet). Study this carefully before beginning to build the drawer.

A clearance of ¹⁄₁₆″ is allowed for the front to extend beyond the sides. The steps in making this joint are as follows:

Step 1. Use a dado head that is ¼″ wide (see pages 291–293). Adjust the dado head to a height of slightly more than ¼″. Set the ripping fence to a distance of twice the width of the dado head measured from the left edge of the blade (double dado), or ½″. Cut dadoes on the inside face of the sides at the front end.

Step 2. Set the height of the dado head to an amount equal to the thickness of the sides plus ¹⁄₁₆″ (for front overlap), or ⁹⁄₁₆″. With the inside face of the front held against the fence, cut a dado across each end of the front.

Step 3. Set the dado head to a height of slightly more than ½″. Adjust the fence to a distance of ⁹⁄₁₆″ from the left edge of the dado head. Use a piece of ¼″ plywood for a stop block. Place the inside face against the table and trim off ⁵⁄₁₆″ from the inside tenon of the drawer front. The joint should slide together easily. Sometimes the joint is made with a narrow dado and thin tenon, as shown in Fig. 18-7.

c. Make a *dovetail joint* by using the portable router as described on pages 353, 354.

d. The *dovetail dado joint* is used for the overlap or overlay drawer. This joint is made with the portable router. The procedure is described in Unit 34.

4. Decide on the back drawer joints. The back can be joined to the sides with a *butt* joint, a *dado* joint or a *rabbet-and-dado* joint. If the dado joint is used, it should

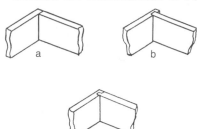

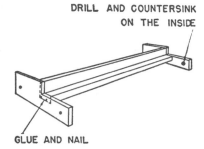

DRILL AND COUNTERSINK
ON THE INSIDE

GLUE AND NAIL

18-13. Common drawer construction joints for joining the sides to the back. (a) Butt, (b) Dado, (c) Dado and rabbet.

18-14. A simple guide and runner.

be located at least ½″ from the back edge of the drawer sides. Fig. 18-13.

5. Cut the pieces for the drawer. If the drawer is to fit flush, the front is cut $\frac{1}{16}$″ narrower and $\frac{1}{8}$″ shorter than the opening measurements. If a lip drawer is being constructed, add ½″ to this width and length. On a lip drawer front a $\frac{3}{8}$″ rabbet is cut all the way around so there is ¼″ clearance built into the front. The length of the sides is found by measuring the overall depth of the drawer and then allowing for the kind of joint used in the front. The back is cut at least $\frac{1}{16}$″ narrower than the sides. Sometimes the back is cut ½″ narrower so that the back rests on the top of the drawer bottom.

6. Make the joints to join the sides to the front and back. Cut a groove ¼″ deep, at least ¼″ from the lower edge of the drawer.

7. Assemble the drawer by fastening the sides to the front with glue and/or nails. Slip the bottom in place but *never* apply glue to the edges. Fasten the back to the sides.

Make the *drawer guides* as follows:

1. There are several kinds of drawer guides. The simplest is the guide and runner which are placed under the lower corners of the drawer. Such a guide and runner arrangement is constructed by cutting two pieces of stock long enough to go between the front and back rails. A rabbet which forms the guide and runner for

the drawer is then cut out. The guide and runner are fastened in place by gluing and/or screws. For this type of drawer guide, a *kicker* is usually placed over the sides of the drawers so that it won't tip too far when it is pulled out. (A kicker is a straight piece of wood fastened in the case over the drawer. There may be just one kicker, over the center of the drawer, or a pair may be used, one on each side.) Fig. 18-14.

2. The side guide and runner are made by cutting a groove along the outside of each side of the drawer. Figs. 18-15a, b, c. This can be located any place on the side, usually toward or slightly above center. Two pieces of stock are then cut long enough to extend between the front and back rails. These pieces fit into the

18-15a. This high quality chest has side guides and runners. Note the groove cut in the side of the drawer.

DRAWER RUNNER

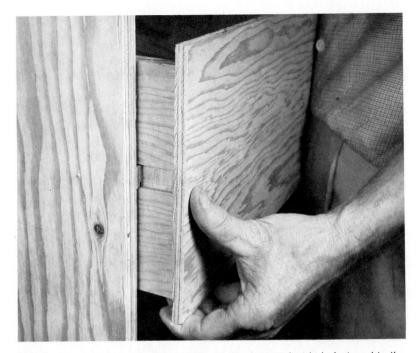

18-15b. Here a groove is cut in the side of the drawer. A strip is fastened to the inside of the chest or cabinet.

DRAWER SIDE

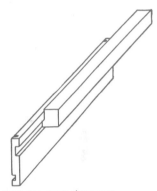

DRAWER SIDE & RUNNER

18-15d. The construction of a side guide and runner for a desk or table on which the drawer runner must be fastened to the underside of the table.

18-15c. This procedure is the reverse of Fig. 18-15b. Here the cabinet or chest side has a dado cut across it. A matching strip is fastened to the side of the drawer. This should be waxed or lubricated with paraffin so that the drawer will slide easily.

grooves on the drawer sides. Then these pieces are fastened between the front and back rails on which the drawer slides. Another method of making a runner for a desk drawer is to cut a rabbet in a larger piece of wood, as shown in Fig. 18-15d.

189

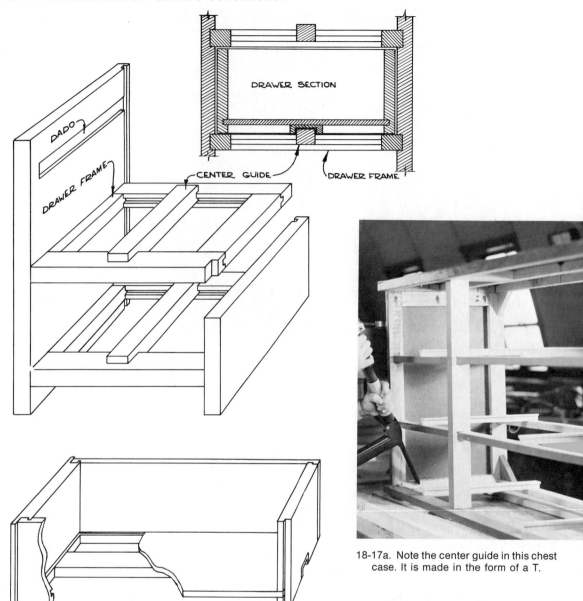

DRAWER SECTION

DADO

DRAWER FRAME

CENTER GUIDE

DRAWER FRAME

18-17a. Note the center guide in this chest case. It is made in the form of a T.

18-16. Center guide and runner.

3. The best drawer guide is the center drawer guide and runner. In this arrangement the guide is fastened to the frame of the chest or desk, or between the front and back rails; the runner or slide is fastened to the center of the drawer bottom. Fig. 18-16. The drawer guide is simply a rectangular piece of stock, usually rounded in the front. A second rectangular piece of stock, which has a groove cut along its length, slides over this guide. When installing the guides to a frame, as in chest construction, a rabbet is cut out on each end of the guide; or a dado can be cut on the back and a rabbet on the front. The guide is then glued and/or screwed in place. The slide or

SYSTEM ASSEMBLED

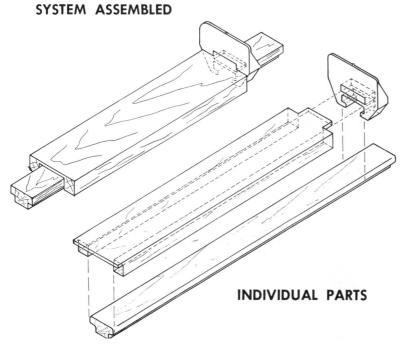

INDIVIDUAL PARTS

18-17b. Here you see the guide and runner. Note that the runner is a groove that gives plenty of clearance on the sides.

18-18. These nylon pins can be used in case construction for allowing the drawer to slide more easily.

18-17c. Plastic bearing for use with T-shaped guide.

runner is glued to the bottom of the drawer. Often a few brads are used to hold the slide snugly in place, thus providing clearance for the guide.

The wood guide is sometimes made in the shape of a T, and at the back a plastic bearing is added to reduce friction to a minimum. Fig. 18-17. Front bearings on the front rail under the drawer sides also help to eliminate friction. Fig. 18-18.

There are many kinds of metal drawer guides. Instructions are furnished by each manufacturer. Fig. 18-19. If commercial guides are used, purchase them before the drawers are constructed, since the amount of clearance necessary varies with the type of guide.

In all drawer construction, it is a good idea to place nylon tacks or tabs at the lower front corners of the case. These will make a drawer slide more easily.

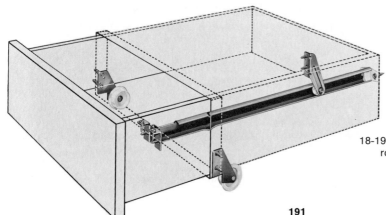

18-19a. Metal center guide with metal and plastic rollers that fit into the side of the case.

18-19b. Metal side guides.

Drawer Hardware

While some drawers are designed to be opened without handles or knobs, most have some kind of metal hardware. Fig. 18-20. When choosing this hardware, be sure that the size and design fit the furniture you are building. Fig. 18-21. A glance through this book will give you good ideas on what to choose. Drawer pulls and knobs should be fitted to the drawer before finishing, and then removed. Give careful attention to the location of this hardware. Drawers without center guides or commercial units should have two drawer knobs. Drawer pulls provide a better appearance if they are placed slightly above center.

18-20a. This chest has no metal hardware. The pulls are slight bevels cut on the undersides of the drawer fronts.

18-20b. Here wood strips are built into the drawers to act as drawer pulls.

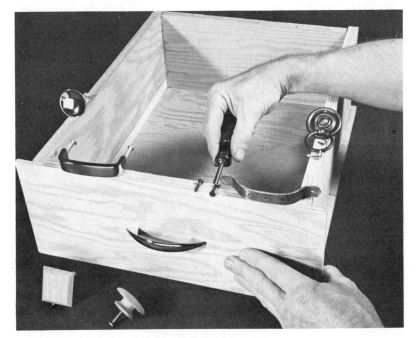

18-21a. Note the variety of pulls and knobs.

PULLS

WOOD SHAPED
FINGER TIP PULL

BRASS KNOB

INSERT PULL

PORCELAIN KNOB
WITH BRASS SLEEVES

18-21b. Be sure to choose the right kind of pulls or knobs. These are designed for Contemporary furniture.

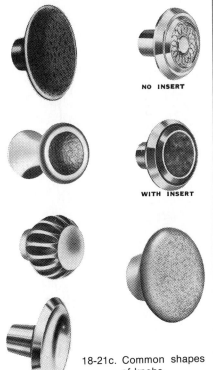

NO INSERT

WITH INSERT

18-21c. Common shapes of knobs.

18-21d. Pulls of different styles. Can you name the styles?

Drawer Dividers

The interior design of drawers is important for proper storage. Many types of drawer dividers can be purchased. These can be arranged for efficient storage of items for which the drawer is intended. Fig. 18-22.

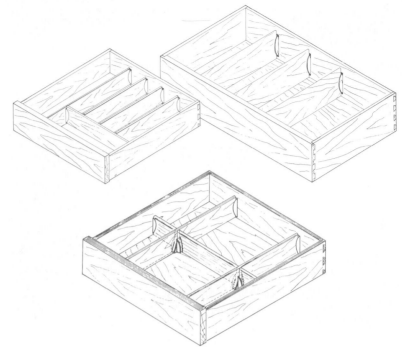

18-22a. Drawer dividers.

For peignoirs, nightgowns.

For shirts, pullovers, pajamas.

For blouses, pajamas.

For hats, handbags, shoes.

For socks, jewelry, belts, handkerchiefs, cosmetics.

For sweaters, scarves, blouses, pajamas.

For slips, girdles, nightgowns.

For gloves, handkerchiefs, lingerie.

18-22b. Note how dividers can increase storage efficiency.

UNIT 19 Doors

Small doors are needed on chests, cabinets, china closets, and many other storage cases. Fig. 19-1. These doors are sometimes called *cupboard doors* to distinguish them from larger doors such as those involved in home construction.

Industry uses a wide variety of methods for constructing these small doors. In cabinet shops the simplest method is to construct a flush door of hardwood plywood or softwood plywood covered with a veneer or plastic laminate. Fig. 19-2. Frequently the front of a plywood door is decorated with molding or some other kind of raised design.

More expensive and time-consuming construction is represented in the frame-and-panel door, typical of Early American and French and Italian Provincial furniture. Fig. 19-3. This door consists of a frame into which a panel is fitted. Fig. 19-4. Usually the panel is raised on one or both sides. Fig. 19-5. Since this type of door construction takes more time and special equipment, it is not included in this text.*

Fitting Swinging Doors

There are three common ways of fitting a swinging door to casework: flush, lip, and overlay. Fig. 19-6. This construction is similar to that for drawers, described in

*Complete details can be found in the book, CABINETMAKING AND MILLWORK, also by John L. Feirer.

19-1. Much of the beauty of this dining room furniture is in the lovely frame and panel doors. The upper doors have glass inserts instead of panels.

19-2. Doors made of plywood covered with plastic laminate.

19-3. The lower doors of this solid cherry buffet are of frame-and-panel construction.

19-4. An example of very simple frame-and-panel doors that could be made in a cabinet shop.

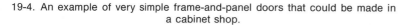

19-5. This corner cupboard makes use of frame and panel doors with the panel raised on one side.

Unit 18. The overlay door which covers two or more edges of the case is frequently found on Contemporary furniture.

Fitting a Flush Door

1. Check with a square to see that the frame of the opening is square. Sometimes the opening is slightly "out of square," in which case the door must be carefully cut to fit.

2. Measure the height at several points and cut off the top and bottom so that it will slip into the frame. It may be necessary to hold the door up to the opening several times and to plane off a little to get it to fit.

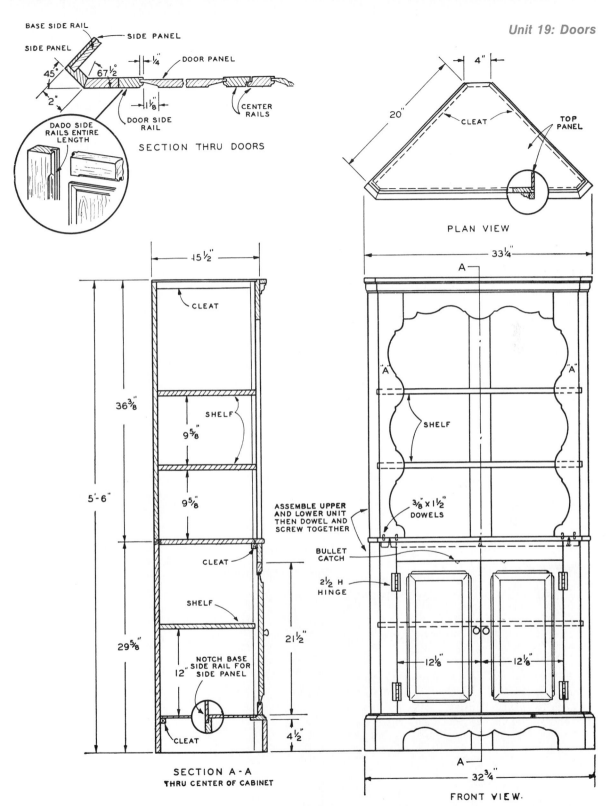

BASE SIDE RAIL

SIDE PANEL

SIDE PANEL

DOOR PANEL

45°

67 1/2°

1/4"

2"

1 1/8"

DOOR SIDE RAIL

CENTER RAILS

DADO SIDE RAILS ENTIRE LENGTH

SECTION THRU DOORS

4"

20"

CLEAT

TOP PANEL

PLAN VIEW

33 1/4"

15 1/2"

CLEAT

A

"A"

"A"

SHELF

SHELF

36 3/8"

9 5/8"

9 5/8"

5'- 6"

CLEAT

ASSEMBLE UPPER AND LOWER UNIT THEN DOWEL AND SCREW TOGETHER

3/8" x 1 1/2" DOWELS

SHELF

BULLET CATCH

2 1/2 H HINGE

29 5/8"

21 1/2"

NOTCH BASE SIDE RAIL FOR SIDE PANEL

12"

12 1/8"

12 1/8"

CLEAT

4 1/2"

SECTION A-A
THRU CENTER OF CABINET

A

32 3/4"

FRONT VIEW.

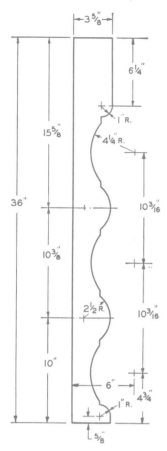

PILASTER "A" DETAIL

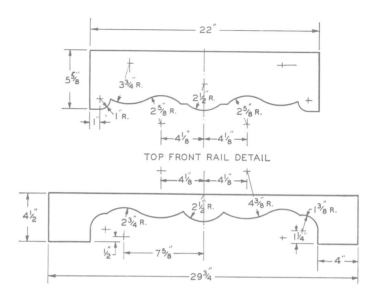

TOP FRONT RAIL DETAIL

BASE FRONT RAIL DETAIL

19-6a. A cabinet with flush doors attached with butt hinges.

3. Measure the width of the opening at top and bottom. Transfer this measurement to the door and cut to fit.

4. Sometimes, in making a double door it is desirable to have the doors overlap at the center by cutting a rabbet on the front edge of one door and the rear edge of the other. In this case, add the width of the rabbet to the door that will have the rabbet on the front edge.

5. Place the door in the frame opening and check it carefully. The edge away from the hinge side is frequently cut at a slight bevel so that, when it swings open or closed, the inside edge will not strike the frame, yet the door will be tight when closed.

19-6c. This small cabinet has overlay doors. Notice how the door fronts cover the sides of the cabinets.

19-6b. These doors are of lip construction and make use of offset surface hinges.

Installing Butt Hinges

Butt hinges are made with the flaps flat or slightly offset (swaged).

Usually a door is hung by two hinges but, if it is to support great weight, a third is installed at the middle. The butt hinges should be proportioned to the size of the door. Fig. 19-7. A 1-inch butt hinge, for example, would be satisfactory for a 1- to 2-foot door, a 2-inch butt hinge for a 2- to 4-foot door, and a 3-inch butt hinge for doors that support considerable weight. See next page.

1. Place the door in the opening and put small wedges below and away from the hinge side to hold the door in place. Measure up from the bottom and down from the top. With a chisel or knife carefully mark a line on the door and frame to indicate the top and bottom of the two hinges. Remove the door from the opening.

2. Continue the line with a try square across the edge of the frame and the door to indicate the position of the hinge.

3. Place the hinge over the edge of the door and determine how far

19-7a. Butt hinges are installed for the doors of this server.

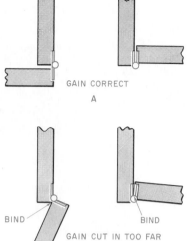

GAIN CORRECT
A

BIND   BIND

GAIN CUT IN TOO FAR
CAUSES HINGE BINDING.
B

19-8. Note the correct (A) and incorrect (B) way of mounting a door. If the hinges are mounted too close, the door will strike the sides of the case.

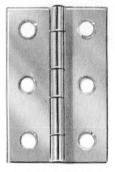

19-7b. Butt hinges are made in many lengths and may have a tight or a loose pin.

A HINGE WITH ONE FLAP
FULL SWAGED

A HINGE WITH BOTH FLAPS
HALF SWAGED

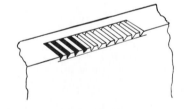

19-9a. Preliminary chisel cuts for a gain.

A HINGE WITH BOTH FLAPS
NOT SWAGED

A HINGE WITH ONE FLAP
HALF SWAGED

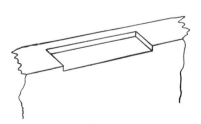

19-9b. A gain ready to receive the hinge.

19-7c. Hinges come in a variety of sizes and with different swaging.

the hinge is to extend beyond the door at the line of the hinge. Fig. 19-8. Draw a line to indicate the depth of the hinge. Do this on both door and frame.

4. Measure the thickness of one leaf of the hinge and set a marking gage to this amount. Mark a line on the door and the frame to indicate this depth.

5. Cut the gain (the opening for the hinge) by hand with a chisel as shown in Fig. 19-9. Outline the gain and then cut small notches in the stock to be removed. Trim out the gain. If a portable router is available, this job can be done quickly.

6. Place the hinge in the door edge, drill pilot holes for the screws, and attach the hinge.

7. Hold the door against the frame, mark the position of one hole on either hinge, and drill a pilot hole. Insert one screw in each hinge.

8. Check to see if the door operates properly. If the door stands away too much from the frame side, it may be necessary to do more trimming. This should be done toward the front edge of the frame. If the door binds on the hinge side, cut a little piece of cardboard to go under the hinge. When the door operates properly, install the other screws.

Using Surface Hinges

The simplest method of hanging a flush door is to use surface hinges. Fig. 19-10. These hinges add to the appearance of a furniture piece. While these hinges are used mostly for flush doors, they can be purchased with a 3⁄8″ offset for installation on lip doors.

19-10a. These cabinet doors have surface hinges.

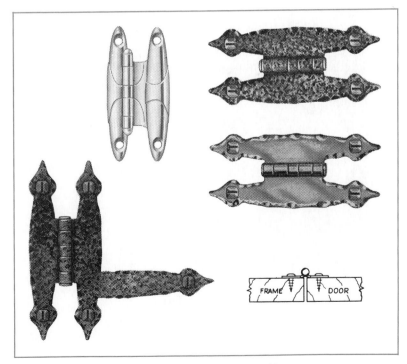

19-10b. Various kinds of surface hinges.

201

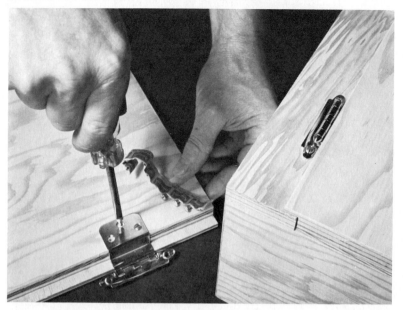

19-11a. Lip doors are neatly hung with semi-concealed hinges. These hinges are made to fit a cut that is half the thickness of the door.

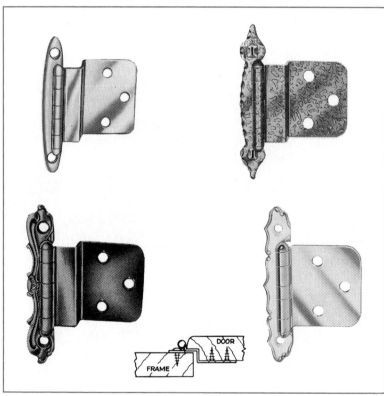

19-11b. Various styles of semi-concealed hinges.

Fitting a Lip Door

It is not necessary to fit a lip door as accurately as a flush door, since the lip will cover part of the frame. Measure the width and height of the opening; then, add twice the amount of the lip or overhang (less the clearance—about $\frac{1}{8}''$ to $\frac{1}{4}''$). Cut a rabbet equal to half this amount around three or four sides of the door. (All four sides should be rabbeted when it is a single door and only three sides when it is a double door.) The rabbet should be at least half the thickness of the stock in depth and equal to the offset of the hinge used. The usual depth is $\frac{3}{8}''$. Usually the front edge of the door is rounded on all sides. This can be done on a shaper or router.

Installing a Semi-Concealed Hinge

The semi-concealed hinge is used most frequently for the lip door. Fig. 19-11. Mark the location of the hinge on the inside of the door and install the hinges on the door itself. Hold the door with the two hinges against the frame, mark the position for the other screws, and fasten in place.

Fitting an Overlay Door

An overlay door that covers the sides and sometimes the top and bottom of the case is a good choice for television and hi-fi cabinets which must be designed so that the doors can swing completely open. Fig. 19-12a. Usually a pivot pin or knife hinge is used, since less of the hinge shows than is true with butt hinges. Fig. 19-12b. A concealed

19-12a. A Contemporary case using pivot or pin hinges.

19-13a. The top doors of this secretary are overlay style and make use of concealed hinges.

19-12b. Common kinds of pivot pin hinges.

hinge can also be used for an overlay door. It is especially good with softwood plywood since the screws can go into the side rather than the edge of the door. Fig. 19-13.

Sliding Doors

Close-fitting sliding doors of plywood or hardboard are made by rabbeting the top and bottom edges of each door. Rabbet the back of the front door and the front of the back door. This lets the door almost touch, leaving a little gap for dust. This also increases the effective depth of the cabinet. For $\frac{3}{8}''$ plywood doors, rabbet half their thickness. Then cut two grooves in the top and

19-13b. A common type of concealed hinge. There is a high knuckle for greater backswing of the overlay doors.

bottom of the cabinet $\frac{1}{2}''$ apart. Always seal the edges and back of the doors with the same material as the front so that the doors will not warp. To make the doors removable, cut the bottom

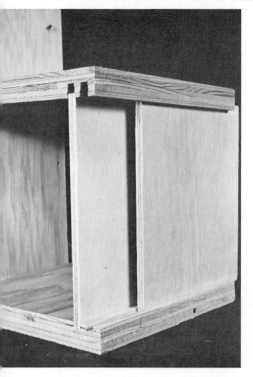

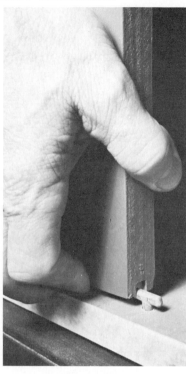

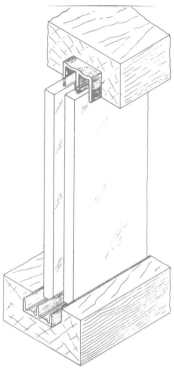

19-14. Note grooves cut deeper at the top than at the bottom so the doors can be easily inserted and removed.

19-15a. This is one type of commercial track that can be used for sliding doors.

19-15b. Another type of plastic door track that fits into grooves at top and bottom.

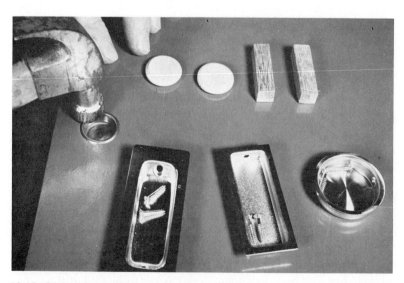

19-16. Sliding doors can be equipped with metal finger cups that are forced into round or rectangular holes. Round or rectangular grips of wood are suitable where clearance between the doors is adequate.

grooves $\frac{3}{16}$" deep and the top grooves $\frac{3}{8}$" deep. Fig. 19-14. After the doors are finished, they can be inserted by slipping them into the excess space in the top grooves. Then they are dropped into the bottom grooves. A metal, plastic, or wood track can also be installed above and below for the sliding doors. Fig. 19-15. Hardboard can also be used for sliding doors. A hole can be drilled near the center right end to serve as an opener. A recessed metal fitting or a surface piece can also be used as a handle. Fig. 19-16.

Catches

There are several types of

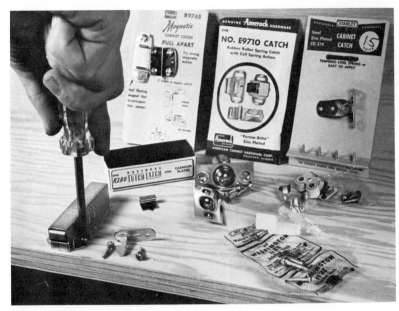

19-17a. Catches come in many varieties. The touch type being installed here allows the door to open at a touch.

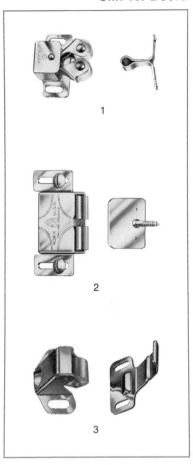

19-17b. Common kinds of catches. 1. Friction. 2. Magnetic. 3. Spring Roller.

catches available, including the friction, clip, ball, and magnetic. Fig. 19-17. These are all in two parts, one to fit on the door and the other to fit on the furniture piece itself. Catches should usually be installed near the handle, for smoother operation.

Locks

There are many different kinds of drawer and cabinet locks that can be purchased. Modern and Early American furniture usually requires a concealed type of lock that fits in or on the back of the door.

UNIT 20 Fasteners

Furniture parts are joined together primarily with machined and glued wood joints. Fig. 20-1. Also, some screws, nails, staples, and other metal fasteners are used by themselves or added to the wood joint for extra strength. Many types of screws are needed for attaching hardware.

Wood Screws

Wood screws are used for many purposes including:
● The installation of corner blocks.
● Fastening a top to the base of a table or cabinet.
● Attaching a frame or trim to the front of a cabinet.

● Installing hardware.

Screws are usually purchased with flat, round, or oval heads with either slotted or recessed (Phillips) heads. Fig. 20-2. They are made of many kinds of materials. Roundhead screws are often blue, while flatheads are bright steel. Screws are often packaged with such items as locks and hinges. Fig. 20-3a.

Screws are available in *lengths* from $3/16''$ to $6''$ and in diameters from 0 to 24 gage. Note that the

20-1. Metal fasteners are used in nearly all furniture construction including tables, chairs, and casework. Except on the hardware, most metal fasteners do not show in the final product.

same length screw can be purchased in several different diameters. Fig. 20-3b.

If screws are to be recessed below a wood surface, it is necessary first to counterbore a hole of the correct size. Fig. 20-4. When joining two wood pieces with screws, two holes are necessary. The hole in the first piece of wood is called a *shank* or *clearance* hole. It should be about the same diameter as the shank of the screw. The hole in the second piece is called the *pilot* or lead hole. Fig. 20-5.

The use of a pilot hole avoids distortion and tearing of wood fibers. The correct sizes of drills for shank and pilot holes are shown in Fig. 20-6. Drill the shank hole first. Then hold the first piece over the second and with a scratch awl mark the location of the pilot hole. When installing screws in hardwood, make sure that the pilot hole is drilled the full depth of the screw. When installing flathead screws, countersink the upper surface so that the head will be flush. Fig. 20-7.

If the size is not shown on your working drawing, choose a screw that will go at least two-thirds of its length into the second piece. Fig. 20-8. If the second piece is end grain, the screw should be even longer since end grain does not hold very well.

d

c

WOOD SCREWS

e

b

f

a

20-2. Common types of wood screws (recessed are also called Phillips head.): (a) Flathead slotted. (b) Flathead recessed. (c) Roundhead slotted. (d) Roundhead recessed. (e) Ovalhead slotted. (f) Ovalhead recessed.

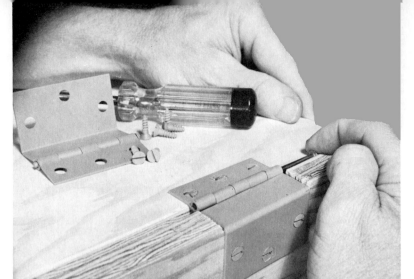

20-3a. The correct sizes and kinds of wood screws are packaged with hardware such as hinges.

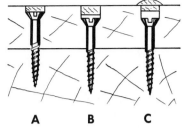

20-4. If the head of a wood screw must be covered, it is necessary first to counterbore the hole. Three methods of covering the heads of screws: (A) With plastic wood. (B) With a plain wood plug. (C) With a fancy wood plug.

20-5. When installing a flathead screw, it is necessary to have the correct size of: (A) Pilot hole. (B) Shank hole. (C) Countersink.

COUNTER SINK (C)

SHANK HOLE (B)

PILOT HOLE (A)

WOOD SCREW SIZE CHART

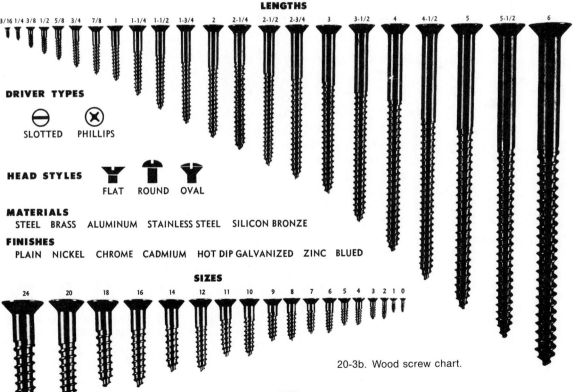

LENGTHS

3/16 1/4 3/8 1/2 5/8 3/4 7/8 1 1-1/4 1-1/2 1-3/4 2 2-1/4 2-1/2 2-3/4 3 3-1/2 4 4-1/2 5 5-1/2 6

DRIVER TYPES

SLOTTED   PHILLIPS

HEAD STYLES

FLAT   ROUND   OVAL

MATERIALS

STEEL   BRASS   ALUMINUM   STAINLESS STEEL   SILICON BRONZE

FINISHES

PLAIN   NICKEL   CHROME   CADMIUM   HOT DIP GALVANIZED   ZINC   BLUED

SIZES

24 20 18 16 14 12 11 10 9 8 7 6 5 4 3 2 1 0

20-3b. Wood screw chart.

LENGTH	\	SHANK NUMBERS →																
¼ inch	0	1	2	3														
⅜ inch			2	3	4	5	6	7										
½ inch			2	3	4	5	6	7	8									
⅝ inch				3	4	5	6	7	8	9	10							
¾ inch					4	5	6	7	8	9	10	11						
⅞ inch							6	7	8	9	10	11	12					
1 inch							6	7	8	9	10	11	12	14				
1 ¼ inch								7	8	9	10	11	12	14	16			
1 ½ inch							6	7	8	9	10	11	12	14	16	18		
1 ¾ inch									8	9	10	11	12	14	16	18	20	
2 inch									8	9	10	11	12	14	16	18	20	
2 ¼ inch										9	10	11	12	14	16	18	20	
2 ½ inch													12	14	16	18	20	
2 ¾ inch														14	16	18	20	
3 inch															16	18	20	
3 ½ inch																18	20	24
4 inch																18	20	24
0 TO 24 DIAMETER DIMENSIONS IN INCHES AT BODY	.060	.073	.086	.099	.112	.125	.138	.151	.164	.177	.190	.203	.216	.242	.268	.294	.320	.372

20-6. Chart for selecting correct-size drills or bits.

TWIST BIT SIZES For Round, Flat and Oval Head Screws in Drilling Shank and Pilot Holes.

SHANK HOLE HARD & SOFT WOOD	$\frac{1}{16}$	$\frac{5}{64}$	$\frac{3}{32}$	$\frac{7}{64}$	$\frac{7}{64}$	$\frac{1}{8}$	$\frac{9}{64}$	$\frac{5}{32}$	$\frac{11}{64}$	$\frac{3}{16}$	$\frac{3}{16}$	$\frac{13}{64}$	$\frac{7}{32}$	$\frac{1}{4}$	$\frac{17}{64}$	$\frac{19}{64}$	$\frac{21}{64}$	$\frac{3}{8}$
PILOT HOLE SOFT WOOD	$\frac{1}{64}$	$\frac{1}{32}$	$\frac{1}{32}$	$\frac{3}{64}$	$\frac{3}{64}$	$\frac{1}{16}$	$\frac{1}{16}$	$\frac{1}{16}$	$\frac{5}{64}$	$\frac{5}{64}$	$\frac{3}{32}$	$\frac{3}{32}$	$\frac{7}{64}$	$\frac{7}{64}$	$\frac{9}{64}$	$\frac{9}{64}$	$\frac{11}{64}$	$\frac{3}{16}$
PILOT HOLE HARD WOOD	$\frac{1}{32}$	$\frac{1}{32}$	$\frac{3}{64}$	$\frac{1}{16}$	$\frac{1}{16}$	$\frac{5}{64}$	$\frac{5}{64}$	$\frac{3}{32}$	$\frac{3}{32}$	$\frac{7}{64}$	$\frac{7}{64}$	$\frac{1}{8}$	$\frac{1}{8}$	$\frac{9}{64}$	$\frac{5}{32}$	$\frac{3}{16}$	$\frac{13}{64}$	$\frac{7}{32}$
AUGER BIT SIZES FOR COUNTERBORED HEADS			#3	#4	#4	#4	#5	#5	#6	#6	#6	#7	#7	#8	#9	#10	#11	#12
MACHINE SPUR BIT SIZES FOR COUNTERBORED HEADS			$\frac{3}{16}$	$\frac{1}{4}$	$\frac{1}{4}$	$\frac{1}{4}$	$\frac{5}{16}$	$\frac{5}{16}$	$\frac{3}{8}$	$\frac{3}{8}$	$\frac{3}{8}$	$\frac{7}{16}$	$\frac{7}{16}$	$\frac{1}{2}$	$\frac{9}{16}$	$\frac{5}{8}$	$1\frac{1}{16}$	$\frac{3}{4}$

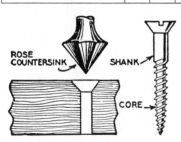

20-7. Countersinking.

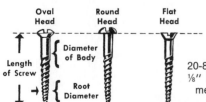

20-8. Screw length should be at least ⅛″ less than the combined measurement of the materials being joined.

Holding strength of screws varies directly with the length of the threaded section that goes into the second part. In hardwood species it is better to use long, thin screws, even though there is a chance of twisting off the screw during installation. Brass screws are more likely to twist off than are steel ones. If the hole has been counterbored, it can be covered after assembly with plastic wood or with a wood plug.

Nails

There is a limited use for nails in furniture construction. Fig. 20-9. In some cases, however, simple, modern furniture is assembled with nails. The ones used are *finishing nails* and *brads*. The most common sizes are shown in Fig. 20-10. When joining parts with nails, always select a nail that is at least twice as long as the thickness of the first piece. If nailing is to be done in hardwood, drill a small pilot hole in both pieces to within one-half the depth of the nail length. When installing nails, drive the nail into the wood until

208

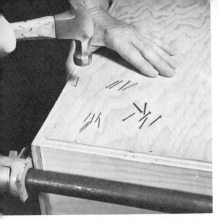

20-9. Nailing a back panel into the rabbet using brads or finishing nails.

20-11. This drawer is assembled with staples. The worker is using an air-operated stapler to attach the back of the drawer to the sides.

FINISHING NAILS

Size	Length	Gauge	Diameter Head Gauge
3d	1¼"	15½	12½
4d	1½"	15	12
6d	2"	13	10
8d	2½"	12½	9½
10d	3"	11½	8½

BRADS

Length in inches	Gauge (Available in following range)
½"	20
⅜"	20
½"	20 to 16
⅝"	20 to 16
¾"	20 to 16
⅞"	20 to 16
1"	20 to 14
1¼"	18 to 14
1½"	17 to 12
1¾"	15 to 12
2"	16 to 12
2½"	13 to 10
3"	12 to 11

Decimal equivalent of gauge number is:

21 = .032	13 = .092
20 = .035	12 = .106
19 = .041	11 = .121
18 = .047	10 = .135
17 = .054	9 = .148
16 = .063	8 = .162
15 = .072	7 = .177
14 = .080	

20-10. Finishing nails and brads.

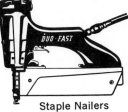
Staple Nailers

Air Tackers

Intermediate Air Tackers

Electric Tackers

Brad and Finish Nailers

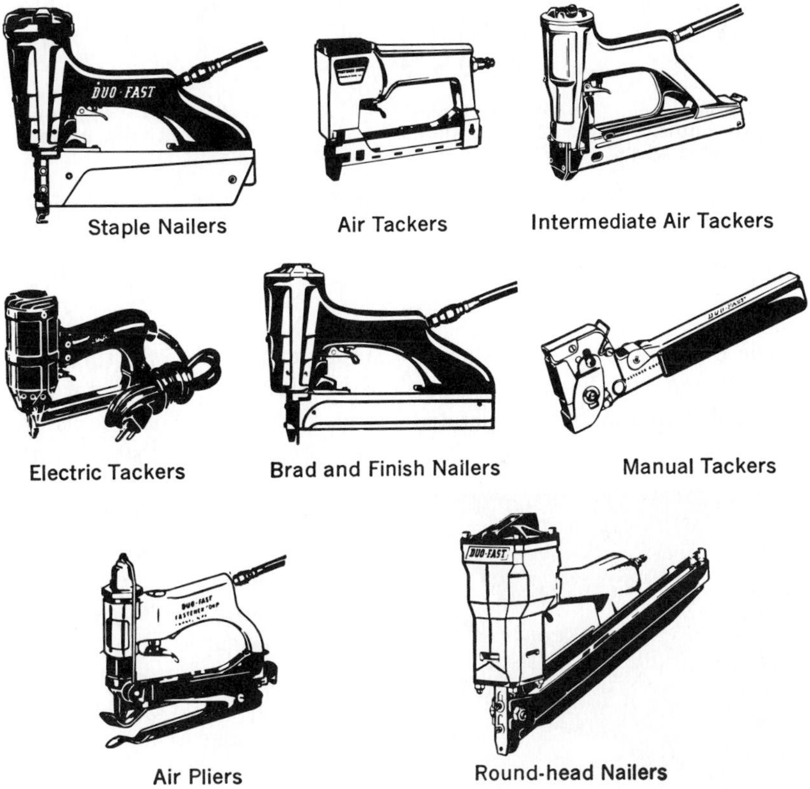

Manual Tackers

Air Pliers

Round-head Nailers

20-12. Common kinds of nailers, tackers, and staplers.

it is within a short distance of the face of the stock; then drive the head slightly below the surface with a nail set. Brads are used most often to join back panels to furniture pieces.

Stapling

Staplers, tackers, and nailers are commonly used in the furniture industry. Fig. 20-11. Many kinds of manual, air, or electric machines are available. Fig. 20-12.

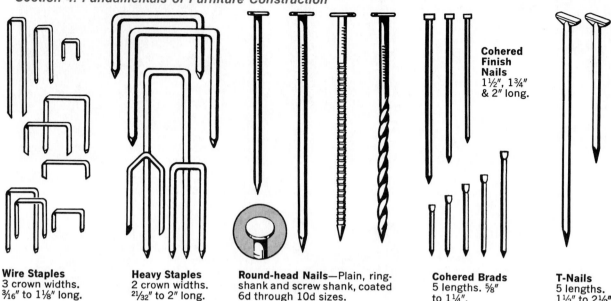

Wire Staples
3 crown widths.
³⁄₁₆″ to 1⅛″ long.

Heavy Staples
2 crown widths.
²¹⁄₃₂″ to 2″ long.

Round-head Nails—Plain, ring-shank and screw shank, coated 6d through 10d sizes.

Cohered Finish Nails
1½″, 1¾″ & 2″ long.

Cohered Brads
5 lengths. ⅝″ to 1¼″.

T-Nails
5 lengths.
1½″ to 2½″.

20-13. Kinds of staples, nails, and brads that can be installed with a machine.

These machines can drive staples, brads, and nails. Fig. 20-13. In the school shop a manually operated stapler can be used for such jobs as installing the back panel of a case. Fig. 20-14. These tools are also used for upholstery work.

Other Common Fasteners

Three other common fasteners are the *clamp nail,* the *chevron,* and the *corrugated fastener.* The *clamp nail* is particularly good for holding lighter joints together. It is flared slightly on both edges so it acts as a wedge to hold the parts firmly together. Fig. 20-15. In installing a clamp nail, a groove is cut in each of the two parts. An extra thin circular saw blade or a back saw or dovetail saw should be used for making these cuts. Each groove is about half the width of the clamp nail. In assembling the joint, the flared end of the clamp nail is driven into the

20-14. Using a manually operated stapler to install a back panel in a cabinet.

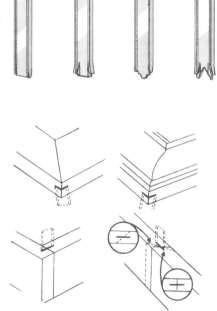

20-15. Clamp nails can be used to fasten many parts together.

20-16. Chevrons are good for assembling a miter joint.

groove. Clamp nails for miter corners can be set below the wood surface to allow for filling.

Chevrons are designed to draw two parts of a miter joint tight together. Fig. 20-16.

Corrugated fasteners also draw two parts together and hold them. These do not require any machining to install. Fig. 20-17. They are driven into solid wood like a staple. Generally, corrugated fasteners are used only on relatively rough wood. They are available in lengths from $\frac{1}{4}''$ to $\frac{3}{4}''$, in units of 100.

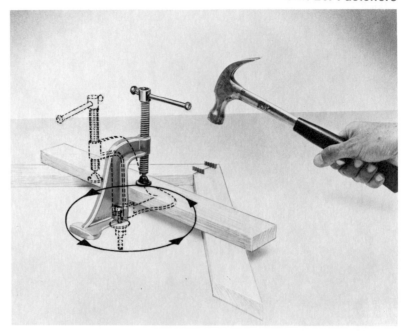

20-17. Installing two corrugated fasteners on a miter corner. The pieces are held by a bench clamp that can be rotated in any direction.

UNIT 21 Assembling Furniture

Furniture assembly involves the use of many joints, such as the dowel, mortise-and-tenon, dovetail, miter, and others, as explained in Unit 14. These joints must be accurately cut with sharp tools. A joint must fit snugly when assembled.

An essential of most good joint construction is the correct selection and use of adhesives. A white glue in the familiar squeeze bottle is best for simple cabinetwork which requires a relatively short assembly time. If a longer assembly time is needed, a liquid hide glue is generally used. Glue is not a filler, although some glues fill minor irregularities better than others. For more information on adhesives, review Unit 13.

The steps in assembling a project are determined largely by how complicated it is. On simple projects, all parts can be assembled at one time. Fig. 21-1. On more complicated ones—such as a table with four legs, rails, and a top—it may be a two- or three-stage job. It is often better to glue the two legs and a rail to form the sides or ends as a sub-assembly and

21-1. This bookcase could be glued up in a single step except for the installation of the back. The shelves fit into the sides with dado joints so the total assembly should be glued at one time. The back can then be installed with wood screws.

21-2. A table such as this one requires several subassemblies which are then put together to make the whole.

21-3a. A simple frame being glued up with only two clamps.

later to glue these to the other two rails. Then the top is fastened in place. Fig. 21-2.

Follow these steps:

1. Get all parts together and check to see that they are completed, including sanding. Make sure that you have identification marks on all pieces so that you know exactly how they are to go together. Check this and see that all joints fit properly.

2. Decide on whether the project is to be assembled with glue, screws, or nails. Most furniture pieces have screws and glue as part of the assembly.

3. Cut a number of cauls (scrap pieces of stock) that will be used to protect the wood from being marred by the clamps.

4. Get out the clamps and adjust them to the correct openings.

21-3b. This larger frame has to have clamps in both directions. Note that a clamp is installed at or near each joint. Rails are fastened to the stiles with mortise-and-tenon joints.

21-3c. Another clamping technique.

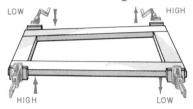

21-4. To correct twist, place the clamps in the direction of the arrows.

Review Unit 13 for information about clamps.

5. If sub-assemblies are to be glued up, decide on which parts are to be assembled first.

Frames are typical sub-assemblies that must be glued up before the final project is assembled. Fig. 21-3. Frames may be used in the interior of cases and also for exterior trim. Clamps should be used at every joint location. Check to see that the frame is square. If not, shift the clamps at a slight angle to correct this. Also check for levelness with a level or straightedge. Twist can be detected by sighting down the frame and can be corrected by moving the clamps. Fig. 21-4.

Frames with miter joints (the kind of joint used in picture frames) are fairly difficult to glue. An adjustable frame clamp can be made that uses a standard hand screw to apply pressure. Fig. 21-5. There is a special type of miter clamp that can be used which requires that $5/8''$ blind holes be bored in the back of the frame. Fig. 21-6, page 215.

21-5a. This adjustable frame clamp can be used for frames of different sizes.

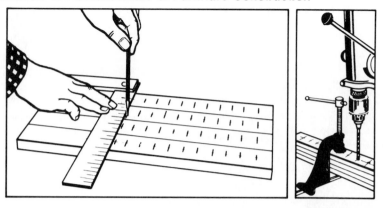

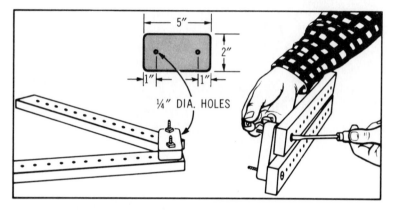

5"

2"

1" 1"

¼" DIA. HOLES

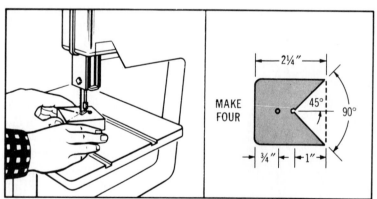

2¼"

MAKE
FOUR

45°

90°

¾" 1"

21-5b. Steps in making an adjustable
frame clamp.

bly of the clamp. This will permit the clamp to lie flat on the bench.

SWIVEL BARS: (two required). Use the same 1" x 2" hardwood stock, cut 5" long. Locate centers 1" in from each end and drill ¼" dia. holes. Round the ends for neat appearance.

CORNER BLOCKS: (four required). Make from the same 1" x 2" hardwood stock, cut 2¼" long. Mark for two ¼" dia. holes, with one of them being 1" in from the end so it will be centered at the bottom of the right-angle "V". This will provide relief for the corners of the frame being clamped so that it will draw up properly, without crushing any sharp corners on the frame. Cut perfect 90° recesses into each block.

ASSEMBLY: You will need eight ¼ x 2¼" flathead machine screws, with nuts or wing nuts to fit. Assemble the swivel bars onto the legs as illustrated. The corner blocks are assembled into each of the legs at positions determined by the size of the frame to be mitered. Make certain that the corner blocks are assembled at the same relative position in each leg.

CLAMPING: With both pairs of legs placed on the bench so that the swivel bars are on top, the four corner blocks can be roughly positioned to fit the frame. The swivel bars should be parallel to each other, and separated by some convenient distance. Pressure is applied by drawing the swivel bars together by means of a "jorgensen" handscrew. On very large frames, the swivel bars may be a considerable distance apart, in which case a "jorgensen" (or "pony") bar clamp can be used.

LEGS: (four required). Use straight, clear hardwood strips 1" thick by 2" wide, 18" long or as much longer as you wish for the jobs intended. Maple, oak, or similar hardwoods are preferred.

With the four strips side by side, carefully mark off 1" intervals along the full length of each. Locate centers at each interval and drill ¼" dia. holes as marked. Accuracy is important. If you prefer, the four legs can be "stacked," clamped, and drilled simultaneously. Corners should be rounded.

Counterbore all holes on the underside of each leg to accommodate the flathead machine screw to be used in the assem-

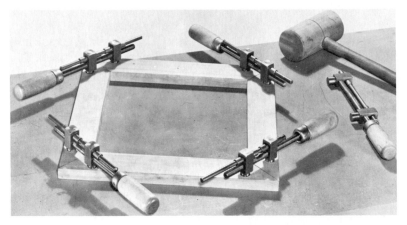

21-6. These special miter clamps require that holes be drilled in the back of the frame.

Fig. 21-6. There are also patented spring clamps with pivoting jaws and serrated teeth along the edge that will hold a miter joint. Fig. 21-7. Still another method is to glue temporary, triangular blocks to the sides of the case and then use standard clamps to hold the case during the gluing. These blocks can later be split off. Fig. 21-8.

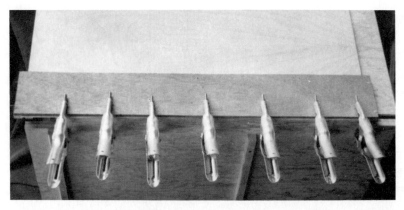

21-7. Note the spacing of these clamps. They have serrated teeth which permit clamping at a 45° angle.

21-8. Note the triangular blocks temporarily glued to the outside of the case. C-clamps can then be used to hold the miter joint in place. This method cannot be used on fine hardwood on which a natural finish will be applied.

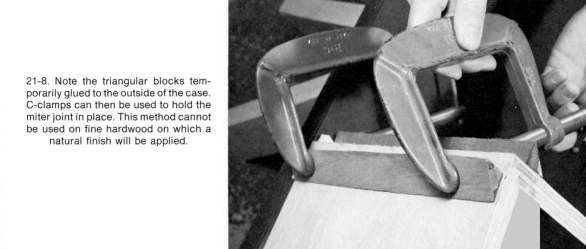

215

A four-corner miter clamp can also be purchased that will clamp all four corners at one time and will not mar the work. This clamp can be used on finished stock and is quickly adjusted to any square or other rectangle desired, limited by the length of the threaded rod. Fig. 21-9. A miter-and-corner clamp is ideal for assembling frames. Fig. 21-10.

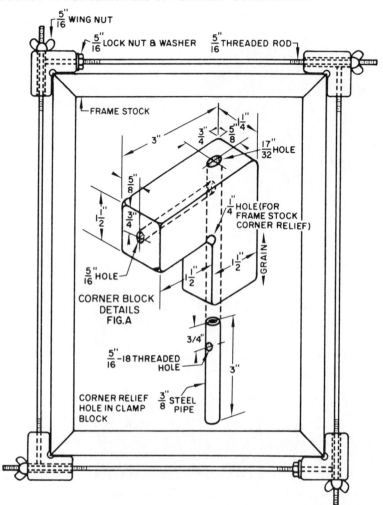

21-9. This frame-gluing clamp is a jig that can be made in the shop. The four clamp blocks are made from such hardwoods as maple, birch, hickory, or oak. Note that 5⁄16″ threaded rods are used for the clamps. A 3⁄8″ steel pipe acts as a bushing that allows the rods easy movement for adjusting the clamp block. A commercial clamp of this type can also be purchased.

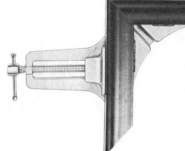

21-10. This miter-and-corner clamp is good for gluing up frames.

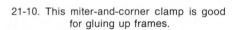

216

21-11. Checking an assembly with a square.

21-12. Checking across the corners for squareness.

21-13. Checking with a straightedge for levelness.

6. Make a temporary assembly of the parts to see that the piece will clamp up properly and the joints fit correctly. Figs. 21-11, 12, 13, and 14. Check with a square and rule to see that the parts are at correct angles to each other and are parallel and level. Be sure to check at several points. A straightedge is also useful for checking levelness. Sometimes it may be necessary to do a little hand trimming or to shift the clamps.

7. When assembling with glue, mix only the amount needed at one time. Cover the top of the workbench with paper. Lay the clamps out in proper position. Have the scrap blocks handy and a rubber mallet ready. Also have a square and rule nearby.

21-14. Make sure that the joints fit perfectly before attempting to glue up the case.

21-15. Applying liquid hide glue with a stick. This kind of glue is good if you need a long time during the assembly of the project.

8. Carefully apply the glue to the joints. Fig. 21-15. Be careful not to put on too much. Apply a little extra glue on the end grain, which soaks it up. Fig. 21-16.

Be careful to keep the exposed sanded surface free of glue. Even a small amount of glue left on the surface will show through the finish.

21-16. White glue in a squeeze bottle is good to use if the assembly time is not too long.

9. Quickly assemble the parts, place the scrap pieces over the project, and apply the clamps. Fig. 21-17. Do not apply too much pressure. Then quickly check with a square and tape to see that everything is true. If necessary, a clamp can be shifted or a joint can be tapped with a rubber mallet to bring it into place. Fig. 21-18.

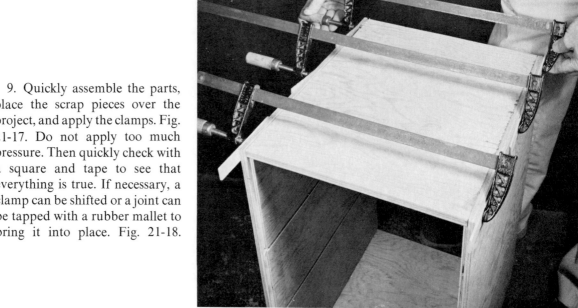

21-17. Clamping up the project. Place cauls (blocks of wood) under the jaws of the clamp to protect the surfaces.

21-18a. Checking the assembly with a square.

21-18b. Checking across the corners of the cabinet with a steel tape. Make sure the measurement is equal in both directions.

21-18c. Shift one or more of the clamps if the test shows that the cabinet is "out of square." Then recheck both levelness and squareness.

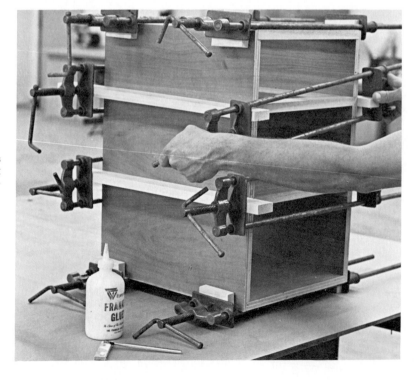

10. When the project is clamped together, remove the excess glue.

There should be a minimum of squeeze out. Remove this excess glue with a stick or sharp tool. Then wipe the surface clean with a sponge or rag that has been dipped in hot water. Another method of protecting the exposed surfaces is to apply masking tape around the joint.

Store the part or piece where it can dry without being bumped. If it is a sub-assembly, after these parts are dry, complete the entire assembly. Irregularly shaped products, such as chair frames used in some types of upholstery, can be held with either a canvas or steel band clamp. Fig. 21-19.

21-19a. A canvas band clamp used to assemble a chair frame.

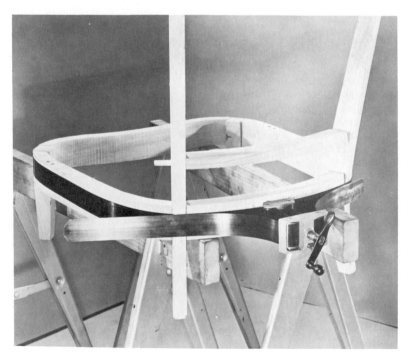

21-19b. A steel band clamp holds irregular parts in place, which makes it useful in upholstery as well as furniture assembly.

DISCUSSION TOPICS

Section Four—FUNDAMENTALS OF FURNITURE CONSTRUCTION

Unit 14. Making Joints

1. Describe four major steps in the construction of all joints.

2. Describe three methods of strengthening joints.

3. Describe the way to install a dowel.

4. State the primary use of edge joints.

5. Where are butt joints commonly used?

6. What is a rabbet joint? Tell where it is used.

7. Describe three types of dado joints.

8. Describe how a miter joint can be strengthened.

9. Name four kinds of lap joints.

10. Why is a mortise-and-tenon joint good in table and chair construction?

11. Where is a dovetail joint most often used?

Unit 15. Tables and Chairs

1. Which is more difficult to build—tables or chairs? Explain.

2. Name some common kinds of tables.

3. What is the most common construction for a table base?

4. Tell how to treat the edges of plywood.

5. What are corner blocks used for?

6. Discuss different methods of fastening tops to tables and desks.

7. Discuss the construction of chairs.

Unit 16. Plastic Laminates

1. What is a plastic laminate?

2. Explain the advantages of plastic laminate.

3. Describe how to install a plastic laminate top on a table.

Unit 17. Casegoods

1. Describe where panel construction is used.

2. Name some kinds of furniture that are classified as casegoods.

3. Explain how to build a frame and panel.

4. Describe the types of panel surfaces.

5. Which is the most common method of installing an adjustable shelf?

Unit 18. Drawers

1. How many parts are there in a drawer? Name them.

2. Describe three basic types of drawer fronts.

3. Name the common joints used in drawer construction.

4. Discuss the different types of drawer guides.

Unit 19. Doors

1. What are small doors called?

2. Describe how to hang a door.

3. Describe the advantages of using a lip door.

Unit 20. Fasteners

1. What are the different shapes of wood screw heads?

2. Identify the different kinds of wood screw heads as to slot.

3. Name some of the common materials used for wood screws.

4. Are nails widely used in furniture construction?

5. Describe common methods of using metal fasteners in industry.

6. What is the difference between a clamp nail and a corrugated fastener?

Unit 21. Assembling Furniture

1. Describe three methods of checking an assembly after it is clamped.

2. Why is it necessary to use protective wood blocks when clamping up furniture?

EXTRA CREDIT

1. Study drawer construction by inspecting some expensive and inexpensive furniture. Describe the differences in construction.

2. Make a list of different types and uses of furniture hardware. Use magazines and catalogs for sources.

3. Write a report on the manufacture of wood screws.

4. Discuss how case construction is done in industry.

Tools and Machines

In the following units many illustrations show dangerous operations being performed on machines without guards. The guards have been removed so that the photographs will show the operations more clearly. NOTE: Whenever this drawing of a guard appears with an illustration, A GUARD MUST BE USED for the operation that is shown.

Safety

In industry, safety is regarded as an important part of the total operation, no less important than production. This is true for at least two reasons. One is the natural concern for people's welfare. Another perfectly valid reason is financial. Industrial managers know that injuries to employees are costly since they reduce the efficiency of the working force and may result in expensive medical bills and law suits.

Therefore many modern industries have safety programs which are intended to protect every employee, from the president on down to the newest trainee.

Safety is of prime importance in the operation of the type of power tools you will be using in woodworking. Therefore you should not just read but really learn the safety rules for any job you do, and *put the rules into practice.* Do this for each piece of equipment you use. Learn to make safety a habit as you develop your skills.

The following is a list of general safety rules to be used in the shop as you work on and around machines. These rules will help to protect you and others who are near you while you work.

● Do not use a machine until you understand it thoroughly. Any tool with a sharp cutting edge can cause serious injury if mishandled.

● Use guards on power equipment. It should be understood that using guards does not necessarily prevent accidents. Guards indicate points of danger, but they must be used correctly if they are to provide fullest protection. Also, it is impossible to do some operations, especially on the circular saw, with the regular guard in place. Therefore there are times when special guards should be used. These are explained at appropriate points in the following units.

● Always wear tight-fitting clothes when working around machines. Tuck in your tie and roll up your sleeves or wear a tight-fitting shop coat or apron.

● Always keep your fingers away from the moving cutting edges. The most common accident is caused by trying to run too small a piece through a machine.

● Keep the floor around the machine clean. The danger from falling or slipping is always great.

● Make all adjustments with the power off and the machine at a dead stop.

● Remove all jewelry from hands and wrists.

● Always wear approved eye protection.

● Always walk—do not run—in the shop.

● Never talk to or interrupt anyone while he is working on a machine.

● Remove power plug or turn off power supply to a machine when changing cutters or blades.

● Never leave tools or pieces of stock lying on the table surface of a machine being used.

● When finished with a machine, turn off the power and wait until the blade or cutter has come to a complete stop before leaving.

● Always carefully check stock for knots, splits, metal objects and other defects before machining.

● Always turn on the dust collector if it is connected to the machine being used.

● Always use a brush to clean the table surface.

● Always keep your eyes focused on where the cutting action is taking place.

● Always use sharp tools.

● When using tools for set up work on a machine: (1) Select the right tool for the job. (2) Keep it in safe condition. (3) Keep it in a safe place.

● Report strange noises or faulty operation of machines to the instructor.

● Follow the suggestions for each machine given in this book.

General Safety Rules for Portable Power Tools

• Never use portable power tools in contact with water, including rain, or if any part of your body is in contact with moisture.

• Be sure the power plug is removed before making any adjustments.

• Portable power tools should be properly grounded with a three-prong grounded plug. If a grounded receptacle is not available, use a three-to-two-prong

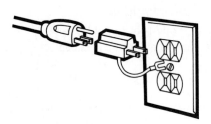

Fig. A. A three-to-two-prong adapter plug.

adapter plug which has been properly grounded. Fig. A.

• Always wear approved eye protection.

• Always disconnect the power plug when the work is completed.

• Be sure the switch is in the "off" position before connecting the power plug.

• Always use the recommended extension cord size. Fig. B.

CORD LENGTH IN FEET

Name-plate Amperes	25	50	75	100	125	150	175	200	225	250	275	300	325	350	375	400	425	450	475	500
1	16	16	16	16	16	16	16	16	16	16	16	16	16	16	16	16	16	16	16	14
2	16	16	16	16	16	16	16	16	16	16	14	14	14	14	14	12	12	12	12	12
3	16	16	16	16	16	16	14	14	14	14	12	12	12	12	12	10	10	10	10	10
4	16	16	16	16	16	14	14	12	12	12	12	12	12	10	10	10	10	10	10	10
5	16	16	16	16	14	14	12	12	12	12	10	10	10	10	10	8	8	8	8	8
6	16	16	16	14	14	12	12	12	10	10	10	10	10	8	8	8	8	8	8	8
7	16	16	14	14	12	12	12	10	10	10	10	8	8	8	8	8	8	8	8	8
8	14	14	14	14	12	12	10	10	10	10	8	8	8	8	8	8	8	8		
9	14	14	14	12	12	10	10	8	8	8	8	8	8	8	8					
10	14	14	14	12	12	10	10	8	8	8	8	8	8	8						
11	12	12	12	12	10	10	10	8	8	8	8	8	8	8						
12	12	12	12	12	10	10	8	8	8	8	8	8	8							
13	12	12	12	12	10	10	8	8	8	8	8	8								
14	10	10	10	10	10	10	8	8	8	8	8									
15	10	10	10	10	10	8	8	8	8	8										
16	10	10	10	10	10	8	8	8	8	8										
17	10	10	10	10	10	8	8	8	8											
18	8	8	8	8	8	8	8	8	8											
19	8	8	8	8	8	8	8	8												
20	8	8	8	8	8	8	8	8												

NOTES: Wire sizes are for 3-CDR Cords, one CDR of which is used to provide a continuous grounding circuit from tool housing to receptacle. Wire sizes shown are A. W. G. (American Wire Gauge). Based on 115V power supply; Ambient Temp. of 30°C, 86°F.

Fig. B. Recommended extension cord sizes for use with portable electric tools.

UNIT 22 Layout, Measuring, and Checking Devices

TOOL	DESCRIPTION	USES
Bench Rule *Fig. 22-1.*	A 12-inch or one-foot rule. One side is divided into eighths, the other into sixteenths.	1. To make simple measurements. 2. To adjust dividers. *Caution.* Never use as a straightedge.

22-1

Zig-Zag Rule *Fig. 22-2.*	A folding rule of six- or eight-foot length.	1. To measure distances greater than 2′, place the rule flat on the stock. 2. To measure less than 2′, it is better to use the rule on edge.

22-2

Flexible Tape Rules *Fig. 22-3.*	A flexible tape that slides into a metal case. Comes in lengths of 6′, 8′, 10′, 12′, 50′, and 100′. The steel tape has a hook on the end that adjusts to true zero.	1. To measure irregular as well as regular shapes. 2. To make accurate inside measurements. (Measurement is read by adding 2″ to the reading on the blade.)

22-3a

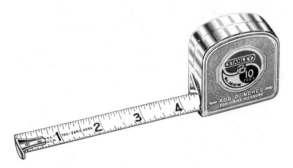

22-3b

TOOL	DESCRIPTION	USES
Try Square *Fig. 22-4.*	A squaring, measuring, and testing tool with a metal blade and a wood or metal handle.	1. To test a surface for levelness. 2. To check adjacent surfaces for squareness. 3. To make lines across the face or edge of stock.

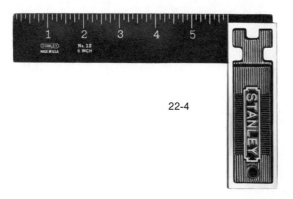

22-4

| Combination Square
Fig. 22-5. | Consists of a blade and handle. The blade slides along in the handle or head. There is a level and a scriber in the handle. | 1. To test a level or plumb surface.
2. To check squareness—either inside or outside.
3. To mark and test a 45-degree miter.
4. To gauge-mark a line with a pencil. |

22-5

| Sliding T Bevel
Fig. 22-6. | A blade that can be set at any angle to the handle. Set with a framing square or protractor. | 1. To measure or transfer an angle between 0 and 180 degrees.
2. To check or test a miter cut. |

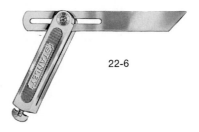

22-6

TOOL	DESCRIPTION	USES
Dividers *Fig. 22-7.*	A tool with two metal legs. One metal leg can be removed and replaced with a pencil. To set the dividers, hold both points on the measuring lines of the rule.	1. To lay out an arc or circle. 2. To step off measurements. 3. To divide distances along a straight line.

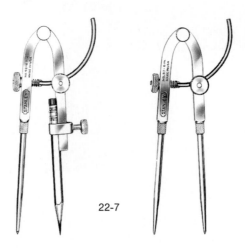

22-7

| Framing or Rafter Square
Fig. 22-8. | A large steel square consisting of a blade, or body, and a tongue. | 1. To check for squareness.
2. To mark a line across a board.
3. To lay out rafters and stairs. |

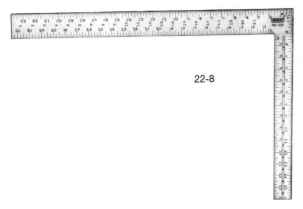

22-8

| Carpenter's Level
Fig. 22-9. | A rectangular metal or wood frame with several level glasses. | To check whether a surface is level or plumb. |

22-9

TOOL	DESCRIPTION	USES
Marking Gage *Fig. 22-10.*	A wood or metal tool consisting of a beam, head, and point.	To mark a line parallel to the grain of wood.

22-10

| Scratch Awl *Fig. 22-11.* | A pointed metal tool with handle. | 1. To locate a point of measurement. 2. To scribe a line accurately. |

22-11

| Trammel Points *Fig. 22-12.* | Two metal pointers that can be fastened to a long bar of wood or metal. | 1. To lay out distances between two points. 2. To scribe arcs and circles, larger than those made with dividers. |

22-12

UNIT 23 Sawing Tools

TOOL	DESCRIPTION	USES
Back Saw *Fig. 23-1.*	A fine-tooth, crosscut saw with a heavy metal band across the back to strengthen the thin blade.	1. To make fine cuts for joinery. 2. To use in a miter box.

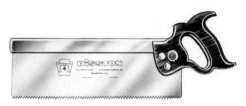

23-1

Crosscut Saw *Fig. 23-2.*	A hand saw in lengths from 20″ to 26″ with from 4 to 12 points per inch. A 22″, 10-point saw is a good one for general purpose work.	1. To cut across grain. 2. Can be used to cut with the grain. *Caution:* Never cut into nails or screws. Never twist off strips of waste stock.

23-2a

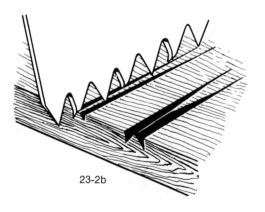

23-2b

TOOL	DESCRIPTION	USES
Rip Saw *Fig. 23-3.*	A hand saw in lengths from 20″ to 28″. A 26″, 5½-point saw is good for general use.	To cut with the grain. *Caution:* Support the waste stock. Never allow end of saw to strike the floor.

23-3a

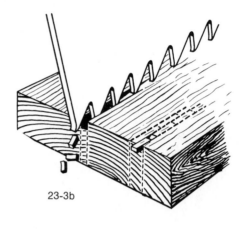

23-3b

| Compass Saw
Fig. 23-4. | A 12″ or 14″ taper blade saw. | 1. To cut gentle curves.
2. To cut inside curves. |

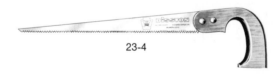

23-4

| Keyhole Saw
Fig. 23-5. | A 10″ or 12″ narrow taper saw with fine teeth. | To cut small openings and fine work. |

23-5

TOOL	DESCRIPTION	USES
Miter Box Saw *Fig. 23-6.*	A longer back saw (24″ to 28″).	Used in a homemade or commercial miter box for cutting miters or square ends.

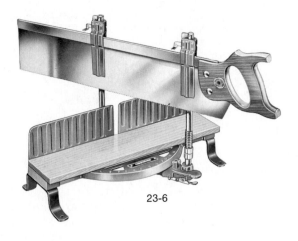

23-6

TOOL	DESCRIPTION	USES
Coping Saw *Fig. 23-7.*	A U-shaped saw frame permitting $4\frac{5}{8}$″ or $6\frac{1}{2}$″ deep cuts. Uses standard $6\frac{1}{2}$″ pin-end blades.	1. To cut curves. 2. To shape the ends of molding for joints. 3. For scroll work.

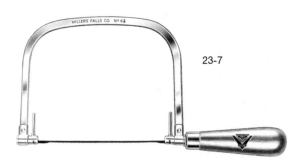

23-7

TOOL	DESCRIPTION	USES
Dovetail Saw *Fig. 23-8.*	An extremely thin blade with very fine teeth.	For smoothest possible joint cuts.

23-8

TOOL	DESCRIPTION	USES
Smooth Plane *Fig. 24-1.*	A 7″ to 9″ plane.	1. For general use. 2. For smaller work.

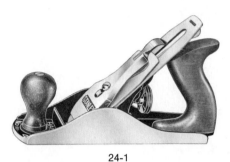

24-1

| Jack Plane
Fig. 24-2. | A 14″ or 15″ plane. | 1. Ideal for rough surfaces where chip should be coarse.
2. Also used to obtain a smooth, flat surface. |

24-2

| Fore Plane
Fig. 24-3. | An 18″ plane. | For fine flat finish on longer surfaces and edges. |

24-3

TOOL	DESCRIPTION	USES
Jointer Plane *Fig. 24-4.*	A 22″ or 24″ plane.	1. To smooth and flatten edges for making a close-fitting joint. 2. For planing long boards such as the edges of doors.

24-4

| Router Plane
Fig. 24-5. | A cutting tool with several cutters. | To surface the bottom of grooves and dadoes. |

24-5

| Block Plane
Fig. 24-6. | A small plane with a single, low-angle cutter with the bevel up. | 1. To plane end grain.
2. For small pieces.
3. For planing the ends of molding, trim, and siding. |

24-6

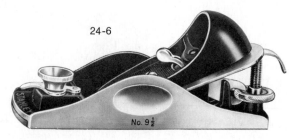

No. 9½

TOOL	DESCRIPTION	USES
Chisels *Fig. 24-7.*	A set usually includes blade widths from $\frac{1}{8}''$ to $2''$.	To trim and shape wood.

24-7

| Draw Knife
Fig. 24-8. | An open-bevelled blade with handles on both ends. | To remove much material in a short time. |

24-8

| Surform Tool
Fig. 24-9. | Available in plane file type. Also round, or block-plane types. A blade with 45-degree cutting teeth. | For all types of cutting and trimming. |

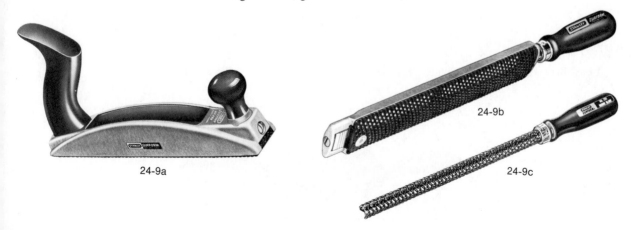

24-9b

24-9a

24-9c

TOOL	**DESCRIPTION**	**USES**
Gouges *Fig. 24-10.*	A chisel with a curved blade. Sharpened on the inside or, more commonly, on the outside.	To cut grooves or to shape irregular openings.

24-10a

24-10b

Spokeshave *Fig. 24-11.*	A small plane-like tool.	To form irregularly shaped objects.

24-11

Hand Scraper *Fig. 24-12.*	A blade-like tool.	To scrape the surface of wood with irregular grain.

24-12

Cabinet Scraper *Fig. 24-13.*	A blade in a holder.	To scrape the surface of furniture woods.

24-13

25 Drilling and Boring Tools

TOOL	DESCRIPTION	USES
Auger Bit *Fig. 25-1.*	May be either single-twist or double-twist bit. Comes in sizes from No. 4 ($\frac{1}{4}''$) to No. 16 (1'').	1. To bore holes $\frac{1}{4}''$ or larger. 2. Single twist bit is better for boring deep holes.

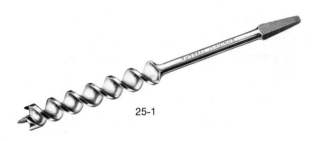

25-1

TOOL	DESCRIPTION	USES
Dowel Bit *Fig. 25-2.*	A shorter bit with a sharper twist.	To bore holes for making dowel joints.

25-2

TOOL	DESCRIPTION	USES
Expansion Bit *Fig. 25-3.*	A bit that holds cutters of different sizes. Sometimes this tool is called an expansive bit.	1. To bore a hole larger than 1''. 2. One cutter will bore holes in the 1'' to 2'' range. 3. A second cutter will bore holes in the 2'' to 3'' range.

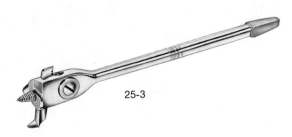

25-3

TOOL	DESCRIPTION	USES
Brace *Fig. 25-4.*	Two common types—the plain for a full swing, and the ratchet for close corners.	To hold and operate bits.

25-4

| Foerstner Bit
Fig. 25-5. | A bit with a flat cutting surface on the end. | 1. To bore a shallow hole with a flat bottom.
2. To bore a hole in thin stock.
3. To bore a hole in end grain.
4. To enlarge an existing hole. |

25-5

| Bit or Depth Gages
Fig. 25-6. | Two types—one is a solid clamp, the other a spring type. | To limit the depth of a hole. |

25-6a

25-6b

TOOL	**DESCRIPTION**	**USES**
Twist Drill (*a*) or Bit Stock Drill (*b*) *Fig. 25-7.*	A fractional-sized set from $\frac{1}{64}''$ to $\frac{1}{2}''$ is best.	To drill small holes for nails, screws, etc.

25-7a

25-7b

Hand Drill *Fig. 25-8.*	A tool with a 3-jaw chuck.	To hold twist drills for drilling small holes.

25-8

Automatic Drill *Fig. 25-9.*	A tool with drill points and handle. Sizes of drill points are: #1 = $\frac{1}{16}''$; #2 = $\frac{5}{64}''$; #3 = $\frac{3}{32}''$; #4 = $\frac{7}{64}''$; #5 = $\frac{1}{8}''$; #6 = $\frac{9}{64}''$; #7 = $\frac{5}{32}''$; #8 = $\frac{11}{64}''$.	To drill many small holes.

25-9

RADIAL-ARM SAW

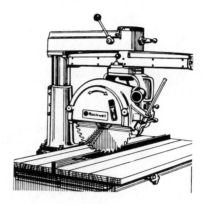

SAFETY

- Always keep the safety guard and the anti-kickback device in position.
- Make sure the clamps and locking handles are tight.
- When crosscutting, adjust the anti-kickback device (sometimes called "fingers") to clear the top of the work by about $\frac{1}{8}''$. This acts as a guard to prevent your fingers from coming near the revolving saw.
- Make sure the stock to be cut is held tightly against the fence.
- For crosscutting, dadoing, and similar operations, pull the saw into the work.
- Return the saw to the rear of the table after each cut.
- For ripping, make sure that the blade is rotating upwards toward you. Use the anti-kickback device to hold work firmly against the table. Feed the stock from the end opposite the anti-kickback device.
- Keep your hands away from the danger area—that is, the path of the saw blade.
- Be sure the power is off and the saw is *not* rotating before making any adjustments.
- Always use a sharp saw or cutter.
- Allow the saw to reach full speed before making a cut.
- Hold the saw to prevent it from coming forward, before turning on the power.
- This saw tends to feed itself into the work. Therefore it is necessary to regulate the rate of cutting by holding back the saw. Otherwise it will feed faster than it can cut, causing the motor to stall.
- Use a brush or stick to keep the table clear of all scraps and sawdust.

UNIT 26 Radial-Arm Saw

The radial-arm saw, Fig. 26-1, is a very versatile machine. It can be used for ripping, dadoing, grooving, and various combinations of these cuts. Many of these operations can be performed more easily on the radial-arm saw than on any other machine. For instance, a long board can be cut into shorter lengths easily because the board remains stationary on the table while the saw is pulled through the stock. Fig. 26-2. Another advantage is that the saw blade is on top of the work so that when dadoes, grooves, and stop cuts are made, the cut is always in sight.

Installing the Saw Blade

Remove the guard by removing the wing nut on top of the motor housing. Fig. 26-3. Raise the blade so it will clear the table top when it is removed.

To remove the arbor nut, hold the arbor with one wrench and turn the nut clockwise with a second wrench. Fig. 26-4. *Do not attempt to hold the blade with a block of wood while you loosen the nut.* If you do, the saw will climb onto the block and will thus be forced out of alignment.

Place the blade on the arbor. Make certain the teeth at the bottom are pointing away from you and toward the column. Replace the collar, recessed side against the blade. Replace and securely tighten the nut. Then replace the guard. Fig. 26-5.

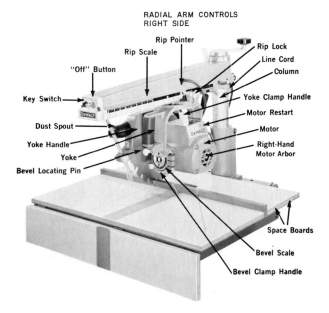

RADIAL ARM CONTROLS RIGHT SIDE

26-1a. Study the names of the parts and controls. You must know them to follow directions for making adjustments and cuts. See Fig. 26-1b.

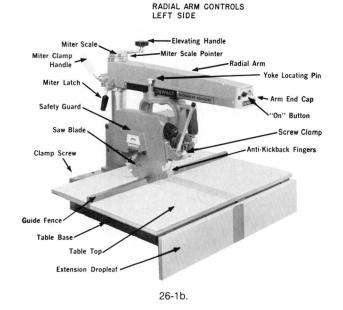

RADIAL ARM CONTROLS LEFT SIDE

26-1b.

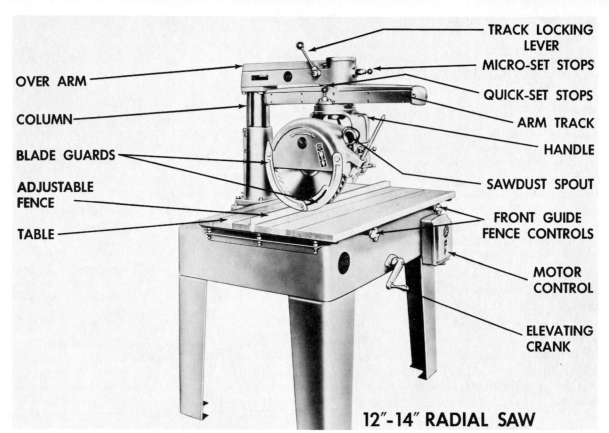

TRACK LOCKING LEVER

MICRO-SET STOPS

OVER ARM

QUICK-SET STOPS

COLUMN

ARM TRACK

HANDLE

BLADE GUARDS

ADJUSTABLE FENCE

SAWDUST SPOUT

TABLE

FRONT GUIDE FENCE CONTROLS

MOTOR CONTROL

ELEVATING CRANK

12″-14″ RADIAL SAW

26-1c. This machine has the double arm with the arm track pivoting from the upper arm directly over the work area. This places the saw cut nearer the center of the table on both the left and right hand miters.

26-2. Regardless of the furniture piece to be made or the complexity of the design, the first operation in the shop is to cut stock to rough length on the radial-arm saw.

26-3. The guard is held firmly on the motor housing by a wing nut.

26-4. The arbor is held in place with a hex wrench. On some machines the arbor is held by using an open-end wrench on a flat area between the blade and motor housing. Use the correct size wrench to turn the arbor nut.

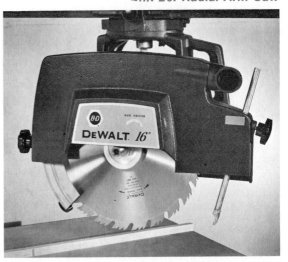

26-5. The teeth on the bottom of the saw blade point away from the operator and toward the column. Not all blades will have an arrow to show the direction of rotation.

Crosscutting

1. Mount a crosscutting or combination saw blade on the arbor.

26-6a. When cutting stock to length, place the workpiece against the fence and slowly pull the saw into the stock. (Note the guard printed over this caption. This means that a guard must be used for this operation.)

2. Adjust the radial arm to zero (at right angles to the guide fence) and set the motor so that the blade will be at right angles to the table top. Lock the radial arm with the miter clamp handle.

3. Turn the elevating handle down until the teeth are about $1/16''$ below the surface of the wood table. (The blade should follow the saw kerf already cut in the table.)

4. Adjust the anti-kickback fingers about $1/8''$ above the work surface.

5. With one hand hold the work on the table firmly against the guide fence. The layout line should be in line with the path of the saw.

6. Turn on the power and allow the saw to come to full speed. Grasp the motor yoke handle and pull the saw firmly but slowly through the work. Fig. 26-6.

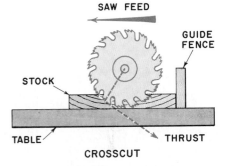

26-6b. In crosscutting, the saw's thrust is downward and to the rear, thus holding the stock firmly against the guide fence.

7. When the cut is completed, return the saw behind the guide fence. Then turn off the power.

Miter Cuts

Flat miter. For miter cuts, loosen the miter clamp handle and lift the miter latch. Swing the arm to the desired angle. Reclamp and make the cut as described

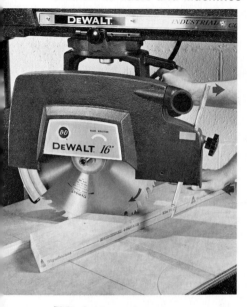

26-7. Cutting a flat miter. The work-piece is held firmly against the fence and the saw is pulled slowly into the stock as in crosscutting.

26-8. When cutting a flat miter on a piece of molding, it is necessary to make a right hand cut on one end, and a left hand cut on the other end. These cuts can be made on some radial-arm saws, such as the one shown here, without swinging the arm to a different side for each of the cuts.

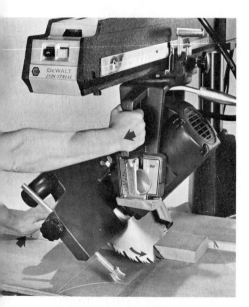

26-9. To make an edge miter (bevel), hold the workpiece with the left hand and pull the saw into the work with the right hand.

under crosscutting. Fig. 26-7. The flat miter can also be cut by clamping or nailing a piece of stock on the table top at the required angle. Fig. 26-8.

Edge miter (Bevel). To make an edge miter, loosen the bevel clamp handle and pull out the bevel locating pin. Tilt the motor to the desired angle and reclamp. The saw will have to be elevated so the blade will clear the table top when the motor is tilted. Proceed with the cut as described under cross-cutting. Fig. 26-9.

Compound miter (Double bevel). To cut the compound miter, the arm is set as described under flat miter cuts and the motor is tilted as for edge miters. The correct settings for the arm and motor can be determined by referring

to Fig. 26-10. The cut is then made as described under crosscutting. Fig. 26-11.

Ripping

1. Mount a combination or ripping blade. Pull the entire motor carriage to the front of the arm. Pull up on the locating pin above the yoke. Rotate the yoke 90 degrees *clockwise* until the blade is parallel to the guide fence. The motor should be "outboard" (that is, away from the column) so it will not obstruct the cutting. Fig. 26-12. When ripping wide panels it is necessary to rotate the yoke counterclockwise so the motor will be "inboard" (that is, toward the column). This will increase the ripping capacity. Fig. 26-13.

The figures in the table below are degrees to nearest quarter-degree, and are for direct setting of track-arm and blade tilt. Taper per inch given in second column applies only to front elevation and only to a 4-side figure.

Tilt of Work	Equivalent Taper per Inch	4-Side Butt		4-Side Miter		6-Side Miter		8-Side Miter	
		Blade Tilt	Track-Arm	Blade Tilt	Track-Arm	Blade Tilt	Track-Arm	Blade Tilt	Track-Arm
5°	.087	½	5°	44¾	5°	29¾	2½	22¼	2
10°	.176	1½	9¾	44¼	9¾	29½	5½	22	4
15°	.268	3¾	14½	43¼	14½	29	8¼	21½	6
20°	.364	6¼	18¾	41¾	18¾	28¼	11	21	8
25°	.466	10	23	40	23	27¼	13½	20¼	10
30°	.577	14½	26½	37¾	26½	26	16	19½	11¾
35°	.700	19½	29¾	35¼	29¾	24½	18¼	18¼	13¼
40°	.839	24½	32¾	32½	32¾	22¾	20¼	17	15
45°	1.000	30	35¼	30	35¼	21	22¼	15¾	16¼
50°	1.19	36	37½	27	37½	19	23¾	14¼	17½
55°	1.43	42	39¼	24	39¼	16¾	25¼	12½	18¾
60°	1.73	48	41	21	41	14½	26½	11	19¾

26-10. Table of compound angles for use on the radial-arm saw. Note that angles are given for both butt and miter joints. NOTE: The track-arm angle given in the chart is the number of degrees off 90°. A four-sided box with mitered corners and with the sides tilted 25° requires a track arm setting of 23° off of 90° (90° − 23° = 67°). The track arm is set at 67°.

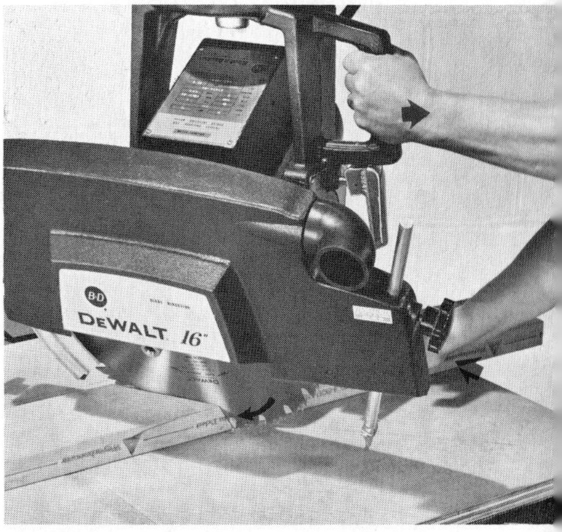

26-11. When making a compound miter cut, the arm or track and motor unit must be carefully set to the correct angles according to the chart in Fig. 26-10.

26-12. When ripping, adjust the "fingers" on the anti-kickback device to project about ⅛" below the surface of the workpiece. As the work is fed, the "fingers" will ride up on the surface of the work. Always use a push stick to feed the workpiece past the saw blade as the cut is finished.

26-13. The ripping capacity can be increased by rotating the saw counterclockwise and ripping with the blade "outboard" (away from the column).

26-14a and b. For your safety and the safety of others working around you, always set the guards properly for maximum protection.

2. Move the motor assembly along the radial arm until the correct width is shown on the rip scale. Tighten the *rip clamp* (on opposite side of radial arm from locating pin). Lower the saw until

26-14c. When ripping stock, always feed it into the rotation of the blade as shown here.

the blade just touches the wood table.

3. Adjust the guard so that the infeed end clears the work slightly (about $\frac{1}{8}''$). Adjust the anti-kickback device so that the points are $\frac{1}{8}''$ below the surface of the workpiece. Fig. 26-14a and b.

4. Turn on the power. Make sure the saw is rotating upwards toward you. Hold the work against the guide fence and feed it into the blade as shown in Fig. 26-14c. Never feed the work from the anti-kickback end. Use a push stick to complete the cut. Fig. 26-15.

Ripping Angles

The motor is positioned as described in ripping. Then the saw is elevated and the motor is tilted

in the yoke to any desired angle from the horizontal to the vertical position. Lower the saw until the teeth are $\frac{1}{16}''$ below the wood table. Make the cut as described under ripping. Several cuts of this type are shown in Fig. 26-16.

Using a Dado Head

The same types of dado heads which are used on the circular saw can be used on the radial-arm saw. Be sure the arbor hole is the correct size. Mount the dado head as described on page 291. Make certain the saw teeth next to the table top are pointed back toward the column, the same as when mounting a saw blade. Fig. 26-17. Replace the guard and rotate the dado head by hand to make sure it turns freely.

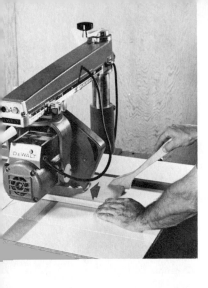

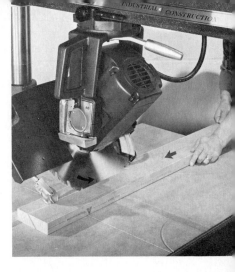

26-15. Use a push stick to complete the cut. Push the stock about 2″ beyond the saw, then pull the stick directly back.

26-16a. Ripping a bevel.

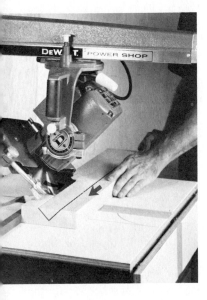

26-16b. A V-block can be made by making two bevel rip cuts to a set depth.

26-16c. A groove can be cut on the edge of a piece of stock by rotating the motor unit to a vertical position. Notice the use of the special guard.

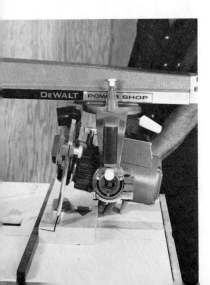

26-16d. A rabbeted edge can be made on an angle by making the first cut as shown in Fig. 26-16c and then setting the saw as shown here to complete the cut.

26-17. Mounting the dado head. Note how the chippers are placed an equal distance apart.

26-18. Cutting a plain dado.

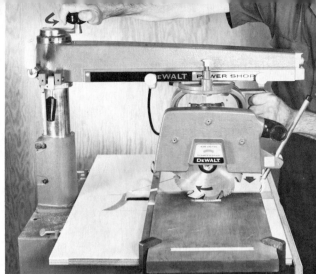

26-19. Cutting a blind dado. Notice the use of two stop clamps on the arm to limit the travel of the saw.

26-20. The shelves in this contemporary bookcase are set in blind dadoes so the joint will not show on front edges of the vertical members.

Plain dado. A dado is cut across the grain of the wood. Mount the correct combination of cutters for the desired width of cut. Take a piece of scrap stock of the same thickness as your finished stock, and lay it on the table top. Lower the blade until it just touches the surface of the scrap stock. Remove the scrap piece. On most radial-arm saws one revolution of the elevation crank lowers the blade $\frac{1}{8}$". If a $\frac{1}{4}$"-deep cut is desired, turn the elevating crank two complete turns; then proceed with the cut as you would for crosscutting. Fig. 26-18.

Blind dado. Place a clamp stop on the radial arm as this will limit the travel of the saw and insure that all dadoes will be the same length. Should you want the dado to be blind on both ends, raise the saw by turning the elevating handle. Clamp the stock in place. Locate the saw over the point where the cut is to begin. Turn on the machine. Lower the blade by

26-21. Making a groove with a dado head. This cut is sometimes called ploughing.

26-22. Cutting a groove with a dado head. Note the plywood placed over the table so the groove just clears the guide fence.

turning the elevating handle to the desired depth. Then pull the saw until the carriage hits the front clamp stop. Turn the power off, then raise the saw and push it back against the rear clamp. Figs. 26-19 and 26-20.

Grooves

Install the dado head as described on page 291 and rotate the motor unit counterclockwise as for ripping. Clamp the rip lock and set the depth of cut. Proceed as in ripping. Fig. 26-21. *Be sure that the direction of feed is as shown in Fig. 26-14c.*

To cut a groove on the edge of a piece of stock, loosen the yoke clamp handle, pull the yoke locating pin, turn the yoke 90 degrees *counterclockwise,* reset the yoke pin, and tighten the yoke clamp handle. Raise the radial arm about 2″ by turning the elevating handle. Then loosen the bevel clamp handle, pull the bevel locating pin, and pivot the motor to the vertical position. Lower the radial arm so the saw is the correct height off the table top. Place the yoke in the correct position and tighten the rip lock. Be sure the blade is properly guarded. Again, refer to Fig. 26-14c to see the direction of feed. Fig. 26-22.

Rabbet

Install the dado head, set up the saw, and make the cut the same as for cutting a groove. Fig. 26-23. The end rabbet can be made with a combination saw blade. Raise the radial arm about 2″, loosen the bevel clamp, pull the bevel pin, and turn the motor unit to the vertical position. Push the pin in, tighten the clamp, and lower the saw to the desired height. The material to be cut should be placed on a wooden auxiliary table, so

26-23. Cutting a rabbet.

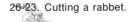

the guard will clear the table top. Figs. 26-24 and 26-25. The shoulder cut is made with the saw in the regular crosscutting position. Adjust the saw blade to the correct depth of cut. Fig. 26-26.

Tenons

The tenon is cut in the same manner as the end rabbet. To cut the tenon, an end rabbet is cut on each side of the stock. Fig. 26-27.

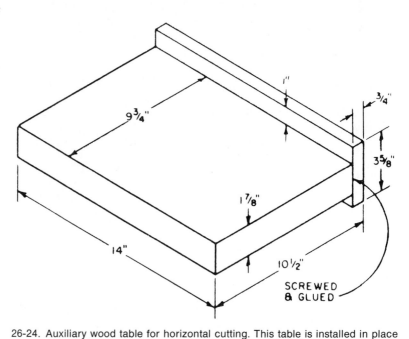

26-24. Auxiliary wood table for horizontal cutting. This table is installed in place of the standard guide fence. To do this, release the clamp screws, lift out the guide fence, slide in the auxiliary table, then retighten the clamp screws.

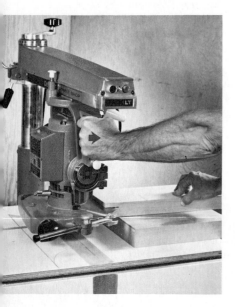

26-25. To make an end rabbet, place the stock flat against the auxiliary table and fence (Fig. 26-24) and then make the first cut with the saw in horizontal position.

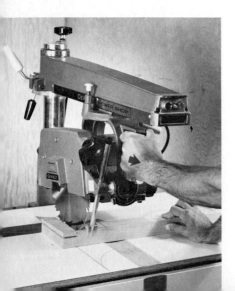

26-26. The second cut for an end rabbet is a simple crosscut with the blade set for correct depth.

26-27. Cutting a tenon. The shoulder cuts are made in the same way as shown for an end rabbet in Fig. 26-26.

JOINTER

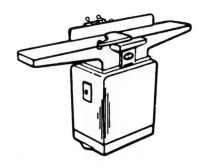

SAFETY

- *Always keep the knives of the jointer sharp.* Dull knives tend to cause kickback and also result in poor planing.
- *The fence should be tight.* Never adjust the fence while the jointer is running.
- Adjust the depth of cut before the jointer is turned on.
- *See that the guard is in place and operating easily.* If the regular guard is removed, a special guard must be provided.
- *Always allow the machine to come to full speed before using it.*
- Check the stock for knots, splits, metal particles, and other imperfections before jointing. Defective stock may break up or be thrown from the jointer.
- *Keep the left hand back from the front end of the board when feeding.*
- *Stand to the side of the jointer, never directly behind it.* In case of kickback you will be out of the way.
- *Cut with the grain, never against it.*
- *Always use a push stick or push block.*
- *Do not try to take too heavy a cut.*
- *Use common sense about when stock is too thin or too short to joint safely.*
- *Never apply pressure to the board with your hand directly over the cutterhead.*
- Use a brush to clean shavings off the table. Never use your hand.

27 Jointer

Although the jointer is not used for a great variety of operations, it is one of the most frequently used machines in a typical shop. Fig. 27-1. Common uses of the jointer are for surfacing a board and for planing an edge or an end. It can also be used for cutting a rabbet, bevel, chamfer, or taper.

The jointer has a circular cutterhead which usually has three or four blades (or knives). The blades rotate, shearing off small chips of wood, thus producing a smooth surface on the workpiece.

27-2. This 6″ jointer (left) and 8″ jointer (right) are popular sizes for edge jointing and specialty cuts. Note that the rear (outfeed) table is adjustable on both of these machines, making them even more versatile.

27-1. A jointer is an essential machine in furniture production. Many of the operations in getting out stock, squaring stock and cutting joints on this buffet were performed on the jointer.

Size

The size of a jointer is indicated by the length of the knives. In small shops most jointing operations are performed on the edge of stock. A 6″ or 8″ jointer is most commonly found in these situations. Fig. 27-2. However, if there is a planer in the shop and rough lumber is used, one face of each board will first have to be surfaced on the jointer. In this event a large jointer (12″ or 16″) is often used. Fig. 27-3.

The length of the bed also affects the usefulness of the jointer, since a longer bed provides better support for jointing longer pieces.

Parts

The *frame or base* of the jointer has two tables—the *front or infeed table* and the *rear or outfeed table*.

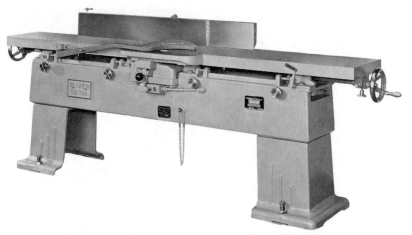

27-3. This 16″ heavy duty jointer is ideally suited for surfacing lumber for the thickness planer. This machine can also be used for edge jointing and other special cuts.

The fence provides support for the work while it is fed, on edge or on end, through the machine. The fence can be adjusted to various angles, usually up to 45 degrees both ways from the vertical position.

The guard is a protective device covering the cutterhead. It either swings out of the way or lifts up. Most operations, except rabbeting on some jointers, and certain tapering, should be done with the guard in place.

The jointer usually operates at about 4000 rpm.

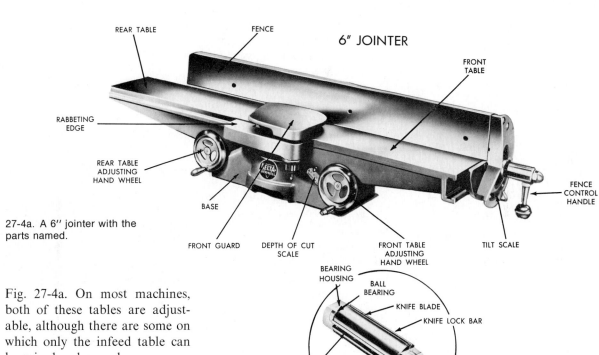

27-4a. A 6″ jointer with the parts named.

27-4b. A 6″ jointer head with the parts named.

Fig. 27-4a. On most machines, both of these tables are adjustable, although there are some on which only the infeed table can be raised or lowered.

The *cutterhead* is the heart of the jointer. As mentioned, it consists of the head itself and three or more knives. This assembly usually operates on two roller bearings. Fig. 27-4b.

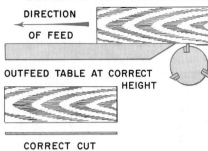

DIRECTION OF FEED

OUTFEED TABLE AT CORRECT HEIGHT

CORRECT CUT

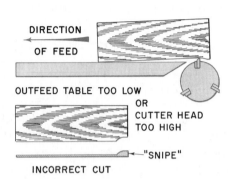

DIRECTION OF FEED

OUTFEED TABLE TOO LOW
OR
CUTTER HEAD TOO HIGH

"SNIPE"

INCORRECT CUT

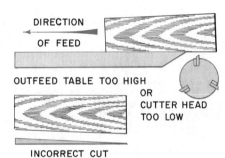

DIRECTION OF FEED

OUTFEED TABLE TOO HIGH
OR
CUTTER HEAD TOO LOW

INCORRECT CUT

27-5. The jointer must be adjusted so the outfeed table is at exactly the same height as the cutterhead knife at its highest point. Otherwise a taper or a recess will be cut. (A recess is sometimes called a "snipe.")

Adjustments

Aligning and Adjusting the Outfeed Table

The top of the outfeed table must be at exactly the same height as the knife blades at their highest point of revolution. If the table is too low, the board will drop down onto the knives as it leaves the infeed table. This will cause a recess to be cut at the end of the board. If the table is too high, the board will be slightly tapered. Fig. 27-5 shows correct and incorrect cuts.

To align the knives with the table as just mentioned, turn the cutterhead until one blade is at its highest point. Release the table locking screw on the side of the jointer. Lower the outfeed table until it is below the blade; then place a straightedge on the outfeed table with one end projecting over the blade. Fig. 27-6. Turn the table up slowly until it is in line with the knife at the highest point. Turn the cutterhead over slowly by hand until there is very light contact between the knives and the bottom of the straightedge. Tighten the lock nut. Once the outfeed table is set, it does not require changing except for certain cuts such as stop chamfers and bevels, and recess cuts. If the outfeed table is the fixed kind, raise or lower the cutterhead until the knives are even with the outfeed table.

Adjusting the Infeed Table

The distance the infeed table is below the knives determines the depth of cut. The depth of cut to be taken will depend on:
• The width of the surface being jointed.
• The kind of wood and grain pattern.
• Whether you are making a rough or finish cut.

Loosen the lock on the side of the infeed table, then turn the

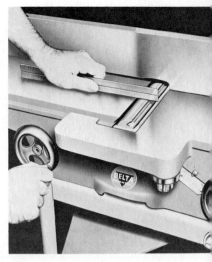

27-6. Adjusting the outfeed table. Raise the table slowly until the straightedge rests evenly on the table and the knife. Always replace the guard after making this adjustment.

27-7. Always check the depth of cut before making a cut on the jointer.

handle beneath the table to raise or lower it. There is a pointer and scale, indicating the depth of cut, which must be checked periodically for accuracy. Fig. 27-7.

Use to make to make

27-8. Use a try square to make sure the fence is set at right angles to the table.

Adjusting the Position of the Fence

For most operations it is desirable to have the fence at an exact right angle to the table. To adjust the fence, loosen the knob or lever that holds it in position; then set the fence at a 90-degree angle to the table. To check that the angle is correct, hold a square against the table and fence. Fig. 27-8. The fence can be moved in or out. When cutting, never expose any more of the blade than necessary.

The fence can also be *tilted* 45 degrees to right or left. This can be set on the tilt scale and checked with a protractor head of a combination square set or a sliding T bevel. There is a pointer and scale to indicate the tilt. Fig. 27-9.

Basic Procedures

1. Check the fence for squareness and the infeed table for depth of cut before turning on the machine. If the jointer has been used for some other operation, make a trial cut after resetting it.

2. Adjust the *depth of cut* with these things in mind:
● The amount of stock to be removed. Take a light cut for such operations as face planing or end planing and a slightly heavier cut for edge planing.
● The kind of wood. A light or heavy cut may be made on soft woods; a light cut is best on hard woods.
● The kind of planed surface. Take a heavier cut for removing stock and a lighter cut for finishing.

3. Change the position of the fence periodically to distribute the wear on the jointer knives.

4. When duplicate parts are needed, do the jointing operations first; then cut the stock into the desired smaller pieces.

5. If you are righthanded, stand to the left of the jointer with your left foot forward and right foot back and beneath the infeed table. Move your body along as you do the planing operation.

6. Always check a board for warp and wind first. Fig. 27-10. Place a concave surface down for the first cuts. If the board has twist, balance it on the high corners to take the first cuts.

Planing a Surface

1. Check the board for warp and for direction of grain. Be certain the jointer is correctly adjusted.

2. Hold the board firmly on the infeed table with your left hand toward the front of the board and your right hand on the push block.

27-9. Loosen the fence control handle to adjust for the angle of cut. The fence can also be moved in and out to distribute the wear on the knives, especially for edge jointing.

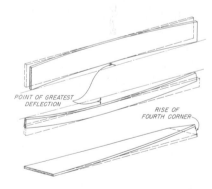

27-10. Common kinds of warp that can be removed on the jointer.

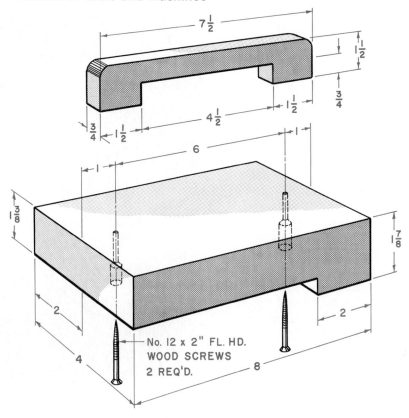

27-11a. A drawing of a one-handed push block.

27-11b. Using the one-handed push block.

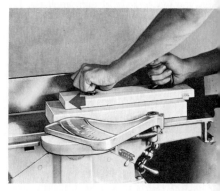

27-11c. Using a push block to do facing on short stock. Note the use of the push block or hold-down. The knob is held in the left hand and the handle in the right.

27-12. Face planing or surfacing on an 8″ jointer. Note how the left hand is kept back from the front edge of the board.

Fig. 27-11a. The push block is hooked on the end of the board over the infeed table. Fig. 27-11b. Apply equal pressure with both hands. Figs. 27-11c and d.

3. Turn on the machine and allow it to come to full speed.

4. Move the stock forward, keeping your left hand back of the cutterhead. When about half to two-thirds of the board has passed the cutterhead, move the left hand to the board over the outfeed table. Fig. 27-12.

5. After most of the board has passed over the cutter, move the right hand to the portion of the

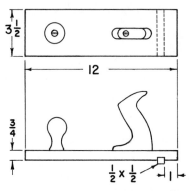

27-11d. Drawing of a push block. This one has a knob and handle from a hand plane.

START THE CUT

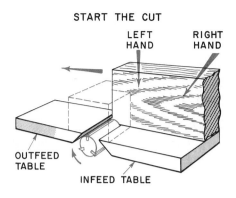

LEFT HAND   RIGHT HAND

OUTFEED TABLE

INFEED TABLE

CONTINUE THE CUT

LEFT HAND   RIGHT HAND

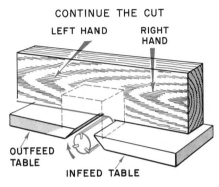

OUTFEED TABLE

INFEED TABLE

27-14a. Jointing the edge of a board.

FINISH THE CUT

LEFT HAND   RIGHT HAND

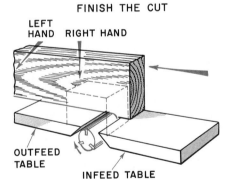

OUTFEED TABLE

INFEED TABLE

27-13. Correct method of feeding when the hands are moved as stock passes across the cutterhead. The danger area is shown in color.

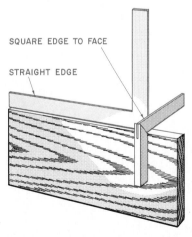

SQUARE EDGE TO FACE

STRAIGHT EDGE

27-14b. A properly jointed edge is straight along its entire length and forms a 90-degree angle with the working face.

board over the outfeed table to finish the cut. *Never place your hand directly over the cutterhead.* Fig. 27-13.

Planing an Edge

The most common use for the jointer is planing or jointing an edge. Fig. 27-14a. An edge is said to be jointed when it is at right angles to the face of the board and is true along its entire length. Fig. 27-14b.

1. Check the fence for squareness. Generally, for safest operation, it is best to set the fence as close as possible to the left side of the machine.

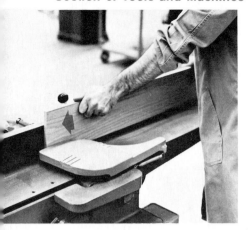

27-15. Three steps in jointing an edge or surface.

2. Select the best edge and determine the grain direction.

3. Adjust for proper depth of cut. To insure parallel edges on the stock, rip to width and allow just enough extra stock to joint off the sawn edges.

4. Hold the stock firmly against the infeed table and the fence. The jointed or planed surface of the board should be against the fence.

5. For the righthanded person, the left hand is a guide and the right hand pushes the stock across the cutterhead. Move the left hand along with the board until the major portion of the board is over the outfeed table; then move the right hand to the other side of the cutterhead, to the stock over the outfeed table. Fig. 27-15. Do not push the board too fast, as this will make a rippled edge.

Planing End Grain

This operation is very dangerous, especially with stock less than 10″ wide. This is because the cutters must shave off the ends of the wood fibers, which are tough. *Always set the machine for a very light cut for this operation.*

If both edges of the board are surfaced, proceed as follows:

1. Take a light cut about 1″ in length along the end grain.

2. Reverse the board and finish the cut.

Make sure you hold the board firmly over the outfeed table as the end of the cut is made. Fig. 27-16. As in hand planing, running the board completely across would split out the edge.

If only one edge of the board is surfaced, the jointing can be

done from the finished edge all the way across, since a splinter can be removed when the rough edge is jointed later. Fig. 27-17.

Cutting a Bevel or Chamfer

1. Adjust the fence to the correct angle. Since the fence can be tilted to the right or left, the cut can be made with the fence tilted either way. Fig. 27-18.

2. Check the fence with a protractor or sliding T bevel.

3. Proceed with the cutting as for edge planing. Examine the cut after each pass to see how much more must be removed. When chamfering or beveling the ends and edges of a board, do the ends first and then the edges. The splinter which occurs when jointing the ends will be removed as the edges are jointed.

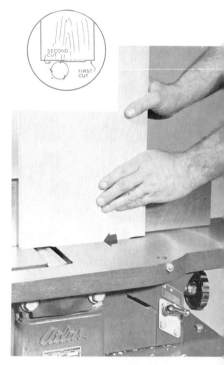

27-16. Planing end grain.

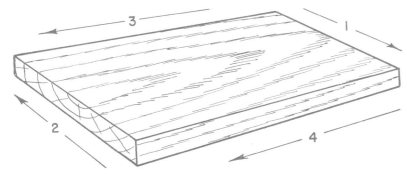

27-17. Steps in jointing the edges and ends of a board.

27-18a. Cutting a chamfer or bevel with the fence tilted in.

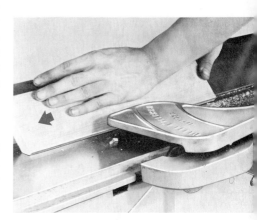

27-18b. Cutting a bevel or chamfer with the fence tilted out.

Cutting a Stop Chamfer

A stop chamfer can be cut only on jointers on which the outfeed table can be lowered.

1. Lower both tables an amount equal to the depth of the chamfer. To make this adjustment, first lower the infeed table to the proper depth. Next, place a straightedge on the rabbeting ledge and extend it over to the edge of the outfeed table. Then lower the outfeed table until it is even with the extended straightedge.

2. With the power turned off, hold the stock with the end of the chamfer over the cutter, and clamp a stop block over the outfeed table. Next hold the stock with the beginning of the chamfer over the cutter and clamp a stop block over the infeed table at the other end of the board.

3. Adjust the fence to the desired angle of cut. Turn the cutter over by hand to make sure that it turns freely and does not strike any part of the machine.

4. Turn on the machine. Hold the end of the stock against the stop block on the infeed table with the *left* hand, and slowly lower it into the cutter with the *right* hand. In this position you will be standing off to the side of the jointer. Push the board along until it strikes the stop block over the outfeed table. Then carefully raise the board.

Cutting a Recess

With the fence set at right angles, follow the same general procedures as for cutting a stop chamfer. Fig. 27-19.

Cutting a Long Taper

1. If the taper to be cut is shorter than the length of the infeed table, lower the infeed table an amount equal to the amount of taper. Make a mark completely around the first piece, to show where the taper will begin. Move the fence as close to the left side of the jointer as possible. Remove the guard and clamp a scrap block

27-19. Cutting a recess in a board.

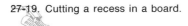

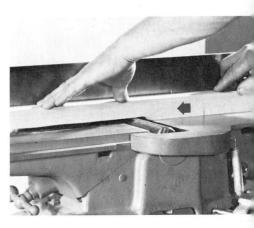

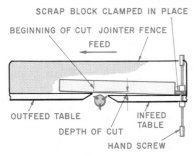

SCRAP BLOCK CLAMPED IN PLACE
BEGINNING OF CUT JOINTER FENCE
FEED
OUTFEED TABLE
INFEED TABLE
DEPTH OF CUT
HAND SCREW

27-20. Setting up the jointer to cut a taper. Note the beginning of the cut is in line with the lip of the outfeed table.

on the fence or the table to serve as a stop as shown in Fig. 27-20.

2. Turn on the machine. Place the portion of the piece that is to be untapered on the outfeed table; then lower the board, with the starting line directly over the lip of the outfeed table. Fig. 27-20. Push the board along to complete the tapered cut. *A push stick should be used.*

3. If the piece to be tapered is longer than the infeed table, di-

vide the tapered section into two or more parts. For example, if the tapered portion is 36", divide it into 18" sections. Fig. 27-21. If the amount of taper is $\frac{3}{8}$", adjust the machine to a $\frac{3}{16}$" cut. Make the first cut from the halfway point and then make a second cut starting at the beginning of the taper. Fig. 27-22.

Cutting a Short Taper

A short, sharp taper should be cut in a slightly different manner.

1. Lay out the location of the taper around the stock. Lower the infeed table to a depth equal to the amount of the taper. Remove the guard and fasten a stop block to the infeed table so that the lip of the outfeed table lines up with the beginning of the cut.

2. Turn on the machine and stand facing the outfeed table, just opposite from the way you would normally stand.

3. Hold the end of the stock against the stop block. Lower the stock, then draw it toward you to cut the taper. Sometimes it is a good idea to slip a block of wood under the stock on the outfeed table to help to support it as the taper is cut. Fig. 27-23.

Cutting a Rabbet

One of the best ways to cut a rabbet with the grain is on the jointer.

1. Adjust the fence so that the distance between the end of the knives and the fence is equal to the width of the rabbet.

2. Lower the infeed table an amount equal to the depth of the rabbet. If the rabbet is quite deep, it may be necessary to cut it in

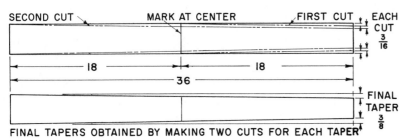

SECOND CUT — MARK AT CENTER — FIRST CUT — EACH CUT $\frac{3}{16}$

18 — 18
36

FINAL TAPER $\frac{3}{8}$

FINAL TAPERS OBTAINED BY MAKING TWO CUTS FOR EACH TAPER

27-21a. When the stock is longer than the infeed table, divide the taper into two or more equal sections.

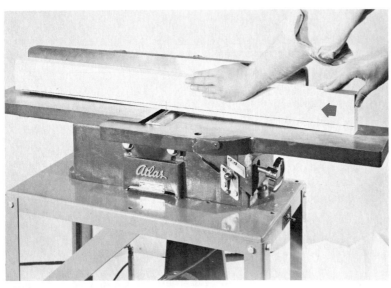

27-21b. Making the first cut on a long taper.

27-22. Tapered legs are found on many pieces of furniture.

two passes. In that event the table is lowered an amount equal to about half the depth of the rabbet for the first pass, then lowered again to the desired depth to complete the cut.

3. Remove the guard, if necessary. Hold the stock firmly on the infeed table and move it along slowly. Fig. 27-24.

Many types of simple moldings can be rabbeted in this way.

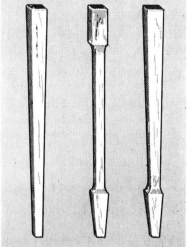

27-23b. Examples of tapered furniture legs.

27-23a. Cutting a short taper.

27-24. Cutting a rabbet. On some machines it is not necessary to remove the guard, as must be done here.

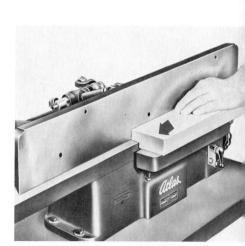

27-25. Making the cheek cut on a tenon.

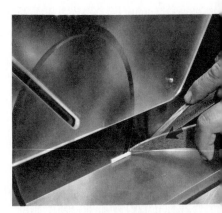

27-26. Rotary jointer-surfacer.

Cutting a Tenon

Lay out the tenon and make the shoulder cut on the circular saw. (See Unit 29.) Then follow these steps:

1. Adjust the fence to equal the length of the tenon.

2. Lower the infeed table to equal the amount of stock to be removed from each side of the tenon.

3. Hold the end of the tenon firmly against the fence and move the stock past the cutter. Fig. 27-25. A wide piece of scrap stock placed behind the workpiece and used as a miter gage will help to hold the workpiece at right angles to the fence. It will also serve as a back-up board to prevent the end grain from tearing out.

Rotary Jointer-Surfacer

This machine, which is sold under the trade name *Uniplane,* will perform many operations not easily done on the conventional jointer. It will safely and accurately plane, joint, bevel, chamfer, trim, and taper. Fig. 27-26.

Capacity. This machine can surface stock up to 6″ wide and can plane pieces as small as $\frac{1}{8}$″ square. Fig. 27-27.

Cutterhead. The cutterhead contains eight cutters. Mounted alternately are four scoring cutters and four shearing cutters. The cutterhead operates at 4000 rpm. Fig. 27-28.

Depth-of-cut adjustment. The depth-of-cut control is located on the front of the machine and is calibrated in 64ths of an inch, with even finer settings possible to five thousandths of an inch. Fig. 27-29.

Table adjustments. By loosening

27-27a. Stock up to 6″ wide can be surfaced on a rotary jointer-surfacer.

27-27b. The rotary jointer-surfacer safely trims pieces that could not be planed on a jointer.

the two table-locking handles, one in the front and one in the rear, the table can be positioned at 90 degrees to the cutterhead or at any angle up to 45 degrees. Fig. 27-30. The table has a slot in which a miter gage can be used to support the stock for trimming narrow pieces, or for cutting miters or compound angles. Fig. 27-31.

With a rotary jointer-surfacer you can work on much smaller pieces of stock than with a jointer. This machine will also do a good job on end grain. Keep in mind, however, that the safety precautions used for the conventional jointer must be employed. Fig. 27-32.

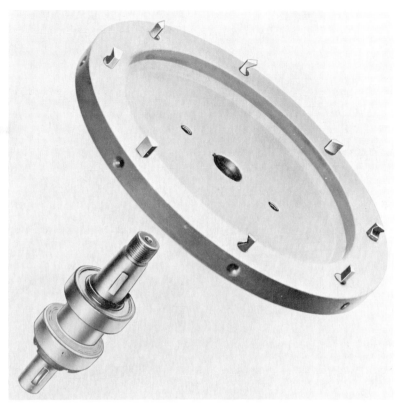

27-28. The rotary jointer-surfacer has a balanced cast-iron cutterhead.

27-31. Trimming a compound miter.

27-29. The depth of cut control is calibrated in 64ths of an inch.

27-30. The table of a rotary jointer-surfacer is fully adjustable and has positive stops at 0 and 45 degrees.

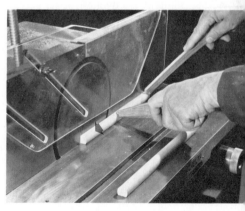

27-32. Cutting a flat side on round stock. Note the use of the push sticks to keep the operator's fingers a safe distance from the cutters.

PLANER

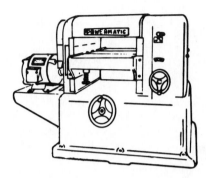

SAFETY

- Keep your fingers away from the underside of the board as it is fed through the planer. Keep your hands away from the top of the board near the infeed roller.
- Never stand directly behind the board when planing.
- Don't look into the planer when the machine is in operation.
- Plane only one thickness at a time if the planer has a solid infeed roll and chip breaker.
- Never plane boards until one surface has been trued on the jointer.
- Make sure the board is longer than the distance between the centers of the infeed and outfeed rolls.
- Scrape all glue off the stock before running it through the surfacer.
- Make all adjustments with the power off and the cutterhead standing still.
- Do not remove shavings while the cutterhead is revolving.
- Do not force stock into the surfacer.
- Do not take too deep a cut.
- Check all stock for knots, splits, metal particles, and other imperfections before surfacing.
- Always use the exhaust system.
- Hold a board flat on the infeed table; do not tip it up to start the cut.
- Never lower the table when a piece of stock will not feed through. Turn off power; then, after the cutterhead is stopped completely, make the necessary corrections.
- Always surface wood with the grain; never run a piece cross grain.

The *thickness planer,* or *surfacer* as it is sometimes called, is a single-purpose machine that produces true, smooth, parallel surfaces on a board. The planer will not correct warp. One face of a warped piece must be surfaced on the jointer before the board is passed through the planer. Fig. 28-1.

Planers are made with either single or double surfacing knives. Most medium and small planers have single surfacing knives, which means that they can surface only one side of a board at a time. A planer is often used for surfacing lumber that has been purchased rough as well as for reducing the thickness of lumber that is to be used on small products. This is necessary to keep the lumber thickness in proportion to the size of the product. Fig. 28-2.

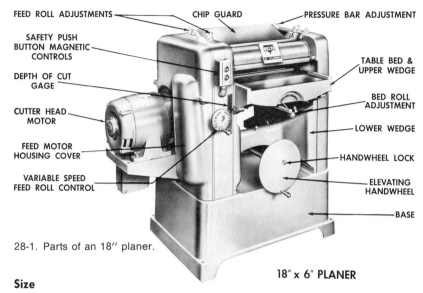

FEED ROLL ADJUSTMENTS — CHIP GUARD — PRESSURE BAR ADJUSTMENT

SAFETY PUSH BUTTON MAGNETIC CONTROLS

DEPTH OF CUT GAGE

CUTTER HEAD MOTOR

FEED MOTOR HOUSING COVER

VARIABLE SPEED FEED ROLL CONTROL

TABLE BED & UPPER WEDGE

BED ROLL ADJUSTMENT

LOWER WEDGE

HANDWHEEL LOCK

ELEVATING HANDWHEEL

BASE

28-1. Parts of an 18″ planer.

18″ x 6″ PLANER

Size

The size of a planer is indicated by the width and thickness of stock it can handle. Common sizes are 13″ x 5″, 20″ x 8″, 24″ x 8″, and 30″ x 8″. Figs. 28-3, 4, 5, and 6. See the next page.

28-3. This planer has a 13″ x 5″ capacity, belt drive, and a screw-type bed for adjusting the table height.

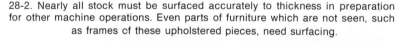

28-2. Nearly all stock must be surfaced accurately to thickness in preparation for other machine operations. Even parts of furniture which are not seen, such as frames of these upholstered pieces, need surfacing.

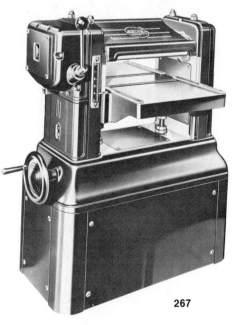

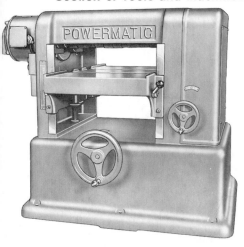

28-4. This is a 20″ x 8″ planer with a variable feed rate.

28-6. This is a 30″ x 8″ planer with a screw type bed adjustment that is power operated. Fine table adjustments are made manually with the handwheel located on the front of the machine.

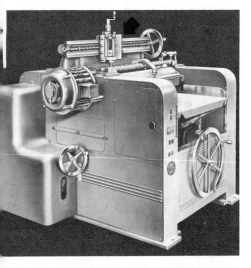

28-5. This is a 24″ x 8″ planer with a variable feed rate and wedge adjusted bed. Note that this planer is also equipped with a carrier for a grinder (arrow).

28-7. Cross-section of a planer showing the parts and their relationships to each other. The two lower rolls are called *table rolls.*

Parts

The main parts are a bed or table, a feed mechanism, a cutter-head, a chipbreaker and a pressure bar. Fig. 28-7. The table moves up and down on two screws or by sliding on a wedge-shaped casting. Figs. 28-8 and 9.

Notice on Fig. 28-7 that there are two table rolls set about $\frac{1}{32}$″ to $\frac{1}{16}$″ above the level of the table. The shafts on which these rolls turn are mounted on springs; as the stock passes over the rolls they are compressed to table level. The infeed roll, directly above one of the table rolls, moves the work into the machine. It is usually corrugated to give a better grip.

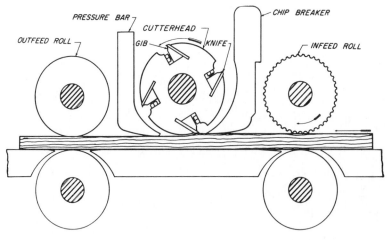

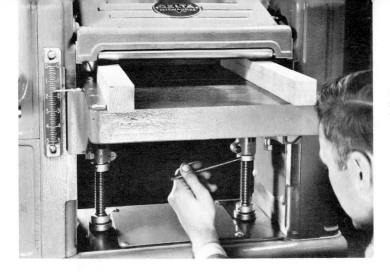

28-8. To compensate for uneven wear, these screws can be adjusted separately to enable the leveling of the table parallel to the cutterhead.

On most machines the corrugated infeed roll is made in sections which are individually spring loaded. Fig. 28-10. This is necessary for a more positive (non-slip) feeding of various thicknesses of lumber, especially on the first cut after surfacing on the jointer. Fig. 28-11.

Located between the cutterhead and the corrugated infeed roll is the chipbreaker, which is also usually made in sections. Fig. 28-12. The chipbreaker presses the stock firmly down on the table and breaks the chips off short, preventing "tear out" below the surface being cut.

28-9. The wedge bed gives greater work support than the screw type bed, and seldom needs adjustment.

28-10. Upper sectional infeed roll. This roll permits you to feed several pieces of stock with slightly different thicknesses at the same time without danger of kickback.

SPRING

OUTER CORRUGATED SECTION
INNER SPIDER SECTION

ROLL SHAFT

LOCKING COLLAR

DIRECTION OF ROTATION

DIVIDING DISK

SECTIONAL ROLL

Section 5: Tools and Machines

The cutterhead is similar to that of a jointer and usually has three or four knives. It revolves in a direction opposite the infeed roll, so the lumber is fed against the rotation of the cutterhead.

Between the cutterhead and the upper outfeed roll is a bar which exerts pressure on the finished surface, holding the board firmly against the table. Fig. 28-13. The top outfeed roll, and the table roll just below it, move the board through the planer.

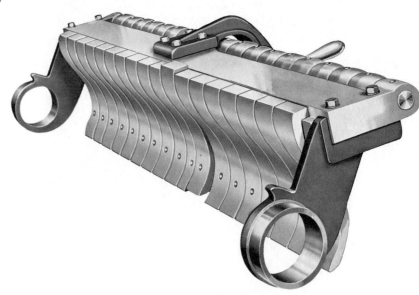

28-12. The sectional chip breaker holds the stock firmly on the bed across its entire width.

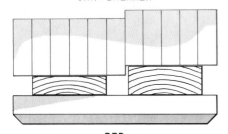

SECTIONAL
CHIP BREAKER

BED

SOLID
CHIP BREAKER

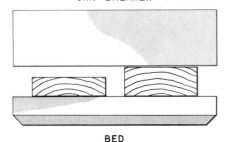

BED

28-11. Note the advantage of a sectional chip breaker when surfacing two or more pieces of slightly different thicknesses. A solid chip breaker puts no pressure on the thinner stock, allowing the cutterhead to tear the grain. A sectional upper infeed roll, Fig. 28-10, has the same advantage with stock of irregular thickness—for instance, when the working face has been surfaced on a jointer.

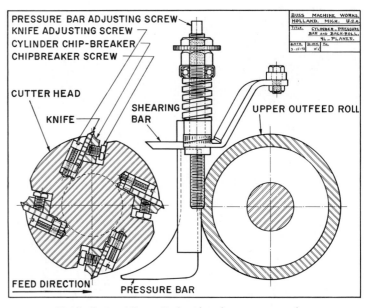

28-13. Parts of the cutterhead and rear pressure bar.

28-14. This push button controls both the separate feed drive and cutterhead motor.

Controls

There are only four or five simple controls on most planers:

• A switch to turn on the machine. Fig. 28-14.

• A hand wheel which elevates or lowers the table. Fig. 28-15.

• A pointer on the table, indicating thickness on a scale attached to the base.

• A feed-control lever which engages or disengages the feed mechanism. Fig. 28-16. On some planers there is a control that regulates the rate of feed from slow to fast. Fig. 28-17. The slower feed gives a smoother cut surface. On all power-driven machines, the switch causes the cutterhead to revolve, but not the feed rolls. The

28-16. The clutch control will permit the operator to stop the feed mechanism without turning off the machine.

feed rolls start when the feed-control lever is engaged.

Operations

1. Surface one side of the board on a jointer.

2. Measure the thickness of the board at its thickest point and adjust the machine for the desired cut.

3. Place the jointed surface against the table and feed the board with the grain. Stand to one side of the machine.

4. Turn the machine on and engage the feed mechanism. Then push the board into the planer. Fig. 28-18. If it should get started at a slight angle, a quick shove will straighten it. If the board sticks as it is part way through the planer, turn off the power first, wait until the cutterhead *stops,* and then release the pressure with the elevating hand wheel.

5. When the major portion of the board has passed through the machine, walk around to the back and support it as it comes through. On long stock it's a good idea to have a helper on the other side to support the board as it comes from the machine.

Always try to plan your cuts so that an equal amount of wood is removed from each side of the board. This will help to keep the moisture content of the lumber the same on both surfaces, equalize the strain, and reduce the chance of warpage.

28-18. This is the correct way to feed stock into the planer. Don't place your fingers under the board. The feed rolls will press the board down onto the bed, pinching your hand and possibly pulling it into the machine.

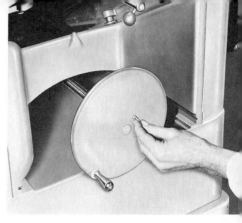

28-15. To adjust for depth of cut, loosen the handwheel lock and turn the elevating handwheel up or down. The finish thickness will register on the depth-of-cut gage.

28-17. The variable feed control lets you change the rate at which the stock is fed past the cutterhead. Slower speeds produce a smoother cut.

If several pieces are to be surfaced, finish only one side of all pieces and then the other side.

If the board being surfaced is made of glued-up sections, always scrape the glue from the joints first. The glue will dull or even nick the knife blades and adhere to the outfeed rolls, causing irregularities in the finished surface of the board. The same problems will arise if wood with too much pitch is surfaced or if old lumber with a finish on it is resurfaced. If this mistake is made, stop the machine and clean the rolls. (Use the solvent recommended by the manufacturer of the planer.)

Squaring Legs on the Surfacer

Another operation that can be performed on the planer is that of squaring stock to be used for legs, especially for Contemporary and Colonial furniture. Fig. 28-19. Colonial furniture legs are usually partially turned on the lathe, leaving equal flat areas on all sides. This requires a perfectly squared leg before turning.

Begin the squaring operation by cutting the stock to rough size; joint one face and then one edge 90 degrees to the jointed face.

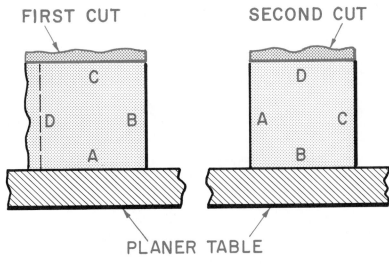

28-20. Squaring stock on the planer.

28-19a. A colonial style chair. These legs must be very accurately squared and centered in the lathe to produce uniform flat areas.

(This face and edge are shown as sides A and B, Fig. 28-20.) Mark these surfaces for identification. Place the stock with jointed surface on the planer table and the jointed edge to the right. Set the planer for the necessary cut. Fig. 28-20, side C. Make the cut. When the stock is retrieved from the outfeed table of the planer, special care should be taken not to alter the position of the pieces. Place the stock on the infeed table in the same position as for the first cut, then turn each piece one-quarter turn clockwise. Don't change the thickness setting. Feed the stock through the planer for the second cut. Fig. 28-20, side D. Measure the stock and, if necessary, repeat the two cuts on sides A and B. It may also be necessary to make additional cuts on sides C and D, continuing until the stock is the correct size. Remember, try to plan your cuts so an equal amount of material is removed from all sides.

28-19b. A contemporary table. These legs are easily made on the planer after two adjacent sides are accurately jointed to 90 degrees.

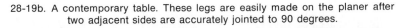

272

CIRCULAR SAW

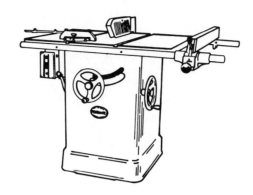

SAFETY

- Make all adjustments when the power is off and the blade has stopped revolving.
- Always adjust the saw blade so it protrudes just enough above the stock to cut completely through.
- Never reach over a revolving saw; instead, bring the cut piece back around the side of the machine.
- Keep your fingers away from the saw blade at all times.
- Always keep the guard and splitter in place unless this is impossible for the kind of cut you are making.
- If the cut you are making doesn't permit use of the regular guard, use a feather board or a special guard.
- When crosscutting with the miter gage, never use the fence for a stop unless a clearance block is used.
- Always push the stock through with a push stick when ripping stock that cannot be fed safely by hand.
- Never stand directly behind the blade.
- Always use a sharp blade.
- When ripping, place the jointed edge against the fence.
- Keep the saw table clean. Remove all scraps with a brush or push stick, *never with your fingers*.
- Remove rings, watches and other items that might catch in the saw. Wear garments with short or tight sleeves.
- Use the proper saw blade for the operation being performed.
- Always hold the stock firmly against the miter gage when crosscutting and against the ripping fence when ripping.
- Be certain the fence is clamped securely.
- When a helper assists you, he should not *pull* the stock. He only *supports* the stock.
- Do not saw warped material on the circular saw.
- If stock must be lowered onto the revolving blade for certain cuts, use stops and guards. Never have your hands in line with the blade.

29 Circular Saw and Portable Power Saw

Many fundamental woodworking operations can be done with the circular saw. It can be used not only for cutting stock to size but also for cutting many joints. Fig. 29-1.

Size

The size of the circular saw is indicated by the diameter of blade recommended for its use. Typical sizes are the 8″ or 10″. These saws are made in either bench or floor type. The large saws frequently have two arbors on which two different blades can be mounted. As one blade is turned into position, the other is below the table, not running. This is called a *uni-versal-type saw*. Fig. 29-2. Most saws, however, have a single arbor and are called *variety saws*. On most models the blade tilts to the right while on some it tilts to the left. The table remains permanently fastened in the horizontal position. Fig. 29-3.

Blades

There are six basic kinds of saw blades. In selecting a blade, make sure that you secure one with the correct diameter arbor hole size. Never attempt to install a blade that has too large a hole.

The six common kinds of blades are:

● The *cutoff* or *crosscut* blade.

29-1b. The circular saw is essential to any well-equipped woodworking shop. The operator should always closely follow the recommended safety procedures in its use.

This has teeth similar to the hand crosscut saw and is used primarily for trimming stock to length and squaring. Fig. 29-4a.

● The *hollow-ground* (or *planer*) blade. This is used for fine cabinetwork. Fig. 29-4b. The teeth of this blade are not set (bent). The necessary side clearance is ground in the body of the blade as the cross section drawing shows. (Most saws have some teeth that are bent to the right and others to the left. The teeth are bent this way to make the kerf, or saw cut, slightly wider than the blade. This provides clearance so the blade will not stick in the kerf.)

● The *ripsaw* blade. This has chisel-like teeth and is used for ripping operations. Fig. 29-4c.

● The *combination saw* blade.

29-1a. In the manufacture of furniture, large numbers of operations are done on the circular saw. Even on furniture as ornate as the pieces pictured here there are many circular saw operations. How many could you list?

29-2. A universal tilting-arbor circular saw. Notice that the left half of the table rolls, so it will carry the workpiece when crosscutting.

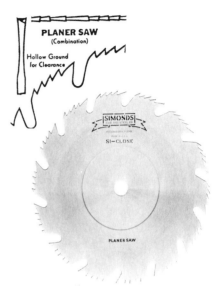

29-4b. Hollow-ground or planer blade. It should be used only where a smooth finish cut is needed.

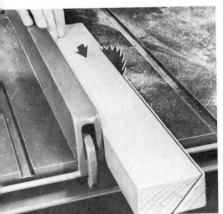

29-3a. Cutting a bevel on a circular saw with a blade that tilts to the left.

29-3b. Cutting a chamfer with a blade that tilts to the right.

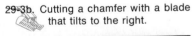

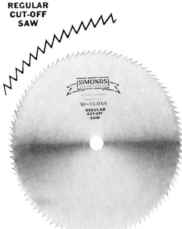

29-4a. Cutoff or crosscut blade. This blade is designed for cutting only across the grain of the lumber.

29-4c. Rip blade. This blade is designed for sawing only with the grain of the lumber.

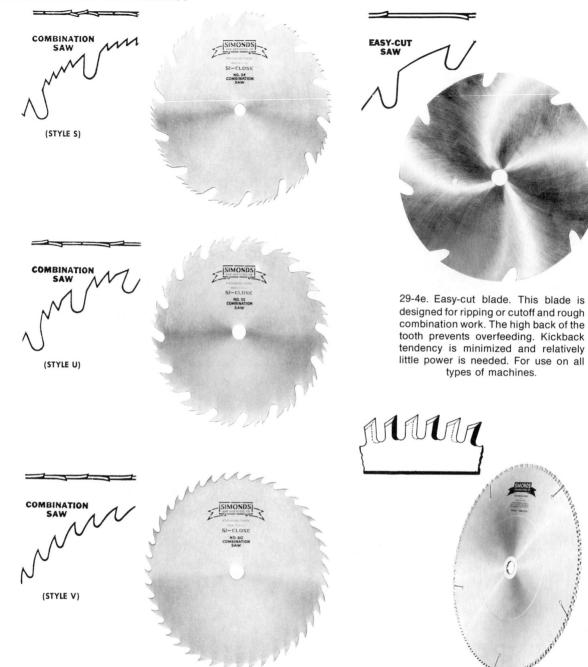

COMBINATION SAW

(STYLE S)

COMBINATION SAW

(STYLE U)

COMBINATION SAW

(STYLE V)

EASY-CUT SAW

29-4e. Easy-cut blade. This blade is designed for ripping or cutoff and rough combination work. The high back of the tooth prevents overfeeding. Kickback tendency is minimized and relatively little power is needed. For use on all types of machines.

29-4d. Combination blades. These blades are designed to be used for either ripping or crosscutting, and are convenient when it is impractical to change blades frequently. Style S teeth are recommended for bench saws which require a fine cut. Style U teeth are recommended for radial-arm saws. Style V teeth are the fastest cutting of the various combination saws and are recommended for use on all types of machines.

29-4f. Plywood blade. This blade is designed for cutting across the grain and can be used for either hard or soft woods, or plywood. When used for plywoods the finer tooth saws are recommended.

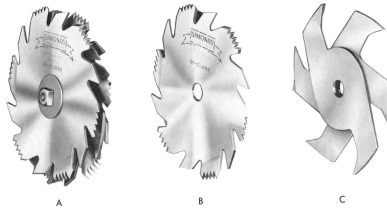

A   B   C

29-4g. An assembled dado head (A); an outside cutter (B); and chippers or inside cutters (C).

This has a combination of ripping and crosscut teeth and is used for a great variety of cutting. Several styles of teeth are available, and each has a particular application. Fig. 29-4d.

● The *easy-cut* blade. This has only a few large teeth and is considered to be the safest blade since it practically eliminates kickback. It does, however, make a rather wide kerf and does not cut so smoothly as the cutoff, hollow-ground, and combination saws. Fig. 29-4e.

● The *plywood saw* blade, as the name indicates, is a special blade for cutting plywood. It cuts with a minimum of chipping and leaves an extremely smooth edge. The steel is specially tempered to give the teeth a longer life for cutting through the many glue lines in plywood. Fig. 29-4f.

Dado Head

In addition to standard equipment, a *dado head* can be purchased that will cut all common widths of grooves or dadoes. Fig. 29-4g. This will be described later.

Parts

Study the parts of the circular saw, as shown in Fig. 29-5. Notice that this is a tilting arbor saw. The table top has two grooves cut in it into which the miter gage fits. These are parallel to the saw blade. The miter gage comes equipped with a stop rod which can be adjusted in length for cutting duplicate parts. A fence clamps to the table for all ripping operations. Also available are table extensions which can be fastened to the sides of the table top and are especially convenient when cutting long or large stock such as a sheet of plywood. An opening in the center of the table is covered by a throat plate. A

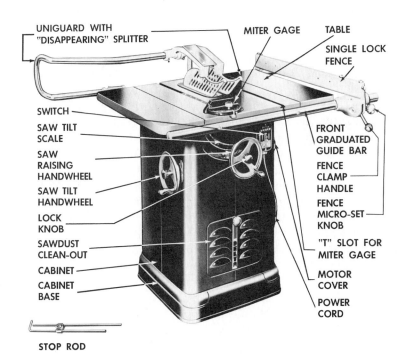

10″ TILTING ARBOR UNISAW®

29-5. Parts of a 10″ tilting-arbor circular saw.

guard, which drops over the blade, is always fastened to the back or side of the table. This should be kept in place whenever possible. (There are some operations for which regular guards cannot be used; a special guard or a feather board should then be used.) There is also a splitter which is usually a part of the back of the guard. This fits directly back of the saw blade and is slightly thicker than the blade. It keeps the saw kerf open as the cutting is done.

Adjustments

Installing or Removing a Saw Blade

1. Remove the throat plate. This usually snaps in and out of position.

2. Select a wrench to fit the arbor nut. On some saws the arbor has a lefthand thread and must be turned clockwise to loosen. However, some saws have a righthand thread. If so, you must turn it counterclockwise to remove. Always check the thread before loosening. A good rule to remember is that the nut always loosens by turning it in the direction the teeth are pointing (direction of blade rotation). If the nut doesn't come off easily, hold a piece of scrap wood against the blade to keep the arbor from turning. Fig. 29-6.

3. Remove the nut and the collar, and take off the old blade.

4. Replace the blade in the correct position, with the saw teeth pointing in the direction of blade rotation. Replace the collar and nut. Tighten it firmly, but not too tight. The nut tightens against

29-6. Hold the blade with a piece of scrap wood. The nut will loosen if turned in the direction the teeth are pointing.

the rotation and will not come off. Replace the throat plate.

Raising the Saw Blade

There is a wheel or lever on the front of the machine to raise or lower the blade. Often, in addition, there is a lock that must be loosened when making this adjustment. To raise the blade to the proper position, hold the workpiece against the side of the blade and carefully turn the blade until the top tooth is at the correct height. For most cutting, the top of the blade should extend no more than $\frac{1}{8}''$ above the stock. On many joint cuts, however, the blade must be set for the exact depth of cut.

Tilting the Saw Blade

A lever or handle on the side of the machine tilts the blade. A pointer or scale on the front indi-

cates the degree of tilt. There is usually a lock to hold the blade in position when it is tilted.

Adjusting the Fence

A ripping fence is fastened to the table for all ripping operations and for many other cutting jobs. It is usually placed to the right of the blade. To adjust the fence to the correct position, first move it to an approximate location. Hold a rule or try square at right angles to the fence and carefully measure the distance from the fence to one tooth bent toward the fence. Fig. 29-7.

On some machines there is a pointer on the fence and a scale on the front of the table to indicate the width of cut. This should be checked frequently to make sure it is accurate. Each time the blade is changed, this scale will have to be checked, because the

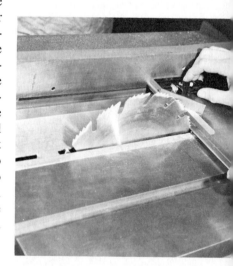

29-7. Adjusting the fence for the correct width of cut. Make a small test cut on the workpiece and measure it to double check the set-up before making the complete cut.

amount of set in the saw blade will affect the distance between the fence and the saw kerf. It is a good practice to use this scale for rough set-ups only. Accurate set-ups should be made by making a test cut and checking it with a rule or by superimposing (mock assembly of parts).

Adjusting the Miter Gage

The miter gage, which is used for crosscutting operations, can be used in either groove of the table but usually is placed in the groove to the left of the blade. There is a pointer and scale on the miter gage for setting it to any degree right or left. Most gages have automatic stop positions at 30, 45, 60, and 90 degrees.

Ripping

Install a ripping, combination, or easy-cut blade for these operations:

Cutting Wide Stock to Width

1. When the width of the board to be cut is 6 inches or more, this is considered a wide cut. Adjust the fence and blade accordingly.

2. Turn on the machine. Place the board over the table. Apply pressure against the fence with the left hand, and push the board forward with the right. If the board is longer than 6 or 8 feet, have a helper stand behind the saw to hold the piece up after it passes the blade. If a helper is not available, use a roller stand as shown in Fig. 29-8.

3. Feed the stock at an even speed into the blade about as fast as it will cut. Do not overload the saw. Hold your right hand close

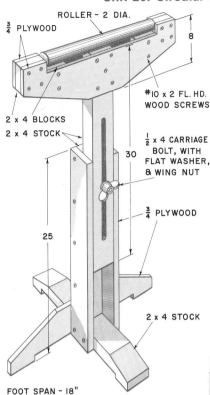

29-8. A roller stand used to support long stock when ripping.

to the fence as you push the end of the board through the saw. Fig. 29-9a.

4. If extremely thick or hard wood is being cut, it is often necessary to cut part way through the board, then turn the board over and complete the cut. (See *Resawing.*)

Cutting Narrower Stock to Width

1. When cutting stock narrower than 6 inches, observe the same general practices as in starting the cut on wide stock.

2. As the end of the board reaches the front of the table, use a push stick to do the work you began with your right hand, guiding the board between the

29-9a. Ripping on the circular saw.

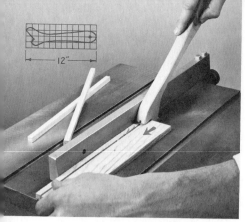

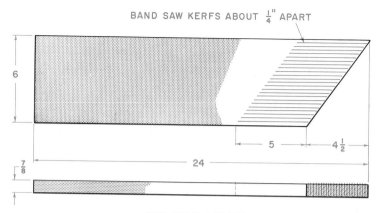

29-9b. Using a push stick in ripping narrow stock.

BAND SAW KERFS ABOUT $\frac{1}{4}$" APART

USE SOLID LUMBER

29-11. A feather board.

blade and the fence. Fig. 29-9b. *Never under any circumstances cut narrow stock without a push stick.* It is good practice to hang the push stick conveniently at the side of the saw so that you don't take a chance and cut without it.

3. If very narrow stock is being cut, it may be a good idea to cut half the length of the stock, pull it back out, reverse it, and complete the cut from the other end. Fig. 29-10.

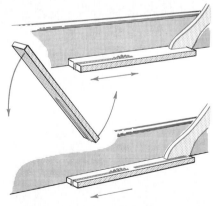

29-10. Another method of ripping narrow stock. Saw halfway through and then move the stock back out of the saw. Turn the stock end for end and complete the cut.

Resawing

Resawing means ripping a board to make one or more thin pieces. This can be done on a circular saw only if the width of the board is less than twice the capacity of the saw. If the board is wider, a kerf can be cut on either side on the circular saw and the resawing completed on a band saw.

For resawing, it is a good idea to make a feather board to help guide the stock. Cut a flat miter at about 30 degrees across the end of a piece of scrap stock; then make a series of saw kerfs with the grain, about 5" long and about ¼" apart. Fig. 29-11. The feather board helps to hold the stock firmly against the fence at all times during the cutting. It is needed because the operator must use both hands to guide and push the board. Clamp this board to the table to apply slight pressure to the stock. Fig. 29-12. Adjust the blade so it will pass through slightly more than half the width of the board. Push the board

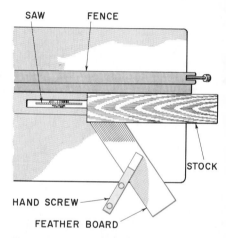

29-12. Note that the feather board is clamped to the table with a hand screw so that the pressure is just ahead of the saw blade. Apply just enough pressure to hold the stock lightly but firmly against the fence. If side pressure is applied next to the saw, it will cause binding which results in kickback.

through the saw, return it, reverse it, and cut the other half.

Crosscutting

Install a crosscutting, hollow-ground, or combination blade. Use the miter gage for all crosscutting operations. For added support of the workpiece some operators like to fasten permanently a long support board to the miter gage. Always remove the ripping fence for crosscutting. Carefully mark a line on the edge of the stock nearest the blade. (You must be able to see the mark easily, so you can begin the cut accurately.) Be sure the miter gage is set to cut the correct angle. It is also a good practice to use the stop rod as an aid to prevent the stock from moving while the cut is made.

Cutting Short Boards

Place the gage in the groove in the side toward the longest portion of the board. Fig. 29-13. Hold the stock firmly against the gage and advance it slowly into the blade. Never drag the cut edge back across the blade.

Cutting Long Pieces

If the board is longer than 6', have a helper support the other end.

29-13. Crosscutting narrow pieces.

Cutting Plywood

Because of its construction, and often because of its size, plywood presents special cutting problems. Since grain directions of alternating plies are at right angles to each other, there is a tendency to split out the ends of cross-grain layers, no matter what the direction of the cut. The glue lines are also a problem in that they dull the blade. Finally, since plywood is glued up in large sheets, the workpiece is often too large to fit conveniently on the table of a circular saw.

To reduce these problems to a minimum, adjust the blade so it will barely clear the top of the plywood, and place the stock with the good side up. Fig. 29-14. Then use one of the three following methods to guide the stock:
• The miter gage can be reversed in the groove when the cut is started, to guide the stock for as long a cut as possible. Fig. 29-15. Then the gage can be removed and slipped into its regular position to complete the cut.
• Another suggestion for sawing plywood is to clamp a straight-edged board on the underside of the plywood. This will act as a guide against the edge of the table. Fig. 29-16.
• The ripping fence can be used as a guide in cutting plywood to size.

29-14. Plywood should be cut with the good face up. Use a combination, crosscut, or plywood blade.

29-15. Starting a cut on a piece of plywood with the miter gage reversed.

29-16. Clamp a piece of scrap stock, with a straight edge, to the underside of a piece of plywood to act as a guide when cutting.

29-17. This method is recommended for cutting several short pieces of the same length from a long piece of stock.

29-18. Using the stop rod on the miter gage is a quick, accurate way of cutting several pieces to the same length. Remember to square one end of each piece first.

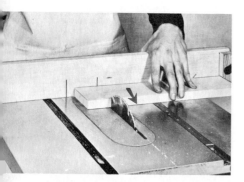

29-19. Using a stop block on an auxiliary board fastened to a miter gage for cutting pieces to identical length.

Cutting Identical Pieces to Length

There are many ways of cutting identical pieces to length:

● For cutting many short pieces, clamp a stop block to the ripping fence in front of the cutting edge of the blade. Adjust the fence to cut the proper length of stock. By placing the end of the board against this stop, you can cut the correct length and there will be plenty of clearance between the fence and the finished pieces to prevent kickback. Fig. 29-17.

● A second method is to adjust the stop rod on the gage for the correct length of the cut. Fig. 29-18.

● A third method is to clamp a stop block to the auxiliary board fastened to the miter gage. Fig. 29-19.

● A fourth method is to clamp a stop block to the table. Fig. 29-20.

Special Cuts

Cutting a Bevel or Chamfer with the Grain

Tilt the blade to the correct angle for the chamfer or bevel. Place the fence on the table so the blade tilts away from the fence. Adjust the height of the blade to clear the top of the board slightly. Hold the work firmly against the fence as the cut is made. Fig. 29-21.

Cutting a Bevel or Chamfer Across Grain

Adjust the blade to the correct angle and place the miter gage in the groove on the side toward which the blade tilts. Hold the stock firmly against the gage to

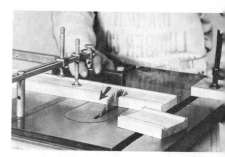

29-20. Using a stop block clamped to the table.

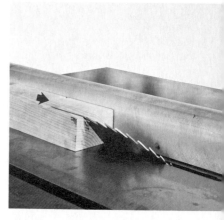

29-21a. Cutting a bevel with the grain.

make the cut. Sometimes it's a good idea to clamp the stock to the gage for making this kind of cut. Fig. 29-22.

Cutting a Taper

A tapering jig must be used. It can be a simple fixed-taper jig or an adjustable jig.

Fixed-taper jigs are quickly and easily made; therefore they are often used. This type of jig must be made for the particular taper to be cut. Each time a different taper is cut, a new jig must be made. A fixed-taper jig consists of

282

29-21b. A bevel cut with the grain forms the inside face of each leg of this table.

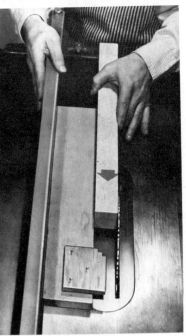

29-23b. Adjusting the fence before cutting the taper.

a *stop block* nailed to a piece of stock called a *guide board.* The stop block is a block of wood with two notches cut in it. The notches are cut to a depth equal to the amount of taper on one side of the workpiece. Fig. 29-23a. The distance from the end of the guide board to the bottom of the first notch in the stop block should be equal to the length of the taper.

Place the jig, with the workpiece alongside, on the saw table next to the blade. Move the fence over

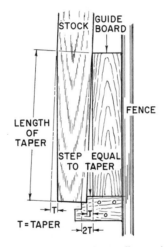

29-23a. A fixed jig. A new jig must be made each time a different taper is cut.

the first cut. If the piece is to be tapered on all four sides, use the second notch to make taper cuts on the sides *opposite* those already tapered. This compensates for the amount of stock already removed by the first taper cut.

until it just touches the guide board of the jig. Fig. 29-23b. Now place the workpiece in the first notch and make the first taper cut. Fig. 29-23c. The second cut is made with the piece in the same notch as for the first cut, and on the side of the stock *adjacent* to

29-22. Cutting a chamfer across grain by tilting the saw blade to 45 degrees.

29-23c. Cutting a taper, using a fixed jig on a circular saw.

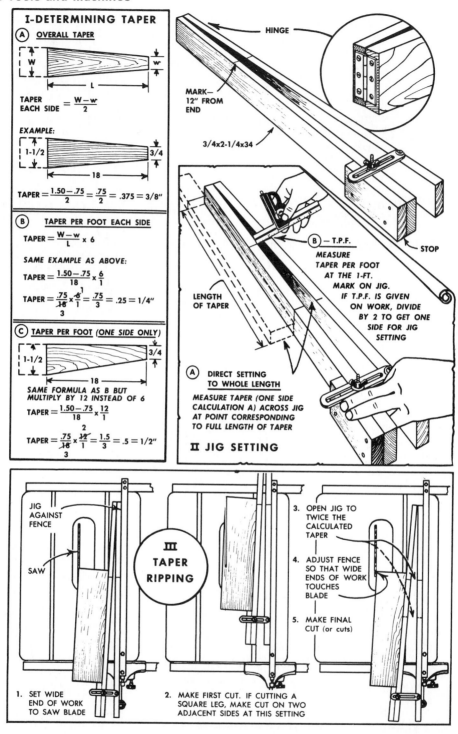

29-24a. Follow these steps in determining the taper, setting the jig, and ripping.

29-24b. Cutting a taper, using an adjustable jig. Hold the stock securely in the jig and hold the jig firmly against the fence as the cut is made.

● *Method A. Making two cuts with a saw blade.*

Lay out the width and depth of the rabbet on the end or edge of stock so that the lines can be easily seen during the cutting. Adjust the saw blade to a height equal to the depth of the rabbet. If the rabbet is cut with the grain, place the stock face down on the table, with the edge against the fence, and make the first cut. Fig. 29-25. If the rabbet is cut across grain, place the stock face down and hold against the miter gage with the end firmly against the fence. Fig. 29-26. For the second cut, adjust the blade to a height equal to the width of the rabbet and adjust the fence with the saw blade just inside the waste stock.

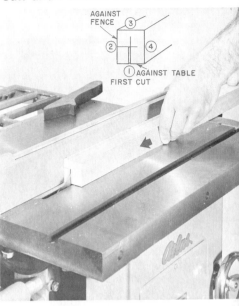

29-25. Making the first cut of a rabbet with the grain. After the cut is started, hold the work against the fence with your left hand and push it along with a push stick. Notice that side No. 1 is against the table and side No. 2 is against the fence.

If several different tapers must be cut, it would be advisable to make an adjustable taper jig. A description of the jig and the procedure for its use is shown in Fig. 29-24a. When cutting a taper, hold the workpiece firmly against the jig and the jig against the fence. Cut the taper as in ripping. Fig. 29-24b.

Joint Cuts

All cuts for making joints should be done with a crosscut, hollow-ground, or combination blade, since it is important to have a very smooth cut.

Cutting a Rabbet

There are two common methods of cutting a rabbet on the circular saw:

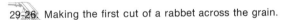

29-26. Making the first cut of a rabbet across the grain.

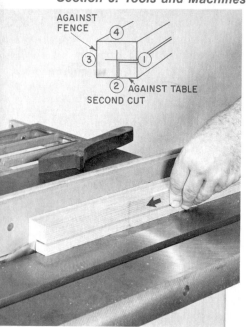

AGAINST FENCE

SECOND CUT
AGAINST TABLE

29-27. Making the second cut of a rabbet with the grain. With this method the waste stock falls away from the blade without binding or kickback. Notice that side No. 2 is against the table and side No. 3 is against the fence.

Fig. 29-27. Hold the surface away from the rabbet firmly against the fence and carefully make the second cut. If the surface or edge of the board that was on the table for the first cut is held against the fence when the second cut is made, the strip of wood which is cut out will kick back with considerable force.

• *Method B. Using a dado head.*

Set up the dado head as described on page 290. Take a piece of wood about the size of the ripping fence and clamp it to the fence. Keep the clamps up off of the table so they will not interfere with the stock during the cut. Set the fence for the desired width of cut, and adjust the height of the dado head for depth of cut. Take

care to hold the stock firmly on the table to avoid an uneven cut. Fig. 29-28.

Cutting a Miter

Miter cuts are usually made at a 45-degree angle, although they can be made at any angle. If any shape other than a rectangle is to be cut, you must find the correct angle for the miter cuts. To do this, divide 180 by the number of sides; then subtract that answer from 90. The result will be the number of degrees for each miter cut. For example, to make cuts for a five-sided figure:

$$180 \div 5 = 36$$
$$90 - 36 = 54$$

Make the cuts at a 54-degree angle.

When cutting mitered corners for picture frames, follow Fig. 29-29 to determine the overall length of the sides. Determine the length of the glass or picture. To this length add twice the width of the frame, measured from the rabbet edge to the outside edge. (This width is shown most clearly as dimension A at lower left of Fig. 29-29.) Lay out this overall measurement along the outside edge of the stock.

Making a flat miter cut: Adjust the miter gage as required, usually to 45 degrees. If two miter gages are available, the cutting will be simplified. Adjust both gages to turn inward toward the saw blade. Place a stop rod on the left miter gage to equal the exact length of the sides to be cut. Hold the stock firmly against the right miter gage and cut the first miter from the inside edge toward the corner.

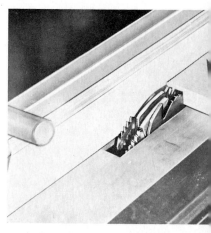

29-28. Cutting a rabbet with a dado head. Hold the workpiece firmly on the table to insure an even cut.

Fig. 29-30. To make the second cut, hold the mitered end against the stop rod and cut as before. Many types of mitering jigs have been developed to aid the woodworker in making an accurate miter joint. Fig. 29-31.

To install a spline in a flat miter, make a jig by cutting a scrap piece of wood at a 45-degree angle. Adjust the height of the blade so the groove for the spline will be cut to the desired depth. Adjust the fence so the cut will be in the correct position from right to left.

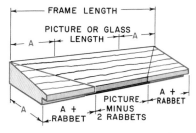

FRAME LENGTH

PICTURE OR GLASS LENGTH

A

A

PICTURE

A + RABBET

A + MINUS 2 RABBETS

A + RABBET

A

29-29. Laying out the proper measurement for cutting miter joints on a picture frame. The length as marked on the outside of the frame is equal to the length of the glass plus twice the width of the stock measured from the rabbet to the outside edge.

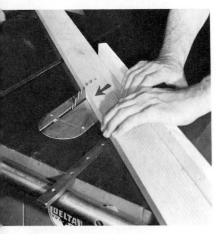

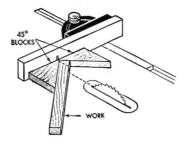

29-31a. A simple jig for cutting miters when only one miter gage is available. When using this jig, all stock is cut to finished length before mitering.

29-31c. Another type of mitering jig, used for cutting a 45-degree edge miter.

29-30. Making a flat miter cut. With wood screws a piece of scrap stock is fastened to the miter gage. This prevents "tear out" as the blade cuts through the edge of the moulding.

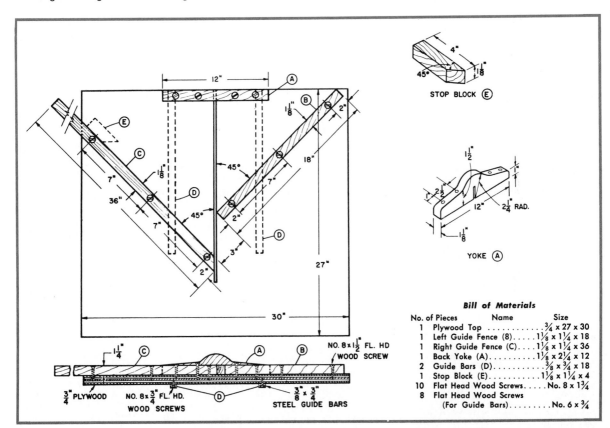

Bill of Materials

No. of Pieces	Name	Size
1	Plywood Top	¾ x 27 x 30
1	Left Guide Fence (8)	1⅛ x 1¼ x 18
1	Right Guide Fence (C)	1⅛ x 1¼ x 36
1	Back Yoke (A)	1⅛ x 2¼ x 12
2	Guide Bars (D)	⅜ x ¾ x 18
1	Stop Block (E)	1⅛ x 1¼ x 4
10	Flat Head Wood Screws	No. 8 x 1¾
8	Flat Head Wood Screws (For Guide Bars)	No. 6 x ¾

29-31b. This mitering jig, made of plywood, is fitted with metal guides that ride in the table slots. Make the screw holes in the guide fences slightly oversize to allow for adjustments.

29-32. Cutting a groove for a spline in a flat miter joint.

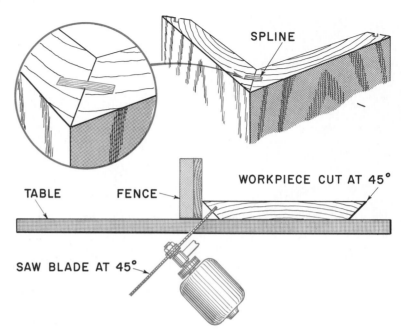

29-34. Cutting a groove for a spline. The workpiece is on the table and rides against the fence.

Hold the stock firmly against the jig as shown in Fig. 29-32, and cut the groove.

Making a miter on edge: Tilt the saw blade to an angle of 45 degrees and set the miter gage at 90 degrees. Place the miter gage in the groove so the blade tilts away from it. Adjust it to the correct height, and make the miter cut as shown in Fig. 29-33.

To install a spline in a miter on edge, set the fence as shown in Fig. 29-34. Adjust the height of the blade and cut the groove as shown.

Making a compound miter cut: This is often used in making picture frames. Adjust the miter gage to the correct angle and tilt the

saw blade to the desired degree. Fig. 29-35. Then make a trial cut of the two pieces on scrap stock. Fig. 29-36. Carefully check the corners.

Putting a feather across a miter corner: Make a small jig, similar to the one in Fig. 29-37, that will support the corner of the frame.

29-33. Making an edge miter.

29-35. This table must be consulted before making a compound miter cut. For example, suppose you wish to cut a four-sided mitered frame with the sides tilted to 20 degrees. Look across the column to the 4-side miter. Note that the tilt of the blade must be 41¾ degrees and that the miter gage must be adjusted to 71¼ degrees.

TABLE FOR COMPOUND MITER CUTS

Tilt of Work	4-Side Butt		4-Side Miter	
	Blade Tilt	Miter Gauge	Blade Tilt	Miter Gauge
5 degrees	½	85	44¾	85
10 degrees	1½	80¼	44¼	80¼
15 degrees	3¾	75½	43¼	75½
20 degrees	6¼	71¼	41¾	71¼
25 degrees	10	67	40	67
30 degrees	14½	63½	37¾	63½
35 degrees	19½	60¼	35¼	60¼
40 degrees	24½	57¼	32½	57¼
45 degrees	30	54¾	30	54¾
50 degrees	36	52½	27	52½
55 degrees	42	50¾	24	50¾
60 degrees	48	49	21	49

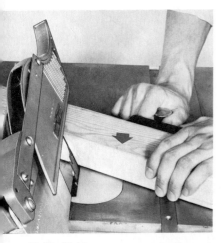

29-36. Making a compound miter cut.

Adjust the blade to the correct height and set the fence so that the cut will be made across the corners.

Cutting a Tenon

There are two common methods of cutting the tenon—with a *single saw blade* and with a *dado*

29-37. Making a saw cut across the corner of a frame to install a feather. Notice the jig for holding the stock in position.

head. Usually there are eight tenons to be cut in making simple tables, chairs, and other four-legged objects.

● *Method A. Cutting with a single saw blade.*

1. Set the fence so the distance from the left edge of the saw to the fence is equal to the length of the tenon.

2. Adjust the height of the saw so it is equal to the thickness of the stock to be removed.

3. Hold the pieces against the miter gage and make the shoulder cut. Fig. 29-38. The critical dimension when cutting tenons is the distance between the shoulders. This dimension establishes the length of the rail and thus the size of the frame. If the tenon is perfectly centered, the stock can be reversed and the other side of the tenon cut. Shoulder cuts may be made on one, two, three, or four sides, depending on the type of tenon.

4. Make all shoulder cuts on all pieces.

5. Readjust the fence so the distance from the right side of the saw to the fence will remove the correct thickness of the material from one side of the tenon. Adjust the saw blade height so it equals the length of the tenon. Make the cheek cuts. This should *not* be done freehand on pieces less than 4″ wide, since it can be a very dangerous operation. Fig. 29-39.

29-38. Making a shoulder cut on a tenon, using the fence for a stop.

29-39. Making the cheek cut freehand. Special care must be exercised when cutting a tenon in this manner.

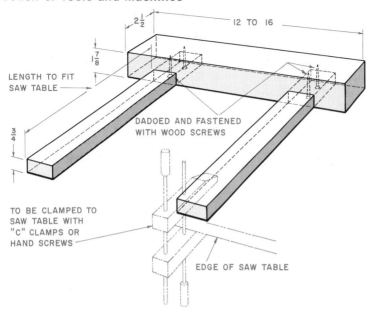

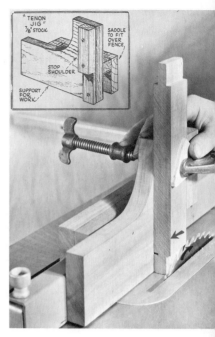

29-40a. Circular saw guard. This guard should be used when making the cheek cuts on a tenon freehand if the conventional saw guard will not function. It should also be used with other special set-ups when the conventional guard cannot be used.

29-41. Making the cheek cut, using a wooden jig.

For added protection, use the guard as shown in Fig. 29-40. The danger can be minimized by using a jig similar to that shown in Fig. 29-41, which will keep the operator's fingers away from the saw

29-40b. Circular saw guard in use.

blade. A commercially made tenoner attachment simplifies this operation and makes it safer. Fig. 29-42.

● *Method B. Cutting with a dado head.*

1. Place a dado head on the saw and adjust it to a height equal to the thickness of stock to be removed on one side of the tenon. (See *Method C* under *Cutting a Groove,* for the use of the dado head.)

2. Adjust the fence so the distance from the left edge of the dado to the fence is equal to the length of the tenon.

3. Hold the stock firmly against the miter gage, with the end held against the fence. Make the first cut; then return the stock to the original position, and move it to the left to make succeeding cuts

until one side is finished. Fig. 29-43. Repeat on the other sides.

This same procedure (Method B) can be followed with a single saw blade, trimming off the waste stock with a hand chisel.

Cutting a Groove

A groove is a rectangular opening cut with the grain of wood. There are three simple ways of doing this operation.

● *Method A. Making two or more cuts with a standard blade.*

Adjust the blade to a height equal to the depth of the groove. Adjust the fence so the blade will remove stock to form one side of the groove. Make the first cut. Turn the stock around so the second face is against the fence and make the second cut. This will insure that the groove will be in

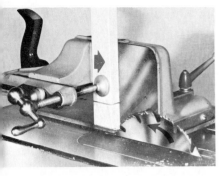

29-42. A tenoning jig is an accessory for making tenons and grooves. This one will take stock up to 2¼'' thick and any width within the capacity of the saw.

29-43. Cutting a tenon, using a dado head.

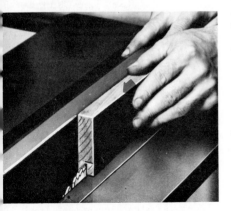

29-44a. Cutting a groove.

the center of stock. When the two outside cuts have been made on all the pieces, move the fence over, if necessary, and make cuts as needed to clean out the remaining stock. Fig. 29-44.

● *Method B. Using wobble washers.*

Wobble washers replace the regular washers that hold the blade on the arbor. These can be set so the blade wobbles and cuts a groove of a specific width. There are marks on the washers for setting the width of cut. Adjust the blade to the correct height. Set the fence and make the cut. *This is somewhat dangerous because the blade does not run smoothly.* Fig. 29-45.

● *Method C. Using a dado head.*

This is the safest and fastest method of cutting grooves. As mentioned, a dado head consists of two outside cutters with chippers placed between them. Fig. 29-46. Remove the throat plate and the saw blade. Place one of the dado head blades on the arbor and then put on the correct number of chippers for the desired width of groove. Finally, add the second blade. (Usually the blades and cutters are ⅟₁₆'', ⅛'' and ¼'' wide, making it possible to cut a groove of any standard width.)

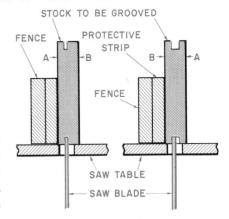

29-44b. Here are the steps for cutting a groove with a single saw blade.

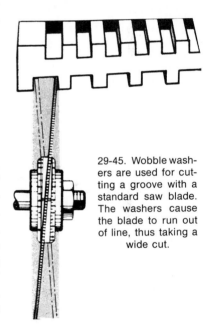

29-45. Wobble washers are used for cutting a groove with a standard saw blade. The washers cause the blade to run out of line, thus taking a wide cut.

29-46. With this dado head set you can cut grooves from ⅛'' to ¹³/₁₆'' in intervals of ⅟₁₆''.

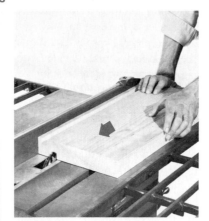

29-49. Cutting a groove, using a dado head.

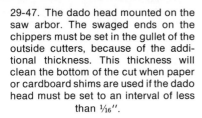

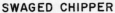

SWAGED CHIPPER

29-47. The dado head mounted on the saw arbor. The swaged ends on the chippers must be set in the gullet of the outside cutters, because of the additional thickness. This thickness will clean the bottom of the cut when paper or cardboard shims are used if the dado head must be set to an interval of less than $\frac{1}{16}$".

Turn the chippers until the points are evenly spaced and the swaged (enlarged) cutting edge of the chipper is in the gullet of the outside cutter. Fig. 29-47. For example, if three cutters are used, they should be set 120 degrees apart. This makes the dado head operate smoothly. Install a throat plate of the type made specially for a dado head. Fig. 29-48. Adjust the dado head and the fence as required, and proceed with the cut. Fig. 29-49.

Adjustable Dado Head

The adjustable dado head is easy to use and will give a clean cut. Fig. 29-50. The width can be set by loosening the arbor nut and rotating the center section of the head until the width mark on this part is opposite the desired dimension. Fig. 29-51a. The cut can be easily and accurately varied to any width from $\frac{1}{4}$" to $\frac{13}{16}$". Fig. 29-51b.

29-51a. An adjustable dado head.

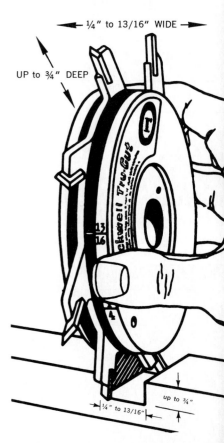

29-51b. Drawing of an adjustable dado head. Note that the depth as well as the width of cut is adjustable.

29-48. A special throat plate is needed for installing a dado head.

29-50. Using the adjustable dado.

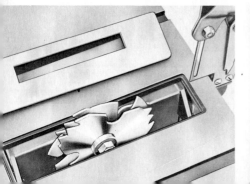

292

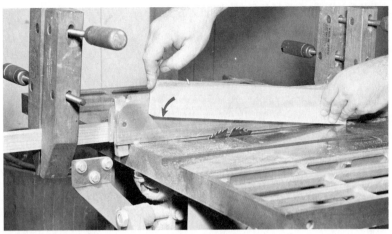

29-52. Cutting a stopped groove. Notice the use of hand screws as stop blocks to control the length of cut.

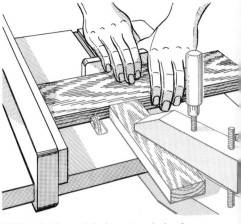

29-54. Cutting a blind or stop dado. A stop block clamped to the table controls the length of cut.

Cutting a Stopped Groove

A stopped groove is not cut along the entire length of the stock. Such grooves are usually toward the center of the stock. Fasten hand screws to the fence to control the length of the cut. Turn on the machine. Hold one end of the stock against the first clamp, and lower it into the saw. Push the stock along until it strikes the second clamp. Carefully raise the stock. Fig. 29-52.

Cutting Dadoes

Plain dado. A dado is a groove cut across grain. It can be done in any of the ways described for

29-53. Cutting a plain dado.

cutting a groove. The fence can serve as a stop block while the work is held against the miter gage. When cutting a regular dado, pass the stock completely across the cutter, then remove the stock. Fig. 29-53. Do not draw the board back across the dado head. This is a very important precaution when using the dado head.

Blind dado. A blind dado or gain is cut only partly across the board. Follow the directions given under dado joints in Unit 14, "Making Joints." Clamp a stop block to the fence to control the length of the dado. Cut the dado as before until the board hits the stop block. Fig. 29-54. Then slowly raise the board or turn off the machine and remove the board.

Corner dado. Make a jig—a simple V block for holding the stock at an angle of 45 degrees to the table. Cut the dado as shown in Fig. 29-55.

29-55. Cutting a corner dado, using a V block to hold the stock.

Cutting Lap Joints

End-lap and half-lap. These joints are actually two tenons with the stock removed from only one side. Lay out the joint so that stock to be removed is exactly half the thickness of the material you are working with. A perfect joint will result with only one set-up on the circular saw. Cut the pieces exactly as you would two tenons— shoulder cuts first and then cheek cuts.

Cross-lap and edge-lap. These joints are cut similar to a dado, except that they are usually wider. Make the layout; then cut by one of the methods described for cutting grooves or dadoes.

PORTABLE POWER SAW

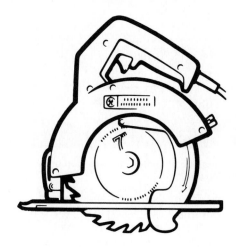

SAFETY

- Make sure the teeth of the blade are sharp and set correctly.
- Never make an adjustment on a saw when it is running.
- Don't stand directly in line with the saw blade. If the blade binds, it has a tendency to kick the saw back out of the cut. If this happens, turn off the switch immediately.
- Always keep the guard in place and the blade adjusted for the correct depth of cut.
- Use the correct blade for the work to be done.
- Disconnect the power source to change a blade. Make sure that the teeth are pointing in the direction of rotation and that the arbor nut is tight.
- Allow the saw to reach full speed before starting a cut.
- Always keep your hands clear of the cutting line.
- Never stand in line with the cut.
- When finished with a cut, release the switch and wait until the blade comes to a dead stop before setting the saw down.

Portable Power Saw

Portable power saws are sometimes called cutoff electric circular hand saws. (Also, these saws are often known by their trade names.) These saws are primarily used for straight cutting on lumber and plywood. They are made in a wide variety of styles and types. Fig. 29-56. One type has a reversible motor with two separate bases so that cuts can be made from either end of a 4 x 8 plywood sheet. Fig. 29-57. With the proper kind of blade, plastic laminate and non-ferrous metals can also be cut. These saws are excellent tools for cabinetmakers, furniture makers and plastic laminate fabricators. Fig. 29-58.

The size of a portable power saw is determined by the blade diameter, which ranges from 6″ to 10″. A common size is a ½-horsepower motor with an 8½-inch blade. Because the saw cuts from the bottom of the material, it leaves a smoother cut at the bottom than at the top. Fig. 29-59. Therefore, plywood should always be cut with the good side down. The blade is on the right side of the motor which makes it convenient for the right-handed person.

29-56b. This saw has a worm gear drive. Notice the saw has two handles, with a switch on each handle.

29-57a. Ripping with the reversible saw from right to left.

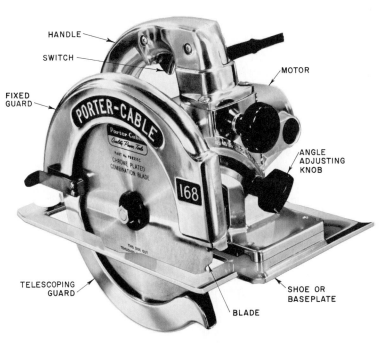

29-56a. Parts of a portable power saw.

HANDLE
SWITCH
FIXED GUARD
MOTOR
ANGLE ADJUSTING KNOB
TELESCOPING GUARD
SHOE OR BASEPLATE
BLADE

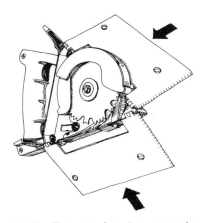

29-57b. The saw has two separate bases so angle cuts can be made from either direction.

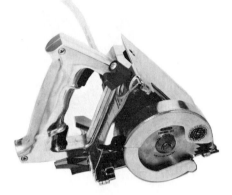

29-58a. The reversible saw turned over and in position to rip from left to right.

29-58b. Making a pocket cut from right to left.

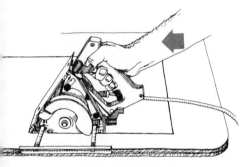

29-58c. This type of blade is specially designed to cut when rotating in either direction, for use on saws with reversible motors.

29-60. Arbor hole bore sizes and shapes for portable power saw blades.

Parts

The saw consists of a motor, a handle, a baseplate or shoe, a fixed and a movable guard, a blade, and a switch. Fig. 29-56a. Blades used are the same type as for the circular saw. Be certain that the blade is of the correct diameter and that the arbor hole in the blade is of the right size and shape. Fig. 29-60.

Straight Cuts

1. Mark the cut-off line on the right end of the board whenever possible. This will give better support as the cut is made. Place the work over the saw horses or support it securely in some other way so that the cut-off line is clear.

2. Loosen the nut or clamp to adjust the depth of cut. Only about $\frac{1}{8}''$ of the blade should show below the stock. Fig. 29-61. Place the baseplate, or shoe, on

D-T
SKIL SAW, THOR

$\frac{1}{2}''$ & $\frac{13}{16}''$
SQUARE
MALL, WAPPAT, CUMMINS, PET

$\frac{5}{8}''$ **ROUND**
PORTER-CABLE, SIOUX, SYNTRON, MILWAUKEE, CRAFTSMAN, STANLEY, MONTGOMERY WARD

$1\frac{1}{8}''$ & $1\frac{3}{8}''$
ROUND
BLACK & DECKER
(also $\frac{5}{8}''$ round)

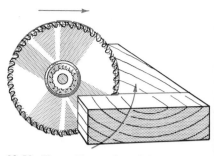

29-59. The cutting action of the portable power saw is different from that of the circular saw. The portable saw cuts from the bottom up.

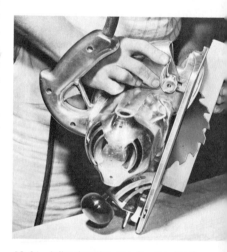

29-61. Adjusting the saw for the depth of cut.

29-62. Straight cutting. Notice that the guard covers nearly all of the blade that is not in contact with the workpiece.

the work with the blade in line with the layout line. Turn on the power and allow it to come up to full speed. Guide the saw across the board firmly but without too much pressure, following the layout line. Fig. 29-62. A guide like the one in Fig. 29-63 will make crosscutting much more accurate. A long ripping cut can be made freehand following the layout line. It is much better, however, to use a ripping fence as shown in Fig. 29-64.

Miter Cuts

Angle or miter cuts can be made freehand except that it is more difficult to start the cut on the layout line. A protractor attachment is ideal to use for making miter cuts. This device is marked in degrees and can be set to cut any angle by moving the projecting arm to the correct degree. To use this attachment, the shoe is lined up with the protractor straightedge. Then saw the same as for any cut.

Bevel Cuts

On most saws the shoe can be adjusted between 45 and 90 degrees. Loosen the wing nut or handle and tilt the shoe to the desired angle. Then retighten the wing nut or handle. Adjust the saw for the correct depth of cut. Make the bevel cut freehand or use a jig to guide the saw. Fig. 29-65.

Compound Angle Cuts

A compound angle cut can be made by tilting the saw blade and using a protractor guide. Fig. 29-66.

29-63. Using a protractor guide for cutting. This can be adjusted to any angle to make miter cuts.

29-64. Ripping with a fence. When ripping a long board, either walk slowly with the saw or stop the saw and pull it back in the kerf a little way, taking a new position to finish the cutting.

29-65. Making a bevel cut.

29-66. Making a compound angle cut.

297

DRILL PRESS

SAFETY

- Keep your fingers away from the revolving tool.
- Never remove chips with your fingers.
- Always make sure that the stock is securely clamped whenever clamping is necessary.
- Always remove the chuck key immediately after installing a tool.
- Keep the cutting tools sharp.
- Make all adjustments with the power off and the cutter standing still.
- Make certain the table and drill are properly adjusted to avoid drilling into the table.
- Make certain the drill is securely clamped in the chuck.
- Do not wear loose clothing or long, unconfined hair.
- Do not hold small pieces of stock by hand. If clamping is impossible, use a pliers.
- If the work has slipped, never attempt to stop it by hand.
- Never use a bit with a lead screw on the drill press.
- Use only straight-shanked tools in the drill press chuck.
- When using the drill press as another machine, such as the router, shaper, or mortiser, be sure to study and follow the appropriate safety rules for the other machine.
- Do not force the drill.
- Back out frequently on deep cuts, to clean and cool the bit.

UNIT 30 Drill Press and Portable Electric Drill

The drill press is one of the most versatile machines in the woodworking shop. It can be used for drilling and boring all standard sizes of holes. Also, with attachments, it can serve as a mortising machine, router, shaper, planer, and sander. Fig. 30-1.

Size

A drill press can be either a *bench* or *floor* type. Fig. 30-2. The size is indicated by the largest diameter of stock through which a hole can be drilled. For example, a 15″ drill press measures $7\frac{1}{2}$″ from the center of the chuck to the column.

Parts

The major parts are shown in Fig. 30-2a. The *base* is heavy cast iron. The *column* is of ground steel, and the *table,* which fastens to the *table bracket,* can be locked in any position. The *head* contains all the operating mechanism. The *chuck* can be removed and other adapters for accessories installed. For most work a *Jacobs chuck* is satisfactory. The *depth gage and stop* will control the amount or depth of the drilling. Most machines have *stop nuts* and a *pointer* to control the amount of movement. The feed is applied by hand with the *feed handle.* If the machine is to double as a shaper and router, it should have a *multispeed attachment* so that speeds from 125 to 5800 rpm can be secured. Fig. 30-3. (See page 301.)

30-1. Making such items as these oak library units requires many operations which can be done with the drill press and attachments.

Adjustments

Installing a Drill or Bit

To fasten a drill or bit in a chuck, open the chuck slightly more than the diameter of the tool. Insert the tool firmly in the chuck and tighten with a key. Remove the key immediately. Never attempt to fasten a tapered shank drill or bit or a squared shank in a chuck. Fig. 30-4. (Page 301.)

Removing the Chuck

It is necessary to remove the chuck for operations other than drilling, since the chuck should

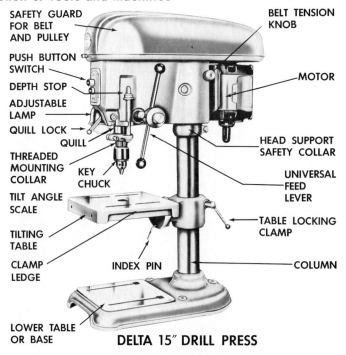

SAFETY GUARD FOR BELT AND PULLEY
PUSH BUTTON SWITCH
DEPTH STOP
ADJUSTABLE LAMP
QUILL LOCK
QUILL
THREADED MOUNTING COLLAR
KEY
CHUCK
TILT ANGLE SCALE
TILTING TABLE
CLAMP LEDGE
INDEX PIN
LOWER TABLE OR BASE

BELT TENSION KNOB
MOTOR
HEAD SUPPORT SAFETY COLLAR
UNIVERSAL FEED LEVER
TABLE LOCKING CLAMP
COLUMN

DELTA 15″ DRILL PRESS

30-2a. Parts of a 15″ bench-type drill press. Four speeds can be obtained by changing the position of the belt.

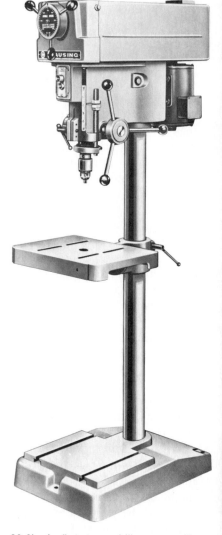

30-2b. A floor-type drill press with variable-speed pulley. The machine must be operating when the speed is changed.

never be used for any cutting that exerts side thrust. Fig. 30-5. Fasten an adapter in place of the chuck to hold the router, shaper, planer, or sanding tool. Fig. 30-6. On some machines, the whole chuck and spindle assembly is a single unit. To remove this, loosen the set screws that hold the spindle in the quill. Insert the new spindle and adapter.

Adjusting the Table

Raise or lower the table by first loosening the clamp that holds it to the column. Always place the table so the clearance hole is directly under the chuck. The space between chuck and table should be slightly more than the length of the cutting tool, plus the thickness of the stock and a backup scrap block. To tilt the table, pull out the pin that locks it to the table bracket. Then loosen the nut and tilt the table to the desired angle. Most models have holes for setting the table with the pin at 45 degrees to right and left as well as horizontally and vertically.

Adjusting the Speed

Speed adjustment on the drill press is of two types—the *step pulley* and the *variable-speed drive*. To change the speed of the drill press with a step pulley:

1. Disconnect the electric power supply.
2. Remove the belt guard.
3. Release the belt tension.

4. Position the belt on the pulleys that will provide the correct speed for the job to be performed.

5. Replace the belt tension, the belt guard, and the electric power plug. You are now ready to proceed with the job. Fig. 30-7.

30-3. The multi-speed attachment provides eight speeds from 125 rpm to 5800 rpm with a 1725 rpm motor.

30-4. Installing a drill in a chuck.

30-5. To remove the chuck, hold it with the chuck key and turn the collar with a spanner wrench. The collar will force the chuck off the tapered spindle.

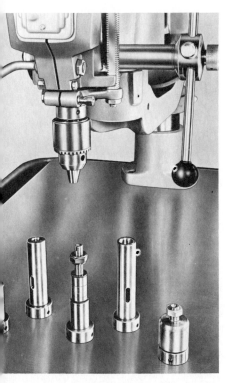

30-6a. The chuck can be replaced with many adapters to hold attachments for such operations as planing, routing, sanding, mortising, and buffing.

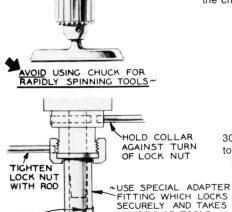

PRESS FIT MAY SHAKE LOOSE AT HIGH R P M

AVOID USING CHUCK FOR RAPIDLY SPINNING TOOLS~

HOLD COLLAR AGAINST TURN OF LOCK NUT

TIGHTEN LOCK NUT WITH ROD

SET SCREW

~USE SPECIAL ADAPTER FITTING WHICH LOCKS SECURELY AND TAKES VARIETY OF TOOLS

30-6b. Installing a special adaptor on the drill press for attachments that exert side thrust.

30-7. Always check the belt tension and adjust it if necessary after changing speeds with a step pulley.

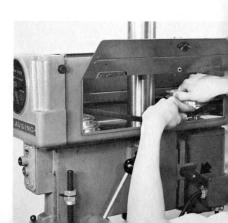

30-8a. Controls for a variable-speed drill press. Never change the speed unless the motor is running.

30-9. A hold-down clamp is an excellent device for safely securing the workpiece.

To change the speed of the variable speed drill press: *Turn the machine on* and turn the speed control handle to the correct speed. Using the correct speed is important for your safety, for a better cut, and for longer lasting cutting tools. Fig. 30-8.

Basic Procedures

• Always make sure that the drill press is set to the proper speed. In general, maintain a slow speed for large drills and bits, and higher speed for small ones. Bits up to about ½″ in size should be operated at a speed of 2000 to 3000 rpm, bits from ½″ to 1″ at about 1000 to 2000 rpm, and above 1″ at about 300 to 500 rpm. For shaper and router operations, a speed of 4000 to 5000 rpm is required.

• Whenever necessary, clamp the work securely. For most drilling and boring of small holes, the work can be held in place with the hand. For other operations, however, hand or C clamps should be used. Fig. 30-9.

• Install the correct kind of tool for the work. There are many styles of wood bits for use in the drill press. The most common are

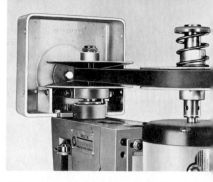

30-8b. Belt tension is automatically maintained when changing speeds on a drill press with variable-speed drive.

the auger bit, twist drill, machine spur bit, multi-spur bit, and the machine Foerstner. Fig. 30-10.

The auger bit is made in either a single or a double twist. Never attempt to use a hand-type auger bit. The machine auger bit must have a brad-type point.

Foerstner bits are used for boring shallow holes. Expansion bits, multi-spur bits, hole saws, and circle cutters are used for cutting large holes. Twist drills, the same as those used in metalworking, can be used for drilling small holes. If a set is to be used exclusively for woodwork, the points should be ground to an included angle of 60 to 80 degrees. *All bits and drills must have straight shanks.*

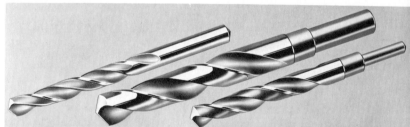

30-10a. Twist drills of several sizes. Other bits and cutters commonly used on the drill press are shown in the illustrations through Fig. 30-10l.

30-10b. Countersink

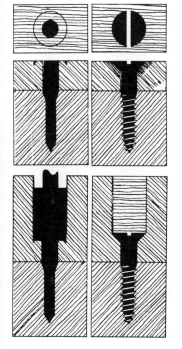

30-10c. "Screwmate." Combination countersink-counterbores.

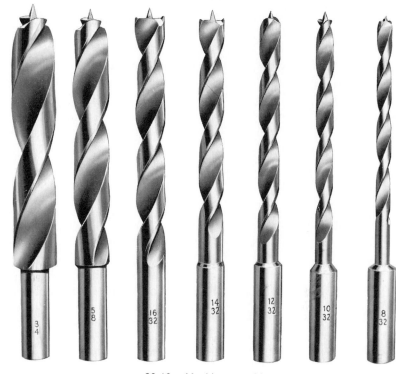

30-10e. Machine spur bits.

30-10f. "Power-bore" bit.

30-10g. Spade-type power bit.

30-10j. Circle cutter.

DOUBLE SPUR BIT *(FLUTED)*

DOUBLE SPUR BIT *(SOLID CENTER)*

30-10d. Double spur bits—fluted (top) and solid center (bottom).

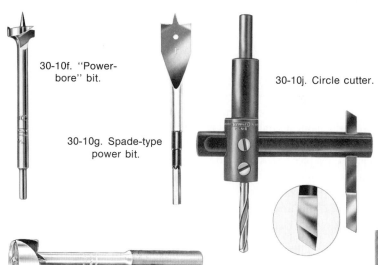

30-10h. Foerstner bit.

30-10l. Hole saw.

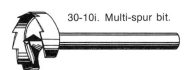

30-10i. Multi-spur bit.

30-10k. Plug cutter.

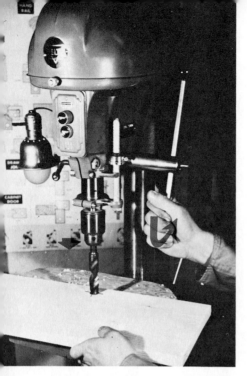

30-11. When boring a hole completely through the workpiece, be sure the bit is lined up with the hole in the table. Back up the workpiece with scrap stock to eliminate tear-out.

Boring Small Holes in Flat Stock

To bore a hole ¾″ or smaller in diameter, use a machine spur bit. Locate the center of the hole and mark it with a center punch or scratch awl. Insert the bit in the chuck. Place a piece of scrap wood on the table and adjust the machine to correct speed. Fig. 30-11. Turn on the machine and slowly bring the point of the bit into the stock. Hold the stock firmly and apply even pressure to the handle. If the stock is hardwood or the hole deep, back up the bit once or twice to remove the chips before finishing the hole. Always bore through the hole and into the scrap wood. If no backup board is used, the wood will split out as

the bit goes through the stock. Fig. 30-12.

Boring Large Holes in Flat Stock

Holes larger than ¾″ must be cut with a multi-spur bit. Fig. 30-13. If the correct size is not available, an expansion bit or a circle cutter should be used. Fig. 30-10. Adjust the cutter until the distance from the center to the spur is equal to the radius of the hole. Fasten the stock to be cut on the table with a piece of scrap stock underneath. It is often necessary to clamp the work for this operation because the cutter is a single-point tool and has a tendency to rotate the work. Make sure that the center of the cutter is directly over the center of the hole. Fig. 30-14. Maintain a low speed and apply slow, even pressure. Thin stock cracks easily when doing this job. The circle cutter can be used to cut small wheels for toys and other objects.

Boring Deep Holes

On most drill presses the spindle will move only 4″; therefore other methods must be used for deeper holes. *If the hole is between 4″ and 8″ deep,* one of the following methods can be followed:

METHOD A: Clamp a piece of scrap stock to the table of the drill press. Select the correct size bit, install it in the chuck, and bore a small hole. Lower the table to accommodate the stock to be drilled. To line up the hole in the

30-14. Always operate the circle cutter at a slow speed and clamp the workpiece to the table.

30-12. Drilling holes in two or more pieces, using clamps.

30-13. Multi-spur bits will bore without tearing. They come in diameters from ½″ to 3″.

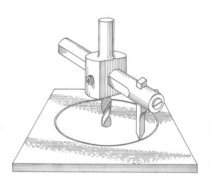

30-15. Boring a deep hole.

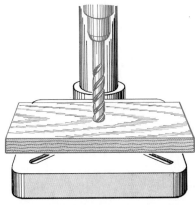

a. Boring a hole in the scrap stock.

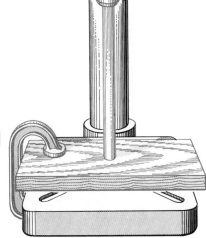

b. Aligning the hole.

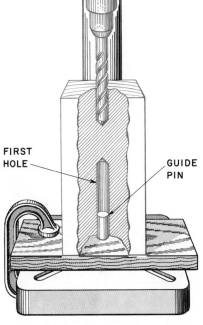

FIRST HOLE

GUIDE PIN

c. Boring from the second end.

30-16. Boring deep holes with the table turned on edge. This same technique can be used for boring holes for dowel joints in leg-and-rail construction.

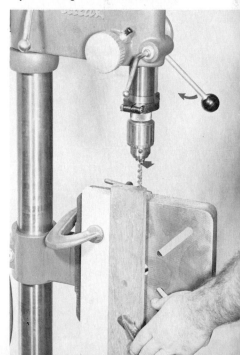

scrap stock with the chuck, it may be necessary to remove the bit and replace it with a long piece of dowel rod. Replace the bit, and bore the hole to the maximum depth. Next, cut a short piece of dowel rod and put it in the hole in the scrap stock; then turn over the material to be bored, with the hole over the dowel rod, and bore the other half of the hole. This will assure the meeting of the holes in the center. Fig. 30-15.

METHOD B: A second method is to turn the table parallel to the column. Fig. 30-16. Fasten a temporary fence to the table, so the hole to be bored aligns with the bit. Then bore from both ends.

If a hole deeper than 8″ is to be bored, a bit extension can be used and one of the above procedures followed, moving the stock as needed.

Boring Equally Spaced Holes Along a Surface or Edge

METHOD A: In a block bore a hole the same size as the holes to

be bored in the work. Insert a dowel, a bolt, or another drill, of the same diameter, to be used as the stop pin. Accurately lay out the location of the first two holes. Bore the first hole, then insert the stop pin with the block attached into the first hole. Position the second hole directly under the point of the bit, and clamp the block to the fence. Turn on the drill press and bore the second hole. Remove the stock and relocate it so that the pin can be reinserted into the second hole. Then bore the third hole. Continue this procedure until the desired number of holes has been bored. Fig. 30-17a. See next page.

METHOD B: A second method is to use a fence with a series of holes in it. Clamp the fence to the table. Place a pin in the first hole and hold the work against it, adjusting the fence to bore the first hole correctly. Move the pin to the next hole and repeat. Fig. 30-17b.

30-17a. The stop pin works through a block and is set in the previously drilled hole to locate the next hole. The distance between the first two holes must be accurately marked.

30-17b. Another method of boring equally spaced holes, using a fence as a jig.

Boring Holes at An Angle

Tilt the table to the desired angle. This can be checked with a sliding T bevel or protractor head, as shown in Fig. 30-18. Clamp the work to the table and proceed. If the hole is fairly large, it may be necessary to cut a piece of scrap stock which has the same angle as the table. Fig. 30-19. This is then clamped to the stock directly over the hole. In this way it is possible to start the hole on a flat surface.

Enlarging Smaller Holes and Counterboring

Frequently in furniture construction the heads of screws must be covered. The preferred method of doing this involves first drilling a large hole for the head of the screw, then making a smaller hole through the center of the larger one. The large hole, which is drilled just deep enough so the screw head will be covered, is called the *counterbored* hole. The smaller hole is for the shank of the screw. Fig. 30-20a.

Sometimes the shank hole is drilled first, then enlarged to a given depth for the head of the screw. One method of enlarging the smaller hole is to use a Foerstner bit. A second method is to obtain a piece of dowel rod equal in diameter to the hole already drilled. Place it in the hole and then bore into the center with the larger bit. This way the drill will not wobble. Fig. 30-20b.

To set up the drill press for counterboring to a specified depth, follow these steps:

1. With the power off, place the workpiece on the table.

30-18. Checking the angle of the table with a sliding T bevel.

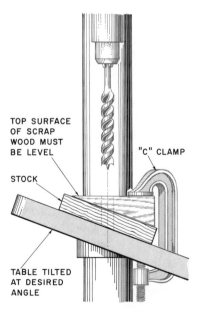

TOP SURFACE OF SCRAP WOOD MUST BE LEVEL

"C" CLAMP

STOCK

TABLE TILTED AT DESIRED ANGLE

30-19. The scrap block serves as a guide to hold the bit as it enters the stock at an angle.

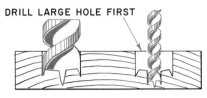

DRILL LARGE HOLE FIRST

30-20a. The best practice when counterboring is to drill the large hole first (left) and then the smaller hole.

DOWEL   HOLE

30-20b. To enlarge a small hole, insert a dowel in the hole and cut with a machine spur bit (left) or use a Foerstner bit (right).

2. Bring the bit down so that the bottom aligns with a mark on the edge of the workpiece, indicating the depth.

3. Clamp the quill.

4. Bring the depth stop into position and lock it. Fig. 30-21.

5. Release the quill lock, turn on the power, and bore the hole.

Boring Holes for Dowel Joints

Edge butt. Lay out the location of the dowel hole. Fasten a temporary fence to the table so that the point of the auger bit lines up with the center of the edge of the stock. Hold the stock firmly against the fence and bore the hole. It is good practice to hold the face surface of both boards against the fence. The hole should always be about ⅛″ deeper than the length of the dowel used. Fig.

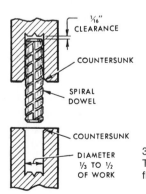

30-21a. To set the drill press for boring holes to a specific depth, first clamp the quill so the bottom of the bit is even with the line indicating the hole depth. Then lock the depth stop.

30-21b. The depth stop on this drill press is calibrated to show changes of two-thousandths of an inch.

30-23a. When preparing to bore a dowel hole, carefully hold the workpiece under the bit and bring the bit down to the center punched mark. Rack the bit up, turn the drill press on, and bore the hole.

30-22. A dowel jig can be used as a guide instead of the fence.

Corner butt. Lay out the holes as described in Unit 14, "Making joints," and center punch the location. Bore the holes in the edge grain as for an edge butt. Turn the table to the vertical position and bore the holes in the end grain.

1/16″ CLEARANCE

COUNTERSUNK

SPIRAL DOWEL

COUNTERSUNK

DIAMETER 1/3 TO 1/2 OF WORK

30-22. Standard dowel construction. The spiral dowel pin allows the glue to flow freely and the air to escape from the hole.

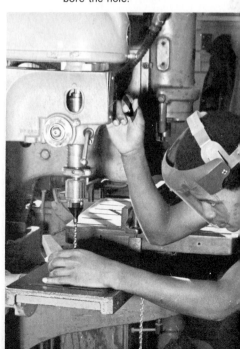

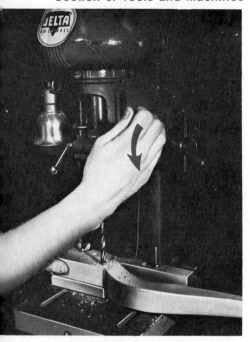

30-23b. Boring dowel holes in a table leg. Because of the shape of the leg, it is necessary to hold the back edge of the leg against the fence.

30-24. Boring holes in the end of a rail for a dowel joint. The table has been turned on edge (to the vertical position.)

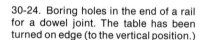

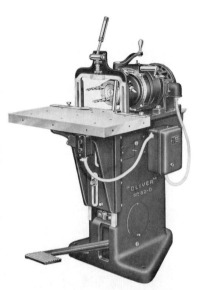

30-25. The horizontal boring machine will bore holes at any angle from the horizontal to the vertical. Bits may be varied from $7/8''$ to $3\frac{1}{2}''$ between centers.

Figs. 30-23 and 30-24. The horizontal boring machine is designed for boring dowel holes. When this machine is available, it is a simple job to handle long stock and to align the holes accurately for a good joint. Fig. 30-25.

Miter Joint

METHOD A: Tilt the table to an angle of 45 degrees. Clamp a temporary fence to it. The edge of the stock should be centered under the chuck. Clamp a stop block to this fence so that the position for the first hole is directly under the chuck. Adjust the depth stop. Bore the first hole in all the pieces. (*For example*, in making frames there would be eight holes.) Then readjust the stop block and bore the second hole in each piece. Fig. 30-26.

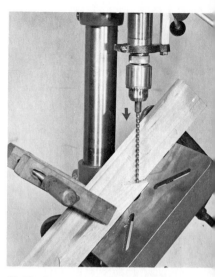

30-26. One method of boring a hole for a miter joint with dowels. Notice that the table is tilted to 45 degrees.

METHOD B: Turn the table to a vertical position. Clamp a fence to the table at an angle of 45 degrees and proceed as shown in Fig. 30-27.

30-27. A second method of boring a hole for a miter joint with dowels. Here the table is turned to a vertical position.

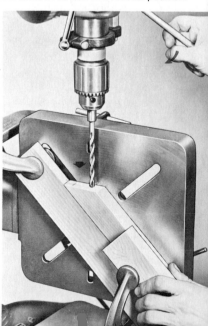

Boring Holes Around a Circle

First, a temporary wood table with a sharp brad point in the center should be clamped over the table. Place the temporary table so that the distance from the brad point to the chuck is equal to the radius of the circle around which the holes are to be bored. Place the work over this brad point and bore the first hole; then swing the work to the next position and repeat until the required number of holes has been bored.

Boring Holes in Round Stock

For small, round stock fasten a V block to the table, with the center of the V directly under the center of the drill or bit. Drill the hole. Fig. 30-28.

A second method is to tilt the table at 45 degrees and clamp a fence to it. The corner formed should be directly under the center of the drill or bit.

30-28. Drilling holes in small rod, using a V block.

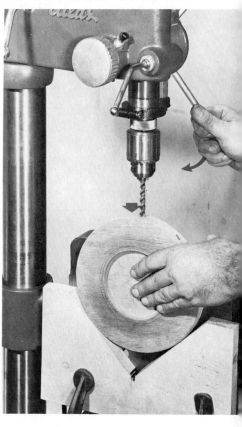

30-29. Boring holes around the edge of a disc, using a V block to hold the work.

To drill or bore holes in the center of wood balls or beads, cut a double V at right angles in a piece of scrap stock. Fasten this to the table with the crossed centers directly under the drill or bit.

If holes must be bored in the edge of a circular piece, turn the table to the vertical position, clamp a large V block in place, and bore the holes. Fig. 30-29. The same technique can be followed in drilling holes in odd-shaped pieces. Fig. 30-30.

Drilling Holes for Wood Screws

Select the correct size drill for the wood screws. Fig. 30-31. The pilot hole is for the threaded portion of the screw. In hardwood, it is good practice to bore the pilot hole the same size as the root diameter. (Consult Fig. 30-31 under heading *Root Diameter.*) In softwood, drill the pilot hole about 15 percent smaller.

Drill the pilot hole through the first piece and into the second piece to the desired depth. Drill the shank hole through the first piece. For flathead screws, use an 82-degree, rose-type countersink to enlarge the end of the shank hole. If the screw is to be covered with a plug, bore the hole for this first, then the shank hole, and finally the root diameter hole.

A second method of drilling holes for screws is to drill the shank hole first. Then hold the first piece over the second and mark the location for the pilot hole with a scratch awl.

30-30. Drilling holes in an irregular shaped piece.

309

Boring Chart for Wood Screws

NO. OF SCREW	MAXIMUM HEAD DIAMETER	SHANK DIAMETER		ROOT DIAMETER		THREADS PER INCH	NO. OF SCREW
		BASIC DEC. SIZE	NEAREST FRACTIONAL EQUIVALENT	AVERAGE DEC. SIZE	NEAREST FRACTIONAL EQUIVALENT		
0	.119	.060	1/16 OVERSIZE .002	.040	3/64 OVERSIZE .007	32	0
1	.146	.073	5/64 OVERSIZE .005	.046	3/64 BASIC SIZE	28	1
2	.172	.086	3/32 OVERSIZE .007	.054	1/16 OVERSIZE .008	26	2
3	.199	.099	7/64 OVERSIZE .010	.065	1/16 UNDERSIZE .002	24	3
4	.225	.112	7/64 UNDERSIZE .003	.075	5/64 OVERSIZE .003	22	4
5	.252	.125	1/8 BASIC SIZE	.085	5/64 UNDERSIZE .007	20	5
6	.279	.138	9/64 OVERSIZE .002	.094	3/32 BASIC SIZE	18	6
7	.305	.151	5/32 OVERSIZE .005	.102	7/64 OVERSIZE .007	16	7
8	.332	.164	5/32 UNDERSIZE .007	.112	7/64 UNDERSIZE .003	15	8
9	.358	.177	11/64 UNDERSIZE .005	.122	1/8 OVERSIZE .003	14	9
10	.385	.190	3/16 UNDERSIZE .002	.130	1/8 UNDERSIZE .005	13	10
11	.411	.203	13/64 BASIC SIZE	.139	9/64 OVERSIZE .001	12	11
12	.438	.216	7/32 OVERSIZE .003	.148	9/64 UNDERSIZE .007	11	12
14	.491	.242	1/4 OVERSIZE .008	.165	5/32 UNDERSIZE .009	10	14
16	.544	.268	17/64 UNDERSIZE .002	.184	3/16 OVERSIZE .003	9	16
18	.597	.294	19/64 OVERSIZE .003	.204	13/64 UNDERSIZE .001	8	18
20	.650	.320	5/16 UNDERSIZE .007	.223	7/32 UNDERSIZE .004	8	20
24	.756	.372	3/8 OVERSIZE .003	.260	1/4 UNDERSIZE .010	7	24

No. 0
No. 1
No. 2
No. 3
No. 4
No. 5
No. 6
No. 7
No. 8
No. 9
No. 10
No. 11
No. 12
No. 14
No. 16
No. 18
No. 20
No. 24

30-31. Drill Size Selection Chart. Root diameters are average dimensions measured at the middle of the threaded portion. Shank diameters are shown as a decimal in thousandths of an inch. To use this chart, read down either of the columns headed *Number of Screw* to the screw size used. For example, if a No. 5 wood screw is used, the shank diameter of the screw will require a ⅛" hole. The pilot hole will need to be 5/64". Note that the pilot hole is .007" undersized. This is about right for softwood. In hardwood the next larger drill size, 3/32", should be used. The column at right shows actual wood screw shank sizes. To determine the size of a screw visually, lay the screw shank on the silhouette.

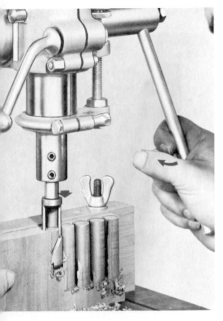

30-32. This plug cutter is being used in an adapter, but such a cutter can be used in the drill press chuck.

Cutting Plugs

Insert the plug cutter in the chuck. Place a piece of scrap wood on the table. Next take a piece of the same kind of wood that is used in the furniture you are making.

30-33. Using the mortising attachment on the drill press.

Place this "good" piece over the scrap piece and cut the plugs. Maintain a spindle speed of 1200 rpm. Try to match the direction and kind of grain of the plug to the place where it will be used. Fig. 30-32.

Cutting a Mortise

A mortising attachment can be fastened to the drill press for this cut. Fig. 30-33.

Using a Shaper Attachment

The drill press can be quickly converted into a shaper. Attach an auxiliary wood table and fence to the table. Replace the chuck with a shaper tool adapter. The head assembly can be kept in its normal position or it can be inverted so that it is below the table. Adjust the speed to 5000 rpm or faster. Attach the cutters and perform the shaper operations as described in the unit beginning on page 355.

Using a Router Attachment

Replace the chuck with a router bit adapter. Attach an auxiliary wood fence. Fig. 30-34. Adjust to 5000 rpm or faster and perform the router operations as described in the unit beginning on page 345.

Using a Planer Attachment

Fasten a planer attachment to an adapter. Install a temporary wood table and fence. Adjust the speed to between 3000 and 5000 rpm. Make the cuts. Move the fence after each cut so a different portion of the workpiece will be surfaced on the next cut. Fig. 30-35.

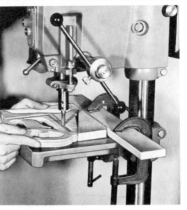

30-34. Routing on the drill press.

30-35a. Using a planer attachment.

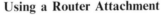

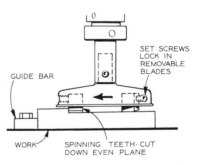

30-35b. Drawing of a planer attachment.

30-36a. Sanding drums. These can be used on the drill press with an adapter or on a wood lathe.

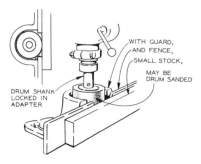

30-36b. Drum sanding the surface of a board.

Using a Sanding Attachment

For sanding the face of a board, fasten a rotary sander attachment to the adapter and adjust to a speed of 3500 rpm. Fig. 30-36. To sand the edge of stock, fasten a drum sander attachment to an adapter and use a temporary wood table. Fig. 30-37.

30-37a. Sanding an irregular edge. Always use the drum diameter which best fits the radius being sanded.

30-37b. The legs on this table can be sanded to fit the center column on a drum sander, (See Fig. 30-37c).

30-37c. Sanding the end of a piece of stock to fit a round column.

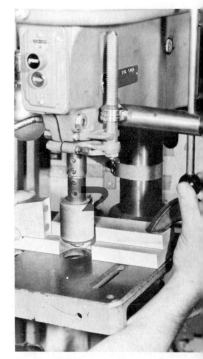

PORTABLE ELECTRIC DRILL

SAFETY

- Review general safety rules for use of portable electric tools.
- Disconnect the power plug before installing or removing drills.
- Make certain the drill is clamped securely in the chuck.
- Be sure the key has been removed.
- Do not force the drill—use an even steady pressure.
- Never use a bit with a square tang or a lead screw.
- When laying the drill down, always have the point away from you, even when it is "coasting" to a stop.
- Never drill through cloth.
- Always clamp small pieces; do not hold them with your fingers when drilling.

Portable Electric Drill

The portable electric drill is an excellent tool for drilling, boring holes, and for many other uses. The tool consists of a housing with a handle, a motor, and a chuck. Most of these drills have a key-type chuck. Fig. 30-38. These tools are made in a variety of shapes. The most common shapes are the pistol-grip drill which usually will hold drill bits up to $\frac{1}{4}''$, and the spade handle drill which usually has a chuck capacity up to $\frac{1}{2}''$. Fig. 30-39.

Some drill housings are made of plastic to reduce the danger from shock. Others have a built-in variable speed unit, the speed varying directly with the amount of pressure exerted on the trigger switch. The cutting tools can be twist drills, auger bits (if they have straight shanks), or spade (speed) bits. Fig. 30-40a.

The combination drill and countersink is a convenient tool for inserting woodscrews. It is always necessary to drill the correct size holes for woodscrews to prevent splitting the workpiece and to get the maximum holding power. This is usually a three-step procedure, if the screw is to be countersunk. The combination drill, however, will drill the pilot hole, shank hole, and countersink, all in one operation. Fig. 30-40b.

Before inserting a bit, make sure that it has a straight shank. Turn the drill chuck by hand until the jaws are open wide enough to take the desired size bit. Insert the

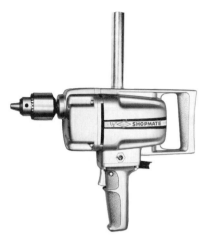

30-39. The $\frac{1}{2}''$ capacity electric hand drill with spade handle.

30-40a. The spade bit is often used to bore large holes with a $\frac{1}{4}''$ capacity hand drill.

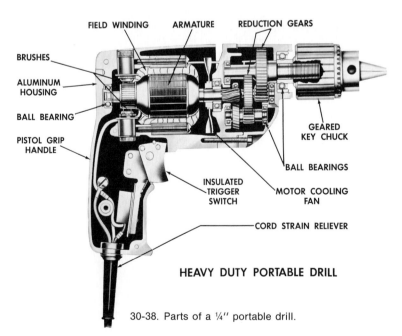

FIELD WINDING   ARMATURE   REDUCTION GEARS

BRUSHES

ALUMINUM HOUSING

BALL BEARING

PISTOL GRIP HANDLE

GEARED KEY CHUCK

BALL BEARINGS

INSULATED TRIGGER SWITCH

MOTOR COOLING FAN

CORD STRAIN RELIEVER

HEAVY DUTY PORTABLE DRILL

30-38. Parts of a $\frac{1}{4}''$ portable drill.

COUNTERSINK
SHANK CLEARANCE
PILOT HOLE

30-40b. Combination drills are available in most of the common woodscrew sizes. For example, if a 1" #8 woodscrew is used, a 1" #8 combination drill should be used.

30-41. Always tighten the chuck securely to prevent the bit from slipping.

bit shank in the chuck as far as possible, then close the jaws by hand. Next, tighten the chuck by inserting the key wrench in each of the key holes in succession. Use all three holes to avoid slippage as much as possible. Fig. 30-41. To release the bit, only one hole needs to be used. Remember, always unplug the drill when changing bits.

Drilling Holes

Always use the correct bit or accessory. Fig. 30-42. Make sure the tool (preferably of high-speed steel) is sharp. Apply just enough pressure to the drill to keep it cutting. Too little pressure will make the drill dull; too much pressure may cause it to stall or break. To prevent break-through splintering, clamp a piece of scrap wood behind the piece being drilled. Always clamp the wood in a vise, or hold it securely with a clamp. Hold the tool at right angles to the work when drilling a straight hole. Fig. 30-43. This can be checked by using a try square to align the tool. If the drill is equipped with a variable speed unit, it can be used as a powerful screwdriver by inserting a screwdriver bit. Fig. 30-44. Start the screw slowly, increase the speed as the screw moves into the stock, and finish by slowing to a stop. On a standard-speed drill, a speed reduction ratchet attachment must be used for installing screws.

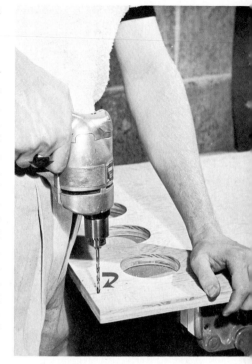

30-43. Drilling a hole in flat stock. Be sure to hold the tool at right angles to the workpiece.

Material or Job	Bit or Accessory	Suggested Speed	
		¼″ Drill	⅜″ Drill
Wood	Twist Drill	High	High
Wood	Spade Bits	High	High
Wood	Auger Bits	Med. to Low	High to Med.
Wood	Hole or Dial Saw	Med. to Low	Medium
Heavy Metal	Twist Drill*	Medium	High
Light Metal	Twist Drill*	High	High
Plastics	Twist Drill	Medium	High
Driving Screws	Driver Bit	Low	Low

* Only high speed steel twist drills should be used for drilling in metal.

30-42. Suggested drilling speeds.

30-44. Using the variable-speed hand drill as a power screwdriver.

MORTISER

- Do not wear loose clothing or long, unconfined hair.
- Remove all chuck keys or wrenches before machine is started.
- Clamp all stock securely.
- Make sure the power is off and the bit is not turning before making adjustments.
- Make sure the clearance is properly set between the bit and chisel.
- Make certain the cutting edges are properly sharpened.
- Do not force the cut, especially on hardwoods.
- Remove all chips with a brush.

Mortisers and
Mortising Attachments

31-1. To manufacture this room of furniture would require over 130 mortise-and-tenon joints.

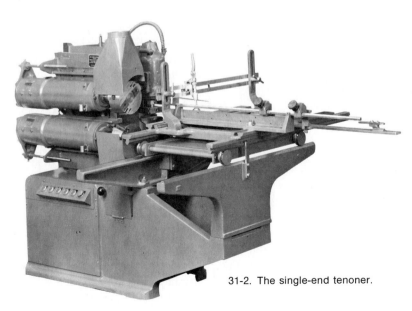

31-2. The single-end tenoner.

The mortise-and-tenon joint is used frequently in furniture construction. Fig. 31-1. Since cutting mortises by hand is a long and tedious job, it is very desirable to have a mortising machine or a mortising attachment for the drill press. This attachment can be purchased very reasonably.

In industry tenons are cut on a tenoner. Fig. 31-2. However, this is an expensive piece of equipment, of limited use in many nonindustrial shops. Therefore in schools and home workshops, tenons are often cut on a circular saw, jointer, or shaper.

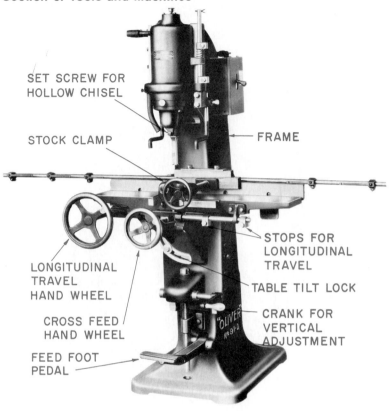

SET SCREW FOR
HOLLOW CHISEL

STOCK CLAMP

FRAME

STOPS FOR
LONGITUDINAL
TRAVEL

LONGITUDINAL
TRAVEL
HAND WHEEL

CROSS FEED
HAND WHEEL

FEED FOOT
PEDAL

TABLE TILT LOCK

CRANK FOR
VERTICAL
ADJUSTMENT

31-3. Parts of a mortiser.

31-4. Mortising chisel and bit: A. Chisel shank diameter. B. Chisel size. C. Mortise depth. D. Bit size.
E. Bit shank diameter.

Mortiser

The mortising machine consists of a vertical column to which a table and motor-driven head are attached. The head moves up and down through the operation of a foot pedal. *The table can be moved up or down* for permanent settings, *in or out* to locate the work in the correct position under the bit, and (on some types) *right or left* for cutting the mortise. Fig. 31-3.

The table has hold-downs which hold the work firmly against the table. Adjustable stops limit the movement of the table, thus controlling the length of the mortise.

Mortising bits fit into the chuck on the end of the motor. There is a bushing for each size chisel to fit into the head of the mortising machine. The common chisel sizes are $\frac{1}{4}''$, $\frac{3}{8}''$, $\frac{1}{2}''$, $\frac{5}{8}''$, $\frac{3}{4}''$, and $1''$. Fig. 31-4.

Using a Mortiser

1. Square up the stock to the desired size and lay out the location for one mortise. The mortises on the other parts will then be in the proper position when the table has been correctly set. When cutting mortises on two sides of a piece, always check the location for each. This is particularly important if the mortise is not centered in the width of the stock. Whenever the mortises are off-center, half will be off-center to the right and half to the left. Care must be taken to keep track of the location of mortises in each piece.

2. Select the correct size of chisel and bit. For example, use a $\frac{1}{2}''$ bit and chisel for a $\frac{1}{2}''$ mortise. Also select the correct size bushing for the chisel. These split bushings all have the same outside diameter, with varying dimensions on the inside to hold chisels with various shank diameters.

3. Insert the bushing for the chisel and then install the chisel itself. Turn the chisel so the open side is to the right (or to the right and left if it is open on both sides). This opening provides an escape for the chips.

4. Hold a square against the side of the chisel and against the fence to align them. Then tighten the set screws that hold the chisel in place. Fig. 31-5.

5. Insert the bit until it extends

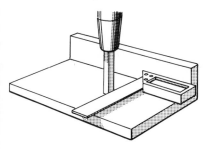

31-5. Use a try square to align the chisel with the fence.

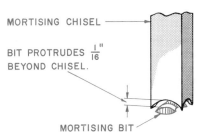

MORTISING CHISEL

BIT PROTRUDES $\frac{1}{16}$" BEYOND CHISEL.

MORTISING BIT

31-6. Always make certain the clearance between the chisel and bit is properly set to avoid overheating the tools and drawing the temper.

about $\frac{1}{16}$" beyond the chisel. Tighten the set screws or chuck. Fig. 31-6.

6. Place the stock to be mortised on the table, with a mark on the end indicating the depth of the mortise. Press the foot pedal down as far as it will go. Turn the screw adjustment on the head until, at the end of the stroke, the chisel is in line with the bottom of the mortise. Release the foot pedal.

7. Place the end of the stock under the chisel and move the table in or out until the chisel is directly over the layout. Now move the work until the mortising chisel is over the extreme right end of the mortise. Place a stop against the end of the stock so that

other identical pieces will be located automatically. Also adjust the stop on the table. Now move the table or the work to the left end of the mortise and adjust the stop. There are two hold-downs to keep the work in place.

8. Move the table back to the starting position, which is the right end. Turn on the machine, press the pedal down, and cut about halfway to depth. Move the table to the right and cut to full depth. Then move it back to the starting position and finish the first hole. This is done to relieve the pressure on the chisel and to provide a way for chips to escape. Continue to make full cuts until the mortise is complete. Fig. 31-7.

9. Cut all identical mortises. Then reset the machine for mortises in a different location.

Mortising Attachment

The mortising attachment for a drill press consists of a fence against which the work is aligned, a clamp to hold the work in position, and a mortising chisel holder which is clamped to the quill. On some machines the mortising chisel bit is held in an adapter. Most often, however, it is fastened into the regular drill chuck. Fig. 31-8.

31-7. Using a mortiser. The operator can move the table from left to right on this mortiser by turning the hand wheel.

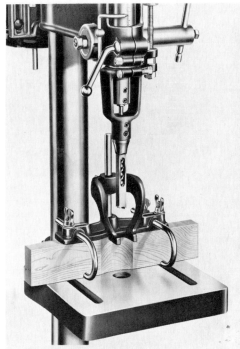

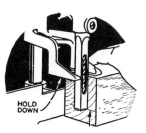

HOLD DOWN

31-8. Mortising attachment for the drill press. Here the bit is held in an adapter.

To install the mortising attachment:

1. Remove the chuck, if necessary, and also the collar from the quill.

2. Install an adapter, if necessary.

3. Replace the stop collar with the mortising chisel socket and clamp it in place. Use the depth stop rod in this chisel socket to keep the quill from turning and to regulate the depth of the chisel cut.

4. Fasten the fence to the table approximately where it should be for the cut. It can be moved in or out to locate the mortise exactly.

5. Install the correct chisel and square up one side of it with the fence. Then install the correct bit. Be sure to allow $\frac{1}{16}''$ clearance between chisel and bit.

6. Turn the drill press over by hand to see that the bit does not scrape the chisel excessively. Adjust the drill press to a speed of about 1000 rpm.

Using a Mortising Attachment

1. Lay out the position of the mortise on all pieces. Place the stock on the table against the fence and move the fence in or out until the chisel is directly over the layout. Then move the stock away from under the chisel, bring the chisel down, and adjust the stop to control the depth of cut. Also place the hold-downs in position to hold the work against the table and the fence.

2. Start at the right end of the mortise and proceed with the cutting as described earlier. The chisel movement is operated by the hand feed lever and the stock must be moved by hand. Fig. 31-9.

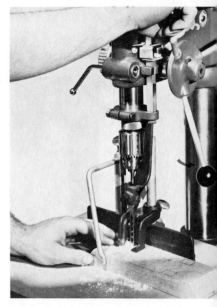

31-9. Using a mortising attachment on the drill press. Here the bit is held in a Jacob's chuck.

BAND SAW

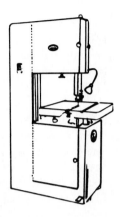

SAFETY

- Keep the upper guide down as close as possible to the top of your work.
- Never line your fingers or thumbs up with the cut.
- Always support round stock in a V-block.
- When doing compound band sawing be sure you have support under the cut. Never attempt to hold the stock up by hand.
- Always make the short cuts first so there will be a minimum of backing out.
- Never stand on the right hand side of a band saw. This is a most dangerous position should a blade break.
- Check before you start your cut to make sure the radius of your cut is not too small for the width of the blade.
- A helper should never pull or guide the work. He just supports the stock.
- If constant, evenly spaced clicks are heard, turn off the machine. Pull the power plug or lock the power supply off and check the blade for a crack.
- The blade should be running at full speed before a cut is started.
- Plan your cuts carefully and make relief cuts before making long curved cuts.
- Be sure there is proper tension on the blade and it is tracking properly before turning the machine on.
- Always use a sharp blade.
- Always feed the stock evenly; never crowd, twist, or jerk the material being sawn.
- If a blade breaks, *turn off the power,* and wait until both wheels stop dead before opening or removing the wheel guards.
- If the saw is equipped with a brake, apply it gently. *Don't jam the brake.*

UNIT **32** Band Saw

The band saw is a simple machine to operate. It gets its name from the fact that *the cutting blade is a continuous band of metal*. It is designed to cut curves and irregular shapes but can also be used for many straight cutting operations. Fig. 32-1.

Size

The size of the band saw is determined by the diameter of the wheel. Sizes from 14″ to 24″ are most common. The size is also indicated by the distance from the top of the table to the bottom of the upper guide. This limits the thickness of stock that the machine can cut.

Parts

The band saw consists of a frame on which two wheels are mounted. The lower wheel is connected to the source of power, and the upper wheel can be moved up or down and tilted for adjustment. The table is fastened to the frame and can be tilted 45 degrees in one direction and, on some types, a few degrees in the other direction. Two guide units, one above and one below the table, keep the blade aligned for cutting. Fig. 32-2. The upper one can be moved up and down as the thickness of stock varies. Guards should cover both upper and lower wheels and all parts of the blade except that part which does the cutting. Fig. 32-3.

Adjustments

The adjusting handles, wheels, and guides are shown in Fig. 32-2a and b.

Installing a New Blade

1. Remove the guards, the throat plate, and the pin or set screw in the table slot. Loosen the upper wheel, open the upper and lower guides, and move the thrust bearing or guide wheels back.

2. Uncoil the blade and slip it through the slot of the table and then over the two wheels. Make

32-1. This drum table would require many band-sawing operations to reproduce. The table is 20″ high and its diameter is 28″.

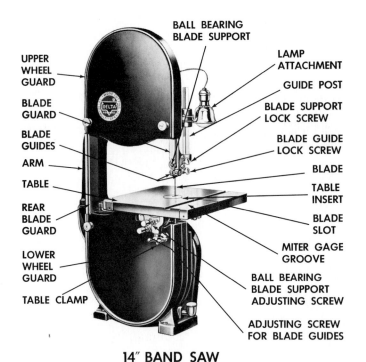

BALL BEARING
BLADE SUPPORT

LAMP
ATTACHMENT

GUIDE POST

BLADE SUPPORT
LOCK SCREW

BLADE GUIDE
LOCK SCREW

BLADE

TABLE
INSERT

BLADE
SLOT

MITER GAGE
GROOVE

BALL BEARING
BLADE SUPPORT
ADJUSTING SCREW

ADJUSTING SCREW
FOR BLADE GUIDES

UPPER
WHEEL
GUARD

BLADE
GUARD

BLADE
GUIDES

ARM

TABLE

REAR
BLADE
GUARD

LOWER
WHEEL
GUARD

TABLE CLAMP

14″ BAND SAW

32-2a. Parts of a 14″ band saw.

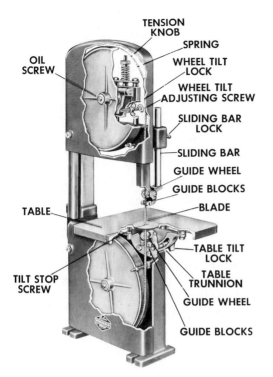

TENSION KNOB

SPRING

OIL SCREW

WHEEL TILT LOCK

WHEEL TILT ADJUSTING SCREW

SLIDING BAR LOCK

SLIDING BAR

GUIDE WHEEL

GUIDE BLOCKS

TABLE

BLADE

TABLE TILT LOCK

TABLE TRUNNION

TILT STOP SCREW

GUIDE WHEEL

GUIDE BLOCKS

32-2b. A cutaway showing the parts and adjusting handles of a 12″ band saw.

32-2c. A 24″ band saw.

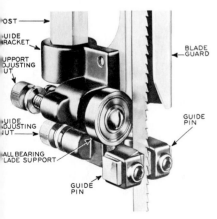

POST

GUIDE BRACKET

SUPPORT ADJUSTING NUT

BLADE GUARD

GUIDE PIN

GUIDE ADJUSTING NUT

BALL BEARING BLADE SUPPORT

GUIDE PIN

32-3a. Parts of the upper blade guide assembly.

sure that the teeth point downward toward the table. If they do not, turn the blade inside out. This is done by holding the blade up in front of you and gripping it with the thumb and index finger on each side. The blade forms a loop. Twist the blade so the edge toward you turns toward the center of the loop and finally snaps through the loop. The blade can then be installed with the teeth pointing downward toward the table. Tighten the upper wheel slightly. Turn the upper wheel over by hand to see if the blade stays in the center of the wheel. If it tends to move to one side or the other, loosen the nut that controls wheel tilt and tilt the wheel until the blade stays on center. Lock the tilt in position.

32-3b. Always keep the upper blade guide as close to the workpiece as possible. Do not expose the blade.

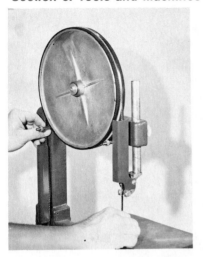

32-4. Installing a new band-saw blade.

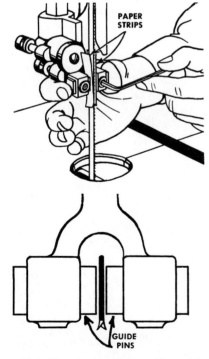

32-5. The pieces of paper will provide the correct clearance between the blade and the guide pins or blocks.

Apply additional tension to the blade. Fig. 32-4. The amount of tension will vary with the width of the blade. Many machines have a scale behind the upper wheel to show the correct tension.

Adjusting the Guide Slides or Pins

Place a piece of paper around the blade and press in the blade guide block. Fig. 32-5. The front of the guide block should be even with the bottom or gullet of the teeth. It may be necessary to move the guide assembly forward or back to make this adjustment. Now lock the guide blocks in position and remove the paper. This will provide just the right amount of clearance. Do this for both the upper and lower guides, making sure that both are aligned vertically. Fig. 32-6. Now move the ball bearing and blade support forward until it just barely clears the back of the blade. (However, when a cut is being made, the blade supports should revolve as soon as pressure is exerted against the blade. When the machine is operating but not cutting, the blade supports should stand still. If the supports revolve continuously the back of the blade will crystallize.) Replace the throat plate and the set screw or pin in the table and the guards. Fig. 32-7.

Folding a Band-Saw Blade

In changing blades, fold the old blade and hang it on a rack. Turn the blade so the teeth point upward, and with your arms outstretched, make an oval shape with it. Now hold and twist the blade as shown in Fig. 32-8. The blade will fold into three circles.

Basic Procedures

● Before operating the band saw, check to see if the correct size

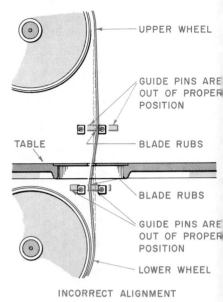

32-6. Incorrect alignment.

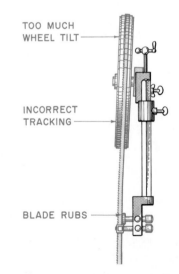

32-7. Incorrect blade support adjustment.

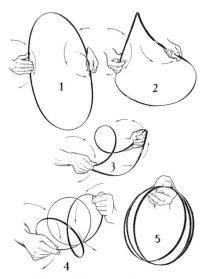

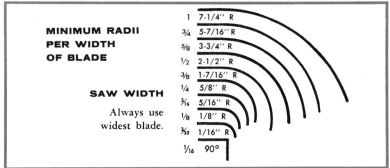

MINIMUM RADII PER WIDTH OF BLADE	1	7-1/4" R
	3/4	5-7/16" R
	5/8	3-3/4" R
	1/2	2-1/2" R
	3/8	1-7/16" R
SAW WIDTH	1/4	5/8" R
	3/16	5/16" R
Always use widest blade.	1/8	1/8" R
	3/32	1/16" R
	1/16	90°

32-9. This chart shows how to select the correct width of blade. For example, a ½" blade cannot cut a circle smaller than 2½" in radius (5" in diameter).

32-8. Folding a band-saw blade.

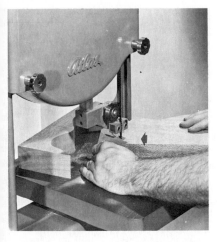

SHORT CUT   LONG CUT

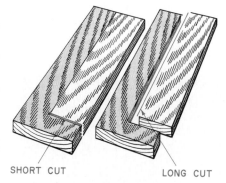

SHORT CUT   LONG CUT

32-11. Always make short cuts before long ones.

32-10. Keep your eyes on the cutting action and never permit your hands to come in line with the path of the blade.

square with the top of the table. Raise the upper guide out of position and check with a square.
● Take the correct cutting position. Right-handed operators should face the blade, standing slightly to the left of it. Guide the stock with the left hand and apply forward pressure with the right. Fig. 32-10. Left-handed operators stand to the right of the blade. They use the right hand for guiding and the left hand for feeding.

Follow these simple suggestions for all cutting:
● Change the position of the upper guide before each cutting so that it just clears the upper surface of the stock.
● Check your layout before cutting. Sometimes you will find that you have the layout on the wrong side of the stock and that the stock will hit the arm of the band saw as the cutting is done.
● Always make short cuts before long ones. When stock is cut from two sides, cut the short side first so that there will be a minimum of backing out. Fig. 32-11. Whenever possible, *cut out through* the waste stock rather than backing out.

blade is on the machine. A small blade is needed to cut sharp curves and a larger one for large circles and straight sawing. Fig. 32-9. A ⅛" or ¼" blade is satisfactory for most cutting.
● Check to see that the blade is

● Make straight cuts before curved ones. This will make the problem of backing out simpler. Fig. 32-12. See next page.
● "Break up" complicated curves and drill clearance holes. If the curve is complex, as for the side of an Early American bookcase or spoon rack, decide how the cuts

325

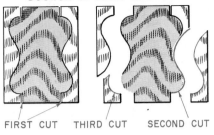

FIRST CUT   THIRD CUT   SECOND CUT

32-12. Break up complicated curves into several simpler cuts.

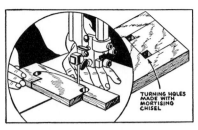

TURNING HOLES MADE WITH MORTISING CHISEL

32-13b. Use turning holes that are a part of the design.

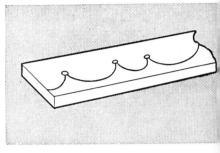

32-13c. Here drilled holes are used to simplify the cutting.

are to be made and drill a clearance hole at the sharp corners in the waste stock. Fig. 32-13. This will make it possible to cut out the design as several simpler pieces.

● Check the band-saw blade for leading. This condition causes the blade to pull to one side or the other, thus cutting a slight taper. It is difficult if not impossible to cut a straight line when this condition exists. It may be caused by

a slight burr on one side of the blade; there may be more set to the teeth on one side than on the other; the guides may be too loose or out of line; or the blade may be too narrow. To correct the first two conditions, hold an abrasive stone lightly against the side toward which the blade leads. For the other conditions, readjust the guide block or change the blade.

Straight Cutting

While the band saw was primarily designed for cutting curves and circles, many straight cutting jobs can also be done with it. One advantage of the band saw is that, if you want to, you can do this cutting freehand, following a guideline. Because the saw kerf is smaller, less material is wasted.

Cutting Freehand

Lay out a guideline on the stock. Guide one edge of the stock with the left hand and apply slow, even pressure with the right. Do not be in a hurry. (Reverse the hands if you are left-handed.) It requires some skill and patience to cut a straight line. Fig. 32-14.

Cutting with the Ripping Fence

Some band saws are equipped

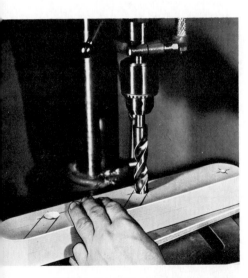

32-13a. Bore the correct diameter hole first as part of the area to be removed. This will insure a radius that is both uniform and smooth at the bottom of the opening.

32-14. Freehand straight cutting. Note the safe position of the thumbs and fingers.

with a ripping fence. If one is not available, a scrap piece of stock with a straightedge can be clamped to the table. Make sure that it is parallel to the blade. Follow the same technique as with a circular saw. Fig. 32-15.

Resawing

Cutting stock to narrower thicknesses is a common operation. The widest possible blade must be installed for this operation. There are several ways to guide the stock. The best way is to clamp a pivot pin to the table as a guide. This is especially desirable because, if the saw tends to lead to one side or the other, the board can be shifted. Fig. 32-16. A ripping fence can also be used but is not satisfactory if the blade tends to lead. When extremely wide stock is to be resawed, it is sometimes wise to make a starter cut on each edge with the circular saw. The disadvantage is, of course, that the circular saw makes a wider kerf.

When feeding the stock through the band saw, hold it firmly against the fence or guide pin. Do not overload the blade. If the lumber is rather green, apply some beeswax to the blade.

Cutting Triangular Pieces

Tilt the table to an angle of 45 degrees and fasten the ripping fence to it so the fence just clears the blade. Start with square stock to cut triangular pieces. Fig. 32-17. This is especially useful in cutting glue blocks used for strengthening adjoining surfaces. The same technique can be followed for (1) cutting quarter-round molding from round stock; (2) cutting a slight kerf across the ends of square or round stock in preparation for wood turning; or (3) for cutting octagonal shapes. A simple V-type jig can be made for performing these same operations with the table in the normal position. Fig. 32-18.

Cutting Compound Curves

Compound sawing is done in making bookends, lamp bases, and other decoratively shaped pieces that are cut on two adjoining surfaces. The cabriole leg found in Traditional and French

32-15. Resawing, using a ripping fence.

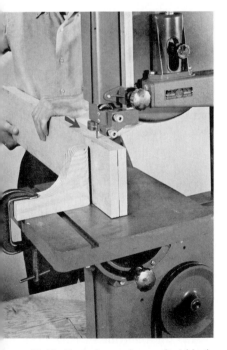

32-16. Resawing, using a pivot block.

32-17. Cutting triangular pieces with the table tilted 45 degrees.

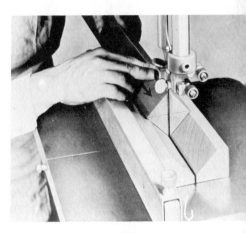

32-18. A fence and V-block can be used for diagonal ripping. This is also a good method of cutting a kerf across the corners to insert the spurs of the live center for wood turning.

32-19a. The furniture industry needs skilled band-saw operators to make such items as these dining room furnishings. Notice the cabriole legs especially.

Provincial furniture is a good example. Fig. 32-19. The most common method of cutting is shown in Fig. 32-20. Follow these steps:

1. Make a pattern of the design on heavy paper. Square up the stock (page 272) and then lay out the pattern for the design on the two adjacent sides.

2. Make the inside and outside cuts from one side, being careful to saw in the waste stock.

3. Nail the waste stock back in position. Make sure you drive the nails in the waste stock. Turn the leg a quarter turn and repeat the cutting. Some operators like to make the first two cuts almost to the end and then back out the blade. Then turn the stock a quarter turn and repeat the cutting.

Cutting a Square Opening from the Edge

Make a straight cut to the bottom of the opening on one side and back out. Then, starting at the other side, cut to the bottom of the opening, backtrack slightly, and make the turn across the bottom of the opening to meet the first cut. Remove the piece of stock and clean out the corner. Fig. 32-21. See page 330.

Cutting Long, Thin Openings

Drill a hole at the end of the opening and then make the straight cut. The end must be trimmed out with a hand chisel, rasp, or similar tool. Fig. 32-22, page 330. A mortising attachment can be used for cutting a square hole at the end of the opening, or the cut can be made as shown in Fig. 32-21.

32-19b. Compound band-saw cuts were used in making the front legs of the chairs in this suite of furniture. This type of cutting is shown in Fig. 32-20.

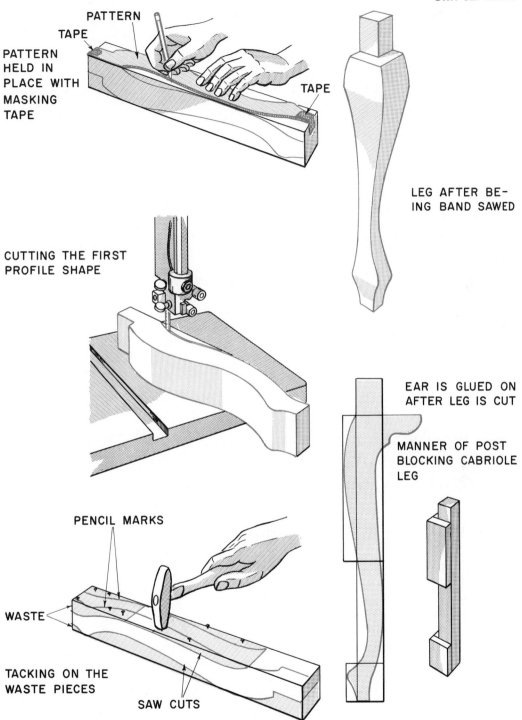

PATTERN

TAPE

PATTERN
HELD IN
PLACE WITH
MASKING
TAPE

TAPE

LEG AFTER BE-
ING BAND SAWED

CUTTING THE FIRST
PROFILE SHAPE

EAR IS GLUED ON
AFTER LEG IS CUT

MANNER OF POST
BLOCKING CABRIOLE
LEG

PENCIL MARKS

WASTE

TACKING ON THE
WASTE PIECES

SAW CUTS

32-20. Steps to follow in laying out and making a compound band-saw cut. The cabriole leg is shown in this example.

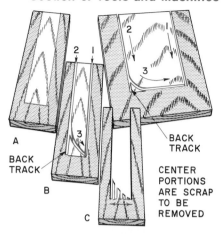

32-21. Cutting rectangular openings. The numbers indicate the order of cuts. It is necessary to backtrack slightly on Cut 2 before the curve is cut to the other corner.

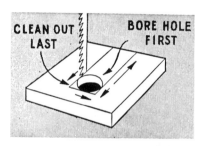

32-22. To cut a long, thin opening, bore a hole at the end of the opening and cut up to it.

Other Kinds of Straight Cutting

Many other kinds of straight cutting can be done in the same manner as with the circular saw. The results, however, will not be as accurate. The band saw is like a tilt-table saw rather than a tilt-arbor. Here are some of the operations:

- Squaring an end with a miter gage.
- Cutting angles with a miter gage.
- Making a compound angle.

- Cutting several pieces to identical length. (There is no need for a clearance block since the blade cuts in one direction and will not kick back.)
- Cutting bevels and chamfers.
- Cutting a miter joint.
- Cutting a cross-lap joint.
- Cutting an open mortise-and-tenon joint.

Cutting Curves and Irregular Shapes

Cutting Shallow Curves

Most curves are shallow and can be cut freehand. Cut up to the layout line, and guide the stock with the left hand, applying even pressure with the right. (Reverse hands if you are left handed.) The cut should be made just outside the layout line. Fig. 32-23.

Cutting Sharp Curves

Remember to install a blade narrow enough to make the cut. If a wider blade is on the machine, sharp curves can be cut by first making many relief cuts to within $1/32''$ of the layout line. Fig. 32-24. The stock will then fall away as the curve is cut.

Cutting Complex Curves

Break up the complex curve into several small cuts. Fig. 32-25.

Cutting Circles

A circular piece can usually be cut freehand, although this is somewhat difficult. Fig. 32-26. If many circular pieces are to be cut, make a simple wood jig. Cut a piece of $3/4''$ plywood slightly smaller than the table. Fasten cleats to two sides. Cut a groove or dado at right angles to the

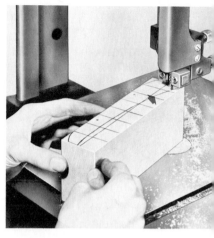

32-23. Cutting curves freehand.

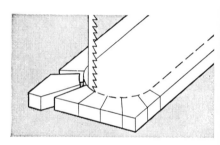

32-24. Cutting a sharp curve by first making several relief cuts.

32-25. This shows the use of relief cuts in making compound cuts for bookends. Notice how the work is held level with a common nail.

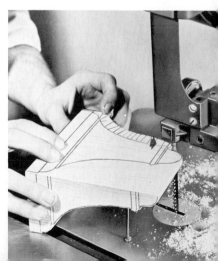

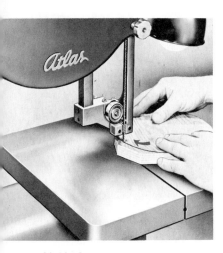

32-26. Cutting a circle freehand.

blade, with the center of the groove at the front of the teeth. Cut a small hardwood stick or aluminum bar that will just slip into the groove and be flush with the top of the wood table. Place a sharp pin or screw at the end of the sliding bar. It's a good idea also to put a small flathead screw next to the bar so that when the screw is tightened down the bar will not move. Remember that the pin must be at right angles to the blade and in line with the front

of the blade. Fig. 32-27. Now adjust the pin equal to the radius of the desired circle. Turn the board slowly as the circle is cut. Fig. 32-28. Beveled circles can be cut by tilting the table. Fig. 32-29.

Cutting Segments of a Circle

Use the temporary wood table and attach an arm to it at right angles to the blade. Cut a pattern of the circle segment. Place two wood screws through the pattern from the underside, with their points exposed. Now fasten the pattern to the temporary table with a single screw located at a point equal to the radius of the arc. Cut the stock, holding the material over the pattern. This same technique can be followed for cutting the arc of a corner. Fig. 32-30.

Cutting Curved Rails or Segments

When it is necessary to cut pieces or segments of a circle for constructing a round table or curved fronts of drawers, lay out the desired curve on thick stock and cut the first curve freehand.

32-29. Cutting a beveled circle freehand.

Then fasten a pivot block or ripping fence to the table at a distance from the blade equal to the thickness of the segments desired. Hold the stock against the fence or pin in making this cut. Fig. 32-31, next page.

331

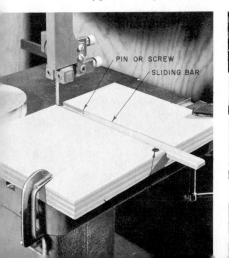

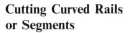

32-27. A jig for cutting circles.

32-28. Using a jig to cut circles.

32-30. Cutting a rounded corner, using a jig.

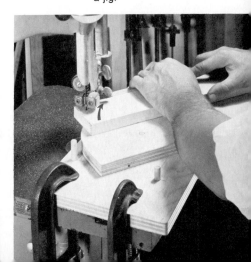

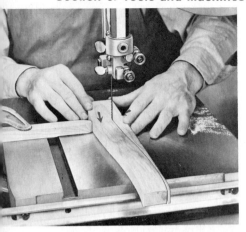

32-31. Cutting parallel curves, using a pivot block or pin. Short sleeves are safer.

Cutting Duplicate Parts

When two or more pieces of the same design must be cut, a simple procedure is to lay out the design on the first piece and then nail the two or more pieces together. The

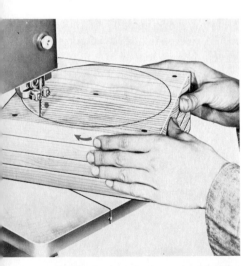

32-32. Cutting duplicate parts by fastening the pieces together with nails in the waste stock. Long, loose sleeves should not be worn around machinery.

nails should be driven into the waste stock. If there is danger of cutting into the nails, small wooden wedges can be band sawn and driven into saw kerfs to hold the pieces together while sawing. Fig. 32-32. Another method is to cut the shape in thick stock and then resaw it into the desired number of pieces. Fig. 32-33.

Cutting Before Lathe Turning

Before doing any turning on the lathe, the band saw often can be used to rough out the shape. This saves time and makes the turning much easier. For example, suppose you want to turn a ball-shaped object on the lathe. First carefully square up the stock. Draw a center line around the adjoining sides. Then carefully lay out the profile of the ball on two adjoining surfaces. Do the compound cutting as described early in this section. After the ball has been roughed out, the finish turning can be done on the lathe. Before spindle turning of large square stock, always rough out the stock to octagonal shape on the band saw.

Cutting off Round Stock

The simplest method for cutting off round stock is to hold it in a V-block or clamp it in an adjustable hand screw. Another method is to drill a hole lengthwise in a piece of scrap stock and shove the round stock through this. It is very dangerous to cut a piece of round stock freehand. Fig. 32-34.

Cutting Grooves in Dowel Rod

Dowel rod with slight grooves holds better for gluing because the

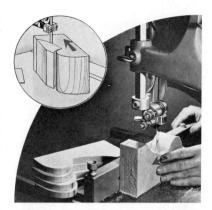

32-33. Cutting duplicate parts by first cutting thicker stock to shape, then resawing to the correct thickness.

glue can penetrate along the entire length. Tilt the table at an angle of about 15 degrees and turn the miter gage to the same angle. Now hold the dowel rod against the miter gage and push it into the saw to the desired depth. The saw will automatically cut a spiral groove along the rod.

32-34. Cutting off round stock, using a V-block.

JIG SAW

SAFETY

- With the hold-down, apply light pressure on the material being cut.
- Tighten the blade securely, with the teeth pointing down, in the lower and upper chucks.
- Apply the correct tension to the blade.
- Always rotate the motor by hand to make sure all adjustments are correct before turning the power on.
- Make all adjustments with the power off.

UNIT 33 Jig, Saber, and Reciprocating Saws

The jig saw, or scroll saw as it is sometimes called, is used primarily for internal and external irregular cutting. It is one of the simplest and safest power saws and will be found most useful in making any parts that involve intricate cutting. Fig. 33-1.

Size

Size is indicated by the distance from the blade to the back of the overarm, the usual sizes being 18″ to 24″. An 18″ machine will cut to the center of a 36″ circle.

Jig saw types vary from simple vibrators to the larger, regular jig saws. Fig. 33-2.

Parts

The main parts of a jig saw include a base and overarm. A

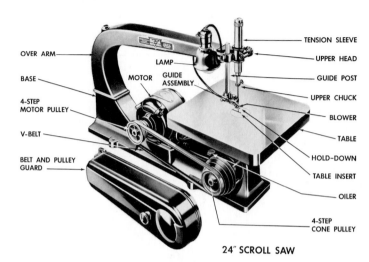

24″ SCROLL SAW

33-2a. Parts of a 24″ jig or scroll saw.

OVER ARM, BASE, 4-STEP MOTOR PULLEY, V-BELT, BELT AND PULLEY GUARD, LAMP, MOTOR, GUIDE ASSEMBLY, TENSION SLEEVE, UPPER HEAD, GUIDE POST, UPPER CHUCK, BLOWER, TABLE, HOLD-DOWN, TABLE INSERT, OILER, 4-STEP CONE PULLEY

driving mechanism changes rotary action to reciprocal or up-and-down motion. A table is fastened to the base which can be tilted 45 degrees to one side. On some models the table can also be turned 90 degrees, and then tilted, for cutting long stock.

An upper and lower chuck hold the saw blade. Fig. 33-3. The lower chuck is connected to the lower plunger which moves the chuck up and down. Fig. 33-4. The upper chuck operates on a spring in the plunger. There is also a guide which can be moved up

33-2b. This type jig saw is used in the furniture industry and is also frequently found in patternmaking shops.

33-1. Making this ornate chest involved many intricate jig saw operations. Note the internal cutting on the front apron. The key escutcheons (arrow) are also an example of fine scroll-saw work. This work precedes the hand carving.

334

33-3. Chucks of a jig saw. Notice that the lower chuck can be turned a quarter turn by loosening a set screw.

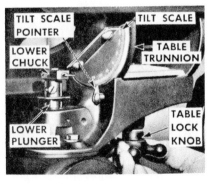

33-4. Parts of the lower unit.

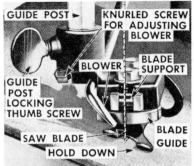

33-5. Parts of the upper unit.

33-6. The spring hold-down can be tilted to hold work firmly on the table when it is set on an angle.

and down to hold the blade in position and to keep the work solid. Some larger jig saws are equipped with an air blower which keeps the sawdust away from the blade and layout line. Fig. 33-5. Most saws operate from an electric motor with a step-pulley arrangement. The pulleys provide for four different speeds ranging from about 600 to 1700 cutting strokes per minute.

Adjustments and Blades

Tilting the Table

A knob or lever located beneath the table can be loosened and the table tilted the desired degree for cutting bevels, chamfers, and other angular work. A pointer and gage indicate the degree of tilt. Fig. 33-4.

Swiveling the Table

On larger jig saws, the table can be turned 90 degrees by loosening two cap screws that hold the frame to the crankcase. Fig. 33-3.

Removing the Overarm

For some jobs in which a saber blade is needed, the overarm is removed. A cap screw located at the upper rear of the overarm holds this to the base.

Adjusting the Blade Guides

On larger machines, the blade guide can be opened or closed for blades with different thicknesses, or the guide can be turned to the correct slot. The guide should just clear the blade, and the front of the guide should be at the bottom of the teeth.

Adjusting the Guide Assembly

The whole guide assembly can be moved up or down by loosening the thumb screw that holds it in place. This guide assembly should always be adjusted so that the hold-downs keep the work firmly on the table. Fig. 33-6.

Blades

There are three major types of blades. Fig. 33-7. See next page.
● *Jig-saw blades* for cutting wood usually have 7 to 10 teeth per inch. However, those used for finer cuts and for cutting veneers may have as many as 18 teeth per

Material Cut	Thick In.	Width In.	Teeth Per Inch	Blade Full Size	Material Cut	Thick In.	Width In.	Teeth Per Inch	Blade Full Size
Steel • Iron Lead • Copper Aluminum	.020	.070	32		Wood Veneer Plus Plastics Celluloid • Hard Rubber Bakelite • Ivory Extremely Thin Materials	.008	.035	20	
Pewter • Asbestos Paper • Felt	.020	.070	20		Plastics • Celluloid Hard Rubber Bakelite • Ivory Wood	.019	.050	15	
Steel • Iron • Lead Copper • Brass	.020	.070	15			.019	.055	12	
Aluminum	.020	.085	15			.020	.070	7	
Pewter • Asbestos Wood	.020	.110	20			.020	.110	7	
Asbestos • Brake Lining • Mica Steel • Iron • Lead Copper • Brass Aluminum Pewter	.028	.250	20		Wall Board • Pressed Wood Wood • Lead Bone • Felt • Paper Copper • Ivory • Aluminum	.020	.110	15	
					Hard and Soft Wood	.020	.110	10	
Wood Panels and Veneers	.010	.048	18			.028	.187	10	
						.028	.250	7	
Plastics • Celluloid Hard Rubber Bakelite • Ivory Wood	.010	.070	14		Pearl • Pewter Mica Pressed Wood Sea Shells Jewelry • Metals Hard Leather	.016	.054	30	
	.010	.055	16			.016	.054	20	
	.010	.045	18			.020	.070	15	
						.020	.085	12	

33-7a. Chart for selecting the correct blade.

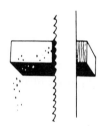

33-7b. Select a blade that will have three or more teeth in contact with the work when cutting.

33-8. The jig saw is used mainly for light work. Heavy work can be done, however, by using the appropriate blade and a slow rate of feed.

inch. These blades are fastened in both upper and lower chucks. The blades are classified by their size and the number of teeth per inch. Fine tooth blades are used for delicate scroll work, and when a smooth cut is desired. Coarse, heavy sawing requires a larger blade with fewer teeth per inch. Fig. 33-8.

• *Jeweler's saw blades,* sometimes called *piercing blades,* are made for cutting metal. They are excellent for cutting parts for hardware or trim. These blades usually have between 15 and 32 teeth per inch.

• *Saber blades* are thicker, shorter blades that are fastened only in the lower jaw, between the V-jaws. They are commonly used for rapid cutting of thick stock and for internal openings. These blades often have 7 to 9 teeth per inch. Fig. 33-9.

Adjusting the Speed

On most jig saws the speed is adjusted by changing the position of the belt on the four-step cone pulley. Remove the power plug and the belt guard, release the belt tension, and reposition the belt for the required speed. Some large jig saws have a variable speed adjustment. The speed on these saws can be changed by turning a handle or crank when the machine is running. Fig. 33-10 shows recommended cutting speeds for various materials.

Installing a Jig-Saw Blade

The regular jig-saw and jeweler's-saw blades are installed in the following manner:

1. Tip the table so you can work on the chuck easily. It may

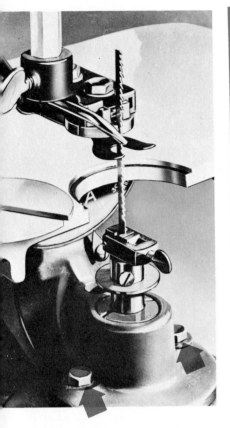

33-9. The lower chuck in position for the saber-saw blade. Note the two hex-head cap screws on the trunnion. (See arrows.) Loosen these to swivel the table 90 degrees.

MATERIAL TO BE CUT	SPEED	MATERIAL TO BE CUT	SPEED
BRAKE LINING	SLOW	ALUMINUM, BRASS	SLOW
MICA	MEDIUM	COPPER	SLOW
FELT	SLOW	JEWELRY METALS	MEDIUM
HARD LEATHER	MEDIUM	LEAD, PEWTER	SLOW
HARD RUBBER	SLOW	SHEET IRON, MILD STEEL	SLOW
INLAYS	SLOW	ASBESTOS	MEDIUM
VENEER	FAST	BAKELITE CELLULOID PLASTICS	SLOW
PRESSED WOOD PLYWOOD WALL BOARD	FAST	LAM'D PLASTICS FIBERTEX MICARTA	SLOW
HARDWOOD	MEDIUM	IVORY	SLOW
SOFTWOOD	FAST	BONE	SLOW
PAPER	FAST	PEARL	MEDIUM

33-10. Jig saw cutting speeds: slow, 650 to 900 rpm; medium, 900 to 1300 rpm; fast, 1300 to 1750 rpm.

33-11. Installing a blade, using an Allen wrench to tighten the chuck.

be desirable also to remove the throat plate. The chuck is opened or closed with either a thumb screw or a set screw. (The latter requires an Allen-type wrench. Fig. 33-11.)

2. Fasten the blade about $\frac{3}{8}''$ deep in the lower chuck and lock it firmly. Turn the machine over by hand until the lower chuck is at the top of the stroke. Loosen the plunger in the overarm and push it down. Pull the upper chuck down over the blade about $\frac{3}{8}''$ and lock firmly. Make sure the

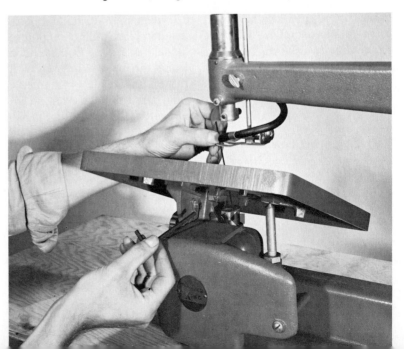

337

33-12. Adjust the blade tension for the type of blade or particular job.

33-14. Cutting a complicated part. Notice the relief cuts.

33-13. Installing a saber blade. Notice that the lower chuck has been turned a quarter turn and the blade fastened in the V-jaws. An extra blade guide has been fastened in place, directly below the table for added support.

guide is adjusted to clear the blade slightly. Pull up on the plunger to apply tension to the spring, and tighten the knurled knob or clamp handle that holds it in the overarm. Fig. 33-12.

3. Adjust the upper guide assembly. The spring hold-down should hold the work firmly on the table, but high enough to permit the workpiece to slide under the front edge easily.

4. Turn the machine over by hand to be sure it runs smoothly. Replace the throat plate and adjust the table.

Installing Saber Saw Blades

On larger machines the lower chuck can be turned a quarter turn. Loosen the set screw that holds the chuck to the shaft, turn it a quarter turn, and retighten. Fasten the saber blade in the V-chuck and tighten it. Sometimes a lower guide attachment is fastened in place to help support the blade. Fig. 33-13. On machines on which the lower chuck cannot be turned, the blade is fastened at right angles to the overarm and the cutting is done from the side.

Basic Procedures

● Assume the correct cutting position. Always stand directly in front of the blade with both hands resting comfortably on the table. Guide the work with both hands, applying forward pressure with the thumbs. Fig. 33-14.

● Select the correct size and type of blade. This depends on the material to be cut, its thickness, and the details of the design. Fig. 33-7. The blade should always be the largest one that will do a good job. Thin blades tend to break too easily or become clogged. *Three teeth should be in contact with the work* at all times while cutting.

● Check all adjustments. Make sure the blade is tight in the chuck, that the correct cutting speed is set, that the table is at right angles to the saw blade, that the saw guides are adjusted properly, and that the hold-down is in a position to keep the work firmly against the table.

● On many saws there is a knob on the end of the motor shaft. Turn this knob over by hand once or twice to make sure everything is adjusted properly.

● Lay out and plan your work before cutting. Have a clean, accurate layout that can be easily followed. When doing complicated cutting, make short cuts first and then long ones. Be careful when cutting corners. This is when blades usually break. If the job is very intricate, rough cut the pattern to the approximate shape and then cut it to the pattern outline.

Cutting

Cutting External Curves

Install the correct size and kind of blade, and adjust the hold-down to the correct position. Place the work on the table, with the forefinger over it on each side and the other fingers on the table. Apply forward pressure with the thumbs. Fig. 33-14. Start in the waste stock and come up to the layout line at a slight angle, applying as much pressure as necessary to keep the cutting going without vibration.

A smooth cut is obtained only when the work is carefully guided. Do not twist the blade, as it is easily broken. When cutting sharp curves, apply almost no forward pressure and turn the work slowly. Fig. 33-15. When it is necessary

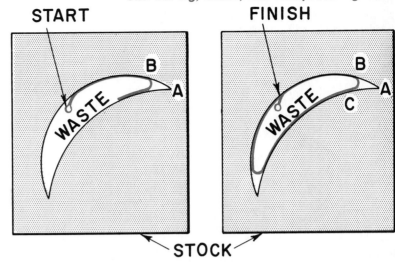

33-16. Cutting a sharp angle. Start from a hole drilled in waste stock. Cut to point B, then make a curve as shown. Follow the layout line from point C to the opposite end, cut another curve, then follow the layout line again until the waste stock drops out. Finally, make the sharp corner by cutting from both B and C to A.

to cut to the end of a long, thin opening, cut to the corner, back out the blade a short way, and "nibble out" the corner until the work can be turned. On some hardwoods, a little soap or wax applied to the blade will help the cutting.

Cutting Duplicate Parts

If it is necessary to cut two or more parts to the same shape, it is a good idea to fasten them together with nails in the scrap stock and cut as before.

Cutting Internal Openings

Bore a hole in the waste stock large enough for the blade. Fig. 33-16. Sometimes it is wise to make the hole a part of the design. Fig. 33-17. For example, if a rectangular opening with rounded corners is needed, bore four holes of the desired radius, one at each

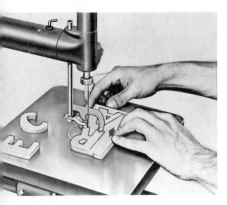

33-15. Cutting external curves.

33-17. The correct-size hole is bored as part of the design. The jig-saw blade is then placed through the hole and the cut is completed.

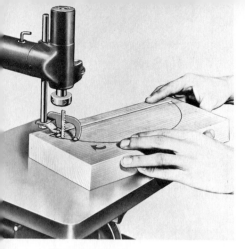

33-18. Cutting an internal opening with a saber blade. Notice that a hole has been drilled in the waste stock to admit the blade.

corner. If a jig-saw blade is used, remove the throat plate, slip the work over the table, put the blade through the opening, and fasten it in the upper and lower chucks. Replace the throat plate and adjust the spring hold-down. If a saber blade is used, it can, of course, be fastened in the machine first and the work placed over it. If the opening is unusual in design, it may be necessary to rough out the waste stock first and then cut up to the pattern outline. Fig. 33-18 shows the method of cutting an internal curved opening.

Cutting Bevels or Chamfers

These can be cut by tilting the table the desired degree.

33-19. Cutting metal on the jig saw.

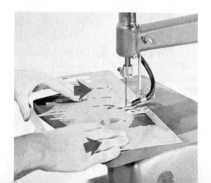

33-20a. A file firmly clamped in the V-jaws of the lower chuck.

Straight Cutting

Straight cutting can be done by fastening a fence to the table to guide the work.

Cutting Metal Hardware and Fittings

A most important use for the jig saw in furniture making is the cutting of fittings such as escutcheon holes, drawer pulls, reinforcement corners, and other decorative metal pieces. For these jobs be sure to install a rather fine jeweler's blade. Set for a medium or slow speed. Fig. 33-19. Small files can be purchased that fasten in the V-chuck to finish the metal edges.

Sanding and Filing

The scroll saw can be used for abrading (sanding) and filing irregular edges of wood and metal. The result will be an edge that is smooth, flat, and at a true right angle to the face of the work. Fig. 33-20.

Special files may be purchased for this purpose; however, a 3″ length taken from the lower portion of a file of the desired shape will do the job. Fig. 33-21. To adapt a standard file, break off the upper portion by placing the lower 3″ of the file in a vise and striking the projecting portion with a hammer. Do this with extreme caution. A good precaution is to place a rag over the portion of the file that is to be hammered off. After breaking the file, grind the tapered shank round and the

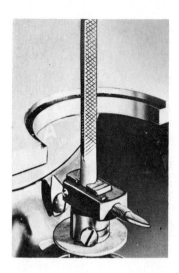

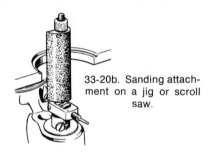

33-20b. Sanding attachment on a jig or scroll saw.

broken end smooth. Install the file in the lower chuck by turning the chuck 90 degrees and placing the file in the V-jaws of the chuck. A special wood insert to fit the table of the jig saw may have to be made to support small pieces.

MACHINE FILES
With ¼″ shank—Overall length 3¼″

	Description
■	Square
▮	Crochet
◖	Half Round
●	Round
◀	Triangle
▮	Oblong

33-21. Common shapes of files.

SABER SAW

SAFETY

- Review general safety rules for use of portable electric tools.
- Select the correct blade for the work and properly secure it in the chuck.
- Be certain the material to be sawn is properly clamped.
- Keep the cutting pressure constant. Do not force the cut.
- When finished, turn off the power switch and allow the saw to come to a dead stop before setting the saw down.
- Hold the base down securely on the work when cutting.

The Portable Electric Jig (Saber) Saw

The *portable jig* (also called *saber* or *bayonet*) *saw* is the best choice for an on-the-job cutting tool for straight or irregular cutting. This tool can do the same cutting as a floor-type jig or band saw, with the added convenience of a hand tool. A larger jig saw can cut through material 2″ thick. It also can cut through a 2″ × 4″ piece in less than 15 seconds. It will cut metal, wood, plastic, and many other materials. Most hand jig saws use orbital action (cutting the material on the up stroke and moving away from it on the down stroke). Because of this, cutting speed is greatly increased and the saw cuts with a cleaner edge.

Parts

The design of this tool varies with the manufacturer. However, all of these tools consist of a motor, a handle, a mechanism to change rotary action into up-and-down action, and a baseplate

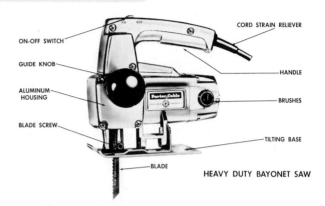

33-22. Parts of the bayonet, saber, or hand jig saw.

Heavy cuts 2″ x 4″ at 45°	6 teeth per inch
General cutting	7, 10
Smooth cuts	12
Plywood	12
Hardboard	12
Cardboard	Knife
Leather	Knife

33-23. Guide for selecting the correct blade.

or shoe. Fig. 33-22. Select the correct blade. Fig. 33-23. At least three teeth must be on the cutting surface at all times. To install the blade, loosen the set screws or clamp, and slip the blade into the slot under the chuck cover until you are sure it is tightly seated. Then tighten the set screw or clamp.

Operations

Straight and Irregular Cutting

Mount the work so it is held rigid. Fig. 33-24. Make a layout line that can be followed. Set the shoe of the tool on the work. Start the motor and allow it to come up to full speed. Then move the saw along slowly. Fig. 33-25. Don't force the cutting. Use only enough pressure to keep the saw cutting at all times. The tool is always held in one hand. The other hand can hold the work or steady the saw. For more accurate straight cutting, a ripping fence can be installed. Fig. 33-26. The ripping fence can also be used for cutting circles. A nail or peg must be driven into the center of the circle.

33-24. Cutting a curve. Notice how the work is clamped to the table.

33-25a. Straight cutting.

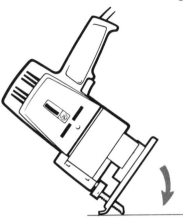

33-27a. Tip the saw up on the front of the baseplate. Turn it on and allow it to come to full speed before lowering the blade into the workpiece.

33-27b. Making an internal cut.

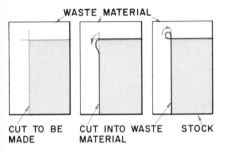

WASTE MATERIAL

CUT TO BE MADE | CUT INTO WASTE MATERIAL | STOCK

33-25b. Two methods of cutting an exterior corner. One way is to make a slightly curved cut at the corner, then trim this off with a second cut. Another method is to make a complete circle in the waste stock.

33-28. Adjusting the shoe, or baseplate, for bevel cutting.

Plunge or Internal Cutting

The portable jig saw can be used to cut out an internal area without first drilling a hole. This is called plunge cutting. With a pencil, mark out the area to be cut. Choose a convenient starting place inside the waste stock. Tip the tool forward with the shoe resting on the surface of the material and the top of the blade clear of the work surface. Fig. 33-27a. Turn on the power. When the blade reaches full speed, slowly lower the back of the machine until the blade cuts through the material to the full depth. Then cut out the opening. Fig. 33-27b.

Bevel Cutting

The shoes of some saws can be adjusted from 0 to 45 degrees for bevel cutting. Fig. 33-28. Such cutting can be done freehand, as shown in Fig. 33-29, or with a guide.

33-26. Using a fence to do ripping.

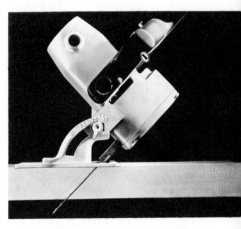

33-29. Cutting a bevel with the saber saw.

Circle Cuts

For circle cuts, remove the guide and turn it over. Set the guide into position for the radius desired and tighten it. Make a pocket cut or drill a pilot hole on the circumference of the desired circle and insert the saw blade. You will find it very difficult to make perfect circles starting from the edge of the board. With the blade on the circumference of the circle, locate the center of the circle and drive a small nail through the hole in the guide at that point. Now begin the cutting, but do not force the saw. Let it do the cutting and you will have a perfect circle. Fig. 33-30.

Reciprocating Saw

Another type of all-purpose saw operates with a back-and-forth movement, like a hacksaw without a frame. This saw is most commonly used for remodeling or cabinetwork, since it can cut wood, plastic, metal, ceramics, and many other materials. Fig. 33-31.

33-31a. The reciprocating saw.

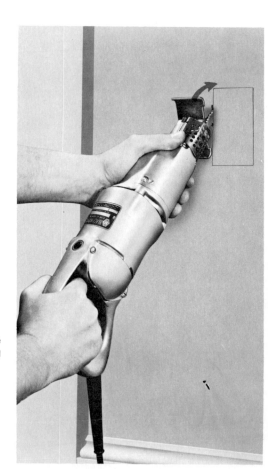

33-31b. Making a plunge cut with a reciprocating saw.

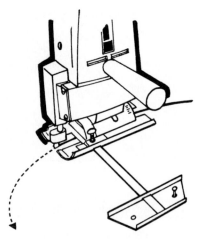

33-30. Making a circle cut.

344

ROUTER

SAFETY

- Review general safety rules for use of portable electric tools.
- Make certain the fence or guide is securely clamped.
- When using the router, keep both hands on the handles.
- Feed in the correct direction.
- Always lay the router down with the cutter pointing away from you and be alert to the coasting cutter.
- Always hold onto the router when it is turned on.
- Be sure that at least $\frac{1}{2}''$ of bit shank is securely tightened in the chuck.
- Make certain the workpiece is securely clamped.
- Make adjustments only when the cutter is at a dead stop.
- Be certain the power switch is off before connecting the power plug.
- When installing or removing cutters, be sure the power plug is disconnected.

Routers and Routing Attachments

Routing is similar to shaping except that the motor and cutters are opposite in arrangement. Fig. 34-1. Production routers, Fig. 34-2, are an essential part of the woodworking industry. Portable routers are usually satisfactory for school and home use. With a router adapter and cutters, many operations can also be done on the drill press.

Portable Router

The portable router consists of a motor with a chuck attached to the spindle. Fig. 34-3. This motor screws into a base to which two handles are attached. A guide for straight or curved routing also can be secured. With an attachment the portable router can be held in

34-1a. The cutting on the end panels of this coffee table was done on a router.

34-2a. A heavy-duty industrial router. This machine has a "floating head" which allows it to rout a contour surface as well as a flat surface.

34-1b. The drawer pulls on this chest were cut on a router.

34-2b. This is an automatic router. The workpiece is clamped to the table, and the table movement is controlled by an electric eye which follows the pattern laid out on the left end of the machine.

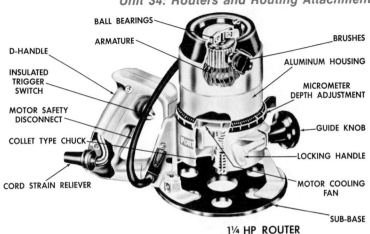

34-3. Portable router with parts named.

1¼ HP ROUTER

BALL BEARINGS
ARMATURE
BRUSHES
D-HANDLE
ALUMINUM HOUSING
INSULATED TRIGGER SWITCH
MICROMETER DEPTH ADJUSTMENT
MOTOR SAFETY DISCONNECT
GUIDE KNOB
COLLET TYPE CHUCK
LOCKING HANDLE
CORD STRAIN RELIEVER
MOTOR COOLING FAN
SUB-BASE

34-2c. This lightweight overarm router can do many of the operations performed by heavy-duty industrial routers.

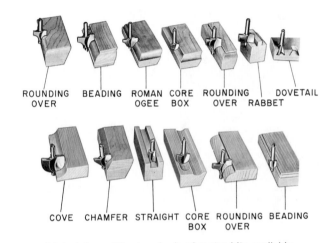

ROUNDING OVER   BEADING   ROMAN OGEE   CORE BOX   ROUNDING OVER   RABBET   DOVETAIL

COVE   CHAMFER   STRAIGHT   CORE BOX   ROUNDING OVER   BEADING

34-4. A few of the hundreds of router bits available.

an inverted position and used as a small shaper. It can also be mounted in a stand which makes it possible for this small machine to do many of the operations performed by the industrial router.

Router Bits

These bits come in many shapes for doing grooved or decorative work in the surface or edge of stock. Some of the common ones are straight, rounding-over, beading, cove, and chamfer bits. Fig. 34-4. In addition, a dovetail bit is needed for cutting a dovetail joint. All router bits cut on their sides rather than on end. Fig. 34-5. See the next page.

34-5a. The amount the router can move sideways can be controlled in five ways: A straightedge can be clamped to the stock and the router base held in contact with it.

34-5b. A straight or circular guide can be attached to the base to control the lateral movement. A guide is used here to make a cut near the edge of a round table top.

34-5c. A template or pattern can be used. A sleeve or guide is attached to the bottom of the base and this rides against the template.

Installing Cutters

1. Disconnect the power plug.

2. Lock the shaft or hold it with a wrench, depending on the kind and size of router.

3. Insert the shank of the bit into the chuck at least $\frac{1}{2}''$.

4. Tighten the chuck with a wrench.

5. Unlock the shaft.

6. Adjust the depth of cut by moving the motor unit up and down in the base.

7. Make a test cut in scrap stock. *Hold onto the router when turning on the power, to overcome the starting torque of the motor.*

Feeding the Hand Router

Always feed against the direction of motor rotation. When making a cut on a straight edge, feed from left to right. When cutting on circular stock, feed in a counterclockwise direction. Fig. 34-6.

Your judgment of how fast to feed will have to be developed by practice. The speed at which the best cut is made will depend on the size cut to be made and on the hardness of the wood. Most hand routers run at speeds of about 21,000 rpm. This is the speed without a load; the motor will slow down when under a work load. If the router is fed too fast, the motor will slow down too much, causing a poor cut. If the router is fed too slowly, the bit will get hot, possibly drawing the temper from the cutting edge or burning the wood. Don't force the cut; allow the bit to cut freely. Listen to the motor for an indication of whether it is working at its most efficient speed.

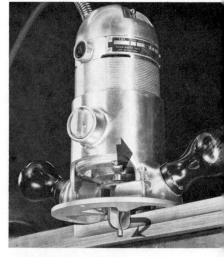

34-5d. Many cutters have pilot edges to control the amount of cut.

34-5e. You can operate the router freehand, as in making this sign.

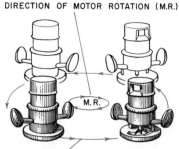

DIRECTION OF MOTOR ROTATION (M.R.)

M. R.

DIRECTION OF FEED

34-6. The router bit revolves clockwise. Therefore, when cutting straight edges, move the router from left to right. When making circular cuts, move the router counterclockwise.

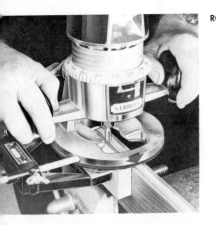

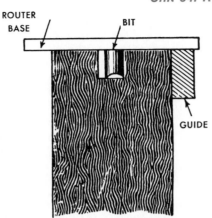

34-7a. Cutting a groove in the edge of a board. Notice the extra piece of wood attached to the guide. This will give the router added support when riding on the narrow edge of the workpiece. (In the photograph, a previous cut removed much of the stock.)

34-7b. Cutting a dado.

Using a Portable Router

Cutting Grooves, Dadoes, Gains, or Mortises

To make these cuts, fasten a straight router bit in the chuck. Screw the motor into the base until the router bit extends the desired depth beyond the base. Attach a guide to the base to control the cut. Lay out the cut and locate the guide. Start at one side or end and move the router along to make the cut. Fig. 34-7.

Cutting Decorative Edges

As mentioned, cutters of many shapes are used for cutting decorative edges. Many of these have a pilot tip which does not cut but merely rides against the uncut edge of the wood. Attach the bit in the machine and adjust for depth. Secure a piece of scrap the same thickness as the finished stock and clamp it to the top of a bench. Hold the router firmly against the top of the work and move the cutter into the stock.

Check to see that the desired shape is being cut. The shape can be changed by moving the motor up and down in the base. Fig. 34-5d.

Freehand Routing

Signs and decorations are sometimes made freehand with the router. Carefully lay out the areas to be removed. Secure a cutter bit of the desired diameter and fasten it into the machine. Clamp the work to the table top, then lower the router into the design. Move the router along to follow the outline. Fig. 34-5e.

Pattern Routing

For irregular-shaped objects of which several duplicates are to be cut, it may be desirable to make a pattern. To do this, lay out on a piece of plywood the areas to be routed out. Cut these areas out on a jig saw. Then fasten this piece to another piece of plywood. Place some small nails through

34-7c. Cutting a mortise.

this template to hold the work. Select a router bit of the desired diameter and fasten it in a drill press as described on page 311.

Clamp a temporary wood board on the table of the drill press and bore a hole in it with the router bit. Place a small pin in this hole. Cut the pin off so that it will be less than $\frac{1}{4}''$ above the table.

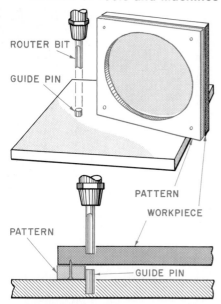

34-8. Pattern routing on a drill press or with a portable router fastened in a stand.

34-9a. Portable router mounted in an overarm machine.

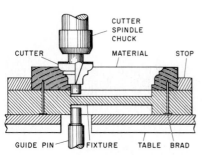

34-9b. Using a fixture and guide pin to do internal routing.

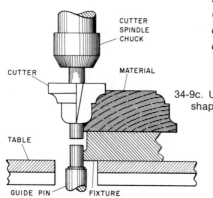

34-9c. Using a fixture and guide pin to shape the entire edge of stock.

Now, to do pattern routing, merely adjust the machine for the correct depth of cut, place the stock to be routed over the template, and place the template over the pin. Then move the stock and pattern around under the router bit. Fig. 34-8.

The portable router can also be clamped in an overarm machine. Fig. 34-9a. In this position, pattern routing can be done in the same manner as on the industrial router. The workpiece is clamped in the fixture for routing out the center. See "A" in Fig. 34-9a. The outline of the cut in the bottom of the fixture is used as a guide against the pin when the cutter is lowered into the workpiece for the cut. Fig. 34-9b. The workpiece is removed from the fixture and inverted over a second fixture ("B" in Fig. 34-9a) for cutting the outside contour of the candy dish. Fig. 34-9c. The square edges of the dish can also be removed by locking the router in position for the proper depth of cut and using a rounding-over bit with a pilot. The finished dish is shown at "C" in Fig. 34-9a.

Pattern or template routing can be done with the portable router by first making a template of tempered hardboard or plywood. Use a straight bit for a sharp corner or a core-box bit for a rounded corner. Attach a template guide to the base of the router. Fig. 34-10. Fasten the template over the work and do the routing as shown in Fig. 34-11.

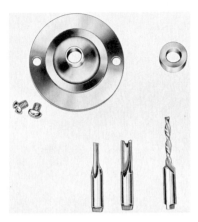

34-10a. Template guide and bits used for template routing.

Beading and Fluting

On many Traditional pieces of furniture, the rails or legs are enriched with beading or fluting. This can be done quickly with the router. Fasten the leg in a wood lathe and place a piece of plywood over the lathe bed as a support. Place the motor of the router in a beading-and-fluting motor bracket. Select a cutter of the desired shape. Adjust the cutter in the attachment so it lines up with the center of the work. Attach a collar above or below the cutter to control the depth of cut. The

34-11. Using a template with the portable router.

indexing attachment on the head of the lathe can control the number of cuts. Turn the router on. Hold the router firmly on the board over the bed and make the cut by moving the router along the workpiece. Fig. 34-12.

Dovetail Joint

The best joint for most drawer construction is the dovetail. This joint is sometimes used for other wooden "box" construction as well. It is a difficult joint to make by hand but simple with a router and dovetail attachment.

1. Clamp the dovetail attachment to a bench or table. Square up the stock to be used for the front and sides of the drawer or box. Fasten a template guide to the base of the router and install a dovetail bit. Adjust the dovetail bit to extend below the base the desired amount. This amount can usually be determined by making a trial cut and readjusting the router to the exact depth.

2. Select a board which will be one side of the box or drawer. Clamp it face side in against the front of the base and protruding $\frac{1}{2}''$ or more above the top surface of the base. This is shown as board B, Fig. 34-13a, next page.

3. Clamp board A, which will be the front or back of the drawer or box, inner side up. Make sure that it is in full contact with board B. It should be set flush with the top end of B. Both boards must be in contact with the locating pins. See arrow "C" on Fig. 34-13b.

4. Place the dovetail template over the two pieces of stock and clamp in place. Fig. 34-13c.

34-10b. The portable router with a bit and template guide attached, ready for use.

34-12. Cutting flutes on a table leg with the portable router, using the lathe as an indexing head.

34-13. Steps in using a Dovetailing Attachment.

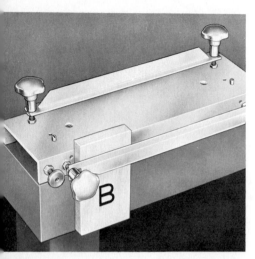

34-13a. Clamp side in place.

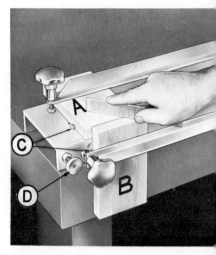

34-13b. Clamp front or back in place.

34-13c. Place template over piece.

34-13d. Cutting the dovetail.

34-13e. Drawer front and side are held on the outside of the fixture, in the same position in which they were cut.

34-13f. Back of drawer side is tipped up and the fit of the joint is checked.

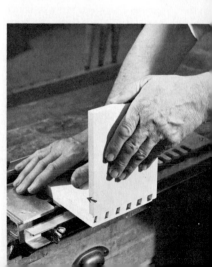

352

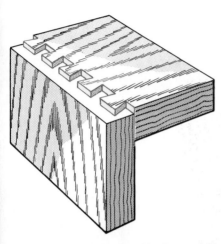

34-14a. If the drawer side does not fit far enough into the front, turn the template adjusting nut *in* to allow a deeper cut in the drawer front.

5. Make a trial cut, being sure that the template guide follows the template. Fig. 34-13d. If the trial joint is too *loose,* adjust to make a *deeper cut.* If the trial joint is too *tight,* adjust for a *shallower cut.* Fig. 34-13e and f.

6. Fig. 34-14a shows a drawer side which does not fit far enough into the front. When this happens, turn *in* the template adjusting nut (D in Fig. 34-13b). This allows a deeper cut into the drawer front. If the drawer side fits in too deeply, Fig. 34-14b, turn the template adjusting nut *out.* Be sure these adjusting nuts on both ends of the fixture are set the same.

7. The completed dovetail should appear as in Fig. 34-14c. The left end of the fixture is used for cutting the right front of the drawer and the left rear corner. The left front and right rear corner are cut on the right end of the dovetail fixture.

34-14c. The dovetail joint is found in the finest drawer construction.

Dovetail Dado

The dovetail dado is a good joint to use where extra strength is needed, because the joint will pull the two pieces together and hold tightly. It is an ideal joint for fastening a drawer side to a front when the front "lips over" the cabinet sides. Fig. 34-15.

Install the dovetail bit in the router and attach the guide. Adjust the depth of cut and set the guide for the first cut. Fig. 34-16a. If the slot is to be cut in a drawer front, it will not be necessary to clamp a piece of wood on either side of the work to support the router. When the first cut has been completed, set the second piece in the vise with a piece of scrap stock

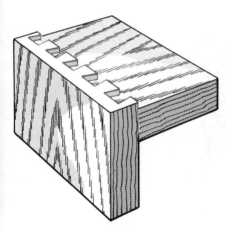

34-14b. If the drawer side fits too deeply into the cuts in the front, turn the template adjusting nut *out.* (Note, however, that sometimes the side will be set low intentionally. This allows for clearance between the drawer side and the cabinet. If this is done, complete the joint by cutting a rabbet on the inside of the drawer front equal to the depth of the projection.)

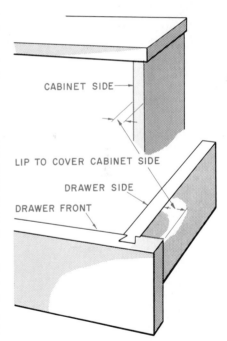

34-15. The dovetail dado joint is an excellent joint to use for drawer construction on Contemporary furniture. This joint is also recommended for attaching the sides of a cabinet to the top, when the cabinet top overhangs the side panels.

353

34-16a. Cutting the dovetail mortise or slot. Note that in the picture it is cut in the edge of the workpiece. For a drawer front or cabinet top the cut would be made on a surface.

34-16b. Cutting the dovetail tenon or stub. A cut is made on each side, leaving the tenon in the center.

on each side. The scrap pieces should be at least $\frac{3}{4}''$ thick and both the same thickness. Leave the depth of cut set the same as for the slot, and readjust the guide so one cut is made on each side

to form the tenon. The width of the tenon is cut to fit the slot by adjusting the guide. Fig. 34-16b. It is recommended that a trial cut be made in scrap stock of the same thickness to insure a good fitting joint.

Dropleaf-Table Joint

A dropleaf-table joint is used frequently in furniture construction, when dropleaf hinges are installed. A set of two bits is needed—one a beading bit to use on the table itself and the other a cove bit to use on the table leaf. Secure some scrap stock the same thickness as the table top. Fig. 34-17. Install the beading bit and adjust to the desired depth. Make the cut on the scrap piece. Install the cove bit, adjust for depth, and cut. Check the two pieces to see that they fit properly. Then make the same cuts on the good stock, using the scraps as guides. Use the router to mortise out the backs of the table top and leaf, to install the dropleaf hinge.

Router Attachment on Drill Press

Remove the chuck and install a router adapter. Set the drill press for highest speed. Install the desired cutter bit. Fasten a fence to the table. Fig. 34-18a. Use a

34-18a. Routing on the drill press, using a fence as a guide.

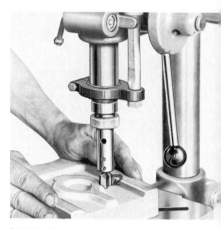

34-18b. Routing on the drill press using a pin in the table as a guide.

template as a guide, Fig. 34-18b, or use a cutter with a pilot to limit the cut. Fig. 34-18c. Lower the cutter bit to the desired depth and do the routing as with a portable router.

34-17. A dropleaf table joint.

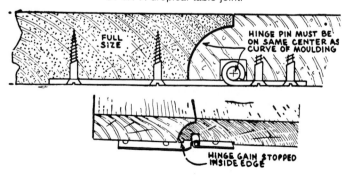
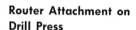
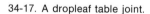

FULL SIZE

HINGE PIN MUST BE ON SAME CENTER AS CURVE OF MOULDING

HINGE GAIN STOPPED INSIDE EDGE

34-18c. Using a pilot on the cutter as a guide to limit the cut.

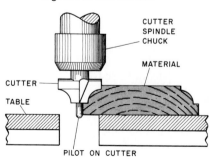

CUTTER SPINDLE CHUCK

MATERIAL

CUTTER

TABLE

PILOT ON CUTTER

SHAPER

SAFETY

- Use the correct guard for the operation to be performed.
- Before making any adjustments, make certain the power is off and the cutter is not rotating.
- Always feed against the rotation of the cutter.
- Never back up the stock being shaped.
- Make certain the fences and guards are clamped securely.
- Use jigs, fixtures, or templates whenever possible.
- Remove all chips from around the knives with a brush.
- Do not wear loose-fitting clothing.
- Make certain the cutter is clamped securely.
- Do not take too deep a cut.
- Install the cutter so the unused portion is below the table surface.
- Be sure the spindle turns freely before turning on the power.
- Before turning on the power, remove all tools and loose accessories from the table.
- When shaping with a depth collar, never start a cut at a corner.
- Use sharp cutters.

The shaper is used primarily for cutting moldings and edge designs, for cutting various types of joints, and for grooving, fluting, and reeding. It is one of the most dangerous machines in the shop and therefore should be used with utmost caution. It will, however, provide the touch of craftsmanship to a piece of furniture. Fig. 35-1. With attachments, the drill press can also serve as a shaper. See page 362.

Size

This is determined by the size of the table and the diameter of the spindle. Most small shapers have a single spindle, while the large production types frequently have two spindles. Fig. 35-2.

35-1. Many shaper operations are readily visible on these pieces of furniture and exemplify fine craftsmanship. The shaper was also used extensively in making the joints.

35-2a. Many shapers have interchangeable spindles. These can be changed by removing the nut on the bottom.

35-2b. A heavy-duty single-spindle shaper.

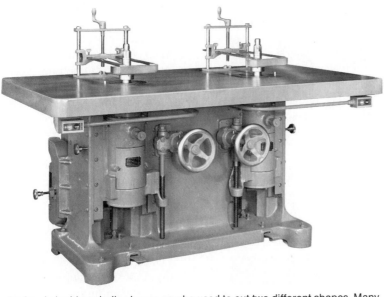

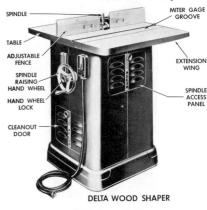

35-3. Parts of a shaper.

35-2c. A double-spindle shaper may be used to cut two different shapes. Many times, however, the operator will run one lefthand and one righthand cutter of the same shape, each in a different direction of rotation. In this way tear-out can be avoided on complex shapes.

35-5. Three-lip shaper cutters.

35-4. Clamp-type shaper cutters with removable flat knives.

Parts

The shaper consists of a base to which a table is attached, and a spindle that operates at a speed of 5,000 to 10,000 rpm. Usually the spindle moves up and down to make adjustments, although sometimes the table moves. A fence can be attached to the table for straight shaping. Fig. 35-3. Most shapers are equipped with a reversing switch. In normal use the shaper should operate in a counterclockwise direction, with the work fed from right to left. For many jobs, though, it is better to reverse this so the work is fed from left to right.

Cutters

There are two common types of cutters—the *clamp type* with removable blades, Fig. 35-4, and the *formed cutters.* Fig. 35-5. When-

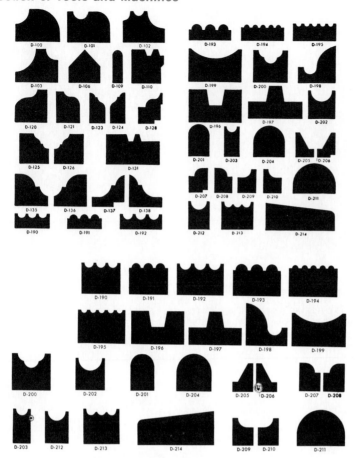

35-6a. A set of three-lip shaper cutters.

ever possible, only formed cutters should be used, because they are the safest. These can be purchased in many different shapes. Fig. 35-6a and b. The clamp type is dangerous because it has only two blades, which can become loose. A third type, the *three-knife safety cutterhead,* has a solid head into which knives can be inserted. Fig. 35-6c, page 359.

Basic Procedures

Selecting the Correct Cutter

When selecting a cutter for a job, hold the flat side of the cutter up against the stock to be shaped. This will give you an approximate indication of the cut which a cutter will make. Fig. 35-7, page 359.

Installing a Cutter

On most shapers there is a flat portion on the spindle, just below the table, over which a wrench can be slipped to keep the spindle from turning. Some shapers have a pin that slips in place to lock the spindle. Remove the nut that holds the cutter. Then install the cutter. Replace the safety washer and the nut, and tighten securely.

If work is to be done without a fence or jig, a depth collar must be placed above, below, or between the cutters to regulate the depth of cut. Sometimes spacers may also be needed, as when shaping a rather complicated edge or making certain types of moldings. Fig. 35-8, next page.

Adjusting Spindle Height

Loosen the spindle lock. Hold the workpiece against the flat side of the cutter and turn the spindle up or down until the desired amount of cutter is exposed. Fig. 35-9. Of course, a different-shaped edge will result with the same cutter, depending upon the position of the spindle.

Checking the Rotation of the Spindle

For most jobs, when feeding from right to left the spindle should rotate counterclockwise as viewed from above. Fig. 35-10. It will sometimes be necessary to remove the cutter, turn it over, replace it on the spindle, and reverse the direction of the spindle. This will enable the operator to feed the stock on the top of the cutter. Fig. 35-8 (center drawing). To feed the stock between the cutter and the table is dangerous because the top of the cutter is exposed. It may also give an uneven cut if there is any irregularity in the stock, as from warp. Also if the stock is not held down securely, especially on a large table top, the cutter will cut too deeply. Fig. 35-8 (left drawing).

Remember, for your safety and for a better job, the cut should be made on the bottom of the stock.

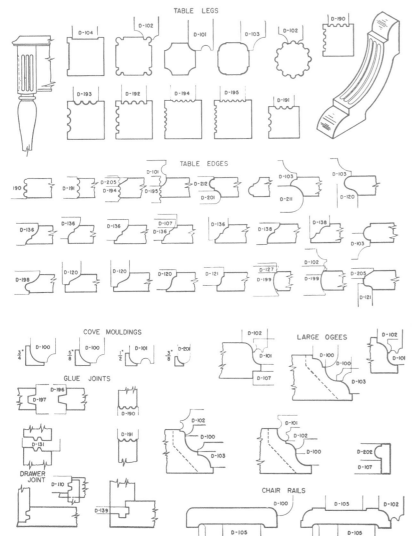

TABLE LEGS

TABLE EDGES

COVE MOULDINGS

GLUE JOINTS

DRAWER JOINT

LARGE OGEES

CHAIR RAILS

35-6b. Applications of three-lip shaper cutters.

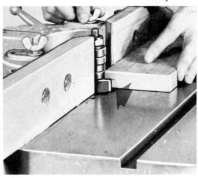

35-7. You can get a good idea of the cut by placing the workpiece in position on the table, with the flat side of the cutter against the material.

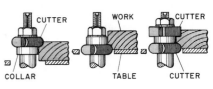

COLLAR   TABLE   CUTTER   WORK   CUTTER

35-8. Limiting the depth of cut by using a depth collar. If at all possible, place the collar on top of the cutter so that the cutter is under the workpiece.

35-9. Adjusting the depth of cut.

35-6c. The three-knife safety cutter-head.

Using the Right Equipment

The correct fence, guard, or jig should always be installed to do the job in the safest possible manner.

Shaping Operations

Shaping with a Fence

1. For most jobs on straight edges, the fence should be in

359

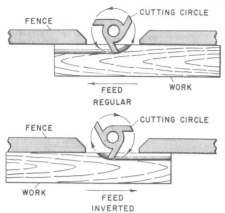

DIRECTION OF FEED FOR SHAPING

35-10. Cutters must rotate so that the *flat side* (not the beveled side) of the cutter hits the workpiece first. Most cutters are designed to rotate counter-clockwise, with the work fed from right to left. This is called regular feed. However, the cutter should also be mounted to do the majority of the cutting on the underside of the board. This may require turning the cutter over and reversing the direction of spindle rotation and feed. This is called *inverted feed.*

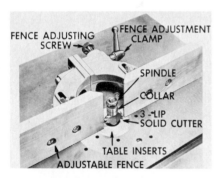

35-11a. Parts of the shaper fence.

place. Fig. 35-11. Fasten the fence to the table and hold a straight-edge as a guide to make sure that both halves of the fence are aligned. Fig. 35-12 (top). If the complete edge must be shaped, the front half of the fence will have to be set back an amount

equal to the depth of the cut, so that the molding or edge will ride on the other half after it is completed. Lock the fence in position. Fig. 35-12 (center and bottom).

2. Whenever possible, fasten a piece of plastic over the spindle as an added protection. When shaping long moldings also use the hold-downs or feather boards to help to hold the work firmly against the fence and the table. Fig. 35-13.

3. Turn the machine on and stand to the side. Never stand directly back of the cutter. Hold the work firmly against the fence and table with the left hand, and feed the work slowly into the revolving cutter, with your right hand applying forward pressure for regular feed. (If left-handed, the left hand is used to feed and the right hand holds the stock.)

4. Always shape end grain first so if the edges tear out the torn portions will be cut away when the edges are shaped. Fig. 35-14.

5. *Never allow your fingers to come anywhere near the cutter.* It is best not to shape a piece shorter than 8″. If this must be done, make a temporary wood jig in which the part can be held as the edge is shaped.

6. To shape end grain on a narrow piece, hold the work against a miter gage. Fig. 35-15. It's a good idea to fasten a temporary wood fence to the miter gage as added protection. This will also help to eliminate tear-out at the end of the cut.

Shaping with Depth Collars

If the entire edge of the stock is not to be shaped, depth collars

35-11b. Shaping a cupboard door with the fence as a guide. Notice the safe work habits used by the operator.

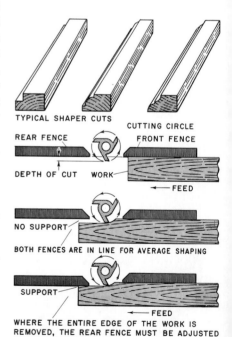

35-12. Properly align the fence as required for the cut to be made.

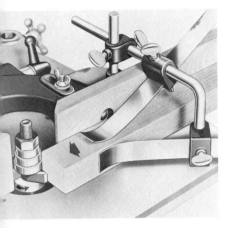

35-13. Use the hold-downs. This will help to make the cut more uniform and also much safer for the operator.

Shaping with a Pattern

If the entire edge of an irregular-shaped object must be formed, a pattern and depth collars are needed. Cut a pattern of the desired shape on a jig or band saw and sand the edge smooth. Any irregularity in the pattern will show up in the object shaped. This pattern must rest against the depth collar and therefore should vary in thickness, depending on how it is to be used. The pattern should also be small enough to allow the cutting to be done to the proper depth. Place several sharp pins through the pattern to hold

35-15. Shaping end grain with the work held against the miter gage.

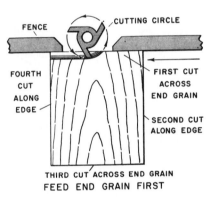

35-14. Always make the first cut on an end and then continue around the board.

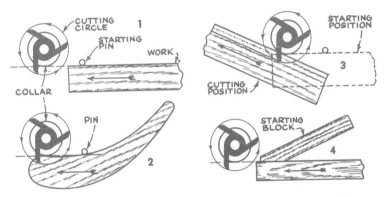

35-16a. Pivot the workpiece into the cutter, using the starting pin as a fulcrum. After the cut is started, the workpiece is swung away from the starting pin and should ride only against the collar.

can be fastened in the spindle to control the depth of cut. These may be above, below, or between the cutters. Fig. 35-8. By this means the edges of irregular-shaped objects can be cut. Install a starting pin; then, using this as a fulcrum, ease the work into the cutters. Fig. 35-16. Then slowly push the stock past the cutters until the edge is shaped.

35-16b. Always use the ring guard, for your protection, when shaping irregular edges with the depth collar as a guide.

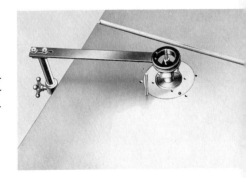

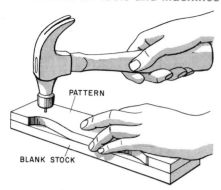

35-17a. Sometimes the pattern is nailed to the back of the workpiece.

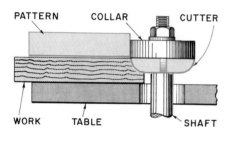

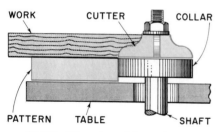

35-17b. The edge of the pattern rides against a collar. The pattern may be either above or below the work.

the stock in place; or, if a heavy cut is to be made, use woodscrews to fasten the pattern to the stock. Adjust the spindle so that the pattern rides on the depth collar. Turn on the shaper and follow the same general techniques as for shaping with depth collars. Fig. 35-17.

Shaping with a Jig

Some shaping jobs can be done with simple jigs. To shape the edge of round stock, cut a large V in a piece of plywood. There should be a clearance hole at the bottom of the V for the cutter. Clamp this to the table. This jig can then be adjusted forward or back until the desired edge can be cut. The stock can then be rotated as it is held against the V-block.

Shaping on a Drill Press

Many simple shaping jobs can be done by fastening an attachment to the spindle of the drill press and attaching the shaper cutters to the spindle. Fig. 35-18.

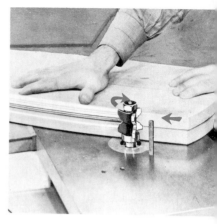

35-17c. Shaping with a pattern.

35-18. Using the shaper attachment on the drill press.

SANDER

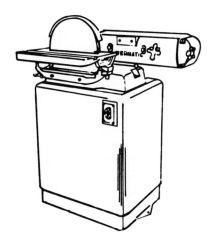

SAFETY

- Be sure the abrasive is in good condition and that the grit is correct for the work to be done.
- Be sure the abrasive belt is installed with the correct tension and is tracking properly.
- Keep your hands away from abrasive surfaces.
- Be sure the abrasive disc is properly secured to the machine.
- Sand only on the down stroke side of the disc sander.
- Be sure the stock is firmly against the stop, fence, or miter gage before applying pressure against the abrasive.
- Never touch the edge of a belt or disc.
- Be sure there are no nicks or tears in the edge of a disc or belt.
- Disconnect the power plug when changing abrasives.
- Make certain the switch is in the "off" position when plugging in the power cord.

UNIT 36 Sanders

In furniture construction, a most important process is finishing. To obtain a really good finish, the wood must be sanded thoroughly. Fig. 36-1. There are many kinds of sanding machines, the most common of which are the floor-type belt sander, the floor-type disc sander, the drum sander, the portable belt sander and the finishing sander. With these machines, all surfaces, edges, and ends can be smoothed.

Kinds of Sanders

Belt and Disc Sanders

Belt and disc sanders may be separate machines. Fig. 36-2. More frequently, however, they are combined in a single machine. Fig. 36-3. Both are equipped with tables on which the work is held. The belt sander can be used in a vertical or horizontal position. Its table has herringbone slots cut in it to keep the underside of the belt free of dust and dirt. The belt sander often comes equipped with a fence similar to that on a jointer. Fig. 36-4a. The disc sander has a rotating disc on which the abrasive paper is fastened. A table can be adjusted at any angle to the vertical surface. Fig. 36-4b. The combination disc-and-belt sander combines these features.

Drum or Spindle Sander

The drum sander has a revolving drum on which an abrasive sleeve is fastened. Fig. 36-5. It is used mostly for sanding the edges of stock. Drill presses, lathes, and shapers can be quickly converted into drum sanders. Fig. 36-6.

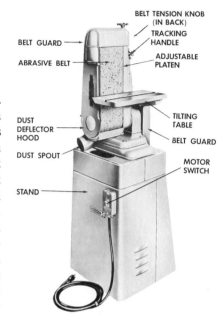

36-2a. Parts of a belt sander.

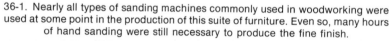

36-1. Nearly all types of sanding machines commonly used in woodworking were used at some point in the production of this suite of furniture. Even so, many hours of hand sanding were still necessary to produce the fine finish.

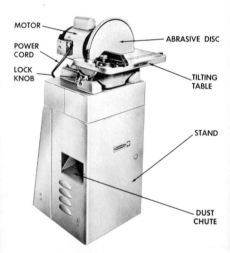

36-2b. Parts of a disc sander.

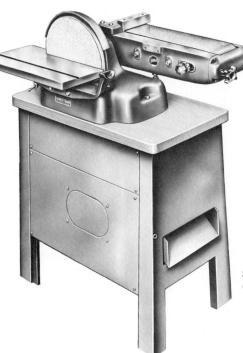

36-4a. Using the fence to support the workpiece when sanding an edge.

36-3. A combination disc-and-belt sander.

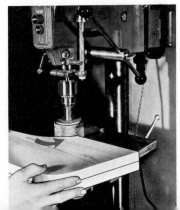

36-4b. The table on the disc sander can be tilted to any angle and held in position by tightening the two lock knobs.

36-5. A heavy-duty drum sander. The drum on this machine oscillates up and down as it rotates. This helps to eliminate sanding scratches.

36-6a. The shaper can be used as a drum or spindle sander.

36-6b. Using a sanding drum on the drill press.

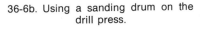

365

36-7. The assembled table is mounted in this semi-automatic stroke sander to sand the table leaves flush with the top.

Hand-Stroke Belt Sander

The hand-stroke belt sander is the best machine for sanding large surfaces such as the tops of desks, tables, and cabinets. Fig. 36-7. A large, continuous belt revolves around two drums. The work table can travel backward and forward. The operator holds a sanding block on the back of the moving belt to control the sanding. Fig. 36-8.

Wide-Belt Sander

The wide-belt sander is relatively new to the wood sanding field. In many instances this single machine is replacing both the drum sander, Fig. 36-9, and the stroke sander. The wide-belt sander uses a belt at least 12″ wide. Fig. 36-10.

An *abrasive planer* is really a heavily constructed wide-belt sander with a large motor. Be-

36-8a. Hand-stroke belt sander.

36-8b. Notice on the machine the operator holds the pad in his hand to apply pressure to the back of the belt.

36-9. Triple-drum sander. The stock is carried on the endless belt under the oscillating drums. The first drum has a coarse abrasive and the succeeding drums have progressively finer abrasive. The stock is sanded in one pass on each side.

Adjustments

Belt Sander

To adjust the belt sander to a vertical, horizontal, or slant position, loosen the two cap screws, move the sander to the desired position, and re-lock. To adjust the tilting table, loosen the clamp handle. Set the table for the desired angle and reclamp. To install a new belt, first remove the drum guard. Release the tension on the belt, slip the old one off, and replace with a new one. Apply a slight amount of belt tension and turn the machine over by hand to see if the belt stays on center. To track the belt, loosen the tracking handle which controls the tilt of the idler arm and tilt in one direction or another. Re-lock. Add

36-10a. The wide-belt sander. This is a slant-head, light-duty machine, with an oscillating belt.

cause of its rapid feed speed and its accuracy, this machine has had an important influence on the furniture industry. Feed speeds may vary from 30 to 200 feet per minute, and the machine will sand to within .005″. In many factories abrasive planers are replacing traditional wood planers because they sharply reduce waste caused by tear-out. A $\frac{1}{8}$″ cut can be taken at speeds of 25–35 feet per minute. Reject rates on the abrasive planer are $\frac{1}{10}$ of 1 percent or less. On a knife planer reject rates for hardwood often are 5 percent, and sometimes as high as 15 percent.

Furniture parts, such as frames and banded tops, can be sanded with accuracy after assembly and without danger of tearout, even on cross-grain cuts.

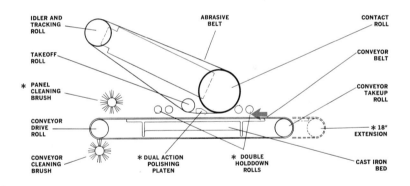

36-10b. Parts of a wide-belt sander. The arrow indicates feed direction.

belt tension as needed. If you start the machine without tracking the belt, it may slide off and be ruined. To remove the back stop for sanding long or wide boards, remove the two cap screws that hold it in place. Fig. 36-11.

36-11. Sanding long flat stock on the belt sander with the backstop removed.

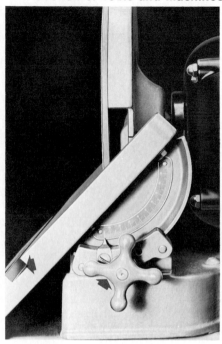

36-12a. To sand angles on the disc sander, loosen the table clamp handle, and tilt the table to the desired angle. A miter gage can be used in the table slot to help guide the workpiece.

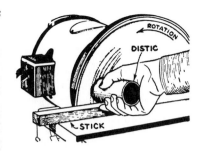

36-13. Installing an abrasive sheet on a disc sander, using a commercial cement. Sheets can also be purchased cut to exact size and with adhesive on the back.

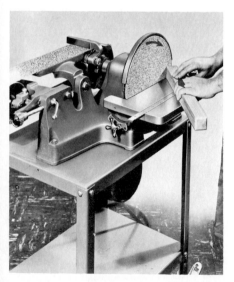

36-12b. Using the miter gage on the disc sander to sand a chamfer.

Disc Sander

Here are some of the common adjustments for the floor-type disc sander. To tilt the table, loosen the handle beneath the table and adjust it to the correct angle. Fig. 36-12a. When using the disc sander, it's a good idea to check the table for squareness frequently. The table is cut with a groove to permit the use of a miter gage. Fig. 36-12b. To remove the disc, hold the spindle firmly and rotate the disc counterclockwise. Sometimes a small piece of wood must be inserted to keep the spindle from revolving.

To install a new sanding disc, first remove the old paper. There are several materials that can be used for fastening the disc in place, among which are glue, rubber cement, or commercial stick cement. If glue is used, the disc must be soaked in water first. If rubber cement or stick cement is used, the machine must be turned on, the end grain of a piece of hardwood held firmly against the disc to heat it, and the old disc pulled off. Cut a new sanding disc if commercial ones are not available. Apply rubber cement or glue, or hold stick cement against the revolving wheel. Fig. 36-13. Put the abrasive paper in place and allow it to dry a short time.

Drum or Spindle Sander

To replace the abrasive paper or cloth on a drum or spindle sander, remove the worn paper. Sometimes a wedge on one side holds the paper in place. In other cases, the drum is made of two half segments that can be separated for replacing the new paper. Spiral sleeves in an assortment of diameters and lengths with various grit sizes can be purchased. These are installed on the hard rubber drums or spindles by loosening the nut on the end of the spindle. Remove the old sleeve, slip the new spiral abrasive sleeve over the spindle, and then tighten the nut to hold the abrasive sleeve in place.

Basic Procedures

● Always select the grade of abrasive for the results you want. See the section on abrasives.
● Make sure that sanding on the disc sander is done on the down side or that the work is fed against the direction in which the belt or spindle sander is rotating.

• Always sand *with the grain* of wood.

• *Do all the cutting operations before sanding.* The sander is designed to finish the surface of the work and not to shape it.

• *Always sand surfaces square.* The tendency in sanding is to round all edges and surfaces. Don't spoil the accuracy of your project by careless sanding.

• Round all edges *slightly* to prevent splintering. The corners should be rounded to about the diameter of the lead in a pencil. This should be done by hand with a fine grit abrasive.

• Apply just enough pressure to get the job done. An inexperienced worker is likely to press too hard, cutting scratches and burning the surface.

• At intervals, clean off the abrasive paper or cloth with a brush.

Using a Belt Sander

• To sand work in a horizontal position, first lower the belt sander into position. For smaller pieces—that is, narrower and shorter than the exposed part of the belt—hold the work lightly but firmly on the belt with one end against the fence or backstop. Fig. 36-14.

• To sand the surface of larger pieces, remove the fence and the backstop and feed the work across the belt at a slight angle.

• To sand edges, fasten a fence or table to the belt sander and remove the fence or backstop. Hold the work against the miter gage, moving it along slowly. Bevels and chamfers can also be sanded accurately in this manner by tilting the table. Fig. 36-15.

36-14. Using the backstop on the belt sander of the combination belt-and-disc sanding machine.

36-15. Sanding a bevel or chamfer on a belt sander.

36-17. Using a disc sander.

36-16a. Form sanding on a belt sander. This form is used to round the corners of stock. The one shown in the inset may be used for sanding a large, concave part.

36-16b. Sanding a concave edge, using the end of the belt sander.

• To do form sanding, make a wood form that is exactly opposite in shape, and cover it with a piece of sheet metal. Fasten this to the sanding table so that the belt runs over the form. Fig. 36-16a.

• To do *concave sanding,* remove the guard and use the end of the drum. Fig. 36-16b. *Convex sanding* can also be done on the back of a sander which has no table. Loosen the tension on the belt slightly. A slash belt, which is one cut into thin ribbons, can be secured for this job, although a regular belt can be used.

• A sanding table can be fastened to the belt sander for smoothing ends and edges.

• To sand an inside corner, remove the guard and hold the stock against the table.

Using a Disc Sander

• Most sanding is done freehand. The table must be square with the sanding disc. The stock is held against the downward side of the rotating disc. Fig. 36-17. Remember that the closer you get to the edge of the disc, the faster the sanding action is.

• To sand the ends of stock ac-curately, hold the work against a miter gage.

• To sand circles or arcs free-hand, hold the work firmly on the table and revolve it slowly.

• A simple jig can be made if many circles or wheels are to be sanded. Use the same kind of jig described for cutting circles on the band saw.

• To sand shaped or bent pieces, such as skis or rail segments of a round table, fasten a stop block on the table at the correct distance from the sanding disc. Then feed the stock between the stop block and the disc.

Using a Drum Sander

• To sand the edges of stock on the drum sander, hold the work freehand, applying equal pressure at all times as you move it along against the rotation of the drum.

• For pattern sanding, turn a block of wood equal in diameter to the drum. Fasten it to the end of the drum. Cut a pattern of the desired size and place two small, sharp screws in it. Place the work over the pattern and adjust the drum sander so that the pattern is held against the collar at the end of the drum sander.

PORTABLE SANDER

SAFETY

- See general safety rules for operation of portable electric tools.
- Be sure the abrasive is in good condition and that its grit is correct for the work to be done.
- Be sure the abrasive belt is installed with the correct tension and is tracking properly.
- Keep your hands away from abrasive surfaces.
- Never touch the edge of a belt or disc.
- Be sure there are no nicks or tears in the edge of a disc or belt.
- Disconnect the power plug when changing abrasives.
- Make certain the switch is in the "off" position when plugging in the power cord.

Portable Electric Sanders

Portable electric sanders are excellent for finish-sanding projects after assembly.

Portable Belt Sander

The portable belt sander operates in a manner similar to the floor-model belt-sanding machine, except that the revolving belt is placed on the work instead of the work against the belt. Fig. 36-18. The size of the machine is determined by length and width of belt.

Replacing a belt is the same as on a floor-type belt sander. Locate the arrow on the inside of the belt and have it point in the same direction as the arrow on the side of the machine.

Using a Portable Belt Sander

The proper technique is to put the cord over your right shoulder, hold the machine with both hands, turn the machine on, and lower the back of it slowly onto the wood. Then do the sanding by moving the machine back and forth, and at the same time moving it slowly from one side to the other. Fig. 36-19.

Finishing (or Pad) Sander

There are many kinds of finishing sanders. Parts of a typical one are shown in Fig. 36-20a. All of these sanders operate on one of the three basic principles shown in Fig. 36-20b. Those with straight-line action are the least likely to leave cross-grain

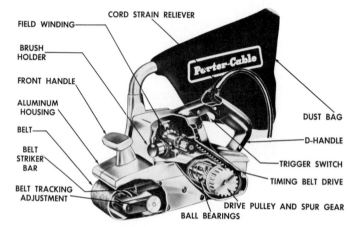

36-18. Parts of a portable belt sander.

36-19a. A two-speed portable belt sander. Note the round knob near the bottom (indicated by arrow) used for tracking the belt. The lever just above this knob is used to release belt tension when replacing a belt.

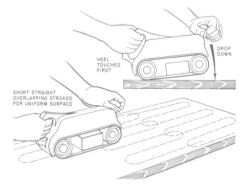

36-19b. Lower the sander slowly to the surface. Move the machine in the pattern shown.

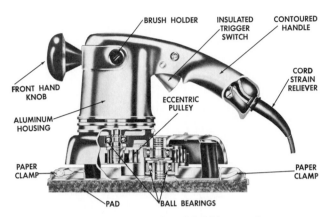

BRUSH HOLDER
INSULATED TRIGGER SWITCH
CONTOURED HANDLE
FRONT HAND KNOB
CORD STRAIN RELIEVER
ECCENTRIC PULLEY
ALUMINUM HOUSING
PAPER CLAMP
PAPER CLAMP
PAD
BALL BEARINGS

36-20a. Parts of a half-pad finishing sander.

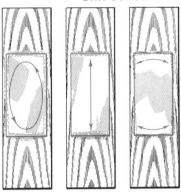

36-20b. Three kinds of action in finishing sanders. Orbital and multi-motion action may cause some cross-grain scratches. Straight-line action is like hand sanding and results in the best surface.

scratches. The size of this machine is determined by the size of the abrasive sheet used. Finishing sanders are primarily used for fine finish-sanding after the project is assembled. To replace a sheet of abrasive, first cut a sheet of paper to the required size. The paper is held on the pad at either end and pressure keys are used to lock the paper in place. Release the pressure keys at either end. Fasten the paper in one end and lock the key at that end. Pull the paper tightly over the pad, slip the loose end under the other clamp, and tighten this lock. The exact method of fastening the paper to the pad will vary with different sanders.

Using a Finishing Sander

The finishing sander should rest evenly on the stock. Apply a moderate amount of pressure and move the sander back and forth, working from one side to the other. Fig. 36-21.

36-21. Using a finishing sander.

LATHE

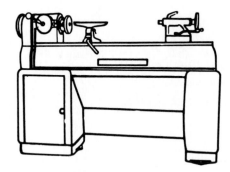

SAFETY

- No one but the operator should stand near the lathe when it is in operation.
- It is especially important that your sleeves be rolled tightly and that your necktie be tucked in.
- Hold all tools firmly.
- Make sure that the wood being turned is free of knots, checks, and other defects.
- Keep the tool rest as close to the work as possible. Check frequently and readjust if necessary.
- Always maintain correct spindle speed.
- Make certain all glued up stock is set before being turned on the lathe.
- Make certain the tool rest and tailstock are clamped securely.
- Do not use a gouge on the inside of bowls when faceplate turning.
- Make certain the tools are sharp.
- Always remove the tool rest for sanding and polishing operations.
- Revolve the work by hand to make sure it turns freely.
- After turning, remove the lathe centers and store them properly.
- Do not attempt anything but scraping cuts on faceplate work.
- Never touch rotating stock with your hands.

UNIT 37 Wood Lathes

37-1a. There are many complex turned parts in this group of furniture pieces.

instance, a manufacturer may produce several hundred Early American chairs, requiring many thousands of turned spindles. An *automatic lathe* is used for this type of work. Even when one-piece items, such as baseball bats or tool handles, are produced in large quantities, they are turned on an automatic lathe. Fig. 37-2. Some lathes can automatically mount a new piece of stock between centers and eject finished pieces.

37-2. Automatic lathe. The knives, set to produce the desired shape, are mounted on an arbor which turns at a high rate of speed. The workpiece is mounted between centers on a counter-balanced unit and is fed slowly into the revolving knives. The finished turning is then removed and another piece of stock is inserted.

Two kinds of wood turning lathes are in common use—the *hand wood lathe* and the *automatic lathe*. The hand wood lathe combines *power operation* with *hand tool skill*. While it is not used very much commercially, it is extremely valuable to the home craftsman for turning many parts for Early American furniture and simple parts for some Modern pieces. Fig. 37-1. It can also be used for making many turned accessories, such as lamp bases, lazy susans, and bowls.

In the woodworking industry, several turned parts may be necessary for a single product. For

37-1b. The simple, tapered legs of this contemporary coffee table were turned on a lathe.

375

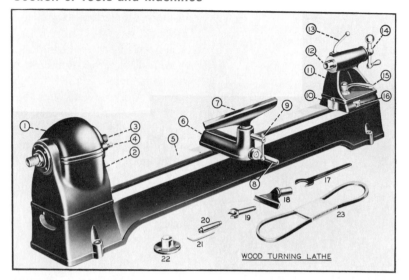

37-3. Parts of a 12″ standard wood-turning lathe: (1) pulley guard, (2) headstock, (3) headstock spindle, (4) index pin, (5) bed, (6) tool-rest base, (7) tool rest, (8) tool-rest base clamp, (9) tool-rest clamp, (10) tailstock base, (11) tailstock, (12) tailstock spindle, (13) tailstock spindle clamp, (14) tailstock spindle feed handle, (15) tailstock clamp handle, (16) set-over adjusting screw, (17) headstock wrench, (18) small tool rest, (19) spur center, (20) cup center, (21) wrench, (22) small faceplate, and (23) belt.

37-4b. A safety shield covers the full lathe work area and slides into position for guarded faceplate turning.

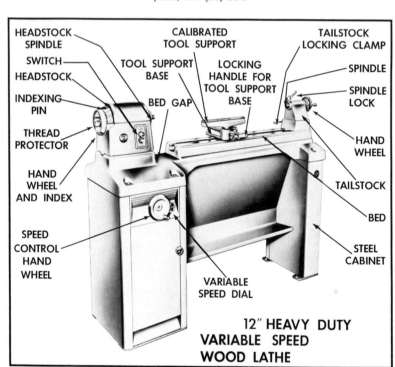

37-4a. Parts of a gap-bed lathe.

Size

The size of the hand wood lathe is indicated by (1) the largest diameter it will turn and (2) the length of the bed. Fig. 37-3. A typical size is the 12″ with 36″ bed. Many lathes now have what is called a *gap bed*. Fig. 37-4a. The gap permits a larger capacity for faceplate turning—usually about a 4″ increase in diameter and $2\frac{1}{2}$ or $3\frac{1}{2}$″ in thickness. Fig. 37-4b.

Parts

The bed is a heavy metal casting. The headstock assembly consists of two items: (1) a hollow spindle that is threaded on each end; and (2) either a step pulley or a variable speed unit, for changing the speed. Fig. 37-5. There are equally spaced holes drilled around the step pulley or hand wheel which act as a divid-

37-5. On a variable-speed lathe the speed is changed by turning the handwheel on the front of the cabinet when the lathe is running. The speed of the other two lathes is changed by turning off the power and repositioning the belt on the cone pulley.

37-7. Kinds of centers: a. Spur or drive. b. Cup or dead. c. 60-degree plain center.

37-6. The spindles in each of these headstocks can be indexed and locked in place by engaging the knob indicated by the arrow.

37-8. Lathe faceplates: a. 6″ faceplate with lefthand and righthand threads, for large faceplate work. b. 3″ faceplate with righthand threads for medium and small faceplate work.

ing head to do many operations. Fig. 37-6a and b. The inside end of the spindle is threaded with a righthand thread and the outside end with a lefthand thread. Faceplates have both righthand and lefthand threads so they can be fastened to either end for faceplate turning. The inside end has a tapered hole (No. 2 Morse taper) into which the spur center fits. Fig. 37-7. The tailstock assembly can be clamped to the bed at any position. A hand wheel can be turned to move the tailstock spindle in or out. This spindle is also hollow, with a No. 2 Morse taper. The cup center fits into this end. Fig. 37-7b. The tool rest and tool rest base are clamped to the bed and can be adjusted for turning any diameter.

Accessories

Many accessories are available. The *regular faceplate* is available in several diameters. It has a hole in the center and three or more equally spaced holes near the outside edge. It is used for all faceplate work. Fig. 37-8. The *single-screw* center is used when turning small bowls and cups. A *sanding drum* or *disc* is available for sanding contour pieces on the lathe. A *steady rest* is used when turning very thin, long stock. The *right angle tool support* is used for faceplate turning. The *knockout*

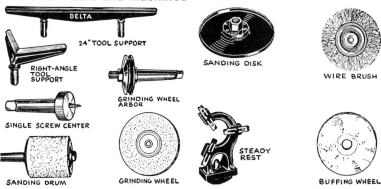

37-9. Common accessories for the lathe.

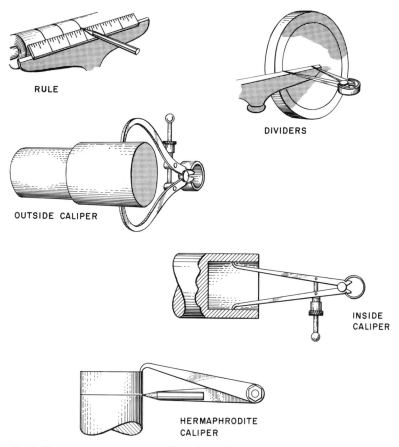

RULE

DIVIDERS

OUTSIDE CALIPER

INSIDE CALIPER

HERMAPHRODITE CALIPER

37-10. Common measuring tools. *Rule,* for making measurements for spindle and faceplate turning and for setting dividers and calipers. *Dividers,* for drawing circles and stepping off measurements. *Outside caliper,* for checking the outside diameter of turned work. *Inside caliper,* for making measurements on the inside diameter. *Hermaphrodite caliper,* for laying out distances from the end of stock and for locating the centers for turning.

bar is used for removing the centers or other accessories from the headstock spindle. Fig. 37-9.

Measuring Tools

The wood turner needs a good one- or two-foot *rule* for measuring distances; inside and outside *calipers* for checking diameters of work; and *dividers* for laying out circles, especially on faceplate work. Fig. 37-10.

Turning Tools

Gouge

The gouge is used for straight turning and for cutting concave and convex surfaces. A bevel is ground on the convex side at an angle of about 30 degrees. This tool is available in several sizes. Usually a large (1″ or 1½″) gouge and a small (½″ or ¾″) gouge are needed. Fig. 37-11.

Skew

Skews are used for finish turning, for cutting shoulders, for trimming ends, and for cutting V's and beads. They get their name from the fact that the cutting edge is askew, usually at an angle of about 60 degrees. The tool is ground from both sides. The upper end is called the toe and the lower end the heel. Usually two sizes, 1″ (large) and ½″ (small) are needed. Fig. 37-11.

Parting Tool

The parting tool is slightly wider at the center and narrower at either edge. The point is ground from both sides. It is used for trimming ends and for marking and turning to various diameters.

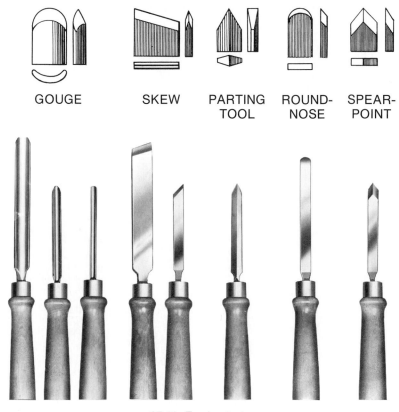

GOUGE   SKEW   PARTING TOOL   ROUND-NOSE   SPEAR-POINT

37-11. Turning tools.

tools, and the wood is removed by wearing away the fibers. It does not produce as smooth a surface but, with sanding, is satisfactory. For the operator who makes only an occasional piece on the wood lathe, this method can be recommended. All faceplate work is done by the scraping method. Fig. 37-12.

● *Cutting or paring.* With this method the wood fibers are sheared off. This requires considerably more practice. It is the method employed by the oldtime, skilled hand wood turners. If one is to do a good deal of wood turning, it would pay to learn this method. Fig. 37-13.

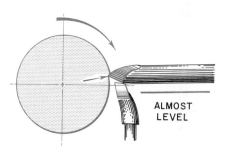

37-12. The scraping method. Note that the tool is held almost level.

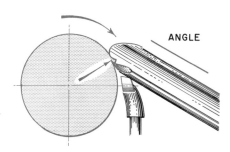

37-13. Cutting produces a much smoother surface than scraping. However, it requires greater skill and much more practice.

When in use it is held on edge and forced into the work. Fig. 37-11.

Square-Nose

A square-nose is shaped like an ordinary wood chisel except that the blade is heavier. It is ground at an angle of about 45 degrees from one side. It is used in scraping operations for straight and taper turning.

Round-Nose

The round-nose is similar to an ordinary chisel except that it is ground with a semicircular end. The bevel is on one side and at an angle of about 40 degrees. It is used for many scraping opera-

tions such as cutting coves or large recesses. Fig. 37-11.

Spear-Point

The spear-point or diamond-point is ground to a sharp point with a bevel on one side at an angle of about 30 degrees. It is used for scraping operations, such as forming sharp V's or corners. Fig. 37-11.

Methods of Turning

There are two basic methods of turning:

● *Scraping.* This is the simplest and easiest method for the beginner to learn. All of the tools are used as ordinary scraping

379

37-14. Draw lines across the corners to locate the center of square stock. To locate the center of an irregularly shaped piece, on the end of the piece and near the center draw a line parallel to each edge. The center of the small enclosed area may then be approximated.

Basic Turning Procedures

Spindle Turning

Turning with the stock held between the spur center and the cup center is called spindle turning.

1. Select a piece of wood of the desired kind. Cut a piece that is slightly larger than the diameter to be turned and about 1″ longer than needed. If the stock measures more than 3″ square, cut it to octagonal shape on the band saw. This can also be done on a circular saw, or on a jointer if the piece is long enough to be jointed safely.

2. Draw lines across the corners of both ends. Fig. 37-14. If it is round, locate the center with a hermaphrodite caliper or a center head.

3. Mark the center with a prick punch or scratch awl.

4. With a knockout bar, remove the spur center from the lathe.

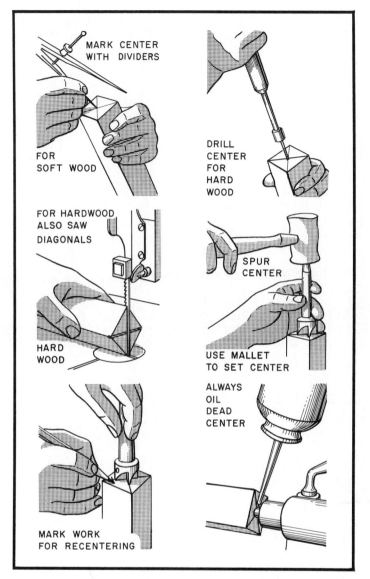

37-15. Preparing the stock for spindle turning.

37-16. Always keep the tool rest properly adjusted. This position may vary slightly for different jobs and operators. Never set the tool rest below the center of the work.

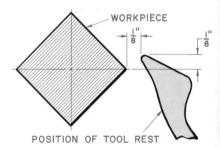

DIA. OF STOCK	ROUGHING TO SIZE	GENERAL CUTTING	FINISHING
Under 2 In. Diameter . . . . . . .900 to 1300 R.P.M.		2400 to 2800	3000 to 4000
2 In. to 4 In. Diameter . . . . . .600 to 1000 R.P.M.		1800 to 2400	2400 to 3000
4 In. to 6 In. Diameter . . . . . .600 to 800 R.P.M.		1200 to 1800	1800 to 2400
6 In. to 8 In. Diameter . . . . . .400 to 600 R.P.M.		800 to 1200	1200 to 1800
8 In. to 10 In. Diameter . . . . .300 to 400 R.P.M.		600 to 800	900 to 1200
Over 10 In. Diameter . . . . . . .200 to 300 R.P.M.		300 to 600	600 to 900

37-17. Speeds for wood turning.

Hold the stock on end over a table and place the spur center in position, striking it several times with a mallet to drive it into the wood. Some operators keep an extra spur center available for this. Never place the wood against the center in the lathe and strike it, since you can ruin the headstock spindle bearings. If the wood is extremely hard, saw a kerf about 1/8″ deep across each corner and drill a small center hole, 1/16″ in diameter and 1/8″ deep, in each end for insertion of the centers.

5. Place the stock over the spur center of the headstock and move the tailstock so that it clears the other end of the wood about 1″. Lock the tailstock in position. Then turn the tailstock handle until the cup center seats firmly in the wood. Release the pressure slightly and apply a little wax or oil. Then apply a little tension to the hand wheel and lock it in position. Fig. 37-15.

6. Adjust the tool rest to clear the stock about 1/8″, when the top of the rest is about 1/8″ above center. Fig. 37-16. If the stock is quite long, adjust the tool rest so that one end is even with the tailstock end of the stock.

7. Set the speed according to the diameter of the stock and the kind of cut to be taken. Fig. 37-17.

8. Turn the lathe over by hand once or twice to make sure that everything clears.

9. Set an outside caliper to measure 1/16″ more than the diameter of the finished stock. Now you are ready to begin.

Rough Turning Between Centers

1. Select a large, well-sharpened gouge. If you are right-handed, hold it in your left hand, using one of the following two methods:

METHOD A: Grasp the gouge about an inch from the cutting end, with the thumb on the inside and the fingers around the outside or convex side. The index finger acts as a stop against the tool rest. Fig. 37-18.

METHOD B: Place the hand over the concave side of the gouge, with the thumb underneath. The wrist must be bent to act as a stop against the tool rest. Fig. 37-19.

2. Hold the handle of the turning tool firmly in the right hand.

3. Turn the machine on. Place the convex side of the gouge against the tool rest about 2″ from the right end. The index finger or your wrist should be held firmly against the rest and the cutting tool against the tool support.

4. Hold the tool at about a 30 degree angle to the revolving stock. Twist the tool slightly in the

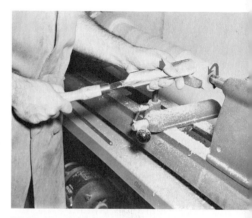

37-18. The underhand method of holding the gouge. Notice the index finger is used as a guide against the tool rest. NOTE: In many photos the shield was removed for a better view. The guard symbol in the captions is a reminder that *you must use the shield when actually doing this work.*

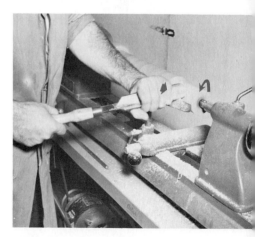

37-19. The overhand method of holding the gouge. Considered safer but awkward.

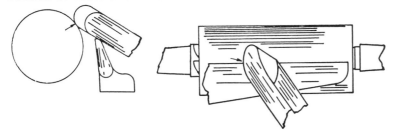

37-20. Correct method of using the gouge for cutting.

direction of the cut to be taken. With beveled edge tangent to the cylinder, make the cut. Fig. 37-20. After each cut move the tool a few inches closer to the headstock. Continue these cuts until 2″ of the left end of the cylinder remain to be turned to the rough size.

5. When the cylinder is formed to within 2″ of the headstock, twist the tool to the left and make the cut toward the headstock. At first the cutting will be done only on the corners. Continue making cuts until the stock is round. It is easy to tell if the stock is round by laying the back of a tool lightly against the revolving surface.

6. When the cylinder is formed,

set the outside caliper $\frac{1}{16}$″ over-size. Hold the caliper in the left hand and a parting tool in the right. Slowly force the parting tool in *near* (but *never at*) the head-stock end and the tailstock end until the caliper just slips over the wood. Make a series of these cuts along the length of the cylinder.

7. With the gouge, cut down to the bottom of the parting tool cuts. The cylinder will now be turned to rough diameter, $\frac{1}{16}$″ oversize.

Finish-Turning a Plain Cylinder

First, adjust an outside caliper to finished size. Then:

● To *scrape* stock to finished size, use a square-nosed tool or a large skew. Use a very high speed. Hold the cutting edge parallel to the cylinder and the tool flat on the tool rest, then force it into the work until the scraping begins. Always start the scraping some distance in from the ends to prevent the tool from catching and splitting the wood; then move it from one side to the other. Fig. 37-21. Check occasionally with an outside caliper until finished size is reached.

● For *cutting*, use a large skew. Place the skew on its flat side, with

the cutting edge slightly above and beyond the cylinder. Start at a point 2″ to 3″ in from the end. Hold the flat side of the tool firmly against the tool rest. Slowly draw the skew back until the cutting edge is over the cylinder at a point about halfway between the heel and toe. Fig. 37-22. Be careful not to catch the toe of the tool in the revolving cylinder. Turn the skew lightly by twisting the handle until the cutting edge can be forced into the wood. Then push the skew along toward the tailstock, taking a shearing cut. Fig. 37-23. You will note that the back portion of the grind or bevel supports the tool, and the handle hand controls

37-22. Use only the lower half of the cutting edge of the skew.

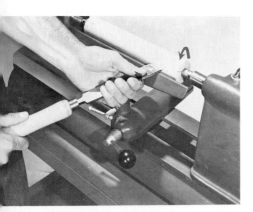

37-21. Using the skew to *scrape* a plain cylinder. Note that the tool is held flat on the tool rest.

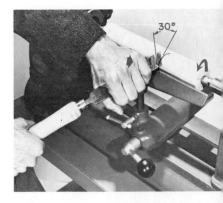

37-23. *Cutting* a plain cylinder with a skew. Note the angle between the chisel's cutting edge and a line drawn around the cylinder.

the depth of cut by rocking the chisel on this pivot point. Reverse the direction and cut toward the headstock. The major difficulties of beginners are that they hold the tool at too great an angle to the work, thus making the tool dig in; or they hold it in one position too long, resulting in too small a diameter.

Using a Parting Tool

The parting tool has many uses. It is a scraping tool, used for cutting a cylinder to length, and for making a shoulder. It is also used in making recesses, tapers, and complex parts (to indicate the depth of turning). Hold the parting tool on edge over the tool rest with your right hand and hold a caliper in your left. Force the parting tool into the revolving stock. At the same time hold the points of the caliper on the cylinder until they just slip over. Fig. 37-24. If the groove to be cut is fairly deep, it's a good idea to move the parting tool back and forth a little to make a slightly wider groove than the tool itself. If further scraping is to be done, allow about $\frac{1}{16}''$ to $\frac{1}{8}''$ beyond the layout line.

Cutting a Shoulder

Turn the cylinder to the desired size; with a rule and pencil mark the position at which the shoulder is to be cut.

● *Scraping method.* Set an outside caliper to the smaller diameter plus $\frac{1}{16}''$. With a parting tool cut a groove at the layout line in the waste stock. The groove should be cut to the caliper measurement. Use a square-nosed tool

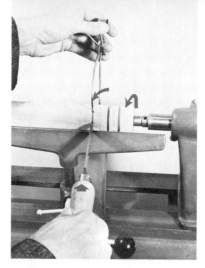

37-24. Using a parting tool and caliper to size the stock.

37-25a. Scraping a shoulder to finished size.

SHOULDERS

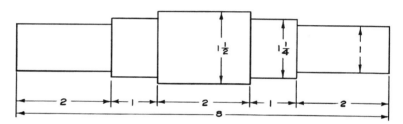

37-25b. A simple turning exercise for straight turning and cutting a shoulder.

or skew and scrape to the finished diameter. Fig. 37-25.

● *Cutting method.* Rough cut the small diameter in the waste stock $\frac{1}{16}''$ from the layout line by using the parting tool and caliper (set $\frac{1}{16}''$ oversize). Remove waste stock with a gouge as described in steps 6 and 7, *Rough Turning Between Centers.* Hold the small skew on edge with the toe down and the heel up. Hold the skew at a slight angle so that one bevel is at right angles to the cylinder. Tip the heel slightly away from the cut. Fig. 37-26. Force the skew into the wood a little at a time

37-26. To cut a shoulder, the toe of the skew is used to remove thin shavings from the side. Hold the skew so that its bottom edge is nearly parallel to the shoulder. Turn the cutting edge away at the top so that only the toe itself does the cutting. Start with the handle low, then raise it slowly during the cut.

INCORRECT   CORRECT

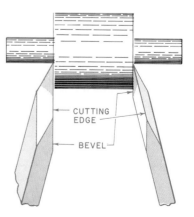

CUTTING EDGE

BEVEL

383

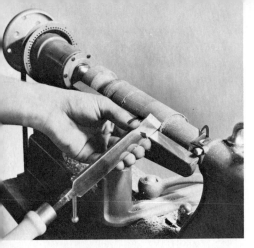

37-27. Making the vertical or side cut of a shoulder with the toe of the skew.

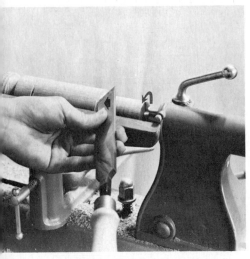

37-28. Making the horizontal cut of a shoulder with the heel of the skew.

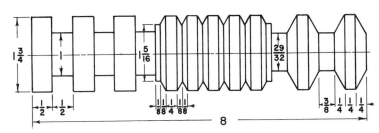

37-30. Turning exercise for V's and recesses.

until the smaller diameter is reached. Fig. 37-27. Then place the skew on its side and finish cutting to the smaller diameter. Fig. 37-28. Use the heel of the skew to cut to the corner. Handling all tools for the wood lathe requires practice.

Cutting a Long Taper

1. Turn the cylinder to the largest diameter. Then place a rule against the tool rest and, with a pencil, mark the beginning and end of the taper.

2. With a parting tool cut a groove to the smallest diameter.

3. Rough cut the cylinder to size with a gouge. Cut from the large diameter toward the small diameter.

4. Turn to finished size. Then use one of these two methods to complete the job:

METHOD A: *Scrape* to finished size with a square-nose or skew. If the taper is long, the tool rest should be set at a slight angle to make it parallel to the tapered surface.

METHOD B: *Cut* to finished size with the skew as in turning a cylinder. Fig. 37-29.

37-29. Cutting a long taper.

Cutting Large Rectangular Recesses

1. Turn the cylinder to the largest finished diameter. Fig. 37-30.

2. Hold a rule on the tool rest and mark the locations of the recesses.

3. With a parting tool, make a groove about $\frac{1}{16}''$ to $\frac{1}{8}''$ inside the layout line at the end of each recess. Scrape to the desired diameter.

4. Turn to finished size. Then use one of these methods:

METHOD A: *Scrape* the recess to size, using a square-nose or skew. Trim the shoulders of the recesses with a parting tool.

METHOD B: *Cut* the recess to rough size with a small gouge. Finish cutting with a skew.

Cutting Stock to Length

Turn the cylinder to the correct diameter and mark the length needed.

● *Scraping method.* Force a parting tool into the stock exactly at the layout line at the tailstock end and cut to a $\frac{1}{8}''$ diameter. Repeat at the headstock end. If you wish to cut the end off completely, hold the parting tool in your right hand and place the left hand loosely around the revolving stock. Continue to force the part-

384

37-31. Using a skew for scraping stock to length.

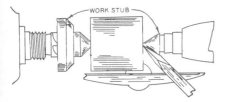

WORK STUB

37-32. The proper method of holding a skew when cutting stock to length.

37-33. Scraping V's with a diamond-point.

ing tool into the wood until the cylinder drops off. Remember to allow enough wood at the head-stock end to keep from hitting the spur center. (This procedure can also be done with a small skew held on its side as shown in Fig.

37-31). Trim off the waste stock on the ends with a saw.

● *Cutting method.* Hold a small skew on edge with the heel up and the toe down. Turn it at an angle so that one bevel is parallel to the cut to be made. Force the skew in slowly; then back it out and cut a half V into the waste stock. Fig. 37-32. Do this on both ends. It's extremely important when cutting with the toe of the skew to keep the heel tipped slightly away from the cut. Review *Cutting Method* under *Cutting a Shoulder*, page 383. It is easy for the tool to dig in and damage the stock.

Cutting V's

● *Scraping method.* Hold a diamond-point tool flat and force it into the wood to cut the V. Fig. 37-33.

● *Cutting method.* Mark the center and edges of the V cut. Hold a skew on edge with the heel down; then force the skew into the stock at the center of the V cut. Use a slight pump-handle action. Fig. 37-34. Work from one side of the V, using the heel of the skew to do the cutting. Continue to force the skew into the center of the cut and cut one side of the V to correct depth. Then cut the opposite side

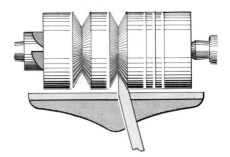

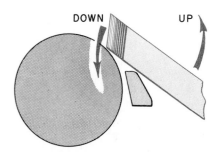

DOWN UP

37-34. Cutting V's with a skew. The skew is pivoted on the tool rest, down into the stock. The cutting is done with the heel.

in a similar manner. Remember when cutting with the heel of the skew chisel to keep the toe tipped slightly away from the cut.

Cutting Beads

● *Scraping method.* Lay out the location of the beads on the workpiece. Fig. 37-35. Make a parting tool cut on each end of

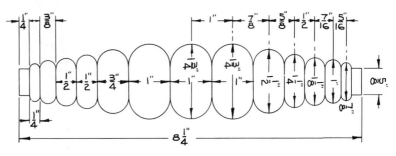

37-35. A bead exercise.

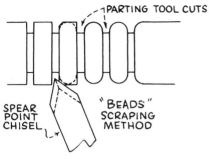

37-36. Shaping a bead by scraping, using a spear-point chisel. The skew may also be used.

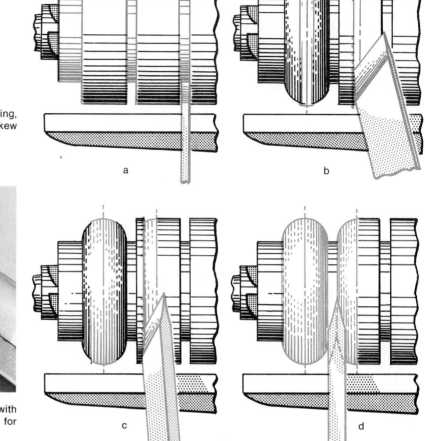

37-37. Making a deep vertical cut with the toe of the skew, in preparation for cutting beads.

37-38. Cutting beads, using the heel to do most of the cutting.

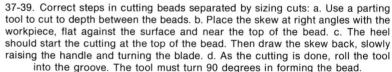

37-39. Correct steps in cutting beads separated by sizing cuts: a. Use a parting tool to cut to depth between the beads. b. Place the skew at right angles with the workpiece, flat against the surface and near the top of the bead. c. The heel should start the cutting at the top of the bead. Then draw the skew back, slowly raising the handle and turning the blade. d. As the cutting is done, roll the tool into the groove. The tool must turn 90 degrees in forming the bead.

the bead, if there is room. Place the tool flat on the tool rest and rotate it horizontally to form the bead. Fig. 37-36.

● *Cutting method.* Beads are rather difficult to cut and will require considerable practice. Mark the position of each bead with a line indicating ends and centers of the beads. Begin the cut as you would a V-cut, using the toe of the skew to start it. Fig. 37-37. Then hold the skew on its side with the heel doing most of the cutting. Fig. 37-38. Start quite high on the cylinder at the center of the bead and turn the tool in the same arc as the bead, at the same time

386

COVES

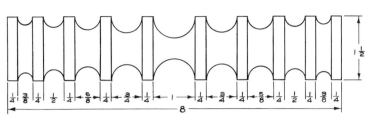

37-40a. A cove exercise.

37-40b. Scraping a cove with a round-nose tool.

drawing it backward and moving it to a vertical position. If the tool is not turned as the cut is made, the heel will dig into the bead. Fig. 37-39.

Cutting Coves

Mark the center and ends of each cove and adjust the caliper to the smaller diameter. Fig. 37-40a.

● *Scraping method.* Force a round-nosed tool into the center of the cove. Swing the tool from one side to the other, using the tool rest as a fulcrum point. Continue to measure the center with a caliper until the desired depth is reached. Fig. 37-40b.

● *Cutting method.* Start at one edge of the cove with a small gouge held on edge, and cut toward the center. Twist the gouge as the cut is made until it lies flat on the tool rest. Cut to the center of the cove, then start on the other edge and repeat. Fig. 37-41.

To develop skill in the use of the turning tools on the lathe will require many hours of practice on the basic cuts. Many students will want to practice using the turning exercises shown earlier. Turning a file handle will give the operator all the basic cuts plus fitting a ferrule and drilling on the lathe. Fig. 37-42, next page.

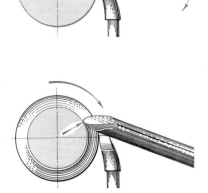

37-41. Making a cove cut with a gouge. Start the cut on one edge, with the gouge vertical. Roll the tool as the cut is made. The tool should be horizontal at the bottom of the cut. Repeat this procedure on the other side of the cove.

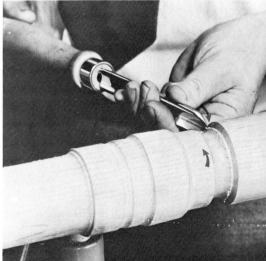

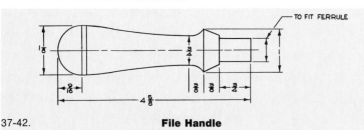

37-42.　　　　　　　　**File Handle**

Plan of Procedure

1. Locate centers.
2. Mount the stock in the lathe, between lathe centers.
3. Rough turn to rough diameter (1³⁄₁₆").
4. Cut to length (4⅝").
5. Lay out the dimensions and cut to size with parting tool and caliper.
6. Fit the ferrule. (Cut a piece of ½" thin-wall conduit ½" long and file the edges smooth.)
7. Install the ferrule. (It should fit tightly.)
8. Make the V cut down to the ferrule.
9. Turn the cove.
10. Turn the taper from the 1⅛" diameter down to the cove cut. Note that this is not a straight line but is slightly concave.
11. Turn the bead on the end.
12. Sand to remove all tool marks and blend the cuts together.
13. Make two V cuts in the handle, using the toe of the skew. Hold the skew on edge, in the vertical position.
14. Remove the file handle from the lathe.
15. Mount a drill chuck in the headstock spindle and install a drill to fit the tang of the file. Hold the end of the file handle against the plain center in the tailstock spindle. Run the lathe at a slow speed and feed the file handle into the drill by turning the tailstock spindle handwheel.
16. Cut off the ends and sand them flush.
17. Apply a finish.

37-43a. Making a template for turning a complicated part.

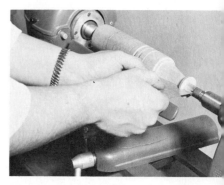

37-43b. Using a template to check the turned part.

Turning Complex Parts

Parts made on a wood lathe usually involve more than one kind of cut. This is true, for example, of turned legs, lamp bases, and other similar objects. Make a full-size drawing of the piece. If it is to be a leg or lamp base, part of which is rectangular, first machine the piece to size. In most cases, the piece can also be cut to the correct length, since the center marks will not ruin the piece.

Turning Duplicate Parts

Many times identical pieces need to be made, as for the legs on a table, spokes in a wheel, or spindles in a chair arm or back.

There are many ways to make this task easier and assure that the pieces produced will be alike. One of the simpler methods for checking the work as the turning progresses is to cut a full-size cardboard or sheet metal template to the required shape. Fig. 37-43. If a large number of identical pieces are to be made, one of the following methods might be used:

METHOD A: First, make a layout pattern, Fig. 37-44, or a layout board. Fig. 37-45. Then size the spindle with a parting tool and calipers or with a diameter gage. Fig. 37-46. The turnings can then be checked for accuracy with a template. Fig. 37-43b.

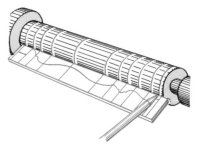

37-44. Using a layout pattern for sizing duplicate turnings.

METHOD B: Use a duplicator on the lathe, as shown in Fig. 37-47. Then proceed as follows:

1. Clamp the duplicator on the lathe bed with the cutter height in line with the middle of the spur center. Fig. 37-48a.

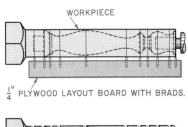

WORKPIECE

$\frac{1}{4}$" PLYWOOD LAYOUT BOARD WITH BRADS.

CUT WITH PARTING TOOL.

37-45. Using a layout board for sizing duplicate turnings.

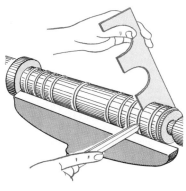

37-46. Using a diameter gage in place of a caliper to size the spindle.

37-47. Colonial and Early American furniture styles require many identically turned spindles. The wood turning duplicator will reproduce these spindles to match a template.

37-48a.

37-48b.

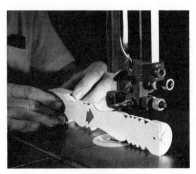

37-48c.

37-48d.

37-48e.

37-48f.

37-48g.

37-48. Using the wood turning duplicator on the wood lathe.

37-48h.

2. Make a template, using one of these three methods:

a. Make a turning freehand, as you would normally. Then trace the turning onto a piece of ⅛" hardboard with a ball-point pen mounted in the duplicator. Fig. 37-48b. Carefully cut it out on the scroll saw or band saw.

b. Make a turning freehand and on the band saw cut a ⅛" section through the center for the template. Fig. 37-48c.

c. With wood screws fasten two pieces of stock together, with a piece of ⅛" hardboard between them. Fig. 37-48d. Turn the piece freehand. Remove the screws and separate the pieces. The hardboard will serve as the template. Fig. 37-48e.

3. Turn the stock to be used for the finished turnings to the rough diameter. Mount one piece in the lathe between centers and set the cutter against the cylinder. Screw the template in position on the duplicator, opposite the stock mounted between centers. Fig. 37-48f.

4. Cut the ends. Fig. 37-48g.

5. Rough turn the outline. Fig. 37-48h. Then take a light cut with the stock turning at 3,000 to 3,300 rpm. (Pieces formed this way will require careful sanding.)

37-49a. Common holding devices for faceplate turning: (1) Screw center. (2) Small (3" diameter) faceplate with three screw holes. (3) Larger (6" diameter) faceplate with special thread that fits both the right-and-left-hand threaded spindles to allow it to be used on either end of the headstock spindle.

Faceplate Turning

There are two common faceplates for turning. The screw center is used for turning stock no larger than 4" in diameter. The regular faceplate usually has a hole in the center and three or more holes spaced around the outside. Faceplates are available in several sizes. Fig. 37-49.

Scraping Tools

All faceplate turning is done with the scraping method. Tools commonly used are the square-nose, round-nose, diamond-point, and parting tool. The skew can also be used as a scraping tool as in spindle turning. Lay the side of the skew flat on the tool support (*never tip it up*) and use it as you would the round-nose, square-nose, or diamond-point.

Simple Turning

1. Select a piece of stock slightly larger and thicker than the desired finished size. Check to see that there is no check or defect in it that will crack or split during the turning. Large pieces, whenever possible, should be cut to octagonal shape or, even better,

37-50. Fastening a faceplate to a lathe.

37-49b. This attractive bowl is an example of faceplate turning.

cut round on a band saw or jig saw. Locate the center of the stock. If it is a small piece and a screw center is used, drill a small hole in the center. Apply a little wax, and screw on the stock. If it is a large piece, place the faceplate over the work and mark the location of the hole. Drill small holes and fasten with short wood screws.

2. Remove the spur center and fasten the work to the spindle. Fig. 37-50.

3. Adjust the tool support across the face of the disc slightly below center so the cutting edge of the tool is exactly at center. Clamp the tool support holder in position, with the tool support about ⅛" from the stock.

4. Adjust the lathe so that it operates at a slow speed.

5. Use a flat- or round-nose tool. Hold it on its side, with the

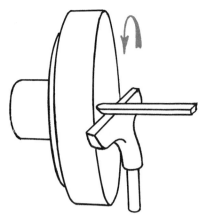

37-51a. Truing a face with a round-nose tool.

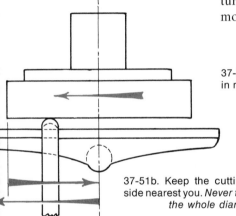

37-51b. Keep the cutting tool on the side nearest you. *Never try to cut across the whole diameter.*

7. Readjust the tool rest until it is parallel to the edge of the stock and also at the same height as the edge. Use the same tool to turn the edge until it has the correct diameter. Fig. 37-52.

8. Lay out the face surface of the disc. Readjust the tool rest across the face and turn to shape. Be sure to select the right tools. Fig. 37-53. For a simple recess, a round-nose tool is usually preferred. Fig. 37-54a. For cutting a bead, choose a square-nose or skew. Sometimes the tool rest must be readjusted at an angle to the work to do certain kinds of turning. Fig. 37-54b. A diamond-point is often used to cut

37-52. Truing the edge of stock. Notice the use of the right-angle tool support.

37-53. Scraping tools can be used in many ways for a variety of cuts.

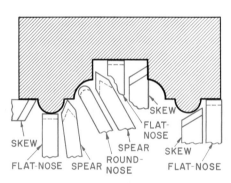

cutting edge parallel to the front of the disc. Start at the center and take a scraping cut toward the outside (the side nearest yourself). Fig. 37-51. Take several cuts until the stock is of the correct thickness. Hold a rule or square against the face surface to make sure that the surface is true.

6. Locate the center of the stock. Adjust the dividers to half the largest diameter that must be turned and mark a circle around the face of the work.

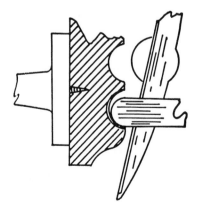

37-54a. Scraping concave curves with a round-nose tool.

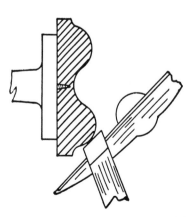

37-54b. Scraping convex curves with a small skew.

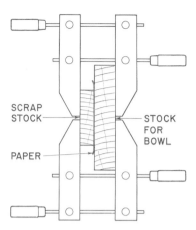

37-56. Gluing scrap stock to the finished piece in preparation for turning.

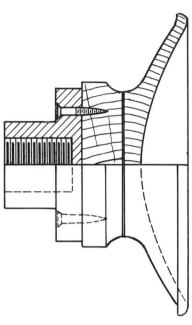

37-57. The front of this bowl has been turned. The workpiece can now be separated from the scrap stock.

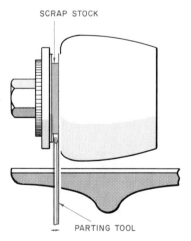

37-58. When undercutting the scrap stock, place the edge of the parting tool right on the paper joint.

37-55. Scraping an edge with a spear-point chisel.

a sharp shoulder on the edge of the work. Fig. 37-55.

Turning Both Sides of Stock

Many faceplate jobs require that both sides of an object be turned. For most work of this kind

there must be no screw holes in the stock. The following steps for turning a simple bowl are an example of this kind of job.

1. Cut a piece of stock slightly larger than the finished bowl. Cut a piece of scrap stock (but not plywood) thick enough to fasten screws into. Glue these two pieces together, with a piece of bond paper between them for easy separation later. Be sure to allow enough time for the glue to cure before mounting the stock on the lathe. Fig. 37-56. Fasten the stock to the faceplate, installing the screws in the scrap piece. Mount the work on the lathe.

2. Turn the front (or inside) and the edge (or outside) of the bowl. Fig. 37-57. Then do all the sanding operations necessary to finish the inside. If mineral oil is to be used as a finish, apply this now.

3. Separate the scrap stock from the finished piece by first undercutting the scrap stock on the lathe. Fig. 37-58. Remove the turning from the lathe. Then have

someone hold the workpiece on the edge of the bench, with both hands. Place a $3/4''$ or $1''$ wood chisel so that its flat surface is next to the bottom of the finished turning. Fig. 37-59. Be sure to drive the chisel in the same direction as the grain in the bowl. Work one end, then turn the bowl around 180 degrees and work the other end. Keep working a few cuts around the circumference. Each time it is turned over, go a little deeper. *Don't hurry.*

4. Make a simple wood chuck to hold the bowl. Cut a piece of scrap stock slightly larger than the diameter of the bowl. Fasten this to the faceplate. Turn the disc and cut a recess in the scrap stock so that the bowl will fit inside. The bowl is then pressed tightly into the recess. This arrangement is

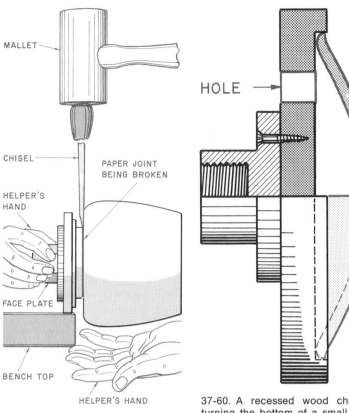

MALLET

CHISEL

PAPER JOINT
BEING BROKEN

HELPER'S
HAND

FACE PLATE

BENCH TOP

HELPER'S HAND

37-59. Do not hit the chisel any harder than necessary. Drive the chisel in the direction of the grain in the workpiece. Take your time.

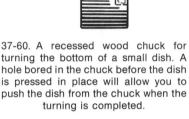

HOLE →

37-60. A recessed wood chuck for turning the bottom of a small dish. A hole bored in the chuck before the dish is pressed in place will allow you to push the dish from the chuck when the turning is completed.

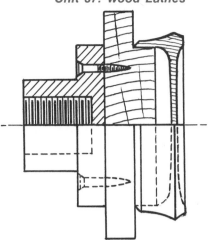

37-61. A spindle chuck for holding a small dish that has an internal surface which can be chucked. (Note that this would not work for the dish shown in Fig. 37-60.)

called a *recessed chuck.* Fig. 37-60. If the recess is slightly oversize, place a piece of paper between the bowl and the recess.

The type of chuck which fits into the workpiece is called a *spindle chuck.* Fig. 37-61. Such chucks are used when the hole is first bored or turned in the stock which is then pressed over the chuck for outside turning. Salt and pepper shakers, for example, or the bottom of a bowl, might be turned with a spindle chuck.

5. Press the stock into the chuck and turn the back side. Fig. 37-62. The work can usually be removed by pulling it out. If necessary, the recessed edge can be cut away to release the bowl.

37-62. Turning the back of a small dish held in a recessed chuck.

393

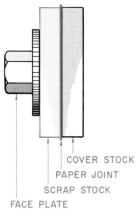

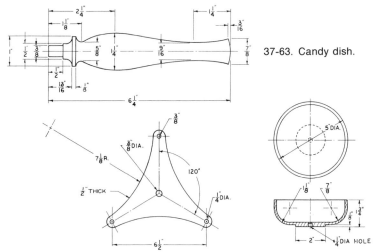

37-63. Candy dish.

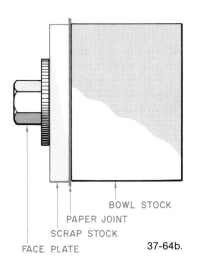

37-64a.

37-64b.

Fig. 37-63 shows a photograph and drawings of a candy dish that can be turned.

Turning a Bowl and Cover

A bowl with a cover has many uses and can be very attractive. Such a bowl might be used for a candy dish, a humidor, a condiment dish, or for holding hairpins, powder, or sewing items. If the bowl is to be used for moist foods, as a condiment dish would, it should have a liner. Obtain a small metal, glass, or plastic dish, and then design the interior shape of the bowl to receive the liner. Bath powder can be purchased in a plastic filler, around which an attractive bowl and cover could be designed. There are any number of possibilities, but the appearance of the finished project will be largely affected by how well the cover is fitted to the bowl. This is a relatively simple task if the following procedure is used:

1. Select the material for the cover and bowl, cut it slightly larger than the finished size. Glue each of these pieces to a piece of scrap stock, with a piece of paper between the workpiece and the scrap. Allow the glue to cure and attach each of these assemblies to a faceplate. Fig. 37-64.

2. Mount the bowl and faceplate on the lathe, and turn the inside of the bowl to the desired shape. If a liner is to be used, carefully fit it to the inside of the bowl. Fig. 37-65. Note that about $3/16''$ of the inside must be turned at 90 degrees to the front face, to receive the cover.

394

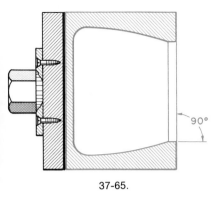

37-65.

Mount the drill chuck, with the correct size drill, in the tailstock spindle. Turn on the power. The drill can then be brought into the revolving cover.

9. Finish-sand the bowl and cover assembly.

10. Remove the cover. Sand the inside of the bowl completely.

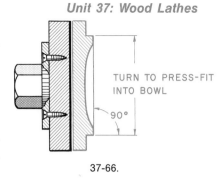

TURN TO PRESS-FIT INTO BOWL

90°

37-66.

3. Mount the cover and faceplate on the lathe. Turn the inside of the cover and the lip to fit into the bowl. When the dimension gets close to the final fit, take light cuts and try the fit often. Fig. 37-66. Sand the inside of the cover completely, but *not* the lip that is to fit into the bowl.

4. Remove the faceplate from the cover. Press the cover into the bowl, and mount the assembled unit on a lathe. Turn the outside contour of the bowl and cover *as a unit.* Fig. 37-67. Note that the tailstock spindle has been set close to the scrap stock on the cover, for safety.

5. Remove the bowl and cover from the lathe and split the scrap stock off the cover as shown in Fig. 37-59.

6. Remount the bowl-and-cover assembly in the lathe and turn the desired shape on the top of the cover. Fig. 37-68. For safety, keep the tool rest as close as possible to the cover.

7. A template can be used to check the contour of the completed turning. Fig. 37-69.

8. If a knob is to be mounted on the cover, the hole can be accurately drilled on the lathe.

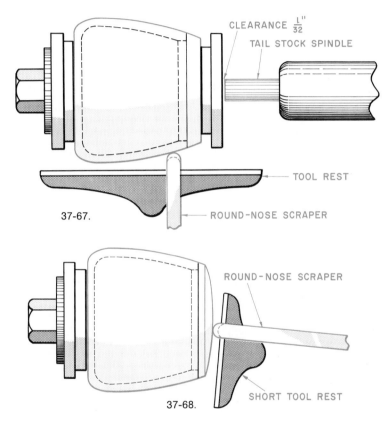

CLEARANCE $\frac{1}{32}$"

TAIL STOCK SPINDLE

TOOL REST

37-67.

ROUND-NOSE SCRAPER

ROUND-NOSE SCRAPER

SHORT TOOL REST

37-68.

(Turning a bowl and cover sequence.)

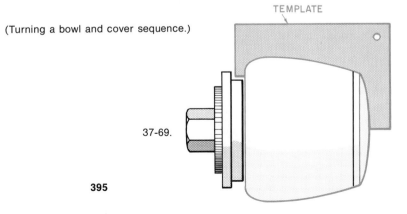

TEMPLATE

37-69.

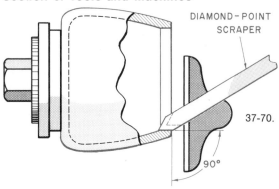

DIAMOND-POINT
SCRAPER

37-70.

90°

Take a light cut on the inside of the bowl to enlarge the opening. Try the cover on the bowl to make sure it fits properly. Fig. 37-70.

11. Remove the bowl from the lathe and split the scrap stock off the bowl as shown in Fig. 37-59.

12. Make a spindle chuck to fit the inside of the bowl. Fig. 37-61. Press the bowl onto the chuck and turn a recess in the bottom of the bowl. Fig. 37-62.

13. Finish as desired.

37-71. Using the screw chuck to turn a knob for a cover. Note the pin end on the knob. This can be glued into a bored hole and eliminate a screw from the inside of the cover.

14. Attach the knob. If the knob is to be turned on the lathe, a screw center can be used to hold the stock. Fig. 37-71.

Mandrel Turning

A mandrel is a tapered spindle that fits into and supports the workpiece. Mandrel turning is done when it is necessary to have a hole completely through the turning, with concentric diameters at each end of the turning. Salt and pepper mill sets are a good example. Fig. 37-72.

1. Obtain a piece of stock slightly longer than the finished dimensions of the turning.

2. Lay out the centers on each end and bore the correct size hole completely through the stock. See Unit 30, page 304, *Boring Deep Holes.*

3. Turn a wooden mandrel with a slight taper (about $\frac{1}{16}''$ per foot) that will fit inside the hole bored in the workpiece.

4. Mount the mandrel in the lathe between centers, large end toward the spur center. The workpiece should be pressed tightly on the mandrel. Fig. 37-73. Place a pencil mark on the end of the work adjacent to a mark

37-72. Salt and pepper mills are a good example of mandrel turning.

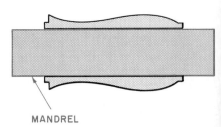

MANDREL

37-73. Workpiece mounted on the mandrel and ready for the lathe.

on the mandrel so the piece can be repositioned if it is removed.

5. Turn the workpiece to the desired shape, using either the cutting or scraping method, as you would a regular spindle turning between centers.

Plug Turning

Plug turning is done when a hole in the workpiece must be concentric with the outside diameter of the turning and is not bored completely through. The candle holders shown in Fig. 37-74 are a good example. To make these candle holders, proceed as follows:

1. Obtain two pieces of stock, $2\frac{1}{4}''$ by $2\frac{1}{4}''$ by $8\frac{1}{4}''$. (If $2\frac{1}{4}''$ stock is not available, the base diameter can be reduced. However, it should be kept as close to $2''$ as possible. If the stock is carefully selected from $\frac{8}{4}$ lumber, it will run a little thicker and the full diameter can be easily turned.) *Make sure the ends are square.*

2. Locate the centers. (Do *not* saw diagonals; the stock is already cut to finished length.) Bore a $1\frac{1}{8}''$ hole, $1\frac{1}{2}''$ deep. This should be done in the lathe, with the chuck mounted in the headstock and the work held against the dead center. This will insure that the center of the hole will align with the center of the turning when the project is finished. This boring operation can be done in the drill press, if the ends of the workpiece are square and the drill press table is at a 90-degree angle to the bit. Fig. 37-75.

3. Using the center of the hole previously bored, bore another hole $\frac{3}{4}''$ in diameter and $\frac{3}{4}''$ deep.

37-74a. Candle holders. These are a good example of plug turning.

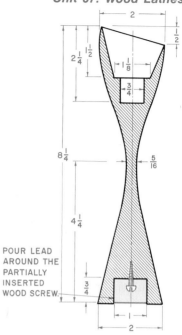

POUR LEAD AROUND THE PARTIALLY INSERTED WOOD SCREW.

TURNED CANDLE HOLDER

37-74b. Drawing of candle holder.

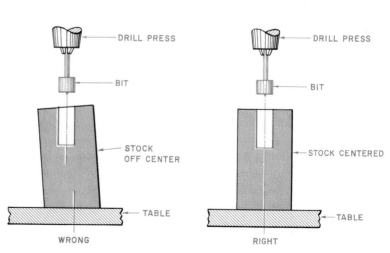

WRONG

RIGHT

37-75. If the stock is not aligned with the bit, the hole will not be concentric with the outside of the workpiece.

PLUG FROM SCRAP WOOD

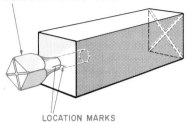

LOCATION MARKS

37-76. Insert the plug in the workpiece and place a location mark on both pieces. This will aid in recentering if the pieces are moved.

4. Turn a plug of hardwood between centers $3\frac{1}{4}$" long and $\frac{3}{4}$" in diameter. The diameter should be accurately turned so that a friction fit is obtained when the plug is inserted into the bored $\frac{3}{4}$" hole. In order that the plug chuck can be properly fitted, turn the $\frac{3}{4}$" end next to the dead center. As the work progresses, try the turning periodically in the bored hole to insure a tight fit. Fig. 37-76.

5. Force the plug into the $\frac{3}{4}$" hole and mount the assembly between centers in the lathe, with the plug on the dead center.

6. Rough turn the piece to slightly over 2".

7. Reach inside with a parting tool and turn the taper on the inside of the top of the holder. This is not a critical dimension, so just make a smooth taper.

8. Turn the outside contour of the top and bottom, and gradually work down to the $\frac{5}{16}$" dimension. (Note: Keep the material as strong as possible as long as you can. It is recommended that the parting tool *not* be used to turn the $\frac{5}{16}$" diameter when shaping.) To shape and size the $\frac{5}{16}$" diame-ter, remove the tool rest; then sand to the finished diameter and shape. When sanding, equalize the pressure applied with the sandpaper by holding the fingers of the other hand against the back of the area being sanded.

9. Complete the turning.

10. Rough sand with $\frac{1}{2}$ or $\frac{1}{0}$ abrasive paper, depending on the species of wood being sanded, and then sand with $\frac{2}{0}$.

11. Finish sand with $\frac{5}{0}$ abrasive paper.

12. Remove the stock from the lathe.

13. Reinsert the drill chuck in the headstock and bore a hole 1" wide and about 1" deep to receive the lead in the bottom of the candle holder.

14. Remove the candle holder from the lathe and insert a wood screw in the bottom of the hole leaving about $\frac{1}{2}$" of the screw projecting so that the lead would be held in place by flowing around the head of the wood screw.

15. Hold the turned candle holder in a V-block; sand the top to the desired angle on either the belt or disc sander.

16. To bring the flat area that resulted from the belt sanding to a sharp edge, hand sand the out-side contour.

17. Make a profile pattern of the first turning. Use this as a template when turning the second candle holder.

18. Pour the lead in the bottom of the candle holders.

19. Carefully hand sand the candle holder with the grain, using fine grit abrasive paper.

20. Finish as desired.

Sanding

Select the correct grade of sandpaper. Usually $\frac{1}{0}$ is used to take out the large imperfections, $\frac{2}{0}$ to smooth the work, and $\frac{5}{0}$ for a very fine surface.

● Cut the paper into strips for sanding long cylinders and pieces held between centers. Fold sand-paper into squares for sanding recesses and for faceplate work.

● Always remove the tool rest and adjust the lathe to a high spindle speed. Never wrap the paper around the work.

● For sanding long stock be-tween centers, hold both ends of the strip of paper and move it back and forth.

● For sanding the inside of a bowl, hold the pad of paper over your fingers and follow the con-tour of the bowl.

Finishing

There are several methods of finishing turned parts. Often the parts are removed from the lathe and the finish is applied as a part of the completed furniture.

For small bowls and other food-serving accessories, mineral oil is rubbed on as a finish.

To apply a French polish, se-cure a piece of fine cotton or linen cloth and fold it into a pad. Apply a solution of about one-half shel-lac and one-half alcohol to the pad. Then place a few drops of mineral oil or machine oil on the pad. Remove the tool support, turn the lathe on, and hold the pad on the work, moving it from side to side. Fig. 37-77. Add shel-lac and oil to keep the pad moist. Continue applying until the de-sired finish is obtained.

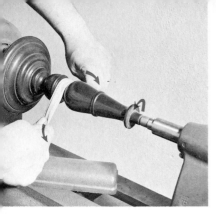

37-77. Applying a French polish.

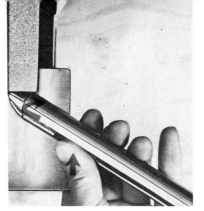

37-79. Grinding a gouge on the face of a flat wheel. In this method, the tool must be rolled to keep the same angle of bevel all around the tool.

37-80a. Honing an outside bevel.

To apply a wax finish, a paste wax is usually used; however, carnauba, beeswax or paraffin wax can be used. The paste wax is applied with a soft cloth directly to the work. Allow the wax to dry for about 10 minutes. Turn the lathe on at a slow speed and polish with a soft cloth. A second coat can be applied in about one hour. Harder waxes, such as carnauba, beeswax and paraffin wax can be applied by holding a piece of the wax directly against the revolving work in the lathe. After an even coat is applied, polish as you would the paste wax.

Sharpening Turning Tools

The correct technique for sharpening turning tools is very similar to that for sharpening chisels and gouges. The proper grinding angle for each tool is shown in Fig. 37-78. If the tools are to be used for cutting (as opposed to scraping), they should be honed. Tools used for scraping should be ground to the correct angle, but *not* honed. The small burr created when grinding should remain. The burr will increase the efficiency of the tool's scraping action.

To sharpen a *gouge,* hold it at an angle of about 30 degrees to the stone and rotate it from side to side, keeping a straight bevel on the outside. Make sure that the corners are rounded so that you can make cove cuts. Fig. 37-79. The concave surface and the beveled edge can be honed with a slipstone. Fig. 37-80.

To sharpen a *skew,* hold it at an angle of about 12½ degrees to the wheel. Turn it to one side to maintain an angle of 60 degrees. Grind each side a little at a time. Fig. 37-81. Hone the edge on a

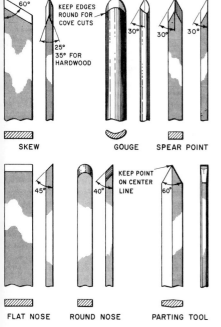

SKEW GOUGE SPEAR POINT

FLAT NOSE ROUND NOSE PARTING TOOL

37-78. Correct shapes for grinding the edges of turning tools.

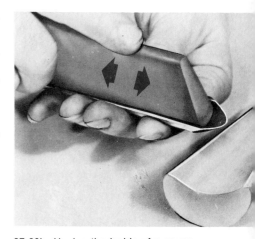

37-80b. Honing the inside of a gouge.

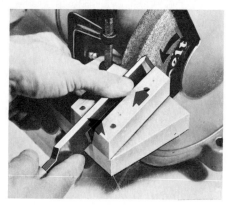

37-81. The bevels on the skew should be ground flat. This simple wood jig will make the work easier.

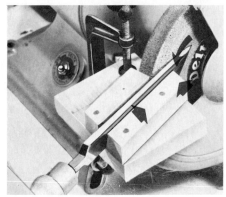

flat oilstone as you would a chisel. Fig. 37-82.

The *flat-nose tool* is ground exactly like an ordinary chisel except that the angle of the bevel is 45 degrees. Fig. 37-78.

The *spear-point* must be ground at two angles from one side. The bevel is 30 degrees and the included angle of the point is 60 degrees. Fig. 37-78.

37-82. Honing a skew. Don't hone a secondary bevel, especially if the tool is used for cutting.

The *round-nose tool* is ground in the same general manner as a gouge, with the bevel at an angle of about 40 degrees. Fig. 37-78.

The *parting tool* must be ground from two edges so that the included angle is 60 degrees. The point of the parting tool should be always kept on the center line of the tool. Fig. 37-78.

DISCUSSION TOPICS

Section Five—TOOLS AND MACHINES

Safety

1. What does understanding a machine have to do with safety?

2. What is the proper dress for operating power tools?

3. In general, when should adjustments on power tools be made? Are there any exceptions?

4. Do guards prevent accidents on power machines? Explain.

5. Describe how safety affects industrial costs.

6. Why should portable power tools be grounded?

7. Explain why it is important to wear proper eye protection in the shop, even when you are not operating power equipment.

Units 22–25. Hand Tools

1. Name several kinds of common rules.

2. What are four uses for the combination square?

3. Why are flexible tapes useful measuring tools?

4. What is the difference between a crosscut saw and a ripsaw? Describe their teeth.

5. Name the hand saws that are used for cutting irregular curves.

6. What is the difference between a back saw and a dovetail saw?

7. Why are planes made in different lengths?

8. Arrange the following planes in order of length: (a) fore, (b) jack, (c) jointer, (d) smooth.

9. What kind of plane is used to clean out the bottoms of grooves and dadoes?

10. How are chisels and gouges similar? How are they different?

11. When would you use a drawknife and when a spokeshave?

12. Name three special-purpose planes.

13. How are chisels and gouges related to carving tools?

14. How does a bit differ from a drill?

15. Name the tool used for operating bits. For operating drills.

16. Describe several uses for the Foerstner bit and the two devices that are used to limit the depth of a hole.

Unit 26. Radial-Arm Saw

1. Describe the main safety precautions to follow in operating a radial-arm saw.

2. Tell how to do crosscutting on a radial-arm saw.

3. In ripping stock on a radial-arm saw, does the work or the saw move? Explain the action.

4. What are the fundamental operations of the radial-arm saw?

5. Explain why it is easier to cut a blind dado on the radial-arm saw than it is on the circular saw.

6. Describe the procedure for cutting a rabbet on the radial-arm saw.

Unit 27. Jointer

1. What function do rotary cutters on a jointer perform?

2. How is the size of a jointer indicated?

3. How is the depth of cut adjusted on a jointer?

4. What happens if the outfeed table of a jointer is too low?

5. What happens if the outfeed table of a jointer is too high?

6. List five safety rules for operating a jointer.

7. What three factors should be considered in adjusting for depth of cut?

8. When should a push block be used?

9. Indicate the most common use for a jointer.

10. When planing end grain, what should be the narrowest width of board?

11. Can a bevel or chamfer be cut on the jointer? Explain.

12. Describe how to cut a taper that is longer than the infeed table.

13. Can the guard be used when cutting a rabbet on the jointer?

14. Describe how to cut a short taper on a jointer.

Unit 28. Planer

1. What is the purpose of a planer?

2. Tell how the size of a planer is indicated.

3. Why must you never stand directly behind a board while planing?

4. What is the shortest length of board that should be surfaced in a planer?

5. Describe the method of setting a planer for thickness.

6. What should you do if a board sticks in a planer?

Unit 29. Circular Saw

1. What is the difference between a universal saw and a variety saw?

2. Name five kinds of blades that can be used on a circular saw.

3. Name the two devices that are used to guide stock when cutting on a circular saw.

4. Tell how to remove a saw blade.

5. List four reasons for kickback.

6. Explain two ways of supporting long stock for ripping.

7. In ripping narrow stock, what safety device should be used?

8. What is meant by resawing?

9. Describe the use of a feather board for resawing.

10. When cutting plywood, should the good side be up or down?

11. What is the purpose of a stop block?

12. Describe the difference between a bevel and a chamfer.

13. Explain how to use an adjustable jig for cutting a taper.

14. How many cuts are necessary to make a rabbet on a circular saw with a single saw blade?

15. Describe the method for finding the length of a picture frame molding.

16. State how to cut a spline for a miter joint on a circular saw.

17. Explain how to adjust the circular saw for a compound miter when the tilt of the work is 45 degrees and a four-side miter must be cut.

18. Describe the two common methods of cutting a tenon on the circular saw.

19. Tell how to cut a groove with a single saw blade.

20. Describe how to assemble a dado head for cutting a $\frac{3}{16}''$ dado.

21. What is a stop groove?

22. What is another name for a blind dado?

23. Tell how to cut a corner dado.

Unit 30. Drill Press

1. Name some of the operations besides drilling that can be performed on a drill press.

2. How is the size of a drill press indicated?

3. Name the principal parts of the drill press.

4. How can the speed of a drill press be regulated?

5. Name six common cutting tools used on the drill press.

6. At what speed should the drill

press be operated for shaper operations?

7. Describe how to bore a 6″ hole with the drill press.

8. When a hole must be bored at an angle of 32 degrees, how should the angle of the table be checked?

9. Describe two methods of boring a hole for miter joints.

10. What is the purpose of a V-block and how is it used?

11. Describe how wood plugs can be cut.

12. List the attachments that can be used on a drill press to convert it to another type of machine.

Unit 31. Mortiser

1. Name the parts of a mortiser.

2. What is the shape of the cutting end of a mortising chisel?

3. Explain how to set up a mortiser for use.

4. How far should the bit extend beyond the mortising chisel?

5. The table on most mortisers can be adjusted three ways. Name them.

6. How do mortising attachments for drill presses differ in the way the bit is held?

Unit 32. Band Saw

1. Describe the principal use of the band saw.

2. Tell how the size of the band saw is determined.

3. When installing a new band-saw blade, how should the teeth point in relation to the top of the table?

4. How should the guide blocks of a band-saw blade be adjusted?

5. Tell how to fold a band-saw blade.

6. What is the diameter of the minimum cutting circle for a $\frac{1}{2}''$ blade?

7. Describe the correct cutting position for a right-handed operator of a band saw.

8. Should short cuts be made before long ones? Explain.

9. What are some of the major causes of "leading" on a band saw?

10. Describe two methods of straight cutting on a band saw.

11. State how to cut a compound curve on a band saw.

12. Describe the steps in cutting a square opening on the band saw.

13. What is the purpose of relief cuts in cutting a sharp curve?

14. How is an auxiliary table used in cutting curves on a band saw?

15. Describe two methods of cutting duplicate parts on the band saw.

16. How should round stock be held for cutting off on the band saw?

Unit 33. Jig Saw

1. What is another name for the jig saw?

2. What is the purpose of the driving mechanism on a jig saw?

3. Describe the purpose of a hold-down on a jig saw.

4. Name the three major types of jig-saw blades.

5. Describe how to install a saber blade.

6. What should be the speed for cutting softwood on a jig saw?

7. Describe how to cut an internal opening on the jig saw.

8. Can metal hardware and fittings be cut on a jig saw? Explain.

Unit 34. Router

1. To what other operations is routing similar?

2. Name six common kinds of router bits.

3. Can a portable router be used for freehand routing? Explain.

4. Can routing be done on the drill press?

5. What accessory is necessary to cut a dovetail joint with a portable router?

Unit 35. Shaper

1. State why the shaper could be a dangerous machine to use.

2. What are the ranges of spindle speed for most shapers?

3. Name the two common types of cutters used on shapers.

4. When should the fence be used for shaping?

5. What is the purpose of a depth collar and how is it used?

6. What is needed to shape the entire edge of an irregularly shaped object.

7. Can simple shaping jobs be done on a drill press? Explain.

Unit 36. Sanders

1. Name five kinds of sanding machines.

2. What is the best machine to use for sanding large surfaces such as the tops of desks and tables?

3. What are the three types of movement (or action) which a finishing or pad sander may have?

4. Tell how to install a new abrasive sheet on a disc sander.

5. Explain why all cutting operations should be completed before sanding.

6. Give the proper technique for using a portable belt sander.

7. Explain how to sand a bevel or chamfer on a belt sander.

Unit 37. Wood Lathe

1. Is the small wood lathe of much commercial value? Explain.

2. Describe the major parts of a lathe.

3. List six accessories that can be used on the lathe.

4. Explain why the headstock spindle on a lathe is hollow.

5. Describe four common kinds of turning tools.

6. Explain the purpose of the spur center and the cup center.

7. Describe the two basic methods of turning.

8. Name the common measuring tools needed in wood turning.

9. At what speed should stock that is 1″ to 2″ in diameter be turned?

10. If stock is larger than 3″ square, what should be done to it before it is turned on the lathe?

11. Describe the two methods of holding a gouge for rough turning between centers.

12. Explain how to use a large skew for scraping a plain cylinder.

13. Name three common uses for a parting tool.

14. Describe the proper method of making a shoulder cut by the scraping method.

15. Explain how to cut a long, true taper.

16. What tool is used to make a V cut by the scraping method?

17. Tell which tool is used to cut beads.

18. What tool is used to make a cove cut by the scraping method?

19. When should a template be used in turning a part?

20. Name the two common kinds of faceplates.

21. Is the scraping or cutting method used for faceplate work?

22. Should a fast speed be used when turning on a faceplate?

23. Describe how to turn both sides of a wood bowl.

24. Why should a piece of paper be placed between the scrap stock and the stock for a bowl before turning?

25. What grade of sandpaper should be used for lathe sanding on walnut to obtain a very fine surface?

26. What is a spindle chuck used for?

27. Describe how to apply a French-type polish on a turned part.

28. At what angle should a gouge be ground?

29. How can the cutting angle of a gouge be honed?

PROBLEMS AND ACTIVITIES

1. Study the history and development of one of the machine tools. Write a report.

2. Study the kinds of cutting tools used in a furniture factory and describe those not commonly found in the school shop.

3. Make a complete list of operations or processes that can be performed on one of the woodworking machines. Describe each operation in some detail.

4. Make a sample of all the kinds of work that can be done on one of the machines.

Finishing

Fine furniture deserves a fine finish. A furniture craftsman will develop wood finishing skills to enhance his products. Sometimes the style of the furniture piece largely determines the finish; for other pieces the craftsman may choose one of several fine finishes. (Baumritter Corporation)

UNIT 38 Preparing Wood for a Finish

38-4a. Roll the knife over and, on the backstroke, drop the material into the defect.

Previous units have explained the materials and procedures for furniture making, including assembly, and have also discussed the tools and machines needed for the various operations. After an item is assembled and the glue has dried, considerable time should be spent in preparing the piece for finishing in order to secure excellent results. Follow these four steps:

1. Remove all excess glue. Use a sharp chisel to remove carefully all traces of glue around the joints. If any glue was spilled on the surface, remove by scraping. Never attempt to remove glue by sanding alone, since this will often force the glue into the wood and make an imperfection in the final finish. Fig. 38-1.

2. Inspect the surface carefully for dents or irregularities. A small dent in the wood can be raised by applying hot water and allowing it to stand for some time. A small soldering copper can also be used with a wet cloth to steam out dents. After the dent has been removed, allow plenty of time for the wood to dry out completely before sanding. If the dent cannot be raised, or if a hole or similar irregularity exists, it can be filled. One of the materials often used is a lacquer or shellac stick which is available in many colors. The stick material is applied to the imperfection by using a small, electric soldering iron or burn-in knife. This knife is heated with an alcohol torch or special electric furnace. Fig. 38-2. The shellac or lacquer is picked up from the stick by placing the heated tool in contact with the stick material. Fig. 38-3. Apply the soft material as shown in Fig. 38-4.

38-4b. Pull the knife forward over the defect. Never allow the hot knife to come to a stop.

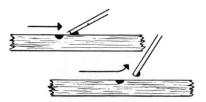

38-4c. Pick up the excess material with the end of the knife. Notice how the knife is brought up to a vertical position at the end of the stroke.

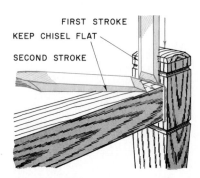

FIRST STROKE
KEEP CHISEL FLAT
SECOND STROKE

38-1. Take care in assembly not to apply too much glue. Use a moist rag to wipe the wet glue that squeezes out. If necessary, use a sharp chisel to remove glue from around a joint.

38-2. An electric furnace is used to heat the burn-in knives when applying stick shellac.

38-3. Use a hot knife to pick up the filler from the stick.

Water putty is another filler. It can be mixed with water stain to obtain the color desired. Fig. 38-5a.

Plastic wood can also be used to fill dents. It is applied directly from the can or tube with a putty knife. Fig. 38-5b. The craftsman can also make a filler by mixing

38-5a. Water putty sets up quickly, so do not mix more than can be used in four or five minutes.

fine sawdust from the sander with liquid glue. This will often match the original wood surface quite closely. Remember, however, that the glue will not absorb a stain the same as the wood.

3. Scrape and/or sand the surface thoroughly. A thoroughly sanded piece is one from which all machine marks, scratches, and similar imperfections have been removed. The final sanding is usually done with ⁴⁄₀ or ⁶⁄₀ paper. Always remember to work *with* the grain, never against it. Fig. 38-6. As you complete the sanding of each piece, soften all edges and corners with a ⁶⁄₀ abrasive. Do *not* round the edges and corners; just remove the sharpness.

4. Dust all surfaces. Brush off all surfaces to remove large accumulations of sanding dust. Then with a commercial tack rag, or with a lint-free cloth slightly moistened with alcohol or turpentine, finish dusting the project. This operation should be done just before the finish is applied, so the project will be free of all

dirt and dust for the finishing operation.

Abrasives Used in Woodworking

Three basic elements are used to make sandpaper—the backing, the adhesive bond, and the abrasive grains.

Backing

The backing for the abrasive may be paper or cloth. Most abrasives have a paper back but cloth is best for power sanding operations, especially belt sanding.

Adhesive Bond

Glues used in the manufacture of coated abrasives are of three types—animal hide glue, resin, and varnish. Animal hide glue is used on most woodworking sandpapers. Synthetic resins are used on wet-or-dry abrasive papers because of their waterproof qualities. In the woodworking industry, the wet-or-dry abrasive is used for sanding finish coats.

Types of Abrasives

Four types of abrasives are used in woodworking:
• *Flint,* a greyish material made of soft sandstone, is good only for simple hand sanding and does not stand up well.
• *Garnet,* a reddish-brown, hard, natural mineral, is excellent for hand sanding and for some kinds of power sanding.
• *Aluminum oxide,* an artificial abrasive, either reddish-brown or white, is used almost exclusively in commercial furniture making. It is excellent for all power-sanding operations.

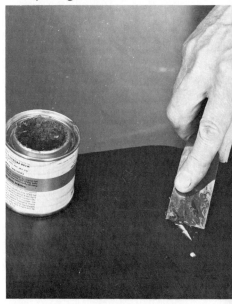

38-5b. Filling a defect with plastic wood. This material shrinks, so build it up above the surface. Allow it to dry thoroughly before sanding flush.

38-6. Support the sandpaper with a block of wood or a commercial sanding block. Never use the fingers alone as a pad. Always sand with the grain.

	SILICON CARBIDE; ALUMINUM OXIDE	GARNET	FLINT	EMERY
	600			
	500			
	400	400 (10/0)		
	360			
VERY FINE	320	320 (9/0)		
	280	280 (8/0)		
	240	240 (7/0)		
	220	220 (6/0)		
			Extra Fine	
	180	180 (5/0)		
				Fine
FINE	150	150 (4/0)		
	120	120 (3/0)	Fine	
	100	100 (2/0)		Medium
MEDIUM	80	80 (0)	Medium	
				Coarse
	60	60 (½)		
	50	50 (1)		
COARSE			Coarse	
	40	40 (1½)		
				Very Coarse
	36	36 (2)		
			Extra Coarse	
	30	30 (2½)		
VERY COARSE	24	24 (3)		
	20	20 (3½)		
	16	16 (4)		
	12			

38-7. This chart compares abrasive grading systems. 0-grade numbers are shown in parentheses after the grit numbers.

● *Silicon carbide,* a black, artificial abrasive, is harder and sharper than aluminum oxide, but not as tough. It is best, therefore, to work with light pressure. In the woodworking field this abrasive is most often used for finish-coat sanding.

Grades of Abrasives

There are two methods of grading abrasives. The more precise one is called the *grit number* system. The numbers indicate the smallest opening through which the abrasive particles will pass. For instance, abrasive particles that will pass through a screen with 80 openings per linear inch are said to be of grit size 80.

The other method, called the *O-grade* system, also uses numbers to indicate abrasive sizes. Fig. 38-7 shows how the two systems compare and also indicates general categories such as "coarse" and "fine."

Abrasive Sheet Sizes

For hand sanding and for the finishing sander, use 9″ × 11″ sheets cut to size. Abrasives can be purchased ready to install on belt and disc sanders, or you can make your own. Use wide rolls for making discs and narrower ones for making belts.

UNIT 39 General Instructions for Wood Finishing

39-1a. To produce the many finishes required for various furniture styles, many years of training and experience are necessary. Wood finishing is one of the most highly skilled occupations in the wood industry. This pecan chest has a low-luster, distressed, antique cherry finish.

39-1b. This commode has a flyspecked, opaque, antique-white finish.

The finishing process varies with the kind of wood and the appearance desired. Fig. 39-1. Today the finisher has many choices of materials, some of which have greatly simplified his job. He can use not only the standard wood finishes such as shellac, varnish, or lacquer, but many specialized commercial finishes that have been especially designed to simplify this work. For example, to add great beauty to the natural wood, a wipe-on finish can be applied with a lint-free cloth. Brushes work better, however, for getting the finish into corners and crevices. The surplus material is then wiped off, also with a lint-free cloth. Wipe-on finish is most effective when used on Contemporary furniture if the wood is not filled and if a low-luster, open-pore finish is desired.

Basic Steps

While the procedure varies for different kinds of wood, the general method to follow in applying standard wood finishes is as follows:

1. *Bleaching.* The first step in many light finishes is to bleach the wood. Fig. 39-2. Many natural or darker finishes do not require bleaching. (For more details see Operation 1, Unit 40, page 412.)

2. *Staining.* This adds color to the wood and enhances the grain. In some light and natural finishes no stain is applied. Use either a

407

39-2. Here you see the results of applying a chemical bleach solution to half of this piece of wood.

39-1c. This dresser has an open-pore oil finish.

39-3a. Brushing on a water stain. Let the stain dry overnight. Scuff-sand to cut raised wood fiber.

39-3b. When using a wiping stain, remove excess stain with a rag. Dry overnight, or according to directions on label.

water or an oil stain. Fig. 39-3. (For more details see Operation 2, Unit 40, page 412.)

3. *Washcoating.* A good washcoat can be made from shellac or lacquer sealer, depending on the top coat to be applied. Fig. 39-4. Washcoats are used to seal a stain and prevent it from bleeding into the top coat. Also, a washcoat should always be applied before filling. This will prevent the wood from absorbing an excessive amount of oil from the filler. (For more details see Operation 3, Unit 40, page 413.)

4. *Filling.* Fillers add color and close the pores of the wood. Fig. 39-5. Close-grained woods, like pine, cherry, poplar, fir, birch, gum, maple, and cedar, require no fillers. Open-grained woods, such as oak, pecan, mahogany, and walnut, require a paste filler. For some natural open-pore finishes, both filler and stain are eliminated. For many blond, bleached, or "decorator" finishes, the filler can be white lead, white zinc, or a natural paste filler colored with

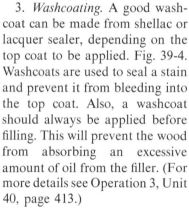

39-4. Applying a washcoat of thinned shellac.

39-5. Wood filler tinted darker than the stain is brushed with the grain.

yellow ochre, raw sienna, burnt sienna, or even red, black, green, or blue. (For more details see Operation 4, Unit 40, page 413.)

5. *Sealing.* A sealer is applied

408

over stain or filler to seal off the surface and provide a smooth foundation for the top coats. Fig. 39-6. A good sealer for finishes is shellac or a diluted mixture of the top-coat material. If the top-coat material is used for a sealer, use the recommended thinner and follow the manufacturer's instructions. Always read the instructions on the can since some of the synthetic varnishes are not compatible with shellac and a diluted solution of the top-coat material *must* be used. If a lacquer finish is to be applied, a regular lacquer sealer should be used. (For more details see Operation 5, Unit 40, page 415.)

6. *Antiquing.* Antiquing gives furniture an aged appearance. This is done by distressing the surface with a series of random marks and indentations of different shapes and sizes. The amount of distressing is determined by how old the furniture should look. Glazing simulates an accumulation of wax and dust. Fig. 39-7. The glaze that settles in the distress marks causes them to stand out in contrast to the finish. Spattering is used to represent flyspecks. (For more details see Operations 6, 7, and 8, Unit 40, pages 415, 416.)

7. *Applying the top coat.* A shellac, varnish, or lacquer top coat can be applied after sealing. Fig. 39-8. Usually, two or more coats are required. Shellac and varnish finishes may be applied with a brush. Lacquer can also be brushed on, but it is more satisfactory when sprayed. (For more details, see Operations 10, 11, and 12, Unit 40, pages 417–420.)

39-6. Applying a sealer coat of varnish. Afterward the workpiece should dry overnight.

39-7. For a glazed finish, brush on thinned colors-in-oil. Wipe off excess glaze with a lint-free cloth.

Sanding. This is not included among the preceding numbered operations because it is not done at any one point in a finishing process, but may be done at several times. The finishing schedules given later in this unit tell when sanding is done in applying certain finishes. Generally speaking, sand with about a 180- or 220-grit abrasive between all finish coats, to remove imperfections and brush marks. When lacquer is used, it is necessary to sand after only the sealer coat and the final coat, unless there is an imperfection, such as a run, that should be sanded out. After the final coat has been sanded with a 400-grit abrasive, it can be rubbed with pumice stone in oil and then rottenstone in oil, using a felt pad. On lacquer a rubbing compound can be used instead of the pumice stone or rottenstone. A final coat of wax should be applied over any finish to protect it.

Finishing Schedules

The finishing schedules which follow include most of the operations used in various finishing processes. The extent to which these schedules are used will be

39-8. Brushing on a coat of varnish.

determined by the finish required for a particular furniture style.

Using Fig. 39-9, you can determine the kind of wood, the stain color, and the texture and luster of finish for many furniture styles. Select the finishing schedule which fits the requirements of the furniture style and top coat to be used. Now write out your schedule, using the chart on page 411. Insert the colors to be used for stain, filler, and glaze. Omit those steps which need not be used, such as distressing or flyspecking on Contemporary walnut. If a natural finish is desired, omit the stain, glaze, distress, and flyspeck; use a natural filler on an open-grained wood. The chart is on page 411.

Style	Wood	Color	Antiquing	Texture	Finish Luster
Mediterranean or Spanish	Pecan Oak Walnut	Cool, dark brown	Distressed and glazed	Open pore	Flat
Early American	Maple Cherry Pine	Warm brown	Distressed and glazed	Smooth	Flat
Traditional or Formal English	Mahogany Walnut	Mellow medium brown or yellow brown	Glazed	Smooth (filled)	Low luster to gloss
French and Italian Provincial	Cherry	Warm medium cherry or tan cherry	Distressed and glazed	Smooth	Flat
Contemporary	Walnut	Dark brown or medium brown	(None)	Open pore or filled	Flat if open pore; low luster if filled
	Pecan	Warm medium brown	Distressed and glazed	Open pore	Low luster

39-9. This chart may be used as an aid in selecting the wood, color, finished texture, and luster for a furniture style. However, if a piece of period furniture is copied and constructed, be sure to duplicate the wood, color, texture, and luster of the period.

Finishing Supplies

Finishing supplies needed depend upon the kind of finishes required. A few of the more common ones are listed here:

• *Brushes.* There are many styles, including flat, round, and oval. The best have a chisel-shaped point. The sizes vary from 1″ to 4″ in width but an average of 2″ is good for most work. An excellent medium-hard bristle is made from Chinese boar hair set in rubber. For varnishing, softer bristles such as fitch hair are good, while camel's hair brushes are desirable for hand lacquering.

• *Turpentine.* Turpentine is made of resin drippings from pine trees and is used as a solvent and thinner for varnish, paints, and enamels.

• *Linseed oil.* Linseed oil is available in raw state or as boiled linseed oil. The boiling improves the drying qualities.

• *Alcohol.* Alcohol is used as a thinner and solvent for shellac.

• *Benzine.* Benzine is used as a solvent and as a cleaning fluid.

• *Pumice.* Pumice, a white powder made from lava, is one of the buffing and polishing compounds needed for smoothing finishes. No. 1 is for coarse rubbing, No. FF or FFF for fine rubbing.

• *Rottenstone.* Rottenstone is a reddish-brown or greyish-black substance for smoother rubbing than pumice.

• *Rubbing oil.* This should be a good quality petroleum or paraffin oil.

• *Steel wool.* Steel wool, sometimes used in place of sandpaper, is used for rubbing after certain finishing operations. It is available in four grades: 0—coarse, 00—medium, 000—fine, and 0000—extra fine.

• *Wet-or-dry abrasive paper.* Waterproof silicon carbide paper in grades from 240 to 600 is used with water for sanding between finishing coats and after the final coat in preparation for rubbing. For sanding the final coat, oil may be substituted for water if a lower luster is desired.

General Finishing Schedules

SCHEDULE A—Lacquer Top Coat on Open-Grained Wood

1. Stain—Operation 2. (See operations in Unit 40.)
2. Washcoat—Operation 3.
3. Sand with a 180-grit sandpaper.
4. Dust—Operation 10, Step 3.
5. Fill with paste wood filler. Allow to dry according to the manufacturer's recommendations—Operation 4.
6. Spray a coat of lacquer sealer—Operation 5.
7. Sand with 180-grit abrasive.
8. Dust—Operation 10, Step 3.
9. Distress (if desired)—Operation 8.
10. Glaze (if desired)—Operation 6.
11. Spray first coat of lacquer—Operation 12.
12. Flyspeck (if desired)—Operation 7.
13. Spray second coat of lacquer—Operation 12.
14. Spray third coat of lacquer—Operation 12.
15. Sand with 400-grit silicon carbide abrasive. Use water or oil as a lubricant.
16. Rub to the desired luster—Operation 13.
17. Clean with a rubber squeegee and wipe with a soft, clean cloth.
18. Wax—Operation 14.

SCHEDULE B—Lacquer Top Coat on Close-Grained Wood

1. Stain—Operation 2. (See operations in Unit 40.)
2. Spray a coat of lacquer sealer—Operation 5.
3. Sand with 180-grit abrasive.
4. Dust—Operation 10, Step 3.
5. Distress (if desired)—Operation 8.
6. Glaze (if desired)—Operation 6.
7. Spray first coat of lacquer—Operation 12.
8. Flyspeck (if desired)—Operation 7.
9. Spray second coat of lacquer—Operation 12.
10. Spray third coat of lacquer—Operation 12.
11. Sand with 400-grit silicon carbide abrasive; use water or oil as a lubricant.
12. Rub to the desired luster—Operation 13.
13. Clean with a rubber squeegee and wipe with a soft, clean cloth.
14. Wax—Operation 14.

SCHEDULE C—Varnish Top Coat on Open-Grained Wood

1. Stain—Operation 2. (See operations in Unit 40.)
2. Washcoat—Operation 3.
3. Scuff-sand with 180-grit abrasive.
4. Dust—Operation 10, Step 3.
5. Fill with paste wood filler. Allow to dry according to the manufacturer's recommendations—Operation 4.
6. Seal—Operation 5.
7. Scuff-sand with 180-grit abrasive.
8. Dust—Operation 10, Step 3.
9. Distress (if desired)—Operation 8.
10. Glaze (if desired)—Operation 6.
11. Apply first coat of varnish. Dry 48 hours—Operation 10.
12. Sand with 220-grit abrasive.
13. Dust—Operation 10, Step 3.
14. Flyspeck (if desired)—Operation 7.
15. Apply second coat of varnish. Dry 48 hours—Operation 10.
16. Sand with 220-grit abrasive.
17. Dust—Operation 10, Step 3.
18. Apply third coat of varnish. Dry 48 hours—Operation 10.
19. Sand with 400-grit abrasive; use water or oil as a lubricant.
20. Rub to the desired luster—Operation 13.
21. Clean with a rubber squeegee and wipe with a soft, clean cloth.
22. Wax—Operation 14.

SCHEDULE D—Varnish Top Coat on Close-Grained Wood

1. Stain—Operation 2. (See operations in Unit 40.)
2. Seal—Operation 5.
3. Scuff-sand with 180-grit abrasive.
4. Dust—Operation 10, Step 3.
5. Distress (if desired)—Operation 8.
6. Glaze (if desired)—Operation 6.
7. Apply first coat of varnish. Dry 48 hours—Operation 10.
8. Sand with 220-grit abrasive.
9. Dust—Operation 10, Step 3.
10. Flyspeck (if desired)—Operation 7.
11. Apply second coat of varnish. Dry 48 hours—Operation 10.
12. Sand with 220-grit abrasive.
13. Dust—Operation 10, Step 3.
14. Apply third coat of varnish. Dry 48 hours—Operation 10.
15. Sand with 400-grit abrasive; use water or oil as a lubricant.
16. Rub to the desired luster—Operation 13.
17. Clean with a rubber squeegee and wipe with a soft, clean cloth.
18. Wax—Operation 14.

UNIT 40 Finishing Procedures

Following are detailed directions for the different steps in the finishing process:

Bleaching—Operation 1

Many furniture pieces that have an extremely light finish require bleaching. The major disadvantage of bleaching is that it weakens the wood cells and removes many of the natural oils.

40-1. The two-part, one-application bleach is most convenient. Always follow the manufacturer's directions for mixing and applying.

40-2. Applying a commercial bleach with a synthetic rubber sponge. Always wear rubber gloves.

Also, many woods will not bleach evenly, resulting in light and dark areas that become more pronounced than when in the natural state. It is necessary, however, to bleach woods to secure light finishes such as blond oak or harvest-wheat mahogany.

For simple bleaching of small articles, a mixture of oxalic acid crystals and hot water is effective. This should be brushed on the wood, allowed to remain 10 to 15 minutes. Then brush on a "hypo" solution such as that used in photography. This is a mixture of 3 ounces sodium hyposulphate to 1 quart of water. Neutralize by applying a mild solution of borax.

To bleach furniture of any size, it is best to use a commercial bleach. There are two kinds. One has two solutions, one of which is applied before the other. The second kind also has two solutions, but they are mixed together just before applying. Fig. 40-1.

Application: Always apply commercial bleaches with a synthetic rubber sponge or a rope brush. Follow the directions given by the manufacturer. *Wear rubber gloves, a rubber apron and goggles,* and always put the bleaching materials in glass or crockery containers only. Also, bleach *from the top down,* since the second application will usually lighten the wood still more. Fig. 40-2.

Bleaching raises the grain and makes it necessary to do further sanding before proceeding with the finishing. Take special precautions not to breathe the sanding dust.

Staining—Operation 2

Stains add color to wood and bring out the grain. While there are many kinds, the two most common are *oil* and *water* stains.

Oil Stains

These can be purchased commercially in colors such as light and dark walnut, light and dark oak, mahogany, cherry, antique pine, fruitwood, and many others. Almost any color is available. Oil stains can also be made by adding universal tinting colors to seven parts linseed oil, two parts turpentine, and one part of drier as follows: raw sienna and chrome yellow to make limed oak; raw sienna, burnt sienna, and burnt umber to make various shades of mahogany; burnt umber and venetian red to make various shades of walnut. Other colors in oil that are useful are lamp black, thalo blue, permanent oxide green, thalo green, dragon red, hansa yellow, and raw umber. Any desired stain color can be mixed using these materials. Begin with the linseed oil, turpentine, and drier. Then add a small amount of the universal tinting color which most closely matches the desired stain color. Test it on a piece of scrap wood which has been sanded. Note the difference between the sample and the desired stain color. Continue adding the universal tinting colors, periodically testing on the scrap stock, until the desired color is obtained.

40-3. Applying stain. Brush on a full, wet coat.

Application: Always begin an unfinished area and work toward the finished part. Use light strokes, brushing the stain evenly. Fig. 40-3. After the stain has been brushed onto a surface, wipe softly with a clean cloth. Allow to dry 24 hours before proceeding, or follow alternative directions, if any, on label. Fig. 40-4.

Water Stains

These stains are available in ready-mixed form or can be made by mixing powdered stain with hot water. Water stains are non-fading, give the clearest color, and penetrate deeply and evenly.

40-4. After the stain loses its wet appearance and looks flat, wipe lightly until the depth of color or desired effect is obtained. Use a clean, lint-free cloth formed into a pad, and follow the grain of the wood.

Application: Water stain raises the grain; therefore it is necessary to sponge the wood surface lightly with water first, allow it to dry, and then sand with 5/0 sandpaper. Fig. 40-5.

Apply the water stain in the same general manner as oil stain. Do not brush it out. Apply as much as the wood will absorb. Then strike off the brush by pressing it against the lip of the can. With a relatively dry brush, "lay-off" the surplus stain on the surfaces by brushing lightly. Sponge the end grain with water just before the stain is applied, to keep it from darkening too much. Allow water stain to dry from 10 to 12 hours. Scuff-sand with a 280-grit abrasive.

Washcoating—Operation 3

Washcoat is a reduced solution of the sealer to be used—usually 7 to 10 parts of thinner to one part of sealer. When shellac is used for the washcoat, the solution is made by mixing 7 parts of alcohol to 1 part of 4-pound cut shellac. Washcoating is necessary before filling, to control the staining action of the filler and to allow the filler to wipe away more cleanly.

Application: Washcoat can be either sprayed or brushed. If brushing, work quickly and take care to avoid runs. Fig. 40-6.

Filling—Operation 4

The purpose of this operation is to fill the wood pores and to add beauty to the wood. For open-grained woods, a commercial paste filler is best. Fig. 40-7. This can often be purchased in the color you desire; or you can buy

40-5. Sponging the surface in preparation for water staining. Do not saturate the surface; moisten it uniformly.

40-6. This coffee table is being sprayed with a washcoat in preparation for the filler.

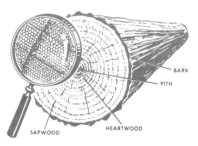

40-7. Many hardwoods contain large vessels and are very porous. When this lumber is surfaced, the cells are broken, leaving tiny troughs that run in the direction of the grain.

40-8. Applying filler. Use a stiff brush and apply with the grain. Then brush across the grain to help pack the filler into the wood pores.

a natural (neutral) color and mix it to various shades, using universal tinting colors. Usually the filler should be slightly darker than the stain; however, white lead and zinc are also used as wood fillers. They may be used as they come from the can for novelty colors or sharp contrast, or they may be tinted.

Application: Mix the paste to the consistency of heavy cream by adding the desired amount of turpentine or oleum spirits. Test to see that the correct consistency is secured. A coarse, open-grained wood, such as oak, will require a heavier consistency than will mahogany or walnut, which are medium, open-grained woods.

1. Apply the filler with a stiff brush, brushing first with the grain and then across it. Cover only a small area at a time. Fig. 40-8.

2. Allow the filler to dry for a few minutes or until it loses its glossy appearance. Wipe off the excess across the grain with rough cloth, burlap, or jute tow. Fig. 40-9 and 40-10.

3. Lightly rub the surface with the grain, using a piece of cheesecloth or other soft cloth to remove the excess. Do not press so hard that the filler is wiped out of the pores. A piece of soft wood, sharpened to a point, can be used to clean out corners. After the

40-9. Wiping the filler. After the filler has lost its shiny appearance, wipe it with a coarse cloth across the grain.

40-10. A rubbing brush is used for removing the excess filler from irregular surfaces, such as a molded edge.

414

40-11. Sanding the sealer coat. Much care, patience, and skill are needed in the sanding steps of a finishing schedule, if the final finish is to be a success.

filler has dried 24 hours (or less if the manufacturer recommends) proceed with the finishing.

Sealing—Operation 5

Sealer is applied over filler on open grained woods and over the stain or natural wood on close grained woods. The sealer gives a good build-up for the top coat, and is lightly sanded with 150- or 220-grit abrasive, to create a smooth surface with good adhesive quality for the top coat.

A one- or two-pound cut shellac will do the job for most finishes. (Reduce four-pound cut shellac with an equal part of alcohol.) If a synthetic varnish is used for a top coat, be sure to read the manufacturer's instructions, as some will not adhere to shellac.

If lacquer is used as a top coat, a lacquer sanding sealer is made especially for this finish.

Application: Sealer can be sprayed or brushed. If brushing, work quickly to lay on a full wet coat, and do not go back over your work with the brush. After the sealer is dry, sand with a 180- or 220-grit abrasive. Fig. 40-11.

Glazing—Operation 6

Glaze is used on nearly all the better finishes. It is applied over the sealer, and it can also be applied over a painted or enameled surface. Glazing gives the furniture piece a highlighted, shaded, or antique appearance. Glazes are available in many colors or can be mixed to any desired color by adding universal tinting colors or inter-mixing the basic colors. Fig. 40-12.

Application: Glaze can be brushed or sprayed onto the surface. It is then allowed to set until the glaze loses its wet appearance. The surplus glaze is then wiped off the surface with a lint-free cloth, and the color is blended with a soft brush (a fitch brush is excellent). Remove as much or as little of the glaze as needed to obtain the desired effect. Fig. 40-13.

Spattering—Operation 7

Spattering is done to simulate flyspecks. A lacquer-base shading stain or a liquid shoe polish will do the job.

Application: Dip a toothbrush into the spatter material. Shake off the surplus and, using a thin piece of wood (popsicle stick) or a piece of metal, flick the brush toward the workpiece. Hold the brush at varying distances from the work for different patterns. Do not try to get a uniform coverage. To get the feel of it, practice on a piece of paper or scrap wood. Fig. 40–14a.

40-12. Glaze is used for shading or highlighting. Notice that more glaze (shown by arrows) is left at the corners and edges.

40-13. Blending the glaze with a soft brush. First, brush across the grain to even out the glaze after wiping. Then blend it by brushing lightly with the grain.

40-14a. Spatter shader or liquid shoe polish is used for flyspecking with a toothbrush and a popsicle stick. A small piece of sheet metal could also be used for flicking the brush.

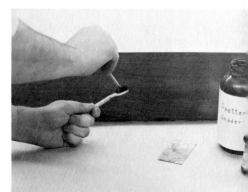

Distressing—Operation 8

Distressing is the technique of making a piece of finished furniture look used. This is usually done after the sealer coat and can be done by making a series of marks of various sizes with a greasless crayon for the purpose of simulating an accumulation of nicks, dents, and scratches from years of use. A more authentic distressing is done by hitting the workpiece in the white (unfinished) wood with a ring of keys, coarse rocks, chain, or small nails laid on the surface and hit with a mallet. Fig. 40-14b. When the glaze is applied later, it will build up in the depressions to resemble dust and wax that have accumulated for years, giving a realistic antique effect.

Applying Wipe-on Finishes— Operation 9

The wipe-on finishes discussed here are of the penetrating type. This type finish is simple to apply and does away with the dust problem. It is frequently used on Contemporary furniture made of walnut or pecan which has not had a filler applied and on which a low luster open-grain appearance is desired.

- Sealacell process. This is a three-step process involving three different materials: Sealacell, Varnowax and Royal Finish. *For application,* see Fig. 40-14c, page 417.
- Danish oil finish. Apply by brush, spray, cloth, roller, or dip. *For application,* see Fig. 40-14d, page 418.

- A home-made wipe-on finish can be mixed from materials commonly found in the finishing room. Mix 6 parts of spar varnish, 2 parts boiled linseed oil, and 2 parts turpentine.

Apply as follows:

1. Apply the finish with a brush, spray gun, cloth, roller, or dip. The material is applied liberally and allowed to penetrate into the wood for 15 or 20 minutes.

2. Wipe off excess oil with a clean, lint-free cloth and allow to dry overnight.

3. Sand lightly with a 180- or 220-grit sandpaper.

4. Apply additional coats, as described in Steps 1 and 2, depending on the amount of build-up desired. Sand between coats with a 180- or 220-grit sandpaper.

40-14b. Distressing is done to imitate the wear marks and other defects found on truly antique furniture. The furniture finisher uses chain, coral rock, and other sharp objects to produce small scratches, dents, and similar defects. A mallet with a nail projecting from the end is used to make imitation worm holes.

Sand with 6/0 Garnet Paper
Sand with 8/0 Garnet Paper

Apply sealer-No. 1-with cloth. BE LIBERAL. Let dry over night.

Buff lightly with "fine" steelwool. Wipe clean with a cloth.

Make small cloth pad 1x2 inches. Apply Varnowax-No. 2 SPARINGLY in a circular motion. Wipe out with the grain. DO NOT SATURATE CLOTH

Buff lightly with steelwool. Apply finishing material-No. 3-in same manner as Step No. 2

40-14c. Sealacell finishing process.

5. After the last coat, rub with 3/0 steel wool and wax.

6. Buff with a clean, lint-free cloth.

Varnishing—Operation 10

Varnish is a transparent finish made from gum, resins, and oils. Many kinds are made, for a variety of purposes. In furniture finishing, select a rubbing varnish or one made especially for this purpose. Complete directions are given by the manufacturer as to drying time and method of application.

Apply as follows:

1. *Secure suitable finishing conditions.* Since varnish is a slow-drying material, it is essential that the room be clean and dry, and that the temperature is between 70 and 80 degrees. Never varnish on a humid day or in dusty conditions.

2. *Select the right kind of varnish* and a good 1½″ to 2″ varnish brush. Pour the desired amount of

1. Sand wood with 4/0 garnet sandpaper using 6/0 for final cut. Wipe clean.

2. Apply oil, completely flooding all surfaces. Let penetrate 30 minutes, adding fresh oil to drying areas.

IMPORTANT: Oiled surfaces must be wiped clean and dry within 1 hour from initial application to prevent finish from becoming tacky. Excessive tackiness may be removed by dissolving with fresh oil and wiping dry immediately.

3. Reapply oil, allowing additional 15 minutes penetration on plywood, 30 minutes on solid wood.

4. Wipe off any excess oil with clean cloth, leaving dry, finished surface.

40-14d. Directions and pictures for Danish oil finishing processes.

varnish into a metal or glass container. Never varnish directly from the can. Fig. 40-15. For the first coat, thin with about one-fourth solvent. (Check the manufacturer's recommendations for solvent.) When this step is completed, discard the remaining varnish mixture.

3. *Brush the surface thoroughly* to remove as much dust as possible, and then wipe with a tack rag. A commercial tack rag can be purchased or one can be made from a lint-free, clean cloth dampened with turpentine into which about 2 or 3 tablespoons of varnish have been worked thor-

oughly. This cloth will pick up dust particles and specks.

4. *Apply the varnish by starting at a corner* and working inward. Dip the brush about one-third into the varnish and apply it with smooth, even strokes. Flow the varnish on; do not brush it out too much. Start at either edge and

brush toward the center. Finally, when the entire surface is covered, without dipping the brush, use only the tip and brush lightly with the grain. Fig. 40-16.

5. *With a small wood splinter, pick out any dust specks.* It isn't necessary to rebrush these spots because varnish will flow in by itself.

6. *Allow the surface to dry thoroughly.* Rub with 220-grit wet-or-dry silicon carbide paper, using a felt-back pad.

7. *Apply a second coat* without thinning the varnish. When it is dry, rub with 220-grit wet-or-dry silicon carbide paper.

8. *For an extremely smooth job, apply a third coat.* Allow it to dry, sand lightly with 400-grit silicon carbide paper and rub with pumice or rottenstone and oil.

Shellacking—Operation 11

Shellac is a very desirable finish for many kinds of projects, although it is not waterproof. Shellac is also a good sealer over a stain or filler, and over knots be-

fore applying paint or enamel. Shellac is available in a natural orange or in bleached white. The orange is tougher but on many light finishes it gives an undesirable yellowish cast. The standard shellac is called a "four-pound cut," which means that there are four pounds of shellac crystals mixed to a gallon of alcohol. Another common mixture is the two-pound cut.

Apply as follows:

1. *Mix an equal amount of four-pound cut shellac and alcohol* in a glass or porcelain container. Four-pound cut shellac will cover about 300 to 350 square feet per gallon. Select a good quality brush 1½″ to 2″ wide.

2. *Dip the brush about one-third and wipe off the excess on the container.* Start near the center and top of a vertical surface or the middle of a horizontal surface. Brush out quickly in long, sweeping strokes. Do not go over the same area several times, since shellac dries very rapidly. Brush toward the edges and be careful

40-15. For a good varnish job, tap the side of the varnish brush against a wire stretched across the pail. Don't rub the varnish brush against the edge of the can.

not to allow the shellac to run over the edges and pile up. The tendency for a beginner is to put shellac on too thick. It is best to apply shellac in several thin coats.

40-16. Brush the varnish both across and with the grain to even the surface. Always finish with the grain.

3. *After the surface is completely covered, allow it to dry three to four hours.* Be sure to soak or clean the brush in alcohol.

4. *Go over the surface with 5/0 sandpaper,* rubbing lightly.

5. *Apply a second coat with a slightly reduced alcohol mixture.* After the last coat dries, sand with a 320-grit abrasive paper and rub with 3/0 steel wool dipped in a paste wax.

Lacquering—Operation 12

Lacquer is the best top coat material available for furniture finishing. It dries dust free in 15 minutes or less. It gives a durable, easily polished surface which is unmatched for luster. Wood lacquers can be formulated to dry to a gloss, semi-gloss, or flat finish sheen. The use of lacquer as a top coat requires that the furniture piece be coated first with a lacquer sanding sealer and sanded with a 180-grit abrasive paper.

Application: Lacquer should be sprayed because it dries rapidly. Fig. 40-17. Brushing requires that a large amount of lacquer thinner be added for better flowing quality. This, however, reduces the body of the lacquer, resulting in

40-17. Spraying a lacquer top coat on a coffee table.

a slow build-up on the surface. Specially formulated brushing lacquers are also available for use in shops without spraying facilities.

Rubbing—Operation 13

After the final coat of finish is applied and allowed to dry thoroughly, rubbing is done to produce a uniform luster. This is done by first sanding the top coat with a 320- or 400-grit silicon carbide abrasive paper, using an oil lubricant. Rubbing compound can then be used to remove the scratches from the sanding operation. The rubbing compound is put on the surface and rubbed with a cloth pad in the direction of the grain. In place of the rubbing compound, pumice stone may be used for a low luster finish. Pumice stone should be followed with rottenstone if a high luster is desired. Pumice stone and rottenstone come in powder form and should be used with water or oil as a lubricant. Apply a puddle of water or oil to the surface to be rubbed, and sprinkle enough abrasive onto the lubricant to make a paste. Use a felt pad to rub with the grain until the sanding scratches have been removed. Always make enough paste to rub the surface completely; if additional abrasive is added, it will be sharp and make new scratches. Check the surface frequently by pushing the rubbing material aside with a small rubber squeegee or the heel of your hand. Rub until the surface has a uniform luster and is free of scratches. Take care *not to rub through* the finish coat. Fig. 40-18.

40-18. Rubbing the final finish coat with a pneumatic (air driven) rubbing machine.

Waxing—Operation 14

Wax is used for protection against moisture and other materials which may be harmful to the finish. Liquid wax or paste wax may be used; however, the paste wax will build up a luster more quickly and give greater protection.

Application: Most waxes are applied with a soft cloth, allowed to dry for 15 or 20 minutes, then

40-19. Applying a paste wax to the finished project.

buffed with a clean, soft cloth. Fig. 40-19.

Sometimes paste wax is applied with a 3/0 or 4/0 steel wool pad after the last coat of finish has been applied and sanded with a 220-grit sandpaper. This will not give as fine a finish as rubbing with pumice stone and rotten-stone, but it will provide an acceptable finish which is reasonably smooth and has uniform luster.

A simple wax finish works well on some small items and particularly on lathe projects. Apply a wash coat of shellac to the wood; then apply several coats of paste wax, buffing each coat. This is popular for lathe work because the wax can be applied while the stock turns in the lathe at about 300 rpm. Drying time can be shortened by speeding up the lathe; then the project can be buffed out at the slower speed. These steps are repeated several times to build up a good finish.

Methods of Application

Brushing

Brushing is the most common method of applying a finish. It is slow compared with the spray gun, but the advantage is that the equipment necessary is simple and far less expensive. With care and patience an equally fine job can be done with a brush.

1. Select a good quality China bristle. (For fast-drying materials a softer brush such as the fitch hair brush is recommended.) A 2″ or 2½″ brush with three rows of bristles, full chisel, and flag ends is excellent. The three rows of bristles make a heavy bodied brush, the full chisel aids in flowing out the finishing material, and the flag ends have a good material-holding capacity. Fig. 40-20.

2. Dip the brush into the material about one-third the length of the bristles, and wipe the surplus material on the edge of the can. Fig. 40-21.

3. Paint should be brushed until the surface film is level and uniform. Varnish, shellac, or lacquer should be flowed on and allowed to level off. Fig. 40-22. Brush out toward the edges to prevent drips. Be careful not to double-coat the surface. Start with the loaded brush on a previously unbrushed area and brush into the coated area.

40-22a. Apply a full, wet coat of varnish, brushing with the grain.

40-22b. Brush across the grain to level out the varnish. Then finish with light strokes in the same direction as the the wood grain.

40-23. Cleaning the brush, using a commercial brush cleaner.

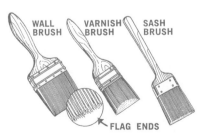

WALL BRUSH   VARNISH BRUSH   SASH BRUSH

FLAG ENDS

40-20. Three commonly used brushes.

40-21. Tap the brush on the side of the can to remove some of the excess material. As mentioned in Fig. 40-15, never rub the bristles on the edge of the can.

40-24. Wash the brush thoroughly with warm water and soap.

40-25. Rinsing the brush in clean water to remove the soap before storing.

Cleaning a brush:

1. Work the proper solvent or a commercial brush cleaner into the heel of the brush. Fig. 40-23. Turpentine is the correct solvent for cleaning brushes used in paints and varnishes. Alcohol should be used to clean shellac brushes, and lacquer thinner is used to clean brushes used in lacquer.

2. Surplus solvent is removed by squeezing the bristles with the thumb and fingers. Continue working clean solvent into the bristles until the solvent that is worked out appears clean.

3. Wash the brush in a mild soap and warm water until the lather is white and free of all traces of the finishing material. Fig. 40-24.

4. Rinse the brush and shape the bristles with a stiff brush or with your thumb and fingers. Fig. 40-25.

5. Either suspend the brush in the correct solvent or wrap the bristles with paper and fold the end up. Fig. 40-26. Be careful not to bend the ends of the bristles when folding up the end of the paper wrapper. Place a rubber band or tie a string around the paper, over the metal ferrule of the brush, to hold the paper wrapper in place.

Spraying

The spray method can be used for applying most types of finishing materials. It is much faster than brushing and can be used to advantage with fast-drying materials.

To do a good job of spraying, work with clean equipment. Wear hard-finished clothing; flannel shirts are poor, because of lint. Practice the following procedure on scrap wood or a piece of paper taped to a support. Develop some skill in the use of spraying equipment before attempting to spray your workpiece.

1. Always work in a spray booth and properly support the workpiece so it does not come in contact with the turntable or floor. Also make sure that it can be easily moved to the drying area when finished. Fig. 40-27.

2. Strain the material and fill

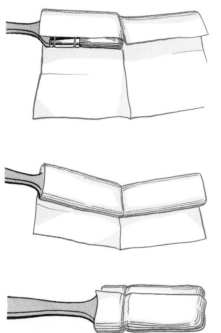

40-26a. Wrapping a brush for storage.

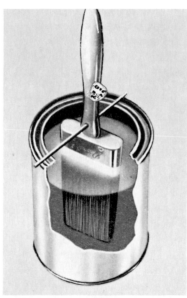

40-26b. Suspend the brush in the solvent. Never set the brush in a solvent with the bristles on the bottom of the can.

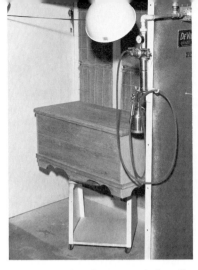

40-27. A cedar chest mounted on the turntable in the spray booth ready to be sprayed.

40-28. Always strain the material to be sprayed, to remove all foreign matter.

40-29a. In this system the material is stored in the pressure tank and is forced through the hose by air pressure to the gun.

the spray gun cup about two-thirds full. Fig. 40-28.

The material to be sprayed is supplied to the gun from (1) a pressure-feed tank through a hose; (2) a pressure-feed cup through a hose; or (3) a suction-feed cup. Fig. 40-29.

3. Adjust the regulator to the desired air pressure. The pressure will be determined by the length of the air hose, the viscosity (ease of flow) of the liquid to be sprayed, and the type of gun. Fig. 40-30. The air pressure should be regulated so that when the gun is moved at a comfortable rate of speed across the work, it will spray a full, wet coat. A *full, wet coat* is all the material that will hang

40-30. The gage at the left indicates the pressure that is set by the regulator knob at the top. The spray system is attached to the hose at the left. The hose at the right is used for a dusting gun. The air pressure for this hose is shown on the gage at the right, which is the main-line pressure. The two smaller knobs on each side are shut-offs for the separate hose connections.

423

40-29b. The material to be sprayed is stored in the two-quart pressure cup. It is forced through the hose to the gun by air pressure.

40-29c. Here the material to be sprayed is stored in the cup attached to the gun. Suction pulls the material out of the cup and through the gun.

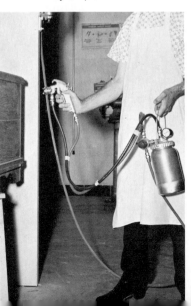

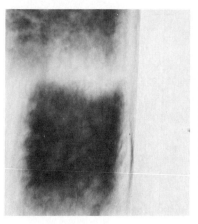

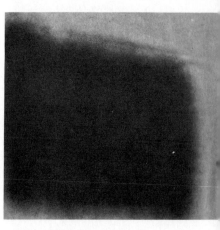

40-31a. Too much material will run or sag.

40-31b. Not enough material will produce a rough surface and insufficient coverage.

40-31c. When the adjustments are properly set, the result will be a smooth, full coat.

40-32. Regulating the fluid-adjusting screw.

on a vertical surface without running. Fig. 40-31. On a suction-feed cup system, the air regulator pressure must be set in a way that will create enough suction to get the material through the gun and atomize (break up) the paint particles. It is necessary, therefore, to regulate the fluid-adjusting screw to obtain a balance between the air pressure and the amount of material coming from the gun. Fig. 40-32.

4. Clamp the cup on the gun and test the spray pattern. Adjust the pattern for the work to be done. Figs. 40-33 and 40-34. Turn the air cap so the horns are horizontal for a vertical pattern or vertical for a horizontal pattern. A vertical pattern is used for spraying horizontally, and vice versa. Fig. 40-35.

5. Hold the gun 6 to 8″ from the work and adjust the spray pattern width so it is about 8″ wide at the work surface. Figs. 40-36 and 40-37. Move the gun

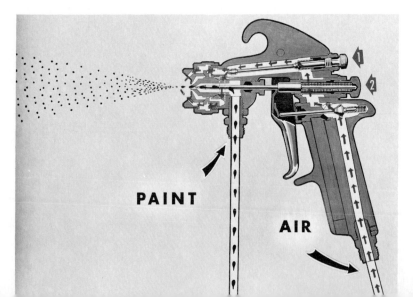

40-33. Arrow 1 points to the spreader adjusting screw. This adjustment changes the size of the spray pattern. Arrow 2 points to the fluid-adjusting screw. Trace the path of the air and the paint to see how they are mixed. Notice how the air atomizes the paint outside the gun. This is an external-mix gun.

424

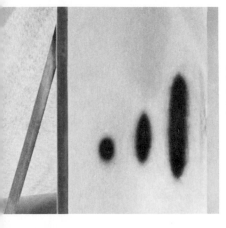

40-34. The spray pattern size can be varied from a small circle to a long oval. This is done by regulating the spreader-adjusting screw. The size of the work to be sprayed will determine the spray pattern size.

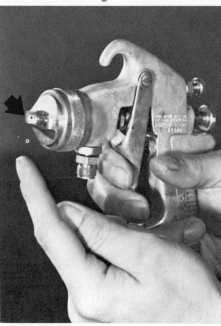

40-35a. The horns (arrow) on the air cap are horizontal for a vertical spray pattern.

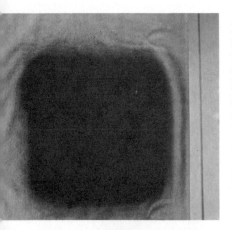

40-35b. Spray horizontally with a vertical pattern.

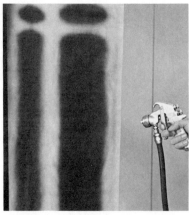

40-35c. Spray vertically with a horizontal pattern.

40-36. One hand-span is usually the correct distance the gun should be held from the work.

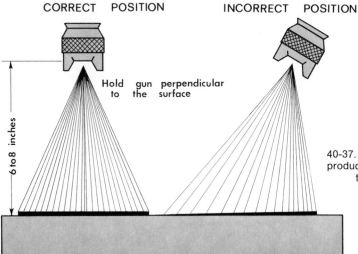

CORRECT POSITION   INCORRECT POSITION

Hold gun perpendicular to the surface

6 to 8 inches

40-37. Holding the gun at an angle will produce an uneven build-up of the material on the work surface.

425

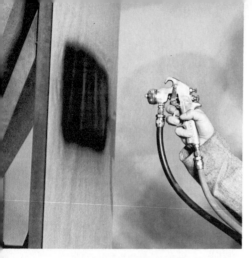

40-38a. The gun is held parallel with the work surface to produce a smooth even build-up of the material.

in a straight line parallel to the work surface. Fig. 40-38. Move your arm, not your wrist, and never use an arcing motion. Fig. 40-39. Band the work first by pointing the gun directly at the

corner so an equal amount of material is deposited on both surfaces. Fig. 40-40.

6. Start your stroke off the end of the work and pull the trigger as the gun approaches the edge of the work. Continue the stroke, as described in Step 5 above, until the end of the workpiece is reached. Release the trigger, but continue the stroke for a few inches before reversing. Move the gun down half the width of the spray pattern so the aiming point is at the bottom of the previous stroke. Start the next pass back across the work the same as you began this stroke. Fig. 40-41.

7. If curved or irregular surfaces are sprayed, keep the air cap about 6 to 8″ from the work and follow the contour of the work surface.

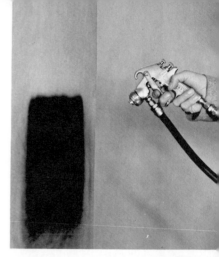

40-38b. This gun is incorrectly held. Notice that the material deposited at the top is quite heavy compared to the extremely light coverage at the bottom.

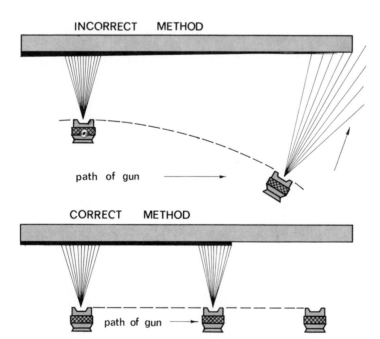

40-39. Always move the gun in a path parallel to the work surface.

40-40. Always band the object to be sprayed before spraying the surfaces. The surfaces should be sprayed starting with those seen least and ending with those seen most; the back, the sides, the front, and last, the top.

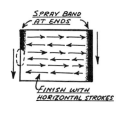
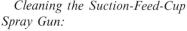
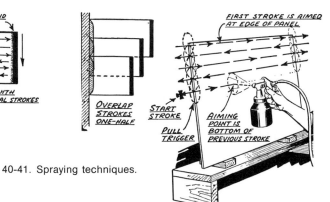

40-41. Spraying techniques.

40-42. Blowing the material out of the gun back into the cup.

Cleaning the Suction-Feed-Cup Spray Gun:

1. Loosen the air cap two or three turns and remove the fluid container. Hold a cloth over the air cap and pull the trigger. This will force the fluid that remains in the gun back into the container. Fig. 40-42.

2. Empty the container and clean it thoroughly with the correct solvent. Fig. 40-43.

3. Pour solvent into the container to a depth of about 1″. Reassemble the gun and spray the solvent to flush out the fluid passages. Fig. 40-44.

4. Remove the container and the air cap; brush and wipe all traces of the finishing material from the gun and air cap. Fig. 40-45. If some of the holes are plugged, use a toothpick or sharpened stick to clean them; never use wire or a nail. Fig. 40-46.

5. Reassemble the gun and set it on the cup. Do not clamp it. Clamping over a long period of time will shorten the life of the cover gasket.

40-43. To clean the cup and gun, use the correct solvent for the material sprayed.

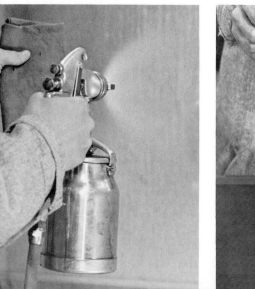

40-44. Spray clean solvent through the gun to clean out the passages.

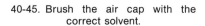
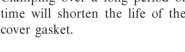

40-45. Brush the air cap with the correct solvent.

40-46. Use a tooth pick or a sharp piece of wood to clean the holes in the air cap.

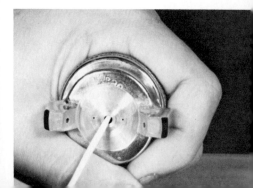

DISCUSSION TOPICS

Unit 38. Preparing Wood for a Finish

1. Describe the four major steps in preparing a project for finishing.

2. Name the three basic kinds of abrasives used in woodworking.

3. An aluminum oxide abrasive with a grit number of 100 is comparable to garnet paper of what O-grade?

4. Name the two common kinds of backing for abrasives.

Unit 39. General Instructions for Wood Finishing

1. Name the basic steps in applying a wood finish. Why is sanding not one of the seven steps numbered in the text?

2. If a light finish is to be applied, what is the first step?

3. What is the purpose of a washcoat?

4. What kind of filler is required for an open-grained wood such as mahogany?

5. What is the purpose of a sealer?

6. Is glazing included in all finishing schedules? Explain.

7. What would be the best top coat for use in your school shop? Discuss.

Unit 40. Finishing Procedures

1. What is the purpose of bleaching?

2. Describe the two common kinds of stains.

3. What is the major difference in the way the two kinds of stain are applied?

4. What two materials are used to make a washcoat? What is the mixture?

5. Describe how filler is applied.

6. What is the purpose of glazing?

7. What is meant by distressing?

8. Describe some methods of distressing.

9. What is the advantage of a wipe-on finish?

10. List the steps in applying a varnish.

11. What are some advantages of lacquer?

12. Why should lacquer be sprayed?

13. List three top coats and their solvents.

14. Explain the difference between brushing paint and brushing varnish.

15. What are the steps in cleaning a brush?

16. What are the three methods of feeding material to a spray gun.

17. What are some factors that affect the setting of the air-regulator pressure?

18. How do the horns of the air cap affect the spray pattern?

19. When the gun is held the proper distance from the work, what should the size of the pattern be at the work surface?

20. How is the width of the pattern changed?

21. Describe the procedure for spraying a coffee table.

22. List the steps in cleaning a suction-feed spray gun.

PROBLEMS AND ACTIVITIES

Section Six-FINISHING

1. Write a report on the source, processing, and use of one common finishing material.

2. Select a particular kind of wood such as oak, mahogany, or walnut, and apply different kinds of finishes to it. Write a report on the results.

3. Write a report on the spray finishing method used in the furniture industry.

Upholstery

Upholstering is an important part of the furniture industry. Even a limited amount of upholstery can make a furniture piece more comfortable and more colorful. In this room the upholstered pieces are the dominating feature. (U. S. Plywood-Champion Papers, Inc.)

Like so many other aspects of fine furniture making, top quality upholstery requires great skill. Fig. 41-1. In an industrial world that has become increasingly mechanized, an upholsterer still does craftsman's work with his hands. It takes a person with aptitude about six years to become a truly accomplished journeyman upholsterer.

However, there are certain relatively simple upholstery methods which produce satisfactory results. Also, many time-consuming upholstery operations, such as webbing, sewing and tying springs, sewing stitched edges, and picking hair, have been all but eliminated by new and improved tools and materials now accepted in the upholstery trade.

There are three basic types of upholstery—pad seat, tight spring, and overstuffed.

● *Pad seats,* sometimes referred to as *slip seats,* have the advantages of being relatively easy to construct and reasonably comfortable. Fig. 41-2. Ordinarily a pad seat is just a sheet of plywood padded by a cushion material and covered with cloth or plastic. The cover is pulled over the padding

41-2. Pad seat. Notice how the fabric is pulled tightly over the edge of the seat to give a smooth edge and avoid hand-stitching the corners.

41-1. Fine upholstery, as shown on this overstuffed sofa and chair, requires the work of a skilled craftsman. Notice the double welt on the chair, used for hiding the tacking of the fabric next to the wood members.

and tacked or stapled on the bottom of the seat. A more comfortable seat can be made by using a frame rather than a plywood sheet for the base, with a webbing material or springs across the

41-3. Tight-spring construction.

41-4. Tight-spring construction with sinuous springs and foam rubber cushioning.

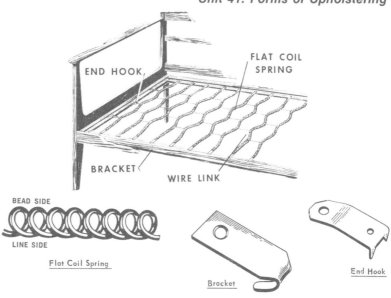

41-5. The flat-coil spring is usually used with the loose cushion.

opening of the frame. (See Fig. 44-12.)

• *Tight-spring* construction is more comfortable than a pad seat, but also a little more complicated to produce. Fig. 41-3. The comfort of the tight-spring seat depends on the size, number, and resiliency of the springs, and the arrangement and amount of compression when tying or clipping them together. Sinuous springs are frequently used for tight-spring seats. Fig. 41-4. A flat-coil steel spring can also be used. Fig. 41-5.

• *Overstuffed* is the most comfortable form of upholstery. It contains two sets of springs—one in the platform under the cushions, and a second set in the cushions. A variation is to use rubber or polyfoam in place of springs in the cushion. Fig. 41-6.

Chairs, benches, footstools, toy chests, footlockers, tie-on cushions for furniture, combination telephone stands and benches, bed headboards, and many other items can be designed to include some form of upholstering.

The upholstery techniques described in this book are primarily simple ones which might be used in the production of a dining room chair. They might also be used in making a living room chair on which most of the exposed surfaces, including the arms and legs, are of wood. Thus the upholstering would be done primarily on just the seat and back of the chair. There are many good books on upholstering that can be studied if you are interested in learning about more complex operations such as upholstering an overstuffed chair or davenport.

41-6. Overstuffed furniture is the most comfortable form of upholstery.

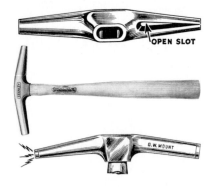

OPEN SLOT

Upholsterer's hammer. The upholsterer's tack hammer has a slightly curved head which is available in various weights from 7 to 12 ounces. There are two types: the solid-end type, and the old-style, slotted type. One end is usually magnetized for holding tacks and the other end is non-magnetic for driving and hammering.

Upholsterer's shears. The upholsterer's shears are usually heavy duty shears with sharp points. They are used to cut webbing, burlap, foam rubber, and similar materials. Good-quality 10″ shears are a must. Upholstery covers are of such a weight that regular sewing shears are not recommended.

Ripping chisel. The ripping chisel is used for removing tacks on the bottom of the frames when recovering. The upholsterer holds the ripper in the left hand and strikes it with a hammer. The tacks are rolled out by driving the blade of the ripper under the head.

Regulator. The regulator is used to reach under the final cover in order to move cotton padding out into corners and into low spots. Be careful not to damage the point of the regulator. A damaged point may damage the final cover and make lumps in the cotton. There are two type of regulators. One has a plastic handle; the other is all steel. Regulators are available in lengths from 6″ to 12″, and in thickness from gage #8 to #10.

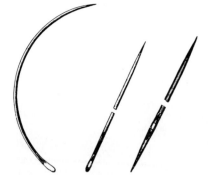

Needles. Two varieties of needles are needed—curved and straight. Curved needles are used for hand stitching. Hand stitching is done on outside backs, outside arms, corners, and front edges. A good, round-point, curved needle is needed for stitching fabric. Sizes from 2″ to 10″ are available. Most commonly used are the 3″ and 4″.

Straight needles, single point and double point, are used for stitching front edges and for putting buttons into backs. Use a round point. Sizes are from 4″ to 18″ in length and from gage #10 to #15 in diameter. Double-pointed needles are used for sewing in both directions without having to turn the needle. These work very well for sewing stuffing materials to the burlap.

Skewers. Skewers, also called *upholsterer's pins,* are used to pin a cover into place during sewing or while making a pattern.

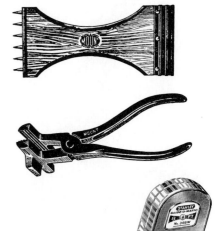

Webbing stretchers. There are several types of stretchers. Every shop should have a minimum of two types—the old wooden stretcher type and the plier type. The stretcher is used to tighten new webbing as it is installed. The plier stretcher is used for repair of webbing that has come loose or for new webbing that has been cut to length. Tin smith's vise-grip, wide nosed, would be a good substitute if the plier stretcher is not available.

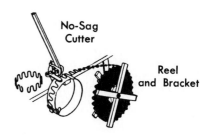

Measuring tape. The upholsterer should have a good steel measuring tape. The 8′ size is adequate.

Sinuous spring cutter. Some device is needed to cut tempered spring wire. The tool should be of adequate capacity to cut No. 8 or No. 9 steel wire. A small bolt cutter will suffice. However, there is a commercially made spring cutter which is better. A reel can be made to hold the coil of sinuous springs. The spring wire is pulled from the reel and fed onto the drum of the cutter, against the stop which is set for the desired length. As many springs as necessary can then be cut to the same length.

No-Sag Cutter

Reel and Bracket

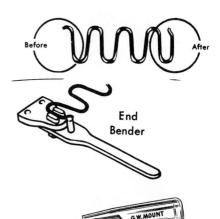

Before   After

End Bender

Spring-end bender. After sinuous springs are cut from the coil, they must have the ends bent to keep them from sliding out of the seat or back clip. The bending tool is simply a combination of two jaw blocks into which the end of the spring is placed. A pin projecting from the handle bears against the extended end of the spring; as pressure is applied manually, the spring end is bent. Care should be taken not to make too sharp a bend; otherwise the end will break off and the spring will not hold in the clip after installation.

Tack lifter. This tool sometimes called the *tack claw,* is used for pulling tacks. The jaws are pushed or driven under the head and the tack is removed by prying.

Button machine. In upholstery, buttons are often used to hold and give shape to materials, and to add beauty to the piece. Buttons are made on a button machine. The machine makes use of a movable plunger which forces the cover over an inner shell, then presses the shell over an inner eye which completes the process to produce a covered button. The button machine is made in several models, some quite elementary and others automatic. Each button size requires a set of matching dies. Sizes range from No. 14 (about $\frac{3}{8}''$ diameter) to No. 100 (about $2\frac{1}{2}''$ diameter).

Spring stretchers. Sinuous springs can be installed by hand. However, because of the sharp ends and the danger of slipping when pulling the spring into the clips, the use of a spring stretcher is recommended. There are two types of spring stretchers—the lever type and the pull type. The lever type is more effective. However, the pull type is necessary when no support or fulcrum is available for the lever. The pull type is also used for installing back and seat helical springs. (Helical springs are coil springs used to tie the sinuous springs together as a unit.)

Gun Tackers   Air Tackers

Hand stapler. This is an excellent tool for fastening tacking tape or cover materials to a base. The use of a power-driven tacker is even more convenient and faster.

Electric Tackers

Sewing machine. The sewing machine is one of the most important pieces of equipment to the upholstery craftsman. A conventional household machine is not recommended, but it can do the job with light materials on a limited basis. Two types of sewing machines are made specially for upholstering. One has a walking foot and the other has a stationary foot. The walking-foot type is recommended. This machine will do both welting and flat sewing. Every upholsterer should know how to sew. This includes proper threading and simple adjustments of tension.

43 Upholstering Materials

Frames

The frame is any wooden or metal assembly over which a cover may be applied to form a seating device. This discussion will be limited to the use of wooden frames. The wood selected for the frame should be straight, close-grained hardwood. Woods that take tacks easily and do not split are recommended, such as walnut, mahogany, soft maple, birch, poplar, beech, and sycamore. Because of their high cost, walnut and mahogany are used primarily where they will be seen.

Frames that are to be fitted with springs should be $1\frac{1}{16}''$ thick, with all surfaces reasonably smooth to prevent snagging or undue wear on the upholstery materials. They should be strongly constructed, with reinforced joints. Dowels, glue, and corner blocks are a necessity. Fig. 43-1. The side rails should butt into the face of the back and front rails so that the pull of the frame will not cause the joint to separate. Fig. 43-2. The corner blocks should be no more than 1″ from the top edge of the frame. Fig. 43-3.

Seats and backs constructed with sinuous springs normally have an arc—that is, the center of the seat or back extends beyond the top edge of the frame. Of course, when someone sits in the upholstered piece, the springs are bent. This bending is called *deflection,* and it equals or slightly exceeds the height of the spring

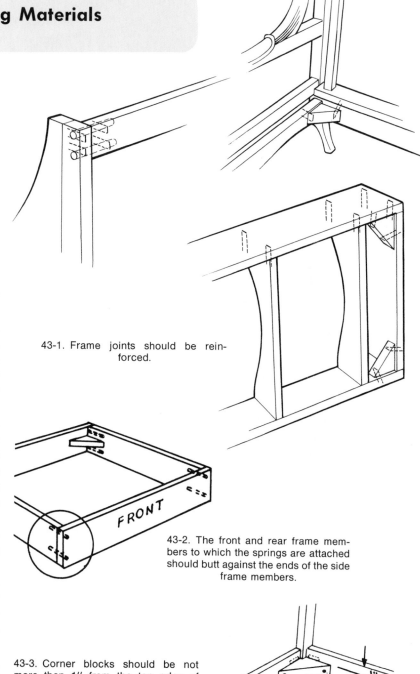

43-1. Frame joints should be reinforced.

43-2. The front and rear frame members to which the springs are attached should butt against the ends of the side frame members.

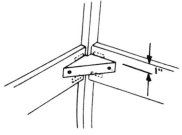

43-3. Corner blocks should be not more than 1″ from the top edge of the frame.

435

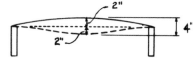

43-4. The arc of the spring is 2″ above the frame edge. It will usually bend down about the same amount when someone sits on it.

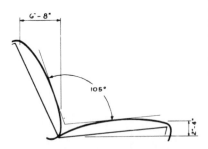

43-5. The rear rail of the seat frame should be 2″ to 4″ lower than the front rail, and the chair back should make about a 105-degree angle with the seat.

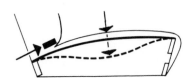

43-6. Arrows show location of bottom back rail (left) and deflection.

arc. Fig. 43-4. This is an important fact to keep in mind when determining the width of the frame members.

Proper design of the frame is essential to the construction of a comfortable spring platform. The rear rail should be 2″ to 4″ lower than the front rail. Fig. 43-5. The bottom back rail should be located 1″ to 3″ ahead of the rear seat rail. This will place the main

43-7. A completed chair frame ready for springing.

weight on the springs at the point of greatest deflection. Fig. 43-6.

After the frame is assembled and the glue is cured, round all sharp edges of the frame with a file to avoid wear on the upholstery where it comes in contact with the frame.

Any wood which is attached to the frame and will show after the final cover is applied should be completely finished before any upholstery operations are started. Fig. 43-7.

Cushioning. Many materials make satisfactory pads. However, professional results are most readily achieved with rubber foam, plastic foam, or rubberized fiber.

Foam rubber is widely used as a cushioning material in upholstery because it is durable, comfortable, attractive, lightweight, allergy free, and easy to work with. While it is somewhat more expensive than other upholstery materials, the fact that it can be

43-8a. Solid-slab foam rubber.

43-8b. Utility foam rubber with cores molded in it.

43-8c. Molded reversible foam rubber cushions.

436

easily cut to shape with an ordinary shears makes it useful for simplified upholstering. Foam rubber is available in three types:

- Solid-slab uncored stock.
- Cored utility stock (with cores molded in it).
- Ready molded or fully molded reversible cushions or molded pieces. Fig. 43-8.

For most simple jobs, foam rubber in the shape of solid slabs or sheets without cored depressions are used. Solid-slab uncored stock is made in varying degrees of softness or compression, ranging from soft to extra firm. Follow these recommendations:

- For small dining room or side chairs, use material from $\frac{3}{4}''$ to 2'' thick, with medium or firm compression.
- For chair backs, use soft or medium compression in thicknesses from $\frac{3}{4}''$ to $1\frac{1}{2}''$.
- For seats with a solid base, such as plywood, use material that is of firm compression and from $1\frac{1}{2}''$ to 2'' thick.
- For seats with a webbing base, use a medium compression and thickness from $\frac{3}{4}''$ to 2''.
- Cored utility stock is used where a deep cushioned effect is desired. For the backs of chairs, cored utility stock should be of soft compression and in thicknesses from $1\frac{1}{2}''$ to 2''.
- For upholstering over no-sag spring seats, use medium to firm compression and thickness from $1\frac{1}{2}''$ to 3''.

Polyurethane foam, better known as "polyfoam," is a manmade spongelike material. Fig. 43-9. Polyfoam is widely used in industry, not only for furniture

43-9. Polyurethane (polyfoam) is available in many sizes.

seating but also for pillows, mattresses, and automobile seats, among other uses.

Rubberized hair is a light, elastic material made from curled hair and rubber with a cotton net backing. It comes in pads or rolls, 1'' or $1\frac{1}{2}''$ thick, 24'' wide, and 75' long. It can also be purchased in 24'' × 72'' sheets. Fig. 43-10. The rubberized fiber is held in place by sewing it to the burlap, using a double-pointed needle and stitching twine. The stitches should be about 2'' long. Plastic or rubber foam is then applied in sufficient quantity to give the desired shape. Cotton, held in place by a muslin cover, can be used instead of the foam. The cover is pulled tight enough to compress the padding slightly and is tacked to the frame.

Edge roll. The edge roll is used around arms and rails where a soft edge is desired. Tacked in place, the roll confines the padding to an area, thus giving the upholstered piece its shape. Edge roll comes in various diameters from $\frac{1}{2}''$ to $1\frac{1}{4}''$. It is sold by the foot or in coils from 50' to 1000'. Fig. 43-11.

43-10. Rubberized hair.

43-11. Edge roll.

43-12a. Tacking strips, cut to length.

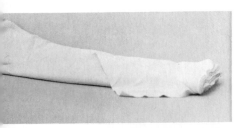

43-13. Cotton muslin.

Tacking strips. Tacking strips are used for blind-tacking on outside arms or backs, or as an aid in holding a straight line on the final cover next to the welt. Tacking strips are made from heavy paper ½″ wide. The strips are available in rolls or cut to length in bundles. Fig. 43-12a. Tacking strips made from metal or fiber are also available with 8 or 10 ounce tacks already in place. Fig. 43-12b.

Muslin. Muslin is used as a temporary covering to hold the padding in place. The final cover is tacked over the muslin. (Actually, the final cover can be put directly over the padding; how-

43-14. Burlap.

43-12b. Metal tacking strips are made with 8 oz. or 10 oz. tacks already in place.

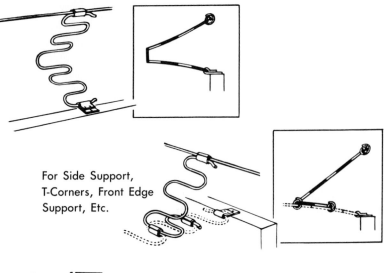

For Side Support, T-Corners, Front Edge Support, Etc.

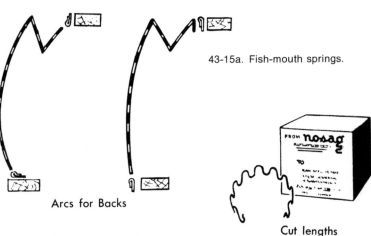

Arcs for Backs

43-15a. Fish-mouth springs.

Cut lengths

Coils

43-15b. Sinuous springs are available in coils or cut to length.

ever, for the beginner this is not recommended. Working with the muslin offers the beginner a means of practicing cutting and tacking. Also, since the muslin holds the padding in place, it allows the beginner to concentrate on a smooth and properly aligned final cover.)

Muslin is a plain-weave cotton material and is available either bleached or unbleached. It can be

438

Gage	Feet per coil
8 & 8½	111
9 & 9½	120
10 & 10½	127 to 128
11, 11½ & 12	140 to 154

43-15c. Specification chart for sinuous spring coils.

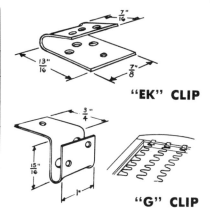

"EK" CLIP

"G" CLIP

43-16. Sinuous spring clips.

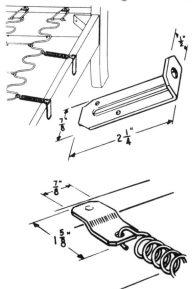

43-17. The upper drawing shows a retainer plate and the lower drawing shows an offset plate used to connect the helical springs to the frame.

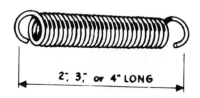

2″, 3″, or 4″ LONG

15 ga. ½″ O.D.

Use 2″ length for 4″ spacing of No-Sag
Use 3″ length for 5″ spacing of No-Sag
Use 4″ length for 6″ spacing of No-Sag

43-18. Seat helical spring.

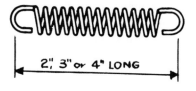

2″, 3″ or 4″ LONG

17 ga. ½″ O.D.

Use 2″ length for 4″ spacing of No-Sag
Use 3″ length for 5″ spacing of No-Sag
Use 4″ length for 6″ spacing of No-Sag

43-19. Back helical springs.

purchased in widths from 36″ to 54″. An inexpensive unbleached muslin 36″ or 40″ wide will make an adequate cover. Fig. 43-13.

Burlap. Burlap is woven in various weights per yard—for example, a 10 oz.-36″ burlap weighs 10 oz. per yard. Burlap is used as a covering over webbing or springs to provide a foundation for felt. Naturally, a better quality of burlap will provide a better base and give better service than an inexpensive material. A good burlap is the 8 oz. or 10 oz. by 40″ wide. Fig. 43-14.

Springs. Sinuous springs are sold under various trade names. They are available in many different shapes and sizes. Special bent shapes can provide soft edges on seats and backs. For instance, the "fish mouth" spring is used on fronts of automotive seats and backs of sofa and chair sets. Fig. 43-15a. Sinuous springs come in gages from 8 to 13, in ½ gage increments. Generally speaking, 9 or 8½ gage should be used on most seats, and 11 to 13 gage used on backs. However, it is a good idea to check the manufacturer's charts for recommendation. Sinuous springs are sold in either coils or cut lengths. Fig. 43-15b.

Clips and fastenings for sinuous springs. Many types of spring clips are available from upholstery supply companies. Of special interest and use to the upholsterer are the "EK" clips and "G" clips.

The "EK" clip is the one general clip that can be used for fastening seat and back springs. The "G" clip is used when a lower profile is desired. Fig. 43-16.

The helical retainer plate or offset plate is another device used to fasten helical springs to the sides of wood frames. The plate is nailed to the frame, and the helical is hooked into the extended end of the clip. Fig. 43-17.

Seat helicals. Seat helicals are small springs used in seating between rows of sinuous springs or fastened to side rails of frames. Lengths available are 2″, 3″, and 4″. Fig. 43-18.

Back helicals. Back helicals are of lighter gage and are used between springs in backs for softness and comfort. Fig. 43-19.

Connecting links. Connecting links are used in between the sinuous springs to give a firm connection. These are frequently used

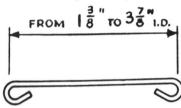

FROM $1\frac{3}{8}''$ TO $3\frac{7}{8}''$ I.D.

43-20. The connecting link

in the center portions of a seat, with helicals on the outsides fastened to the frame. Lengths range from $1\frac{3}{8}''$ to $3\frac{7}{8}''$, in increments of $\frac{1}{8}''$. Fig. 43-20. See Fig. 45-3 to determine correct size.

Spring nails. A good-quality nail is required to hold spring clips to wood frames. Recommended is a forged nail $\frac{7}{8}''$ to $1\frac{1}{8}''$ long x 14 gage. These nails are barbed to give maximum holding power. Fig. 43-21.

Talcum powder. When working with foam rubber, talcum powder can be used to reduce friction, especially when applying the covering materials. Powder can also be dusted on seams that have been cemented unnecessarily, to prevent sticking.

Tacking tape. This is a cloth tape which is available in widths from 2'' to 6''. It is used to fasten foam cushioning to the base. Muslin can be used as a substitute. It should be cut into strips of the desired width, coated with foam cement, and left to dry.

Foam cement. Manufacturers of foam rubber and polyfoam also make cement that is used to fasten tacking tape to the foam or to

43-21. Barbed nail.

fasten pieces of foam together. Make certain to use the correct cement for the specific work you are doing. Fig. 43-22.

Tailor's chalk. Some type of chalk is needed to mark the cover for cutting. White, tailor's chalk is often used; however, ordinary school chalk may also be used. Fig. 43-23.

Upholstery and webbing tacks. These are flat-head tacks, used for holding materials in place. The smaller sizes, 4 to 8 oz., are used for general upholstering. For blind tacking, an 8 or 10 oz. tack should be used. Fig. 43-24. The larger sizes, 12 to 14 oz., are needed for applying webbing. Webbing tacks differ from upholstery tacks in that they have barbs which project from the shank, providing more holding power. Fig. 43-25.

43-22. Spray adhesive for foam rubber and polyfoam.

43-23. Tailor's chalk is used to mark the fabric for cutting.

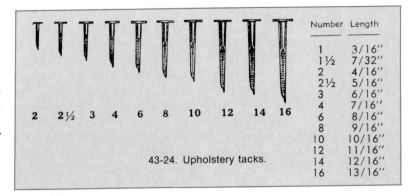

Number	Length
1	3/16''
1½	7/32''
2	4/16''
2½	5/16''
3	6/16''
4	7/16''
6	8/16''
8	9/16''
10	10/16''
12	11/16''
14	12/16''
16	13/16''

2   2½   3   4   6   8   10   12   14   16

43-24. Upholstery tacks.

43-25. Webbing tacks.

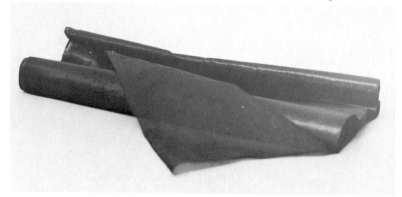

43-26. Cambric.

Cambric. Cambric is a lightweight material used for a dust cloth under the bottom of chairs. It also provides a covering for the frame so that the inside of the chair will not be visible.

Most supply houses list a 29″ medium weight and a 36″ heavy weight. Cambric is much like cheesecloth with a shiny, transparent filler applied. Fig. 43-26.

Welt cord. Welt cord is used extensively in covering work. It serves as a decorative joining agent between two pieces of cover. A regular 4-ply jute twine can be used; it serves as a strong, flexible cord that can be pulled without breaking. More sophisticated types of welt cording are available in sizes of $\frac{4}{32}$″ to $\frac{8}{32}$″. These cords, although not as strong as jute, give a smoother welt that is very pliable. They are made of a soft tissue encased in nylon netting. The size selected will be determined by the style of furniture it is to be used on; however, $\frac{5}{32}$ is applicable to many styles. Fig. 43-27.

Cotton padding. This type of padding (called cotton or felt) is processed into rolls of various thicknesses and widths. The most common width that is stocked is 27″. The weight of felt is indicated by ounces per yard, with the 16-oz. variety commonly used. Fig. 43-28.

43-27. Welt cord.

43-28. Cotton padding.

43-29. Spring twine.

43-30. Stitching twine.

43-31. Colored nylon stitching threads.

Twines and threads. Spring twine is used to tie springs in place. Always use a good quality twine. Italian No. 60 linen is excellent, or any pure flax twine measuring about $\frac{1}{8}''$ to $\frac{3}{16}''$ in cross section. Binder twine and cheap twines should not be used, because they will not withstand wear. Fig. 43-29.

Stitching twine is sometimes referred to as mattress twine. It is sold in spool-like tubes or in balls weighing from $\frac{1}{2}$ to 3 lbs. It is used for stitching front edges, sewing down front edge covers to springs and burlap, and also in tufting and fastening buttons. Its color is beige or light brown. Fig. 43-30.

A colored nylon stitching thread is used for hand stitching of cover and cushions. It is heavier than sewing machine thread, extremely tough, and does not break readily. This thread is available in a large variety of colors and is sold in 2-oz. tubes. Fig. 43-31.

Buttons. Buttons add much to the appearance of a piece of fur-niture. They consist of two parts—the shell, over which the upholstery material is stretched, and the back, by which the button is fastened to the upholstered piece. Several types of backs are available, including *wire loop* (or *wire eye*), tack, tuft, and clinch. Fig. 43-32. The wire loop is the most versatile.

Buttons with the types of backs listed above must be assembled with a button machine. Such buttons are sold by the gross and are available in sizes from No. 14 (about $\frac{3}{8}''$ in diameter) to No. 100 (about $2\frac{1}{2}''$ in diameter). However, if a button machine is not available, buttons can be purchased at a local sewing center and assembled by hand with a hammer and a small tool which comes in the package.

Jute webbing. Webbing is used as a foundation for many types of chair seats. Jute webbing is like strips of woven burlap in $3\frac{1}{2}''$ and $4''$ widths, in rolls 72 yards long. Care should be taken to choose a good quality webbing; poor

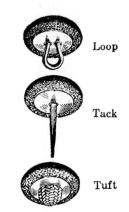

Loop

Tack

Tuft

43-32. Buttons showing some of the various types of backs available.

webbing will soon break down. Jute webbing that is interwoven on the top of the chair seat frame makes an excellent semiflexible base for a pad seat when upholstering with foam rubber. Fig. 43-33.

Rubber webbing. Rubber webbing is 2″ wide by 100′ per roll. It may be nailed as jute webbing is, or it can sometimes be fastened by using clips that fit into grooves cut in the frame. This type of

442

43-33. Jute webbing.

43-34. Rubber webbing. Notice that clips are available which can be pressed onto the end for insertion into a groove which has been cut in the frame.

fastening is generally done on hardwood finished frames that have loose cushions similar to Danish-Modern furniture. Fig. 43-34.

Final cover. The final cover can be selected from sample books of fabrics or plastics available from an upholstery supply company. Care should be taken to select the pattern which is in keeping with the style of furniture. Do not select large patterns of rough-textured fabrics for small projects. This will make the furniture look out of proportion or heavy. The selection of the final fabric is of utmost importance in the appearance of the finished product. Fig. 43-35.

43-35. Final cover material can be selected from a large variety of fabrics or plastics.

44-2. Plywood used in a pad seat makes a simple but durable base.

Using Plywood for a Pad Seat

As mentioned earlier, the simplest upholstered seat is made of a plywood base that is padded with foam rubber and covered with cloth, plastic, or leather. This type of upholstery is often found on dining room chairs and side chairs. Figs. 44-1 and 44-2. To make such a seat, the following tools and materials are needed:

• Plywood, $\frac{1}{4}''$ to $\frac{3}{4}''$ thick, large enough to form the base and back of the chair.
• Foam rubber, slab stock, $1\frac{1}{2}''$ to $2''$ thick, firm compression.
• Tacking tape, $3''$ or $4''$ wide.
• Rubber cement.
• No. 6 upholsterer's tacks or a hand stapler.

Proceed as follows:

1. Cut the plywood base to fit the chair. Drill several $\frac{1}{4}''$ holes in it, about $3''$ apart, for ventilation.

2. Place the base over the foam rubber. With a ballpoint or felt-tip pen, outline the shape of the base on the foam rubber. Add at least $\frac{1}{4}''$ allowance on all sides. (If the foam rubber is to have a cushioned edge, as explained later, add another $\frac{1}{2}''$ allowance, making a total of $\frac{3}{4}''$. Fig. 44-3.

The following steps vary, depending on the type of edge which you plan to form on the foam rubber. There are three common types:

• The *cushioned edge* has the bottom edge of the foam rubber tucked under to round it off. Fig. 44-4.

• For a *feathered edge,* the lower edge is chamfered with shears; thus the edge is contoured to the base. Fig. 44-5.

44-1. The three chairs in this reception area are examples of pad seats with plastic covers.

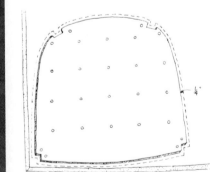

44-3. The foam rubber is cut at least $\frac{1}{4}''$ larger than the pad seat base.

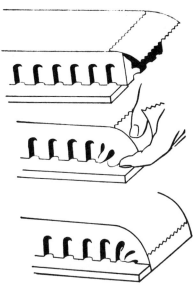

44-4. Cushioned edge.

44-5a. Trim the edge of the foam rubber for a feathered edge.

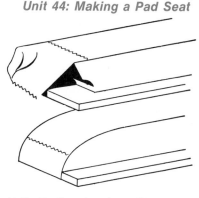

44-5b. Feathered edge. Place the trimmed edge of the foam rubber down against the base and tack the tape underneath.

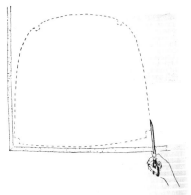

44-7. Cutting the foam rubber to size with scissors.

• The *square edge* provides a straight, vertical surface around the upholstered face. Fig. 44-6.

3a. *For a cushioned edge.* Cut the foam rubber to shape with shears. As mentioned, allow about $\frac{1}{4}''$ extra all around, plus an extra $\frac{1}{2}''$ on the cushion edge or edges. Fig. 44-7. The shears should be lubricated with clear water for easy cutting. Apply rubber cement along about 1″ of the upper surface of the foam rubber around all sides. Fig. 44-8. The tacking tape comes with a 1″ coating of adhesive. If muslin strips have been used, apply cement to about 1″ width along the muslin strip. Allow the surfaces to dry one or two minutes and then apply the tacking tape or muslin as shown in Fig. 44-8. Tuck the foam rubber under so that its thickness is held flat against the base. Keep the tape taut to avoid wrinkling. Tack the tape on the underside with

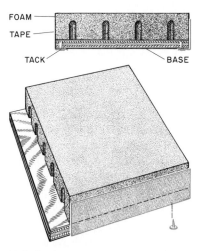

44-6. Square edge. Note that the tacking tape has been glued to the edge of the foam rubber and then tacked to the base.

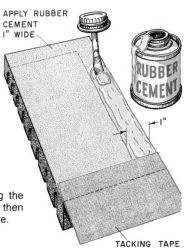

44-8. Apply rubber cement along the upper edge of the foam rubber and then fasten the tacking tape in place.

upholsterer's tacks or staples. You are now ready to apply the final covering.

3b. *For a feathered edge.* Cut the foam rubber to shape with shears. Remember, the stock was marked to allow about an extra $\frac{1}{4}''$ all around. Lubricate the shears with clear water for easy cutting. Trim the underside of the foam rubber as shown in Fig. 44-5a. Then proceed as for a cushioned edge, through the application of the tacking tape or muslin.

3c. *For a square edge.* Cut the foam rubber to size, allowing about $\frac{1}{4}''$ extra all around. Then apply the tacking tape to the vertical edge of the foam rubber. Apply rubber cement around the edges and in the form of an X on the plywood base, and also on the underside of the foam rubber. Fig. 44-9. Cement the tacking tape to the vertical edge and then tack the tape to the bottom or edge of the base or frame.

4. If the final cover is to be of unsupported plastic, leather, or a loosely woven material, it is a good idea to cover the surface with muslin. However, for most other materials, the final cover can be applied directly over the foam rubber.

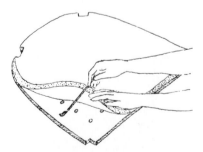

44-9. Applying rubber cement to the plywood base.

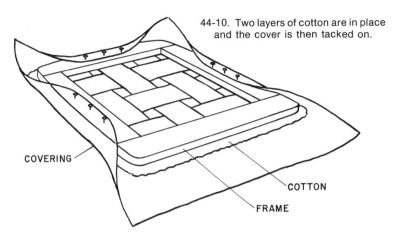

44-10. Two layers of cotton are in place and the cover is then tacked on.

5. *Applying the final cover to the pad seat.* Cut a piece of the final covering about 2″ larger than the seat in all directions.

6. Place the covering, good side down, on a bench. Place the seat, face down, in the center of the cover material.

7. Pull the cover up over the frame and slip tack the cover at the center of the frame on each edge. Fig. 44-10. Continue to tack until the cover is pulled taut and even. Place the tacks about 1″ apart. Tack the corners last, as shown in Fig. 44-11. Special care should be taken to pull all the wrinkles out. This is the reason the cover is first slip tacked. The cover can then be repulled, the tacks knocked out, and new tacks inserted in the repulled area. Continue to repull and retack until a smooth surface results.

Using a Frame and Webbing for a Pad Seat

Instead of plywood, webbing that is interwoven on the top of the chair seat frame can be used as an excellent semi-flexible base

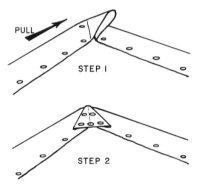

44-11. Tack the sharp corners carefully.

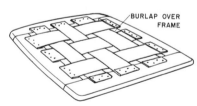

44-12. A webbed frame. Burlap must now be fastened over the webbing.

for foam rubber. The webbing may be of the jute or rubberized types. It can be attached directly to the chair frame, or a frame made independently of the chair can be used. Fig. 44-12. If a separate frame is made, the corners should be reinforced with dowel

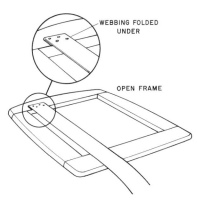

WEBBING FOLDED UNDER

OPEN FRAME

44-13. Turn the loose end of the webbing under and tack in place.

WEBBING STRETCHER

WEBBING FOLDED OVER

44-14. Stretch the webbing and tack to the other side.

44-15. The webbing is interwoven with the first strips of webbing for added strength.

joints, lap joints, or open mortise-and-tenon joints. The upper edge should be rounded so that it will not cut the upholstery fabric.

Using Jute Webbing

The following materials and tools are needed:

- Jute webbing, $3\frac{1}{2}''$ to 4" wide.
- No. 8 upholstery tacks.
- Webbing stretcher.
- Tack hammer.

Before starting to apply the webbing, check to see how many strips are needed in each direction. There should be about 1" or $1\frac{1}{2}''$ space between strips. Mark the location of each piece in both directions. Then follow these steps for attaching jute webbing to a frame made independently of the chair:

1. Start at the back of the chair frame and, without cutting a piece from the roll, place the end of the webbing on the center mark about 1" from the outer edge of the seat. Allow about $1\frac{1}{2}''$ of extra material.

2. Nail four No. 8 tacks about $1\frac{1}{2}''$ from the cut edge of the webbing. Stagger the tacks so that they will not split the frame.

3. Fold over the cut end twice (each fold about $\frac{3}{4}''$) and add four more tacks in a staggered arrangement. Fig. 44-13. (Sometimes three tacks will be adequate for Steps 2 and 3.)

4. Use the webbing stretcher to draw the webbing toward the front of the frame, making it as tight as possible. Hold the webbing tight with the stretcher and stagger about four tacks about 1" away from the front edge of the frame.

5. Cut the webbing about $1\frac{1}{2}''$ beyond the tacked area. Fold it over twice, about $\frac{3}{4}''$ each time, and add four more tacks. Fig. 44-14.

6. Add the strips from the front and back in the same manner. Then interweave a piece of webbing from side to side and fasten in the same manner until the webbing base is complete. Fig. 44-15.

For attaching jute webbing directly to the chair frame, follow the same six steps just listed, with these exceptions: (1) Allow less

extra material in Step 1 for smaller folds in Steps 2 and 5, as required by the narrow edge of the chair frame. (2) Use fewer tacks and stagger them near the center of the frame edge in Steps 2, 3, 4, and 5.

Using Rubber Webbing

Rubber webbing, which is virtually a flat spring made from two layers of fabric rubberized together, can also be used to increase the comfort of a pad seat when applied to the frame members. Fig. 44-16. In Contemporary

44-16. Using rubber webbing as a base for a pad seat with foam rubber cushioning will provide a resilient seat.

447

44-17. Rubber webbing is frequently used under loose cushions.

Seat span	2″ Standard			2″ Super			2″ Extraflex		
	Hard	Medium	Soft	Hard	Medium	Soft	Hard	Medium	Soft
18″	16½″	17″	17½″	16″	16½″	17″	14″	14″	15″
19″	17½″	18″	18½″	16½″	17″	17½″	14″	15″	16″
20″	18½″	19″	19½″	17½″	18″	18½″	15″	16″	17″
21″	19½″	20″	20½″	18½″	19″	19″	16″	17″	17″
22″	20″	20½″	21½″	19″	19½″	20″	16″	17″	18″
23″	21″	21½″	22″	20″	20½″	21″	17″	18″	19″
24″	22″	22½″	23″	21″	21½″	22″	18″	18″	19″

N.B. The recommended strand lengths above are the overall lengths required, and include overlap beyond tacks or inside clips.

44-20. Recommended cut lengths of resilient webbing.

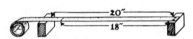

44-18. Rubber webbing should be tensioned. The webbing is stretched ten percent of the distance it must span.

A

B

44-19. Hold the webbing under tension and tack it to the frame. Cut the webbing ¼″ beyond the tack.

seating, rubber webbing is often used under cushions in place of springs. Fig. 44-17.

To attach rubber webbing to wooden frames, the following tools and materials are needed:

- Tack hammer.
- 2″ rubber webbing.
- Steel tape.
- Felt pen.
- Scissors.
- Nails with rounded stems and $\frac{3}{16}$″ to $\frac{5}{16}$″ heads.

To attach the webbing, follow these steps:

1. Tack one end to the frame by placing the nails at least ¼″ from the end of the webbing.

2. Determine the correct dimension by measuring the distance the webbing will span between the frame members, and make a mark on the webbing which is ten percent less than this length. Fig. 44-18.

3. Pull the webbing until the mark you have made aligns with the inside edge of the frame.

4. Tack the loose end and trim off the surplus webbing ¼″ beyond the tacking. Fig. 44-19. You can also consult Fig. 44-20 to determine the proper lengths of webbing required for various size frames.

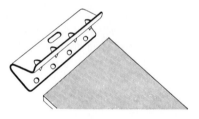

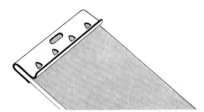

44-21. Attaching metal clips to the ends of the webbing strands is the most popular method of installation.

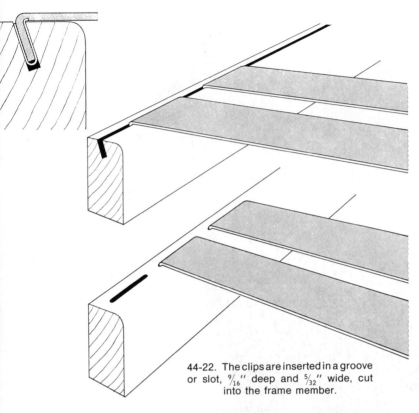

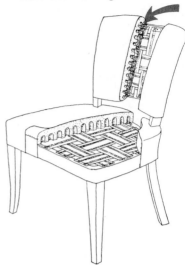

44-23. Burlap (arrow) over the webbing base helps to support the cushioning materials.

44-22. The clips are inserted in a groove or slot, $\frac{9}{16}''$ deep and $\frac{5}{32}''$ wide, cut into the frame member.

Steel clips may be used in place of tacks to attach the webbing to the frame. These clips are pressed onto the end of the webbing strand in a vise. Fig. 44-21. The clips are then inserted in grooves or mortises cut into the rails. Fig. 44-22.

Padding with Foam Rubber

Foam rubber can be added directly over a webbing base; however, it is better first to tack a burlap covering over the frame and webbing. Fig. 44-23. First, use a heavy piece of paper to make a pattern for the seat of the chair. Fig. 44-24. Then follow these steps:

1. Add $\frac{1}{2}''$ to the pattern and cut the pattern to size.

2. Fasten the pattern to the foam rubber with masking tape, or hold the pattern in place and trace around it with a felt pen. Fig. 44-25.

44-24. Making a pattern for the foam rubber.

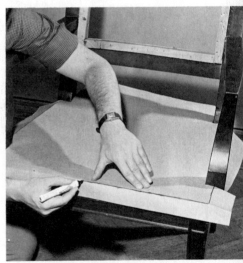

44-25. Tracing the pattern onto the foam rubber. Note that $\frac{1}{2}''$ was added to the pattern as an upholstery allowance.

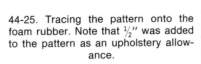

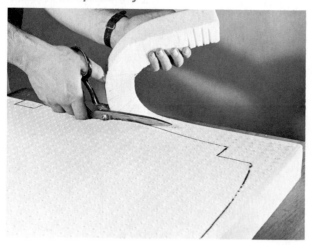

44-26. The foam rubber is cut to size with a pair of sharp shears lubricated in water.

44-27. Apply cement to the edge of the cushion for attaching the tacking tape.

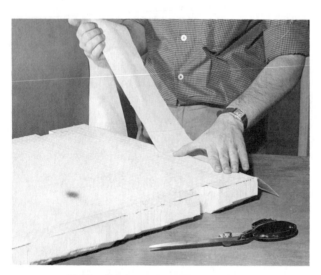

44-28a. It is best to apply two coats of rubber cement to the edges of both the cushion and the tacking tape. Allow the first coat to dry before applying the second coat. Press the tacking tape to the rubber when the second coat is tacky. Be sure to get a firm bond.

44-28b. If the tacking tape is applied to a curved edge, cut V-shaped notches in the tape to form a smooth edge.

3. Use sharp scissors lubricated in water to cut the foam rubber to size. Fig. 44-26. The foam rubber can also be cut on a band saw. If openings or notches are to be cut in the foam rubber to clear a frame part or chair rung, place a piece of adhesive tape about 3″ wide over this area before cutting such openings.

4. Test the foam rubber on the chair to see if it fits properly. When proper fit is obtained, remove the foam rubber cushion and apply rubber cement along its top in a band about 1″ wide. Fig. 44-27.

5. Apply about a 1″ band of cement around a 3″ or 4″ wide muslin strip.

6. When the cement becomes tacky, apply the muslin to the

44-29a. When the rubber cement is dry, place the cushion on the piece of furniture and prepare it for tacking.

upper edge of the cushion. Fig. 44-28.

7. Apply rubber cement to the edge of the chair and the underside of foam rubber.

8. When the cement is dry, place the cushion on the chair,

44-29b. Pull the muslin down and tack or staple it to the frame. Be careful to keep the top edge of the cushion straight and parallel with the bottom of the frame.

pull the muslin down, and tack around the side of the chair frame. Fig. 44-29. The webbed frame pad seat can now be covered with the fabric of your choice, as described on page 446.

UNIT 45 Upholstering with Sinuous Springs

Sinuous springs are known by names such as Sagless, Zig zag, or No-Sag springs and are widely used in upholstery today. They are particularly good to use when upholstering a chair on which most of the exposed legs and arms are of wood, but when the seat and back need a flexible base for the upholstery material. Fig. 45-1.

Installing Sinuous Springs

Normally, the sinuous spring is installed front to rear on seats, and top to bottom on backs. However, side to side springing can be used and would be recommended for installation on an

irregular-shaped piece, such as a chaise lounge.

Measure the distance between the inside of the rails, Fig. 45-2,

45-2. Measure the distance between the inside of the rails. The dimensions indicated by arrows A, B, C, and D are used to determine the springing requirements for the frame.

45-1. Sinuous springs installed in a chair frame.

TABLE FOR DETERMINING NUMBER OF NO-SAG STRANDS, PROPER SPACING OF CLIPS AND CORRECT SIZE CONNECTING LINKS

Distance Between Arms Along Front Seat Rail	Number of No-Sag Strands	Center to Center Spacing for Clips	Center Spacing of Two Outside Clips From Inside Arm Posts	Size of Connecting Links
21" Chair	5	4¼"	2"	2⅝"
22" Chair	5	4½"	2"	2⅞"
23" Chair	5	4¾"	2"	3⅛"
24" Chair	5	5"	2"	3⅜"
25" Chair	6	4¼"	1⅞"	2⅝"
40" Sectional	9	4½"	2"	2⅞"
50" Love Seat	11	4½"	2½"	2⅞"
52" Love Seat	11	4¾"	2¼"	3⅛"
58" Sofa	12	5"	1½"	3⅜"
59" Sofa	12	5"	2"	3⅜"
60" Sofa	13	4¾"	1½"	3⅛"
61" Sofa	13	4¾"	2"	3⅛"
62" Sofa	13	4¾"	2½"	3⅛"
63" Sofa	14	4½"	2¼"	2⅞"
64" Sofa	14	4½"	2¾"	2⅞"
65" Sofa	14	4¾"	1⅝"	3⅛"
66" Sofa	14	4¾"	2⅛"	3⅛"

NOTE: A practical method of spacing springs for any frame consists of marking the center of the rails and locating clips from there following the above spacings.

For Backs follow the same pattern, although springs may be spaced ¼" to ½" further apart in many installations.

45-3.

and refer to Figs. 45-3 and 45-4, to determine the gage, length, recommended number of springs, and spacing. For comfortable seating, the normal arc should be 1¼" to 2" high when the spring is installed. Fig. 45-5. To measure the cut spring, uncoil the spring, lay it flat on the bench top, and measure from end to end. (Never measure around the curve of the sinuous spring with a flexible tape.) Fig. 45-6.

When cutting the springs from continuous coils, the coil should be placed on a reel, for ease and safety in handling, and pulled off to the desired length. The ends of cut springs should then be bent to prevent the spring from slipping out of the clip. Springs with bent ends in the clip can be seen in Fig. 45-7.

Nail the spring clips in position on the frame as Fig. 45-3 indicates. Place one nail (⅞", 14 gage, barbed and blued) through the

SEATS

Inside Seat dimension	Normal arc	Gauge No-Sag	Length
12"	1¼"	11	11¾"
13	1¼	10½	12¾
14	1⅜	10	13¾
15	1½	10	14¾
16	1⅝	10	15¾
17	1⅝	9½	16¾
18	1¾	9	17¾
19	1¾	9	18¾
20	1⅞	9	20
21	1⅞	9	21
22	1⅞	8½	22
23	2	8½	23
24	2	8½	24
25	2	8	24⅞
26	2	8	25¾
27	2	8	26¾

BACKS

Inside back dimension	No-Sag ARC	Gauge No-Sag	Length
16"	1½"	12 or 13	16"
17	1⅝	12 or 13	17
18	1¾	12 or 13	18¼
19	1⅞	12	19¼
20	2	12	20¼
21	2	12	21¼
22	2	12	22¼
23	2¼	11½ or 12	23½
24	2¼	11½	24½
25	2½	11	25½
26	2½	11	26½

45-4. Tables for determining the arc, the gage and the length of the No-Sag spring recommended for seats and backs.

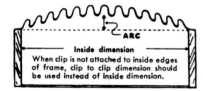

Inside dimension
When clip is not attached to inside edges of frame, clip to clip dimension should be used instead of inside dimension.

45-5. The arc is measured from a line drawn between the clips to the highest point of the spring.

45-6. The length of the spring is the distance between the outsides of each end. Be careful to hold the spring firmly when measuring. The spring may snap back and could cause injury.

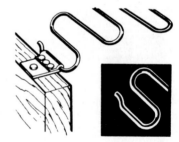

45-7. The end of the spring is bent to prevent it from coming out of the clip.

rear center hole in the clip. The front edge of the clip should be flush with the inside of the frame member. Fig. 45-8(A). When the clips have all been nailed in place, hook one end of the spring into the clip on the rear rail and pull it forward into the clip on the front rail. Fig. 45-9. Be careful to

alternate the ends of the springs in the clips to allow for straight cross tying. Fig. 45-8(B). Permanently nail the sinuous springs in place by placing nails in the forward

45-8. The clips are located on the frame according to Fig. 45-3.

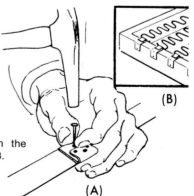

(B)

(A)

45-9. Installing the springs by hand. It is much safer to use one of the spring stretchers to install the springs.

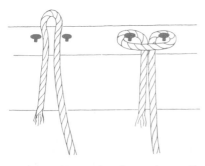

45-11a. When tying the springs with twine, attach the twine to the frame by winding it around two 14 oz. tacks.

holes of the clip. When nailing, be sure to slant the nails in toward the center of the frame member to avoid splitting the wood.

Tying the Sinuous Springs

The springs can now be tied with spring twine or clipped together with connecting links of the proper length as shown in Fig. 45-10.

If the springs are tied with twine, put two rows of twine across and tie a knot in each place as it crosses the spring. Anchor the twine on the frame with two 14-oz. tacks by winding the twine around one tack once; then do the same around the other tack in the opposite direction. Hold the twine tight and drive the tacks down. Fig. 45-11a. If connecting links are used in place of the spring twine, the correct length may be determined by referring to Fig. 45-3.

For a softer seat, helical springs may be used. The helicals of the correct length are placed with the open end of the spring toward the inside of the frame. This prevents the sharp end from snagging the padding and cover. When all the helicals are in place, the open ends are closed with a pair of

45-10. A frame with springs installed. In this cutaway, connecting links and helical springs have both been used to tie the sinuous springs together. Notice also that rubberized hair and padding have been used as a cushion material.

pliers. The number of helicals used will in part determine the resiliency of the seat.

The outside sinuous springs are connected to the frame with a helical spring which can be nailed in place or attached by means of an offset plate or retainer plate. Fig. 45-11b and c.

Applying Burlap

Burlap is now tacked to the top edge of the frame over the springs. This prevents the padding from

45-11b. The helical springs on this frame are simply nailed to the rail.

45-11c. In this frame mock-up, the helicals have been attached to the frame with an offset plate. It retainer plates are used, do not allow them to project more than ½'' above the frame.

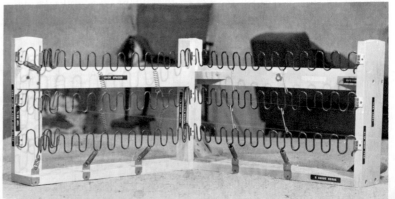

working down between the springs. When latex or plastic foam is used as padding, an insulator of cotton should be used to reduce the friction between the padding and the burlap.

Cut a piece of burlap 2″ to 3″ larger than the measurement of the seat or back. Place the burlap over the springs and smooth it out. Do not pull it taut; leave it loose enough to give with the action of the springs. Place a temporary tack at the center of the back, front, and each side. The burlap should overlap about 1″ or 1½″ on each side. Then tack it evenly around the frame. Fold the extra material over twice with the raw edge under and retack. Fig. 45-12.

Padding Seats with Cotton Felt

Generally speaking, three or four layers of cotton padding are sufficient on seats. The first layer should just cover the seat. Do not let it overhang on the sides or front. It need not be tacked or fastened. Apply it directly on top of the burlap.

Sometimes it may be advisable to use an additional insulating pad to take up the feel of the springs. A curled or rubberized hair is excellent for this. It comes in thicknesses of 1″ or 1½″ and in various densities. If this insulator is used, it should be placed on top of the burlap and sewn to the springs to keep it from moving. Put the curled hair side up. No more than two layers of cotton padding should be placed over a layer of curled hair. Fig. 45-10.

The second layer of cotton padding should be slightly larger

than the frame; let it overhang the sides about 1″. The front may come down about halfway on the rail.

If four layers are to be used, the third layer may overhang the sides about the same as the second layer. Let the last (third or fourth) layer come down near the bottom of the front rail. This, of course, depends on the style of the furniture. No felt should be placed under the bottom edge of the rail, as this makes it difficult to keep out dimples in the final cover at each tack. With the fingers, pluck off the edge of the felt to feather it out along the bottom edge of the rail and give it a smooth, tapered effect along the side of the rails.

Padding Backs with Cotton Felt

Two layers of cotton padding are generally enough in a back. However, if a soft insulator pad of rubberized hair is used, then one layer of felt may be sufficient. This again depends on the furniture style. The cotton padding on the back should come only about halfway around the side of the back, and then be feathered out as it was on the seat.

Padding with Foam

Padding with a foam, either rubber or plastic, will give the most comfortable seating and is probably the easiest method to use. Foam padding is applied over the burlap covered springs in the same manner as over the webbed pad seat described on page 449. Various thicknesses of foam may be used from ¼″ to 4″, depending

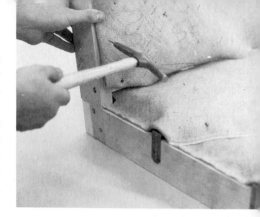

45-12. The seat of this frame has been covered with burlap and is ready for the padding.

on the seat of the chair. If foam is used on a back, it should always be soft density. The density customarily used on a seat will be too firm for a back.

When just a thin layer of foam is used, it should always be placed on top of all other padding, next to the cover. If cotton padding is placed over foam, it has a tendency to creep on the foam and will eventually cause a roll or unevenness in the seat.

Applying Cotton Muslin

In industry, cotton muslin is not used between the padding and the final cover. The final cover is usually applied directly over the padding. It is a good idea, however, to apply a covering of muslin before the final cover, especially when using loosely woven material, leather, or cut velvets for the final covering. The application of the muslin affords the beginner an excellent and inexpensive means of practicing the various cuts necessary to fit the fabric around the frame members. When the cotton padding is used, the muslin holds the padding in place and allows

45-13. This tight-spring seat has the cover applied, using the simple pull-over method. Note that there are no welts and the corners have been pulled, folded, and sewn.

the upholsterer to concentrate on doing a good job of applying the final cover.

The cotton muslin is cut large enough to allow the material to be pulled and tacked on the bottom edges of the seat rails and on the back edges of the back rails. A No. 6 upholstery tack is used to apply the muslin.

The cover is first tacked at the midpoint of each side and then worked (stretched) equally on all four sides away from these midpoints to within 2″ or 3″ of the corner. The corners are then folded under and tacked. The muslin is first slip tacked. This is a temporary tacking. The tacks are not driven all the way down. As the cover is pulled tight, the tack is removed by striking it on the side and "rolling it out," and another tack is driven in to hold the material after it is repulled. When the cover is pulled taut, the pull marks can be avoided by tacking halfway between the existing tack and the point where the hand is pulling the cover taut.

Final Cover

Selecting the material for the final cover is one of the most important decisions to be made in upholstering. The pattern, color, and texture of the material will affect the appearance and function of the final product. The final cover is usually the most expensive single item in upholstering. Because of its importance and expense, this material deserves great care and patience in selecting, laying out, cutting, sewing, and applying. Also, all the operations performed before applying the final cover need to be well done.

The appearance of the finished piece can be varied considerably by the method used to attach the final cover. The simple-pull-over cover, one that is not sewn or tailored, uses large pieces of fabric and gives the upholstered piece a heavier look than the other methods. Fig. 45-13. A second method is to sew a welt into the edge of the cushion. This connects the seat or back piece to the banding at the welt. Fig. 45-14. The third method uses a welt, but it is tacked to the frame rather than sewn into the cover. Fig. 45-15. This method has the advantage of making it possible to use slightly smaller pieces of fabric and does not require a sewing machine except to sew the welt.

Laying Out the Material

The amount of material required for the project can be determined by making a paper scale plan of the fabric and outlining the necessary pieces on this plan. (See Fig. 45-38e on page 470.)

45-14. This overstuffed chair has the welt sewn into the cushion at the junction between the band and seat. In tight-spring construction, when this method is used for attaching the cover, the bottom of the band is tacked under the frame and a welt is tacked along the bottom edge to simulate the cushion.

The warp threads run lengthwise of the goods; therefore the warp threads should run from front to back and top to bottom on a piece of furniture, whenever possible, to realize the greatest wearing potential. Also, when planning the cutting, allow ½″ for

45-15. The tight-spring construction in this seat has the seat cover sewn to the band with a welt at the junction. The band is then tacked near the top edge of the frame, with a welt tacked along this edge. A second band is blind tacked, then pulled and tacked to the bottom of the frame. The seat cover need not have a welt sewn in at the top edge.

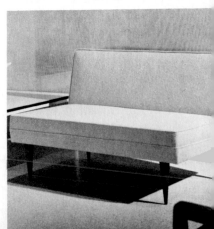

45-16. This chair has welt sewn into the cushion edge and tacked as trim along the joints between the fabric and chair parts.

lineal yard or fraction therof. The pieces can be moved and arranged on the 54″ scaled graph paper so that the least amount of cloth can be calculated.

By using this method, a complete cutting layout can be made that will save time when the cover is to be cut. This layout should be kept until the cover is marked and cut. Be sure to lay out the material so that the pattern direction on the seat is the same as the inside back. Cut the final cover to size according to the patterns and iron out the creases before it is applied.

Welt

Welt is a rolled edge that is used to hide a seam, to finish the edge of a cushion, or to trim the intersection of the parts of a piece of furniture. Fig. 45-16. Welt should be cut from the final cover about 1½″ wide and may be in short pieces that are sewn together to make a long piece. It should always be cut in the same direction, either along the side of the piece or across the width.

Sew the pieces of welting material into one long piece by laying them face to face and stitching them together ½″ from the end.

45-17. Joining short pieces of welt together on the sewing machine. When long pieces of banding are not available, the short pieces are sewn together at the corner of the furniture or cushion in the same way.

Fig. 45-17. With welt cord in one hand, place the cover around the cord and place it in the sewing machine, with the roll (made by the cord and cover) to the left of the needle. The machine has a groove in the welt foot that permits the cord to pass through, forcing the cover tightly around the cord to make a nice tight welt. Fig. 45-18. Welting can be sewn on a standard sewing machine with a zipper foot. Extra care will have to be taken to guide the work, however, when a welting foot is not available.

seams, 3″ for pulling and tacking the fabric, and enough strips 1½″ wide for welt. With a tape, measure the various parts of the padded frame. Allow for seams and pull tabs, and list the dimensions on a material bill form.

After the cover sizes have been established, lay these out to scale on paper. (Graph paper works well for this. Let each square represent 1″.) Then cut out the individual pieces and place them on another piece of graph paper that will be large enough to represent 54″ width. Upholstery cover comes 54″ wide and is sold by the

45-18. Sewing welt cord into the fabric. Note that the seam joining the pieces is laid flat. This prevents the cord from showing through.

457

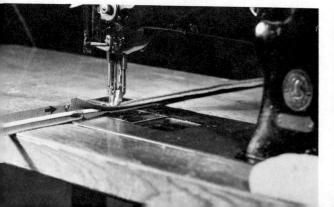

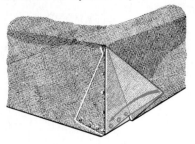

TACKED INSIDE AND
PINNED OUTSIDE.

TACKED 8 FOLD
BEING MADE.

45-19. The corner of the final cover is prepared for sewing.

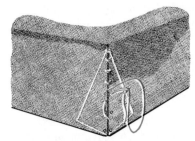

45-20. The corner is sewn from the top down, with stitches about ¼″ apart. Be sure to keep the stitches directly opposite each other.

Fabricating and Applying the Final Cover

METHOD A. The pull-over cover in Fig. 45-13, requires no machine sewing unless a welt is tacked along the bottom and back for trim. Be sure the cover is running in the proper direction. (This is important if the seat is almost square). Place the cover on the chair seat or back, centering it so as to have enough cover to pull over the side rails. Slip tack it in the center of the front. Pull it tight in the center of the back and slip tack it. Duplicate this operation on the sides. Continue pulling the cover down and working toward the outside corners. Be sure the cover is pulled tight enough. It may be necessary to remove tacks in the front or on the side and repull the cover tighter. The corners are always left till the last. Corners should be made so that the open side of the fold is to the side of the chair, not to the front.

To make a corner, divide the surplus material at the corner equally between the front and the side. Fold the material back under and tack the inside piece to the frame. Pull the top piece taut so the fold is right at the corner and pin it. Repeat this operation on the other half of the corner. Fig. 45-19. Stitch the corner with a curved needle and a nylon thread. Fig. 45-20. The color of the thread should match the background color of the fabric.

If the seat is thin, no corner fold will need to be made. A pull right on the corner should remove all fullness. Fig. 45-21. Some experimentation and practice will be necessary before nice corners are achieved.

METHOD B. Sewing a welt into the edge of the cushion requires a good commercial sewing machine and a degree of skill in its operation. Fig. 45-22. Before attempting to sew the final cover, some time should be spent practicing sewing welt, and sewing the band, cover, and welt together. Be sure also to practice turning some corners.

Cut the seat and back cover to the exact size of the frame plus ½″ for seams. Sew the necessary welting as described earlier. Lay the cover on the machine table,

45-21. This chair has several corners where the fabric has been pulled tightly for smoothness without hand stitching.

face up. Place the welt on top of the cloth, on the desired edge, with the raw edge of the welt facing the cut edge of the cloth, allowing ½″ for the seam. Move both pieces into position under the welting foot and sew the welt

45-22. In an upholstery factory these women are sewing welt and banding onto the final cover for a chair.

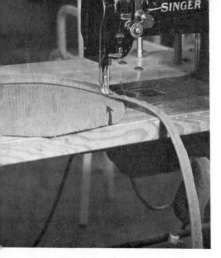

45-23. Sewing welt on a round cover.

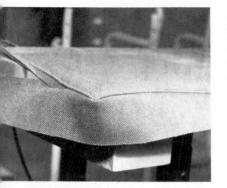

45-25. A welt sewn into the edge of a cushion with a square corner.

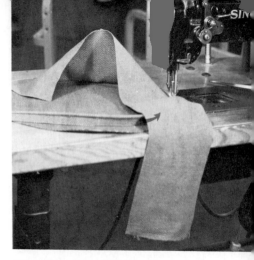

45-24. After the welt is sewn on the cover, then sew the band on the welt and cover.

to the cover. Fig. 45-23. Next, place the band to be sewn, face down on top of the first piece (or face to face). Again, line up the band with the edge of the first piece and the welt, allowing for the $\frac{1}{2}''$ seam. Sew the band in place from end to end. Fig. 45-24. When the cover is removed from the machine and opened up, a nice seam has been formed with the welt between the cover and the band. Fig. 45-25.

Note that some of these separate operations can be done at the same time, in a single operation, as one gains in experience and practice. Fig. 45-26. To sew a square corner in a cover as shown in Fig. 45-25, position the cover in the machine with the welt the same as described above. In the case of a loose cushion, the welt will be sewn onto the cover on all sides of the piece. When the cover is being sewn together for tacking to a padded frame, welt is sewn to three sides only. The fourth side or back tab of the seat and the bottom tab of the inside back is pulled between the junction of the seat and back, and is tacked to the appropriate rail. Always begin to sew several inches from the corner. When the corner is reached, which will be $\frac{1}{2}''$ back from the

edge of the cover, leave the needle down; then with scissors cut a notch in the back or raw edge of the welt about $\frac{1}{4}''$ to $\frac{3}{8}''$ deep. Be sure not to cut too deeply; otherwise the cut will show on the finished side. Fig. 45-27. Keep the needle down and raise the foot. Pivot the cover on the needle and bend the welt to make a 90-degree corner. With the hand on the sewing machine hand wheel, sew

45-27. When sewing the welt onto a cover with a square corner, stop the needle $\frac{1}{2}''$ from the corner and notch the welt before turning the corner.

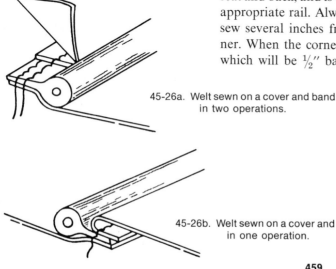

45-26a. Welt sewn on a cover and band in two operations.

45-26b. Welt sewn on a cover and band in one operation.

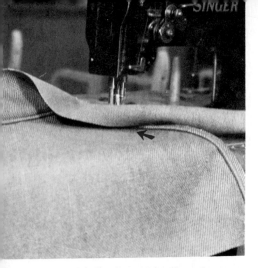

45-28. Sewing the band on the cover and welt. Method B.

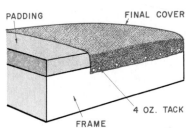

PADDING   FINAL COVER

4 OZ. TACK

FRAME

45-29. First step, Method C. The cover is pulled over the padding and tacked to the frame.

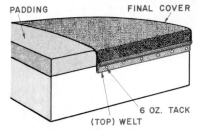

PADDING   FINAL COVER

6 OZ. TACK
(TOP) WELT

45-30. Second step, Method C. Tack the welt in place.

about two stitches along past the new corner. Now lower the foot and continue to sew normally. Fig. 45-28. The sewn cover is then pulled over the padding and tacked along the bottom and back. When tacking, be careful to keep the welt, sewn into the cover, parallel to the bottom and the back of the frame. Mark-off this distance on a piece of cardboard and use it as a gage to check the distance, making sure it is uniform all the way around.

METHOD C. This method of applying the cover is an excellent choice for the beginner. It usually is not necessary to hand sew the corners as described in Method A, and the sewing machine is used only to sew up a length of welting which is tacked on as a trim piece. The seat cover and the back cover are pulled taut and tacked in place as described in Method A, with the exception that the tacks are placed near the top edge of the frame. Fig. 45-29. Position the welt, usually on or near the top edge of the frame member; slip

tack a corner, pull the welt tight, and tack the opposite corner. Continue the welt on around the frame, being careful to keep it parallel to the bottom edge. Fig. 45-30. After the welt has been tacked in place, lay the banding so its face is against the top cover, with the edge to be tacked even with the raw edge of the welt. Tack one end. Pull gently on the other end and tack it in place. It may be advisable to place another tack in the center to be sure it is held in place. Cut a piece of tack strip long enough to reach from one side to the other. Tack one end of the strip in place, covering $\frac{1}{2}$" of the edge of the cloth. Pull gently and tack the other end. Place a tack in the center of the strip to keep it in line. With 10-oz. tacks, tack the strip about every inch. Turn the band back over the tack strip; pull the band taut and tack it in place on the bottom of the frame. Sometimes a piece of welt is also tacked along the bottom to finish off the edge. Fig. 45-31a–d; a, b, c shown here; d on the next page.

45-31c. Third step, contd. A second piece of welt is sometimes tacked under the frame for trim.

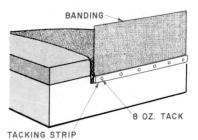

BANDING

8 OZ. TACK

TACKING STRIP

45-31a. Third step, Method C. The band is tacked on with a blind tacking strip.

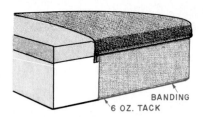

BANDING
6 OZ. TACK

45-31b. Third step, contd. The band is pulled over and tacked under the frame.

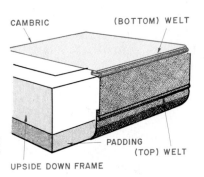

CAMBRIC   (BOTTOM) WELT

PADDING
(TOP) WELT

UPSIDE DOWN FRAME

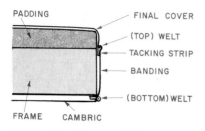

45-31d. Third step, contd. The cambric (dust cover) is tacked to the bottom of the frame.

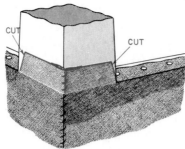

45-32. The cover is sewn at the corner and tacked to the bottom of the frame. Then the cover is cut at the junction between the leg and the rail.

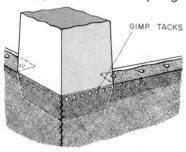

45-33. The cover is folded back under and tacked or glued in place.

Upholstering Around an Arm or Leg

If the legs are constructed so as to be a part of the frame, the final cover will have to be treated differently at these points. Hand stitch the corner as shown in Fig. 45-20, and cut the cover at the inside corner of the arm or leg. Fig. 45-32. Carefully fold the cover back under and tuck the edge down between the cover and the frame. Be sure to keep the folded edge in line with the edge of the frame. The cover may be glued or gimp tacks may be used to hold the cover in place. Fig. 45-33. If an arm is supported by a post coming up out of the front corner of the frame, the cover is cut and folded as described in Fig. 45-34. Should the arm post be built into the frame side rail, the final cover will be cut and folded as shown in Fig. 45-35, page 462.

Attaching the Outside Back

Take the piece of material cut for the outside back and lay it face down on the top of the inside back, centered from side to side. Allow about $\frac{1}{2}''$ of the edge to fall down the outside back below the top edge. Place a 6-oz. tack in one corner and pull gently on the

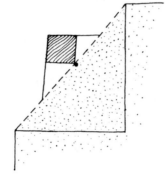

45-34a. Fitting a cover around a corner post. Place the cover on the seat and pull it tight. Fold the cover back as shown and mark the cover where it touches the post.

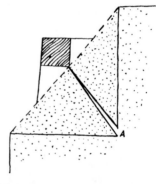

45-34b. Make a cut from point A to the mark made previously at the corner post.

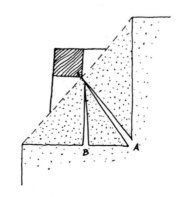

45-34c. Make a second cut from point B to within 1" of the mark made at the corner post.

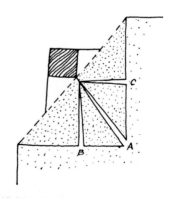

45-34d. Make a third cut from point C to within 1" of the mark made at the corner post.

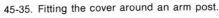
45-35. Fitting the cover around an arm post.

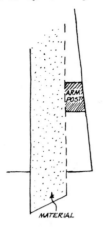

45-35a. Place the cover on the seat and pull it tight. Fold the material back as shown.

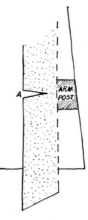

45-35b. Make a cut centered on the post, beginning at point A and cutting to within 1½" of the post.

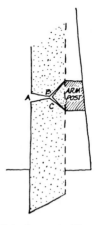

45-35c. Make two cuts (B and C) from the bottom of the first cut to the corners of the post. Fold the triangles back under and pull the cover down firmly past the post.

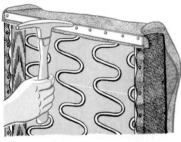

45-36. Tacking the outside back on with a tacking strip.

45-37. Pull the fabric down over the tacking strip and sew the back to the band at the corner. The needle is pulled through right at the fold in the cover material. Note also that the stitches are straight across from each other at the corner.

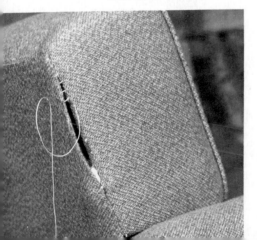

other corner. Now place a second tack in the opposite corner. Place a piece of tacking strip, cut to length, along the top edge and tack in place with 8-oz. tacks about 1" apart. Fig. 45-36. Next take the outside back cover and pull it back over the tacking strip. Pull the back cover taut and tack it under the bottom of the frame. Fold in the two edges about ½" to 1". Thread a 3" curved needle with a piece of colored nylon stitching thread to match the background of the cover material. Tie a knot in one end; begin sewing at the top and work toward the bottom. Take the first stitch from the inside to hide the knot in the end of the twine. Always bring the needle out through the folded edge of the cover. Pass the needle through the second piece of cover directly opposite the previous stitch. Move down under the fold about ¼" and come out through the face edge. Move directly across and pass the needle

through the other edge of the fold. Continue this, moving down about ¼" each time. Be sure to keep each stitch straight across from the previous stitch. Pull on the thread, and the two pieces of cover will pull together like a zipper. Do not stitch diagonally or the thread will show. Fig. 45-37.

Attaching the Bottom Lining

Use a cambric or a cheap denim as a bottom lining. Cut the piece about 2" larger than the actual size of the frame bottom. Fold the excess under and tack the center of the front, back and each side. Work toward the outside corners; pull just enough tension on the cambric to keep out wrinkles. For legs, make cuts similar to those made for arm posts. Figs. 45-34 and 45-35. When the cambric is tacked down, the chair should be complete. Figs. 45-38, 45-39, and 45-40 are suggested chair frame projects. See pages 463–475.

1. Obtain stock:
   a) Front seat rail and top back rail, 2 pieces, $1\frac{1}{8}''$ by $2\frac{3}{4}''$ by $21''$.
   b) Rear seat rail, 1 piece, $1\frac{1}{8}''$ by $3''$ by $21''$, rip 15-degree bevel on top and bottom edges.
   c) Seat side rail, 2 pieces, $1\frac{1}{8}''$ by $2\frac{3}{4}''$ by $23\frac{15}{16}''$; cut 15-degree angle on one end when cutting to length.
   d) Back side rails, 2 pieces, $1\frac{1}{8}''$ by $2\frac{3}{4}''$ by $21\frac{5}{16}''$; cut 15-degree angle on one end when cutting to length.
   e) Spring rail, 1 piece, $1\frac{1}{8}''$ by $1\frac{3}{4}''$ by $18\frac{3}{4}''$.
   f) Corner blocks, 8 pieces, $1\frac{3}{4}''$ by $2''$ by $4''$.
2. Cut $\frac{9}{16}''$ by $\frac{9}{16}''$ dadoes as per drawing on the front seat rail, back top rail, and rear seat rail.
3. Cut $\frac{9}{16}''$ by $\frac{9}{16}''$ rabbets in the seat and back side rails as per drawing. (NOTE: The location of this cut will determine the rights and lefts of these parts.)
4. Cut the half-lap joint in the ends of the seat and back side rails as per drawing (see detail No. 1 Fig. 45-38b).
5. Notch the end of the back side rails as per drawing.
6. Lay out and bore the dowel holes in the back side rails and the spring rail as per drawing.
7. Drill ($\frac{3}{16}''$) and countersink for No. 10 wood screws in the back side rails as per drawing.
8. Drill ($\frac{3}{16}''$) and countersink for No. 10 wood screws in corner blocks as per drawing.
9. Assemble the frames.
10. Spring the seat with 9-gage sinuous wire springs.
11. Spring the back with 11-gage sinuous wire springs.
12. Apply burlap.
13. Pad as desired.
14. Apply the muslin cover.
15. Apply the final cover. See fabric layout, Fig. 45-38e, page 470.

45-38a. Procedure for making chair frame.

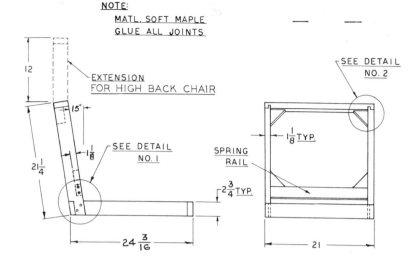

EXTENSION FOR HIGH BACK CHAIR

SEE DETAIL NO. 1

SEE DETAIL NO. 2

SPRING RAIL

$1\frac{1}{8}$ TYP.

$2\frac{3}{4}$ TYP.

CHAIR FRAME

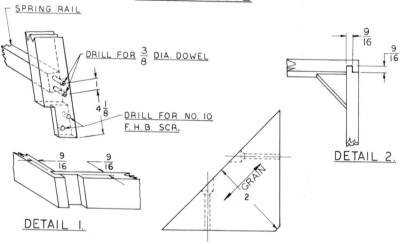

SPRING RAIL

DRILL FOR $\frac{3}{8}$ DIA. DOWEL

DRILL FOR NO. 10 F.H.B. SCR.

DETAIL 1.

CORNER BLOCK
6 REQD. $\frac{3}{4}$ THICK
2 REQD. $1\frac{1}{8}$ THICK

GRAIN

DETAIL 2.

45-38b. Chair frame drawings.

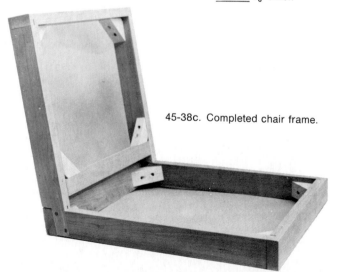

45-38c. Completed chair frame.

463

PROJECT NAME	DATE	FINISHED PIECES		ROUGH	FINISH	T	W	L	SCALE 1"=1"	NO.	OPERATION PROCEDURE
CHAIR FRAME		PER UNIT 6				T 2	W 7/8	L 4		1	Cut to rough length
ASSEMBLY 1	PARTS USED	MATERIAL PINE				T 1 3/4	W 3/4	L 4	CK BY:	2	Surface to thickness
										3	Rip to width
										4	Cut to finish size-45°
										5	Bore 2--3/16" diameter holes countersunk

CORNER BLOCK

NOTE: 2 PCS. 1⅛ THICK

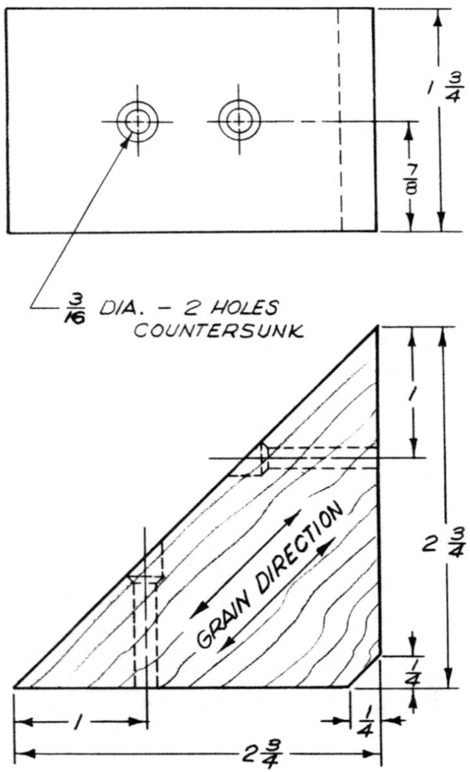

3/16 DIA. - 2 HOLES COUNTERSUNK

GRAIN DIRECTION

1 3/4   7/8   2 3/4   1   1/4   2 3/4   1

45-38d. Route sheets for chair frame.

PROJECT NAME CHAIR FRAME	DATE	FINISHED PIECES PER UNIT 2	ROUGH	T /⁴	W 2⁷⁄₈	L 22	SCALE —=1″	NO.	OPERATION PROCEDURE
ASSEMBLY 2	PARTS USED	MATERIAL SOFT MAPLE	FINISH	T /⁸	W 2³⁄₄	L 21	CK BY:	1	Cut to rough length
								2	Surface to thickness
								3	Rip to width
								4	Joint to finish width
								5	Cut to finish length
								6	Cut 9/16″ x 9/16″ dado both ends

BACK TOP AND FRONT SEAT RAIL

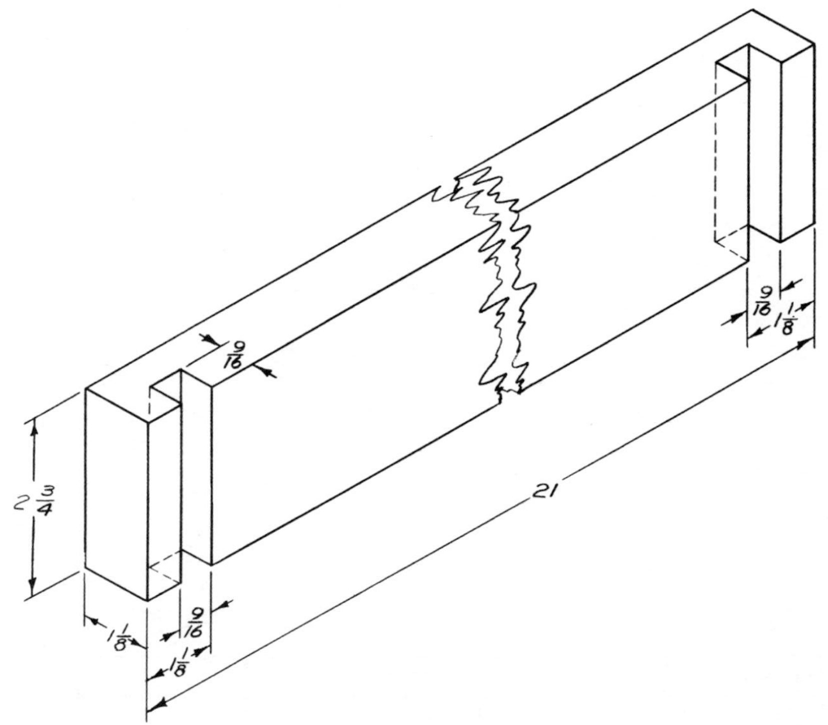

45-38d cont'd.

465

PROJECT NAME CHAIR FRAME	DATE	FINISHED PIECES PER UNIT 2 (1R & 1L)	ROUGH	T 1/4	W 2 7/8	L 24 1/2	SCALE 6"=1'
ASSEMBLY 3	PARTS USED	MATERIAL SOFT MAPLE	FINISH	T 1/8	W 2 3/4	L 23 5/8	CK BY:

NO.	OPERATION PROCEDURE
1	Cut to rough length
2	Surface to thickness
3	Rip to width
4	Joint to finished width
5	Square one end
6	Cut 9/16" × 9 1/6" rabbet on squared end
7	Cut to length at 15° cut
8	Make shoulder cut at 15°
9	Make cheek cut

SEAT RAIL – RIGHT SIDE

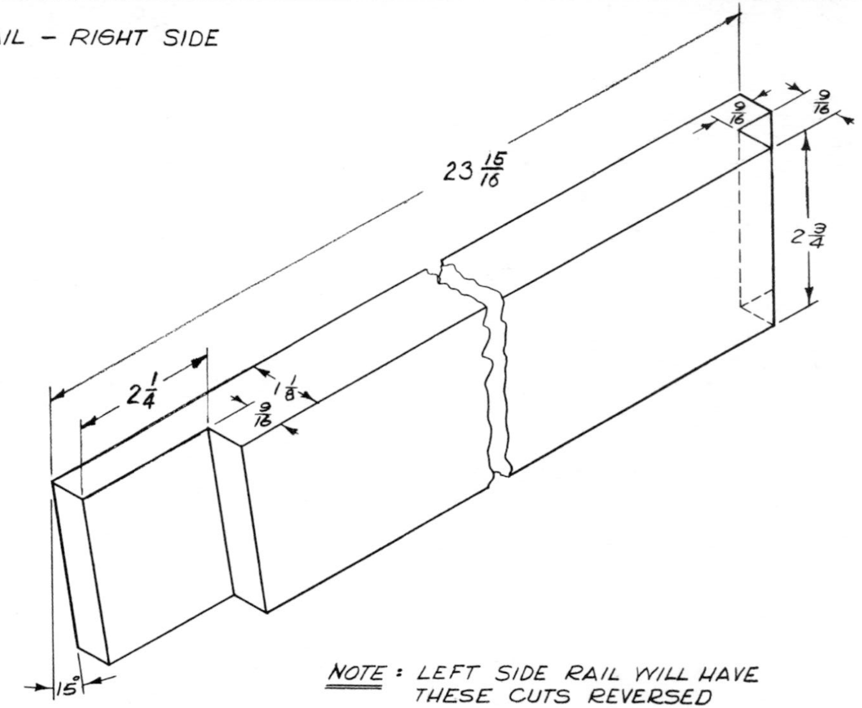

9/16

2 3/4

9/16

23 15/16

1/8

9/16

2 1/4

15°

NOTE : LEFT SIDE RAIL WILL HAVE
THESE CUTS REVERSED

45-38d cont'd.

PROJECT NAME CHAIR FRAME	DATE	FINISHED PIECES PER UNIT 1		ROUGH	T $\frac{1}{4}$	W $3\frac{1}{8}$	L $21\frac{1}{2}$	SCALE	NO.	OPERATION PROCEDURE
ASSEMBLY 4	PARTS USED	MATERIAL *SOFT MAPLE*	FINISH		T $1\frac{1}{8}$	W 3	L 21	CK BY:	1	Cut to rough length
									2	Surface to thickness
									3	Rip to width
									4	Cut to length
									5	Cut 9/16" x 9/16" dado. Both ends
									6	Cut 15° bevel, both edges
									7	Joint to finished width

REAR SEAT RAIL

NOTE 15° ANGLE

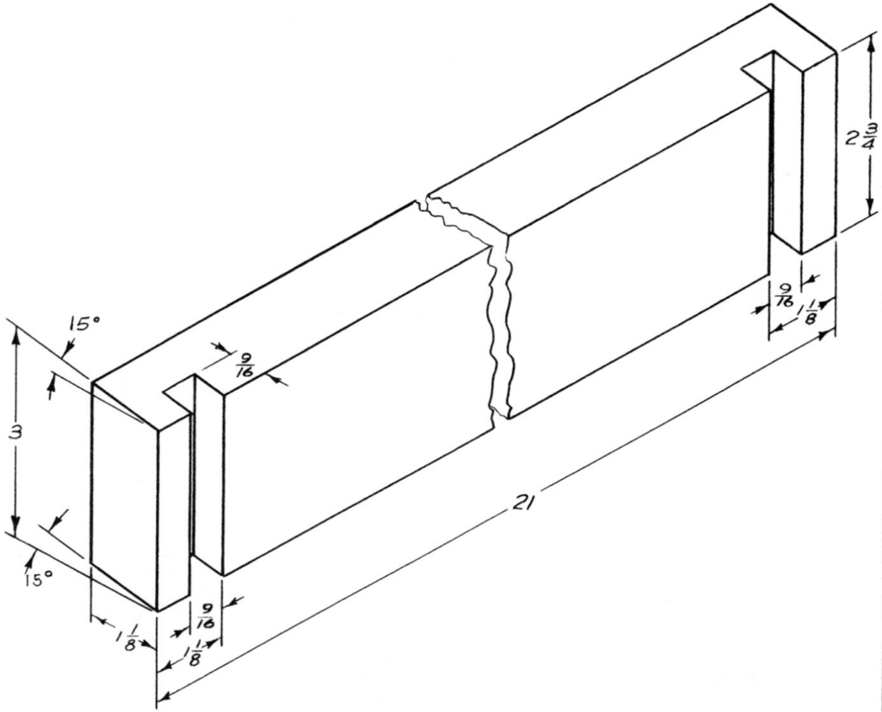

2 $\frac{3}{4}$

$\frac{9}{16}$ 1 $\frac{1}{8}$

21

$\frac{9}{16}$

$\frac{9}{16}$ 1 $\frac{1}{8}$

15°

15°

3

1 $\frac{1}{8}$

45-38d cont'd.

467

PROJECT NAME *CHAIR FRAME*	DATE	FINISHED PIECES PER UNIT 2 (1R & 1L)	ROUGH	T $\frac{1}{4}$	W $2\frac{7}{8}$	L 22	SCALE	NO.	OPERATION PROCEDURE
ASSEMBLY 5	PARTS USED	MATERIAL SOFT MAPLE	FINISH	T $1\frac{1}{8}$	W $2\frac{3}{4}$	L $21\frac{5}{8}$	CK BY:	1	Cut to rough length
								2	Surface to thickness
								3	Rip to width
								4	Joint to finish width
								5	Square one end
								6	Cut to length with 15° cut
								7	Cut 15° angle shoulder cut, 9/16 deep
								8	Cut cheek cut 2 3/4" deep
								9	Cut cheek cut 2 3/4" deep
								10	Cut 15° angle shoulder cut 1 1/8" deep
								11	Cut rabbet on top 9/16" x 9/16"
								12	Drill 2—3/8" diameter holes for dowels
								13	Drill 2—3/16" diameter hole for #10 FH screw

BACK SIDE RAIL — RIGHT

NOTE 15° ANGLE
OVERALL LENGTH 21 5/8

NOTE : LEFT — BACK SIDE RAIL WILL HAVE THESE CUTS REVERSED

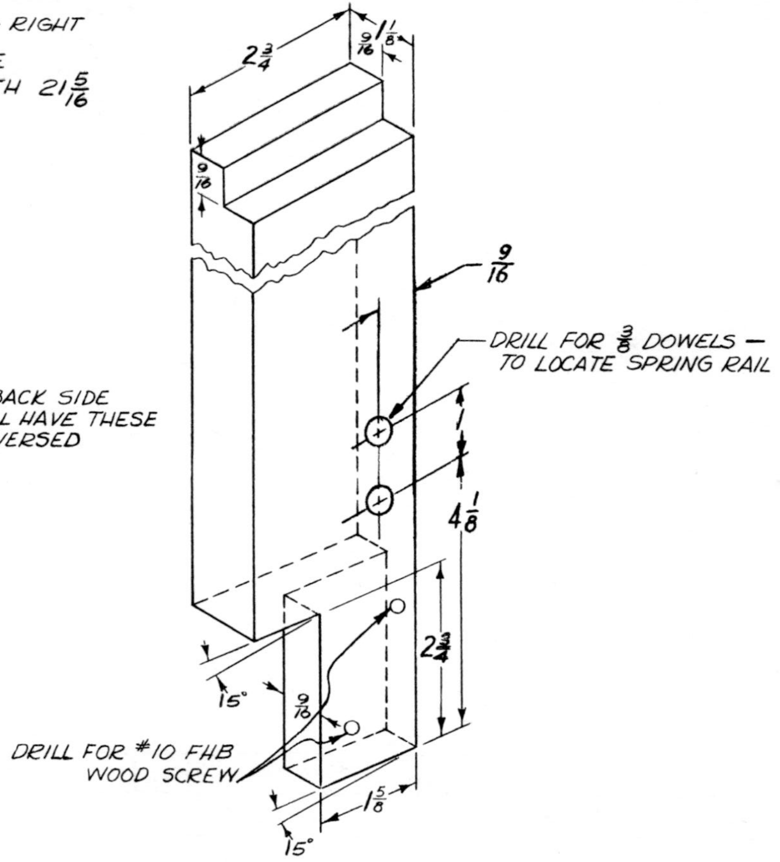

DRILL FOR $\frac{3}{8}$ DOWELS — TO LOCATE SPRING RAIL

DRILL FOR #10 FHB WOOD SCREW

45-38d cont'd.

PROJECT NAME CHAIR FRAME	DATE	FINISHED PIECES PER UNIT 1	ROUGH				SCALE 1/4"=1"
ASSEMBLY 6	PARTS USED	MATERIAL SOFT MAPLE		T	W	L	CK BY:
			FINISH	T 1/8	W 3/4	L 18 3/4	
				T 1/4	W 7/8	L 19	

NO.	OPERATION PROCEDURE
1	Cut to rough length
2	Surface
3	Rip to width
4	Cut to finish length
5	Bore 2--3/8" diameter holes 1 1/4" deep, both ends

SPRING RAIL

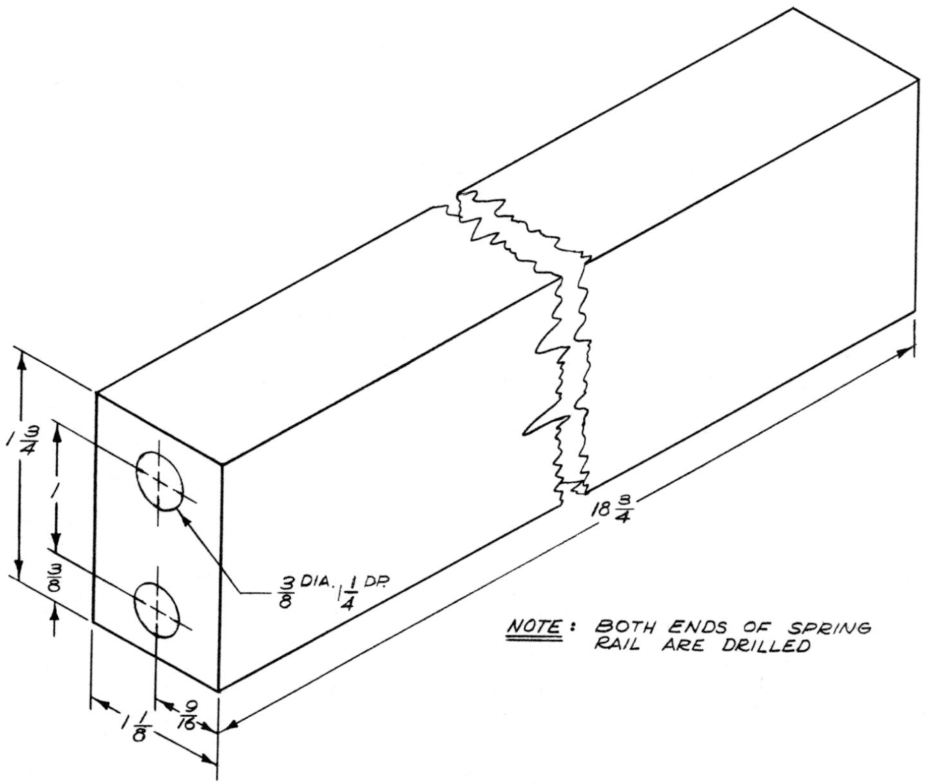

$18\frac{3}{4}$

$\frac{9}{16}$ $\frac{1}{8}$

$\frac{3}{8}$ DIA. $\frac{1}{4}$ DP.

$1\frac{3}{4}$ 1 $\frac{3}{8}$

NOTE: BOTH ENDS OF SPRING RAIL ARE DRILLED

45-38d cont'd.

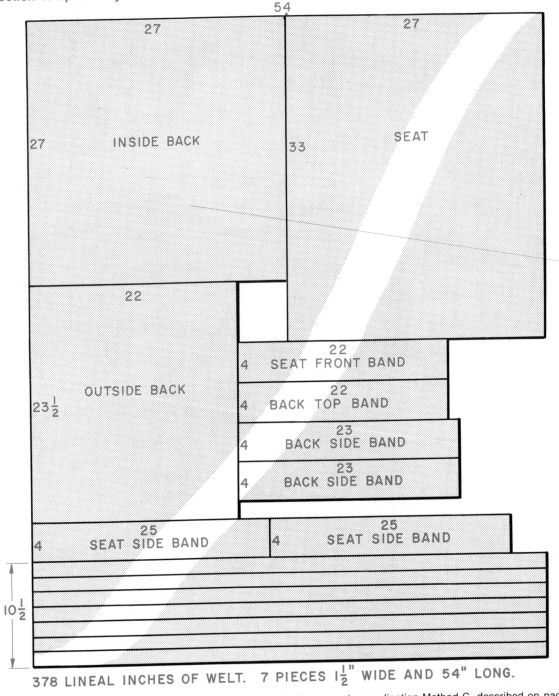

54

| 27 | 27 |

27   INSIDE BACK   33   SEAT

22

OUTSIDE BACK

23½

22
4   SEAT FRONT BAND

22
4   BACK TOP BAND

23
4   BACK SIDE BAND

23
4   BACK SIDE BAND

25
4   SEAT SIDE BAND

25
4   SEAT SIDE BAND

10½

378 LINEAL INCHES OF WELT. 7 PIECES 1½" WIDE AND 54" LONG.

45-38e. Fabric layout. This is the cutting layout for the final cover using application Method C, described on page 460. This layout indicates that 65" or 1⅞ yards of 54" material is required to cover the chair.

45-39b. Colonial style chair made with same basic frame shown and discussed in Fig. 45-38.

45-39a. Contemporary style chair made with same basic frame shown and discussed in Fig. 45-38.

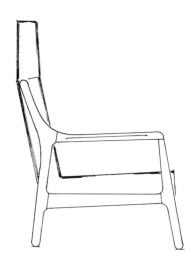

45-39c. Profile drawings of high and low back chairs made with same basic frame shown in Fig. 45-38.

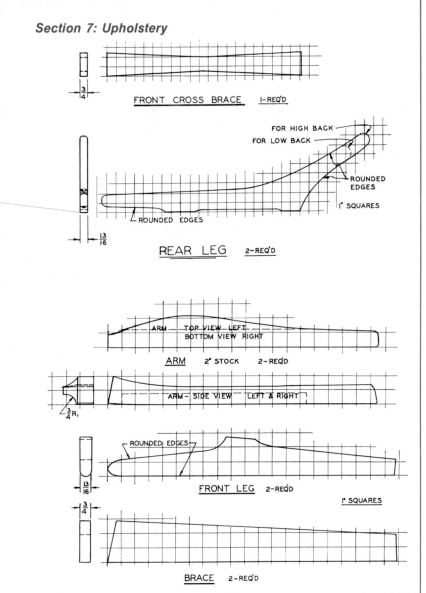

FRONT CROSS BRACE   1-REQ'D

REAR LEG   2-REQ'D

ARM   2" STOCK   2-REQD

FRONT LEG   2-REQD

BRACE   2-REQ'D

45-39d. Detail drawings of arms and legs for use with frame in Fig. 45-38.

3. Joint and plane all stock to finished thickness as per drawings. (When machining the arms, maintain maximum thickness from the 2″ stock.)
4. Joint one edge square to a working face on all stock.
5. Trace the patterns on to the stock. (NOTE: Align the straight edges of the patterns with the jointed edges on the stock. This edge may then be used against the miter gage on the circular saw when cutting the angles on the ends of the arms, leg braces, and front brace. In the case of the legs, place the edge of the pattern which will be joined to the arm and leg brace on the jointed edge of the stock to insure good dowel joints.)
6. Band-saw the legs and leg braces to size.
7. Joint the front edge of the front leg straight.
8. Place this jointed edge of the front leg against the miter gage and cut the angle on the top end of the leg.
9. Cut the angles on the ends of the leg braces and arms.
10. Band-saw the side profile of the arm to the desired contour.
11. Replace the sawn piece on the top of the arm and insert a couple of nails next to the edge which will be sawn off (keeping the nails away from the line on which you will saw).
12. Band-saw the top profile of the arm to the desired contour.
13. Shape the underside of the arm. If this is done on a shaper, place the jointed edge on the shaper table with the flat bottom surface against the fence.
14. File and sand all edges and surfaces as necessary.
15. Shape all rounded edges as per drawing on the front and rear legs.
16. Lay out and bore all dowel holes at right angles to the surface in which they are bored. (NOTE: The

The Procedure

1. Obtain stock: (rough dimensions) arms, 2 pieces, walnut, 2″ by 2¼″ by 20″; leg brace, 2 pieces, walnut, 1″ by 3″ by 21″; front legs, 2 pieces, walnut, 1″ by 3″ by 21″; (high back chair) rear legs, 2 pieces, walnut, 1″ by 8½″ by 29½″; (low back chair) rear legs, 2 pieces, walnut, 1″ by 8½″ by 27″; and front cross brace, 1 piece, walnut, 1″ by 2¾″ by 21½″.
2. Lay out and cut patterns to size.

45-39e. Procedure for making and installing arms and legs on basic chair frame shown in Fig. 45-38.

leg brace is joined to the leg flush on the inside of the assembly. This will leave a $\frac{1}{16}''$ shadow line (offset) on the outside. There are two $\frac{3}{8}''$ dowels at each joint except where the arm attaches to the front leg. Use one $\frac{1}{2}''$ dowel for this joint.)

17. Glue and clamp the two arm and leg assemblies together.

18. Clamp the arm and leg assembly to the upholstered frame. Adjust it as necessary to obtain the most comfortable position. Mark and cut the front brace to length. (This will give you the correct allowance for the fabric thickness on each side of the chair.)

19. Position the front brace tightly under the chair frame and between the front legs, and lay out the dowel holes.

20. Locate and lay out the position of the $\frac{1}{4}''$ by $2\frac{1}{4}''$ FH stove bolt in the rear leg near the base of the chair frame.

21. Locate and lay out the position of the $1\frac{1}{4}''$ No. 10 FH wood screw near the top of the rear leg.

22. Counterbore and drill all holes for the bolts and screws.

23. Bore two $\frac{3}{8}''$ dowel holes in each end of the front brace and on the inside of the front legs.

24. Band-saw the front brace to the desired contour, and file and sand as necessary.

25. Glue and clamp the two arm and leg assemblies together with the front brace.

26. Finish-sand as necessary.

27. Apply an oil finish.

28. Place upholstered frame in the arm and leg assembly and attach with bolts and screws.

29. Locate and drill for two $2\frac{3}{4}''$ No. 10 FH wood screws through the bottom of the front brace and into the upholstered chair frame.

30. Plug the bolt and screw counterbored holes in the arm and leg structures and apply oil finish to the plugged areas.

45-40a. Chair with loose cushions.

IMPORTANT: All dimensions are *finished* size.

No. of Pieces	Part Name	Thickness	Width	Length	Material
2	Back Legs	$1\frac{1}{4}''$	$4\frac{5}{16}''$*	$31\frac{1}{8}''$	White Oak
2	Side Rails	$1\frac{1}{4}''$	$3\frac{1}{8}''$	$28\frac{7}{8}''$	White Oak
1	Front Rail	$1\frac{1}{4}''$	$1\frac{3}{4}''$	$24\frac{1}{2}''$	White Oak
1	Back Rail	$1''$	$3\frac{1}{2}''$	$22''$	White Oak
1	Top Rail	$1\frac{1}{4}''$	$1\frac{1}{4}''$	$23''$	White Oak
2	Arms	$1\frac{1}{4}''$	$1\frac{3}{4}''$	$22''$	White Oak
2	Front Legs	$1\frac{1}{4}''$	$2\frac{1}{8}''$	$20\frac{1}{4}''$	White Oak
2	Seat Frames — Front and Back	$1''$	$2\frac{1}{4}''$	$22\frac{3}{4}''$	White Oak
2	Seat Frames — Side	$1''$	$2\frac{1}{4}''$	$20\frac{1}{8}''$	White Oak
8	Spindles	$\frac{1}{2}''$ dia.		$10\frac{1}{8}''$	Dowel
1	Rung	$\frac{3}{4}''$ dia.		$23\frac{1}{2}''$	Dowel
1	Cleat	$\frac{3}{4}''$	$1\frac{1}{4}''$	$22''$	Hardwood
1	Cleat	$\frac{3}{4}''$	$1\frac{1}{4}''$	$16''$	Hardwood
2	Corner Blocks	$1''$	$3''$	$3''$	Hardwood
2	Batten Strips	$\frac{1}{4}''$	$1''$	$9\frac{1}{2}''$	White Oak
16	Dowels	$\frac{3}{8}''$ dia.		$2''$	Hardwood
4	Dowels	$\frac{1}{2}''$ dia.		$2''$	Hardwood

24 yds. 2" Wide Webbing
8 No. 8 x $1\frac{1}{2}''$ F. H. Wood Screws
10 No. 10 x $1\frac{1}{2}''$ F. H. Wood Screws
2 3" x 21" x 22" Flat Foam Rubber Cushions
Brads and Tacks

* *Two legs can be cut from standard 8" board.*

45-40b. Bill of materials for chair shown in 45-40a.

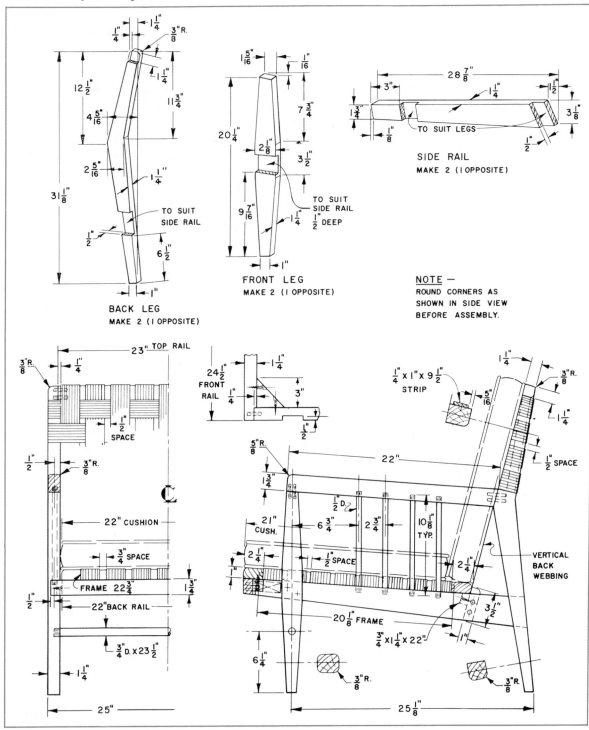

45-40c. Working drawings for chair.

1. Lay out and cut back legs on band saw. Dress front edges on jointer and back edges on disc sander.
2. Cut all other pieces to size on circular saw.
3. Cut tapers on front legs and side rails with taper jig on circular saw. Cut necessary angles and bevels on ends of these pieces, and on top and bottom edges of front rail and seat frame cleats, on circular saw.
4. Locate and bore all dowel, rung and spindle holes.
5. Make trial assembly of front leg, arm and back leg. Place this assembly on side rail and mark cross lap joints on front leg and side rail, and on back leg and side rail. Set up dado head on circular saw and cut these joints. Notch top end of back legs and ends of front rail.
6. Round necessary corners and edges of arms, legs, top rail and back rail with a spindle shaper, or with a file and sandpaper. Sand smooth.
7. Glue up side assemblies.
8. Glue rung, front, back and top rails in place with side assemblies. Drill and countersink screw holes in corner blocks and install.
9. Cut tongue and groove joints on seat frame members and assemble with glue. Round edges with a shaper, or with hand router or file and sandpaper. Sand all pieces smooth.
10. Finish sand entire project and apply finish.
11. Stretch and nail webbing to seat frame and chair back. Install batten strips.
12. Drill and countersink screw holes in seat frame cleats. Install one cleat over webbing on back rail and one over webbing on seat frame to keep it from sliding forward.
13. Make up or purchase cushions, or use chair without cushions, as desired.

45-40d. Procedure for constructing chair.

DISCUSSION TOPICS

Section Seven-UPHOLSTERY

Unit 41. Forms of Upholstering

1. Explain why the upholstering trade would be one of the most difficult to automate.
2. What makes it possible for an inexperienced person to realize a degree of success in such a highly skilled trade as upholstering?
3. List some things you could make that would involve some upholstering.
4. What are the three basic forms of upholstery?
5. How can a pad seat be made more comfortable?
6. What determines the comfort of a tight spring seat?
7. Which is the most comfortable form of upholstery? Explain why.
8. What can be used in place of springs in a cushion?

Unit 42. Upholstering Tools

1. How does an upholsterer's tack hammer differ from the regular carpenters hammer?
2. What are the two styles of tack hammers?
3. What kind of work is the ripping tool usually used for?
4. Why must the upholsterer be careful not to bend the point on the regulator?
5. Why do some upholsterers needles have a point on each end?
6. What are skewers?
7. Name the two types of webbing stretchers.
8. Why would it be necessary to have two types of webbing stretchers in an upholstery shop?
9. What is the best method for cutting sinuous springs to length?
10. Why must the sinuous spring ends be bent after they are cut to length from a coil?
11. Which of the two spring stretchers is most effective? Why?
12. What is the most important machine to the upholsterer?

Unit 43. Upholstering Materials

1. What kind of wood is recommended for upholstery frames. Why?
2. Name four woods that could be used for making frames.
3. Why are the edges on the frame rounded?
4. List three cushion materials.
5. What is edge roll?
6. What are two kinds of tacking strips?
7. What is a tacking strip used for?
8. Tell why muslin is usually used by the beginner in upholstery.
9. Name the material that is used as a covering over webbing or springs as a support for the cushion.
10. What gage sinuous springs are used for backs.
11. There are many styles of clips available for springing a frame with sinuous springs. Which one is used most often?
12. Why are there two kinds of helical springs?
13. Name a good substitute for tailor's chalk.
14. Why is nylon thread used for hand stitching?

15. Describe the difference between an upholstery tack and a webbing tack.

16. Which kind of welt cord gives the smoother, more pliable edge on a cushion?

17. What is another name for cotton padding?

18. What style of furniture is rubber webbing usually used on?

19. How does the selection of the final cover affect the appearance of the furniture on which it is installed?

Unit 44. Making a Pad Seat

1. Name the three kinds of edges used when applying foam rubber, and describe how they differ.

2. Describe briefly the steps in covering a pad seat with the final cover.

3. Describe three kinds of bases used for pad seats.

4. What is used to lubricate the scissors when cutting foam rubber?

Unit 45. Upholstering with Sinuous Springs

1. What are some of the trade names for sinuous springs?

2. Describe how the sinuous spring is measured? How can this be dangerous?

3. Why are sinuous springs tied?

4. What is the most comfortable padding to use when upholstering a piece of furniture?

5. What is slip tacking?

6. When laying out the final cover, what are the allowances for seams and pull tabs?

7. What is a pull tab?

8. Describe the three methods, discussed in the text, for applying the final cover.

9. What is usually the last step in upholstering a piece of furniture?

Problems and Activities

Section Seven

1. Study the history and development of upholstering and its relationship to the social and economic conditions of the times. Write a report.

2. Study the development of some upholstery materials, such as cushioning or springs. Write a report on how new materials have influenced the upholstery industry.

3. Write a report on the manufacture of some upholstery material. Discuss the manufacturing processes and the kinds of skills needed by the workers.

4. Make some mock-ups or samples of many of the operations performed by the upholsterer.

Mass Production

Large, complicated machinery is needed for mass production. A multiple cut-off saw of the type shown here will trim long boards into short pieces, cut large-size sheets, and make a large number of grooves or dadoes with ease and precision. The operation and set-up of this type of equipment in a computerized furniture plant of the future will require skilled craftsmen with a technical background. (Mereen-Johnson Machine Company)

46 Mass-Producing Furniture

The two largest industries in which wood is the prime raw material are residential building and furniture production. Residential building is part of the construction and manufacturing industry while furniture production is part of the manufacturing world. Furniture is produced in less volume than automobiles, but it still represents one of the major areas of mass production.

The 50 largest furniture companies in the United States produce over one-third of all the case goods, one-quarter of the upholstered goods, and over 50 percent of all the metal furniture. Most furniture manufacturers are located in the South Atlantic states and in the East, North, and Central areas of the United States. Fig. 46-1.

A major problem faced by furniture manufacturers is the rising cost of labor, raw materials, plant equipment, advertising, and selling expenses. Another difficulty is that a wide variety of styles in all furniture pieces must be produced. Some large manufacturers, for example, make products in Early American, English, French Provincial, Italian Provincial, and Spanish designs. Other manufacturers concentrate on only one style, such as Early American or Colonial, but even these may make 250 to 300 different items, including as many as 50 kinds of tables, 20 kinds of chairs, and a wide variety of case goods.

While the major material used in the furniture industry today is still wood, there is an increasing use of plastics and metals. Improvements in plastics technology have provided the furniture industry with plastic molded components which serve as wood substitutes for some furniture parts. Sculptured panels and trim of molded plastic, which closely resemble wood, are being produced. Improved plastic finishes, veneers, plastic laminates, and wood-grain plastic coverings allow the production of an attractive, more durable product. Research continues on processes that impregnate woods with plastics and then subject them to irradiation to improve quality. Plastic-treated wood and plastic laminates can give superior strength to a furniture piece and help make it resistant to burns, scuff marks, and scratches.

All mass production involves two major steps:
- The production of a large number of parts of identical size and quality. Fig. 46-2.
- The assembly of these parts on some type of production line. Fig. 46-3.

There are several distinct differences between mass production in the automotive industry and in the furniture industry. In the first, only a few basic body shells are used to permit greater automation. For example, as many as a million cars of one brand name may be manufac-

46-1. Persons with many different abilities are needed in a modern furniture factory. Those shown here work on the design and development of furniture pieces.

46-2a. Many kinds of furniture pieces, such as those shown here, are mass-produced in quantities ranging to thousands.

46-2b. These furniture parts are produced in large quantity to a high standard of accuracy. Parts like these may be shipped to several manufacturers of finished furniture pieces.

tured, each with the same body shell. By contrast, in furniture manufacturing there are a great many different styles and designs. Also, furniture is less complicated as to the number of parts, kinds of materials used, and the precision involved in its manufacture.

Elements of Furniture Manufacturing

Production Facilities

The manufacture of wooden furniture is done in two basic types of factories or plants. The first is sometimes called the *case goods* or *bedroom* furniture plant. Here, all-wood or almost all-wood pieces, such as case goods, chairs with no upholstery, tables, chests,

46-3a. Part of a production line for the manufacture of cedar chests.

46-3b. Sub-assemblies of chairs produced in large quantities.

479

46-4a. Wood furniture parts on stock carts.

46-4c. Assembling furniture, using a power stapler.

and bedroom sets, are made. Fig. 46-4. The second basic type of plant specializes in *upholstered pieces*. In the case-goods type, much more automated equipment is needed and the mass-production operation is more complex. In plants where much upholstery is done, production is less automated since only the frames are made of wood and much more hand work is involved. Fig. 46-5. (Other types of plants specialize in plastic and metal furniture and are not of concern in a woodworking course.)

Management

To be able to produce furniture, it is necessary to have a company or organization. There are approximately 5,500 plants in the United States that produce household furniture. However, over two-thirds of these employ fewer than twenty people. The smaller companies usually are privately owned businesses or are operated as partnerships. Large companies are established as corporations, with many *stockholders*. (People who own shares of a corporation's stock are called stockholders. They are actually the

46-4b. Machining duplicate parts in a furniture factory.

46-4d. Production finishing on an assembly line.

owners of the corporation.) In the large companies, the stockholders select the board of directors. This board, in turn, hires a management group that is responsible for making such important decisions as what products to make, how many to produce, and how to sell the products.

Other Personnel

People with many different skills are needed to produce furniture. These include designers, engineers, drafters, skilled cabi-

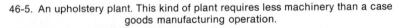

46-5. An upholstery plant. This kind of plant requires less machinery than a case goods manufacturing operation.

netmakers, semi-skilled production workers, millwrights, and many others. Those who work as designers and engineers usually must be college graduates. Often the factory workers must be high school graduates. Many become skilled workers by starting as apprentices.

Capital

Capital is the money that is invested in buildings, machines, tools, materials, wages, and other things necessary to make the product.

In the furniture industry, even small companies require fairly large plants. This is because of the bulky raw material and the need for storage of parts and assembled goods. Large modern companies invest in a great deal of automated equipment for mass production.

Materials

As mentioned, the materials for furniture making are primarily wood and manufactured wood materials such as plywood, particle board and hardboard, Fig. 46-6, although increasing amounts of metals and plastics as well as upholstery materials are being used.

From Idea to Market

Nearly all modern furniture manufacturers follow similar planning, production, and marketing procedures. The total operation can be divided into five basic steps: *market research, product design and development, production control, manufacturing,* and *marketing.* These steps are explained in the discussion which follows.

1. *Market Research.* A survey is made by the sales and marketing staff to determine what the trends are in furniture design, what items sell best, what woods are most desirable, and what are the most popular finishes. Management, along with sales people and designers, must determine the general style that will be produced. Fig. 46-7. Frequently, trips are made to see if furniture retailers would like to purchase this kind of product.

2. *Product Design and Development.* Most companies begin the production of a piece of furniture with pictorial sketches showing several variations of proposed pieces to be manufactured. These sketches are usually *isometric, cabinet,* or *perspective* drawings. Fig. 46-8. Small companies that cannot afford full-time designers may hire an outside professional designer on a contract basis. Larger companies have a designing staff including specialists in furniture upholstery, finishing, color coordinating, and similar assignments.

The proposed designs are then discussed by management, which has final approval. Among things that affect this decision are what the production costs are, what the sale price will be, and how much profit can be made. For any product, management must know the exact costs involved. Three main factors must be considered:
- *Materials* costs.
- *Labor* costs.
- A combination of *overhead* and *profit.*

46-6. Stockpiling rough lumber that will be used to produce furniture.

46-7. This man is responsible for choosing the design for a new piece of furniture to be produced.

Materials costs can be quite easily established, provided there isn't an excessive amount of waste. Labor costs are also carefully analyzed. Overhead refers to the fixed cost of running the business. In addition to these items, management must do its best to make sure that a profit will be made on the items that are manufactured. An analysis must be made of the total cost and how it can be reduced through careful planning or through minor design changes.

46-8. Typical sketches that might be developed by a designer as the first step in furniture production.

For example, plastic legs may have to be substituted for hand-carved wooden legs.

Once a final design is approved, the sketch is made into an orthographic projection drawing, usu-ally having two views. Full-size drawings are used, particularly for products that involve curved and irregular-shaped parts. In this way the final shape can be easily seen. At this point, the engineers and designers determine the materials needed, the processes to be followed, the standard of quality, and many other factors.

There are two basic ways of getting the drawings ready—

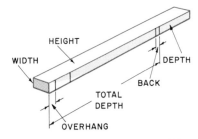

46-9. A simple rod used in building cabinets for a kitchen. All the measurements for width, height, and depth would be marked on three sides of this rod.

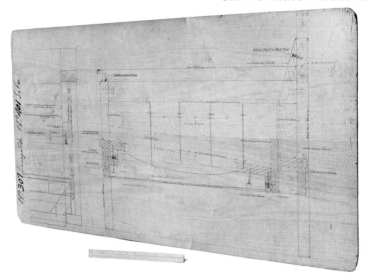

46-10a. The device shown here is also called a rod. It is a drawing on a panel, to show an original design of a chair. All details are drawn in full scale. This type of rod is used when there are curved parts. The rod takes the place of prints and is used for laying out and cutting. Note its size in comparison with the 12″ rule.

namely *rod* and *route sheet.* Some small companies still place measurements on wooden *rods.* There are two types of rods:

● One type of rod consists of a smooth stick of wood on which the actual sizes of parts are laid out on three sides. One side is used for the *width,* another for the *depth,* and a third for the *height.* This type of rod is most commonly used in simple cabinetmaking such as kitchen cabinets. Fig. 46-9.

● The other type of rod has a full scale drawing of the furniture piece on the surface of a smooth piece of wood. Fig. 46-10.

The main idea behind both types of rods is to eliminate errors in measurement. When rods are used, the actual piece of material can be placed against or on the rod to check its dimension.

Few large companies make use of rods because of the difficulty of keeping track of the rod as the pieces move through the production process. Instead, they utilize route sheets which are similar to a plan of procedure. Fig. 46-11. A separate route sheet is made for each individual furniture part, with a drawing or sketch at any scale that is convenient to fit the paper. Fig. 46-12. In addition to the drawing, the route sheet lists the procedures that must be completed for that part as well as such other information as cost and number of parts to be produced. These route sheets are used throughout the manufacture of the part and actually follow the parts along as they are processed.

Once the drawing and route sheets are completed, they are sent to sample or experimental rooms where enough parts are made to produce several sample furniture pieces. These are sometimes called *pilot cuttings.* (Large plants have separate sample plants that produce a few new furniture pieces that can be shown at furniture marts.) One of these

46-10b. Chair shown in the rod drawing.

sample pieces is usually put together without glue by designers and engineers, to check for errors. Another piece is often assembled and left in white wood (without a finish). Once the sample is approved, production may start.

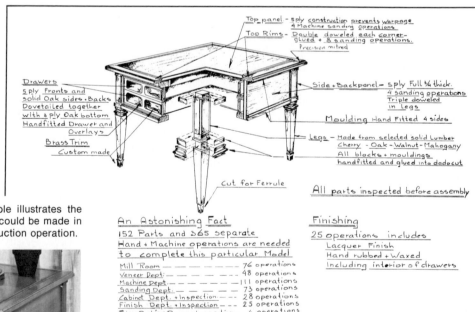

ITEM NO.		NAME OF PART		
NO. PIECES		MAT.		
		LENGTH	WIDTH	THICKNESS
ROUGH				
NET				
NO.		OPERATION		
CHECKED BY			SCALE	
DRAWN BY		DATE	DRAWING NO.	

46-11. A route sheet that could be used in a school lab.

46-12a. This end table illustrates the kind of product that could be made in a school mass-production operation.

Top panel - 5 ply construction prevents warpage 4 Machine sanding operations

Top Rims - Double doweled each corner - glued + 8 sanding operations. Precision mitred

Drawers 5 ply fronts and solid Oak sides + Backs Dovetailed together with ½ ply Oak bottom Handfitted Drawer and Overlays

Brass Trim Custom made

Side + Backpanel - 5 ply Full ¾ thick. 4 sanding operations Triple doweled in legs

Moulding Hand Fitted 4 sides

Legs - Made from selected solid Lumber Cherry - Oak - Walnut - Mahogany All blocks + mouldings handfitted and glued into dado cut

Cut for Ferrule

All parts inspected before assembly

An Astonishing Fact
152 Parts and 365 separate Hand + Machine operations are needed to complete this particular Model

Mill Room	76 operations
Veneer Dept.	48 operations
Machine Dept.	111 operations
Sanding Dept.	73 operations
Cabinet Dept. + Inspection	28 operations
Finish Dept. + Inspection	25 operations
Trim + Packing Room + Inspection	4 operations
	365 operations

Finishing
25 operations includes
Lacquer Finish
Hand rubbed + Waxed
Including interior of drawers

46-12b. Pictorial drawing showing construction. This is one of 22 similar drawings that would be used for mass-producing the end table.

484

Stock No.	105 105-3	Amt.			Job No.	18-144
Pcs. in one	16		500 cherry		Item No.	14
Part	Fill block in Posts.					

	Mah.		S. Maple		Chipcore	
1000	Cherry		Birch			
	Walnut		Oak			

ROUGH SIZE	LENGTH 20	WIDTH 5/8	THICK 4/4	NET SIZE —	LENGTH	WIDTH 3/8 1/32	THICK 13/16

Routing	Check off	pcs. in job	8000 Blocks
Cut	1		
Face	2		
Rip	3		
Stick Square	4		
Plane			
Veneer			
Size			
Cut Net + Mitre	7		
Moulding Sand			
Sand 3 dr. 2 sides	5		
Polish 2 sides	6		

46-12c. Selected route sheet for certain parts of the end table.

46-13. Fully machined parts manufactured by a hardwood dimension plant to be shipped to another plant for use in final furniture production.

46-14a. Using a drilling jig. Notice that this jig both holds the stock in place and guides the drill.

However, more samples are sometimes made to test the market before the piece goes into full production.

3. *Production Control.* After a design has been tested, plans are made to produce the item in the main plant. Production Control must deal with all the problems involved in actually manufacturing the product. Some large manufacturers start with raw lumber and produce all of their own solid and veneer stock. Others have found it less expensive to purchase machined parts from hardwood dimension plants. Fig. 46-13. Items such as hardboard and particle board are also purchased from other plants. In addition, manufacturers must purchase such items as hardware, finishing material, and upholstery material.

Before production can start, the planner must also develop the necessary specialized devices needed for manufacturing. These include the following:

● A *jig* is used to hold and locate a piece of work and also to guide, control, and limit the cutting tool. A drilling jig is a good example. Fig. 46-14a.

485

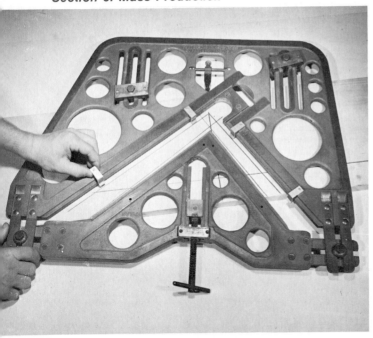

46-14b. A fixture used in assembling frame parts.

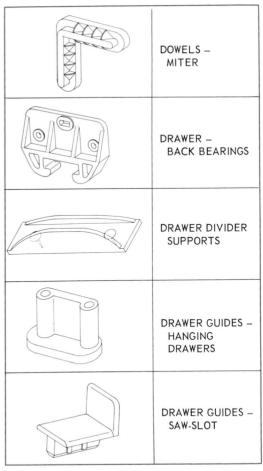

	DOWELS – MITER
	DRAWER – BACK BEARINGS
	DRAWER DIVIDER SUPPORTS
	DRAWER GUIDES – HANGING DRAWERS
	DRAWER GUIDES – SAW-SLOT

46-16. Dies are needed to make these plastic parts which are used in furniture production.

46-15a. A gage used to measure the thickness of paint.

● A *fixture* is a work-holding device that is used on a machine for making duplicate parts. A fixture does not guide the tool. Sometimes the words "jig" and "fixture" are used interchangeably, although a fixture holds the work in a fixed relationship to the cutting tool but does not guide the cutting tool as does the jig. Fig. 46-14b.

● A *gage* is an instrument for measuring or checking a part before, during, or after it has been manufactured. There are two types of gages—*measurement* and *fixed*. A micrometer, for example, is a measurement gage, while a

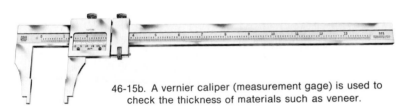

46-15b. A vernier caliper (measurement gage) is used to check the thickness of materials such as veneer.

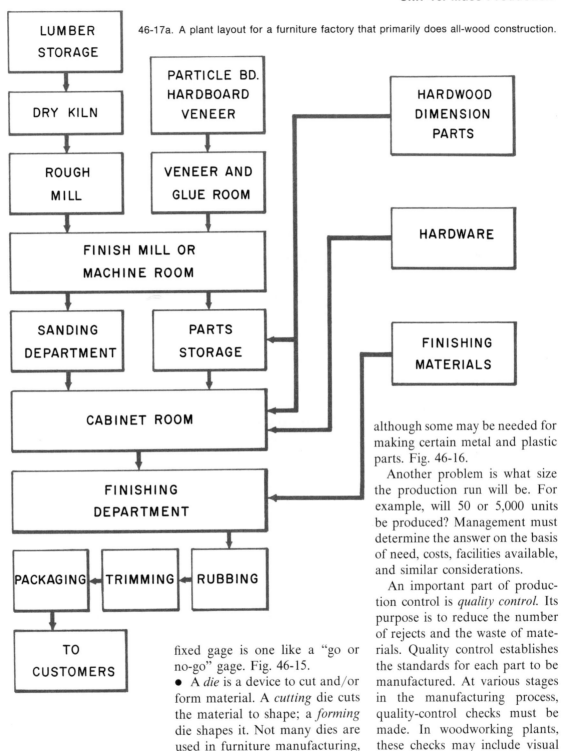

46-17a. A plant layout for a furniture factory that primarily does all-wood construction.

although some may be needed for making certain metal and plastic parts. Fig. 46-16.

Another problem is what size the production run will be. For example, will 50 or 5,000 units be produced? Management must determine the answer on the basis of need, costs, facilities available, and similar considerations.

An important part of production control is *quality control*. Its purpose is to reduce the number of rejects and the waste of materials. Quality control establishes the standards for each part to be manufactured. At various stages in the manufacturing process, quality-control checks must be made. In woodworking plants, these checks may include visual

fixed gage is one like a "go or no-go" gage. Fig. 46-15.

● A *die* is a device to cut and/or form material. A *cutting* die cuts the material to shape; a *forming* die shapes it. Not many dies are used in furniture manufacturing,

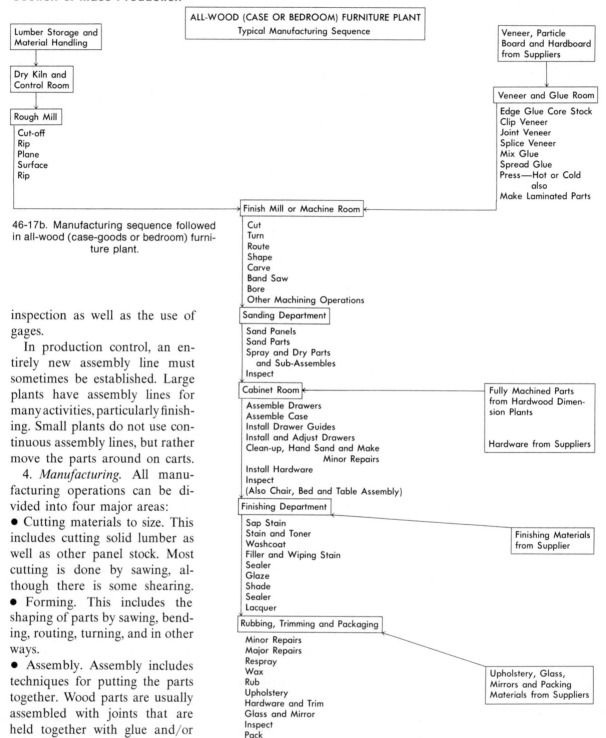

ALL-WOOD (CASE OR BEDROOM) FURNITURE PLANT
Typical Manufacturing Sequence

Lumber Storage and
Material Handling

Dry Kiln and
Control Room

Rough Mill
Cut-off
Rip
Plane
Surface
Rip

Veneer, Particle
Board and Hardboard
from Suppliers

Veneer and Glue Room
Edge Glue Core Stock
Clip Veneer
Joint Veneer
Splice Veneer
Mix Glue
Spread Glue
Press—Hot or Cold
    also
Make Laminated Parts

Finish Mill or Machine Room
Cut
Turn
Route
Shape
Carve
Band Saw
Bore
Other Machining Operations

Sanding Department
Sand Panels
Sand Parts
Spray and Dry Parts
  and Sub-Assembles
Inspect

Cabinet Room
Assemble Drawers
Assemble Case
Install Drawer Guides
Install and Adjust Drawers
Clean-up, Hand Sand and Make
                Minor Repairs
Install Hardware
Inspect
(Also Chair, Bed and Table Assembly)

Fully Machined Parts
from Hardwood Dimen-
sion Plants

Hardware from Suppliers

Finishing Department
Sap Stain
Stain and Toner
Washcoat
Filler and Wiping Stain
Sealer
Glaze
Shade
Sealer
Lacquer

Finishing Materials
from Supplier

Rubbing, Trimming and Packaging
Minor Repairs
Major Repairs
Respray
Wax
Rub
Upholstery
Hardware and Trim
Glass and Mirror
Inspect
Pack
Ship

Upholstery, Glass,
Mirrors and Packing
Materials from Suppliers

46-17b. Manufacturing sequence followed in all-wood (case-goods or bedroom) furniture plant.

inspection as well as the use of gages.

In production control, an entirely new assembly line must sometimes be established. Large plants have assembly lines for many activities, particularly finishing. Small plants do not use continuous assembly lines, but rather move the parts around on carts.

4. *Manufacturing.* All manufacturing operations can be divided into four major areas:

● Cutting materials to size. This includes cutting solid lumber as well as other panel stock. Most cutting is done by sawing, although there is some shearing.

● Forming. This includes the shaping of parts by sawing, bending, routing, turning, and in other ways.

● Assembly. Assembly includes techniques for putting the parts together. Wood parts are usually assembled with joints that are held together with glue and/or some kind of metal fastener.

• Finishing. Finishing includes all processes necessary to give the product a good appearance and to protect it. Most furniture finishing is transparent, although some opaque materials such as paints and enamels are used.

The actual organization of a manufacturing plant and the production sequence followed is determined somewhat by what kind of plant it is. Also, the size of the plant affects actual production practices. In an *all-wood* (case goods or bedroom) furniture plant, the general procedure is as follows: Fig. 46-17, pages 487, 488.

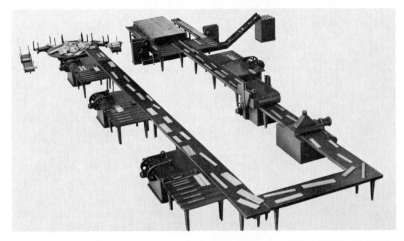

46-18a. This rough mill system is typical of equipment used in a furniture factory for production economy. With the machines and conveyors shown, rough stock is cut to length, surfaced, ripped, and sorted. With this system seven men can do the work formerly done by 16.

46-18b. Schematic drawing of the rough mill system. Notice how the system is kept within minimum space by having the stock turn two right-angle corners.

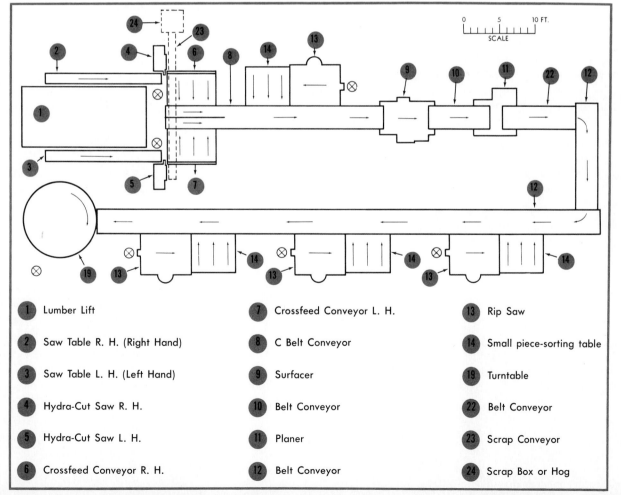

1 Lumber Lift	7 Crossfeed Conveyor L. H.	13 Rip Saw
2 Saw Table R. H. (Right Hand)	8 C Belt Conveyor	14 Small piece-sorting table
3 Saw Table L. H. (Left Hand)	9 Surfacer	19 Turntable
4 Hydra-Cut Saw R. H.	10 Belt Conveyor	22 Belt Conveyor
5 Hydra-Cut Saw L. H.	11 Planer	23 Scrap Conveyor
6 Crossfeed Conveyor R. H.	12 Belt Conveyor	24 Scrap Box or Hog

46-18c. Here you see the stock going first into the surfacer and then into the planer on a conveyor system. This photograph shows numbers 9 and 11 on the schematic drawing, Fig. 46-18b.

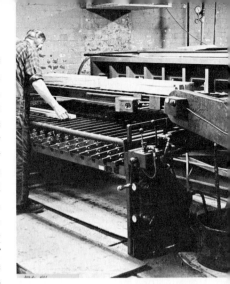

46-19a. Electronic gluing of core stock.

Raw lumber is brought to the plant site and *stored* in the open air or under a shed for air drying. Next it is brought into a *dry kiln* where it is conditioned to the proper moisture content, usually from 6 to 8 percent. From the dry kiln the lumber is moved into the *rough mill* where it is processed into dimensioned stock by cutting, ripping, surfacing, and planing. Fig. 46-18. Some of this dimension stock is moved into the *veneer and glue* room. Veneer, particle board and hardboard also go into the *veneer and glue* room, where the manufacturer actually makes the plywood parts needed. Sometimes plywood is made with a lumber core. Fig. 46-19. At other times particle board is used for the core. Curved and laminated parts are also produced in this area. Fig. 46-20.

Since most furniture contains both solid lumber and veneer or plywood, both of these must go into the *finish mill* or *machine room*. Solid material is cut, shaped, routed, and otherwise formed for items such as legs, rails and other solid parts. Fig. 46-21.

46-19b. Glue spreader for making plywood.

46-19c. Tapeless veneer splicer for joining veneers in making plywood.

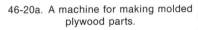

46-19d. Electronic gluing of panels and frames.

46-20a. A machine for making molded plywood parts.

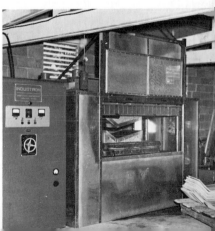

46-20b. Molded plywood parts being removed from electronic gluing equipment.

46-21a. Multiple-spindle boring machine.

46-21b. Double-spindle shaper being used on solid wood parts.

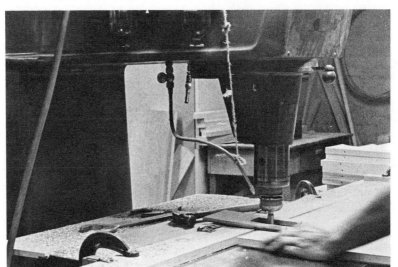

46-21c. Industrial router.

46-21d. Thickness planer.

46-22a. Sanding on a pneumatic-bag sander.

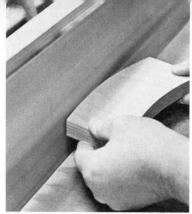

46-22b. Edge belt sanding.

46-23a. Drawer assembly. Note that the multiple dovetail joint is used at all corners.

46-23b. Assembling the sides of a chair.

46-23d. Lines of chests moving on conveyor from final assembly to finishing room get a critical inspection.

Plywood is used for tops and sides of chests, inserts for case goods, and similar items. Materials are then moved into a *sanding department* where all preliminary sanding is done. Fig. 46-22. For some pieces, simple spraying and drying of parts are also done. At times, more parts are made than are needed, and the extras are stored in the *cabinet room* as white wood (unfinished) until they are needed. The parts are inspected (quality control) at each step of production. First the sub-assemblies, such as a drawer assembly, are put together and, finally, the entire product is assembled, including the hardware. Fig. 46-23. From here the product moves to the *finishing* department, where the hardware is removed and then all of the steps necessary to apply the finish are done. Fig. 46-24. Often separate departments are established for such activities as *rubbing, trimming,* (installing glass, mirrors, etc.) *upholstering,* and *packaging.* Fig. 46-25.

5. *Marketing.* The marketing operation involves such matters as accounting, advertising, sales, and service.

46-23c. Doing final sanding and touch-up.

46-24a. Applying sealer to the inside of drawers on an assembly line.

492

46-24b. Applying top coat in the finishing process.

Mass Production in the School Lab

In deciding whether or not to establish a mass-production line for a product, the class must first determine what to make and why. One way of approaching the problem is to organize a company to produce an item for sale. This procedure would involve selling stock to shareholders, electing directors, establishing management, doing production, and providing

for sales and marketing. Another way of mass-producing is to have the class agree on a basic product such as a commode that each would like to take home.

The square commodes were all made on the same production line. Fig. 46-26. The variations for the many styles were made by changing the design of the door, not using shaped edges (Contemporary style); using a heavier shaper cut and building up the thickness of the top (Spanish style); and using different woods. Styles of furniture are usually identified with a particular species of wood and finish. Italian Provincial style cabinet was made of cherry, with a rubbed lacquer and lightly distressed fruitwood finish. To alter it for Spanish style, the cabinet was made from oak with an open-pore, heavily distressed, dark oak finish. The Modern cabinet was made from walnut with an open-pore, natural oil finish. See pages 494–497.

46-25a. Hand rubbing a finish.

46-25b. Applying tacks in upholstering a wood chair.

46-25c. Packaging a chair for shipment.

46-26a. Drawing of a square commode. (Note: Complete plans for mass-producing this commode are included in a set of transparency masters prepared for use with this book and available from the publisher.)

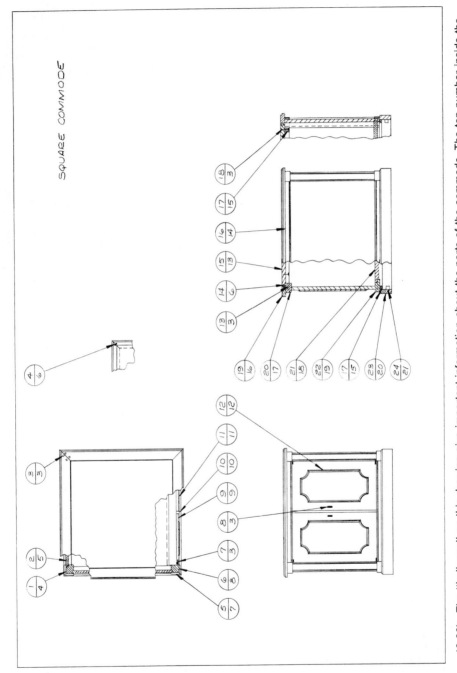

46-26b. The "balloons" on this drawing give important information about the parts of the commode. The top number inside the balloon corresponds to the part number in the column at left on the materials list (Fig. 46-26c). The bottom number tells which of the route sheets shows this particular part. For example, the side and back panels are part No. 2 on the materials list, and their construction is described on route sheet No. 5 (Fig. 46-26d).

ITEM NO.: 200		ITEM NAME: Commode													
NO. OF ITEMS TO BE PRODUCED:															
PART		REQ.	TOTAL REQ.	MAT'L.	ROUGH			FINISH			BD. FT. PER PIECE	TOTAL BD. FT.	TOTAL COST	REMARKS
NO.	NAME				T	W	L	T	W	L				
1	Rear Corner Posts	2		Cherry	8/4	2	18¼	1 3/4	1 3/4	17 3/4	.507	1.014		
2	Side & Back Panels	3		Cherry Veneer	9/16	20	18	9/16	19¼	17 3/4	2.57	7.71		3 pcs. from one 18 x 60 1/2" core; .560" fin.
3	Dowel Pins	8		Maple	3/8		1							
4 & 14	Top Spline	4		Oak	1/4	1/2	19½	3/16	3/8	19	.017	.068		
5	Corner Post Fill Strip	16		Cherry	1/2	1¼	2¼	3/8	1	1 15/16	.010	.16		
6	Front Corner Posts	2		Cherry	8/4	2	18¼	1 3/4	1 3/4	17 3/4	.507	1.014		
7	T. V. Hinges	2pr		#260										
8	Door Pulls	2		#119										
9 & 11	Doors	2		Cherry Veneer	3/4	9 3/4	17	3/4	9 5/16	15 13/16	1.3	2.6		9 pieces from 30 x 60 5/8" core; .685" fin.
10	Door Strip	1		Cherry	4/4	5/8	16½	13/16	1/2	15 13/16	.072	.072		
12	Front Panel	2		Cherry Veneer	5/16	7	13½	5/16	6 3/8	12 3/4	.328	.656		
13	Magnetic Catch	1		#9793PT										
15	Top Panel	1		Cherry Veneer	11/16	20	20	11/16	19 3/4	19 3/4	3.06	3.06		3 pcs. from 20 x 60 5/8" core; .685" fin.
16	Accent Strip	6		Cherry	5/4	1¼	19¼	¼	1	Fit	.209	1.25		
17	Base Support	7		Bass	4/4	3/4	23	3/4	3/4	20 7/8	.120	.48		
18	Wood Screws	28		F.H.B.	#8 1¼									
19	Top Rails	4		Cherry	4/4	2¼	26	3/4	2	24	.406	1.62		
20	Top Door Rail	1		Cherry	5/4	2¼	20	1	1 3/4	18 3/4	.703	.703		
21	Bottom	1		Cherry Veneer	7/16	20	21¼	7/16	19 7/8	21	2.98	2.98		3 pcs. from 60 x 22 3/8" core; .439" fin.
22	Bottom Dr. Rail	1		Cherry	5/4	3	20	1	2¼	18 3/4	.521	.521		
23	Base Rail	4		Cherry	4/4	2 3/4	24 3/4	3/4	2¼	23½	.473	1.89		
24	Corner Block	4		Bass	4/4	1	Random	3/4	1	1	.005	.02		

46-26c. Materials list for the commode.

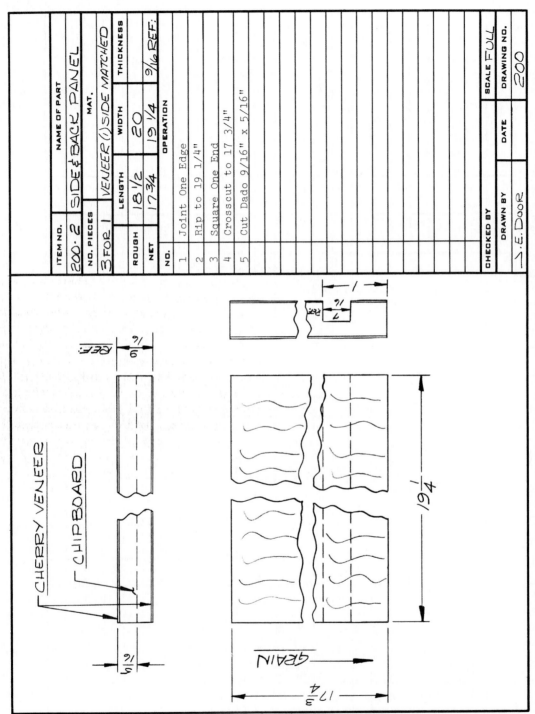

ITEM NO.	NAME OF PART		
200.2	SIDE & BACK PANEL		
NO. PIECES	MAT.		
3 FOR 1	VENEER (1) SIDE MATCHED		
	LENGTH	WIDTH	THICKNESS
ROUGH	18 1/2	20	9/16 REF.
NET	17 3/4	19 1/4	
NO.	OPERATION		
1	Joint One Edge		
2	Rip to 19 1/4"		
3	Square One End		
4	Crosscut to 17 3/4"		
5	Cut Dado 9/16" x 5/16"		

SCALE FULL
DRAWING NO. 200
CHECKED BY
DRAWN BY J. E. DOOR
DATE

46-26d. Route sheet for the side and back panels of the commode. Construction details are shown in the drawing, and step-by-step instructions are given for producing the panels. Note that the item is listed as No. 200-2. The 200 is simply a code number used to identify the commode, for the manufacturer's purposes. The 2 indicates that this is part No. 2 on the materials list (Fig. 46-26c).

ITEM NO.	NAME OF PART					
200·20	TOP DOOR RAIL					
NO. PIECES	MAT.					
1 FOR 1	CHERRY					
		LENGTH	WIDTH	THICKNESS		
	ROUGH	20	2 1/4	5/4		
	NET	18 3/4	1 3/4	1		
NO.	OPERATION					
1	Saw to Rough Length					
2	Joint and Surface to 1"					
3	Rip and Joint to 1-3/4"					
4	Shape (3/32" Rad. Bead)					
5	Saw to Finished Length 18-3/4"					
6	Bore Dowel Holes					

CHECKED BY				SCALE *FULL*
DRAWN BY	DATE			DRAWING NO.
D. E. DooR				*200*

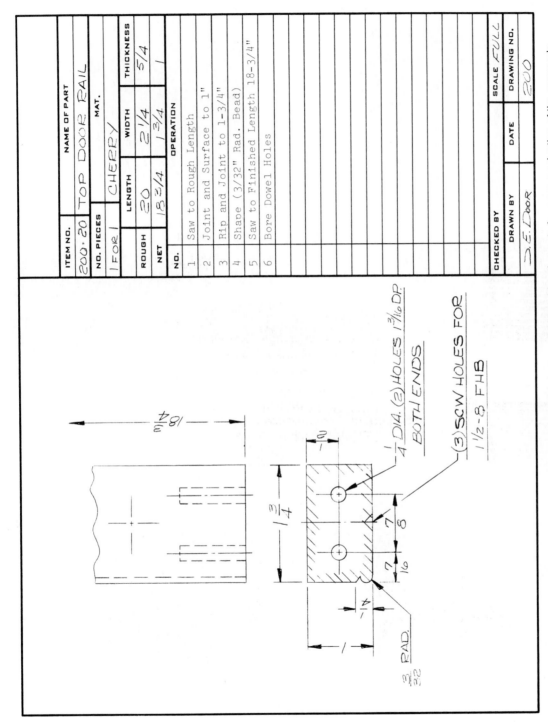

46-26e. Route sheet for top door rail. Twenty-one route sheets are used in making the parts for mass production of the commode.

497

46-27. Here you see how the style of the commode can be altered through relatively minor production changes. a. Italian Provincial (walnut). b. Italian Provincial (cherry). c. Spanish or Mediterranean. d, e, and f. Contemporary styles. g. Colonial.

46-28a. Jig for cutting short pieces to length and mitering in one operation.

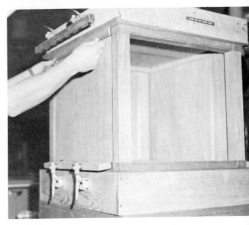

46-28b. Fixture for assembling the commode.

ments can be made to move the parts in logical manner from raw material through the manufacturing process, including assembly, finishing, and inspection areas.

Personnel must be chosen to do each of the jobs and to supervise the overall manufacturing process. Some determination must be made as to how long each operation will take and how many persons are needed for each aspect of production. If the product is to be sold, the price must be arrived at, allowing for raw materials, labor costs, overhead, and profit. However, if each class member is to take home a product, then only the cost of materials need be considered.

Many kinds of products can be mass-produced in the school lab. See Fig. 46-29 for one excellent suggestion, pages 500–505.

As can be seen in Fig. 46-27, the many cabinet styles are quite different, even though most of the machining operations were identical to facilitate the mass production of a class project. To carry out such an operation in your class an analysis must be made to determine the operations involved. Route sheets must be developed for each part of the product. Tooling up for production must be undertaken, including making the necessary jigs and fixtures and other special tools and devices. Fig. 46-28. Orders for materials must be placed and methods of storing and handling the materials established. In the average school shop, some type of rolling cart or pallet must be used to move the parts around. Another matter that must be considered is that of plant layout. While the school laboratory cannot be reorganized into a production line for each new product, arrange-

46-29a. This coffee table would make an attractive and useful addition to many homes. It would be relatively simple to mass-produce in the school.

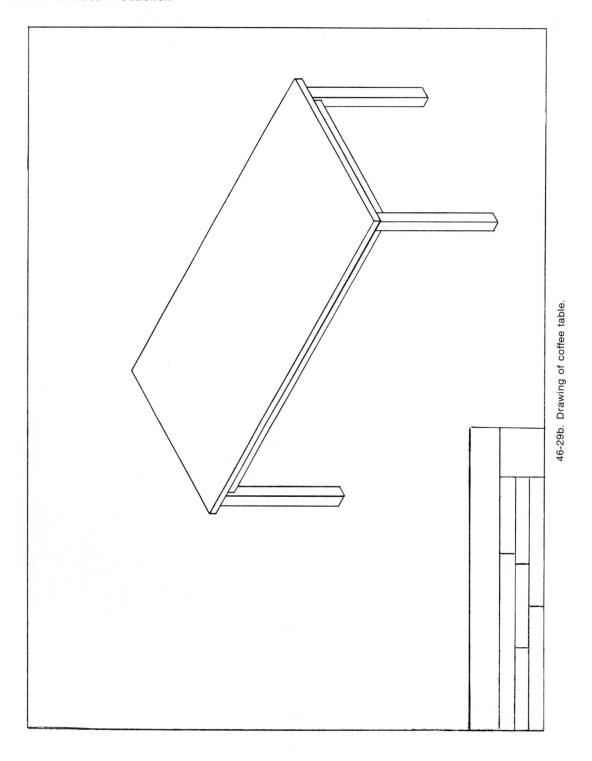

46-29b. Drawing of coffee table.

ITEM NO.: 100   ITEM NAME: KNOCK DOWN COFFEE TABLE

NO. OF ITEMS TO BE PRODUCED:

NO.	PART NAME	REQ. TOTAL REQ.	MAT'L.	ROUGH T	ROUGH W	ROUGH L	FINISH T	FINISH W	FINISH L	BD. FT. PER PIECE	TOTAL BD. FT.	TOTAL COST	REMARKS
1	Top	1	Fir				3/4	19-1/2	39	5.28 sq. ft			
2	Legs	4	Walnut	1-1/2	1-1/2	15-1/2	1-1/4	1-1/4	15-1/4	.24	.96		
3	End Rails	2	Walnut	4/4	2-1/4	16-1/4	3/4	2	16	.25	.50		
4	Side Rails	2	Walnut	See note on detail						A .25 / B .56	.50 / 1.12		
	Hanger bolts	4		1/4 x 3-1/2									
	Corner brackets	4											

46-29c. Materials list for coffee table.

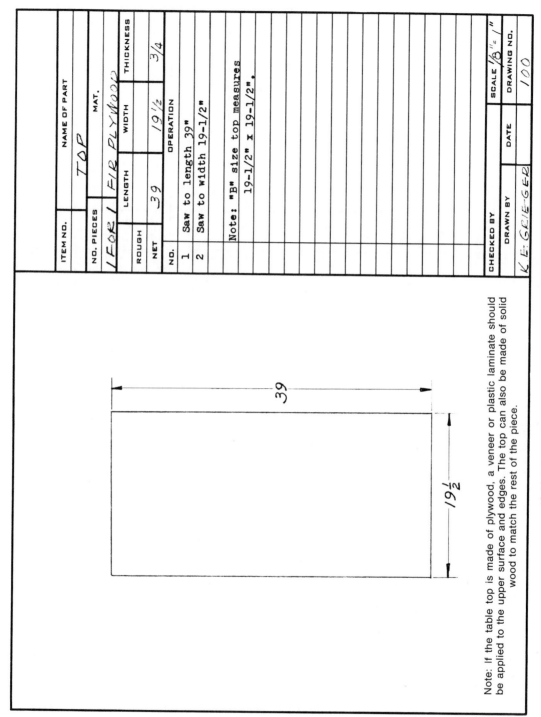

ITEM NO.	NAME OF PART
	TOP

MAT. FIR PLYWOOD

NO. PIECES 1 FOR 1

ROUGH	LENGTH	WIDTH	THICKNESS
NET	39	19 1/2	3/4

NO.	OPERATION
1	Saw to length 39"
2	Saw to width 19-1/2"
	Note: "B" size top measures 19-1/2" x 19-1/2".

CHECKED BY	SCALE 1/8" = 1"
DRAWN BY	DATE	DRAWING NO. 100
K. E. GEIGER		

Note: If the table top is made of plywood, a veneer or plastic laminate should be applied to the upper surface and edges. The top can also be made of solid wood to match the rest of the piece.

46-29d. Route sheet for producing coffee table. (1 of 4)

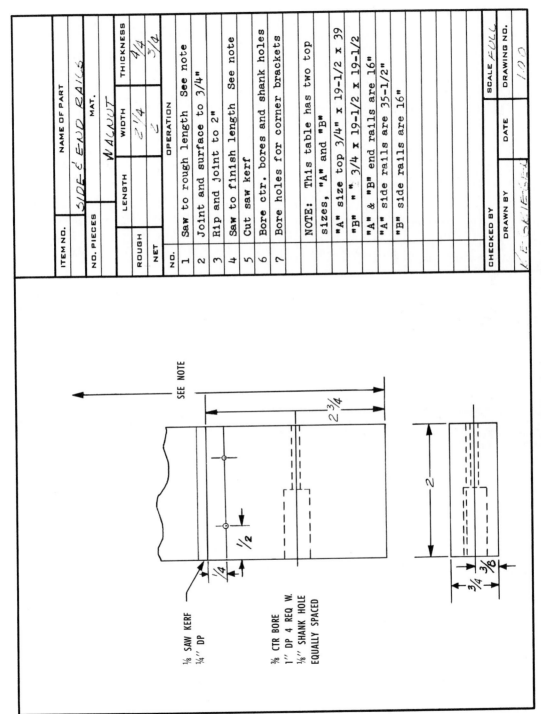

ITEM NO.	NAME OF PART	SIDE & END RAILS		
NO. PIECES	MAT.	WALNUT		
		LENGTH	WIDTH	THICKNESS
	ROUGH		2 1/4	4/4
	NET		2	3/4

NO.	OPERATION
1	Saw to rough length See note
2	Joint and surface to 3/4"
3	Rip and joint to 2"
4	Saw to finish length See note
5	Cut saw kerf
6	Bore ctr. bores and shank holes
7	Bore holes for corner brackets

NOTE: This table has two top sizes, "A" and "B"
"A" size top 3/4" x 19-1/2 x 39
"B" " " 3/4 x 19-1/2 x 19-1/2
"A" & "B" end rails are 16"
"A" side rails are 35-1/2"
"B" side rails are 16"

CHECKED BY
DRAWN BY
DATE
SCALE FULL
DRAWING NO. 100

SEE NOTE

2 3/4

1/2

1/4

1/8 SAW KERF
1/4" DP

3/8 CTR BORE
1" DP 4 REQ W.
1/8" SHANK HOLE
EQUALLY SPACED

2

3/4   3/8

46-29d. Route sheet for producing coffee table. (2 of 4)

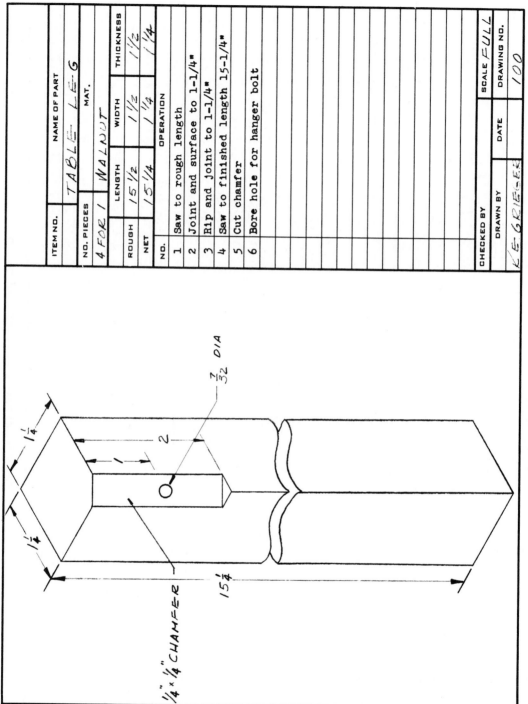

ITEM NO.	NAME OF PART			
	TABLE LEG			
NO. PIECES	MAT.			
4 FOR 1	WALNUT			
		LENGTH	WIDTH	THICKNESS
ROUGH		15 1/2	1 1/2	1 1/2
NET		15 1/4	1 1/4	1 1/4
NO.	OPERATION			
1	Saw to rough length			
2	Joint and surface to 1-1/4"			
3	Rip and joint to 1-1/4"			
4	Saw to finished length 15-1/4"			
5	Cut chamfer			
6	Bore hole for hanger bolt			

CHECKED BY		SCALE *FULL*
DRAWN BY	DATE	DRAWING NO.
L E GRIEGER		*100*

46-29d. Route sheet for producing coffee table. (3 of 4)

$\frac{7}{32}$ DIA

$1\frac{1}{4}$

2

1

$1\frac{1}{4}$

$\frac{1}{4}$" x $\frac{1}{4}$" CHAMFER

$15\frac{1}{4}$

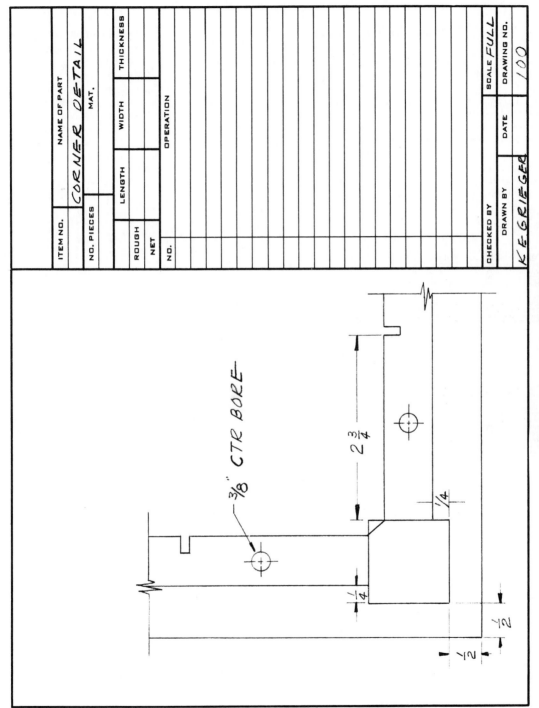

ITEM NO.	NAME OF PART					OPERATION																									
	CORNER DETAIL																														
	NO. PIECES	MAT.																													
			LENGTH	WIDTH	THICKNESS																										
			ROUGH			NO.																									
			NET																												

CHECKED BY

DRAWN BY *K. E. GRIEGER*

DATE

SCALE *FULL*

DRAWING NO. *100*

46-29d. Route sheet for producing coffee table. (4 of 4)

DISCUSSION TOPICS

Section Eight—MASS PRODUCTION

1. Name the two largest industries in which wood is the prime raw material.

2. What are the two major steps in all mass production?

3. How does mass production in the furniture industry differ from that in the automotive industry?

4. List the basic steps followed by furniture manufacturers in mass producing a product.

5. Discuss differences between a rod and route sheet.

6. Explain a jig, a fixture, a gage, and a die.

7. Name the four major manufacturing operations.

8. What is the major purpose of a rough mill?

9. How can a basic wood product be varied in style?

EXTRA CREDIT ACTIVITIES

1. Write a report on one of the major furniture designers.

2. Review articles on a specific subject such as mass production or wood finishing in one or more of the trade magazines, such as *Furniture Production, Furniture World, Furniture Design and Manufacturing,* or *Industrial Woodworking.* Write a report.

3. Visit a furniture factory and write a report of your trip.

Metrics

---

unit **47** **Metrics in Furniture Construction**

Cabinetmakers and furniture builders use two systems of measurement to produce their products. Until recently, all of the English-speaking countries, including the United States, Canada, England, Australia, and New Zealand, used the *customary* sys-

47-1. Furniture produced in Europe, such as this Danish modern chair, is built to metric standards of measurement.

tem. This is sometimes called the *English* system in the United States and *imperial* in the former British Empire countries. Almost all other people of the world use the *metric* system, including the European countries that export furniture and other products to the United States. For example, furniture made in Denmark, Sweden, Italy, and Spain is produced in the metric system. Fig. 47-1.

The customary system continues in use in most woodworking activities in the U. S. However, all English-speaking countries, including the U. S., are committed to changing to the metric system of measurement. Many large American corporations manufacture for world trade and have production facilities throughout the world. Most of these corporations are already designing their

new products in the metric system. This is particularly true of manufacturers of automobiles, computers, and farm machinery. Conversion is less urgent in the furniture field since only a small portion of American furniture is shipped abroad. Then too, the problem of wood replacement parts is less critical than in metal manufacture. For example, the broken leg of a table is usually repaired or replaced on an individual basis, rather than from stock. Eventually, all furniture manufacturing will be done to metric measurement. You should learn the use of the metric system to add to your experience with the customary system.

The SI System

Let's look at the measuring system used by most of the world. This is the updated metric system

507

INTERNATIONAL SYSTEM OF UNITS (SI)

Seven Base Units	Symbol
1. Metre: unit of length	m
2. Kilogram: unit of mass	kg
3. Second: unit of time	s
4. Ampere: unit of electric current	A
5. Kelvin (or degrees Celsius): unit of temperature	K (or °C)
6. Candela: unit of luminous intensity	cd
7. Mole: unit of amount of substance	mol

47-2. The seven base units. For scientific work the kelvin scale is used to record temperatures. For everyday use the temperature is given in degrees Celsius (formerly called Centigrade).

of units, called SI (Systéme International d'Unités) or the modernized metric system. It consists of seven *base* units, Fig. 47-2,

plus many *derived* units. A *derived* unit is one that originates from one or more of the base units. For example, the litre, used for liquid capacity, is derived from the unit of length.

For practical purposes, only three base units are used in everyday life: the metre, the kilogram, and degrees Celsius. The *metre,* the unit of length, is slightly longer than a yard (about 39.37 inches). The *kilogram,* the unit of weight (mass), is a little more than twice a pound (2.2). The unit of temperature is degrees Celsius. (Kelvin is used for scientific work.) In addition, a number of derived units are commonly used in furniture construction. Some of these derived units, such as the square metre (m^2), the cubic metre (m^3), and the litre (l or L)* do not have special names. These symbols are designated with lowercase letters. Others, such as the newton (N), the pascal (Pa), the joule (J), and the watt (W), use a capital letter for the

symbol because they are named after famous people.

The metric system is a decimal system like our money, Fig. 47-3. All larger and smaller units are based on multiples of 10, Fig. 47-4. There are 100 centimetres (cm) in a metre and 1000 millimetres (mm) in a metre (m). There are 1000 metres in a kilometre (km), which is used to measure longer distances. The three most common prefixes are kilo- (1000 times), centi- (1/100 times), and milli- (1/1000 times). These prefixes are used for all units, not just for length. For example, 1/1000 metre is a millimetre (1 mm) and 1/1000 litre is 1 millilitre (1 ml or 1 mL). A comparison of the common units used in the customary and metric systems is shown in Fig. 47-5.

Common Base Units

Three base units commonly used in furniture production are metre, kilogram, and degrees Celsius.

Length. The base unit of length, the metre (m), is about 39.37 inches, or 10 percent longer than a yard. Fig. 47-6a, b. A metre is divided into 10 equal parts called decimetres, 100 equal parts called centimetres (cm), and 1000 equal parts called millimetres (mm). One inch is about 2.5 centimetres or about 25 millimetres. For all industrial production, including furniture manufacturing, the millimetre is used for length measurement. For example, an exact conversion for a 20-inch table leg is 508 mm. Fig. 47-7. Some European countries that have been on the old metric system for many

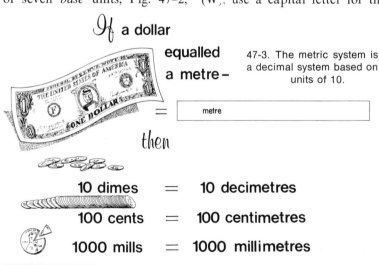

If a dollar equalled a metre –

= | metre |

47-3. The metric system is a decimal system based on units of 10.

then

10 dimes	=	10 decimetres
100 cents	=	100 centimetres
1000 mills	=	1000 millimetres

*The National Bureau of Standards (NBS) has adopted the capital (L) as the symbol for the litre. All other countries use the lower case vertical (l) or the script (ℓ).

TABLE OF SI UNIT PREFIXES

Multiple or Submultiple	Prefix	Symbol	Pronunciation*	Means
$1\ 000\ 000\ 000 = 10^9$	giga	G**	jig' a (a as in about)	One billion times
$1\ 000\ 000 = 10^6$	mega	M**	as in <u>mega</u>phone	One million times
$1\ 000 = 10^3$	kilo	k**	as in <u>kilo</u>watt	One thousand times
$100 = 10^2$	hecto	h	heck' toe	One hundred times
$10 = 10^1$	deka	da	deck' a (a as in about)	Ten times
Base unit $1 = 10^0$		**		
$0.1 = 10^{-1}$	deci	d	as in <u>deci</u>mal	One tenth of
$0.01 = 10^{-2}$	centi	c**	as in <u>centi</u>pede	One hundredth of
$0.001 = 10^{-3}$	milli	m**	as in <u>mili</u>tary	One thousandth of
$0.000\ 001 = 10^{-6}$	micro	μ**	as in <u>micro</u>phone	One millionth of
$0.000\ 000\ 001 = 10^{-9}$	nano	n**	nan' oh (an as in ant)	One billionth of

*The first syllable of every prefix is accented to make sure that the prefix will keep its identity. For example, the preferred pronunciation of kilometre places the accent on the first syllable, not the second.

**Most commonly used and preferred prefixes. Centimetre is used mainly for measuring the body, clothing, sporting goods, and some household articles.

47-4. All metric units share the same prefixes.

years use the centimetre as the unit of length. However, with the updated metric system, only clothing and such common household products as fabrics, bedding, and towels are measured in centimetres. Therefore all furniture drawings show dimensions in millimetres only.

Weight (mass). A kilogram is slightly more than twice a pound in weight, or about 2.2 pounds. Fig. 47-8. A kilogram is divided into 1000 grams. A gram is a very small unit. There are about 28 grams in one ounce. Fig. 47-9. Five hundred grams, or 0.5 kilogram, is a little more than a pound (about 10 percent). Such things as upholstery, stuffing, and plastics will be sold by the kilogram. For example, a 50 kilogram sack of plastic beads is the same as a 110-pound sack.

Temperature. Temperatures are given in metrics in degrees Celsius (°C). On this scale, water

47-5. A comparison of the common measuring units used in the customary and metric systems.

Unit	Customary	Metric	Approximate Comparison
Length	feet—ft or ' inches—in or " fractions of an inch	metres—m centimetres—cm millimetres—mm	3 feet = 1 metre 1 in = 2.5 cm $\frac{1}{8}$ in = 3 mm
Weight	pounds—lb ounces—oz	kilograms—kg grams—g	1 lb = 0.5 kg 1 oz = 28 g
Volume	cubic yard—yd^3 cubic feet—ft^3 cubic inches—in^3	cubic metres—m^3 cubic metres—m^3 cubic centimetres—cm^3	1 yd^3 = 0.76 m^3 1 ft^3 = 0.028 m^3 1 in^3 = 16.4 cm^3
Liquid capacity	quarts—qt pints—fl pt	litres—l millilitres—ml	1 quart = 0.95 l 1 liq pt = 475 ml
Temperature	Fahrenheit—°F	degree Celsius—°C	70 °F = 21 °C

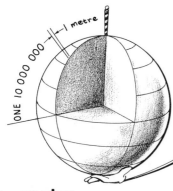

The metre is defined as equal to 1 650 763.73 wave lengths of orange-red light given off by krypton 86.

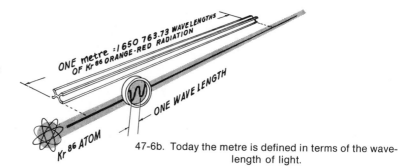

The **metre**
is equal to
$\frac{1}{10,000,000}$ of
the distance from
the north pole
to the equator.

47-6a. The original definition of the metre was based on a measurement of the earth.

47-6b. Today the metre is defined in terms of the wavelength of light.

freezes at 0 °C and boils at 100 °C, and the normal body temperature is 37 °C. Fig. 47-10. For scientific work the kelvin scale is used. Ten degrees Celsius (10 °C) is equal to 50 degrees Fahrenheit. For every 9 degree increase in the Fahrenheit temperature above 50 degrees, add 5 degrees to the Celsius temperature. For example, a good working temperature for a furniture plant might be 20 °C, which is equal to 68 °F.

Derived Units

There are many derived units in the metric system. Some do not have special names, while others are named after famous men of history. Units such as the newton (N), joule (J), pascal (Pa) and watt (W) have symbols with capital letters in contrast to other units

for which the symbols (not abbreviations) are lowercase.

Derived units without special names:

1. square metre (m^2). The square metre is based on the metre and is about 10 percent larger than the square yard. All coverage of finishing materials will be given in square metres. Also panel material may be sold by thickness in millimetres times area in square metres.

2. cubic metre (m^3). The base unit of volume is the cubic metre. This is a large unit (about 30 percent larger than the cubic yard). Lumber will be sold in bulk by the cubic metre rather than by 1000 board feet. There are about 424 board feet in a cubic metre. A cube that measures one decimetre (1/10 of a metre or 10 centimetres) on each side is called a cubic decimetre (dm^3). Fig. 47-11. A cubic decimetre when used as a unit of liquid capacity is called a litre (l or L).

3. litre (l or L). The *litre*, the

unit of liquid capacity, is slightly larger than the quart (about 6 percent more). It is the unit used for liquids such as paints, oils, and other finishing materials. Since most finishing materials are normally packaged in quart and pint sizes, the metric equivalent will be the litre and the half litre (500 millilitres). Gallon size (4 quarts) may be replaced by the 3 litre size [0.8 gallon] or 4 litres [1.06 gallons]. Coverage with the metric units will be just a little more than with the customary units we have been using.

4. metres per second (m/s). Speed in SI is given in metres per second (m/s). However, most machine speeds are shown in metres per minute (m/min). Fig. 47-12 shows speed in metric units for common woodworking machines and how to find the correct rpm.

Derived units with special names:

1. newton (N). The unit of force in metrics is given in new-

Customary (English)	Actual	Accurate Woodworkers' Language	Tool Sizes	Lumber Sizes Thickness	Width
1/32 in	0.8	1 mm bare			
1/16 in	1.6 mm	1.5 mm			
1/8 in	3.2 mm	3 mm full	3 mm		
3/16 in	4.8 mm	5 mm bare	5 mm		
1/4 in	6.4 mm	6.5 mm	6 mm		
5/16 in	7.9 mm	8 mm bare	8 mm		
3/8 in	9.5 mm	9.5 mm	10 mm		
7/16 in	1.1 mm	11 mm full	11 mm		
1/2 in	12.7 mm	12.5 mm full	13 mm	12 mm	
9/16 in	14.3 mm	14.5 mm bare	14 mm		
5/8 in	15.9 mm	16 mm bare	16 mm	16 mm	
11/16 in	17.5 mm	17.5 mm	17 mm		
3/4 in	19.1 mm	19 mm full	19 mm	19 mm	
13/16 in	20.6 mm	20.5 mm	21 mm		
7/8 in	22.2 mm	22 mm full	22 mm	22 mm	
15/16 in	23.8 mm	24 mm bare	24 mm		
1 in	25.4 mm	25.5 mm	25 mm	25 mm	
1 1/4 in	31.8 mm	32 mm bare	32 mm	32 mm	
1 3/8 in	34.9 mm	35 mm bare	36 mm	36 mm	
1 1/2 in	38.1 mm	38 mm full	38 mm	38 mm	
1 3/4 in	44.5 mm	44.5 mm	44 mm	44 mm	
2 in	50.8 mm	51 mm bare	50 mm	50 mm	50 mm
2 1/2 in	63.5 mm	63.5 mm	63 mm	63 mm	
3 in	76.2 mm	76 mm full		75 mm	75 mm
4 in	101.6 mm	101.5 mm		100 mm	100 mm
5 in	127.0 mm	127 mm			125 mm
6 in	152.4 mm	152.5 mm			150 mm
7 in	177.8 mm	178 mm bare			
8 in	203.2 mm	203 mm full			200 mm
9 in	228.6 mm	228.5 mm			
10 in	254.0 mm	254 mm			250 mm
11 in	279.4 mm	279.5 mm			
12 in	304.8 mm	305 mm bare			300 mm
18 in	457.2 mm	457 mm full	460 mm		
24 in	609.6 mm	609.5 mm			
36 in	914.4 mm	914.5 mm			
48 in—4'	1219.2 mm	1220 mm			
96 in—8'	2438.4 mm	2440 mm			

Panel Stock Sizes
1220 mm width
2440 mm length

Present Length, ft	6	8	10	12	14	16	18	20
Replacement Length, m	1.8	2.4	3.0	3.6	4.2	4.8	5.5	6.0

47-7. Conversion table for woodwork.

47-8. A kilogram equals about 2.2 pounds, and a litre of water weighs about 1 kilogram.

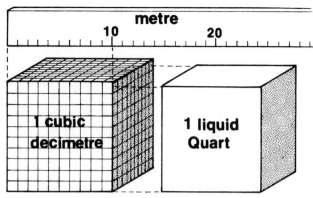

47-11. A cubic decimetre is the same as a litre.

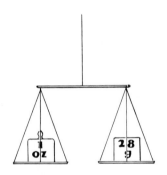

1 ounce = 28.35 grams
1 gram = 0.03527 ounces

47-9. An ounce equals 28.35 grams.

tons (N). The force of gravity on a 1 kilogram mass is 9.8 newtons at sea level and 1.6 newtons on the Moon. The force of gravity on a person with a mass of 100 kilograms [220 lb] is 980 newtons on Earth and 160 newtons on the Moon.

2. pascal (Pa). The unit of pressure is the pascal (Pa). Because this is a very small amount, pressure is given in kilopascals (kPa). One psi (pounds per square inch) is equal to about seven kilopascals. For example, if the air pressure specified for paint spraying is 60 psi, the equivalent in metrics is about 420 kPa.

3. joule (J). The joule is the unit of energy or work. This is a very small unit so the kilojoule (kJ) is used. One kilojoule is about equal to one Btu in the customary system.

4. watt (W). The unit for all power in metrics (not just electricity) is the watt (W). However, the kilowatt (kW) is more common. A popular size electric lamp consumes 100 watts per hour.

47-10. Comparison of the two common scales used for temperature.

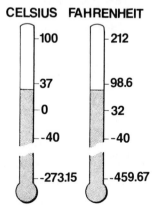

CELSIUS   FAHRENHEIT

CELSIUS	FAHRENHEIT
100	212
37	98.6
0	32
-40	-40
-273.15	-459.67

47-12. Cutting speeds in metres per minute.

Type of Lumber	Cutting Speeds in Metres per Minute						
	Drill-ing	Turn-ing	Sawing			Sand-ing	Plan-ing
			Circular	Band	Jig		
Hard	80	150	2500	650	30	850	1250
Soft	120	300	3000	1000	100	1000	1750
Very soft	160	450	4000	1250	200	1250	2000

$$CS = \frac{RPM \times \pi \times D}{1000}$$

$$RPM = \frac{CS \times 1000}{\pi \times D}$$

CS: Cutting speed in metres per minute

RPM: Revolutions per minute

D: Diameter in milli-metres

METRIC UNITS FOR COMMON USE

Quantity	Metric unit and symbol	Conversion Factors (approximate)	
		Customary to Metric Units	Metric to Customary Units
Length	millimetre (mm)	1 in = 25.4 mm*	1 mm = 0.0394 in
	centimetre (cm)	1 in = 2.54 cm*	1 cm = 0.394 in
		1 ft = 30.5 cm	
	metre (m)	1 yd = 0.914 m	1 m = 3.28 ft
	kilometre (km)	1 mi = 1.61 km	1 km = 0.62 mi
Weight (Mass)	gram (g)	1 oz = 28.3 g	1 g = 0.0353 oz
	kilogram (kg)	1 lb = 454 g	1 kg = 2.2 lb
	metric ton or tonne (t)	1 long ton = 1.02 t	1 t = 0.98 long ton
Area	square centimetre (cm^2)	1 in^2 = 6.45 cm^2	1 cm^2 = 0.155 in^2
	square metre (m^2)	1 ft^2 = 929 cm^2	1 m^2 = 10.8 ft^2
		1 yd^2 = 0.836 m^2	1 m^2 = 1.2 yd^2
	hectare (ha)	1 acre = 0.405 ha	1 ha = 2.47 acres
	square kilometre (km^2)	1 mi^2 = 2.59 km^2	1 km^2 = 0.386 mi^2
Volume	cubic centimetre (cm^3)	1 in^3 = 16.4 cm^3	1 cm^3 = 0.061 in^3
	cubic metre (m^3)	1 ft^3 = 28 300 cm^3	1 m^3 = 35.3 ft^3
		1 yd^3 = 0.765 m^3	1 m^3 = 1.31 yd^3
Volume (liquids and gases)	millimetre (ml)	1 fl oz = 29.6 ml	1 ml = 0.033 8 fl oz
	litre (L or l)	1 liq qt = 0.946 litre	1 litre = 1.057 liq qt
	kilolitre (kl)	1 gal = 3.79 litres	1 kl = 264 gal
Time Interval	second (s)		
	minute (min)		
	hour (h)		
Speed	metre per minute (m/min)	1 ft/min = 0.305 m/min	1 m/min = 3.28 ft/min
Pressure	kilopascal (kPa)	1 psi = 6.89 kPa	1 kPa = 0.145 psi
Energy	kilojoule (kJ)	1 Btu = 1.06 kJ	1 kJ = 0.948 Btu
Power	kilowatt (kW)	1 hp = 0.746 kW	1 kW = 1.34 hp
Temperature	degree Celsius (°C)	°C = 5/9 (°F-32)	°F = 9/5°C + 32

* Accurate

47-13. Conversion of metric units to customary units and the reverse.

One horsepower equals about 3/4 (0.75) of a kilowatt (kW). Therefore a 2 horsepower motor on a circular saw is listed as 1.5 kilowatts in metric units. Fig. 47-13.

Furniture Manufacturing

Most furniture plants are largely self-contained in the production of wood products. Companies buy the hardwood lumber in rough sizes in random widths and lengths. From this hardwood lumber, furniture parts are machined to correct dimensions. Manufacturers also make their own hardwood plywood to specific sizes to fit the furniture being manufactured. There are relatively easy ways for any furniture manufacturer to convert to the metric measuring system:

● Change the drawings to give all dimensions in millimetres.
● Use rules and other measuring instruments marked in metric units.
● Add metric scales to the adjustments on machines.
● Train workers to use the metric system.

There is little need for *metric standards* in furniture since com-

513

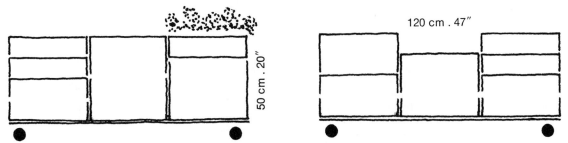

50 cm . 20"

120 cm . 47"

47-14a. This modular European furniture gives the dimensions in centimetres and equivalent inches.

47-14b. The layout of modular furniture is based on the square centimetre.

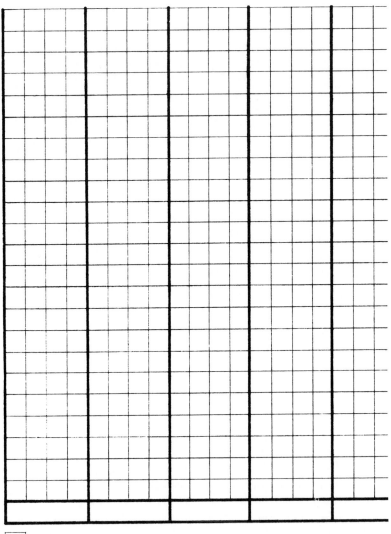

☐ = 10×10 cm . $3^{15}/_{16}$×$3^{15}/_{16}$"

panies do not provide replacement parts as is done in the metal industry. The timing for conversion will depend on the interest and desire of each company. Furniture imported from European countries is designed and manufactured to metric measurement. As more international trade in furniture develops, metric measurement will become the predominant way of measuring. Normally, all furniture drawings use the millimetre dimensions only. However, some countries that have been on the metric system for many years use the centimetre as the basic unit of measurement. Fig. 47-14.

Conversion to metrics may extend over many years. There are three major steps involved in this conversion.

1. Changing to the metric measuring system only.

2. Developing metric standards for materials based on metric modules.

3. Producing standard materials based on these metric modules.

The first step is called a soft conversion. This can be illustrated as follows: A board surfaced on a planer to 1" in thickness is shown on a drawing as 1", or 25.4 mil-

47-15. A plastic rule of this type can be glued on one side of a bench rule so that the rule can be used for both customary and metric measurement.

limetres (mm). The thickness hasn't changed, since 1″ equals 25.4 mm. Another example, if a bench top is 24″ by 30″, the size could be shown as 610 mm by 762 mm without actually changing the top.

The second and third conversion steps, which are very complex, are called hard conversion. Hard conversion means that metric standards must be established and products produced to these standards. For example, production of all panel stock—plywood, hardboard, and particle board—will eventually be based on the 100 millimetre module for use in house construction. The size of a 4′ x 8′ sheet will be changed from 1220 x 2440 mm to 1200 x 2400 mm. All metal fasteners such as bolts and nuts will have metric diameters and threads. *These are not interchangeable with customary fasteners.*

Comparison of Customary and Metric Rules

Rules with customary markings used in woodworking are the 6″, 12″ (foot), and 36″ (yard). Similar rules in the metric system are 150 mm (15 cm), 300 mm (30 cm), and 1 metre. The 300 mm (30 cm) rule is slightly shorter than the 12″ rule. Fig. 47-15. The bench rule is divided into 12 inches.

Each inch is divided into fractions of either eighths ($\frac{1}{8}$″) or sixteenths ($\frac{1}{16}$″). The smallest division on the bench rule is $\frac{1}{16}$″. Each numbered line on the metric rule is marked (graduated) 10, 20, 30, or 40 mm. If the rule is marked 10, 20, 30, and 40, these numbered lines represent millimetres. It is more difficult to use the centimetre rule. For example, if there are two small divisions beyond the 1, you must change the 1 to 10 by adding a zero and then counting the number of small divisions beyond that number line to make a total of 12. You do not have to convert when using a rule with numbered lines graduated in millimetres. Three small divisions beyond 10 is 13

millimetres, with no figuring needed. Fig. 47-16. Therefore select a rule marked in millimetres as your first choice.

Note that on the metric rule the smallest division is 1 mm, which is about $\frac{1}{25}$″ while the smallest division on the customary woodworking rule is $\frac{1}{16}$″. The 1 mm division is smaller than the $\frac{1}{16}$″ but larger than the $\frac{1}{32}$″. Since woodworking is not a precise craft like machine shop, you should measure to the nearest millimetre for average work. You should measure to a half millimetre (0.5 mm) for more precise work such as in patternmaking. Fig. 47-17. This is more accurate than if you measure to the nearest $\frac{1}{16}$″ since 1 millimetre is about $\frac{1}{25}$″.

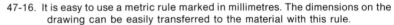

47-16. It is easy to use a metric rule marked in millimetres. The dimensions on the drawing can be easily transferred to the material with this rule.

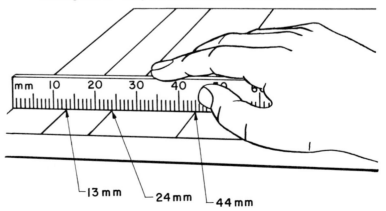

515

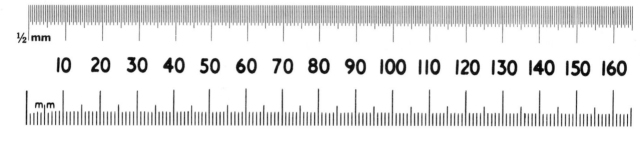

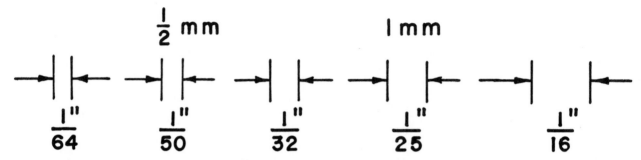

47-17. Some metric rules are graduated in millimetres on one edge and half millimetres (0.5 mm) on the other. A millimetre is about halfway between 1/32″ and 1/16″. One-half millimetre is about halfway between 1/32″ and 1/64″.

Rules are available in three different types: customary only (English), metric only, and customary-metric combination. The customary-metric rule is usually divided into inches and fractions of an inch on the top half of the rule and in millimetres on the bottom half. Fig. 47-18.

Materials. Lumber for furniture production is purchased in random widths and lengths with no size specification except thickness. Fig. 47-19. Hardwoods are purchased either surfaced one side or surfaced two sides. Therefore the actual thickness is always less than the nominal thickness. A nominal 1″ board could be listed as 25 mm with the equivalent metric sizes of surfaced lumber shown in Fig. 47-20. Plywood and other panel stock used throughout the United States, England, and Canada is based on the 4′x8′ module, and is listed in metric terms as 1220 x 2440 mm. Furniture manufacturers make their own hardwood plywoods to sizes needed for production. Wood screws, nails, staples, dowel rods, and many other woodworking materials will not change in size for many years. These items may be shown in metric measurement. Therefore a 6 mm (1/4″) drill can be used to install a 6 mm (1/4″) dowel. A 2″ wood screw can be listed as a 50 mm screw.

Painting and Finishing

Metric conversion will have relatively little effect on painting and wood finishing except for a change in the container size. The standard unit of fluid volume or liquid capacity is the litre, which is about six percent larger than the quart. Therefore coverage of areas using a litre would be somewhat greater than with a quart. Coverage information will be given in square metres (m^2). Paints and other finishing materials may be produced in one and four litre sizes, plus multiples of these for the larger containers. A three litre container would be somewhat smaller than one gallon. A four litre container would be somewhat larger than a gallon.

Converting Tools and Machines

It is relatively simple in woodworking to convert to the metric

516

47-18. Flexible tape should be graduated like this.

47-19. Lumber is delivered to a furniture plant in random widths and lengths.

47-20. Comparison of the nominal or rough sizes and the surface sizes of hardwood in customary and metric units.

THICKNESS (widths vary with grades)

Nominal (rough)	Exact mm	Rounded mm	Surfaced 1 Side (S1S)	Exact mm	Rounded mm	Surfaced 2 Sides (S2S)	Exact mm	Rounded mm
$3/8''$	9.5	10	$1/4''$	6.4	6	$3/16''$	4.8	5
$1/2''$	12.7	13	$3/8''$	9.5	9	$5/16''$	7.9	8
$5/8''$	15.9	16	$1/2''$	12.7	13	$7/16''$	11.1	11
$3/4''$	19.1	19	$5/8''$	15.9	16	$9/16''$	14.3	14
$1''$	25.4	25	$7/8''$	22.2	22	$13/16''$	20.6	21
$1 1/4''$	31.8	32	$1 1/8''$	28.6	29	$1 1/16''$	27.0	27
$1 1/2''$	38.1	38	$1 3/8''$	34.9	35	$1 5/16''$	33.3	33
$2''$	50.8	50	$1 13/16''$	46.0	46	$1 3/4''$	44.5	44
$3''$	76.2	75	$2 13/16''$	71.4	71	$2 3/4''$	69.9	70
$4''$	101.6	100	$3 13/16''$	96.8	97	$3 3/4''$	95.3	95

METRIC EQUIVALENTS SHOWN ARE THE EXPECTED REPLACEMENT SIZES TO BE AVAILABLE IN THE FUTURE.

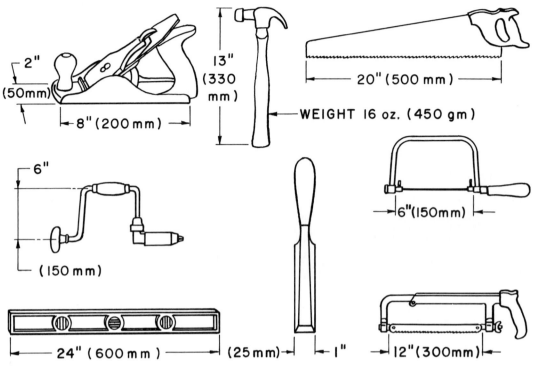

47-21. Tools that will not need replacement.

system. The only hand tools that need replacement are rules and other measuring instruments. It isn't necessary to replace such tools as boring bits, planes, or drills. Countries going to the metric system merely use the metric measurement to identify tools. For example, a 2″ plane becomes a 50 mm plane. A 1″ boring tool becomes a 25 mm tool, and a 1½″ wood screw becomes a 75 mm length. Fig. 47-21.

Converting woodworking machines is simple. A piece of plastic paste-on metric tape or a metal metric scale is placed over the customary scale. Fig. 47-22.

Reading Metric Drawings

The three common ways of making a furniture drawing so that the product can be built are as follows:

Dual dimensioning. In this method both the metric and the customary dimensions are shown directly on the drawing. For example, if the design dimension is 2 inches, it would be shown as $\frac{2}{[51]}$. A symbol on the drawing such as $\frac{in}{[mm]}$ indicates that the top dimension is in inches and the dimension in brackets is in milli-

metres. Note that the actual conversion would be 50.8 mm, but it is rounded to 51 mm. With dual dimensioning, the drawing looks more complicated. If the design dimensions are in metric, the customary dimensions are in brackets. Fig. 47-23a, b. For example, if the dimension is 14 millimetres, it would be shown as $\frac{14}{[9/16]}$.

Metric dimension with customary read-out. On this type of drawing, the dimensions shown on the drawing are in metric and a small chart is added giving the equivalent sizes in the customary system. For example, if the metric

518

MACHINE WOODWORK
GAGE AND SCALE CONVERSION

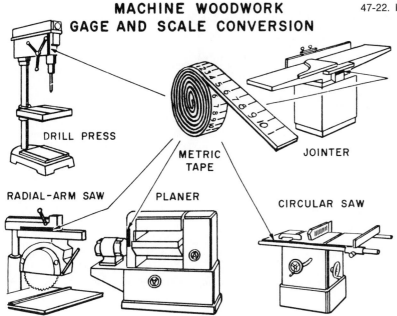

DRILL PRESS

METRIC TAPE

JOINTER

RADIAL-ARM SAW

PLANER

CIRCULAR SAW

47-22. It is relatively easy to convert power tools for metric use.

47-23a. This game table can be built using either customary or metric measuring units.

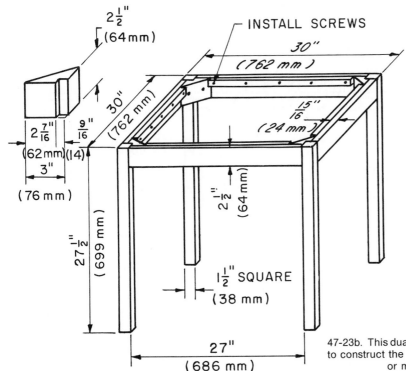

INSTALL SCREWS

$2\frac{1}{2}$" (64mm)

30" (762 mm)

30" (762 mm)

$\frac{15}{16}$" (24 mm)

$2\frac{7}{16}$" (62mm)

$\frac{9}{16}$" (14)

3" (76 mm)

$2\frac{1}{2}$" (64 mm)

$27\frac{1}{2}$" (699 mm)

$1\frac{1}{2}$" SQUARE (38 mm)

27" (686 mm)

47-23b. This dual-dimensioned drawing can be used to construct the game table using either customary or metric measuring tools.

519

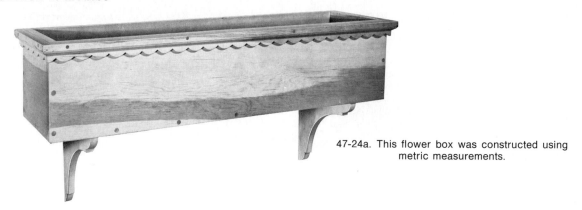

47-24a. This flower box was constructed using metric measurements.

47-24b. This drawing of a flower box uses only metric measurements.

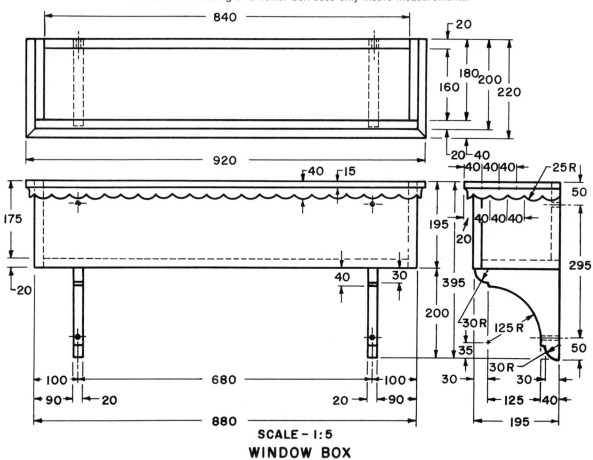

SCALE – 1:5

WINDOW BOX

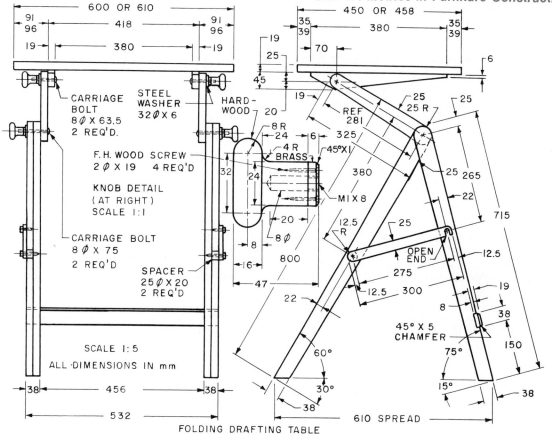

47-25. This drawing of a folding drafting table uses only metric measurements.

size is 13 mm, the chart would show that this measurement equals about ½".

All-metric drawings. Eventually, all drawings will show metric measurements only. Two examples are the flower box in Fig. 47-24a, b and the drafting table in Fig. 47-25.

Converting from Customary to Metric

Any woodworking product can be built to metric dimensions by using Fig. 47-7 to change the cus-tomary dimensions from inches and fractions of an inch to milli-metres. For most projects, convert to full millimetres: round UP for metric dimensions 0.5 and above; round DOWN for dimensions below 0.5 mm. For example, round ³⁄₁₆" to 5 mm and 1" to 25 mm. The only exception to this might be to round ½" lumber to 12 mm instead of 13 mm since lumber thickness tends to run smaller than the stated sizes. However, if a dado is to be cut that calls for a ½" width, then

13 mm will be a better conversion than 12 mm. A customary chisel for trimming the dado measures 12.7 mm and couldn't be used to trim a 12 mm dado. For more precise work, it is just as easy to work to 0.5 millimetre as it is to the full millimetre since many metric rules are graduated to the half millimetre. Remember that 1 millimetre is about ¹⁄₂₅", which is more precise than ¹⁄₁₆". One-half millimetre (0.5 mm) is about ¹⁄₅₀", which is about halfway between ¹⁄₃₂" and ¹⁄₆₄".

DISCUSSION TOPICS

Section Nine—METRICS IN FURNITURE CONSTRUCTION

1. What are the seven basic units of the SI metric system?

2. Which three of the seven base units are most frequently used in everyday life?

3. List the ways in which a furniture manufacturer can convert to the metric measuring system.

4. What are the three steps in metric conversion?

5. Discuss the effect of metric conversion on painting and wood finishing.

6. Describe the two measurement systems used to produce wood products.

7. What is SI?

8. How is speed of machinery given in metric units?

9. If air pressure for spraying is 50 psi, what is the equivalent in kilopascals?

10. Describe soft conversion. Describe hard conversion.

11. What are the three methods of giving dimensions on a drawing so that a product can be built to metric dimensions?

EXTRA CREDIT ACTIVITIES

1. Convert an existing drawing from the customary to the metric system. Then build the product using metric measuring tools.

2. Secure a set of woodworking drawings from a country using the metric system—such as Sweden or Denmark. Compare these drawings with a set from an American furniture manufacturer.

10

Furniture Repairs

Many problems are encountered in caring for, repairing, and refinishing fine wood furniture. A common problem is sticking doors and drawers. This is caused by changes in humidity. Other problems, such as loose joints or a broken leg on chairs and tables, are usually the result of misuse. For example, leaning back on a chair places too much weight on the joints between legs and rails. Repairs to the finish are often needed due to normal, everyday wear and tear. Exposed parts of furniture, such as the edge of a desk or the top of a dining table, eventually require refinishing.

Unlike other mass-produced products, such as cars and appliances, replacement parts for furniture cannot be bought. The skilled woodworker has to be able to make a new part, fit, and refinish it. Fig. 48-1.

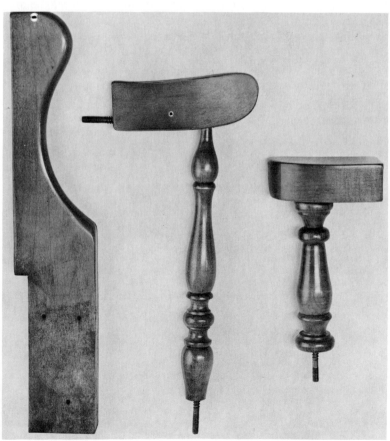

48-1. The skilled woodworker must be able to make replacement parts for a piece of furniture that is broken.

523

Care of Furniture Surfaces

First aid for minor scratches, blemishes, and stains:

● *Minor scratches.* Rub the scratch well with a wax stick in a matching color. Wax sticks are inexpensive and are usually available at paint, hardware, and furniture stores. Fill the scratch and then wipe with a soft, dry cloth. Apply your preferred polish. Tan, brown, and black shoe polish can also be used for this purpose. Fig. 48-2.

● *White spots, cause unknown.* Rub the blemish with cigar or cigarette ashes using a cloth dipped in wax, lubricating oil, vegetable shortening, lard, or salad oil. Wipe off immediately and rewax with your preferred polish.

● *Alcohol spots.* Method A: Rub with finger dipped in paste wax, silver polish, linseed oil, or moistened cigar ash. Rewax with your preferred polish. Method B: On some finishes a quick application of ammonia will do the trick. Put a few drops on a damp cloth and rub the spot. Follow immediately with an application of polish.

● *Water marks.* Marks or rings from wet glasses are common on tables, especially if these surfaces have not been waxed. Wax will keep liquid from being absorbed immediately, giving you time to wipe it up before it damages the finish. However, even wax cannot prevent damage when liquids are allowed to stand on the finish indefinitely. If water marks appear, here are some remedies to try.

Method A: Apply preferred wax or polish with fine 3/0 steel wool, rubbing *lightly.* Method B: Place a clean thick blotter over the ring and press with a warm (not hot) iron. Repeat until ring disappears.

● *Candle wax.* Hold an ice cube on the wax for a few seconds to harden it. Wipe up melted ice immediately. Crumble off as much wax as can be removed with the fingers and then scrape gently with a dull knife. Rub briskly with clean cloth saturated with liquid wax, wiping dry with another clean cloth. Repeat until mark disappears.

● *Milk spots.* When milk or foods containing milk or cream are allowed to remain on furniture, the effect of the lactic acid is like that of a paint or varnish remover. Wipe up the spilled food as quickly as possible. If spots show, clean with wax. Then follow procedure for alcohol spots.

● *Plastic place mats or tablecloths.* Since some plastics contain chemicals which are not compatible with fine furniture finishes, plastic place mats and tablecloths should be fabricbacked.

Minor Repairs

● *Door and drawer handles or pulls.* If the door or drawer handles or pulls are broken, purchase new ones that will cover the exposed wood area. If you don't plan to refinish the whole piece of furniture, buy door or drawer pulls with a *large backplate.* Fig. 48-3. You can drill new holes for the pulls and attach them. In this way they will cover the area around the old holes and the unfinished portion of the furniture.

● *Drawers.* When a drawer will not move in and out smoothly, do the following:

1. Remove the drawer from the case. If the drawer is stuck fast, it may be necessary to re-

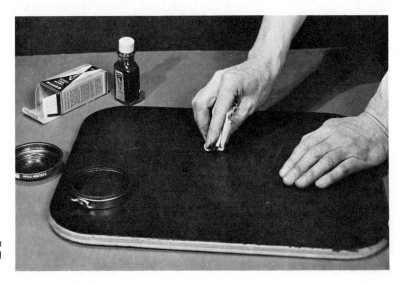

48-2. Liquid or paste shoe polish can be used to cover scratches and small blemishes on furniture.

move the back of the case. Then tap the drawer with a rubber mallet until the drawer is removed.

2. Carefully inspect the drawer to see what has caused it to stick. Sometimes the center guide does not operate smoothly. If the center guide is of wood, make sure that the two parts do not bind. If necessary, sand and wax the runner. Fig. 48-4. If the guide is metal, apply *slip spray.* If the drawer fits into a simple runner on each side, there may be wear between the bottom of the drawer and the frame. In still other cases, the sides of the drawer may bind at the exposed frame. Fig. 48-5. Sanding the drawer frame or side of the drawer will help. It may be necessary to plane the bottom edge of the drawer *sides* and *front* to make it operate freely. If the drawer has a simple side runner, place nylon-headed tacks, strips of nylon, or pads on the frame directly under the sides of the drawer. Fig. 48-6. This makes for smooth operation.

● *Hinges.* Remove the hinge and plug the hole with either match-

48-4. Sometimes the center guide, or runner, must be sanded lightly and rewaxed to make the drawer operate smoothly.

sticks (softwood) or toothpicks (hardwood). Replace the hinge using wood screws that are slightly longer but the same diameter.

● *Joints on leg-and-rail (frame) construction.* The leg-and-rail joints on most tables and chairs are either dowels or mortise-and-tenon joints. Corner blocks add strength to joints. Joints frequently become loose, particularly on chairs, because of misuse. Repair as follows:

48-3. By installing a new handle with a large backplate, the original unfinished area can be covered.

48-5. Often the drawer sides will bind on the face frame. Sand either the frame or the drawer sides to improve the drawer operation.

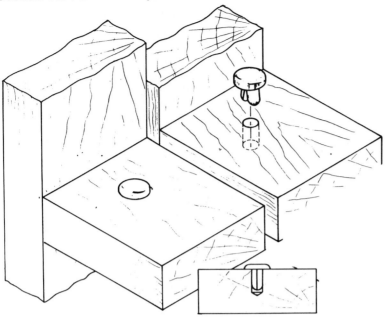

48-6a. Nylon buttons or tacks installed on the frame under the side of the drawer will make it operate more smoothly.

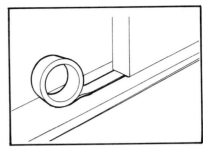

48-6b. Nylon tape can be used to eliminate friction. This material has an adhesive back. Simply peel the paper backing from the tape and press it in place.

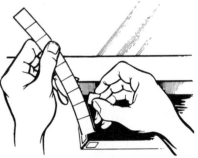

48-6c. Nylon pressure-sensitive antifriction pads.

1. Remove the top of the table or the seat (usually a pad seat) from the chair. Fig. 48-7. Sometimes the corner block should be completely removed. Fig. 48-8. However, if one side of the leg-and-rail and the corner block is solid, remove only one wood screw from one side of the corner block. Separate the leg and rail enough so that some of the old glue can be scraped off.

When the joint is loose but cannot be separated, the best method of regluing is to use a tool called a glue injector (an old medical syringe can also be used). Bore a $\frac{1}{16}''$ hole at an angle in the leg from the underside of the rail. The hole should go into the area of the dowels or mortise-and-tenon joint. Insert the tip of the injector in the hole and squeeze white glue into the joint. Reclamp the leg and rail. Fig. 48-9.

48-7. Remove the tabletop or the seat from the chair before attempting repairs.

48-8a. If the corner block is loose, completely remove it. This corner block on the inside of the chair frame was glued to improve stability for the unit.

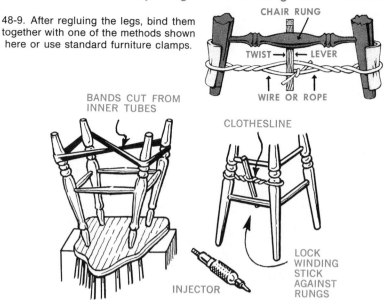

48-9. After regluing the legs, bind them together with one of the methods shown here or use standard furniture clamps.

48-8b. Here the corner block has been removed so that the old glue can be cleaned out. Corner blocks on high-quality furniture are grooved to increase the holding power of the glue.

If the corner block has been completely removed, scape off all the old glue and reglue in place. Sometimes slightly larger and longer wood screws must be used to fasten the corner block. If that isn't possible, redrill the holes in the corner block at a different location. In this way the corner block will be as secure as when first installed.

Repairing Cracks

Cracks in horizontal surfaces, such as the tops of tables or chests, can usually be repaired by injecting some glue into the cracked surfaces and then reclamping until dry.

Most cracks occur at an angle in the leg of a table or chair that has been misused. The best method of making this repair is to refit the cracked surface together carefully. Clamp the two parts while they are dry. Bore a hole from the back of the leg, at an angle, through the cracked surface for a dowel pin. Apply glue to the cracked surface. Reclamp and allow to dry. The dowel should not show on the two exterior surfaces of the leg.

Another method of repairing a crack in a leg is to bore a dowel hole in each portion of the leg and insert the dowel between the portions before regluing. Carefully apply glue to the cracked surface and to the hole for the dowel. Drive the dowel into one side and then into the other. Reclamp the cracked surface together. Allow the glue to dry; then trim off the excess dowel from the inside of the leg. The repaired area can be refinished in the same color as the furniture piece.

If the crack in the leg is very severe and there is a damaged section, repair can often be made by cutting out the damaged section. Recut a new piece for the leg, and then bore a hole between the old part and the new. Insert dowels and reglue the leg. The new section can then be shaped the same as the old leg and refinished. Fig. 48-10.

48-10a. The letters indicate typical areas in a chair that may need repairs.

If only a small portion of the leg is damaged, this can be cut out and a piece glued in before it is trimmed and finished.

Patching

Often the surface or edge of a table covered with veneer or plastic laminate will be damaged or become loose. If the edge is loose, clean off the glue on both surfaces with a sharp knife. Apply contact cement to both surfaces, allow to dry properly, and then reglue in place. If a portion of the edge is broken, carefully cut off the broken section and replace it with an identical piece of veneer or plastic laminate.

When the suface blemish on a tabletop is too large to be filled with some repair material, a patch is required. Patches should normally be made in the shape of a diamond or parallelogram. To do top-quality patching on veneer work, the sides that are cut

out and the patch should be tapered in opposite directions so that the patch will show as little

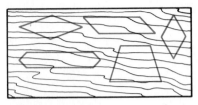

PATCHES MAY BE MADE FROM VENEER OR PLASTIC LAMINATE

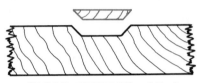

CROSS SECTION OF A TABLE TOP CUT OUT TO RECEIVE A PATCH

48-11a. Methods of cutting patches of veneer or plastic laminate. When possible, the patch should be at an angle to the cutout area.

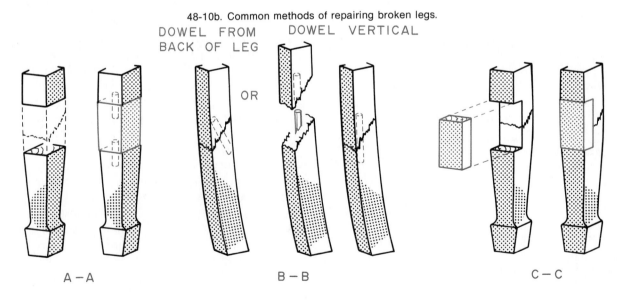

48-10b. Common methods of repairing broken legs.

DOWEL FROM BACK OF LEG

DOWEL VERTICAL

OR

A – A

B – B

C – C

48-11b. A carbide cutter is the best tool to use for cutting plastic laminate.

as possible. Fig. 48-11a. The grain structure or design of the patch should match the top as closely as possible, and it should be of the same thickness. To match either veneer or plastic laminate, first make a cardboard template of the needed size and shape. Trace around it with a knife (for veneer) or a carbide cutter (for plastic laminate). Fig. 48-11b. The veneer can easily be cut out with a

wood chisel. Plastic laminate must be cut with a metal-cutting saw or a carbide cutter. Put the patch in the hole without glue to make sure that it is correct. Then apply contact cement to both the back surface of the patch and the tabletop. Place the patch in position and put a heavy weight over it until it is dry.

Removing Old Finish

Commercial paint and finish removers are the best products for removing old furniture finish down to the bare wood. These materials are a mixture of various chemicals that soften the old paint or finish. They will not injure the surface of the wood, loosen glue, or raise wood grain. Some kinds are thin liquids, while others are thicker, often like syrup in consistency. Always fol-

low the label directions for applying the remover. *CAUTION: Wear rubber gloves when using these chemicals.*

Allow the chemical remover to work and then gently scrape off the old finish with a putty knife. Fig. 48-12a. For small areas, such as around moldings or carvings, use an old toothbrush, cotton swab, or small strips of cloth to scrape the old finish away. Fig. 48-12b. Some chemical removers require that the surface be washed with water; other chemical removers don't have to be washed off. Sand lightly before refinishing as described in Section 6.

Repairing Finishes

Repairing furniture finish is a full-time occupation for many people. Several companies pro-

48-12b. Small scraps of rug or other rough material can be used to clean out the finish in small areas.

48-12a. Using a putty knife to remove the old finish.

48-13. Putty-type filler sticks can be used to fill joints, holes, and scratches. No need to lacquer over. They are available in a broad selection of wood colors.

48-14. Quick-drying, touch-up coatings in felt-tipped pen form are available. No need to lacquer over. This material seals and finishes in one step. Most furniture colors can be matched with these pens.

vide complete touch-up service kits as well as workshops to learn the techniques of repairing damaged furniture finishes.*

Damage to furniture finish can occur during manufacture, storage, shipping, in the furniture store, and in use. Many different kinds and types of patching materials are available to repair this damage. Most of these repair products are available in paint and hardware stores along with color charts for matching furniture finishes.

There are several ways to repair furniture finishes.

• Use *putty-type filler sticks* for small repairs. These can be rubbed on to fill open joints, holes, and scratches. They come in a variety of colors. Fig. 48-13.

• *Marker pens* with convenient felt tips contain a quick-drying touch-up coating that seals and finishes in one step. These pens are available in a variety of colors to match almost any wood finish. Fig. 48-14.

• More extensive repairs are made by applying *finishing liquids* with a brush, spray, or pad. Spray lacquer in aerosol cans, available in popular furniture colors, can be used to spray over a damaged section. Fig. 48-15. Also available are liquid blended stains and finishes that can be applied with a brush or pad. Fig. 48-16. One of the best ways to repair a damaged finish is to use a pad and a proper padding-type finish as follows:

1. Cut a one-foot-square piece of lint-free cloth and fold twice to form a 6″ square. Place two-thirds of a full ball of cotton in the center of the cloth and fold the corners around it as tightly as possible. Tie a string around the open end of the ball. Fig. 48-17.

2. Hold this pad in one hand and pour about one-third ounce

*Two companies that provide workshops and materials are the Star Chemical Co., Inc., 360 Shore Drive, Hinsdale, IL 60521 and Mohawk Finishing Products, Inc., Amsterdam, NY 12010.

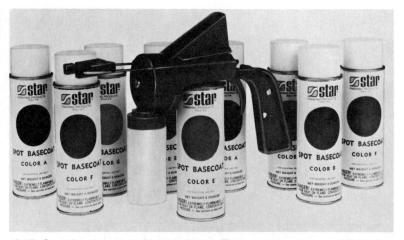

48-15. Spray lacquer comes in areosol cans. These are commonly used by professional finishers for touching up small areas.

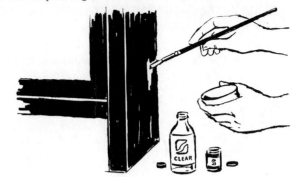

48-16. Combination liquid stain and finish can be used for most patching and touch-up. These can be applied with a brush or padding. These materials are available in a wide variety of colors and can be intermixed for more careful color matching.

of the proper finishing material onto the pad. Never soak the pad.

3. Tap the pad as it is held in the palm of your open hand to make sure that the finishing material is spread throughout the pad.

4. To use the pad, move it in a swinging motion like the pendulum of a large clock, just touching the damaged surface. Fig. 48-18. Never wipe the pad back and forth with a brush stroke. Always pad with the grain, never across

it. Continue padding until the defective spot is filled with the finish.

48-17. A polishing pad.

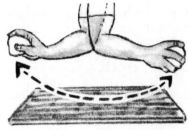

48-18. Using a polishing pad to apply stain and finish in one operation.

DISCUSSION TOPICS

Section Ten—REPAIRING AND REFINISHING WOOD FURNITURE

Unit 48. Repairing and Refinishing Wood Furniture

1. Name some of the common problems encountered in caring for, repairing, and refinishing fine furniture.

2. Describe some of the best methods of removing water marks.

3. List some of the steps that might have to be done in order to make a drawer work smoothly in a case.

4. Describe the method of repairing joints in leg-and-rail construction.

5. What are two methods of repairing a cracked leg on a table or chair?

6. Which is the more difficult material to repair on a tabletop: a veneer surface or a plastic laminate surface? Explain your answer.

7. What precautions should be observed in removing an old finish?

8. What are some of the common kinds of repair materials used by professional furniture refinishers?

EXTRA CREDIT ACTIVITIES

1. Obtain color charts of refinishing products and make a display board showing the various color materials available.

2. Visit a major furniture store and discuss the problems of furniture refinishing with a person there who is professionally responsible for fixing damaged furniture.

Index